Relational Database Design and Implementation

FOURTH EDITION

Jan L. Harrington

AMSTERDAM • BOSTON • HEIDELBERG • LONDON
NEW YORK • OXFORD • PARIS • SAN DIEGO
SAN FRANCISCO • SINGAPORE • SYDNEY • TOKYO

Morgan Kaufmann is an imprint of Elsevier

British Library Cataloguing-in-Publication Data
A catalogue record for this book is available from the British Library

Library of Congress Cataloging-in-Publication Data
A catalog record for this book is available from the Library of Congress

ISBN: 978-0-12-804399-8

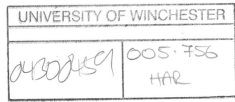
For information on all Morgan Kaufmann publications
visit our website at https://www.elsevier.com/

 Working together
to grow libraries in
developing countries

www.elsevier.com • www.bookaid.org

Publisher: Todd Green
Acquisition Editor: Todd Green
Editorial Project Manager: Amy Invernizzi
Production Project Manager: Punithavathy Govindaradjane
Designer: Greg Harris

Typeset by Thomson Digital

Relational Database Design
and Implementation

 THE UNIVE[

Contents

PART IV   USING INTERACTIVE SQL TO MANIPULATE A RELATIONAL DATABASE

PART V   DATABASE IMPLEMENTATION ISSUES

PART VI   BEYOND THE RELATIONAL DATA MODEL

Preface to the Fourth Edition

One of my favorite opening lines for the database courses I taught during my 32 years as a college professor was: "Probably the most misunderstood term in all of business computing is *database*, followed closely by the word *relational*." At that point, some students would look a bit smug, because they were absolutely, positively sure that they knew what a database was and that they also knew what is meant for a database to be relational. Unfortunately, the popular press, with the help of some PC software developers, long ago distorted the meaning of both these terms, which led many small business owners to think that designing a database was a task that could be left to a clerical worker who had taken a few days training in using database software.

At the other end of the spectrum, we found large businesses that had large data management systems that they called databases, but depending on the software being used and the logical structuring of the data, may or may not have been. Even 45 years later, the switch to the relational data model continues to cause problems for companies with significant investments in prerelational legacy systems.

There are data models older than the relational data model and even a couple of new ones (object-oriented and NoSQL) that are postrelational. Nonetheless, the vast majority of existing, redesigned, and new database systems are based on the relational data model, primarily because it handles the structured data that form the backbone of most organizational operations. That's why this book, beginning with the first edition, has focused on relational design, and why it continues to do so.

This book is intended for anyone who has been given the responsibility for designing or maintaining a relational database (or whose college degree requirements include a database course). It will teach you how to look at the environment your database serves and to tailor the design of the database to that environment. It will also teach you ways of designing the database so that it provides accurate and consistent data, avoiding the problems that are common to poorly designed databases. In addition, you will learn about design compromises that you might choose to make in the interest of database application performance and the consequences of making such choices.

For the first time, this edition also includes coverage of using SQL, the international standard for a relational database query language. What you have in your hands is therefore a complete treatment of the relational database environment. There is also an appendix on prerelational data models and two chapters on the postrelational data models.

Changes in the Fourth Edition

The core of this book—the bulk of the content of the previous edition—remains mostly unchanged from the third edition. Relational database theory has been relatively stable for more than 45 years (with the exception of the addition of sixth normal form) and requires very little updating from one edition to the next, although it has been nearly seven years since the third edition appeared.

By far the biggest change in this edition, however, is the addition of full SQL coverage. Previous editions did include material on using SQL to implement a relational design, but nothing about querying the database. Now readers will have everything they need in a single volume.

Note: Because not everyone who studies database design will be fluent in a high-level programming language, SQL programming has been placed in Appendix B and easily can be skipped if desired.

There is also a new chapter about NoSQL databases. This trend goes hand-in-hand with the analysis of "big data," especially that found in data ware-houses. Readers should be aware of the special needs of large, unstructured data sets and why the relational data model may not be the best choice for data analytics.

What You Need to Know

When the first edition of this book appeared in 1999, you really didn't need much more than basic computer literacy to understand just about everything in the book. However, the role of networking in database architectures has grown so much in the past decade that, in addition to computer literacy, you need to understand some basic network hardware and software concepts (eg, the Internet, interconnection devices such as routers and switches, and servers).

Note: It has always been a challenge to decide whether to teach students about systems analysis and design before or after database management. Now we worry about where a networking course should come in the sequence. It's tough to understand databases without networking, but, at the same time, some aspects of networking involve database issues.

Teaching Materials

A packet of materials to support a college-level course in database manage-ment can be found on the Morgan Kaufmann Web site. In it, you will find sample syllabi, assignments and associated case studies, exams and exam scenarios, and text files to paste into a SQL command processor to create and populate the databases used in the SQL examples in this book.

Acknowledgments

As always, getting this book onto paper involved an entire cast of characters, all of whom deserve thanks for their efforts. First are the people at Morgan Kaufmann:

- Todd Green (Publisher)
- Amy Invernizzi (Editorial Project Manager)
- Punithavathy Govindaradjane (Production Manager)

And I am always grateful for the keen eyes of the reviewer. For this book, I want to thank Raymond J. Curts, PhD.

Finally, let's not forget my mother and my son, who had to put up with me through all the long days I was working.

Part

I

Introduction

The first part of this book deals with the organizational environment in which databases exist. In these chapters, you will find discussions of various hardware and network architectures on which databases operate and an introduction to database management software. You will also learn about alternative processes for discovering exactly what a database needs to do for an organization.

Chapter

1

The Database Environment

Can you think of a business that doesn't have a database that is stored on a computer? It's hard. I do know of one, however. It is a small used paperback bookstore. A customer brings in used paperbacks and receives credit for them based on the condition, and in some cases, the subject matter, of the books. That credit can be applied to purchasing books from the store at approximately twice what the store pays to acquire the books. The books are shelved by general type (for example, mystery, romance, and non-fiction), but otherwise not organized. The store doesn't have a precise inventory of what is on its shelves.

To keep track of customer credits, the store has a 4 × 6 card for each customer on which employees write a date and an amount of credit. The credit amount is incremented or decremented based on a customer's transactions. The cards themselves are stored in two long steel drawers that sit on a counter. (The cabinet from which the drawers were taken is nowhere in evidence.) Sales slips are written by hand and cash is kept in a drawer. (Credit card transactions are processed by a stand-alone terminal that uses a phone line to dial up the processing bank for card approval.) The business is small, and its system seems to work, but it certainly is an exception.

Although the bookstore just described doesn't have a computer or a database, it does have data. In fact, like a majority of businesses today, it relies on data as the foundation of what it does. The bookstore's operations require the customer credit data; it couldn't function without it.

Data form the basis of just about everything an organization that deals with money does. (It is possible to operate a business using bartering and not keep any data, but that certainly is a rarity.) Even a Girl Scout troop selling cookies must store and manipulate data. The troop needs to keep track of how many boxes of each type of cookie have been ordered, and by whom.

They also need to manage data about money: payments received, payments owed, amount kept by the troop, amount sent to the national organization. The data may be kept on paper, but they still exist and manipulation of those data is central to the group's functioning.

In fact, just about the only "business" that doesn't deal with data is a lemonade stand that gets its supplies from Mom's kitchen and never has to pay Mom back. The kids take the entire gross income of the lemonade stand without worrying about how much is profit.

Data have always been part of businesses.[1] Until the mid-twentieth century, those data were processed manually. Because they were stored on paper, retrieving data was difficult, especially if the volume of data was large. In addition, paper documents tended to deteriorate with age, go up in smoke, or become water-logged. Computers changed that picture significantly, making it possible to store data in much less space than before, to retrieve data more easily, and usually to store it more permanently.

The downside to the change to automated data storage and retrieval was the need for at some specialized knowledge on the part of those who set up the computer systems. In addition, it costs more to purchase the equipment needed for electronic data manipulation than it does to purchase some file folders and file cabinets. Nonetheless, the ease of data access and manipulation that computing has brought to businesses has outweighed most other considerations.

Defining a Database

Nearly 35 years ago, when I first started working with databases, I would begin a college course I was teaching in database management with the following sentence: "There is no term more misunderstood and misused in all of business computing than 'database.'" Unfortunately, that is still true to some extent, and we can still lay much of the blame on commercial software developers. In this section, we will explore why that is so, and provide a complete definition for a database.

Lists and Files

A portion of the data used in a business is represented by lists of things. For example, most of us have a contact list that contains names, addresses, and

---

[1]The phrase "data have" is correct. Although people commonly use "data" as singular, the actual singular form of the word is "datum"; "data" is the plural form. Therefore, "data are" is correct, as are "the datum is" and "the piece of data is."

phone numbers. Business people also commonly work with planners that list appointments. In our daily lives, we have shopping lists of all kinds as well as "to do" lists. For many years, we handled these lists manually, using paper, day planners, and a pen. It made sense to many people to migrate these lists from paper to their PCs.

Software that helps us maintain simple lists stores those lists in files, generally one list per physical file. The software that manages the list typically lets you create a form for data entry, provides a method of querying the data based on logical criteria, and lets you design output formats. List management software can be found not only on desktop and laptop computers, but also on our handheld computing devices.

Unfortunately, list management software has been marketed under the name "database" since the advent of PCs. People have therefore come to think of anything that stores and manipulates data as database software. Nonetheless, a list handled by list-management software is not a database.

Databases

There is a fundamental concept behind all databases: There are things in a business environment about which we need to store data, and those things are related to one another in a variety of ways. In fact, to be considered a *database*, the place where data are stored must contain not only the data but also information about the relationships between those data. We might, for example, need to relate our customers to the orders they place with us and our inventory items to orders for those items.

The idea behind a database is that the user—either a person working interactively or an application program—has no need to worry about the way in which data are physically stored on disk. The user phrases data manipulation requests in terms of data relationships. A piece of software known as a *database management system* (DBMS) then translates between the user's request for data and the physical data storage.

Why, then, don't the simple "database" software packages (the list managers) produce true databases? Because they can't represent relationships between data, much less use such relationships to retrieve data. The problem is that list management software has been marketed for years as "database" software and many purchasers do not understand exactly what they are purchasing. Making the problem worse is that a rectangular area of a spreadsheet is also called a "database." Although you can use spreadsheet functions to reference data stored outside a given rectangular area, this is not the same as relationships in a real database. In a database, the relationships are between those things mentioned earlier (the customers, orders, inventory items, and so on) rather than between individual pieces of data. Because this problem of terminology remains, confusion about exactly what a database happens to be remains as well.

Note: A generic term that is commonly used to mean any place where data are stored, regardless of how those data are organized, is "data store."

Systems that Use Databases

Databases do not exist in a vacuum in any organization. Although they form the backbone for most organizational data processing, they are surrounded by information systems that include application software and users.

There are two major types of systems that use databases in medium to large organizations:

- Transaction processing: Transaction processing systems (*online transaction processing*, or OLTP) handle the day-to-day operations of an organization. Sales, accounting, manufacturing, human resources—all use OLTP systems. OLTP systems form the basis of information processing in most organizations of any size. (In fact, typically OLTP is the only type of information system used by a small business.) The data are dynamic, changing frequently as the organization sells, manufactures, and administers.
- Analytical processing: Analytic processing systems (*online analytical processing*, or OLAP) are used in support of the analysis of organizational performance, making high-level operational decisions, and strategic planning. Most data are extracted from operational systems, reformatted as necessary, and loaded into the OLAP system. However, once part of that system, the data values are not modified frequently.

Relational databases, which form the bulk of databases in use today (as well as the bulk of this book), were developed for transaction processing. They handle the data that organizations need to stay in business. The data needed by the organization are well known and are usually structured in a predictable and stable manner. In other words, we know generally what we need and how the data interact with one another. Our needs may change over time, but the changes are relatively gradual and, in most cases, changes to the data processing system do not have to be made in a hurry.

Some OLAP systems also use relational databases, including some large data warehouses (see Chapter 24). However, in recent years, volumes of unstructured data (data without a predictable and stable structure) have become important for corporate decision making. A new category of databases has arisen to handle these data. You will read about them in Chapter 28.

Data "Ownership"

Who "owns" the data in your organization? Departments? IT? How many databases are there? Are there departmental databases or is there a centralized, integrated database that serves the entire organization? The answers to these questions can determine the effectiveness of a company's database management.

The idea of data ownership has some important implications. To see them, we must consider the human side of owning data. People consider exclusive access to information a privilege and are often proud of their access: "I know something you don't know." In organizations where isolated databases have cropped up over the years, the data in a given database are often held in individual departments that are reluctant to share that data with other organizational units.

One problem with these isolated databases is that they may contain duplicated data that are inconsistent. A customer might be identified as "John J. Smith" in the marketing database but as "John Jacob Smith" in the sales database. It also can be technologically difficult to obtain data stored in multiple databases. For example, one database may store a customer number as text while another stores it as an integer. An application therefore may be unable to match customer numbers between the two databases. In addition, attempts to integrate the data into a single, shared data store may run into resistance from the data "owners," who are reluctant to give up control of their data.

In yet other organizations, data are held by the IT department, which carefully doles out access to those data as needed. IT requires supervisor signatures on requests for accounts and limits access to as little data as possible, often stating requirements for system security. Data users feel as if they are at the mercy of IT, even though the data are essential to corporate functioning.

The important psychological change that needs to occur in either of the above situations is that data belong to the organization and that they must be shared as needed throughout the organization without unnecessary roadblocks to access. This does not mean that an organization should ignore security concerns, but that where appropriate, data should be shared readily within the organization.

Service-Oriented Architecture (SOA)

One way to organize a company's entire information systems functions is *Service-Oriented Architecture* (SOA). In an SOA environment, all information systems components are viewed as services that are provided to the organization. The services are designed so that they interact smoothly, sharing data easily when needed.

An organization must make a commitment to implement SOA. Because services need to be able to integrate smoothly, information systems must be designed from the top down. (In contrast, organizations with many departmental databases and applications have grown from the bottom up.) In many cases, this may mean replacing most of an organization's existing information systems.

SOA certainly changes the role of a database in an organization: The database becomes a service provided to the organization. To serve that role, a database must be designed to integrate with a variety of departmental applications. The only way for this to happen is for the structure of the database to be well documented, usually in some form of *data dictionary*. For example, if a department needs an application program that uses a customer's telephone number, application programmers first consult the data dictionary to find out that a telephone number is stored with the area code separate from the rest of the phone number. Every application that accesses the database must use the same telephone number format. The result is services that can easily exchange data because all services are using the same data formats.

Shared data also place restrictions on how changes to the data dictionary are handled. Changes to a departmental database affect only that department's applications, but changes to a database service may affect many other services that use the data. An organization must therefore have procedures in place for notifying all users of data when changes are proposed, giving the users a chance to respond to the proposed change, and deciding whether the proposed change is warranted. As an example, consider the effect of a change from a five- to nine-digit zip code for a bank. The CFO believes that there will be a significant savings in postage if the change is implemented. (The post office charges discounted rates for pre-stamped bulk mail that is sorted by nine-digit zip codes.) However, the transparent windows in the envelopes used to mail paper account statements are too narrow to show the entire nine-digit zip code. Envelopes with wider windows are very expensive, so expensive that making the change will actually cost more than leaving the zip codes at five digits. The CFO was not aware of the cost of the envelopes; the cost was noticed by someone in the purchasing department.

SOA works best for large organizations. It is expensive to introduce because typically organizations have accumulated a significant number of independent programs and data stores that will need to be replaced. Just determining where all the data are stored, who controls the data, which data are stored, and how those data are formatted can be a daunting task. It is also a psychological change for those employees who are used to owning and controlling data.

Organizations undertake the change to SOA because in the long run it makes information systems easier to modify as corporate needs change.[2] It does not change the process for designing and maintaining a database, but does change how applications programs and users interact with it.

Database Software: DBMSs

There is a wide range of DBMS software available today. Some, such as Microsoft Access[3] (part of the Windows Microsoft Office suite) are designed for single users only.[4] The largest proportion of today's DBMSs, however, are multiuser, intended for concurrent use by many users. A few of those DBMSs are intended for small organizations, such as FileMaker Pro[5] (cross-platform, multiuser) and Helix[6] (Macintosh multiuser). Most, however, are intended for enterprise use. You may have heard of DB2[7] or Oracle,[8] both of which have versions for small businesses but are primarily intended for large installations using mainframes. As an alternative to these commercial products, many businesses have chosen to use open source products, a list of which can be found at the end of this chapter.

For the most part, enterprise-strength commercial DBMSs are large, expensive pieces of software. (This goes a long way when explaining interest in

---

[2]Some organizations implement SOA because they think it will solve all their data problems. This is not necessarily the case. Packaged SOA solutions are based on industry "best practices" that may not match a company's needs.

[3]http://office.microsoft.com/en-us/access/default.aspx

[4]It is possible to "share" an Access database with multiple users, but Microsoft never intended the product to be used in that way. Sharing an Access database is known to cause regular file corruption. A database administrator working in such an environment once told me that she had to rebuild the file "only once every two or three days."

[5]http://www.filemaker.com

[6]http://www.qsatoolworks.com

[7]http://www-306.ibm.com/software/data/db2/

[8]http://www.oracle.com

open source software.) They require significant training and expertise on the part of whoever will be implementing the database. It is not unusual for a large organization to employ one or more people to handle the physical implementation of the database along with a team (or teams) of people to develop the logical structure of the database. Yet more teams may be responsible for developing application programs that interact with the database and provide an interface for those who cannot, or should not, interact with the database directly.

Regardless of the database product you choose, there are some capabilities that you should expect to find:

- A DBMS must provide facilities for creating the structure of the database. Developers must be able to define the logical structure of the data to be stored, including the relationships among data.
- A DBMS must provide some way to enter, modify, and delete data. Small DBMSs typically focus on form-based interfaces; enterprise-level products begin with a command-line interface. The most commonly used language for interacting with a relational database (the type we are discussing in this book) is SQL (originally called Structured Query Language), which has been accepted throughout much of the world as a standard data manipulation language for relational databases.
- A DBMS must also provide a way to retrieve data. In particular, users must be able to formulate queries based on the logical relationships among the data. Smaller products support form-based querying while both small and enterprise-level products support SQL. A DBMS should support complex query statements using Boolean algebra (the AND, OR, and NOT operators) and should also be able to perform at least basic calculations (for example, computing totals and subtotals) on data retrieved by a query.

Note: You will find references to SQL throughout this book, even in chapters that don't discuss the language specifically. The emphasis on SQL isn't promotion of a particular company's product. In fact, SQL isn't a product; it's a set of standards, the most recent of which is SQL:2011. DBMS developers must add code to their software that implements what is described in the standards. There are a myriad of SQL implementations available that vary somewhat in which portions of the standard are supported. Nonetheless, if you are familiar with basic SQL, you will know at least 90% of what it takes to manipulate data in any DBMS that uses SQL.

- Although it is possible to interact with a DBMS either with basic forms (for a smaller product) or at the SQL command line (for enterprise-level products), doing so requires some measure of specialized training. A business usually has employees who need to manipulate data, but either don't have the necessary expertise, can't or don't want to gain the necessary expertise, or shouldn't have direct access to the database for security reasons. Application developers therefore create programs that simplify access to the database for such users. Most DBMSs designed for business use provide some way to develop such applications. The larger the DBMS, the more likely it is that application development requires traditional programming skills. Smaller products support graphic tools for "drawing" forms and report layouts.

- A DBMS should provide methods for restricting access to data. Such methods often include creating user names and passwords specific to the database, and tying access to data items to the user name. Security provided by the DBMS is in addition to security in place to protect an organization's network.

What DBMSs are Companies Really Using

There are a lot of DBMSs on the market, so what products are really being used? Recent surveys[9] have uncovered relatively consistent results, which are summarized in Table 1.1. Notice that the percentages add up to far more than 100% because many companies run multiple DBMSs.

Table 1.1 DBMS Use in Medium to Large Businesses

Relational DBMSs	Percent Companies Using	Non-Relational DBMSs	Percent Companies Using
Microsoft SQL Server	60–90%	MongoDB	10–15%
Oracle	40–80%	Hadoop	8%
MySQL	80%	Cassandra	4%
IBM DB2	15–30%	Riak	2%
PostgreSQL	15%	Couchbase	1%

Sources: King, Dr Elliott, Research Analyst, Unisphere Research. The Real World of the Database Administrator; Tesora. Database Usage in the Public and Private Cloud: Choices and Preferences.

[9]See http://www.infoworld.com/article/2607910/database/not-so-fast--nosql----sql-still-reigns.html, http://db-engines.com/en/ (updated monthly), and http://www.zdnet.com/article/as-dbms-wars-continue-postgresql-shows-most-momentum/.

Database Hardware Architecture

Because databases are almost always designed for concurrent access by multiple users, database access has always involved some type of computer network. The hardware architecture of these networks has matured along with more general computing networks.

Centralized

Originally, network architecture was centralized, with all processing done on a mainframe. Remote users—who were almost always located within the same building, or at least the same office park—worked with dumb terminals that could accept input and display output but had no processing power of their own. The terminals were hard-wired to the mainframe (usually through some type of specialized controller) using coaxial cable, as in Figure 1.1.

During the time that the classic centralized architecture was in wide use, network security also was not a major issue. The Internet was not publically available, there was no World Wide Web, and security threats were predominantly internal.

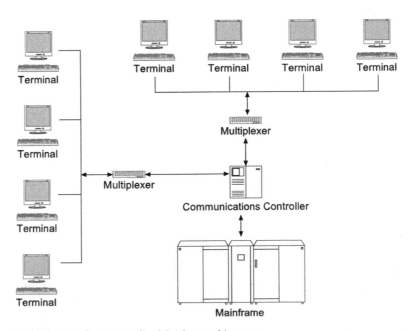

■ FIGURE 1.1 Classic centralized database architecture.

Centralized database architecture, in the sense we have been describing, is rarely found today. Instead, those organizations that maintain a centralized database typically have both local and remote users connecting using PCs, local area networks (LANs), and a wide area network (WAN) of some kind. As you look at Figure 1.2, keep in mind that although the terminals have been replaced with PCs, the PCs are not using their own processing power when interacting with the database. All processing is still done on the mainframe.

From the point of view of an IT department, there is one major advantage to the centralized architecture: control. All the computing is done on one computer to which only IT has direct access. Software management is easier because all software resides and executes on one machine. Security efforts can

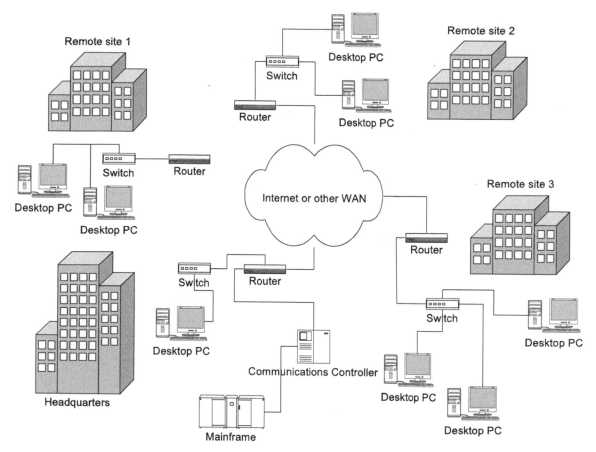

■ FIGURE 1.2 A modern centralized database architecture including LAN and WAN connections.

be concentrated on a single point of vulnerability. In addition, mainframes have the significant processing power to handle data-intensive operations as well as the capacity to handle large volumes of I/O.

One drawback to a centralized database architecture is network performance. Because the terminals (or PCs acting as terminals) do no processing power on their own, all processing must be done on the mainframe. The database needs to send formatted output to the terminals, which consumes more network bandwidth than would sending just the data.

A second drawback to centralized architecture is reliability. If the database goes down, the entire organization is prevented from doing any data processing.

Mainframes are not gone, but their role has changed as client/server architecture has become popular.

Client/Server

Client/server architecture shares the data processing chores between a server—typically, a high-end workstation but quite possibly a mainframe—and clients, which are usually PCs. PCs have significant processing power and therefore are capable of taking raw data returned by the server and formatting the result for output. Application programs and query processors can be stored and executed on the PCs. Network traffic is reduced to data manipulation requests sent from the PC to the database server and raw data returned as a result of that request. The result is significantly less network traffic and theoretically better performance.

Today's client/server architectures exchange messages over LANs. Although a few older Token Ring LANs are still in use, most of today's LANs are based on Ethernet standards. As an example, take a look at the small network in Figure 1.3. The database runs on its own server (the database server), using additional disk space on the network attached storage device. Access to the database is controlled not only by the DBMS itself, but by the authentication server.

A client/server architecture is similar to the traditional centralized architecture in that the DBMS resides on a single computer. In fact, many of today's mainframes actually function as large, fast servers. The need to handle large data sets still exists although the location of some of the processing has changed.

Because a client/server architecture uses a centralized database server, it suffers from the same reliability problems as the traditional centralized

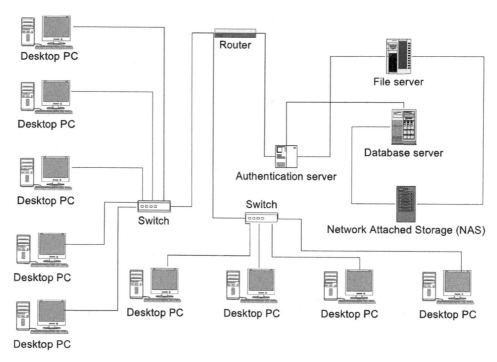

■ FIGURE 1.3 Small LAN with network-accessible database server.

architecture: if the server goes down, data access is cut off. However, because the "terminals" are PCs, any data downloaded to a PC can be processed without access to the server.

Distributed

Not long after centralized databases became common—and before the introduction of client/server architecture—large organizations began experimenting with placing portions of their databases at different locations, each site running a DBMS against part of the entire data set. This architecture is known as a *distributed database*. (For example, see Figure 1.4.) It is different from the WAN-using centralized database in Figure 1.2 in that there is a DBMS and part of the database at each site as opposed to having one computer doing all of the processing and data storage.

A distributed database architecture has several advantages:

■ The hardware and software placed at each site can be tailored to the needs of the site. If a mainframe is warranted, then the organization uses a mainframe. If smaller servers will provide enough capacity,

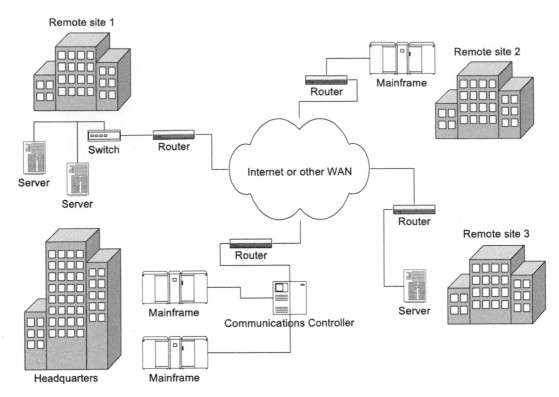

Remote site 1

Remote site 2

Mainframe

Router

Switch

Router

Server

Internet or other WAN

Server

Router

Remote site 3

Router

Mainframe

Server

Communications Controller

Mainframe

Headquarters

Mainframe

■ **FIGURE 1.4 Distributed database architecture.**

then the organization can save money by not needing to install excess hardware. Software, too, can be adapted to the needs of the specific site. Most current distributed DBMS software will accept data manipulation requests from mores than one DBMS that uses SQL. Therefore, the DBMSs at each site can be different.

■ Each site keeps that portion of the database that contains the data that it uses most frequently. As a result, network traffic is reduced because most queries stay on a site's LAN rather than needing to use the organization's WAN.

■ Performance for local queries is better because there is no time lag for travel over the WAN.

■ Distributed databases are more reliable than centralized systems. If the WAN goes down, each site can continue processing using its own portion of the database. Only those data manipulation operations that require data not on site will be delayed. If one site goes down, the other sites can continue to process using their local data.

Despite the advantages, there are reasons why distributed databases are not widely implemented:

- Although performance of queries involving locally stored data is enhanced, queries that require data from another site are relatively slow.
- Maintenance of the data dictionary (the catalog of the structure of the database) becomes an issue: Should there be a single data dictionary or a copy of it at each site? If the organization keeps a single data dictionary, then any changes made to it will be available to the entire database. However, each time a remote site needs to access the data dictionary, it must send a query over the WAN, increasing network traffic, and slowing down performance. If a copy of the data dictionary is stored at each site, then changes to the data dictionary must be sent to each site. There is a significant chance that, at times, the copies of the data dictionary will be out of sync.
- Some of the data in the database will exist at more than one site, usually because more than one site includes the same data in the "used most often" category. This introduces a number of problems in terms of ensuring that the duplicated copies remain consistent, some of which may be serious enough to prevent an organization from using a distributed architecture. (You will read more about this problem in Chapter 25.)
- Because data are traveling over network media not owned by the company (the WAN), security risks are increased.

Web

The need for Web sites to interact with database data has introduced yet another alterative database architecture. A Web server needing data must query the database, accept the results, and format the result with HTML tags for transmission to the end user and display by the user's Web browser. Complicating the picture is the need to keep the database secure from Internet intruders.

Figure 1.5 provides an example of how a Web server affects the hardware on a network when the Web server must communicate with a database server. For most installations, an overriding concern is security. The Web server is isolated from the internal LAN and a special firewall is placed between the Web server and the database server. The only traffic allowed through that firewall is traffic to the database server from the Web server and from the database server to the Web server.

Some organizations prefer to isolate an internal database server from a database server that interacts with a Web server. This usually means that there

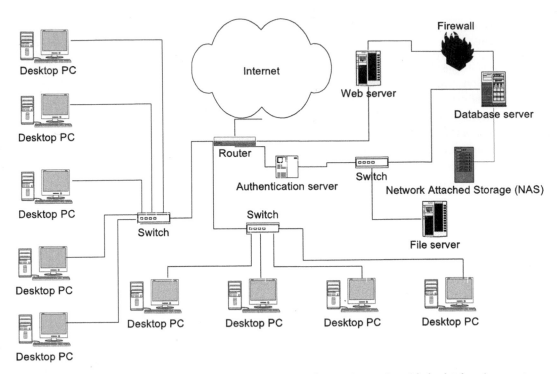

■ **FIGURE 1.5** The placement of a database server in a network when a Web server interacting with the database is present.

will be two database servers: The database server that interacts with the Web server is a copy of the internal database that is inaccessible from the internal LAN. Although more secure than the architecture in Figure 1.5, keeping two copies of the database means that those copies must be reconciled at regular intervals. The database server for Web use will become out-of-date as soon as changes are made to the internal database, and there is the chance that changes to the internal database will make portions of the Web-accessible database invalid or inaccurate. Retail organizations that need live, integrated inventory for both physical and Web sales cannot use the duplicated architecture. You will see an example of such as organization in Chapter 15.

Remote Access

In addition to the basic architecture we have chosen for our database hardware, we often have to accommodate remote users. Salespeople, agents in the field, telecommuters, executives on vacation—all may have the need to access a database that is usually available only over a LAN. Initially, remote access involved using a phone line and a modem to dial into the office network. Today, however, the Internet (usually with the help of a virtual private network (VPN)) provides cheaper and faster access, along with serious security concerns.

As you can see in Figure 1.6, the VPN creates a secure encrypted tunnel between the business's internal network and the remote user.[10] The remote user must also pass through an authentication server before being granted access to the internal LAN. Once authenticated, the remote user has the same access to the internal LAN—including the database server—as if he or she were present in the organization's offices.

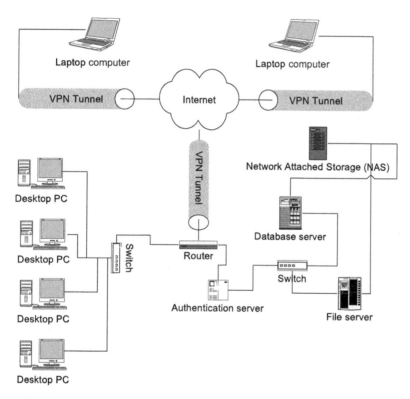

■ FIGURE 1.6   Using a VPN to secure remote access to a database.

Cloud Storage

All of the architectures you have seen to this point assume that the database is stored on hardware at one or more business-owned locations. However, the past few years have seen a migration to *cloud storage*. The term "cloud" has long been used as a generic term for the Internet. (Notice that the Internet

---

[10]To be totally accurate, there are two kinds of VPNs. One uses encryption from end-to-end (user to network and back). The other encrypts only the Internet portion of the transmission.

is represented in Figures 1.5 and 1.6 by a picture of an amorphous cloud.) When databases are stored in the cloud, they are hosted on hardware not owned by the organization that owns the data. The data reside on servers maintained by another organization that is in the business of storing software and data for other organizations.[11]

You can find a sample architecture for a cloud-stored database in Figure 1.7. The most important characteristic of this architecture is that the DBMS and the database to which it provides access are not located on the company's premises: They are stored on hardware owned and maintained by the cloud service provider. Someone who needs to use the data in the database communicates with the database using the Internet as the communications pathway.

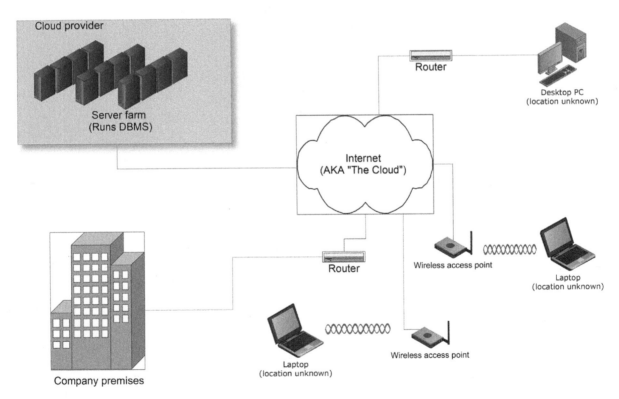

■ FIGURE 1.7 **Storing a database in the cloud.**

---

[11]The biggest players in enterprise-level cloud computing include Amazon and Google, both of which maintain huge server farms throughout the country. Although you may not think of it as such, you probably use cloud storage yourself: iCloud, GoogleApps, Dropbox, and Amazon Cloud Drive are all examples of end-user cloud computing.

Advantages of Cloud Storage

There are some tangible benefits of moving a database to the cloud:

- The owner of the data does not need to maintain database hardware or a DBMS. That becomes the responsibility of the cloud service provider. This can significantly reduce the cost of supporting the database, not only because the data owner does not need to purchase hardware and software, but because it does not need to hire staff members or consultants who can maintain the database environment.
- The database can scale seamlessly. If new/larger/faster hardware is needed, the cloud service provider purchases and installs the replacement hardware. The cloud service provider may also be responsible for upgrading the DBMS. (Responsibility for application software that interacts with the DBMS may be the responsibility of the owner of the data or application development may be included in cloud service package.)
- The company using the cloud has fixed, predictable expenses for database maintenance that are negotiated up front.
- The database is accessible from anywhere the Internet is available.

The bottom line is that in most cases, cloud storage can save money and a lot of effort.

Problems with Cloud Storage

As ideal as cloud storage may sound initially, there are some serious issues that a company must consider:

- Because the database is not located on company premises, security becomes an enormous challenge. The company that owns the data no longer has complete control over security measures. It must rely on the cloud service provider to secure the database from unauthorized access; it must also implicitly trust the service provider's employees.
- Access to the database requires a live Internet connection. Unlike architectures where the database is located on the company's internal network, no processing can continue when the Internet is unavailable.
- The company that owns the data must rely on the cloud storage provider for consistent up-time. The responsibility for ensuring that the database is accessible is no longer with the company; it lies with a third party.

Overall, the owner of the data loses a great deal of control over the data when the data are stored in the cloud. The more important the security of the data, the riskier cloud storage becomes.

Other Factors in the Database Environment

Choosing hardware and software to maintain a database and then designing and implementing the database itself was once enough to establish a database environment. Today, however, security concerns loom large, coupled with government regulations on the privacy of data. In addition, a new database is unlikely to be the first database in an organization that has been in business for a while; the new database may need to interact with an existing database that cannot be merged into the new database. In this section, we will briefly consider how those factors influence database planning.

Security

Before the Internet, database management was fairly simple in that we were rarely concerned about security. A user name and password were enough to secure access to a centralized database. The most significant security threats were internal, from employees who either corrupted data by accident or purposely exceeded their authorized access.

Most DBMSs provide some type of internal security mechanism. However, that layer of security is not enough today. Adding a database server to a network that has a full-time connection to the Internet means that database planning must also involve network design. Authentication servers, firewalls, and other security measures therefore need to be included in the plans for a database system.

There is little benefit to the need for added security. The planning time and additional hardware, and software increase the cost of implementing the database. The cost of maintaining the database also increases as network traffic must be monitored far more than when we had classic centralized architectures. Unfortunately, there is no alternative. Data are the lifeblood of almost every modern organization and must be protected.

The cost of a database security breach—the loss of trade secrets, the release of confidential customer information—can be devastating to a business. Even if there is no effect of the actual unauthorized disclosure of data, security breaches can be a public relations nightmare, causing customers to lose confidence in the organization and, therefore, to take their business elsewhere. Even worse, the unauthorized disclosure of personal data may lead to widespread identity theft, one of the banes of our digitized lives.

Note: Because database security is so vitally important, this book devotes an entire chapter to the topic (see Chapter 23).

Government Regulations and Privacy

Until the past 15 years or so, decisions about which data need to be secured to maintain privacy have been left up to the organization storing the data. In the United States, that is no longer the case for many types of data. Government regulations determine who can access the data and what they may access (although the provisions of many of those laws are difficult to interpret). Among the US laws that may affect owners of databases are:

- Health Insurance Portability and Accountability Act (HIPPA): HIPPA is intended to safeguard the privacy of medical records. It restricts the release of medical records to the patient alone (or the parent/guardian in the case of those under 18) or to those the patient has authorized in writing to retrieve records. It also requires the standardization of the formats of patient records so they can be transferred easily among insurance companies and the use of unique identifiers for patients. (The social security number may not be used.) Most importantly for database administrators, the law requires that security measures be in place to protect the privacy of medical records.

- Family Educational Rights and Privacy Act (FERPA): FERPA is designed to safeguard the privacy of educational records. Although the US Federal government has no direct authority over most schools, it does wield considerable power over funds that are allocated to schools. Therefore, FERPA denies Federal funds to those schools that do not meet the requirements of the law. It states that parents have a right to view the records of children under 18 and that the records of older students (those 18 and over) cannot be released to anyone but the student without the written permission of the student. Schools therefore have the responsibility to ensure that student records are not disclosed to unauthorized people, thus the need for secure information systems that store student information.

- Children's Online Privacy Protection Act: Provisions of this law govern which data can be requested from children (those under 13) and which of those data can be stored by a site operator. It applies to Web sites, "pen pal services," e-mail, message boards, and chat rooms. It general, the law aims to restrict the soliciting and disclosure of any information that can be used to identify a child—beyond information required for interacting with the Web site—without approval of a parent or guardian. Covered information includes first and last name, any part of a home address, e-mail address, telephone number, social security number, or any combination of the preceding.

If covered information is necessary for interaction with a Web site—for example, registering a user—the Web site must collect only the minimally required amount of information, ensure the security of that information, and not disclose it unless required to do so by law. The main intent of this law is to restrict data that might be accessed by Internet predators (in other words, to make it harder for predators to obtain data that pinpoint a child's location).[12]

Legacy Databases

Many businesses keep their data "forever." They never throw anything out nor do they delete electronically stored data. For a business that has been using computing since the 1960s or 1970s, this typically means that there are old database applications still in use. We refer to such databases that use pre-relational data models as *legacy databases*. The presence of legacy databases presents several challenges to an organization, depending on the need to access and integrate the older data.

If legacy data are needed primarily as an archive (either for occasional access or retention required by law), then a company may choose to leave the database and its applications as they stand. The challenge in this situation occurs when the hardware on which the DBMS and application programs run breaks down and cannot be repaired. The only alternative may be to recover as much of the data as possible and convert it to be compatible with newer software.

Businesses that need legacy data integrated with more recent data have to answer the following question: Should the data be converted for storage in the current database or should intermediate software be used to move data between the old and the new as needed? Because we are typically talking about large databases running on mainframes, neither solution is inexpensive.

The seemingly most logical alternative is to convert legacy data for storage in the current database. The data must be taken from the legacy database and reformatted for loading into the new database. An organization can hire one of a number of companies that specialize in data conversion or perform the transfer itself. In both cases, a major component of the transfer process is a program that reads data from the legacy database, reformats them as necessary so that they match the requirements of the new database, and then loads them into the new database. Because the structure of legacy databases varies

---

[12]But let's get real here: Any kid who is savvy enough to be registering for Web accounts can subtract well enough to ensure that his or her birth year is more than 13 years ago.

so much among organizations, the transfer program is usually custom-written for the business using it.

Just reading the procedure makes it seem fairly simple, but keep in mind that because legacy databases are old, they often contain "bad data" (data that are incorrect in some way). Once bad data get in to a database, it is very hard to get them out. Somehow, the problem data must be located and corrected. If there is a pattern to the bad data, then the pattern needs to be identified so further bad data can be caught before they get into the database. The process of cleaning the data therefore can be the most time consuming part of data conversion. Nonetheless, it is still far better to spend the time cleaning the data as they come out of the legacy database than attempting to find errors and correct them once they enter the new database.

The bad data problem can be compounded by missing mandatory data. If the new database requires that data be present (for example, requiring a zip code for every order placed in the United States) and some of the legacy data are missing the required values, there must be some way to "fill in the blanks" and provide acceptable values. Supplying values for missing data can be handled by conversion software, but in addition, application programs that use the data must then be modified to identify and handle the instances of missing data.

Data migration projects also include the modification of application programs that ran solely using the legacy data. In particular, it is likely that the data manipulation language used by the legacy database is not the same as that used by the new database.

Some very large organizations have determined that it is not cost effective to convert data from a legacy database. Instead, they choose to use some type of middleware that moves data to and from the legacy database in real time as needed. An organization with a widely-used legacy database can often find middleware that it can purchase. For example, IBM markets software that translates and transfers data between IMS (the legacy product) and DB2 (the current, relational product). When such an application does not exist, it will need to be custom-written for the organization.

Note: One commonly used format for transferring data from one database to another is XML. You will read more about it in Chapter 26.

Open Source Relational DBMSs

Commercial DBMSs often require a significant financial investment in software. If you want to explore how DBMSs work, however, there are some very robust open-source products. Some have been deployed in significant commercial environments. All of the following have precompiled distributions for Windows, Mac OS X, and a variety of flavors of UNIX:

DBMS	Download URL
Firebird	http://www.firebirdsql.org/en/firebird-2-5-4/
MySQL	http://dev.mysql.com/downloads/
PostgreSQL	http://www.postgresql.org/download/
SQLite	https://www.sqlite.org/download.html

For Further Reading

Adebiaye, Richmond, Owusu, Theophilus, 2013. Network Systems and Security (Priniciples and Practices): Computer Networks, Architecture and Practices. CreateSpace Independent Publishing.

Barton, Blain, 2015. Microsoft Public Cloud Services: Setting Up Your Business in the Cloud. Microsoft Press.

Berson, Alex., 1996. Client/Server Architecture, second ed. McGraw-Hill.

Chong, Raul F., Wang, Xiamei, Dang, Michael, Snow, Dwaine R., 2008. Understanding DB2: Learning Visually with Examples, second ed. IBM Press.

Erl, Thomas, 2007. SOA Principles of Service Design. Prentice Hall.

Erl, Thomas, Cope, Robert, Naserpour, Amin, 2015. Cloud Computing Design Patterns. Prenctice Hall.

Feller, J., 2009. FileMaker Pro 10 in Depth. Que.

Greenwald, R., Stackowiak, R., Stern, Jonathan, 2007. Oracle Essentials: Oracle Database 11g. O'Reilly Media.

Kofler, M., 2005. The Definitive Guide to MySQL 5, third ed. Apress.

McDonald, M., 2006. Access 2007: The Missing Manual. Pogue Press.

McGrew, P.C., McDaniel, W.D., 2001. Wresting Legacy Data to the Web & Beyond: Practical Solutions for Managers & Technicians. McGrew & Daniel Group, Inc.

2

Systems Analysis and Database Requirements

As you will discover, a large measure of what constitutes the "right" or "correct" database design for an organization depends on the needs of that organization. Unless you understand the meaning and uses of data in the database environment, you can't produce even an adequate database design.

The process of discovering the meaning of a database environment and the needs of the users of that data is known as *systems analysis*. It is part of a larger process that involves the creation of an information system from the initial conception all the way through the evaluation of the newly implemented system. Although a database designer may indeed be involved in the design of the overall system, for the most part, the database designer is concerned with understanding how the database environment works and, therefore, in the results of the systems analysis.

Many database design books pay little heed to how the database requirements come to be. In some cases, they seem to appear out of thin air! Clearly, that is not the case. A systems analysis is an essential precursor to the database design process, and it benefits a database designer to be familiar with how an analysis is conducted and what it produces. In this chapter, you will be introduced to a classic process for conducting a systems analysis. The final section of the chapter provides an overview two alternative methods.

The intent of this chapter is not to turn you into a systems analyst—it would take a college course and some years of on-the-job experience to do that—but to give you a feeling of what happens before the database designer goes to work.

Dealing with Resistance to Change

Before we look at systems analysis methodologies, there is one additional very important thing we need to consider: A new system or modifications to an existing system may represent significant change in the work environment, something we humans usually don't accept easily. We become comfortable with the way we operate and any change creates some level of discomfort. (How much discomfort depends, of course, on the individual.)

Even the best designed and implemented information system will be useless if users don't accept it. This means that as well as discovering what the data management needs of the organization happen to be, those in charge of system change need to be very sensitive to how users react to modifications.

The simplest way to handle resistance to change is to understand that if people have a stake in the change, then they will be personally invested in seeing that the change succeeds. Many of the needs assessment techniques that you read about in this chapter can foster that type of involvement: Ask the users what they need and really listen to what they are saying. Show the users how you are implementing what they need. For those requests that you can't satisfy, explain why they are infeasible. Users who feel that they matter, that their input is valued, are far more likely to support procedural changes that may accompany a new information system.

There are also a number of theoretical models for managing change, including the following

- ADKAR: ADKAR's five components make up the model's name's acronym:
  - **A**wareness: Make users aware of why there must be a change.
  - **D**esire: Involve and educate users so that they have a desire to be part of the change process.
  - **K**nowledge: Educate users and system development personnel in the process of making the change.
  - **A**bility: Ensure that users and system development personnel have the skills necessary to implement the change. This may include training IT staff in using new development tools and training users to use the new system.
  - **R**einforcement: Continue follow-up after the system is implemented to ensure that the new system continues to be used as intended.

- Unfreeze–Change–Refreeze: This is a three stage model with the following components:
  - Unfreezing: Overcome inertia by getting those who will be affected by the change to understand the need for change and to take steps to accept it.
  - Change: Implement the change, recognizing that users may be uneasy with new software and procedures.
  - Refreeze: Take actions to ensure that users are as comfortable with the new system as they were with the one it replaced.

The Structured Design Life Cycle

The classic method for developing an information system is known as the *structured design life cycle*. It works best in environments where it is possible specify the requirements of a system, where the requirements are fairly well known, before developing the system.

There are several ways to describe the steps in the structured design life cycle. Typically, the process includes the following activities:

1. Conduct a needs assessment to determine what the new or modified system should do. (This is the portion of the process typically known as a *systems analysis*.)
2. Assess the feasibility of implementing the new/modified system.
3. Generate a set of alternative plans for the new/modified system. (At this point, the team involved with designing and developing the system usually prepares a *requirements document*, which contains specifications of the requirements of the system, the feasibility analysis, and system development alternatives.)
4. Evaluate the alternatives and choose one for implementation.
5. Design the system.
6. Develop and test the system.
7. Implement the system. This includes various strategies for phasing out any existing system.
8. Evaluate the system.

The reason the preceding process is known as a "cycle" is that when you finish Step 8, you go right back to Step 1 to modify the system to handle any problems identified in the evaluation (see Figure 2.1). If no problems were found during the evaluation, then you wait a while and evaluate again. However, the process is also sometimes called the *waterfall method* because the project falls from one step to another, like the waterfall in Figure 2.2.

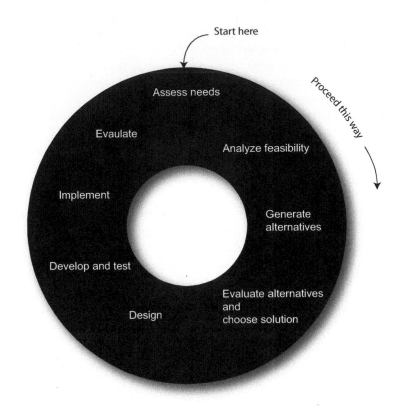

■ FIGURE 2.1   The traditional systems development life cycle.

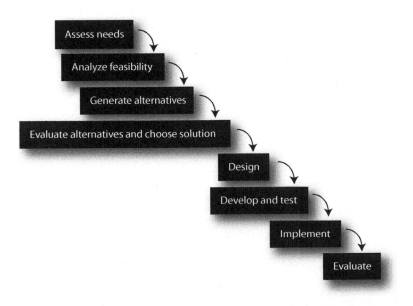

■ FIGURE 2.2   The waterfall view of the traditional systems development life cycle.

Database designers are typically involved in Steps 1 through 5. The database design itself takes place during Step 5, but that process can't occur until the preceding steps are completed.

Conducting the Needs Assessment

The needs assessment, in the opinion of many systems analysts, is the most important part of the systems development process. No matter how well developed, even the best information system is useless if it doesn't meet the needs of its organization. A system that is not used represents wasted money.

A systems analyst has many tools and techniques available to help identify the needs of a new or modified information system:

- Observation: The systems analyst observes employees without interference. This allows users to demonstrate how they actually use the current system (be it automated or manual).
- Interviews: The systems analyst interviews employees at various levels in the organizational hierarchy. This process allows employees to communicate what works well with the current system and what needs to be changed. During the interviews, the analyst attempts to identify the differences among the perceptions of managers and those who work for them.

Sometimes a systems analyst will discover that what actually occurs is not what is supposed to be standard operating procedure. If there is a difference between what is occurring and the way in which things "should" happen, then either employee behavior will need to change or procedures will need to change to match employee behavior. It is not the systems analyst's job to make the choice, but only to document what is occurring and to present alternative solutions.

Occasionally observations and interviews can expose informal processes that may or may not be relevant to a new system. Consider what happened to a systems analyst who was working on a team that was developing an automated system for a large metropolitan library system. (This story is based on an incident that actually occurred in the 1980s.) The analyst was assigned to interview staff of the mobile services branch, the group that provided bookmobiles as well as individualized service to home-bound patrons. The process in question was book selection and ordering.

Here is how it was supposed to happen. Each week, the branch received a copy of a publication called *Publishers Weekly*. This magazine, which is still available, not only documents the publishing trade, but also lists and reviews forthcoming media (at the time, primarily books). The librarians (four adult librarians and one children's librarian) were to go through the magazine and place a checkmark by each book the branch should order. Once a month, the branch librarian was to take the marked up magazine to the central order meeting with all the other branch librarians in the system. All books with three or more checks should be ordered, although the branch librarian was to exercise her own judgment and knowledge of the branch patrons to help make appropriate choices.

The preceding is what the systems analyst heard from the branch librarian. The five librarians, however, told a different story. At one point, they concluded that the branch librarian wasn't exercising any judgment at all but was simply ordering all books with three checks. There was only one children's librarian and therefore children's books almost never received three checks. Few children's books were being ordered.

To test their theory, the librarians placed four checkmarks next to a significantly inappropriate title—a coffee table book that was too heavy for many of their elderly patrons and that exceeded the branch's price limit—and waited to see what would happen. The coffee table book was ordered. It was clear to them that no professional judgment was being used at the order meeting.

The librarians, therefore, took the situation into their own hands. When the branch librarian returned from the order meeting, she gave the copy of the *Publishers Weekly* to one of the clerks, who created cards for each ordered book. The cards were to be matched to the new books when they arrived. However, the librarians arranged for the clerk to let them see the cards as soon as they were made. The librarians removed books that shouldn't be ordered and added those that had been omitted (primarily, children's books). The clerk then phoned the changes to the order department.

What should the analyst have done? The process was clearly broken. The branch librarian wasn't doing her job. The librarians had arranged things so that the branch functioned well, but they were circumventing standard operating procedure (SOP) and were probably placing their jobs in danger by doing so. This was a case of "the end justifies the means." No one was being harmed and the branch patrons were being helped. How should the analyst have reported her findings? Should she have exposed what was really happening or should she simply have documented how the procedure was *supposed* to work? What would happen when the ordering process was automated and there were no longer any centralized order meetings? There would be no order cards held at the branch and no opportunity for the librarians to correct the book order.

This was a very delicate situation because if it were exposed either the branch librarian and/or the other librarians would face significant problems. A systems analyst's job is to observe, interview, and record, not to intervene in employee relations. The book ordering process would be changing anyway with an automated system. If the librarians were to need to continue to work around the branch librarian, they would need to change their informal process as well. Therefore, the best strategy for the analyst probably was to remove herself from the personnel problems and report the process as it was supposed to work.

In other cases, where informal procedures do not violate SOP, an analyst can feel free to report what is actually occurring. This will help in tailoring the new information system to the way in which the business actually operates.

- Questionnaires: The systems analyst prepares questionnaires to be completed by employees. Like interviews, questionnaires give the systems analyst information about what is working currently and what needs to be fixed. The drawback to questionnaires, however, is that they are limited by the questions asked—even if they include open-ended questions—and may miss important elements of what a system needs to do.
- Focus groups: The systems analyst conducts a focus group to hear from employees who don't use the system directly and those who may not be employees, but who use the system in some way. For example, accountants may not use the payroll system directly, but may receive output from that system as input to the accounting system. A focus group can give them a forum to express how well the input meets their needs and how it might be changed to better suit them. A retail firm that sells through a Web site may conduct a focus group for customers to find out what changes should be made to the catalog and shopping cart interfaces.

Focus groups can be a double-edged sword. The members of the focus group are not privy to many of the constraints under which a business operates and the limitations of technology. Their suggestions may be impractical. The analyst conducting the focus session needs to be careful not to make promises to group members that can't be kept. Participants in a focus group can have their expectations raised so high that those expectations can never be met, creating disappointment and disaffection with the business.

- Brainstorming sessions: When employees know that something is not right with the current system, but are unable to articulate how it should be changed, a brainstorming session allows people to toss about ideas that may or may not be feasible. The intent is to stimulate everyone's thinking about the needs of a new or modified system without being critical.

The results of the needs assessment are collected into a *requirements document* or a requirements database. At this point in the process, the needs identified by the analyst are expressed in general terms. For example, the requirements document might include a need for a new Web site shopping cart that allowed users to check out on one page rather than three. The fact that the redesigned Web page needs to include the customer's area code as a separate piece of data is not documented at this point.

Assessing Feasibility

Once the operational requirements of a new system have been documented, the systems analyst turns to assessing the feasibility of the required system. There are three types of feasibility that systems analysts consider:

- Operational feasibility: Is it possible to develop a system that will fit within the organization's way of doing business or are any business process changes required realistic?
- Technical feasibility: Does the technology exist to implement a system to meet the organization's needs? (This includes not only the technology to implement the system, but the technology to provide adequate security.)
- Financial feasibility: Are the costs of implementing the system in a range that the organization is able/willing to pay?

Operational feasibility looks at whether it makes sense for the company to change any part of its operating procedures to accommodate a new system. If payroll employees enter data currently from time cards by hand, a change to a machine-readable system is operationally feasible. The procedure for entering hours worked changes slightly, but the employees will still use some sort of time card, and payroll employees will still be processing the data. In contrast, consider the situation where a new system would require all purchase requisitions to be placed using an online form. However, some offices in remote locations do not have consistent Internet access. It is therefore not feasible to shut down paper-based requisitions entirely.

Operational feasibility also relies to a large extent on an organization's and its employees' willingness to change. Assume, for example, that insurance company representatives fill out currently paper forms when making a sale at a customer's home. The company would like to replace the paper with laptops or tablets to exchange data with the home office. Certainly, this is a reasonable choice given the way in which the company operates, but if many of the salespeople are resistant to working with the mobile hardware, then a project to introduce the new devices may fail. Sometimes the introduction of new technology, especially in a manufacturing environment, is crucial to maintaining a company's competitive position and therefore its ability to stay in business. Employees who are resistant to the new technology (either unwilling or unable to be retrained) may need to be laid off to ensure that the company survives.

Technological feasibility is relatively easy to assess. Can the necessary technology be purchased? If not, is it possible to develop that technology in a reasonable amount of time and at a reasonable cost? Consider, for example, the situation of a rural library cooperative in the mid-1980s. Most library information systems used minicomputers. However, the rural cooperative was interested in a client-server architecture, with small servers at each library. Before proceeding, the cooperative needed to determine whether such a system actually existed or whether one was soon to become available.[1]

Financial feasibility means asking the question: "Can we afford it?" Often the answer is "We can't afford not to do this." In such a situation, an organization will spend as much as it can to implement a new information system. To assess financial feasibility, an organization will undertake some type of cost/benefit analysis to answer the question "Do the benefits justify the costs?".

Because no specific system alternative has been selected at this point, financial feasibility assessment is often very general. It can be conducted in-house or an outside firm can be hired to conduct the analysis. The analysis includes market research to describe the market, its size, and typical customers as well as competition in the marketplace. From those data, the analyst can estimate demand for the company's product and generate an estimate of revenue. In addition to hardware and software costs, the cost estimates include facility expenses (rental, construction, and so on), financing (loan costs), and personnel expenses (hiring, training, salaries, and so on). The result is a projection of how a new information system will affect the bottom line of the company. As with the needs assessment, the results of the feasibility analysis are presented as part of the requirements document.

One thing to keep in mind during a feasibility analysis is that the systems analyst—whether an employee of the company contemplating a new system or an employee of an outside firm hired specifically to conduct the analysis—will not be making the decision as to whether an entire project will proceed. The decision is made by the organization's management.

Generating Alternatives

The third section in the system requirements document is a list of two or more system design alternatives for an organization to consider. Often they will be distinguished by cost (low cost, medium cost, and high cost). However, the first alternative is almost always "do nothing": Keep the current system.

A low-cost alternative generally takes advantage of as much existing facilities, hardware, and software as possible. It may rely more on changing employee behavior than installing new technology.

---

[1]The final decision was to become beta-testers for the first library client-server hardware/software combination. Although the cooperative did have to deal with some bugs in the system, they paid less than would have otherwise.

A moderate-cost alternative includes some new hardware and software purchases, some network modification, and some changes of employee behavior. It may not, however, include the top-of-the-line hardware or software. It may also use off-the-shelf software packages rather than custom-programmed applications. Employee training may include sending users to take classes offered by hardware and software vendors, either in person or online.

The high-cost solution usually includes the best of everything. Hardware and software are top-of-the-line and include a significant amount of excess capacity. Custom-programming is included where appropriate. Employee training includes on-site seminars tailored specifically to the organization.

Labor is an ongoing cost. Regardless of the alternative, the cost of personnel to keep the system running over time needs to be included. Labor costs, however, continue to increase and therefore are often underestimated.

Evaluating and Choosing an Alternative

Evaluating alternatives involves assigning numeric values for costs and benefits to of each alternative. Some costs are easy to quantify, especially the cost of hardware and prepackaged software. Labor can be estimated relatively easily as well (although as noted earlier, costs may rise significantly over time).

However, assigning dollar values to the benefits of a systems development project can be difficult because they are often intangible:

- When a system is being designed to generate an increase in sales volume, the amount of increase is by its very nature an estimate.
- Increased customer satisfaction and better employee attitudes are difficult to measure.
- Impact on system maintenance costs and future system development costs are at best an estimate.

Note: Doing nothing may not be the cost-free alternative that it at first appears to be. When doing nothing means losing customers because they can't order online, then doing nothing has a negative cost.

The analyst completes the requirements document by adding the cost/benefit analyses of the proposed alternatives and then presents it to company management. Although the requirements document typically includes specific groups of hardware, software, and labor for each alternative, management may decide to use part of one alternative (for example, existing hardware) and part of another (for example, custom-written application programs).

Once company management agrees to the project and its specifications, the requirements document can become a contract between IT and management, defining what IT will provide and what management should expect. The more seriously all parties view the document as a contract, the more likely the system development project is to succeed.

Creating Design Requirements

The alternative chosen by an organization is usually expressed as a general strategy such as "implement a new Web site backed by an inventory database." Although many of the exact requirements of the database were collected during the systems analysis phase of the life cycle, company management usually doesn't really care about the details of which specific data will be in the database. The system that they chose has been specified as a series of outputs, the details of which may not have been designed as of yet.

Therefore, the first job in the design phase is to document exactly what data should be in the database and the details of application programs. This is the time when user interfaces are designed and an organization begins to build its data dictionary. Once the data specifications are in place, actual database design can begin.

Alternative Analysis Methods

As mentioned at the beginning of this chapter, the structured design life cycle works best when the requirements of an information system can be specified before development of the system begins. However, that is not always possible. Users may be able to express a general need—such as "It is imperative that we speed up the order entry process"— but are unable to articulate exactly what they want to see. In that situation, users may need the system developer to produce something to which they can react. They may not be able to articulate their needs in detail, but can indicate whether an existing piece of software works for them and if it does not, how the software should be changed to better meet their needs.

Prototyping

Prototyping is a form of systems development that is appropriate particularly in many situations where the exact requirements of an information system are not known in advance. Often the potential users know that help is needed, but can't articulate exactly what they want. The developer therefore begins by creating a shell for the system, consisting of user interface components but not necessarily any of the programs or databases behind them. This is the *prototype.*

The developer shows the users the prototype and lets them react to it. Based on user comments, the developer refines the prototype. The next version shown to the users may include user interface changes and some of the background programming.

The process can be summarized as:

1. Get a general idea of what the new information system should do.
2. Create a prototype.
3. Let the users react to the prototype.
4. Refine the prototype based on user input.
5. Return to step 3.
6. Repeat as many times as necessary until the users are satisfied.

A prototype may be missing some of the features of the final system. For example, initial programming may not include some of the security features or integrity controls that are likely to appear in the production product.

A prototype may be enhanced until it becomes the final system (*evolutionary prototyping*). In contrast, the prototype may be discarded once system requirements have been determined and the final system developed from scratch (*throwaway prototyping*). The latter is particularly useful when the code underlying the prototype has become difficult to follow (and thus maintain) because of the many changes that have been made during the prototyping process. Throwaway prototyping is also a very fast form of system development because it doesn't have to be "clean."

There are several drawbacks to prototyping. First, users may become confused between a prototype and a production system. They may expect the prototype to be a functioning whole and are therefore frustrated and disappointed when it is not. Second, prototyping doesn't include an analysis phase and relies solely on interaction between the users and the system developers to identify system requirements. Requirements that management may want to add to the system may not be included; users may leave out necessary system functions. Finally, prototyping may be expensive if the costs for developing the prototype are not controlled.

Database designers are usually involved after the first prototype is developed, and users have responded to it. The database design is created to provide whatever is needed to generate the outputs in the prototype and changes as the prototype is refined. The flexibility of relational database design is an enormous help to this methodology because of the ease in modifying the database structure.

Note: You will see an example of prototyping used in the case study in Chapter 14.

Spiral Methodology

The *spiral methodology* of systems analysis and design, which employs prototyping in a more formal way than the prototyping method, uses a gradual process in which each cycle further refines the system, bringing it closer to the desired end point. As you can see in Table 2.1, the methodology has four broad stages, each of which represents one trip around the spiral. The same type of activities is performed in each quadrant during each cycle. As you examine the table, also look at Figure 2.3. The activity numbers in the table correspond to the numbers on the spiral in the illustration.

Table 2.1 The Steps in the Spiral Systems Analysis and Design Methodology

Cycle	Quadrant	Specific Activities
Cycle 1	Quadrant 1: Plan next phases Quadrant 2: Determine objectives, abstractions, and constraints Quadrant 3: Evaluate alternatives; identify, resolve risks Quadrant 4: Design, verify next-level product	1. Requirements plan; life cycle plan 2. Risk analysis 3. Prototype #1 4. Concept of operation
Cycle 2	Quadrant 1: Plan next phases Quadrant 2: Determine objectives, abstractions, and constraints Quadrant 3: Evaluate alternatives; identify, resolve risks Quadrant 4: Design, verify next-level product	5. Development plan 6. Risk analysis 7. Prototype #2 8. Simulations 9. System requirements 10. Requirements validation 11. Integration and test plan
Cycle 3	Quadrant 1: Plan next phases Quadrant 2: Determine objectives, abstractions, and constraints Quadrant 3: Evaluate alternatives; identify, resolve risks Quadrant 4: Design, verify next-level product	12. Risk analysis 13. Prototype #3 14. Models 15. System design 16. Design validation and verification
Cycle 4	Quadrant 1: Plan next phases Quadrant 2: Determine objectives, abstractions, and constraints Quadrant 3: Evaluate alternatives; identify, resolve risks Quadrant 4: Design, verify next-level product	17. Determine process objectives, alternatives, and constraints. 18. Evaluate process alternatives, modify, resolve product risks 19. Design, verify next-level process plans 20. Risk analysis 21. Operational prototype 22. Benchmarks 23. Detailed design 24. Code 25. Unit test 26. Integration and test 27. Acceptance test 28. Implementation

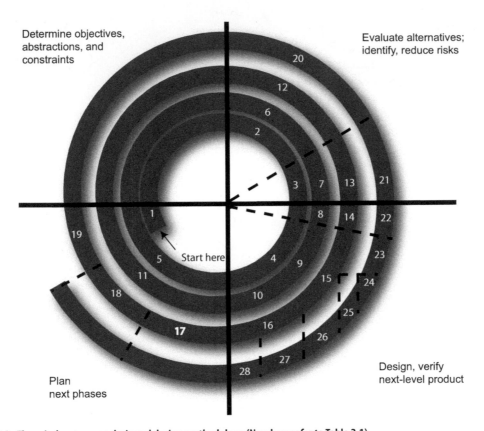

FIGURE 2.3 The spiral systems analysis and design methodology (Numbers refer to Table 2.1).

Notice that there are no specific activities listed for Quadrant 2 in any of the cycles. Systems analysis occurs in this quadrant, using the same techniques that are used to gather information for needs assessment in the traditional systems life cycle.

The spiral model is intended to address a perceived failing in the traditional system design cycle: analysis of the risk of the project. Although the traditional systems life cycle includes a feasibility analysis, there is no specific provision for looking at the chances that the system development project will succeed.

Because there are prototype systems created during every cycle, database designers may be involved from throughout the entire process, depending on the characteristics of each prototype. The flexibility of a database design to change during the iterative development process becomes essential so that the database can be refined just as the other parts of the new system.

Object-Oriented Analysis

Object-oriented analysis is a method for viewing the interaction of data and manipulations of data that is based on the object-oriented programming paradigm. The traditional systems lifecycle looks at the outputs the system requires and then assembles the database so that it contains the data needed to produce those outputs. Documentation reflects the "input–process–output" approach, such that the inputs are identified to achieve a specified output; the process of translating the inputs into desired outputs is where the database and the programs that manipulate the database are found. Where the traditional systems analysis life cycle looks at data and data manipulation as two distinct parts of the system, object-oriented analysis focuses on units (*classes*) that combine data and procedures.

Although a complete discussion of object-oriented analysis and design is well beyond the scope of this book, a small example might help to make the distinction between traditional and object-oriented analysis clearer.[2] Assume that you are developing a system that will provide an employee directory of a company. Both forms of analysis begin with the requirements, such as the ability to search for employees in the directory and the ability to update employee information. Then the two approaches diverge.

Traditional analysis indicates the specifics of the application programs that will provide the updating and searching capabilities. The database specifications include the data needed to support those applications. The requirements document might contain something like Figure 2.4. The database itself

```
%NAME prepare_online_directory
%DEFINITION
Format and display an electronic version of the employee directory

%NAME prepare_print_directory
%DEFINITION
Format a directory for hard copy output

%NAME search_for_employee
%DEFINITION
Find an employee using the format "Last name, first name"

%NAME update_employee_information
%DEFINITION
Insert, modify, and delete employee information
```

■ **FIGURE 2.4** Requirements for the employee directory.

---

[2]Details of the object-oriented paradigm and its role in relational databases can be found in Chapter 27.

```
        Employee
------------------------
      employee_id
       first_name
       last_name
     street_address
          city
          state
           zip
        birthdate
           ssn
       home_phone
      office_number
     office_extension
         e_mail
```

■ **FIGURE 2.5 A graphic representation of the data describing an employee for the employee directory.**

would not have been designed. When it is, an employee might be represented something like Figure 2.5.

In contrast, object-oriented analysis specifies both the data and procedures together. In Figure 2.6 you will find a graphic representation of the employee directory environment. The rectangle labeled Employee is a class representing a single employee. The middle section of the rectangle contains the data that describe an employee for the directory. The bottom portion lists the things that an employee *object* (an instance of the class containing actual data) knows how to do.

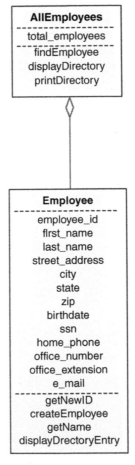

■ **FIGURE 2.6 A graphic representation of the object-oriented approach to the employee directory.**

The rectangle labeled AllEmployees is a class that gathers all the employee objects together (an *aggregation*). Procedures that are to be performed on all of the employees are part of this class. Diagrams of this type form the basis of an object-oriented requirements document and system design.

Object-oriented analysis is well-suited for large projects, especially those where requirements are likely to change as the system is being designed and developed. As object-oriented software development has replaced structured programming, object-oriented systems analysis has become increasingly popular.

For Further Reading

Arnowitz, J., Arent, M., Berger, N., 2006. Effective Prototyping for Software Makers. Morgan Kaufmann.

Boehm, B., 1998. A Spiral Model of Software Development and Enhancement. IEEE Computer 21, 5, 61–72.

Clegg, B., Birch, P., 2007. Instant Creativity: Techniques to Ignite Innovation & Problem Solving. Kogan Page.

Dennis, A., Wixom, B.H., Roth, R.M., 2014. Systems Analysis and Design, sixth ed. Wiley.

Hiatt, J., Creasey, T., 2012. Change Management: The People Side of Change, second ed. Prosci Learning Center Publications.

Hoffer, J.A., George, J., VAlacich, J.A., 2013. Modern Systems Analysis and Design, seventh ed. Prentice Hall.

Kendall, K.E., Kendall, J.E., 2013. Systems Analysis and Design, ninth ed. Prentice Hall.

Kock, N.F., 2006. Systems Analysis & Design Fundamentals: A business Process Redesign Approach. Sage Publications.

Kotter, J.P., Harvard Business Review, 2011. HBR's 10 Must Reads on Change Management. Harvard Business Review Press.

Krueger, R.A., 2008. Focus Groups: A Practical Guide for Applied Research, fourth ed. Sage Publications.

Luecke, R., 2003. Managing Change and Transition. Harvard Business School Press.

Shoval, P., 2006. Functional and Object Oriented Analysis and Design: An Integrated Methodology. IGI Global.

Whitten, J., 2005. Systems Analysis and Design Methods, seventh ed. McGraw-Hill/Irwin.

Part II

Relational Database Design Theory

This part of the book considers the theoretical aspects of relational database design. You will read about identifying data relationships in your database environment, the details of the relational data model, and how to translate data relationships into a well-designed relational database that avoids most of the problems associated with bad designs.

Chapter
3

Why Good Design Matters

Many of today's businesses rely on their database systems for accurate, up-to-date information. Without those repositories of mission-critical data, most businesses are unable to perform their normal daily transactions, much less create summary reports that help management make corporate decisions. To be useful, the data in a database must be accurate, complete, and organized in such a way that data can be retrieved when needed and in the format desired.

Well-written database application programs—whether they execute locally, run over a local area network, or feed information to a Web site—are fundamental to timely and accurate data retrieval. However, without a good underlying database design, even the best program cannot avoid problems with inaccurate and inconsistent data.

Effects of Poor Database Design

To make it a bit clearer why the design of a database matters so much, let's take a look at a business that has a very bad design, and the problems that the poor design brings. The business is named *Antique Opticals and DVDs* (called *Antique Opticals* for short by its regular customers).

Note: Remember the definition of a database that was presented in Chapter 1. As you will see, the data storage used by Antique Opticals and DVDs isn't precisely a database.

Back in the early 1980s, when most people were just discovering videotapes, Mark Watkins and Emily Stone stumbled across a fledgling technology known as the laser disc. There were several competing formats, but by 1986 the industry had standardized on a 12-inch silver platter on which either 30 or 60 minutes of video and audio could be recorded on each side. Although the market was still small, it was at that time that Watkins and

Stone opened the first incarnation of their business, originally named *Lasers Only*, to sell and rent laser discs. Some of its income came from sales and rentals directly from its single retail store. However, the largest part of its revenue came from mail-order sales.

The appearance of DVDs in 1995 put a quick end to the release of new laser discs. The last new title was released in 2000, but the number of new titles had decreased significantly even before that time. Watkins and Stone saw their business dwindling rapidly in the late 1990s.

The owners of *Lasers Only* realized that they needed to change their merchandise focus, if they were to continue in business. Laser discs were now the "antiques" of the optical media world, with DVDs—and most recently Blu-ray high-definition discs—the currently technology.

Antique Opticals and DVDs now sells and rents DVDs and Blu-ray discs from the retail store. It also sells used laser discs it purchases, used, from those who wish to sell them.

The company has a primitive Web site for mail order sales. The current catalog is updated weekly and uploaded to the site, where users place orders. However, the catalog is not integrated with any live data storage. An employee must take the order from the Web site and then shop for the customer. As a result, customers occasionally do not receive their entire order, when ordered items have been sold at the retail store. This is particularly true in the case of used laser discs, where the quantity in stock is rarely more than one per title.

In 1990, when the store began its mail order business, Watkins create a "database" to handle the orders and sales. Customers were (and still are) enticed to order titles before the official release date by offering a 15–20 percent discount on preorders. (All titles are always discounted 10 percent from the suggested retail price.) The mail order database (which has evolved into today's Web order database) therefore needed to include a way to handle backorders so that preordered items could be shipped as soon as they came into the store.

At the time we visit *Antique Opticals*, it is still using the software Watkins created. The primary data entry interface is a form like that in Figure 3.1.

Customer numbers are created by combining the customer's zip code, the first three letters of his or her last name, and a three-digit sequence number. For example, if Stone lives in zip code 12345 and she is the second customer in that zip code with a last name beginning with STO, then her customer number is 12345STO002. The sequence numbers ensure that no two customer numbers will be the same.

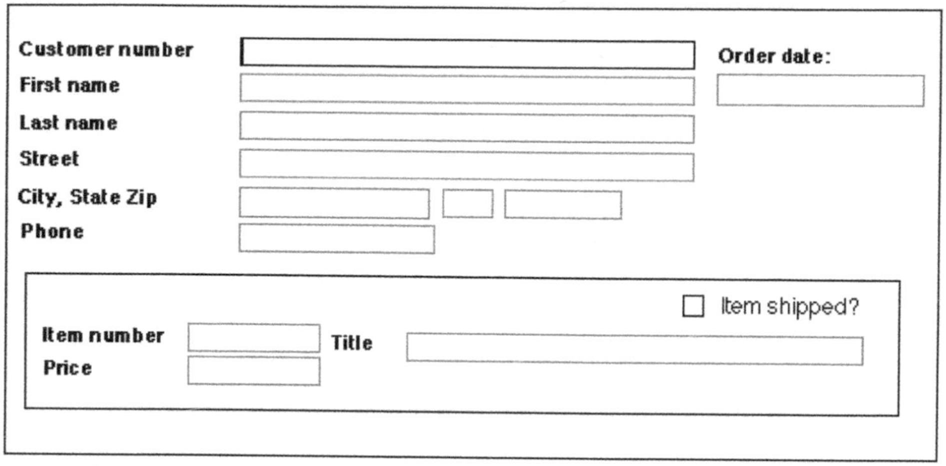

■ FIGURE 3.1   The data entry form used by *Antique Opticals* and DVDs for their mail order business.

Let's assume that Ms. Stone places an order for three items. One copy of all the data collected on the data entry form for each item ordered will be stored in the database. Therefore, an *Antique Opticals* employee fills out the form three times with the data found in Figure 3.2. The most important thing to notice is that the customer number, customer name, customer address, and customer phone number are duplicated for each item on the order. Those data will be stored three times.

When a new title comes into the store, an employee searches the database to find all people who have preordered that title. The employee prints a packing slip from the stored data and then places an X in the "item shipped" check box.

At first glance, *Antique Opticals'* software seems pretty simple and straightforward. Should work just fine, right? (This is assuming we ignore the issue of integration with the Web site.) Well, it worked well for a while, but as the business expanded, problems began to arise.

Unnecessary Duplicated Data and Data Consistency

The *Antique Opticals* database has a considerable amount of duplicated data that probably don't need to be duplicated:

- A customer's name, address, and phone number are duplicated for every item the customer orders.
- A merchandise item's title is duplicated every time the item is ordered.

Customer number	12345STO002		Order date:
First name	Emily		
Last name	Stone		
Street	89 Main Street		
City, State Zip	Anytown	NY	12345
Phone	914-555-1234		

☐ Item shipped?

| Item number | 15992345 | Title | Return of the Jedi |
| Price | 52.99 | | |

Customer number	12345STO002		Order date:
First name	Emily		
Last name	Stone		
Street	89 Main Street		
City, State Zip	Anytown	NY	12345
Phone	914-555-1234		

☐ Item shipped?

| Item number | 19339900 | Title | Lawrence of Arabia |
| Price | 75.99 | | |

Customer number	12345STO002		Order date:
First name	Emily		
Last name	Stone		
Street	89 Main Street		
City, State Zip	Anytown	NY	12345
Phone	914-555-1234		

☐ Item shipped?

| Item number | 56892144 | Title | Gone with the Wind |
| Price | 63.00 | | |

■ FIGURE 3.2 The data entered by an *Antique Opticals* employee for a three-item order.

What is the problem with this duplication? When you have duplicated data in this way, the data should be the same throughout the database. In other words, every order for a given customer should have the same name, address, and phone number, typed exactly the same way. Every order for a single title should have the exact same title, typed exactly the same way. We want the duplicated data to be consistent throughout the database.

As the database grows larger, this type of consistency is very hard to maintain. Most business-oriented database software is *case sensitive*, in that it considers upper- and lowercase letters to be different characters. In addition, no one is a perfect typist. A difference in capitalization, or even a single mistyped letter, will cause database software to consider two values to be distinct.

When an *Antique Opticals* employee performs a search to find all people who have ordered a specific title, the database software will retrieve only those orders that match the title entered by the employee exactly. For example, assume that a movie named *Summer Days* is scheduled to be released soon. In some orders, the title is stored correctly as "Summer Days." However, in others it is stored as "summer days" or even "sumer days." When an employee searches for all the people to whom the movie should be shipped, the orders for "summer days" and "sumer days" will not be retrieved. Those customers will not receive their orders, resulting in disgruntled customers and, probably, lost business.

The current *Antique Opticals* software has no way to ensure that duplicated data are entered consistently. There are two solutions. The first is to eliminate as much of the duplicated data as possible. (As you will see, it is neither possible nor desirable to eliminate all of it.) The second is to provide some mechanism for verifying that, when data must be duplicated, they are entered correctly. A well-designed database will do both.

Note: Unnecessary duplicated data also take up extra disk space, but given that disk space is relatively inexpensive today, that isn't a major reason for getting rid of redundant data.

Data Insertion Problems

When operations first began, the *Lasers Only* staff generated the catalog of forthcoming titles by hand. By 1995, however, Stone realized that this was a very cumbersome process and thought it would be much better if the catalog could be generated from the database.

Why not get a list of forthcoming titles from the database and have an application program generate the entire catalog? As Stone discovered, it could not be done from the existing database. There were two major reasons.

First, the database did not contain all of the information needed for the catalog, in particular a synopsis of all the content of the disc. This problem could be remedied by adding that information to the database. However, doing so would only exacerbate the problem with unnecessary duplicated data if the company were to include the summary with every order. If the summary were to be included only once, how would the company know which order contained the summary?

Second, and by far more important, there is no way to enter data about a title unless someone has ordered it. This presents a large Catch-22. The company could not insert data about a title unless it had been ordered at least once, but customers would not know that it was available to be ordered without seeing it in the catalog. But the catalog could not contain data about the new title until someone was able to get the data into the database, and that could not happen until the title has been ordered.

Note: This problem is more formally known as an "insertion anomaly," and you will learn about it more formally throughout this book.

Antique Opticals solved the problem by creating a second database for forthcoming titles from which the catalog could be generated. Unfortunately, the second database produced problems of its own, in particular because it introduced yet another source of duplicated data. The catalog database and the orders database did not communicate to verify that duplicated data are consistent, creating another potential source of errors in the orders database.

Data Deletion Problems

Antique Opticals also has problems when it comes to deleting data. Assume, for example, that a customer orders only one item. After the order has been processed, the item is discontinued by the manufacturer. *Antique Opticals* therefore wants to delete all references to the item from its database because the item is no longer available.

When the orders containing the item are deleted, information about any customer who has ordered only that item is also deleted. No other orders remain in the database for that customer. *Antique Opticals* will be unable to e-mail that customer any more catalogs and must hope that the customer visits the Web site without being contacted by the company. A very real potential exists that *Antique Opticals* has lost that individual as a customer.

Note: This problem is more formally known as a "deletion anomaly." It, too, will be discussed in greater depth throughout this book.

Meaningful Identifiers

The *Antique Opticals* orders database has another major problem: those customer numbers. It is very tempting to code meaning into identifiers, and it usually works well—until the values on which the identifiers are based change.

Consider what happens when an *Antique Opticals* customer moves into a different zip code. The person's customer number must change. At that point, there will be orders for the same customer with two different customer numbers in the same database.

If a customer who has moved since first ordering from the store calls and asks for a list of all items he or she has on order, the first thing the employee who answers the telephone does is ask the customer for his or her customer number. The customer, of course, provides the current value, which means that anything ordered under the old customer number will be missed during a search. The customer may assume that titles ordered under the old customer number are not on order. As a result, the customer may place another order, causing two copies of the same item to be shipped. *Antique Opticals* is then faced with another disgruntled customer who has to make the effort to send back the duplicate, and get the second charge removed from his or her credit card.

The Bottom Line

The bottom line is that what might initially seem like a simple, good design for data storage may present problems that will affect the consistency and accuracy of the data in the long run. Don't forget that the major goal with a database is to retrieve data accurately when it is needed. A bad design can make achieving that goal very difficult, especially because you may not always know that a problem exists. It is therefore worth the time and effort needed to design your database well from the start.

Chapter
4

Entities and Relationships

In this chapter, we will look at the basis for all database systems: the relationships between elements in the database environment. The formal way in which you express data relationships to a database management system (DBMS) is known as a *data model*. The relational data model, about which you will learn in this book, is just such a formal structure. However, the underlying relationships in a database are independent of the data model and, therefore, also independent of the DBMS you are using. Before you can design a database for any data model, you need to be able to identify data relationships.

Note: Most DBMSs support only one data model. Therefore, when you choose a DBMS, you are also choosing your data model.

Entities and Their Attributes

Most database designs begin by identifying entities. An *entity* is something about which we store data. A customer is an entity, as is a merchandise item stocked by *Antique Opticals*. Entities are not necessarily tangible. For example, an event such as a concert is an entity; an appointment to see a doctor is an entity.

Entities have data that describe them (their *attributes*). For example, a customer entity is usually described by a customer number, first name, last name, street, city, state, zip code, and phone number. A concert entity might be described by a title, date, location, and name of the performer.

When we represent entities in a database, we actually store only the attributes. Each group of attributes that describes a single real-world occurrence of an entity acts to represent an *instance* of an entity. For example, in Figure 4.1, you can see four instances of a customer entity stored in a database. If we have 1000 customers in our database, then there will be 1000 collections of customer attributes.

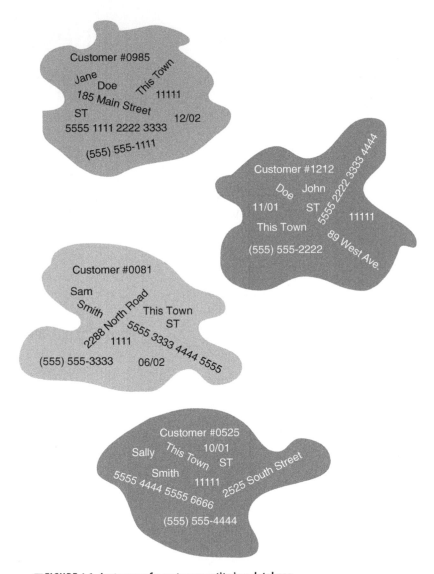

■ FIGURE 4.1 Instances of a customer entity in a database.

Note: Keep in mind that we are not making any statements about how the instances are physically stored. What you see in Figure 4.1 is purely a conceptual representation.

Entity Identifiers

The only purpose for putting the data that describe an entity into a database (an instance of the entity) is to retrieve the data at some later date. This means that we must have some way of distinguishing one entity instance from another, so that we can always be certain that we are retrieving the precise instance we want. We do this by ensuring that each entity instance has some attribute values that distinguish it from every other instance of the same entity in the database (an *entity identifier*).

Assume, for example, that *Antique Opticals* has only two customers named John Smith. If an employee searches for the items John Smith has on order, which John Smith will the DBMS retrieve? In this case, both of them. Because there is no way to distinguish between the two customers, the result of the query will be inaccurate.

Antique Opticals solved the problem by creating unique customer numbers. That is indeed a common solution to identifying instances of entities where there is no simple unique identifier suggested by the data themselves.

Another solution would be to pair the customer's first and last names with his or her telephone number. This combination of pieces of data (a *concatenated identifier*) would also uniquely identify each customer. There are, however, two drawbacks to doing so. First, the identifier is long and clumsy; it would be easy to make mistakes when entering any of the parts. Second, if the customer's phone number changes, then the identifier must also change. As you read in Chapter 3, changes in an entity identifier can cause serious problems in a database.

Some entities, such as invoices, come with *natural identifiers* (the invoice number). We assign unique, meaningless numbers to others—especially accounts, people, places, and things. Still others require concatenated identifiers.

Note: We will examine the issue of what makes a good unique identifier more closely in Chapter 5, when we talk about "primary keys."

When we store an instance of an entity in a database, we want the DBMS to ensure that the new instance has a unique identifier. This is an example of a *constraint* on a database, a rule to which data must adhere. The enforcement of a variety of database constraints helps us to maintain data consistency and accuracy.

Single-Valued Versus Multivalued Attributes

Because we are eventually going to create a relational database, the attributes in our data model must be *single-valued*. This means that for a given instance of an entity, each attribute can have only one value. For example, the customer entity shown in Figure 4.1 allows only one telephone number for each customer. If a customer has more than one phone number, and wants them all included in the database, then the customer entity cannot handle them.

Note: While it is true that the conceptual data model of a database is independent of the formal data model used to express the structure of the data to a DBMS, we often make decisions on how to model the data based on the requirements of the formal data model we will be using. Removing multivalued attributes is one such case. You will also see an example of this when we deal with many-to-many relationships between entities, later in this chapter.

The existence of more than one phone number turns the phone number attribute into a *multivalued attribute*. Because an entity in a relational database cannot have multivalued attributes, you must handle those attributes by creating an entity to hold them.

In the case of the multiple phone numbers, we could create a phone number entity. Each instance of the entity would include the customer number of the person to whom the phone number belonged, along with the telephone number. If a customer had three phone numbers, then there would be three instances of the phone number entity for the customer. The entity's identifier would be the concatenation of the customer number and the telephone number.

Note: There is no way to avoid using the telephone number as part of the entity identifier in the telephone number entity. As you will come to understand as you read this book, in this particular case, there is no harm in using it in this way.

Note: Some people view a telephone number as made of three distinct pieces of data: an area code, an exchange, and a unique number. However, in common use, we generally consider a telephone number to be a single value.

What is the problem with multivalued attributes? Multivalued attributes can cause problems with the meaning of data in the database, significantly slow down searching, and place unnecessary restrictions on the amount of data that can be stored.

Assume, for example, that you have an Employee entity, with attributes for the name and birthdates of dependents. Each attribute is allowed to store multiple values, as in Figure 4.2, where each gray blob represents a single instance of the Employee entity. How will you associate the correct birthdate with the name of the dependent to which it applies? Will it be by the position of a value stored in the attribute (in other words, the first name is related to the first birthdate, and so on)? If so, how will you ensure that there

■ **FIGURE 4.2** Entity instances containing multivalued attributes.

is a birthdate for each name, and a name for each birthdate? How will you ensure that the order of the values is never mixed up?

When searching a multivalued attribute, a DBMS must search each value in the attribute, most likely scanning the contents of the attribute sequentially. A sequential search is the slowest type of search available.

In addition, how many values should a multivalued attribute be able to store? If you specify a maximum number, what will happen when you need to store more than the maximum number of values? For example, what if you allow room for 10 dependents in the Employee entity just discussed, and you encounter an employee with 11 dependents? Do you create another instance of the Employee entity for that person? Consider all the problems that doing so would create, particularly in terms of the unnecessary duplicated data.

Note: Although it is theoretically possible to write a DBMS that will store an unlimited number of values in an attribute, the implementation would be difficult, and searching much slower than if the maximum number of values were specified in the database design.

As a general rule, if you run across a multivalued attribute, this is a major hint that you need another entity. The only way to handle multiple values of the same attribute is to create an entity of which you can store multiple instances, one for each value of the attribute (for example, Figure 4.3). In the case of the Employee entity, we would need a Dependent entity that could be related to the Employee entity. There would be one instance of the Dependent entity related to an instance of the Employee entity, for each of an employee's dependents. In this way, there is no limit to the number of an employee's dependents. In addition, each instance of the Dependent entity would contain the name and birthdate of only one dependent, eliminating any confusion about which name was associated with which birthdate. Searching would also be faster, because the DBMS could use fast searching techniques on the individual Dependent entity instances, without resorting to the slow sequential search.

Avoiding Collections of Entities

When you first begin to work with entities, the nature of an entity can be somewhat confusing. Consider, for example, the merchandise inventory handled by *Antique Opticals*. Is "inventory" an entity? No. Inventory is a collection of the merchandise items handled by the store. The entity is actually the merchandise item. Viewing all of the instances of the merchandise item entity as a whole provides the inventory.

To make this a bit clearer, consider the attributes you would need if you decided to include an inventory entity: merchandise item number, item title, number in stock, retail price, and so on. But because you are trying to describe an entire inventory with a single entity, you need multiple values for each of those attributes. As you read earlier, however, attributes should not be multivalued. This tells you that inventory cannot stand as an entity. It must be represented as a collection of instances of a merchandise item entity.

As another example, consider a person's medical history maintained by a doctor. Like an inventory, a medical history is a collection of more than one entity. A medical history is made up of appointments and the events that occur during those appointments. Therefore, the history is really a collection of instances of appointment entities and medical treatment entities. The "history" is an output that a database application can obtain by gathering the data stored in the underlying instances.

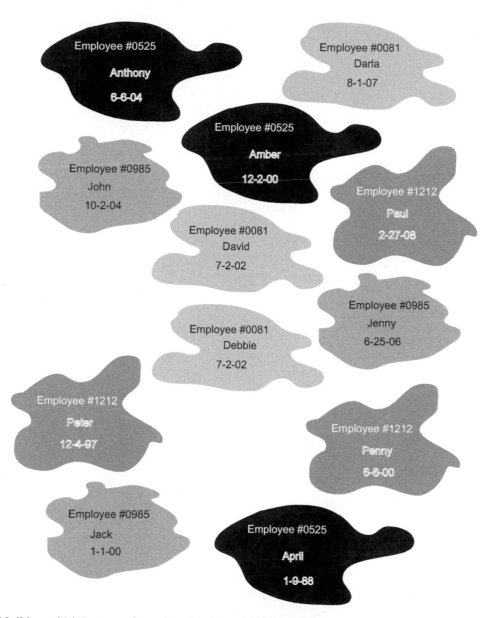

■ FIGURE 4.3 Using multiple instances of an entity to handle a multivalued attribute.

Documenting Entities and Their Attributes

Entity-relationship (ER) diagrams (ERDs) provide a way to document the entities in a database, along with the attributes that describe them. There are actually several styles of ER diagrams. Today, there are three major methods: the Chen model (named after the originator of ER modeling, Dr. Peter P.S. Chen), Information Engineering (IE, or "crows feet"), and Unified Modeling Language (UML). If you are not including object-oriented concepts in a data model, it really doesn't matter which you use, as long as everyone who is using the diagram understands the symbols. However, UML is specifically intended for the object-oriented environment, and is usually the choice when objects are included.

All three diagramming styles use rectangles to represent entities. Each entity's name appears in the rectangle, and is expressed in the singular, as in

customer

The original Chen model has no provision for showing attributes on the ER diagram itself. However, many people have extended the model to include the attributes in ovals:

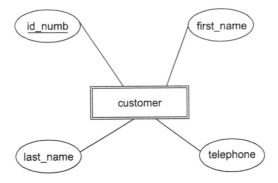

The entity's identifier is underlined (id_numb).

The IE and UML styles of ER diagramming include the attributes in the rectangle with the entity; the entity identifier is preceded by an asterisk (*):

Customer
*customer_numb customer_first_name customer_last_name customer_street customer_city customer_state customer_zip customer_phone

Because the IE and UML approaches tend to produce a less cluttered diagram, and because they are the more flexible styles, we will be using IE for most of the diagrams in this book, although you will be introduced to elements of the Chen style and the UML style throughout this chapter. When we introduce object-oriented concepts, we will be using the UML diagramming style.

Entities and Attributes for *Antique Opticals*

The major entities and their attributes for the *Antique Opticals* database can be found in Figure 4.4. As you will see, the design will require additional entities as we work with the relationships between those already identified. In particular, there is no information in Figure 4.4 that indicates which items appear on which orders, and no information about which used laser discs are purchased by the store during a single transaction. This occurs because the missing information is a part of the logical relationships between customers, orders, purchases, and items.

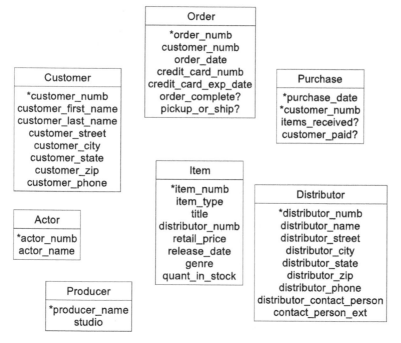

■ **FIGURE 4.4** Major entities and their attributes for the *Antique Opticals* database.

Note: The entities in Figure 4.4 and the remainder of the diagrams in this book were created with a special type of software known as a CASE tool (computer-aided software engineering). CASE tools provide a wide range of data and systems modeling assistance. You will find more details on how CASE tools support the database design process in Chapter 12.

Figure 4.4 demonstrates some of the choices made for the *Antique Opticals* database. Notice, for example, that there is only one entity for merchandise items, yet the store carries new DVDs, new blue-ray discs, and used laserdiscs. The *item_type* attribute distinguishes the three types of merchandise. Because all merchandise items are stored as the same type of entity, queries such as "Show me *Star Wars IV* in any format" will be easy to satisfy using just the item name, and queries such as "Do you have a used *Star Wars IV* laserdisc?" will be easy to satisfy using both the title of the item and its type.

Domains

Each attribute has a *domain*, an expression of the permissible values for that attribute. A domain can be very small. For example, a T-shirt store might have a Size attribute for its merchandise items, with the values L, XL, and XXL comprising the entire domain. In contrast, an attribute for a customer's first name is very large and might be specified only as "text" or "human names."

A DBMS enforces a domain through a *domain constraint*. Whenever a value is stored in the database, the DBMS verifies that it comes from the attribute's specified domain. Although in many cases we cannot specify small domains, at the very least the domain assures us that we are getting data of the right type. For example, a DBMS can prevent a user from storing 123×50 in an attribute whose domain is currency values. Most DBMSs also provide fairly tight domain checking on date and time attributes, which can help you avoid illegal dates, such as Feb. 30.

Documenting Domains

The common formats used for ER diagrams do not usually include domains on the diagrams themselves, but store the domains in an associated document (usually a *data dictionary*, something about which you will read much more throughout this book). However, the version of the Chen method that includes attributes can also include domains underneath each attribute. Notice in Figure 4.5 that three of the domains are fairly general (integer and character), while the domain for the telephone number attribute includes a very specific format. Whether a domain can be constrained in this way depends on the DBMS.

Note: There is no specific syntax for indicating domains. However, if you know which DBMS you will be using, consider using the data types supported by that product as domains in an ERD to simplify the later conversion to the DBMS's representation.

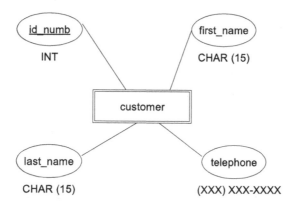

■ **FIGURE 4.5**   Indicating domains on an ER diagram.

Practical Domain Choices

The domains that *Antique Opticals* chooses for its attributes should theoretically be independent of the DBMS that the company will use. In practical terms, however, it makes little sense to assign domains that you cannot implement. Therefore, the database designer working for *Antique Opticals* takes a look at the DBMS to see what data types are supported.

Most relational DBMSs that use SQL as their query language provide the following among their data types, any of which can be assigned as a domain to an attribute:

- CHAR: A fixed-length string of text, usually up to 256 characters.
- VARCHAR: A variable-length string of text, usually up to 256 characters.
- INT: An integer, the size of which varies, depending on the operating system.
- DECIMAL and NUMERIC: Real numbers, with fractional portions assigned to the right of the decimal point. When you assign a real number domain, you must specify how many digits the number can contain (including the decimal point) and how many digits should be to the right of the decimal point (the value's *precision*). For example, currency values usually have a precision of two, so a number in the format XXX.XX might have a domain of DECIMAL (6,2).
- DATE: A date.
- TIME: A time.
- DATETIME: The combination of a date and a time.
- BOOLEAN: A logical value (true or false).

Many of today's DBMSs also support a data type known as a binary large object (BLOB) that can store anything binary, such as a graphic.

Choosing the right domain can make a big difference in the accuracy of a database. For example, a US zip code is made up of five or nine digits. Should an attribute for a zip code, therefore, be given a domain of INT? No, for two reasons. First, it would be nice to be able to include the hyphen in nine-digit zip codes. Second, and more importantly, zip codes in the northeast begin with a zero. If they are stored as a number, the leading zero disappears. Therefore, we always choose a CHAR domain for zip codes. Since we never do arithmetic with zip codes, nothing is lost by using character, rather than numeric storage.

By the same token, it is important to choose domains of DATE and TIME for chronological data. As an example, consider what would happen if the dates 01/12/2017 and 08/12/2016 were stored as characters. If you ask the DBMS to choose which date comes first, the DBMS will compare the character strings in alphabetical order and respond the 01/12/2017 comes first, because 01 alphabetically precedes 08. The only way to get character dates to order correctly is to use the format YYYY/MM/DD, a format that is rarely used anywhere in the world. However, if the dates were given a domain of DATE, then the DBMS would order them properly. The DBMS would also be able to perform date arithmetic, finding the interval between two dates or adding constants (for example, the correct number of days in a month) to dates.

Domains for Numbers

Does it really matter if you choose character or numeric domains for numbers? Yes, it matters a great deal. A computer's internal representation for characters and numbers are very different. When you use an integer or decimal domain, the computer stores a quantity that can be used in computations. Comparisons between values with numeric domains and the ordering of values work in correct numeric order as well. However, if you store a number as a character, the computer encodes the individual digits—typically using the ASCII coding scheme—as text. The ASCII code for a number is not equivalent to the mathematical value of a number. If you try to perform arithmetic using character-coded digits, the result will not be correct. Use character storage for numbers that will never be used in mathematic operations, such as ID numbers and zip codes. If there is even the slightest chance that a computation will be performed using a value, give it a numeric domain.

Basic Data Relationships

Once you have a good idea of the basic entities in your database environment, your next task is to identify the relationships among those entities. There are three basic types of relationships that you may encounter: one-to-one (1:1), one-to-many (1:M), and many-to-many (M:N or M:M).

Before turning to the types of relationships themselves, there is one important thing to keep in mind: The relationships that are stored in a database are between instances of entities. For example, an *Antique Opticals* customer is related to the items he or she orders. Each instance of the customer entity is related to instances of the specific items ordered (Figure 4.6).

■ FIGURE 4.6 Relationships between instances of entities in a database.

When we document data relationships, such as when we draw an ER diagram, we show the types of relationships among entities. We are showing the possible relationships that are allowable in the database. Unless we specify that a relationship is mandatory, there is no requirement that every instance of every entity be involved in every documented relationship. For example, *Antique Opticals* could store data about a customer without the customer having any orders to which it is related.

One-to-One Relationships

Consider, for a moment, an airport in a small town and the town in which the airport is located, both of which are described in a database of small town airports. Each of these might be represented by an instance of a different type of entity. The relationship between the two instances can be expressed as "The airport is located in one and only one town, and the town has one and only one airport."

This is a true *one-to-one relationship* because at no time can a single airport be related to more than one town and no town can be related to more than one airport. (Although there are municipalities that have more than one airport, the towns in the database are too small for that to ever happen.)

If we have instances of two entities (A and B) called A_i and B_i, then a one-to-one relationship exists if at all times A_i is related to no instances of entity B or one instance of entity B, and B_i is related to no instances of entity A or one instance of entity A.

True one-to-one relationships are very rare in business. For example, assume that *Antique Opticals* decides to start dealing with a new distributor of DVDs. At first, the company orders only one specialty title from the new distributor. If we peered inside the database, we would see that the instance of the distributor entity was related to just the one merchandise item instance. This would then appear to be a one-to-one relationship. However, over time, *Antique Opticals* may choose to order more titles from the new distributor, which would violate the rule that the distributor must be related to no more than one merchandise item. (This is an example of a one-to-many relationship, which is discussed in the next section of this chapter.)

By the same token, what if *Antique Opticals* created a special credit card entity to hold data about the credit cards that customers use to place orders? Each order can be charged to only one credit card. There would therefore seem to be a one-to-one relationship between an instance of an order entity and an instance of a credit card entity. However, in this case, we are really dealing with a single entity. The credit card number and the credit card's expiration date can become attributes of the order entity. Given that only one credit card is allowed per order, the attributes are not multivalued; no separate entity is needed.

If you think you are dealing with a one-to-one relationship, look at it very carefully. Be sure that you are not really dealing with a special case of a one-to-many relationship or two entities that should really be one.

One-to-Many Relationships

The most common type of relationship is a *one-to-many relationship.* (In fact, relational databases are constructed from the rare one-to-one relationship and numerous one-to-many relationships.) For example, *Antique Opticals* typically orders many titles from each distributor, and a given title comes from only one distributor. By the same token, a customer places many orders, but an order comes from only one customer.

If we have instances of two entities (A and B), then a one-to-many relationship exists between two instances (A_i and B_i) if A_i is related to zero, one, or more instances of entity B, and B_i is related to zero or one instance of entity A.

Other one-to-many relationships include that between a daughter and her biological mother. A woman may have zero, one, or more biological daughters; a daughter can have only one biological mother. As another example, consider a computer and its CPU. A CPU may not be installed in any computer, or it may be installed in at most one computer; a computer may have no CPU, one CPU, or more than one CPU.

The example about which you read earlier, concerning *Antique Opticals* and the distributor from which the company ordered only one title, is actually a one-to-many relationship where the "many" is currently "one." Remember that, when we are specifying data relationships, we are indicating possible relationships, and not necessarily requiring that all instances of all entities participate in every documented relationship. There is absolutely no requirement that a distributor be related to any merchandise item, much less one or more merchandise items. (It might not make much sense to have a distributor in the database from which the company does not order, but there is nothing to prevent data about that distributor from being stored.)

Many-to-Many Relationships

Many-to-many relationships are also very common. There is, for example, a many-to-many relationship between an order placed by an *Antique Opticals* customer and the merchandise items carried by the store. An order can contain multiple items; each item can appear on more than one order. The same is true of the orders placed with distributors. An order can contain multiple items, and each item can appear on more than one order.

A many-to-many relationship exists between entities A and B if for two instances of those entities (A_i and B_i), A_i can be related to zero, one, or more instances of entity B, and B_i can be related to zero, one, or more instances of entity A.

Many-to-many relationships present two major problems to a database's design. These issues, and the way in which we solve them, are discussed in the next major section of this chapter (Dealing with Many-to-Many Relationships).

Weak Entities and Mandatory Relationships

As we have been discussing types of data relationships, we have defined those relationships by starting each with "zero," indicating that the participation by a given instance of an entity in a relationship is optional. For example, *Antique Opticals* can store data about a customer in its database before the customer places an order. Therefore, an instance of the customer entity does not have to be related to any instances of the order entity.

However, the reverse is not true in this database. An order *must* be related to a customer. Without a customer, an order cannot exist. An order is, therefore, an example of a *weak entity*, one that cannot exist in the database, unless a related instance of another entity is present and related to it. An instance of the customer entity can be related to zero, one, or more orders. However, an instance of the order entity must be related to one and only one customer. The "zero" option is not available to a weak entity. The relationship between an instance of the order entity and an instance of the customer entity is, therefore, a *mandatory* relationship.

Identifying weak entities and their associated mandatory relationships can be very important for maintaining the consistency and integrity of the database. Consider the effect, for example, of storing an order without knowing the customer to whom it belongs. There would be no way to ship the item to the customer, causing a company to lose business.

By the same token, we typically specify the relationship between an order and the order lines (the specific items on the order) as mandatory, because we don't want to allow an order line to exist in the database without it being related to an order. (An order line is meaningless without knowing the order to which it belongs.)

In contrast, we can allow a merchandise item to exist in a database without indicating the supplier from which it comes (assuming that there is only one source per item). This lets us store data about new items before we have decided on a supplier. In this case, the relationship between a supplier and an item is not mandatory (sometimes described as zero-to-many, rather than one-to-many).

Documenting Relationships

The Chen, IE, and UML methods of drawing ER diagrams have different ways of representing relationships, each of which has its advantages in terms of the amount of information it provides and its complexity.

The Chen Method

The Chen method uses diamonds for relationships and lines with arrows to show the types of relationships between entities. For example, in Figure 4.7 you can see the relationship between an *Antique Opticals* customer and an order. The single arrow pointing toward the customer entity indicates that an order belongs to at most one customer. The double arrow pointing toward the order entity indicates that a customer can place one or more orders. The word within the relationship diamond gives some indication of the meaning of the relationship.

There are two alternative styles within the Chen method. The first (for example, Figure 4.8) replaces the arrows with numbers and letters. A "1" indicates that an order comes from one customer. The "M" (or an "N") indicates that a customer can place many orders.

FIGURE 4.7 Using the Chen method with relationship diamonds and arrows.

■ **FIGURE 4.8 A Chen ER diagram using letters and numbers rather than arrows to show relationships.**

The second alternative addresses the problem of trying to read the relationship in both directions when the name of the relationship is within the diamond. "Customer places order" makes sense, but "order places customer" does not. To solve the problem, this alternative removes the relationship name from the diamond and adds both the relationship and its inverse to the diagram, as in Figure 4.9. This version of the diagram can be read easily in either direction: "A customer places many orders" and "An order is placed by one customer."

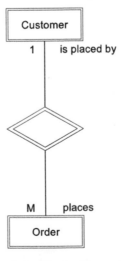

■ **FIGURE 4.9 Adding inverse relationships to a Chen method ER diagram.**

There is one major limitation to the Chen method of drawing ER diagrams: There is no obvious way to indicate weak entities and mandatory relationships. For example, an order should not exist in the database without a customer. Therefore, order is a weak entity, and its relationship with a customer is mandatory.

IE Style Diagrams

The IE diagramming style exchanges simplicity in line ends for added information. As a first example, consider Figure 4.10. This is the same one-to-many relationship we have been using to demonstrate the Chen method ER diagrams. However, in this case, the ends of the lines (some of which look a bit like "crow's feet") indicate which relationships are mandatory.

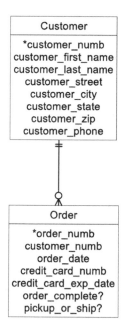

■FIGURE 4.10   A one-to-many relationship using the IE method.

The double line below the customer entity means that each order is related to one and only one customer. Because zero is not an option, the relationship is mandatory. In contrast, the 0 and crow's foot connected to the order entity mean that a customer may have zero, one, or more orders.

There are four symbols used at the ends of lines in an IE diagram:

- ||: One and one only (mandatory relationship)
- 0|: Zero or one

■ >1: One or more (mandatory relationship)

■ >0: Zero, one, or more

Although we often see the symbols turned 90 degrees, as they are in Figure 4.10, they are actually readable if viewed sideways as in the preceding list.

An IE method ER diagram often includes attributes directly on the diagram. As you can see in Figure 4.10, entity identifiers are marked with an asterisk.

UML Style Diagrams

UML notation for entity relationships is very similar to IE notation. However, the symbols at the ends of lines are replaced by numeric representations of the type of relationship (Figure 4.11).

The possible relationships are:

■ 1: One and only one (mandatory)

■ 1...*: One or more (mandatory)

■ 0...1: Zero or one

■ 0...*: Zero, one, or more

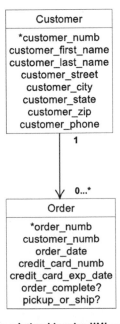

■FIGURE 4.11 A one-to-many relationship using UML notation.

Basic Relationships for Antique Opticals

The major entities in the *Antique Opticals* database are diagrammed in Figure 4.12. You read the relationships in the following way:

- One customer can place zero, one or more orders. An order comes from one and only one customer.
- The store may make many purchases of used discs from each customer. A purchase transaction comes from one and only one customer.
- An order has one or more items on it. An item can appear in zero, one, or more orders.
- A purchase is made up of one or more items. An item can be purchased zero, one, or more times.

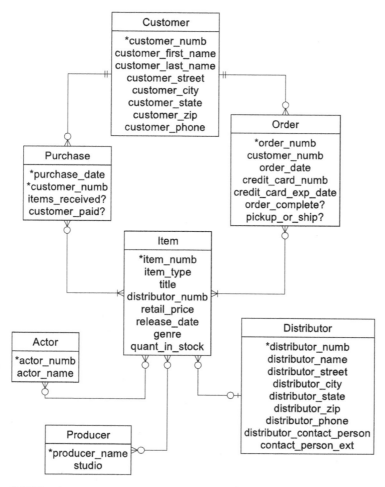

■ FIGURE 4.12 The major entities and the relationships between them in the *Antique Opticals* database.

- An actor appears in zero, one, or more items. An item has zero, one, or more actors in it. (There may occasionally be films that feature animals rather than human actors; therefore, it is probably unwise to require that every merchandise item be related to at least one actor.)
- Each item has zero, one, or more producers. Each producer is responsible for zero, one, or more items. (Although in practice you would not store data about a producer unless that producer was related to an item, leaving the relationship between a producer and an item as optional means that you can store producers without items, if necessary.)
- Each item comes from zero or one distributors. Each distributor supplies zero, one, or more items.

The major thing to notice about this design is that there are four many-to-many relationships: order to item, purchase to item, actor to item, and producer to item. Before you can map this data model to a relational database, they must be handled in some way.

Dealing with Many-to-Many Relationships

As you read earlier, there are problems with many-to-many relationships. The first is fairly straightforward: The relational data model cannot handle many-to-many relationships directly; it is limited to one-to-one and one-to-many relationships. This means that you must replace the many-to-many relationships that you have identified in your database environment with a collection of one-to-many relationships if you want to be able to use a relational DBMS.

The second is a bit more subtle. To understand it, consider the relationship between an order an *Antique Opticals* customer places with the store and the merchandise items on the order. There is a many-to-many relationship between the order and the item because each order can be for many items, and each item can appear on many orders (typically orders from different customers). Whenever a customer orders an item, the number of copies of the item varies, depending on how many copies the customer needs. (Yes, typically people order only one copy of a movie, but we need to allow them to order as many as they want. It certainly would be poor business practice to do otherwise.)

Now the question: Where should we store the quantity being ordered? It cannot be part of the order entity, because the quantity depends on the item being ordered. By the same token, the quantity cannot be part of the item entity, because the quantity depends on the specific order.

What you have just seen is known as *relationship data*, data that apply to the relationship between two entities, rather than to the entities themselves. In the relational data model, however, relationships cannot have attributes. We must therefore have some entity to represent the relationship between the two entities participating in the M:M relationship, an entity to which the relationship data can belong.

Composite Entities

Entities that exist to represent the relationship between two or more other entities are known as *composite entities*. As an example of how composite entities work, consider once again the relationship between an order placed by an *Antique Opticals* customer and the items on that order.

What we need is an entity that tells us that a specific title appears on a specific order. If you look at Figure 4.13, you will see three order instances, and three merchandise item instances. The first order for customer 0985 (Order #1) contains only one item (item 02944). The second order for

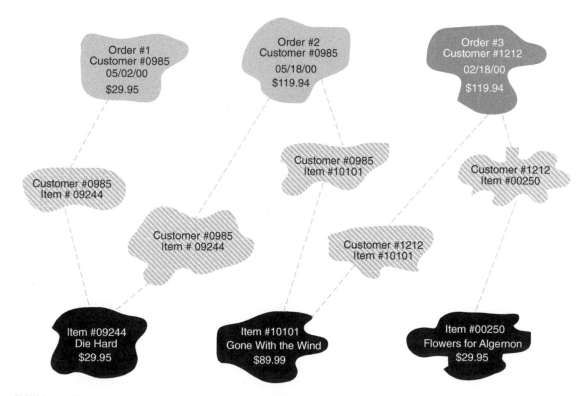

■ FIGURE 4.13 Using instances of composite entities to change many-to-many relationships into one-to-many relationships.

customer 0985 (Order #2) contains a second copy of item 02944, as well as item 10101. Order #3, which belongs to customer 1212, also has two items on it (item 10101 and item 00250).

There are five items ordered among the three orders. The middle of the diagram, therefore, contains five instances of a composite entity we will call a "line item" (thinking of it as a line item on a packing slip or invoice). The line item entity has been created solely to represent the relationship between an order and a merchandise item.

Each order is related to one line item instance for each item on the order. In turn, each item is related to one line item instance for each order on which it appears. Each line item instance is related to one and only one order; it is also related to one and only one merchandise item. As a result, the relationship between an order and its line items is one-to-many (one order has many line items) and the relationship between an item and the orders on which it appears is one-to-many (one merchandise item appears in many line items). The presence of the composite entity has removed the original many-to-many relationship.

If necessary, the composite entity can be used to store relationship data. In the preceding example, we might include an attribute for the quantity ordered, a flag to indicate whether it has been shipped, and a shipping date.

Documenting Composite Entities

In some extensions of the Chen method for drawing ER diagrams, the symbol for a composite entity is the combination of the rectangle used for an entity, and the diamond used for a relationship:

The IE and UML styles, however, have no special symbol for a composite entity.

Resolving *Antique Opticals'* Many-to-Many Relationships

To eliminate *Antique Opticals'* many-to-many relationships, the database designer must replace each many-to-many relationship with a composite entity, and two one-to-many relationships. As you can see in Figure 4.14, the four new entities are as follows:

■ Order item: An instance of the order item entity represents one item appearing on one order. Each order can have many "order items," but

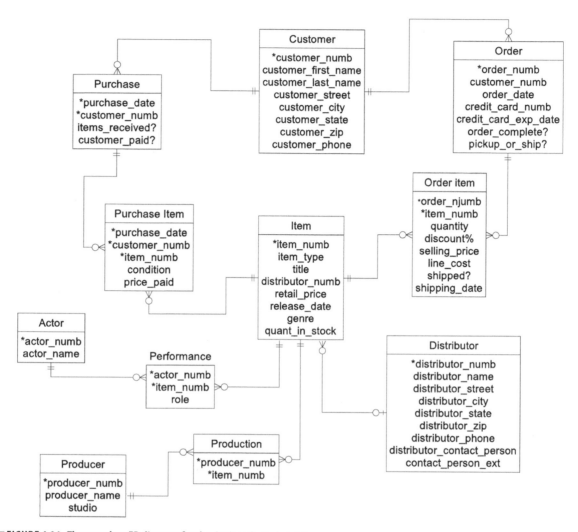

■FIGURE 4.14 The complete ER diagram for the *Antique Opticals* database.

an ordered item must appear on one and only one order. By the same
token, an ordered item contains one and only one item, but the same
item can appear in many order item instances, each of which is related
to a different order.

■ Purchase item: An instance of the purchase item entity represents one
used laser disc purchased from one customer as part of a purchase
of one or more discs. Many items can be purchased during a single
transaction, but each item purchased is purchased during only
one transaction. The purpose of the purchase item entity is therefore

the same as the order item entity: to represent specific items in a single transaction.

- Performance: The performance entity represents one actor appearing in one film. Each performance is for one and only one film, although a film can have many performances (one for each actor in the film). Conversely, an actor is related to one performance for each film in which he or she appears, although each performance is in one and only one film.
- Production: The production entity represents one producer working on one film. A producer may be involved in many productions, although each production relates to one and only one producer. The relationship with item indicates that each film can be produced by many producers, but that each production relates to only one item.

Note: If you find sorting out the relationships in Figure 4.14 a bit difficult, keep in mind that if you rotate the up-and-down symbols 90 degrees, you will actually be able to read the relationships from the symbols at the ends of the lines.

Because composite entities exist primarily to indicate a relationship between two other entities, they must be related to both of their parent entities. This is why the relationship between each composite entity in Figure 4.14 and its parents is mandatory.

N-Way Composite Entities

There is no reason a composite entity can't represent a relationship between more than two parent entities. As an example, assume that we are creating a database for a community theater group. We want to keep track of which actors performed which roles during the run of each play. To do this, we need entities for the roles, the actors, and the scheduled plays. A scheduled play is a specific play performed at a specific location, during a specific range of dates. (There are other entities in the database, such as the theater and the play, but they don't factor in to this discussion.)

The relationships are as follows:

- A role may be performed by many actors, and an actor may perform many roles.
- An actor may appear in many scheduled plays, and a scheduled play may have many actors.
- A role may appear in many scheduled plays, and a scheduled play may have many roles.

When we draw the ER diagram, we end up with circular many-to-many relationships (Figure 4.15). These relationships are indeed correct, but they don't capture one very important piece of information: which actor performed

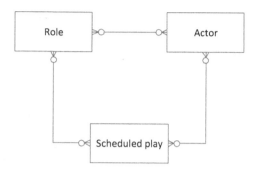

■ FIGURE 4.15 Circular many-to-many relationships.

which role, in which scheduled play. The M:M relationship between a role and an actor tells us who performed which role, but can't tell us the scheduled play. The M:M relationship between an actor and a scheduled play tells us who was in each performance, but can't tell us the role the actor portrayed. Finally, the M:M relationship between a role and a scheduled play can tell us what the roles were in a scheduled play, but not who performed each role during a specific performance.

A performance—who performed what role, during what scheduled play—needs three pieces of data to describe it: the actor, the role, and the scheduled play. The only way to capture this is to create a single composite entity that has for its parents one actor, one role, and one scheduled play. As you can see in Figure 4.16, when we introduce the performance entity, all the relationships become 1:M, with the performance on the "many" end. Each performance, therefore, represents one actor performing one role in one scheduled play.

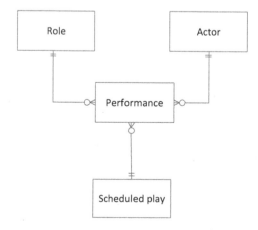

■ FIGURE 4.16 A three-way composite entity.

Relationships and Business Rules

In many ways, database design is as much an art as a science. Exactly what the "correct" design for a specific business happens to be depends on the business rules; what is correct for one organization may not be correct for another.

As an example, assume that you are creating a database for a small establishment that has more than one store. One of the things you are being asked to model in the database is an employee's schedule. Before you can do that, you need to answer the question of the relationship between an employee and a store: Is it one-to-many or many-to-many? Does an employee always work at one store—in which case the relationship is one-to-many—or can an employee split his or her time between more than one store, producing a many-to-many relationship? You can see two possible relationships in Figure 4.17. The diagram on the left says that a store has one or more employees, and an employee can work at zero or one store. In contrast, the diagram on the right says that a store may have zero or more employees, and that an employee may work at zero or more stores. Choosing one is not a matter of right or wrong database design, but an issue of how the business operates.

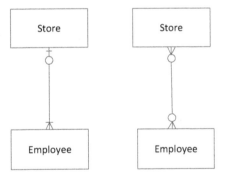

■ FIGURE 4.17 Two possible relationships requiring a decision based on business rules.

Data Modeling Versus Data Flow

One of the most common mistakes people make when they are beginning to do data modeling is to confuse data models with data flows. A *data flow* shows how data are handled within an organization, including who handles the data, where the data are stored, and what is done to the data. In contrast, a *data model* depicts the internal, logical relationships between the data, without regard to who is handling the data or what is being done with them.

Data flows are often documented in *data flow diagrams* (DFDs). For example, in Figure 4.18 you can see a top-level data flow diagram for *Antique Opticals*. The squares with drop shadows represent the people who are handling the data. Simple rectangles with numbers in them represent *processes*, or things that are done with the data. A place where data are stored (a *data store*) appears as two parallel lines, in this example containing the words "Main database." The arrows on the lines in the diagram show the way in which data pass from one place to another. For example, "Take order" is a process. Two people generate the data, the Customer and the Employee. Notice that the arrows on the lines between those two and the "Take order" process point to the process, showing that the data flows from the people to the process.

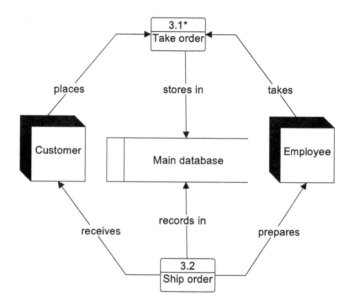

■ **FIGURE 4.18**   A top-level data flow diagram for *Antique Opticals*.

Data flow diagrams are often exploded to show more detail. For example, Figure 4.19 contains an explosion of the "Take order" process from Figure 4.18. You can now see that the process of taking an order involves two major steps: getting customer information, and getting item information.

Each of the processes in Figure 4.19 can be exploded even further to show additional detail (Figures 4.20 and 4.21). At this point, the diagrams are almost detailed enough so that an application designer can plan an application program.

Where do the database and the ER diagram fit into all of this? The entire ER diagram is buried inside the "Main database." In fact, most CASE software

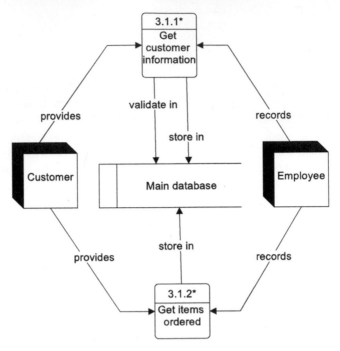

■ FIGURE 4.19 An explosion of the "Take order" process from Figure 4.18.

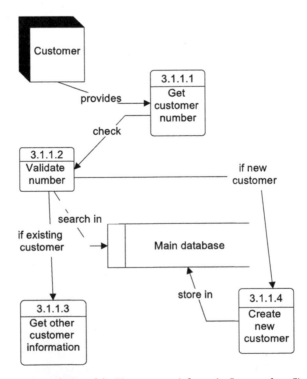

■ FIGURE 4.20 An explosion of the "Get customer information" process from Figure 4.19.

allows you to link your ER diagram to a database's representation on a data flow diagram. Then, you can simply double-click on the database representation to bring the ER diagram into view.

There are a few guidelines you can use to keep data flows and data models separate:

- A data flow shows who uses or handles data. A data model does not.
- A data flow shows how data are gathered (the people or other sources from which they come). A data model does not.
- A data flow shows operations on data (the process through which data are transformed). A data model does not.
- A data model shows how entities are interrelated. A data flow does not.
- A data model shows the attributes that describe data entities. A data flow does not.

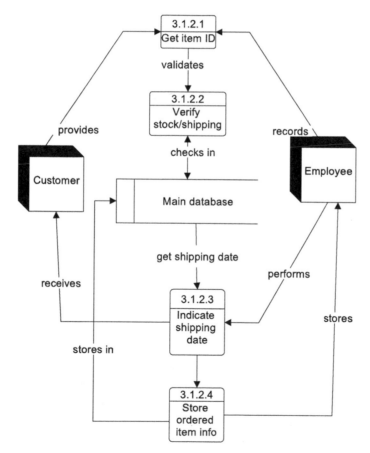

■ **FIGURE 4.21   An explosion of the "Get items ordered" process from Figure 4.19.**

The bottom line is this: A data model contains information about the data being stored in the database (entities, attributes, and entity relationships). If data about an entity are not going to be stored in the database, then that entity should not be part of the data model. For example, although the *Antique Opticals* data flow diagrams show the employee who handles most of the data, no data about employees are going to be stored in the database. Therefore, there is no employee entity in the ER diagram.

Schemas

A completed entity-relationship diagram represents the overall, logical plan of a database. In database terms, it therefore is known as a *schema*. This is the way in which the people responsible for maintaining the database will see the design. However, users (both interactive users and application programs) may work with only a portion of the logical schema. And both the logical schema and the users' views of the data are at the same time distinct from the physical storage.

The underlying physical storage managed by the DBMS is known as the *physical schema*. It is for the most part determined by the DBMS. (Only very large DBMSs give you any control over physical storage.) The beauty of this arrangement is that both database designers and users do not need to be concerned about physical storage, greatly simplifying access to the database, and making it much easier to make changes to both the logical and physical schemas.

Because there are three ways to look at a database, some databases today are said to be based on a *three-schema architecture* (Figure 4.22). Systems programmers, and other people involved with managing physical storage, deal with the physical schema. Most of today's relational DBMSs provide very little control over the file structure used to store database data. However, DBMSs designed to run on mainframes to handle extremely large datasets do allow some tailoring of the layout of internal file storage.

Note: DBMSs based on earlier data models were more closely tied to their physical storage than relational DBMSs. Therefore, systems programmers were able to specify physical file structures to a much greater extent. An overview of the older database models can be found in Appendix A.

Data designers, database administrators, and some application programmers are aware of and use the logical schema. End users working interactively, and application programmers who are creating database applications for them, work with user views of the database.

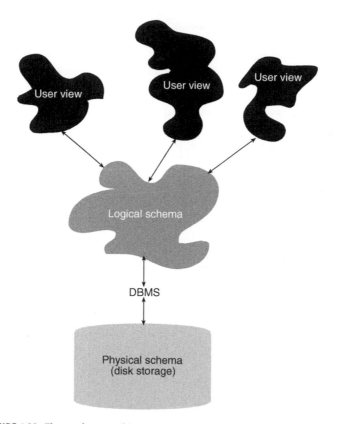

■ **FIGURE 4.22** **Three-schema architecture.**

Throughout most of the first portion of this book we will be focusing on the design of the logical schema. You will also learn how to create and use database elements that provide users with limited portions of the database.

For Further Reading

The entity-relationship model was developed by Peter P.S. Chen. If you want to learn more about its early forms and how the model has changed, see the following:

Chen, P., 1976. The entity-relationship model: toward a unified view of data. ACM Trans Database Sys 1 (1), 9–36.

Chen, P., 1977. The Entity-Relationship Approach to Logical Database Design. QED Information Sciences, Data Base Monograph Series, No. 6.

Chen, P., 1981. Entity-Relationship Approach to Information Modeling. E-R Institute.

The original work that described the Information Engineering approach can be found in the following:

Martin, J., 1989. Information Engineering, Book I: Introduction, Book II: Planning and Analysis, Book III: Design and Construction. Prentice Hall, New Jersey.

Finkelstein, C., 1989. An introduction to Information Engineering. Addison-Wesley, Australia.

For information on UML, see:

Chonoles, M.J., Schardt, J.A., 2003. UML 2 for Dummies. For Dummies Press.

Fowler, M., 2003. UML Distilled: A Brief Guide to the Standard Object Modeling Language, third ed. Addison-Wesley Professional.

Pilone, D., Pitman, N., 2005. UML 2.0 in a Nutshell, second ed. O'Reilly Media, Inc.

For more in-depth coverage of ER modeling, see any of the following:

Baqui, S., Earp, R., 2003. Database Design Using Entity-Relationship Diagrams. Auerbach.

Batini, C., Ceri, S., Navathe, S.B., 1991. Conceptual Database Design: An Entity-Relationship Approach. Addison-Wesley.

Earp, R., 2007. Database Design Using Entity-Relationship Diagrams. Taylor & Francis.

Thalheim, B., 2000. Entity-Relationship Modeling: Foundations of Database Technology. Springer.

Chapter

5

The Relational
Data Model

Once you have a completed ER diagram, you can translate that conceptual logical schema into the formal data model required by your DBMS. Today, most new database installations are based on the relational data model. We call databases that adhere to that model *relational databases*.

Note: The older data models that are described in Appendix A are still in use, in many legacy database systems. However, it is extremely rare to find a business creating a new one. On the other hand, the object-oriented data model is still current and although it has not replaced the relational data model and does not appear to be doing so, some new installations use either object-oriented or a combination of relational and object-oriented (see Chapter 27). The existence of extremely large data stores has also led to the development of post-relational DBMSs known as NoSQL. You will read about them in Chapter 28.

A relational database is a database whose logical structure is made up of nothing but a collection of *relations*. Although you may have read somewhere that a relational database has "relationships between files," nothing could be further from the truth. In this chapter, you will learn exactly what a relational database is, and how relations provide representations of data relationships.

Note: Remember from Chapter 4 that we said that a DBMS isolates database users from physical storage. A logical data model, therefore, has absolutely nothing to do with how the data are stored in files on disk.

The relational data model is the result of the work of one man—Edgar (E. F.) Codd. During the 1960s, Dr. Codd, although trained as a mathematician, was working with existing data models. His experience led him to believe that they were clumsy and unnatural ways of representing data relationships. He therefore went back to mathematical set theory and focused on the construct known as a relation. He extended that concept to produce the relational database model, which he introduced in a paper in 1970.

Note: You will find the citations for Codd's original paper and his other writings on the relational data model in the For Further Reading section at the end of this chapter.

Note: E. F. Codd was born in England in 1923 and later migrated to the United States, where he did most of his work on the relational data model at IBM's Watson Research Center. He died in 2003.

Understanding Relations

In mathematical set theory, a *relation* is the definition of a table with columns (*attributes*) and rows (*tuples*). (The word "table" is used synonymously with "relation" in the relational data model, although, to be strictly correct, not every table is a relation.) The definition specifies what will be contained in each column of the table, but does not include data. When you include rows of data, you have an *instance* of a relation, such as the small *customer* relation in Figure 5.1.

Customer Number	First Name	Last Name	Phone
0001	Jane	Doe	(555) 555-1111
0002	John	Doe	(555) 555-2222
0003	Jane	Smith	(555) 555-3333
0004	John	Smith	(555) 555-4444

■ FIGURE 5.1 A simple *customer* relation.

At first glance, a relation looks much like a flat file or a rectangular portion of a spreadsheet. However, because it has its underpinnings in mathematical set theory, a relation has some very specific characteristics that distinguish it from other rectangular ways of looking at data. Each of these characteristics forms the basis of a constraint that will be enforced by the DBMS.

Columns and Column Characteristics

A column in a relation has the following properties:

■ A name that is unique within the table: Two or more tables within the same relational database schema may have columns with the same names—in fact, as you will see shortly, in some circumstances this is highly desirable—but a single table must have unique column names. When the same column name appears in more than one table, and tables that contain that column are used in the same data manipulation operation, you qualify the name of the column by preceding it with the name of its table and a period, as in:

```
customer.customer_number
```

- A domain: The values in a column are drawn from one and only one domain. As a result, relations are said to be *column homogeneous.* In addition, every column in a table is subject to a domain constraint. Depending on your DBMS, the domain constraint may be as simple as a data type, such as integers or dates. Alternatively, your DBMS may allow you to create your own, very specific, domains that can be attached to columns.
- There are no "positional concepts." In other words, the columns can be viewed in any order without affecting the meaning of the data.

Rows and Row Characteristics

In relational design theory, a row in a relation has the following properties:

- Only one value at the intersection of a column and row: A relation does not allow multivalued attributes.
- Uniqueness: There are no duplicate rows in a relation.

Note: for the most part, DBMSs do not enforce the unique row constraint automatically. However, as you will see in the next bullet, there is another way to obtain the same effect.

- A primary key: A *primary key* is a column or combination of columns with a value that uniquely identifies each row. As long as you have unique primary keys, you will ensure that you also have unique rows. We will look at the issue of what makes a good primary key in great depth in the next major section of this chapter.
- There are no positional concepts. The rows can be viewed in any order without affecting the meaning of the data.

Note: You can't necessarily move both columns and rows around at the same time and maintain the integrity of a relation. When you change the order of the columns, the rows must remain in the same order; when you change the order of the rows, you must move each entire row as a unit.

Types of Tables

A relational database works with two types of tables. *Base tables* are relations that are actually stored in the database. These are the tables that are described by your schema.

However, relational operations on tables produce additional tables as their result. Such tables, which exist only in main memory, are known as *virtual tables*. Virtual tables may not be legal relations—in particular, they may have no primary key—but because virtual tables contain copies of data in the base tables and are never stored in the database, this presents no problem in terms of the overall design of the database.

The use of virtual tables benefits a DBMS in several ways. First, it allows the DBMS to keep intermediate query tables in main memory, rather than storing them on disk, enhancing query performance. Second, it allows tables that violate the rules of the relational data model to exist in main memory without affecting the integrity of the database. Finally, it helps avoid fragmentation of database files and disk surfaces by avoiding repeated write, read, and delete operations on temporary tables.

Note: SQL, the language used to manage most relational databases, also supports "temporary base tables." Although called base tables, temporary tables are actually virtual tables in the sense that they exist only in main memory for a short time and are never stored in the physical database.

A Notation for Relations

You will see instances of relations throughout this book, used as examples. However, we do not usually include data in a relation, when documenting that relation. One common way to express a relation is as follows:

```
relation_name (primary_key, non_primary_key_column …)
```

For example, the *customer* relation that you saw in Figure 5.1 would be written as:

```
customer (customer_numb, first_name last_name, phone)
```

The preceding expression is a true relation, an expression of the structure of a relation. It correctly does not contain any data. (As mentioned earlier, when data are included, you have an instance of a relation.)

Primary Keys

As you have just read, a unique primary key makes it possible to uniquely identify every row in a table. Why is this so important? The issue is the same as with entity identifiers: You want to be able to retrieve every single piece of data you put into a database.

As far as a relational database is concerned, you should need only three pieces of information to retrieve any specific bit of data: the name of the table, the name of the column, and the primary key of the row. If primary keys are unique for every row, then we can be sure that we are retrieving exactly the row we want. If they are not unique, then we are retrieving only *some* row with the primary key value, which may not be the row containing the data for which we are searching.

Along with being unique, a primary key must not contain the value *null*. Null is a special database value meaning "unknown." It is not the same as a zero or a blank. If you have one row with a null primary key, then you are actually alright. However, the minute you introduce a second one, you have lost the property of uniqueness. We therefore forbid the presence of nulls in any primary key columns. This constraint, known as *entity integrity*, will be enforced by a DBMS whenever data are entered or modified.

Selecting a good primary key can be a challenge. As you may remember from Chapter 4, some entities have natural primary keys, such as purchase order numbers. These are arbitrary, meaningless unique identifiers that a company attaches to the orders it sends to vendors and are therefore ideal primary keys.

Occasionally, you will run across a relation that has two or more attributes (or combinations of attributes) that can serve as a primary key. Each of these possible primary keys is known as a *candidate key*. You will therefore need to choose from among the candidate keys: A relation can have only one primary key.

Primary Keys to Identify People

What about a primary key to identify people? The first thing that pops into your mind might be a social security number (or, for those outside the United States, a national identification number). Every person in the United States is supposed to have a social security number (SSN); parents apply for them in the hospital when a baby is born, right? And the US government assigns them, so they are unique, right? Unfortunately, the answer to both questions is "no."

The Social Security Administration has been known to give everyone in an entire town the same SSN; over time, SSNs are reused. However, these are minor problems, compared to the issue of the social security number being null.

Consider what happens at a college that uses social security numbers as student numbers when international students enroll. Upon entry into the country, the international students do not have SSNs. Because primary keys cannot be null, the international students cannot sign up for classes or even be enrolled in the college, until they have some sort of SSN.

The college's solution is to give them "fake" numbers in the format 999-99-XXXX, where XXXX is some number currently not in use. Then, when the student receives a "real" SSN from the government, the college supposedly replaces the fake value with the real one. Sometimes, however, the process doesn't work. A graduate student ended up with his first semester's grades being stored under the fake SSN, but the rest of his grades under his real number. (Rather than changing the original data, someone created an entire new transcript for the student.) When the time came to audit his transcript to see if he had satisfied all his graduation requirements, he was told that he was missing an entire semester's worth of courses.

This example leads us to two important desirable qualities of primary keys:

- A primary key should be some value that is highly unlikely ever to be null.
- A primary key value should never change. (It should be *immutable*.)

In addition, there is significant concern of security problems that can arise from the use of social security numbers as identifiers in a database. The danger of identity theft has made it risky to store a national identifier. Many US state governments, for example, have mandated that publicly-supported organizations use something other than the SSN as a customer/client/student ID to help protect individual privacy.

Although SSNs initially look like good natural identifiers, you will be much better off in the long run using arbitrary numbers for people—such as student numbers or account numbers—rather than relying on government-issued identification numbers.

Avoiding Meaningful Identifiers

It can be very tempting to code meaning into a primary key. For example, assume that *Antique Opticals* wants to assign codes to its distributors, rather than giving them arbitrary distributor numbers. Someone might create codes such as TLC for *The Laser Club*, and JS for *Jones Services*. At first, this might seem like a good idea. The codes are short and by looking at them, you can figure out which distributor they represent.

But what happens if one of the companies changes its name? Perhaps *Jones Services* is renamed *Jones Distribution House*. Do you change the primary key value in the distributor table? Do you change the code so that it reads

JDH? If the distributor table were all that we cared about, that would be the easy solution.

However, consider that the table that describes merchandise items contains the code for the distributor, so that *Antique Opticals* can know which distributor provides the item (you will read a great deal more about this concept in the next major section of this chapter.) If you change the distributor code value in the distributor table, you must change the value of the code for every merchandise item that comes from that distributor. Without the change, *Antique Opticals* will not be able to match the code to a distributor and get information about the distributor. It will appear that that the item comes from a nonexistent distributor!

Note: This is precisely the same problem about which you read in Chapter 3, concerning Antique Opticals' identifiers for its customers.

Meaningful primary keys tend to change and therefore introduce the potential for major data inconsistencies between tables. Resist the temptation to use them, at all costs. Here, then, is yet another property of a good primary key:

- A primary key should avoid using meaningful data. Use arbitrary identifiers or concatenations of arbitrary identifiers wherever possible.

Many of the Web sites on which you have accounts will use your e-mail address as your user ID. This is another example of why primary keys should be immutable. Our e-mail addresses change occasionally. (By this time, most of us dread having to change our primary e-mail address, but doing so can be forced on us by circumstances.) If a company is using a relational database with an e-mail address as the primary key for its customer table, a change in that key becomes a major event. Should the company keep a history of all the user's e-mail addresses and leave references from old orders intact? Should the all the user's orders (even those that have been filled) be changed to reflect the new e-mail address? If the company doesn't do one or the other, orders with an old e-mail address will be left hanging with no connection to a customer. No matter what the company decides to do, it will require some significant data modification and tight controls to ensure that the data remain consistent.

It is not always possible to use completely meaningless primary keys. You may find, for example, that you need to include dates or times in primary keys to distinguish between events. The suggestion that you should not use meaningful primary keys is therefore not a hard-and-fast rule, but a guideline to which you should try to adhere whenever it is realistic to do so.

Concatenated Primary Keys

Some tables have no single column in which the values never duplicate. As an example, look at the *order items* table in Figure 5.2. Because
there is more than one item on an order, order numbers are repeated;
because the same item can appear on more than one order, item numbers
are repeated. Therefore, neither column by itself can serve as the table's
primary key.

Order Number	Item Number	Quantity
10991	0022	1
10991	0209	2
10991	1001	1
10992	0022	1
10992	0486	1
10993	0209	1
10993	1001	2
10994	0621	1

■ **FIGURE 5.2** A sample order items table.

However, the combination of an order number and an item number *is*
unique. We can, therefore, concatenate the two columns to form the table's
primary key.

It is true that you could also concatenate all three columns in the table, and
still ensure a unique primary key. However, the quantity column is not necessary to ensure uniqueness and therefore should not be used. We now have
some additional properties of a good primary key:

- A concatenated primary key should be made up of the smallest number
  of columns necessary to ensure the uniqueness of the primary key.
- Whenever possible, the columns used in a concatenated primary key
  should be meaningless identifiers.

All-Key Relations

It is possible to have a table in which every column is part of the primary
key. As an example, consider a library book catalog. Each book title owned
by a library has a natural unique primary key—the ISBN (International
Standard Book Number). Each ISBN is assigned to one or more subject
headings in the library's catalog; each subject heading is also assigned to
one or more books. We therefore have a many-to-many relationship between
books and subject headings.

A relation to represent this relationship might be:

```
subject_catalog (isbn, subject heading)
```

All we need to do is pair a subject heading with a book identifier. No additional data are needed. Therefore, all columns in the table become part of the primary key.

There is absolutely no problem with having all-key relations in a database. In fact, they occur whenever a database design contains a composite entity that has no relationship data. They are not necessarily an error, and you can use them wherever needed.

Representing Data Relationships

In the preceding section we alluded to the use of identifiers in more than one relation. This is the one way in which relational databases represent relationships between entities. To make this concept clearer, take a look at the three tables in Figure 5.3.

Items

Item Number	Title	Distributor Number	Price
1001	Gone with the Wind	002	39.95
1002	Star Wars IV: Special Edition	002	59.95
1003	Die Hard	004	29.95
1004	Bambi	006	29.95

Orders

Order Number	Customer Number	Order Date
11100	0012	12/18/09
11101	0186	12/18/09
11102	0056	12/18/09

Order Item

Order Number	Item Number	Quantity	Shipped?
11100	1001	1	Y
11100	1002	1	Y
11101	1002	2	Y
11102	1002	1	N
11102	1003	1	N
11102	1001	1	N

■ FIGURE 5.3 Three relations from the *Antique Opticals* database.

Each table in the illustration is directly analogous to the entity by the same name in the *Antique Opticals* ER diagram. The *orders* table (the Order entity) is identified by an order number, an arbitrary unique primary key assigned by *Antique Opticals*. The *items* table (the Item entity) is identified by an item number, which could be another arbitrary unique identifier assigned by the company (often called an SKU, for stock keeping unit) or a UPC.

The third table—*order item* (the Order Item entity)—tells the company which items are part of which order. As you saw earlier in this chapter, this table requires a concatenated primary key because multiple items can appear on multiple orders. The columns in this primary key, however, have more significance than simply uniquely identifying each row. They also represent a relationship between the order items, the orders on which they appear, and the items being ordered.

The *item number* column in the *order item* relation is the same as the primary key of the *item* table. This indicates a one-to-many relationship between the two tables. By the same token, there is a one-to-many relationship between the *order* and *order item* tables because the *order number* column in the *order item* table is the same as the primary key of the *orders* table.

When a table contains a column (or concatenation of columns) that is the same as the primary key of some table in the database, the column is called a *foreign key*. The matching of foreign key values to primary key values represents data relationships in a relational database. As far as the user of a relational database is concerned, there are no structures that show relationships other than the matching column's values.

Note: This is why the idea that relational databases have "relationships between files" is so absurd. The relationships in a relational database are between logical constructs—tables—and nothing else. Such structures make absolutely no assumptions about physical storage.

Foreign keys may be part of a concatenated primary key, or they may not be part of their table's primary key at all. Consider, for example, a pair of simple *Antique Opticals customer* and *order* relations:

```
customer (customer_numb, first_name, last_name, phone)

order (order_numb, customer_numb, order_date)
```

The customer number column in the *order* table is a foreign key that matches the primary key of the *customer* table. It represents the one-to-many relationship between customers and the orders they place. However, the customer number is not part of the primary key of its table; it is a nonkey attribute that is nonetheless a foreign key.

Technically, foreign keys need not have values unless they are part of a concatenated primary key; they can be null. For example, there is no theoretical reason that the *orders* relation above must have a value for the customer number. It is not part of the primary key of the table. However, in this particular database, *Antique Opticals* would be in serious trouble if customer numbers were null: There would be no way to know which customer placed an order!

A relational DBMS uses the relationships indicated by matching data between primary and foreign keys. For example, assume that an *Antique Opticals* employee wanted to see what titles had been ordered on order number 11102. First, the DBMS identifies the rows in the *order item* table that contain an order number of 11102. Then, it takes the item numbers from those rows and matches them to the item numbers in the *item* table. In the rows where there are matches, the DBMS retrieves the associated data.

Referential Integrity

The procedure described in the preceding paragraph works very well—unless, for some reason, there is no order number in the *order* table to match a row in the *order item* table. This is a very undesirable condition, because there would be no way to ship the ordered items because there would be no way to find out which customer placed the order.

This relational data model therefore enforces a constraint called *referential integrity*, which states that *every nonnull foreign key value must match an existing primary key value*. Of all the constraints on a relational database, this is probably the most important, because it ensures the consistency of the cross-references among tables.

Referential integrity constraints are stored in the database, and enforced automatically by the DBMS. As with all other constraints, each time a user enters or modifies data, the DBMS checks the constraints, and verifies that they are met. If the constraints are violated, the data modification will not be allowed.

Concatenated Foreign Keys

A foreign key does not necessarily need to be made up of a single column. In some cases, you may have a concatenated foreign key that references a concatenated primary key. As an example, let us consider a very small accounting firm that uses the following relations:

```
accountant (acct_first_name, acct_last_name, date_hired,
     office_ext)

customer (customer_numb, first_name, last_name, street,
     city, state_province, zip_postcode, contact_phone)

job (tax_year, customer_numb, acct_first_name,
     acct_last_name)

form (tax_year, customer_numb, form_id, is_complete)
```

Because the firm is so small, the database designer decides that employee numbers are not necessary and, instead, uses the accountants' first and last names as the primary key of the *accountant* table. The *job* table, used to gather data about one accountant preparing one year's tax returns for one customer, uses the tax year and the customer number as its primary key. The *form* table that stores data about the forms that are part of a specific tax return uses the concatenation of the form's ID and the primary key of the project table for its primary key.

A foreign key is the same as the *complete* primary key of another table. Therefore, the *acct_first_name* attribute by itself in the *job* table is not a foreign key; neither is the *acct_last_name* attribute. If you concatenate them, however, then they are the same as the primary key of the *accountant* table and, in fact, this is the unit with which referential integrity should be enforced.

Assume that "Jane Johnson" is working on customer 10100's 2017 tax return. It is not enough to ensure that "Jane" appears somewhere in the first name column in the *accountant* table and "Johnson" appears anywhere in the last name column in the *accountant* table. There could be many people named "Jane" and many with the last name of "Johnson." What we need to ensure is that there is one person named "Jane Johnson" in the *accountant* table, the concatenation of the two attributes that make up the primary key.

The same holds true for the concatenated foreign key in the *form* table: the tax year and the customer number. A row with a matching pair must exist in the *job* table before referential integrity is satisfied.

Foreign Keys That Reference the Primary Key of Their Own Table

Foreign keys do not necessarily need to reference a primary key in a different table; they need only reference a primary key. As an example, consider the following *employee* relation:

```
employee (employee_ID, first_name, last_name, department,
     manager_ID)
```

A manager is also an employee. Therefore, the manager ID, although named differently from the employee ID, is actually a foreign key that references the primary key of its own table. The DBMS will, therefore, always ensure that whenever a user enters a manager ID, that manager already exists in the table as an employee.

Views

The people responsible for developing a database schema and those who write application programs for use by technologically unsophisticated users typically have knowledge of and access to the entire schema, including direct access to the database's base tables. However, it is usually undesirable to have end users working directly with base tables, primarily for security reasons.

The relational data model therefore includes a way to provide end users with their own window into the database, one that hides the details of the overall database design and prohibits direct access to the base tables: *views*.

The View Mechanism

A view is not stored with data. Instead, it is stored under a name in a database table, along with a database query that will retrieve its data. A view can therefore contain data from more than one table, selected rows, and selected columns.

Note: Although a view can be constructed in just about any way that you can query a relational database, many views can only be used for data display. As you will learn in Chapter 20, only views that meet a strict set of rules can be used to modify data.

The real beauty of storing views in this way, however, is that whenever the user includes the name of the view in a data manipulation language statement, the DBMS executes the query associated with the view name and recreates the view's table. This means that the data in a view will always be current.

A view table remains in main memory only for the duration of the data manipulation statement in which it was used. As soon as the user issues another query, the view table is removed from main memory to be replaced by the result of the most recent query. A view table is therefore a virtual table.

Note: Some end user DBMSs give the user the ability to save the contents of a view as a base table. This is a particularly undesirable feature, as there are no provisions for automatically updating the data in the saved table whenever the tables on which it was based change. The view table therefore quickly will become out of date and inaccurate.

Why Use Views?

There are three good reasons to include views in the design of a database:

- As mentioned earlier, views provide a significant security mechanism by restricting users from viewing portions of a schema to which they should not have access.
- Views can simplify the design of a database for technologically unsophisticated users.
- Because views are stored as named queries, they can be used to store frequently used, complex queries. The queries can then be executed by using the name of the view in a simple query statement.

Like other structural elements in a relational database, views can be created and destroyed at any time. However, because views do not contain stored data, but only specification of a query that will generate a virtual table, adding or removing view definitions has no impact on base tables or the data they contain. Removing a view will create problems when that view is used in an application program and the program is not modified to work with a different view or base table. A problem may also occur if a view used in the definition of another view is deleted.

The Data Dictionary

The structure of a relational database is stored in the database's *data dictionary*, or *catalog*. The data dictionary is made up of a set of relations, identical in properties to the relations used to hold data. They can be queried using the same tools used to query data-handling relations. No user can modify the data dictionary tables directly. However, data manipulation language commands that create, modify, and destroy database structural elements work by modifying rows in data dictionary tables.

You will typically find the following types of information in a data dictionary:

- Definitions of the columns that make up each table.
- Integrity constraints placed on relations.
- Security information (which user has the right to perform which operation on which table).
- Definitions of other database structure elements such as views and user-defined domains.

When a user attempts to access data in any way, a relational DBMS first goes to the data dictionary to determine whether the database elements the user has requested are actually part of the schema. In addition, the DBMS verifies that the user has the access right to whatever he or she is requesting.

When a user attempts to modify data, the DBMS also goes to the data dictionary to look for integrity constraints that may have been placed on the relation. If the data meet the constraints, then the modification is permitted. Otherwise, the DBMS returns an error message and does not make the change.

Because all access to a relational database is through the data dictionary, relational DBMSs are said to be *data dictionary driven*. The data in the data dictionary are known as *metadata*: data about data.

Sample Data Dictionary Tables

The precise tables that make up a data dictionary depend somewhat on the DBMS. In this section, you will see one example of a typical way in which a DBMS might organize its data dictionary.

The linchpin of the data dictionary is actually a table that documents all the data dictionary tables (often named *syscatalog*, the first few rows of which can be found in Figure 5.4). From the names of the data dictionary tables, you can probably guess that there are tables to store data about base tables, their columns, their indexes, and their foreign keys.

creator	tname	dbspace	tabletype	ncols	Primary_key
SYS	SYSTABLE	SYSTEM	TABLE	12	Y
SYS	SYSCOLUMN	SYSTEM	TABLE	14	Y
SYS	SYSINDEX	SYSTEM	TABLE	8	Y
SYS	SYSIXCOL	SYSTEM	TABLE	5	Y
SYS	SYSFOREIGNKEY	SYSTEM	TABLE	8	Y
SYS	SYSKCOL	SYSTEM	TABLE	4	Y
SYS	SYSFILE	SYSTEM	TABLE	3	Y
SYS	SYSDOMAIN	SYSTEM	TABLE	4	Y
SYS	SYSUSERPERM	SYSTEM	TABLE	10	Y
SYS	SYTSTABLEPERM	SYSTEM	TABLE	11	Y
SYS	SYSCOLPERM	SYSTEM	TABLE	6	Y

■ FIGURE 5.4 **A portion of a *syscatalog* table.**

The *syscolumn* table describes the columns in each table (including the data dictionary tables). In Figure 5.5, for example, you can see a portion of a *syscolumn* table that describes the *Antique Opticals* merchandise item table.

creator	cname	tname	coltype	nulls	length	Inprimarykey	Colno
DBA	item_numb	items	integer	N	4	Y	1
DBA	title	items	varchar	Y	60	N	2
DBA	distributor_numb	items	integer	Y	4	N	3
DBA	release_date	items	date	Y	6	N	4
DBA	retail_price	items	numeric	Y	8	N	5

■ FIGURE 5.5 Selected rows from a *syscolumn* table.

Keep in mind that these data dictionary tables have the same type of structure as all other tables in the database, and must adhere to the same rules as base tables. They must have non-null unique primary keys; they must also enforce referential integrity among themselves.

A Bit of History

When Codd published his paper describing the relational data model in 1970, software developers were bringing databases based on older data models to market. The software was becoming relatively mature and was being widely installed. Although many theorists recognized the benefits of the relational data model, it was some time before relational systems actually appeared.

IBM had a working prototype of its *System R* by 1976. This product, however, was never released. Instead, the first relational DBMS to feature SQL—an IBM development—was *Oracle*, released by the company of the same name in 1977. IBM didn't actually market a relational DBMS until 1981, when it released *SQL/DS*.

Oracle debuted on minicomputers running UNIX. *SQL/DS* ran under the VM operating environment (often specifically using CMS on top of VM) on IBM mainframes.[1] There was also a crop of early products that were designed specifically for PCs, the first of which was *dBase II*, from a company named Ashton-Tate. Released in 1981, the product ran on IBM PCs and Apple II + s.

Note: It is seriously questionable whether dBase was ever truly a relational DBMS. However, most consumers saw it as such and it is therefore considered the first relational product for PCs.

Oracle was joined by a large number of competing products in the UNIX market, including *Informix* and *Ingres*. *Oracle* has been the biggest winner

---

[1] VM (an acronym for "virtual machine") was an environment that ran on IBM mainframes. It was designed primarily to run other operating systems, such as CMS. Users rarely interacted with VM directly.

in this group because it now runs on virtually every OS/hardware platform combination imaginable and has scaled well (down to PCs and up to main-frames). Prior to the widespread deployment of the open source DBMS *mySQL* as a database server for Web sites, it was safe to say that there were more copies of *Oracle* running on computers than any other DBMS.

The PC market for relational DBMSs has been flooded with products. As often happens with software, the best has not necessarily become the most successful. In 1983, Microrim released its *R:BASE* product, the first truly relational product for a PC. With its support for standard SQL, a powerful integrity rule facility, and a capable programming language, *R:BASE* was a robust product. It succumbed, however, to the market penetration of *dBASE*. The same can be said for *Paradox* (originally a Borland product and later purchased by Corel) and *FoxPro* (a *dBase*-compatible product originally developed by Fox Software).

dBase faded from prominence after being purchased by Borland in 1991. *FoxPro*, *dBase*'s major competitor, was purchased by Microsoft in 1992. It, too, has faded from the small computer DBMS market. Instead, the primary end user desktop DBMS for Windows today is *Access*, first released by Microsoft in 1993.

For Further Reading

If you want to follow the history of Codd's specifications for relational databases, consult the following:

Codd, E.F., 1970. A relational model of data for large shared databanks. Commun. ACM 13 (6), 377–387.

Codd, E.F., 1979. Extending the relational model to capture more meaning. Trans. Data-base Sys. 4 (4), 397–434.

Codd, E.F., 1982. Relational database: a practical foundation for productivity. Commun. ACM 25 (2), 109–117.

Codd, E.F., 1990. The Relational Data Model, Version 2. Addison-Wesley, ISBN 978-0201141924.

There are also literally hundreds of books that discuss the details of specific relational DBMSs. After you finish reading this book, you may want to consult one or more books that deal with your specific product to help you learn to develop applications using that product's tools.

Other titles of interest:

Date, C.J., 2013. Relational Theory for Computer Professionals. O'Reilly Media.

Lightstone, S.S., Teorey, T.J., Nadeau, T., 2007. Physical Database Design: the database professional's guide to exploiting views, storage and more. Morgan Kaufmann.

Chapter

6

Relational Algebra

When we use SQL to manipulate data in a database, we are actually using something known as the *relational calculus*, a method for using a single command to instruct the DBMS to perform one or more actions. The DBMS must then break down the SQL command into a set of operations that it can perform one after the other to produce the requested result. These single operations are taken from the *relational algebra*.

Why look at relational algebra here, rather than when we look at SQL in depth? Because relational algebra also underlies some of the theory of relational database design, which we will discuss in Chapter 7.

Note: Don't panic. Although both the relational calculus and the relational algebra can be expressed in the notation of formal logic, there is no need for us to do so. You won't see anything remotely like mathematic notation in this chapter.

In this chapter we will look at seven relational algebra operations. The first five—restrict,[1] project, join, union, and difference—are fundamental to SQL and database design operations. In fact, any DBMS that supports them is said to be *relationally complete*. The remaining operations (product and intersect) are useful for helping us understand how SQL processes queries.

It is possible to design relational databases and use SQL without understanding much about relational algebra. However, you will find it easier to formulate effective, efficient queries if you have an understanding of what the SQL syntax is asking the DBMS to do. There is often more than one way to write a SQL command to obtain a specific result. The commands will often differ in the underlying relational algebra operations required

---

[1]Restrict is a renaming of the operation that was originally called "select." Because SQL's main retrieval command is SELECT (a relational calculus command), restrict was introduced by C. J. Date for the relational algebra operation to provide clarity. It is used in this book to help avoid confusion.

to generate results and therefore may differ significantly in performance. Understanding relational algebra can also help you to resolve some difficult relational database design problems.

Note: The bottom line is: You really do need to read this chapter. Once you've finished reading Chapter 7, where relational algebra gives us the tools to create well designed databases, you can put it aside until we get to material about using SQL to retrieve data. (Notice that the preceding doesn't give you permission to forget about it entirely...)

The most important thing to understand about relational algebra is that each operation does one thing and one thing only. For example, one operation extracts columns while another extracts rows. The DBMS must do the operations one at a time, in a step-by-step sequence. We therefore say that relational algebra is *procedural*. SQL, on the other hand, lets us formulate our queries in a logical way, without necessarily specifying the order in which relational operations should be performed. SQL is, therefore, *non-procedural*.

There is no official syntax for relational algebra. What you will see in this chapter, however, is a relatively consistent way of expressing the operations, without resorting to mathematical symbols. In general, each command has the following format:

```
OPERATION parameters FROM source_table_name(s)
   GIVING result_table_name
```

The parameters vary, depending on the specific operation. They may specify a second table that is part of the operation or they may specify which attributes are to be included in the result.

The result of every relational algebra operation is another table. In most cases, the table will be a relation, but some operations—such as the outer join—may have nulls in primary key columns (preventing the table from having a unique primary key) and therefore will not be legal relations. The result tables are virtual tables that can be used as input to another relational algebra operation.

The Relational Algebra and SQL Example Database: Rare Books

The relational algebra examples in this chapter and most of the SQL examples in this book are taken from a portion of a relational database that supports a rare book dealer. You can find the ER diagram in Figure 6.1. The rare book dealer handles rare fiction editions and some modern fiction. Because many of books are one-of-a-kind, he tracks each volume individually.

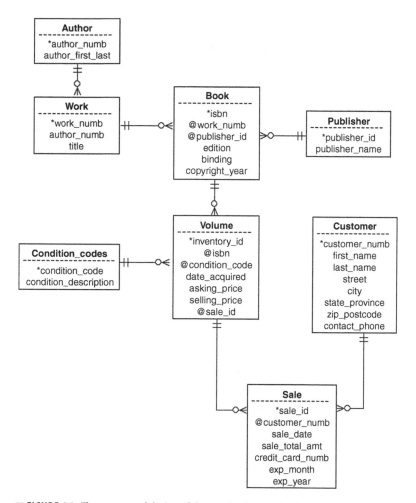

■ FIGURE 6.1 The conceptual design of the rare book store database.

The portion of the database we will be using contains data on customers and the volumes that they purchase. Notice, however, that it really takes three entities to describe a physical volume that is sold. The *work* entity describes a text written by one author, with one title. A *book* is a specific published version of a work (an edition); it is identified by an ISBN.[2] A *volume* is one physical copy of a book. This is the unit that is being sold.

Notice also that many of the text attributes of a *work/book/volume* are represented by numeric codes that act as foreign keys. For example, a book has

---

[2]It is true that some very old books do not have ISBNs. If that occurs, the rare book store gives the book a unique, arbitrary ID number.

a *work_id* that relates it to the work. It also has a *publisher_id* that connects to a table that contains the text of publisher names. Why design the database this way? Because it is very easy to make mistakes when typing text, especially long text, such as names and titles. Not only is a pain in the neck to type the same text repeatedly, but the chance of typos is fairly high. As you might expect, this is a very undesirable situation: Queries may not return accurate results. For this particular business, we store the text just once, and relate it to *works/books/volume* using integer codes.

The Sample Data

To make it easier to understand the relational algebra and SQL examples, we have loaded the rare bookstore database with tables. The data can be found in Tables 6.1–6.8.

Table 6.1 Publisher

```
publisher_id |                         publisher_name
-------------+-----------------------------------------------------
           1 | Wiley
           2 | Simon & Schuster
           3 | Macmillan
           4 | Tor
           5 | DAW
```

Table 6.2 Author

```
author_numb |                     author_last_first
------------+------------------------------------------------------
          1 | Bronte, Charlotte
          2 | Doyle, Sir Arthur Conan
          3 | Twain, Mark
          4 | Stevenson, Robert Louis
          5 | Rand, Ayn
          6 | Barrie, James
          7 | Ludlum, Robert
          8 | Barth, John
          9 | Herbert, Frank
         10 | Asimov, Isaac
         11 | Funke, Cornelia
         12 | Stephenson, Neal
```

Table 6.3 Condition Codes

```
condition_code  |           condition_description
----------------+-----------------------
              1 | New
              2 | Excellent
              3 | Fine
              4 | Good
              5 | Poor
```

Table 6.4 Work

```
work_numb  | author_numb |                  title
-----------+-------------+-----------------------------------------
         1 |           1 | Jane Eyre
         2 |           1 | Villette
         3 |           2 | Hound of the Baskervilles
         4 |           2 | Lost World, The
         5 |           2 | Complete Sherlock Holmes
         7 |           3 | Prince and the Pauper
         8 |           3 | Tom Sawyer
         9 |           3 | Adventures of Huckleberry Finn, The
         6 |           3 | Connecticut Yankee in King Arthur's Court, A
        13 |           5 | Fountainhead, The
        14 |           5 | Atlas Shrugged
        15 |           6 | Peter Pan
        10 |           7 | Bourne Identity, The
        11 |           7 | Matarese Circle, The
        12 |           7 | Bourne Supremacy, The
        16 |           4 | Kidnapped
        17 |           4 | Treasure Island
        18 |           8 | Sot Weed Factor, The
        19 |           8 | Lost in the Funhouse
        20 |           8 | Giles Goat Boy
        21 |           9 | Dune
        22 |           9 | Dune Messiah
        23 |          10 | Foundation
        24 |          10 | Last Foundation
        25 |          10 | I, Robot
        26 |          11 | Inkheart
        27 |          11 | Inkdeath
        28 |          12 | Anathem
        29 |          12 | Snow Crash
        30 |           5 | Anthem
        31 |          12 | Cryptonomicon
```

Table 6.5 Books

isbn	work_numb	publisher_id	edition	binding	copyright_year
978-1-11111-111-1	1	1	2	Board	1857
978-1-11111-112-1	1	1	1	Board	1847
978-1-11111-113-1	2	4	1	Board	1842
978-1-11111-114-1	3	4	1	Board	1801
978-1-11111-115-1	3	4	10	Leather	1925
978-1-11111-116-1	4	3	1	Board	1805
978-1-11111-117-1	5	5	1	Board	1808
978-1-11111-118-1	5	2	19	Leather	1956
978-1-11111-120-1	8	4	5	Board	1906
978-1-11111-119-1	6	2	3	Board	1956
978-1-11111-121-1	8	1	12	Leather	1982
978-1-11111-122-1	9	1	12	Leather	1982
978-1-11111-123-1	11	2	1	Board	1998
978-1-11111-124-1	12	2	1	Board	1989
978-1-11111-125-1	13	2	3	Board	1965
978-1-11111-126-1	13	2	9	Leather	2001
978-1-11111-127-1	14	2	1	Board	1960
978-1-11111-128-1	16	2	12	Board	1960
978-1-11111-129-1	16	2	14	Leather	2002
978-1-11111-130-1	17	3	6	Leather	1905
978-1-11111-131-1	18	4	6	Board	1957
978-1-11111-132-1	19	4	1	Board	1962
978-1-11111-133-1	20	4	1	Board	1964
978-1-11111-134-1	21	5	1	Board	1964
978-1-11111-135-1	23	5	1	Board	1962
978-1-11111-136-1	23	5	4	Leather	2001
978-1-11111-137-1	24	5	4	Leather	2001
978-1-11111-138-1	23	5	4	Leather	2001
978-1-11111-139-1	25	5	4	Leather	2001
978-1-11111-140-1	26	5	1	Board	2001
978-1-11111-141-1	27	5	1	Board	2005
978-1-11111-142-1	28	5	1	Board	2008
978-1-11111-143-1	29	5	1	Board	1992
978-1-11111-144-1	30	1	1	Board	1952
978-1-11111-145-1	30	5	1	Board	2001
978-1-11111-146-1	31	5	1	Board	1999

Making Vertical Subsets: Project

The first relational algebra operation we will consider is one that is used by every SQL query that retrieves data: project. A *projection* of a relation is a new relation created by copying one or more the columns from the source relation into a new table. As an example, consider Figure 6.2. The result table (arbitrarily called *names_and_numbers*) is a projection of the *customer* relation, containing the attributes *customer_numb*, *first_name*, and *last_name*.

Table 6.6 Volume (continues)

inventory_id	isbn	condition_code	date_acquired	asking_price	selling_price	sale_id
1	978-1-11111-111-1	3	12-JUN-19 00:00:00	175.00	175.00	1
2	978-1-11111-131-1	4	23-JAN-20 00:00:00	50.00	50.00	1
7	978-1-11111-137-1	2	20-JUN-19 00:00:00	80.00		
3	978-1-11111-133-1	2	05-APR-18 00:00:00	300.00	285.00	1
4	978-1-11111-142-1	1	05-APR-18 00:00:00	25.95	25.95	2
5	978-1-11111-146-1	1	05-APR-18 00:00:00	22.95	22.95	2
6	978-1-11111-144-1	2	15-MAY-19 00:00:00	80.00	76.10	2
8	978-1-11111-137-1	3	20-JUN-19 00:00:00	50.00		
9	978-1-11111-136-1	1	20-DEC-19 00:00:00	75.00		
10	978-1-11111-136-1	2	15-DEC-19 00:00:00	50.00		
11	978-1-11111-143-1	1	05-APR-20 00:00:00	25.00	25.00	3
12	978-1-11111-132-1	1	12-JUN-20 00:00:00	15.00	15.00	3
13	978-1-11111-133-1	3	20-APR-20 00:00:00	18.00	18.00	3
15	978-1-11111-121-1	2	20-APR-20 00:00:00	110.00	110.00	5
14	978-1-11111-121-1	2	20-APR-20 00:00:00	110.00	110.00	4
16	978-1-11111-121-1	2	20-APR-20 00:00:00	110.00		
17	978-1-11111-124-1	2	12-JAN-21 00:00:00	75.00		
18	978-1-11111-146-1	1	11-MAY-20 00:00:00	30.00	30.00	6
19	978-1-11111-122-1	2	06-MAY-20 00:00:00	75.00	75.00	6
20	978-1-11111-130-1	2	20-APR-20 00:00:00	150.00	120.00	6
21	978-1-11111-126-1	2	20-APR-20 00:00:00	110.00	110.00	6
22	978-1-11111-139-1	2	16-MAY-20 00:00:00	200.00	170.00	6
23	978-1-11111-125-1	2	16-MAY-20 00:00:00	45.00	45.00	7
24	978-1-11111-131-1	3	20-APR-20 00:00:00	35.00	35.00	7
25	978-1-11111-126-1	2	16-NOV-20 00:00:00	75.00	75.00	8
26	978-1-11111-133-1	3	16-NOV-20 00:00:00	35.00	55.00	8
27	978-1-11111-141-1	1	06-NOV-20 00:00:00	24.95		
28	978-1-11111-141-1	1	06-NOV-20 00:00:00	24.95		
29	978-1-11111-141-1	1	06-NOV-20 00:00:00	24.95		
30	978-1-11111-145-1	1	06-NOV-20 00:00:00	27.95		
31	978-1-11111-145-1	1	06-NOV-20 00:00:00	27.95		
32	978-1-11111-145-1	1	06-NOV-20 00:00:00	27.95		
33	978-1-11111-139-1	2	06-OCT-20 00:00:00	75.00	50.00	9
34	978-1-11111-133-1	1	16-NOV-20 00:00:00	125.00	125.00	10
35	978-1-11111-126-1	1	06-OCT-20 00:00:00	75.00	75.00	11
36	978-1-11111-130-1	3	06-DEC-19 00:00:00	50.00	50.00	11
37	978-1-11111-136-1	3	06-DEC-19 00:00:00	75.00	75.00	11
38	978-1-11111-130-1	2	06-APR-20 00:00:00	200.00	150.00	12
39	978-1-11111-132-1	3	06-APR-20 00:00:00	75.00	75.00	12
40	978-1-11111-129-1	1	06-APR-20 00:00:00	25.95	25.95	13
41	978-1-11111-141-1	1	16-MAY-20 00:00:00	40.00	40.00	14
42	978-1-11111-141-1	1	16-MAY-20 00:00:00	40.00	40.00	14
43	978-1-11111-132-1	1	12-NOV-20 00:00:00	17.95		
44	978-1-11111-138-1	1	12-NOV-20 00:00:00	75.95		
45	978-1-11111-138-1	1	12-NOV-20 00:00:00	75.95		
46	978-1-11111-131-1	3	12-NOV-20 00:00:00	15.95		
47	978-1-11111-140-1	3	12-NOV-20 00:00:00	25.95		
48	978-1-11111-123-1	2	16-AUG-20 00:00:00	24.95		
49	978-1-11111-127-1	2	16-AUG-20 00:00:00	27.95		
50	978-1-11111-127-1	2	06-JAN-21 00:00:00	50.00	50.00	15
51	978-1-11111-141-1	2	06-JAN-21 00:00:00	50.00	50.00	15
52	978-1-11111-141-1	2	06-JAN-21 00:00:00	50.00	50.00	16

(Continued)

Table 6.6 Volume (*cont.*)

53	978-1-11111-123-1	2	06-JAN-21 00:00:00	40.00	40.00	16
54	978-1-11111-127-1	2	06-JAN-21 00:00:00	40.00	40.00	16
55	978-1-11111-133-1	2	06-FEB-21 00:00:00	60.00	60.00	17
56	978-1-11111-127-1	2	16-FEB-21 00:00:00	40.00	40.00	17
57	978-1-11111-135-1	2	16-FEB-21 00:00:00	40.00	40.00	18
59	978-1-11111-127-1	2	25-FEB-21 00:00:00	35.00	35.00	18
58	978-1-11111-131-1	2	16-FEB-21 00:00:00	25.00	25.00	18
60	978-1-11111-128-1	2	16-DEC-20 00:00:00	50.00	45.00	
61	978-1-11111-136-1	3	22-OCT-20 00:00:00	50.00	50.00	19
62	978-1-11111-115-1	2	22-OCT-20 00:00:00	75.00	75.00	20
63	978-1-11111-130-1	2	16-JUL-20 00:00:00	500.00		
64	978-1-11111-136-1	2	06-MAR-20 00:00:00	125.00		
65	978-1-11111-136-1	2	06-MAR-20 00:00:00	125.00		
66	978-1-11111-137-1	2	06-MAR-20 00:00:00	125.00		
67	978-1-11111-137-1	2	06-MAR-20 00:00:00	125.00		
68	978-1-11111-138-1	2	06-MAR-20 00:00:00	125.00		
69	978-1-11111-138-1	2	06-MAR-20 00:00:00	125.00		
70	978-1-11111-139-1	2	06-MAR-20 00:00:00	125.00		
71	978-1-11111-139-1	2	06-MAR-20 00:00:00	125.00		

Table 6.7 Customer

customer_numb	first_name	last_name	street	city	state_province	zip_postcode	contact_phone
1	Janice	Jones	125 Center Road	Anytown	NY	11111	518-555-1111
2	Jon	Jones	25 Elm Road	Next Town	NJ	18888	209-555-2222
3	John	Doe	821 Elm Street	Next Town	NJ	18888	209-555-3333
4	Jane	Doe	852 Main Street	Anytown	NY	11111	518-555-4444
5	Jane	Smith	1919 Main Street	New Village	NY	13333	518-555-5555
6	Janice	Smith	800 Center Road	Anytown	NY	11111	518-555-6666
7	Helen	Brown	25 Front Street	Anytown	NY	11111	518-555-7777
8	Helen	Jerry	16 Main Street	Newtown	NJ	18886	518-555-8888
9	Mary	Collins	301 Pine Road, Apt. 12	Newtown	NJ	18886	518-555-9999
10	Peter	Collins	18 Main Street	Newtown	NJ	18886	518-555-1010
11	Edna	Hayes	209 Circle Road	Anytown	NY	11111	518-555-1110
12	Franklin	Hayes	615 Circle Road	Anytown	NY	11111	518-555-1212
13	Peter	Johnson	22 Rose Court	Next Town	NJ	18888	209-555-1212
14	Peter	Johnson	881 Front Street	Next Town	NJ	18888	209-555-1414
15	John	Smith	881 Manor Lane	Next Town	NJ	18888	209-555-1515

Using the syntax for relational algebra, the projection in Figure 6.2 is written:

```
PROJECT customer_rows, first_name, last_name
    FROM customer GIVING names_and_numbers
```

The order of the columns in the result table is based on the order in which the column names appear in the project statement; the order in which they are defined in the source table has no effect on the result. Rows appear in the order in which they are stored in the source table; project does not include sorting or ordering the data in any way. As with all relational algebra operations, duplicate rows are removed.

Table 6.8 Sale

sale_id	customer_ numb	sale_date	sale_total_ amt	credit_card_ numb	exp_month	exp_year
3	1	15-JUN-21 00:00:00	58.00	1234 5678 9101 1121	10	18
4	4	30-JUN-21 00:00:00	110.00	1234 5678 9101 5555	7	17
5	6	30-JUN-21 00:00:00	110.00	1234 5678 9101 6666	12	17
6	12	05-JUL-21 00:00:00	505.00	1234 5678 9101 7777	7	16
7	8	05-JUL-21 00:00:00	80.00	1234 5678 9101 8888	8	16
8	5	07-JUL-21 00:00:00	90.00	1234 5678 9101 9999	9	15
9	8	07-JUL-21 00:00:00	50.00	1234 5678 9101 8888	8	16
10	11	10-JUL-21 00:00:00	125.00	1234 5678 9101 1010	11	16
11	9	10-JUL-21 00:00:00	200.00	1234 5678 9101 0909	11	15
12	10	10-JUL-21 00:00:00	200.00	1234 5678 9101 0101	10	15
13	2	10-JUL-21 00:00:00	25.95	1234 5678 9101 2222	2	15
14	6	10-JUL-21 00:00:00	80.00	1234 5678 9101 6666	12	17
15	11	12-JUL-21 00:00:00	75.00	1234 5678 9101 1231	11	17
16	2	25-JUL-21 00:00:00	130.00	1234 5678 9101 2222	2	15
17	1	25-JUL-21 00:00:00	100.00	1234 5678 9101 1121	10	18
18	5	22-AUG-21 00:00:00	100.00	1234 5678 9101 9999	9	15
2	1	05-JUN-21 00:00:00	125.00	1234 5678 9101 1121	10	18
1	1	29-MAY-21 00:00:00	510.00	1234 5678 9101 1121	10	18
19	6	01-SEP-21 00:00:00	95.00	1234 5678 9101 7777	7	16
20	2	01-SEP-21 00:00:00	75.00	1234 5678 9101 2222	2	15

Note: It is important to keep in mind that relational algebra is first and foremost a set of theoretical operations. A DBMS may not implement an operation the same way that it is described in theory. For example, most DBMSs don't remove duplicate rows from result tables unless the user requests it explicitly. Why? Because to remove duplicates the DBMS must sort the result table by every column (so that duplicate rows will be next to one another), and then scan the table from top to bottom, looking for the duplicates. This can be a very slow process if the result table is large.

Whenever you issue a SQL command that asks for specific columns—just about every retrieval command—you are asking the DBMS to perform the *project* operation. Project is a very fast operation because the DBMS does not need to evaluate any of the data in the table.

There is one issue with project with which you need to be concerned. A DBMS will project any columns that you request. It makes no judgment as to whether the selected columns produce a meaningful result. For example, consider the following operation:

```
PROJECT sale_total_amt, exp_month FROM sale GIVING invalid
```

In theory, there is absolutely nothing wrong with this projection. However, it probably doesn't mean much to associate a dollar amount with a credit

```
customer_ | first_ | last_ |        street       |    city     | state_   | zip_     | contact_
numb      | name   | name  |                     |             | province | postcode | phone
----------+--------+-------+---------------------+-------------+----------+----------+----------------
        1 | Janice | Jones | 125 Center Road      | Anytown     | NY       | 11111    | 518-555-1111
        2 | Jon    | Jones | 25 Elm Road          | Next Town   | NJ       | 18888    | 209-555-2222
        3 | John   | Doe   | 821 Elm Street       | Next Town   | NJ       | 18888    | 209-555-3333
        4 | Jane   | Doe   | 852 Main Street      | Anytown     | NY       | 11111    | 518-555-4444
        5 | Jane   | Smith | 1919 Main Street     | New Village | NY       | 13333    | 518-555-5555
        6 | Janice | Smith | 800 Center Road      | Anytown     | NY       | 11111    | 518-555-6666
        7 | Helen  | Brown | 25 Front Street      | Anytown     | NY       | 11111    | 518-555-7777
        8 | Helen  | Jerry | 16 Main Street       | Newtown     | NJ       | 18886    | 518-555-8888
        9 | Mary   | Collins| 301 Pine Road, Apt. 12 | Newtown   | NJ       | 18886    | 518-555-9999
       10 | Peter  | Collins| 18 Main Street      | Newtown     | NJ       | 18886    | 518-555-1010
       11 | Edna   | Hayes | 209 Circle Road      | Anytown     | NY       | 11111    | 518-555-1110
       12 | Franklin| Hayes| 615 Circle Road      | Anytown     | NY       | 11111    | 518-555-1212
       13 | Peter  | Johnson| 22 Rose Court       | Next Town   | NJ       | 18888    | 209-555-1212
       14 | Peter  | Johnson| 881 Front Street    | Next Town   | NJ       | 18888    | 209-555-1414
```

```
                    PROJECT customer_numb, first_name, last_name
                    FROM customer GIVING Names_and_numbers
```

```
customer_ | first_  | last_   |
numb      | name    | name    |
----------+---------+---------+-
        1 | Janice  | Jones   |
        2 | Jon     | Jones   |
        3 | John    | Doe     |
        4 | Jane    | Doe     |
        5 | Jane    | Smith   |
        6 | Janice  | Smith   |
        7 | Helen   | Brown   |
        8 | Helen   | Jerry   |
        9 | Mary    | Collins |
       10 | Peter   | Collins |
       11 | Edna    | Hayes   |
       12 | Franklin| Hayes   |
       13 | Peter   | Johnson |
       14 | Peter   | Johnson |
```

■ **FIGURE 6.2 Taking a projection.**

card expiration month. Notice in Figure 6.3 that because there is more than one sale with the same total cost (for example, $110), the same sale value is associated with more than one expiration month. We could create a concatenated primary key for the result table using both columns, but that still would not make the resulting table meaningful in the context of the database environment. There is no set of rules as to what constitutes a meaningful projection. Judgments as to the usefulness of projections depend solely on the meaning of the data the database is trying to capture.

Making Horizontal Subsets: Restrict

The *restrict* operation asks a DBMS to choose rows that meet some logical criteria. As defined in the relational algebra, restrict copies rows from the source relation into a result table. Restrict copies all attributes; it has no way to specify which attributes should be included in the result table.

```
sale_id | customer_| sale_date | sale_total_amt |     credit_card_numb      | exp_month | exp_year
        |   numb   |           |                |                           |           |
--------+----------+-----------+----------------+---------------------------+-----------+----------
      3 |        1 | 15-JUN-13 |          58.00 | 1234 5678 9101 1121       |        10 |       18
      4 |        4 | 30-JUN-13 |         110.00 | 1234 5678 9101 5555       |         7 |       17
      5 |        6 | 30-JUN-13 |         110.00 | 1234 5678 9101 6666       |        12 |       17
      6 |       12 | 05-JUL-13 |         505.00 | 1234 5678 9101 7777       |         7 |       16
      7 |        8 | 05-JUL-13 |          80.00 | 1234 5678 9101 8888       |         8 |       16
      8 |        5 | 07-JUL-13 |          90.00 | 1234 5678 9101 9999       |         9 |       15
      9 |        8 | 07-JUL-13 |          50.00 | 1234 5678 9101 8888       |         8 |       16
     10 |       11 | 10-JUL-13 |         125.00 | 1234 5678 9101 1010       |        11 |       16
     11 |        9 | 10-JUL-13 |         200.00 | 1234 5678 9101 0909       |        11 |       15
     12 |       10 | 10-JUL-13 |         200.00 | 1234 5678 9101 0101       |        10 |       15
     13 |        2 | 10-JUL-13 |          25.95 | 1234 5678 9101 2222       |         2 |       15
     14 |        6 | 10-JUL-13 |          80.00 | 1234 5678 9101 6666       |        12 |       17
     15 |       11 | 12-JUL-13 |          75.00 | 1234 5678 9101 1231       |        11 |       17
     16 |        2 | 25-JUL-13 |         130.00 | 1234 5678 9101 2222       |         2 |       15
     17 |        1 | 25-JUL-13 |         100.00 | 1234 5678 9101 1121       |        10 |       18
     18 |        5 | 22-AUG-13 |         100.00 | 1234 5678 9101 9999       |         9 |       15
      2 |        1 | 05-JUN-13 |         125.00 | 1234 5678 9101 1121       |        10 |       18
      1 |        1 | 29-MAY-13 |         510.00 | 1234 5678 9101 1121       |        10 |       18
     19 |        6 | 01-SEP-13 |          95.00 | 1234 5678 9101 7777       |         7 |       16
     20 |        2 | 01-SEP-13 |          75.00 | 1234 5678 9101 2222       |         2 |       15
```

```
PROJECT sale_total_amt, exp_month
FROM sale GIVING invalid
```

```
sale_total_amt | exp_month
---------------+----------
         58.00 |        10
        110.00 |         7
        110.00 |        12
        505.00 |         7
         80.00 |         8
         90.00 |         9
         50.00 |         8
        125.00 |        11
        200.00 |        11
        200.00 |        10
         25.95 |         2
         80.00 |        12
         75.00 |        11
        130.00 |         2
        100.00 |        10
        100.00 |         9
        125.00 |        10
        510.00 |        10
         95.00 |         7
         75.00 |         2
```

■ **FIGURE 6.3 An invalid projection.**

Restrict identifies which rows are to be included in the result table, with a logical expression known as a *predicate*. The operation, therefore, takes the following general form:

```
RESTRICT FROM source_table_name
   WHERE predicate GIVING result_table_name
```

For example, suppose we want to retrieve data about customers who live in zip code 11111. The operation might be expressed as

```
RESTRICT FROM customer WHERE zip_postcode = '11111'
   GIVING one_zip
```

The operation appears in Figure 6.4. The result table includes the entire row for each customer that has a value of 11111 in the *zip_postcode* column.

```
customer_ | first_   | last_    |         street          |    city     | state_   | zip_     | contact_
numb      | name     | name     |                         |             | province | postcode | phone
----------+----------+----------+-------------------------+-------------+----------+----------+--------------
        1 | Janice   | Jones    | 125 Center Road         | Anytown     | NY       | 11111    | 518-555-1111
        2 | Jon      | Jones    | 25 Elm Road             | Next Town   | NJ       | 18888    | 209-555-2222
        3 | John     | Doe      | 821 Elm Street          | Next Town   | NJ       | 18888    | 209-555-3333
        4 | Jane     | Doe      | 852 Main Street         | Anytown     | NY       | 11111    | 518-555-4444
        5 | Jane     | Smith    | 1919 Main Street        | New Village | NY       | 13333    | 518-555-5555
        6 | Janice   | Smith    | 800 Center Road         | Anytown     | NY       | 11111    | 518-555-6666
        7 | Helen    | Brown    | 25 Front Street         | Anytown     | NY       | 11111    | 518-555-7777
        8 | Helen    | Jerry    | 16 Main Street          | Newtown     | NJ       | 18886    | 518-555-8888
        9 | Mary     | Collins  | 301 Pine Road, Apt. 12  | Newtown     | NJ       | 18886    | 518-555-9999
       10 | Peter    | Collins  | 18 Main Street          | Newtown     | NJ       | 18886    | 518-555-1010
       11 | Edna     | Hayes    | 209 Circle Road         | Anytown     | NY       | 11111    | 518-555-1110
       12 | Franklin | Hayes    | 615 Circle Road         | Anytown     | NY       | 11111    | 518-555-1212
       13 | Peter    | Johnson  | 22 Rose Court           | Next Town   | NJ       | 18888    | 209-555-1212
       14 | Peter    | Johnson  | 881 Front Street        | Next Town   | NJ       | 18888    | 209-555-1414
```

```
RESTRICT FROM customer WHERE zip_postcode = '11111'
GIVING one_zip
```

```
customer_ | first_   | last_    |      street       |  city   | state_   | zip_     | contact_
numb      | name     | name     |                   |         | province | postcode | phone
----------+----------+----------+-------------------+---------+----------+----------+--------------
        1 | Janice   | Jones    | 125 Center Road   | Anytown | NY       | 11111    | 518-555-1111
        4 | Jane     | Doe      | 852 Main Street   | Anytown | NY       | 11111    | 518-555-4444
        6 | Janice   | Smith    | 800 Center Road   | Anytown | NY       | 11111    | 518-555-6666
        7 | Helen    | Brown    | 25 Front Street   | Anytown | NY       | 11111    | 518-555-7777
       11 | Edna     | Hayes    | 209 Circle Road   | Anytown | NY       | 11111    | 518-555-1110
       12 | Franklin | Hayes    | 615 Circle Road   | Anytown | NY       | 11111    | 518-555-1212
```

■ **FIGURE 6.4** Restricting rows from a relation.

Note: There are many operators that can be used to create a restrict predicate, some of which are unique to SQL. You will begin to read about constructing predicates in Chapter 16.

Choosing Columns and Rows: Restrict and Then Project

As we said at the beginning of this chapter, most SQL queries require more than one relational algebra operation. We might, for example, want to see just the names of the customers that live in zip code 11111. Because such a query requires both a *restrict* and a *project*, it takes two steps:

1. Restrict the rows to those with customers that live in zip code 1111.
2. Project the first and last name columns.

In some cases, the order of the restrict and project may not matter. However, in this particular example, the restrict must be performed first. Why?

Because the project removes the column needed for the restrict predicate from the intermediate result table, which would make it impossible to perform the restrict.

It is up to a DBMS to determine the order in which it will perform relational algebra operations to obtain a requested result. A *query optimizer* takes care of making the decisions. When more than one series of operations will generate the same result, the query optimizer attempts to determine which will provide the best performance, and will then execute that strategy.

Note: There is a major tradeoff for a DBMS when it comes to query optimization. Picking the most efficient query strategy can result in the shortest query execution time, but it is also possible for the DBMS to spend so much time figuring out which strategy is best that it consumes any performance advantage that might be had by executing the best strategy. Therefore, the query strategy used by a DBMS may not be the theoretically most efficient strategy, but it is the most efficient strategy that can be identified relatively quickly.

Union

The *union* operation creates a new table by placing all rows from two source tables into a single result table, placing the rows on top of one another. As an example of how a union works, assume that you have the two tables at the top of Figure 6.5. The operation

```
in_print_books UNION out_of_print_books GIVING union_result
```

produces the result table at the bottom of Figure 6.5.

For a union operation to be possible, the two source tables must be *union compatible*. In the relational algebra sense, this means that their columns must be defined over the same domains. The tables must have the same columns, but the columns do not necessarily need to be in the same order or be the same size.

In practice, however, the rules for union compatibility are stricter. The two source tables on which the union is performed must have columns with the same data types and sizes, in the same order. As you will see, in SQL the two source tables are actually virtual tables created by two independent retrieval statements, which are then combined by the union operation.

Join

Join is arguably the most useful relational algebra operation, because it combines two tables into one, usually via a primary key–foreign key relationship. Unfortunately, a join can also be an enormous drain on database performance.

in_print_books

isbn	author_name	title
0-153-2345-0	Jones, Harold	My Life
0-154-2020-X	Smith, Kathryn	Autobiographical Tales
0-456-2946-0	Johnson, Mark	About Me

out_of_print_books

isbn	author_name	title
0-391-3847-2	Jones, Harold	Growing Up
0-381-4819-X	Jones, Harold	My Childhood
0-149-3857-5	Clark, Maggie	Horrible Teen Years, The

in_print_books UNION out_of_print_books GIVING union_result

isbn	author_name	title
0-149-3857-5	Clark, Maggie	Horrible Teen Years, The
0-153-2345-0	Jones, Harold	My Life
0-154-2020-X	Smith, Kathryn	Autobiographical Tales
0-381-4819-X	Jones, Harold	My Childhood
0-391-3847-2	Jones, Harold	Growing Up
0-456-2946-0	Johnson, Mark	About Me

■ FIGURE 6.5 The union operation.

A Non-Database Example

To help you understand how a join works, we will begin with an example that has absolutely nothing to do with relations. Assume that you have been given the task of creating manufacturing part assemblies by connecting two individual parts. The parts are classified as either A parts or B parts.

There are many types of A parts (A1 through A*n,* where *n* is the total number of types of A parts) and many types of B parts (B1 through B*n*). Each B is to be matched to the A part with the same number; conversely, an A part is to be matched to a B part with the same number.

The assembly process requires four bins. One contains the A parts, one contains the B parts, and one will hold the completed assemblies. The remaining bin will hold parts that cannot be matched. (The unmatched parts bin is not strictly necessary; it is simply for your convenience.)

You begin by extracting a part from the B bin. You look at the part to determine the A part to which it should be connected. Then, you search the A bin for the correct part. If you can find a matching A part, you connect the two pieces and toss them into the completed assemblies bin. If you cannot find a matching A part, then you toss the unmatched B part into the bin that holds unmatched B parts. You repeat this process until the B bin is empty. Any unmatched A parts will be left in their original location.

Note: You could just as easily have started with the bin containing the A parts. The contents of the bin holding the completed assemblies will be the same.

As you might guess, the A bins and B bins are analogous to tables that have a primary to foreign key relationship. This matching of part numbers is very much like the matching of data that occurs when you perform a join. The completed assembly bin corresponds to the result table of the operation. As you read about the operation of a join, keep in mind that the parts that could not be matched were left out of the completed assemblies bin.

The Equi-Join

In its most common form, a join forms new rows when data in the two source tables match. Because we are looking for rows with equal values, this type of join is known as an *equi-join* (or a *natural equi-join*). It is also often called an *inner join*. As an example, consider the join in Figure 6.6.

Notice that the *customer_numb* column is the primary key of the *customer_data* table, and that the same column is a foreign key in the *sale_data* table. The *customer_numb* column in *sale_data* therefore serves to relate sales to the customers to which they belong.

customer_data

```
 customer_numb | first_name | last_name
---------------+------------+-----------
             1 | Janice     | Jones
             2 | Jon        | Jones
             3 | John       | Doe
             4 | Jane       | Doe
             5 | Jane       | Smith
             6 | Janice     | Smith
             7 | Helen      | Brown
             8 | Helen      | Jerry
             9 | Mary       | Collins
            10 | Peter      | Collins
            11 | Edna       | Hayes
            12 | Franklin   | Hayes
            13 | Peter      | Johnson
            14 | Peter      | Johnson
            15 | John       | Smith
```

sale_data

```
 sale_id | customer_numb |      sale_date       | sale_total_amt
---------+---------------+----------------------+----------------
       3 |             1 | 15-JUN-13 00:00:00 |          58.00
       4 |             4 | 30-JUN-13 00:00:00 |         110.00
       5 |             6 | 30-JUN-13 00:00:00 |         110.00
       6 |            12 | 05-JUL-13 00:00:00 |         505.00
       7 |             8 | 05-JUL-13 00:00:00 |          80.00
       8 |             5 | 07-JUL-13 00:00:00 |          90.00
       9 |             8 | 07-JUL-13 00:00:00 |          50.00
      10 |            11 | 10-JUL-13 00:00:00 |         125.00
      11 |             9 | 10-JUL-13 00:00:00 |         200.00
      12 |            10 | 10-JUL-13 00:00:00 |         200.00
      13 |             2 | 10-JUL-13 00:00:00 |          25.95
      14 |             6 | 10-JUL-13 00:00:00 |          80.00
      15 |            11 | 12-JUL-13 00:00:00 |          75.00
      16 |             2 | 25-JUL-13 00:00:00 |         130.00
      17 |             1 | 25-JUL-13 00:00:00 |         100.00
      18 |             5 | 22-AUG-13 00:00:00 |         100.00
       2 |             1 | 05-JUN-13 00:00:00 |         125.00
       1 |             1 | 29-MAY-13 00:00:00 |         510.00
      19 |             6 | 01-SEP-13 00:00:00 |          95.00
      20 |             2 | 01-SEP-13 00:00:00 |          75.00
```

JOIN cusstomer_data TO sale_data OVER customer_numb GIVING joined_table

joined_table

```
 customer_numb | first_name | last_name | sale_id |      sale_date       | sale_total_amt
---------------+------------+-----------+---------+----------------------+----------------
             1 | Janice     | Jones     |       3 | 15-JUN-13 00:00:00 |          58.00
             4 | Jane       | Doe       |       4 | 30-JUN-13 00:00:00 |         110.00
             6 | Janice     | Smith     |       5 | 30-JUN-13 00:00:00 |         110.00
            12 | Franklin   | Hayes     |       6 | 05-JUL-13 00:00:00 |         505.00
             8 | Helen      | Jerry     |       7 | 05-JUL-13 00:00:00 |          80.00
             5 | Jane       | Smith     |       8 | 07-JUL-13 00:00:00 |          90.00
             8 | Helen      | Jerry     |       9 | 07-JUL-13 00:00:00 |          50.00
            11 | Edna       | Hayes     |      10 | 10-JUL-13 00:00:00 |         125.00
             9 | Mary       | Collins   |      11 | 10-JUL-13 00:00:00 |         200.00
            10 | Peter      | Collins   |      12 | 10-JUL-13 00:00:00 |         200.00
             2 | Jon        | Jones     |      13 | 10-JUL-13 00:00:00 |          25.95
             6 | Janice     | Smith     |      14 | 10-JUL-13 00:00:00 |          80.00
            11 | Edna       | Hayes     |      15 | 12-JUL-13 00:00:00 |          75.00
             2 | Jon        | Jones     |      16 | 25-JUL-13 00:00:00 |         130.00
             1 | Janice     | Jones     |      17 | 25-JUL-13 00:00:00 |         100.00
             5 | Jane       | Smith     |      18 | 22-AUG-13 00:00:00 |         100.00
             1 | Janice     | Jones     |       2 | 05-JUN-13 00:00:00 |         125.00
             1 | Janice     | Jones     |       1 | 29-MAY-13 00:00:00 |         510.00
             6 | Janice     | Smith     |      19 | 01-SEP-13 00:00:00 |          95.00
             2 | Jon        | Jones     |      20 | 01-SEP-13 00:00:00 |          75.00
```

■ **FIGURE 6.6** An equi-join.

Assume that you want to see the names of the customers who placed each order. To do so, you must join the two tables, creating combined rows wherever there is a matching *customer_numb*. In database terminology, we are joining the two tables *over customer_numb*. The result table, *joined_table*, can be found at the bottom of Figure 6.6.

An equi-join can begin with either source table. (The result should be the same, regardless of the direction in which the join is performed.) The join compares each row in one source table with the rows in the second. For each row in the first source table that matches data in the second source table in the column or columns over which the join is being performed, a new row is placed in the result table.

Assume that we are using the *customer_data* table as the first source table, producing the result table in Figure 6.6. The join might, therefore, proceed conceptually as follows:

1. Search *sale_data* for rows with a *customer_numb* of 1. There are four matching rows in *sale_data*. Create four new rows in the result table, placing the same customer information in each row, along with the data from *sale_data*.
2. Search *sale_data* for rows with a *customer_numb* of 2. Because there are three rows for customer 2 in *sale_data*, add three rows to the result table.
3. Search *sale_data* for rows with a *customer_numb* of 3. Because there are no matching rows in *sale_data*, do not place a row in the result table.
4. Continue as established until all rows from *customer_data* have been compared to *sale_data*.

If the value from the *customer_numb* column does not appear in both tables, then no row is placed in the result table. This behavior categorizes this type of join as an inner join. (Yes, there is such a thing as an outer join. You will read about it shortly.)

What's Really Going On: Product and Restrict

From a relational algebra point of view, a join can be implemented using two other operations: product and restrict. As you will see, this sequence of operations requires the manipulation of a great deal of data and, if implemented by a DBMS, can result in slow query performance. Many of today's DBMSs therefore use alternative techniques for processing joins. Nonetheless, the concept of using product followed by restrict underlies the original SQL join syntax.

The *product* operation (the mathematical Cartesian product) makes every possible pairing of rows from two source tables. The product of the tables in Figure 6.6 produces a result table with 300 rows (the 15 rows in *customer_data* times the 20 rows in *sale_data*), the first 60 of which appear in Figure 6.7.

Note: Although 300 rows may not seem like a lot, consider the size of a product table created from tables with 10,000 and 100,000 rows! The manipulation of a table of this size can tie up a lot of disk I/O and CPU time.

customer_numb	first_name	last_name	sale_id	customer_numb	sale_date	sale_total_amt
1	Janice	Jones	3	1	15-JUN-13 00:00:00	58.00
2	Jon	Jones	3	1	15-JUN-13 00:00:00	58.00
3	John	Doe	3	1	15-JUN-13 00:00:00	58.00
4	Jane	Doe	3	1	15-JUN-13 00:00:00	58.00
5	Jane	Smith	3	1	15-JUN-13 00:00:00	58.00
6	Janice	Smith	3	1	15-JUN-13 00:00:00	58.00
7	Helen	Brown	3	1	15-JUN-13 00:00:00	58.00
8	Helen	Jerry	3	1	15-JUN-13 00:00:00	58.00
9	Mary	Collins	3	1	15-JUN-13 00:00:00	58.00
10	Peter	Collins	3	1	15-JUN-13 00:00:00	58.00
11	Edna	Hayes	3	1	15-JUN-13 00:00:00	58.00
12	Franklin	Hayes	3	1	15-JUN-13 00:00:00	58.00
13	Peter	Johnson	3	1	15-JUN-13 00:00:00	58.00
14	Peter	Johnson	3	1	15-JUN-13 00:00:00	58.00
15	John	Smith	3	1	15-JUN-13 00:00:00	58.00
1	Janice	Jones	4	4	30-JUN-13 00:00:00	110.00
2	Jon	Jones	4	4	30-JUN-13 00:00:00	110.00
3	John	Doe	4	4	30-JUN-13 00:00:00	110.00
4	Jane	Doe	4	4	30-JUN-13 00:00:00	110.00
5	Jane	Smith	4	4	30-JUN-13 00:00:00	110.00
6	Janice	Smith	4	4	30-JUN-13 00:00:00	110.00
7	Helen	Brown	4	4	30-JUN-13 00:00:00	110.00
8	Helen	Jerry	4	4	30-JUN-13 00:00:00	110.00
9	Mary	Collins	4	4	30-JUN-13 00:00:00	110.00
10	Peter	Collins	4	4	30-JUN-13 00:00:00	110.00
11	Edna	Hayes	4	4	30-JUN-13 00:00:00	110.00
12	Franklin	Hayes	4	4	30-JUN-13 00:00:00	110.00
13	Peter	Johnson	4	4	30-JUN-13 00:00:00	110.00
14	Peter	Johnson	4	4	30-JUN-13 00:00:00	110.00
15	John	Smith	4	4	30-JUN-13 00:00:00	110.00
1	Janice	Jones	5	6	30-JUN-13 00:00:00	110.00
2	Jon	Jones	5	6	30-JUN-13 00:00:00	110.00
3	John	Doe	5	6	30-JUN-13 00:00:00	110.00
4	Jane	Doe	5	6	30-JUN-13 00:00:00	110.00
5	Jane	Smith	5	6	30-JUN-13 00:00:00	110.00
6	Janice	Smith	5	6	30-JUN-13 00:00:00	110.00
7	Helen	Brown	5	6	30-JUN-13 00:00:00	110.00
8	Helen	Jerry	5	6	30-JUN-13 00:00:00	110.00
9	Mary	Collins	5	6	30-JUN-13 00:00:00	110.00
10	Peter	Collins	5	6	30-JUN-13 00:00:00	110.00
11	Edna	Hayes	5	6	30-JUN-13 00:00:00	110.00
12	Franklin	Hayes	5	6	30-JUN-13 00:00:00	110.00
13	Peter	Johnson	5	6	30-JUN-13 00:00:00	110.00
14	Peter	Johnson	5	6	30-JUN-13 00:00:00	110.00
15	John	Smith	5	6	30-JUN-13 00:00:00	110.00
1	Janice	Jones	6	12	05-JUL-13 00:00:00	505.00
2	Jon	Jones	6	12	05-JUL-13 00:00:00	505.00
3	John	Doe	6	12	05-JUL-13 00:00:00	505.00
4	Jane	Doe	6	12	05-JUL-13 00:00:00	505.00
5	Jane	Smith	6	12	05-JUL-13 00:00:00	505.00
6	Janice	Smith	6	12	05-JUL-13 00:00:00	505.00
7	Helen	Brown	6	12	05-JUL-13 00:00:00	505.00
8	Helen	Jerry	6	12	05-JUL-13 00:00:00	505.00
9	Mary	Collins	6	12	05-JUL-13 00:00:00	505.00
10	Peter	Collins	6	12	05-JUL-13 00:00:00	505.00
11	Edna	Hayes	6	12	05-JUL-13 00:00:00	505.00
12	Franklin	Hayes	6	12	05-JUL-13 00:00:00	505.00
13	Peter	Johnson	6	12	05-JUL-13 00:00:00	505.00
14	Peter	Johnson	6	12	05-JUL-13 00:00:00	505.00
15	John	Smith	6	12	05-JUL-13 00:00:00	505.00

■ **FIGURE 6.7** The first 60 rows of a 300 row product table.

Notice first that the *customer_numb* is included twice in the result table, once from each source table. Second, notice that in some rows the *customer_numb* is the same. These are the rows that would have been included in a join. We can therefore apply a restrict predicate (a *join condition*) to the product table to end up with same table provided by the join you saw earlier. The predicate can be written:

```
customer.customer_numb = sale.customer_numb
```

The rows that are selected by this predicate from the first 60 rows in the product table appear in black in Figure 6.8; those eliminated by the predicate are gray.

Note: The "dot notation" that you see in the preceding join condition is used throughout SQL. The table name is followed by a dot, which is followed by the column name. This makes it possible to have the same column name in more than one table and yet be able to distinguish among them.

It is important that you keep in mind the implication of this sequence of two relational algebra operations when you are writing SQL joins. If you are using the traditional SQL syntax for a join, and you forget the predicate for the join condition, you will end up with a product. The product table contains bad information; it implies facts that are not actually stored in the database. It is therefore potentially harmful, in that a user who does not understand how the result table came to be might assume that it is correct and make business decisions based on the bad data.

Equi-Joins over Concatenated Keys

The joins you have seen so far have used a single-column primary key and a single-column foreign key. There is no reason, however, that the values used in a join can't be concatenated. As an example, let us look again at the four relations from the accounting firm database that was used as an example in Chapter 5:

```
accountant (acct_first_name, acct_last_name, date_hired,
    office_ext)
```

```
customer (customer_numb, first_name, last_name, street,
    city, state_province, zip_postcode, contact_phone)
```

```
job (tax_year, customer_numb, acct_first_name,
    acct_last_name)
```

```
form (tax_year, customer_numb, form_id, is_complete)
```

Suppose we want to see all the forms, and the year that the forms were completed for the customer named Peter Jones by the accountant named

customer_numb	first_name	last_name	sale_id	customer_numb	sale_date	sale_total_amt
1	Janice	Jones	3	1	15-JUN-13 00:00:00	58.00
2	Jon	Jones	3	1	15-JUN-13 00:00:00	58.00
3	John	Doe	3	1	15-JUN-13 00:00:00	58.00
4	Jane	Doe	3	1	15-JUN-13 00:00:00	58.00
5	Jane	Smith	3	1	15-JUN-13 00:00:00	58.00
6	Janice	Smith	3	1	15-JUN-13 00:00:00	58.00
7	Helen	Brown	3	1	15-JUN-13 00:00:00	58.00
8	Helen	Jerry	3	1	15-JUN-13 00:00:00	58.00
9	Mary	Collins	3	1	15-JUN-13 00:00:00	58.00
10	Peter	Collins	3	1	15-JUN-13 00:00:00	58.00
11	Edna	Hayes	3	1	15-JUN-13 00:00:00	58.00
12	Franklin	Hayes	3	1	15-JUN-13 00:00:00	58.00
13	Peter	Johnson	3	1	15-JUN-13 00:00:00	58.00
14	Peter	Johnson	3	1	15-JUN-13 00:00:00	58.00
15	John	Smith	3	1	15-JUN-13 00:00:00	58.00
1	Janice	Jones	4	4	30-JUN-13 00:00:00	110.00
2	Jon	Jones	4	4	30-JUN-13 00:00:00	110.00
3	John	Doe	4	4	30-JUN-13 00:00:00	110.00
4	**Jane**	**Doe**	**4**	**4**	**30-JUN-13 00:00:00**	**110.00**
5	Jane	Smith	4	4	30-JUN-13 00:00:00	110.00
6	Janice	Smith	4	4	30-JUN-13 00:00:00	110.00
7	Helen	Brown	4	4	30-JUN-13 00:00:00	110.00
8	Helen	Jerry	4	4	30-JUN-13 00:00:00	110.00
9	Mary	Collins	4	4	30-JUN-13 00:00:00	110.00
10	Peter	Collins	4	4	30-JUN-13 00:00:00	110.00
11	Edna	Hayes	4	4	30-JUN-13 00:00:00	110.00
12	Franklin	Hayes	4	4	30-JUN-13 00:00:00	110.00
13	Peter	Johnson	4	4	30-JUN-13 00:00:00	110.00
14	Peter	Johnson	4	4	30-JUN-13 00:00:00	110.00
15	John	Smith	4	4	30-JUN-13 00:00:00	110.00
1	Janice	Jones	5	6	30-JUN-13 00:00:00	110.00
2	Jon	Jones	5	6	30-JUN-13 00:00:00	110.00
3	John	Doe	5	6	30-JUN-13 00:00:00	110.00
4	Jane	Doe	5	6	30-JUN-13 00:00:00	110.00
5	Jane	Smith	5	6	30-JUN-13 00:00:00	110.00
6	**Janice**	**Smith**	**5**	**6**	**30-JUN-13 00:00:00**	**110.00**
7	Helen	Brown	5	6	30-JUN-13 00:00:00	110.00
8	Helen	Jerry	5	6	30-JUN-13 00:00:00	110.00
9	Mary	Collins	5	6	30-JUN-13 00:00:00	110.00
10	Peter	Collins	5	6	30-JUN-13 00:00:00	110.00
11	Edna	Hayes	5	6	30-JUN-13 00:00:00	110.00
12	Franklin	Hayes	5	6	30-JUN-13 00:00:00	110.00
13	Peter	Johnson	5	6	30-JUN-13 00:00:00	110.00
14	Peter	Johnson	5	6	30-JUN-13 00:00:00	110.00
15	John	Smith	5	6	30-JUN-13 00:00:00	110.00
1	Janice	Jones	6	12	05-JUL-13 00:00:00	505.00
2	Jon	Jones	6	12	05-JUL-13 00:00:00	505.00
3	John	Doe	6	12	05-JUL-13 00:00:00	505.00
4	Jane	Doe	6	12	05-JUL-13 00:00:00	505.00
5	Jane	Smith	6	12	05-JUL-13 00:00:00	505.00
6	Janice	Smith	6	12	05-JUL-13 00:00:00	505.00
7	Helen	Brown	6	12	05-JUL-13 00:00:00	505.00
8	Helen	Jerry	6	12	05-JUL-13 00:00:00	505.00
9	Mary	Collins	6	12	05-JUL-13 00:00:00	505.00
10	Peter	Collins	6	12	05-JUL-13 00:00:00	505.00
11	Edna	Hayes	6	12	05-JUL-13 00:00:00	505.00
12	**Franklin**	**Hayes**	**6**	**12**	**05-JUL-13 00:00:00**	**505.00**
13	Peter	Johnson	6	12	05-JUL-13 00:00:00	505.00
14	Peter	Johnson	6	12	05-JUL-13 00:00:00	505.00
15	John	Smith	6	12	05-JUL-13 00:00:00	505.00

■ **FIGURE 6.8** The four rows of the product in Figure 6.6 that are returned by the join condition in a restrict predicate.

Edgar Smith. The sequence of relational operations would go something like this:

1. Restrict from the customer table to find the single row for Peter Jones. Because some customers have duplicated names, the restrict predicate would probably contain the name and the phone number. (We are assuming that the person setting up the query doesn't know the customer number.)
2. Join the table created in Step 1 to the *job* table over the customer number. The result table contains one row for each job that the accounting firm has performed for Peter Jones. The primary key of the result table will be the customer number and the tax year.
3. Restrict from the table created in Step 2 to find the jobs for Peter Jones that were handled by the accountant Edgar Smith. (Because a restrict does not specify which columns appear in the result table, the result table will have the same primary key as the result table from Step 2.)
4. Now, we need to get the data about which forms appear on the jobs identified in Step 3. We therefore need to join the table created in Step 3 to the *form* table. There is a concatenated foreign key in the *form* table—the tax year and customer number—which just happens to match the primary key of the result table produced by Step 3. The join is therefore over the concatenation of the tax year and customer number, rather than over the individual values. When making its determination whether to include a row in the result table, the DBMS puts the tax year and customer number together for each row and treats the combined value as if it were one.
5. Project the tax year and form ID to present the specific data requested in the query.

To see why treating a concatenated foreign key as a single unit when comparing to a concatenated foreign key is required, take a look at Figure 6.9. The two tables at the top of the illustration are the original *job* and *form* tables created for this example. We are interested in customer number 18 (our friend Peter Jones), who has had jobs handled by Edgar Smith in 2006 and 2007.

Result table (a) is what happens if you join the tables (without restricting for customer 18) only over the tax year. This incorrect join expands the 10 row *form* table to 20 rows. The data imply that the same customer had the same form prepared by more than one accountant in the same year.

Result table (b) is the result of joining the two tables just over the customer number. This time, the incorrect result table implies that, in some cases, the same form was completed in two years, which may or may not be correct.

job

tax_year	customer_numb	acct_first_name	acct_last_name
2006	12	Jon	Johnson
2007	18	Edgar	Smith
2006	18	Edgar	Smith
2007	6	Edgar	Smith

form

tax_year	customer_numb	form_id	is_complete
2006	12	1040	t
2006	12	Sch. A	t
2006	12	Sch. B	t
2007	18	1040	t
2007	18	Sch. A	t
2007	18	Sch. B	t
2006	18	1040	t
2006	18	Sch. A	t
2007	6	1040	t
2007	6	Sch. A	t

(a) project JOIN form OVER tax_year GIVING invalid_1

tax_year	customer_numb	acct_first_name	acct_last_name	tax_year	customer_numb	form_id	is_complete
2006	18	Edgar	Smith	2006	12	1040	t
2006	12	Jon	Johnson	2006	12	1040	t
2006	18	Edgar	Smith	2006	12	Sch. A	t
2006	12	Jon	Johnson	2006	12	Sch. A	t
2006	18	Edgar	Smith	2006	12	Sch. B	t
2006	12	Jon	Johnson	2006	12	Sch. B	t
2007	6	Edgar	Smith	2007	18	1040	t
2007	18	Edgar	Smith	2007	18	1040	t
2007	6	Edgar	Smith	2007	18	Sch. A	t
2007	18	Edgar	Smith	2007	18	Sch. A	t
2007	6	Edgar	Smith	2007	18	Sch. B	t
2007	18	Edgar	Smith	2007	18	Sch. B	t
2006	18	Edgar	Smith	2006	18	1040	t
2006	12	Jon	Johnson	2006	18	1040	t
2006	18	Edgar	Smith	2006	18	Sch. A	t
2006	12	Jon	Johnson	2006	18	Sch. A	t
2007	6	Edgar	Smith	2007	6	1040	t
2007	18	Edgar	Smith	2007	6	1040	t
2007	6	Edgar	Smith	2007	6	Sch. A	t
2007	18	Edgar	Smith	2007	6	Sch. A	t

(b) job JOIN form OVER tax_year GIVING invalid_2

tax_year	customer_numb	acct_first_name	acct_last_name	tax_year	customer_numb	form_id	is_complete
2006	12	Jon	Johnson	2006	12	1040	t
2006	12	Jon	Johnson	2006	12	Sch. A	t
2006	12	Jon	Johnson	2006	12	Sch. B	t
2006	18	Edgar	Smith	2007	18	1040	t
2007	18	Edgar	Smith	2007	18	1040	t
2006	18	Edgar	Smith	2007	18	Sch. A	t
2007	18	Edgar	Smith	2007	18	Sch. A	t
2006	18	Edgar	Smith	2007	18	Sch. B	t
2007	18	Edgar	Smith	2007	18	Sch. B	t
2006	18	Edgar	Smith	2006	18	1040	t
2007	18	Edgar	Smith	2006	18	1040	t
2006	18	Edgar	Smith	2006	18	Sch. A	t
2007	18	Edgar	Smith	2006	18	Sch. A	t
2007	6	Edgar	Smith	2007	6	1040	t
2007	6	Edgar	Smith	2007	6	Sch. A	t(

(c) job JOIN form OVER tax_year + customer_numb GIVING correct_result

tax_year	customer_numb	acct_first_name	acct_last_name	tax_year	customer_numb	form_id	is_complete
2006	12	Jon	Johnson	2006	12	1040	t
2006	12	Jon	Johnson	2006	12	Sch. A	t
2006	12	Jon	Johnson	2006	12	Sch. B	t
2006	18	Edgar	Smith	2006	18	1040	t
2006	18	Edgar	Smith	2006	18	Sch. A	t
2007	18	Edgar	Smith	2007	18	Sch. B	t
2007	18	Edgar	Smith	2007	18	1040	t
2007	18	Edgar	Smith	2007	18	Sch. A	t
2007	6	Edgar	Smith	2007	6	1040	t
2007	6	Edgar	Smith	2007	6	Sch. A	t

■ **FIGURE 6.9 Joining using concatenated keys.**

The correct join appears in result table (c) in Figure 6.9. It has the correct 10 rows, one for each form. Notice that *both* the tax year and customer number are the same in each row, as we intended them to be.

Note: The examples you have seen so far involve two concatenated columns. There is no reason, however, that the concatenation cannot involve more than two columns if necessary.

Θ-Joins

An equi-join is a specific example of a more general class of join known as a Θ-*join* (*theta-join*). A Θ-join combines two tables on some condition, which may be equality or may be something else. To make it easier to understand why you might want to join on something other than equality and how such joins work, assume that you're on vacation at a resort that offers both biking and hiking. Each outing runs a half day, but the times at which the outings start and end differ. The tables that hold the outing schedules appear in Figure 6.10. As you look at the data, you will see that some ending and starting times overlap, which means that if you want to engage in two outings on the same day, only some pairings of hiking and biking will work.

```
hiking                                      biking

tour_numb | start_time | end_time          tour_numb | start_time | end_time
----------+------------+---------          ----------+------------+---------
       6 | 01:00:00   | 16:00:00                  1 | 09:00:00   | 12:00:00
       8 | 09:00:00   | 11:30:00                  2 | 09:00:00   | 11:30:00
       9 | 10:00:00   | 14:00:00                  3 | 09:00:00   | 12:30:00
      10 | 09:00:00   | 12:00:00                  4 | 12:00:00   | 15:00:00
       7 | 12:00:00   | 15:30:00                  5 | 13:00:00   | 17:00:00
```

■ **FIGURE 6.10 Source tables for the Θ-join examples**.

To determine which pairs of outings you could do on the same day, you need to find pairs of outings that satisfy either of the following conditions:

```
hiking.end_time < biking.start_time
```

```
biking.end_time < hiking.start_time
```

A Θ-join over either of those conditions will do the trick, producing the result tables in Figure 6.11. The top result table contains pairs of outings where hiking is done first; the middle result table contains pairs of outings where biking is done first. If you want all the possibilities in the same table, a union operation will combine them, as in the bottom result table. Another way to generate the combined table is to use a complex join condition in the Θ-join:

```
hiking.end_time < biking.start_time OR
    biking.end_time < hiking.start_time
```

Note: As with the more restrictive equi-join, the "start" table for a Θ-join does not matter. The result will be the same, either way.

```
hiking

tour_numb | start_time | end_time
----------+------------+----------
        6 | 01:00:00   | 16:00:00
        8 | 09:00:00   | 11:30:00
        9 | 10:00:00   | 14:00:00
       10 | 09:00:00   | 12:00:00
        7 | 12:00:00   | 15:30:00
```

```
biking

tour_numb | start_time | end_time
----------+------------+----------
        1 | 09:00:00   | 12:00:00
        2 | 09:00:00   | 11:30:00
        3 | 09:00:00   | 12:30:00
        4 | 12:00:00   | 15:00:00
        5 | 13:00:00   | 17:00:00
```

```
hiking JOIN biking OVER hiking.end_time < biking.start_time GIVING hiking_first

tour_numb | start_time | end_time | tour_numb | start_time | end_time
----------+------------+----------+-----------+------------+----------
        4 | 12:00:00   | 15:00:00 |         8 | 09:00:00   | 11:30:00
        5 | 13:00:00   | 17:00:00 |         8 | 09:00:00   | 11:30:00
        5 | 13:00:00   | 17:00:00 |        10 | 09:00:00   | 12:00:00
```

```
hiking JOIN biking OVER biking.end_time < hiking.start_time gIVING biking_first

tour_numb | start_time | end_time | tour_numb | start_time | end_time
----------+------------+----------+-----------+------------+----------
        2 | 09:00:00   | 11:30:00 |         7 | 12:00:00   | 15:30:00
```

```
hiking JOIN biking OVER hiking.end_time < biking.start_time GIVING hiking_first
UNION
hiking JOIN biking OVER biking.end_time < hiking.start_time GIVING biking_first
tour_numb | start_time | end_time | tour_numb | start_time | end_time
----------+------------+----------+-----------+------------+----------
        4 | 12:00:00   | 15:00:00 |         8 | 09:00:00   | 11:30:00
        5 | 13:00:00   | 17:00:00 |         8 | 09:00:00   | 11:30:00
        5 | 13:00:00   | 17:00:00 |        10 | 09:00:00   | 12:00:00
        7 | 12:00:00   | 15:30:00 |         2 | 09:00:00   | 11:30:00
```

■ **FIGURE 6.11** **The results of Θ-joins of the tables in Figure 6.10.**

Outer Joins

An *outer join* (as opposed to the inner joins we have been considering so far) is a join that includes rows in a result table even though there may not be a match between rows in the two tables being joined. Wherever the DBMS can't match rows, it places nulls in the columns for which no data exist. The result may therefore not be a legal relation because it may not have a primary key. However, because they query's result table is a virtual table that is never stored in the database, having no primary key does not present a data integrity problem.

Why might someone want to perform an outer join? An employee of the rare book store, for example, might want to see the names of all customers along with the books ordered in the last week. An inner join of the customer table to the sale table would eliminate those customers who had not purchased anything during the previous week. However, an outer join will include all customers, placing nulls in the sale data columns for the customers who have not ordered. An outer join, therefore, not only shows you matching data, but also tells you where matching data *do not* exist.

There are really three types of outer join, which vary depending on the table or tables from which you want to include rows that have no matches.

The Left Outer Join

The *left outer join* includes all rows from the first table in the join expression, along with rows with matching foreign keys from the second:

```
Table1 LEFT OUTER JOIN table2 GIVING result_table
```

For example, if we use the data from the tables in Figure 6.6 and perform the *left outer join* as

```
customer LEFT OUTER JOIN sale GIVING left_outer_join_result
```

then the result will appear as in Figure 6.12: There is a row for every row in *customer*. For the rows that don't have orders, the columns that come from sale have been filled with nulls.

The Right Outer Join

The *right outer join* is the precise opposite of the left outer join. It includes all rows from the table on the right of the outer join operator. If you perform

```
customer RIGHT OUTER JOIN sale GIVING right_outer_join_result
```

using the data from Figure 6.6, the result will be the same as an inner join of the two tables. This occurs because there are no rows in sale that don't appear in customer. However, if you reverse the order of the tables, as in

```
sale RIGHT OUTER JOIN customer GIVING right_outer_join_result
```

you end up with the same data as Figure 6.12.

customer_numb	first_name	last_name	sale_id	customer_numb	sale_date	sale_total_amt
1	Janice	Jones	1	1	29-MAY-13 00:00:00	510.00
1	Janice	Jones	2	1	05-JUN-13 00:00:00	125.00
1	Janice	Jones	17	1	25-JUL-13 00:00:00	100.00
1	Janice	Jones	3	1	15-JUN-13 00:00:00	58.00
2	Jon	Jones	20	2	01-SEP-13 00:00:00	75.00
2	Jon	Jones	16	2	25-JUL-13 00:00:00	130.00
2	Jon	Jones	13	2	10-JUL-13 00:00:00	25.95
3	John	Doe	null	null	null	null
4	Jane	Doe	4	4	30-JUN-13 00:00:00	110.00
5	Jane	Smith	18	5	22-AUG-13 00:00:00	100.00
5	Jane	Smith	8	5	07-JUL-13 00:00:00	90.00
6	Janice	Smith	19	6	01-SEP-13 00:00:00	95.00
6	Janice	Smith	14	6	10-JUL-13 00:00:00	80.00
6	Janice	Smith	5	6	30-JUN-13 00:00:00	110.00
7	Helen	Brown	null	null	null	null
8	Helen	Jerry	9	8	07-JUL-13 00:00:00	50.00
8	Helen	Jerry	7	8	05-JUL-13 00:00:00	80.00
9	Mary	Collins	11	9	10-JUL-13 00:00:00	200.00
10	Peter	Collins	12	10	10-JUL-13 00:00:00	200.00
11	Edna	Hayes	15	11	12-JUL-13 00:00:00	75.00
11	Edna	Hayes	10	11	10-JUL-13 00:00:00	125.00
12	Franklin	Hayes	6	12	05-JUL-13 00:00:00	505.00
13	Peter	Johnson	null	null	null	null
14	Peter	Johnson	null	null	null	null
15	John	Smith	null	null	null	null

■ **FIGURE 6.12** The result of a left outer join.

Choosing a Right versus Left Outer Join

As you have just read, outer joins are directional: The result depends on the order of the tables in the command. (This is in direct contrast to an inner join, which produces the same result regardless of the order of the tables.) Assuming that you are performing an outer join on two tables that have a primary key–foreign key relationship, then the result of left and right outer joins on those tables is predictable (Table 6.9). Referential integrity ensures that no rows from a table containing a foreign key will ever be omitted from a join with the table that contains the referenced primary key. Therefore, a

Table 6.9 The Effect of Left and Right Outer Joins on Tables with a Primary Key–Foreign Key Relationship

Outer Join Format	Outer Join Result
`primary_key_table LEFT OUTER JOIN foreign_key_table`	All rows from primary key table retained; matching rows from foreign key table included
`foreign_key_table LEFT OUTER JOIN primary_key_table`	Same as inner join
`primary_key_table RIGHT OUTER JOIN foreign_key_table`	Same as inner join
`foreign_key_table RIGHT OUTER JOIN primary_key_table`	All rows from primary key table retained; matching rows from foreign key table included

left outer join where the foreign key table is on the left of the operator and a right outer join where the foreign key table is on the right of the operator are no different from an inner join.

When choosing between a left and a right outer join, you therefore need to pay attention to which table will appear on which side of the operator. If the outer join is to produce a result different from that of an inner join, then the table containing the primary key must appear on the side that matches the name of the operator.

The Full Outer Join

A full outer join includes all rows from both tables, filling in rows with nulls where necessary. If the two tables have a primary key–foreign key relationship, then the result will be the same as that of either a left outer join, when the primary key table is on the left of the operator or a right outer join, when the primary key table is on the right side of the operator. In the case of the full outer join, it does not matter on which side of the operator the primary key table appears; all rows from the primary key table will be retained.

Valid Versus Invalid Joins

To this point, all of the joins you have seen (with the exception of some outer joins) have involved tables with a primary key–foreign key relationship. These are the most typical types of join and always produce valid result tables. In contrast, most joins (other than outer joins) between tables that do not have a primary key–foreign key relationship are not valid. This means that the result tables contain information that is not represented in the database, conveying misinformation to the user. Invalid joins are therefore far more dangerous than meaningless projections.

As an example, let us temporarily add a table to the rare book store database. The purpose of the table is to indicate the source from which the store acquired a volume. Over time, the same book (different physical volumes) may come from more than one source. The table has the following structure:

```
book_sources (isbn, source_name)
```

Someone looking at this table and the *book* table might conclude that, because the two tables have a matching column (*isbn*), it makes sense to join the tables to find out the source of every volume that the store has ever had in inventory. Unfortunately, this is not the information that the result table will contain.

To keep the result table to a reasonable length, we will work with an abbreviated *book_sources* table that does not contain sources for all volumes (Figure 6.13). Let's assume that we go ahead and join the tables over the

```
           isbn           |       source_name
-------------------------+--------------------------
      978-1-11111-111-1  |  Tom Anderson
      978-1-11111-111-1  |  Church rummage sale
      978-1-11111-118-1  |  South Street Market
      978-1-11111-118-1  |  Church rummage sale
      978-1-11111-118-1  |  Betty Jones
      978-1-11111-120-1  |  Tom Anderson
      978-1-11111-120-1  |  Betty Jones
      978-1-11111-126-1  |  Church rummage sale
      978-1-11111-126-1  |  Betty Jones
      978-1-11111-125-1  |  Tom Anderson
      978-1-11111-125-1  |  South Street Market
      978-1-11111-125-1  |  Hendersons
      978-1-11111-125-1  |  Neverland Books
      978-1-11111-130-1  |  Tom Anderson
      978-1-11111-130-1  |  Hendersons
```

■ **FIGURE 6.13 The** *book_source* **table.**

ISBN. The result table (without columns that are not of interest to the join itself) can be found in Figure 6.14.

If the store has ever obtained volumes with the same ISBN from different sources, there will be multiple rows for that ISBN in the *book_sources* table. Although this doesn't give us a great deal of meaningful information, in

```
inventory_id |          isbn          | sale_id |       source_name
-------------+------------------------+---------+----------------------
           1 | 978-1-11111-111-1      |      1  | Church rummage sale
           1 | 978-1-11111-111-1      |      1  | Tom Anderson
          20 | 978-1-11111-130-1      |      6  | Hendersons
          20 | 978-1-11111-130-1      |      6  | Tom Anderson
          21 | 978-1-11111-126-1      |      6  | Betty Jones
          21 | 978-1-11111-126-1      |      6  | Church rummage sale
          23 | 978-1-11111-125-1      |      7  | Neverland Books
          23 | 978-1-11111-125-1      |      7  | Hendersons
          23 | 978-1-11111-125-1      |      7  | South Street Market
          23 | 978-1-11111-125-1      |      7  | Tom Anderson
          25 | 978-1-11111-126-1      |      8  | Betty Jones
          25 | 978-1-11111-126-1      |      8  | Church rummage sale
          35 | 978-1-11111-126-1      |     11  | Betty Jones
          35 | 978-1-11111-126-1      |     11  | Church rummage sale
          36 | 978-1-11111-130-1      |     11  | Hendersons
          36 | 978-1-11111-130-1      |     11  | Tom Anderson
          38 | 978-1-11111-130-1      |     12  | Hendersons
          38 | 978-1-11111-130-1      |     12  | Tom Anderson
          63 | 978-1-11111-130-1      |         | Hendersons
          63 | 978-1-11111-130-1      |         | Tom Anderson
```

■ **FIGURE 6.14 An invalid join result.**

and of itself, the table is valid. However, when we look at the result of the join with the volume table, the data in the result table contradict what is in *book_sources*. For example, the first two rows in the result table have the same inventory ID number yet come from different sources. How can the same physical volume come from two places? That is just impossible. This invalid join therefore implies facts that simply cannot be true.

The reason this join is invalid is that the two columns over which the join is performed are not in a primary key–foreign key relationship. In fact, in both tables, the *isbn* column is a foreign key that references the primary key of the *book* table.

Are joins between tables that do not have a primary key–foreign key relationship ever valid? On occasion, they are, in particular if you are joining two tables with the same primary key. You will see an example of this type of join when we discuss joining a table to itself, when a predicate requires that multiple rows exist before any are placed in a result table.

For another example, assume that you want to create a table to store data about your employees:

```
employees (id_numb, first_name, last_name,
  department, job_title, salary, hire_date)
```

Some of the employees are managers. For those individuals, you also want to store data about the project they are currently managing and the date they began managing that project. (A manager handles only one project at a time.) You could add the columns to the employees table and let them contain nulls for employees who are not managers. An alternative is to create a second table just for the managers:

```
managers (id_numb, current_project, project_start_date)
```

When you want to see all the information about a manager, you must join the two tables over the *id_numb* column. The result table will contain rows only for the manager because employees without rows in the managers table will be left out of the join. There will be no spurious rows such as those we got when we joined the *volume* and *book_sources* tables. This join therefore is valid.

Note: Although the id_numb column in the managers table technically is not a foreign key referencing employees, most databases using such a design would nonetheless include a constraint that forced the presence of a matching row in employees for every manager.

The bottom line is that you need to be very careful when performing joins between tables that do not have a primary key–foreign key relationship. Although such joins are not always invalid, in most cases they will be.

Difference

Among the most powerful database queries are those phrased in the negative, such as "show me all the customers who have not purchased from us in the past year." This type of query is particularly tricky because it is asking for data that are not in the database. The rare book store has data about customers who *have* purchased but not those who have not, for example. The only way to perform such a query is to request the DBMS to use the *difference* operation.

Difference retrieves all rows that are in one table but not in another. For example, if you have a table that contains all your products and another that contains products that have been purchased, the expression—

```
all_products MINUS products_that_have_been_purchased
    GIVING not_purchased
```

—is the products that have *not* been purchased. When you remove the products that *have* been purchased from all products, what are left are the products that *have not* been purchased.

The difference operation looks at entire rows when it makes the decision whether to include a row in the result table. This means that the two source tables must be union compatible. Assume that the *all_products* table has two columns—*prod_numb* and *product_name*—and the *products_that_have_been_purchased* table also has two columns—*prod_numb* and *order_numb*. Because they don't have the same columns, the tables aren't union-compatible.

As you can see from Figure 6.15, this means that a DBMS must first perform two projections to generate the union-compatible tables before it can perform the difference. In this case, the operation needs to retain the product number. Once the projections into union-compatible tables exist, the DBMS can perform the difference.

Intersect

As mentioned earlier in this chapter, to be considered relationally complete, a DBMS must support restrict, project, join, union, and difference. Virtually every query can be satisfied using a sequence of those five operations. However, one other operation is usually included in the relational algebra specification: *intersect*.

In one sense, the intersect operation is the opposite of union. Union produces a result containing all rows that appear in either relation, while intersect produces a result containing all rows that appear in both relations. Intersection can therefore only be performed on two union-compatible relations.

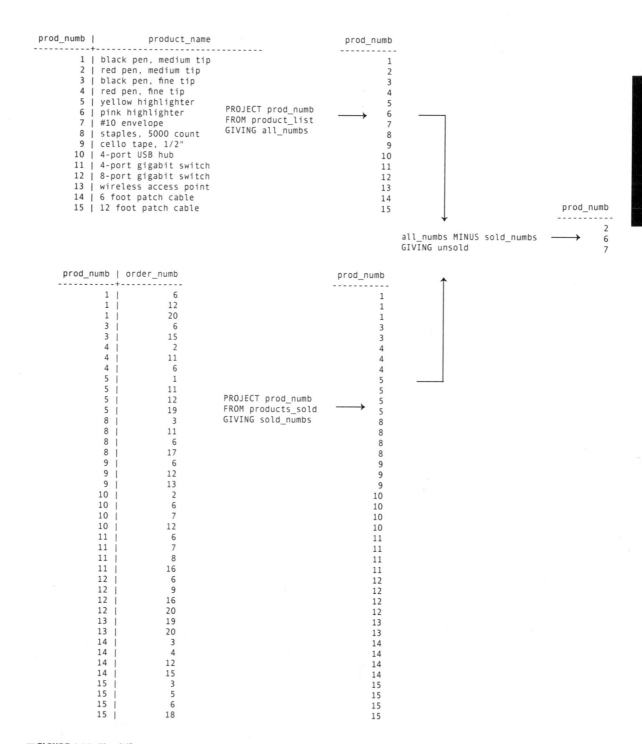

■ **FIGURE 6.15** The difference operation.

Assume, for example, that the rare book store receives data listing volumes in a private collection that are being offered for sale. We can find out which volumes are already in the store's inventory using an intersect operation:

```
books_in_inventory INTERSECT books_for_sale
  GIVING already_have
```

As you can see in Figure 6.16, the first step in the process is to use the project operation to create union-compatible operations. Then, an intersect will provide the required result.

Note: A join over the concatenation of all the columns in the two tables produces the same result as an intersect.

Divide

An eighth relational algebra operation—*divide*—is often included with the operations you have seen in this chapter. It can be used for queries that need to have multiple rows in the same source table for a row to be included in the result table. Assume, for example, that the rare book store wants a list of sales on which two specific volumes have appeared.

There are many forms of the divide operation, all of which except the simplest are extremely complex. To set up the simplest form you need two relations, one with two columns (a *binary* relation) and one with a single column (a *unary* relation). The binary relation has a column that contains the values that will be placed in the result of the query (in our example, a sale ID) and a column for the values to be queried (in our example, the ISBN of the volume). This relation is created by taking a projection from the source table (in this case, the *volume* table).

The unary relation has the column being queried (the ISBN). It is loaded with a row for each value that must be matched in the binary table. A sale ID will be placed in the result table for all sales that contain ISBNs that match all of the values in the unary table. If there are two ISBNs in the unary table, then there must be a row for each of them with the same sale ID in the binary table to include the sale ID in the result. If we were to load the unary table with three ISBNs, then three matching rows would be required.

You can get the same result as a divide using multiple restricts and joins. In our example, you would restrict from the volume table twice, once for the first ISBN and once for the second. Then, you would join the tables over the sale ID. Only those sales that had rows in both of the tables being joined would end up in the result table.

Because divide can be performed fairly easily with restrict and join, DBMSs generally do not implement it directly.

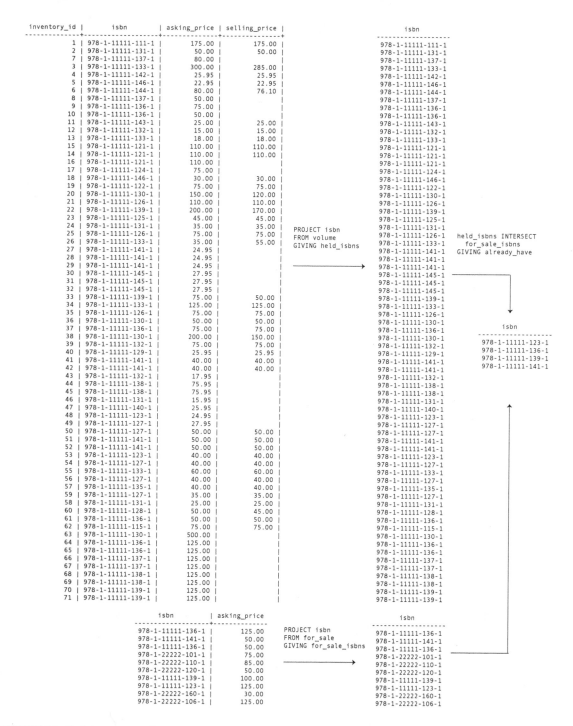

■ **FIGURE 6.16** The intersect operation.

For Further Reading

deHaan, L., 2007. Applied Mathematics for Database Professionals. Apress.

Maddux, R.D., 2006. Relation Algebras. Elsevier Science.

Molkova, L., 2012. Theory and Practice of Relational Algebra: Transforming Relational Algebra to SQL. LAMBERT Academic Publishing.

Chapter

7

Normalization

Given any pool of entities and attributes, there is a large number of ways you can group them into relations. In this chapter, you will be introduced to the process of *normalization*, through which you create relations that avoid most of the problems that arise from bad relational design.

There are at least two ways to approach normalization. The first is to work from an ER diagram. If the diagram is drawn correctly, then there are some simple rules you can use to translate it into relations that will avoid most relational design problems. The drawback to this approach is that it can be difficult to determine whether your design is correct. The second approach is to use the theoretical concepts behind good design to create your relations. This is a bit more difficult than working from an ER diagram, but often results in a better design.

Normalization theory relies heavily on the relational algebra operation project. When moving a relation from one design stage to another, we *decompose* a relation by taking projections to create more than one relation. Normalization also occasionally uses the join operation.

In practice, you may find it useful to use a combination of both the ER diagram and theoretical approaches. First, create an ER diagram, and use it to design your relations. Then, check those relations against the theoretical rules for good design, and make any changes necessary to meet the rules.

Translating an ER Diagram into Relations

An ER diagram in which all many-to-many relationships have been transformed into one-to-many relationships, through the introduction of composite entities, can be translated directly into a set of relations. To do so:

- Create one table for each entity.
- For each entity that is only at the "one" end of one or more relationships, and not at the "many" end of any relationship, create a single-column primary key, using an arbitrary unique identifier if no natural primary key is available.
- For each entity that is at the "many" end of one or more relationships, include the primary key of each parent entity (those at the "one" end of the relationships) in the table as foreign keys.
- If an entity at the "many" end of one or more relationships has a natural primary key (for example, an order number or an invoice number), use that single column as the primary key. Otherwise, concatenate the primary key of its parent with any other column or columns needed for uniqueness to form the table's primary key.

Following these guidelines, we end up with the following tables for the *Antique Opticals* database:

```
customer (customer_numb, customer_first_name,
     customer_last_name, customer_street, customer_city,
     customer_state, customer_zip, customer_phone)

distributor (distributor_numb, distrbutor_name,
     distrbutor_street, distrbutor_city, distrbutor_state,
     distrbutor_zip, distrbutor_phone,
     distrbutor_contact_person, contact_person_ext)

item (item_numb, item_type, title, distributor_numb,
     retail_price, release_date, genre, quant_in_stock)

order (order_numb, customer_numb, order_date, credit_card_numb,
     credit_card_exp_date, order_complete?, pickup_or_ship?)

order item (order_numb, item_numb, quantity, discount_percent,
     selling_price, line_cost, shipped?, shipping_date)

purchase (purchase_date, customer_numb, items_received?,
     customer_paid?)

purchase item (purchase_date, customer_numb, item_numb,
     condition, price_paid)

actor (actor_numb, actor_name)

performance (actor_numb, item_numb, role)

producer (producer_name, studio)

production (producer_name, item_numb)
```

Note: You will see these relations reworked a bit throughout the remainder of the first part of this book to help illustrate various aspects of database design. However, the preceding is the design that results from a direct translation of the ER diagram.

Normal Forms

The theoretical rules that the design of a relation must meet are known as *normal forms.* Each normal form represents an increasingly stringent set of rules. Theoretically, the higher the normal form, the better the design of the relation.

As you can see in Figure 7.1, there are six nested normal forms, indicating that if a relation is in one of the higher, outer normal forms, it is also in all of the normal forms inside it.

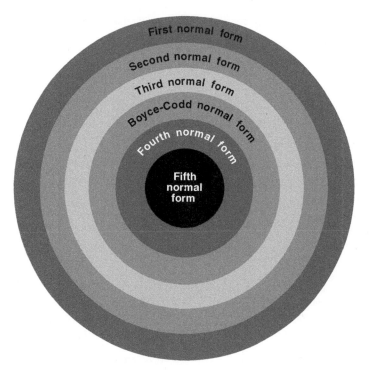

■ **FIGURE 7.1 Nested normal forms.**

In most cases, if you can place your relations in third normal form (3NF), then you will have avoided most of the problems common to bad relational designs. The three higher normal forms—Boyce–Codd, fourth normal form (4NF), and fifth normal form (5NF)—handle special situations that arise only occasionally. However, the situations that these normal forms handle are conceptually easy to understand, and can be used in practice, if the need arises.

In recent years, sixth normal form has been added to relational database design theory. It is not precisely a more rigorous normal form than fifth normal form, although it uses the same principles to transform relations from one form to another. You will be introduced to it briefly at the end of this chapter.

Note: In addition to the six normal forms in Figure 7.1 and sixth normal form, there is another normal form—domain/key normal form—that is of purely theoretical importance and to this date, has not been used as a practical design objective.

First Normal Form

A table is in first normal form (1NF) if it meets the following criteria:

- The data are stored in a two-dimensional table.
- There are no repeating groups.

The key to understanding 1NF therefore is understanding the nature of a repeating group of data.

Understanding Repeating Groups

A *repeating group* is an attribute that has more than one value in each row of a table. For example, assume that you were working with an employee relation, and needed to store the names and birthdates of the employees' children. Because each employee can have more than one child, the names of children and the children's birthdates each form a repeating group.

Note: A repeating group is directly analogous to a multivalued attribute in an ER diagram.

There is actually a very good reason why repeating groups are disallowed. To see what might happen if they were present, take a look at Figure 7.2, an instance of an *employee* table containing repeating groups.

Note: The table in Figure 7.2 is not a legal relation, because it contains those repeating groups. Therefore, we should not call it a relation.

emp#	first	last	children's names	children's birthdates
1001	Jane	Doe	Mary, Sam	1/9/02, 5/15/04
1002	John	Doe	Lisa, David	1/9/00, 5/15/01
1003	Jane	Smith	John, Pat, Lee, Mary	10/5/04, 10/12/00, 6/6/2006, 8/21/04
1004	John	Smith	Michael	7/4/06
1005	Jane	Jones	Edward, Martha	10/21/05, 10/15/99

■ FIGURE 7.2 A table with repeating groups.

Notice that there are multiple values in a single row in both the children's names and children's birthdates columns. This presents two major problems:

■ There is no way to know exactly which birthdate belongs to which child. It is tempting to say that we can associate the birthdates with the children by their positions in the list, but there is nothing to ensure that the relative positions will always be maintained.

■ Searching the table is very difficult. If, for example, we want to know which employees have children born before 2005, the DBMS will need to perform data manipulation to extract the individual dates themselves. Given that there is no way to know how many birthdates there are in the column for any specific row, the processing overhead for searching becomes even greater.

The solution to these problems, of course, is to get rid of the repeating groups altogether.

Handling Repeating Groups

There are two ways to get rid of repeating groups to bring a table into conformance with the rules for first normal form—a right way and a wrong way. We will look first at the wrong way so you will know what *not* to do.

In Figure 7.3 you can see a relation that handles repeating groups by creating multiple columns for the multiple values. This particular example includes three pairs of columns for a child's name and birthdate.

emp#	first	last	child name 1	child bdate 1	child name 2	child bdate 2	child name 3	child bdate 3
1001	Jane	Doe	Mary	1/1/02	Sam	5/15/04		
1002	John	Doe	Lisa	1/1/00	David	5/15/01		
1003	Jane	Smith	John	10/5/04	Pat	10/12/00	Lee	6/6/06
1004	John	Smith	Michael	7/4/06				
1005	Joe	Jones	Edward	10/21/05	Martha	10/15/99		

■ **FIGURE 7.3** A relation handling repeating groups in the wrong way.

The relation is Figure 7.3 does meet the criteria for first normal form. The repeating groups are gone and there is no problem identifying which birthdate belongs to which child. However, the design has introduced several problems of its own:

■ The relation is limited to three children for any given employee. This means that there is no room to store Jane Smith's fourth child. Should you put another row for Jane Smith into the table? If so, then the primary key of this relation can no longer be just the employee number. The primary key must include one child's name as well.

- The relation wastes space for people who have less than three children. Given that disk space is one of the least expensive elements of a database system, this is probably the least of the problems with this relation.
- Searching for a specific child becomes very clumsy. To answer the question "Does anyone have a child named Lee?" the DBMS must construct a query that includes a search of all three child name columns because there is no way to know in which column the name might be found.

The right way to handle repeating groups is to create another table (another entity) to handle multiple instances of the repeating group. In the example we have been using, we would create a second table for the children, producing something like Figure 7.4.

employee

emp#	first	last
1001	Jane	Doe
1002	John	Doe
1003	Jane	Smith
1004	John	Smith
1005	Joe	Jones

children

emp#	c_first	c_birthdate
1001	Mary	1/1/02
1001	Sam	5/15/04
1002	Lisa	1/1/00
1002	David	5/15/01
1003	John	10/5/04
1003	Pat	10/12/00
1003	Lee	6/6/06
1003	Mary	8/21/04
1004	Michael	7/4/06
1005	Edward	10/21/05
1005	Martha	1015/99

■ FIGURE 7.4 The correct way to handle a repeating group.

Neither of the two new tables contains any repeating groups and this form of the design avoids all the problems of the preceding solution:

- There is no limit to the number of children that can be stored for a given employee. To add another child, you simply add another row to the *children* table.

- There is no wasted space. The children table uses space only for data that are present.
- Searching for a specific child is much easier because children's names are found in only one column.

Problems with First Normal Form

Although first normal form relations have no repeating groups, they are full of other problems. To see what these problems are, we will look at the table underlying the data entry form in Chapter 3. (This table comes from *Antique Opticals'* original data management system, rather than the new and improved design you saw earlier in this chapter.) Expressed in the notation for relations that we have been using, the relation is:

```
orders (customer_numb, first_name, last_name, street,
    city, state, zip, phone, order_numb, order_date,
    item_numb, title, price, has_shipped?)
```

The first thing we need to do is determine the primary key for this table. The customer number alone will not be sufficient, because the customer number repeats for every item ordered by the customer. The item number will also not suffice, because it is repeated for every order on which it appears. We cannot use the order number, because it is repeated for every item on the order. The only solution is a concatenated key, in this example, the combination of the order number and the item number.

Given that the primary key is made up of the order number and the item number, there are two important things we cannot do with this relation:

- We cannot add data about a customer until the customer places at least one order because, without an order and an item on that order, we do not have a complete primary key.
- We cannot add data about a merchandise item we are carrying without that item being ordered. There must be an order number to complete the primary key.

The preceding are *insertion anomalies*, a situation that arises when you are prevented from inserting data into a relation because a complete primary key is not available. (Remember that *no* part of a primary key can be null.)

Note: To be strictly correct, there is a third insertion anomaly in the orders relation. You cannot insert an order until you know one item on the order. In a practical sense, however, no one would enter an order without there being an item ordered.

Insertion anomalies are common in first normal form relations that are not also in any of the higher normal forms. In practical terms, they occur because there are data about more than one entity in the relation. The anomaly forces you to insert data about an unrelated entity (for example, a merchandise item) when you want to insert data about another entity (such as a customer).

First normal form relations can also give us problems when we delete data. Consider, for example, what happens if a customer cancels the order of a single item and the business rules state that cancelled items and orders are to be deleted:

- In cases where the deleted item was the only item on the order, you lose all data about the order.
- In cases where the order was the only order on which the item appeared, you lose data about the item.
- In cases where the deleted item was the item ordered by a customer you lose all data about the customer.

These *deletion anomalies* occur because part of the primary key of a row becomes null when the merchandise item data are deleted, forcing you to remove the entire row. The result of a deletion anomaly is the loss of data that you would like to keep. In practical terms, you are forced to remove data about an unrelated entity when you delete data about another entity in the same table.

Note: Moral to the story: More than one entity in a table is a bad thing.

One of the most important things to keep in mind about insertion and deletion anomalies is that they affect entire entities. If you want to insert customer data but can't because the customer has not placed an order, for example, you can't insert *any* customer data. The anomaly does not just prevent you from entering a primary key value, but also anything else you want to store about an instance of the customer entity.

There is a final type of anomaly in the *orders* relation that is not related to the primary key: a *modification*, or *update*, *anomaly*. The *orders* relation has a great deal of unnecessary duplicated data, in particular, information about customers. When a customer moves, then the customer's data must be changed in every row for every item on every order ever placed by the customer. If every row is not changed, then data that should be the same are no longer the same. The potential for these inconsistent data is the modification anomaly.

Second Normal Form

The solution to anomalies in a first normal form relation is to break the relation down so that there is one relation for each entity in the 1NF relation. The *orders* relation, for example, will break down into four relations (*customers*, *items*, *orders*, and *line items*). Such relations are in at least second normal form (2NF).

In theoretical terms, second formal form relations are defined as follows:

- The relation is in first normal form.
- All nonkey attributes are functionally dependent on the entire primary key.

The new term in the preceding is *functionally dependent*, a special relationship between attributes.

Understanding Functional Dependencies

A functional dependency is a one-way relationship between two attributes, such that at any given time, for each unique value of attribute A, only one value of attribute B is associated with it throughout the relation. For example, assume that A is the customer number from the *orders* relation. Each customer number is associated with one customer first name, one last name, one street address, one city, one state, one zip code, and one phone number. Although the values for those attributes may change at any moment, there is only one.

We therefore can say that first name, last name, street, city, state, zip, and phone are functionally dependent upon the customer number. This relationship is often written:

```
customer_numb ->> first_name, last_name, street, city, state,
     zip, phone
```

and read "customer number determines first name, last name, street, city, state, zip, and phone." In this relationship, customer number is known as the *determinant* (an attribute that determines the value of other attributes).

Notice that the functional dependency does not necessarily hold in the reverse direction. For example, any given first or last name may be associated with more than one customer number. (It would be unusual to have a customer table of any size without some duplication of names.)

The functional dependencies in the orders table are:

```
customer_numb ->> first_name, last_name, street, city, state,
     zip, phone

item_numb ->> title, price

order_numb ->> customer_numb, order_date

item_numb + order_numb ->> has_shipped?
```

Notice that there is one determinant for each entity in the relation and the determinant is what we have chosen as the entity identifier. Notice also that, when an entity has a concatenated identifier, the determinant is also concatenated. In this example, whether an item has shipped depends on the combination of the item and the order.

Using Functional Dependencies to Reach 2NF

If you have correctly identified the functional dependencies among the attributes in a database environment, then you can use them to create second normal form relations. Each determinant becomes the primary key of a relation. All the attributes that are functionally dependent upon it become non-key attributes in the relation.

The four relations into which the original *orders* relation should be broken are:

```
customer (customer_numb, first_name, last_name, street, city,
     state, zip, phone)

item (item_numb, title, price)

order (order_numb, customer_numb, order_date)

order_items (order_numb, item_numb, has_shipped?)
```

Each of these should, in turn, correspond to a single entity in your ER diagram.

Note: When it comes to deciding what is driving database design—functional dependencies or entities—it is really a "chicken and egg" situation. What is most important is that there is consistency between the ER diagram and the functional dependencies you identify in your relations. It makes no difference whether you design by looking for functional dependencies or for entities. In most cases, database design is an iterative process in which you create an initial design, check it, modify it, and check it again. You can look at either functional dependencies and/or entities at any stage in the process, checking one against the other for consistency.

The relations we have created from the original orders relation have eliminated the anomalies present in the original:

- It is now possible to insert data about a customer before the customer places an order.
- It is now possible to insert data about an order before we know an item on the order.

- It is now possible to store data about merchandise items before they are ordered.
- Line items can be deleted from an order without affecting data describing that item, the order itself, or the merchandise item.
- Data describing the customer are stored only once and therefore any change to those data needs to be made only once. A modification anomaly cannot occur.

Problems with 2NF Relations

Although second normal form eliminates problems from many relations, you will occasionally run into relations that are in second normal form, yet still exhibit anomalies. Assume, for example, that each new DVD title that *Antique Opticals* carries comes from one distributor, and that each distributor has only one warehouse, which has only one phone number. The following relation is therefore in second normal form:

```
item (item_numb, title, distrib_numb, warehouse_phone_number)
```

For each item number, there is only one value for the item's title, distributor, and warehouse phone number. However, there is one insertion anomaly—you cannot insert data about a distributor until you have an item from that distributor—and a deletion anomaly—if you delete the only item from a distributor, you lose data about the distributor. There is also a modification anomaly: the distributor's warehouse phone number is duplicated for every item the company gets from that distributor. The relation is in second normal form, but not third.

Third Normal Form

Third normal form is designed to handle situations like the one you just read about in the preceding section. In terms of entities, the item relation does contain two entities: the merchandise item and the distributor. That alone should convince you that the relation needs to be broken down into two smaller relations, both of which are now in third normal form:

```
item (item_numb, distrib_numb)
```

```
distributor (distrib_numb, warehouse_phone_number)
```

The theoretical definition of third normal form says:

- The relation is in second normal form.
- There are no transitive dependencies.

The functional dependencies found in the original relation are an example of a *transitive dependency*.

Transitive Dependencies

A transitive dependency exists when you have the following functional dependency pattern:

```
A –>> B and B –>> C therefore A –>> C
```

This is precisely the case with the original items relation. The only reason that the warehouse phone number is functionally dependent on the item number is because the distributor is functionally dependent on the item number, and the phone number is functionally dependent on the distributor. The functional dependencies are really:

```
item_numb –>> distrib_numb
distrib_numb –>> warehouse_phone_number
```

Note: Transitive dependencies take their name from the transitive property in mathematics, which states that if a > b and b > c, then a > c.

There are two determinants in the original items relation, each of which should be the primary key of its own relation. However, it is not merely the presence of the second determinant that creates the transitive dependency. What really matters is that the second determinant is not a candidate key (could be used as a primary key) for the relation.

Consider, for example, this relation:

```
Item (item_numb, upc, distrib_numb, price)
```

The item number is an arbitrary number that *Antique Opticals* assigns to each merchandise item. The UPC is an industry-wide code that is unique to each item as well. The functional dependencies in this relation are:

```
item_numb –>> upc, distrib_numb, price

upc –>> item_numb, distrib_numb, price
```

Is there a transitive dependency here? No, because the second determinant is a candidate key. (*Antique Opticals* could just as easily have used the UPC as the primary key.) There are no insertion, deletion, or modification anomalies in this relation; it describes only one entity—the merchandise item.

A transitive dependency therefore exists only when the determinant that is not the primary key is not a candidate key for the relation. For example, in the *items* table we have been using as an example, the distributor is a determinant, but not a candidate key for the table. (There can be more than one item coming from a single distributor.)

When you have a transitive dependency in a 2NF relation, you should break the relation into two smaller relations, each of which has one of the determinants in the transitive dependency as its primary key. The attributes determined by the determinant become nonkey attributes in each relation. This removes the transitive dependency—and its associated anomalies—and places the relation in third normal form.

Note: A second normal form relation that has no transitive dependencies is, of course, automatically in third normal form.

Boyce–Codd Normal Form

For most relations, third normal form is a good design objective. Relations in that state are free of most anomalies. However, occasionally you run into relations that exhibit special characteristics where anomalies still occur. Boyce–Codd normal form (BCNF), fourth normal form (4NF), and fifth normal form (5NF) were created to handle such special situations.

Note: If your relations are in third normal form and do not exhibit the special characteristics that BCNF, 4NF, and 5NF were designed to handle, then they are automatically in 5NF.

The easiest way to understand BCNF is to start with an example. Assume that *Antique Opticals* decides to add a relation to its database to handle employee work scheduling. Each employee works one or two 4-hour shifts a day at the store. During each shift, an employee is assigned to one station (a place in the store, such as the front desk or the stockroom). Only one employee works a station during the given shift.

A relation to handle the schedule might be designed as follows:

```
schedule (employee_id, date, shift, station, worked_shift?)
```

Given the rules for the scheduling (one person per station per shift), there are two possible primary keys for this relation: *employee_ID + date + shift* or *date + shift + station*. The functional dependencies in the relation are:

```
employee_id + date + shift ->> station, worked_shift?

date + shift + station ->> employee_id, worked_shift?
```

Keep in mind that this holds true only because there is only one person working each station during each shift.

Note: There is very little difference between the two candidate keys as far as the choice of a primary key is concerned. In cases like this, you can choose either one.

This schedule relation exhibits *overlapping candidate keys*. (Both candidate keys have date and shift in common.) BCNF was designed to deal with relations that exhibit this characteristic.

To be in BCNF, a relation must meet the following rules:

- The relation is in third normal form.
- All determinants are candidate keys.

BCNF is considered to be a more general way of looking at 3NF because it includes those relations with the overlapping candidate keys. The sample *schedule* relation we have been considering does meet the criteria for BCNF because the two determinants are indeed candidate keys.

Fourth Normal Form

Like BCNF, fourth normal form was designed to handle relations that exhibit a special characteristic that does not arise too often. In this case, the special characteristic is something known as a *multivalued dependency*.

As an example consider the following relation:

```
movie info (title, star, producer)
```

A given movie can have more than one star; it can also have more than one producer. The same star can appear in more than one movie; a producer can also work on more than one movie (for example, see the instance in Figure 7.5). The relation must therefore include all columns in its key.

Because there are no nonkey attributes, this relation is in BCNF. Nonetheless, the relation exhibits anomalies:

- You cannot insert the stars of a movie without knowing at least one producer.
- You cannot insert the producer of a movie without knowing at least one star.

title	star	producer
Great Film	Lovely Lady	Money Bags
Great Film	Handsome Man	Money Bags
Great Film	Lovely Lady	Helen Pursestrings
Great Film	Handsome Man	Helen Pursestrings
Boring Movie	Lovely Lady	Helen Pursestrings
Boring Movie	Precocious Child	Helen Pursestrings

■ **FIGURE 7.5 A relation with a multivalued dependency.**

- If you delete the only producer from a movie, you lose information about the stars.
- If you delete the only star from a movie, you lose information about its producers.
- Each producer's name is duplicated for every star in the movie. By the same token, each star's name is duplicated for each producer of the movie. This unnecessary duplicated data forms the basis of a modification anomaly.

There are at least two unrelated entities in this relation: one that handles the relationship between a movie and its stars and another that handles the relationship between a movie and its producers. In a practical sense, that is the cause of the anomalies. (Arguably, there are also movie, star, and producer entities involved.)

However, in a theoretical sense, the anomalies are caused by the presence of a multivalued dependency in the same relation, which must be eliminated to get to fourth normal form. The rules for fourth normal form are:

- The relation is in BCNF.
- There are no multivalued dependencies.

Multivalued Dependencies

A multivalued dependency exists when for each value of attribute A, there exists a finite set of values of attribute B that are associated with it, and a finite set of values of attribute C that are also associated with it. Attributes B and C are independent of each other.

In the example we have been using, there is just such a dependency. First, for each movie title, there is a group of actors (the stars) who are associated with the movie. For each title, there is also a group of producers who are associated with it. However, the actors and the producers are independent of one another. As you can see in the ER diagram in Figure 7.6, the producers and stars have no direct relationship (despite the relationships being M:M).

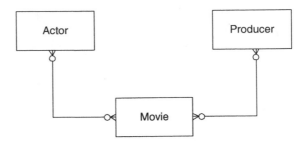

■ FIGURE 7.6 An ER diagram of the multivalued dependency.

Note: At this point, do not let semantics get in the way of database theory. Yes, it is true that producers fund the movies in which the actors are starring, but in terms of database relationships, there is no direct connection between the two.

The multivalued dependency can be written:

```
title  ->> star
```

```
title  ->> producer
```

and read "title multidetermines star and title multidetermines producer."

Note: To be strictly accurate, a functional dependency is a special case of a multivalued dependency where what is being determined is one value rather than a group of values.

To eliminate the multivalued dependency and bring this relation into fourth normal form, you split the relation placing each part of the dependency in its own relation:

```
movie_stars (title, star)
```

```
movie_producers (title, producer)
```

With this design, you can independently insert and remove stars and producers without affecting the other. Star and producer names also appear only once for each movie with which they are involved.

Another way to look at this is to notice that *movie_stars* and *movie_producers* are actually composite entities. When we add them to the ER diagram, they resolve the M:M relationships (Figure 7.7).

Fifth Normal Form

Fifth normal form—also known as projection-join normal form—is designed to handle a general case of a multivalued dependency known as a *join dependency.*

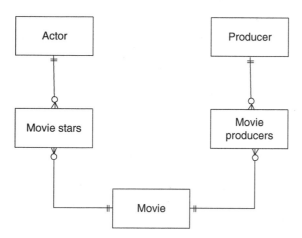

■ **FIGURE 7.7 Creating fourth normal form with composite entities.**

Consider the following relation that is in fourth normal form, but not fifth:

```
selections (customer_numb, series, item_numb)
```

This relation represents various series of discs, such as Star Trek or Rambo. Customers place orders for a series; when a customer orders a series, he or she must take all items in that series. Determining fifth normal form becomes relevant only when this type of rule is in place. If customers could request selected titles from a series, then the relation would be fine. Because it would be all-key and would have no multivalued dependencies, it would automatically fall through the normal form rules to 5NF.

To make the problems with this table under the preceding rule clearer, consider the instance of the relation in Figure 7.8.

Because this table has no multivalued dependencies, it is automatically in fourth normal form. However, there is a great deal of unnecessary duplicated data in this relation—the item numbers are repeated for every customer that orders a given series. The series name is also repeated for every item in the series and for every customer ordering that series. This relation will therefore be prone to modification anomalies.

There is also a more subtle issue: under the rules of this relation, if customer 2180 orders the first Harry Potter movie and indicates that he or she would like more movies in the series, then the only way to put that choice in the table is to add rows for all five Harry Potter movies. You may be forced to add rows that you don't want to add and introduce data that are not accurate.

customer number	series	item number
1005	Star Wars	2090
1005	Star Wars	2091
1005	Star Wars	2092
1005	Star Wars	4689
1005	Star Wars	4690
1005	Star Wars	4691
1010	Harry Potter	3200
1010	Harry Potter	3201
1010	Harry Potter	3202
1010	Harry Potter	3203
1010	Harry Potter	3204
2180	Star Wars	2090
2180	Star Wars	2091
2180	Star Wars	2092
2180	Star Wars	4689
2180	Star Wars	4690
2180	Star Wars	4691

■ **FIGURE 7.8 A relation in 4NF but not 5NF.**

Note: There is no official term for the preceding anomaly. It is precisely the opposite of the insertion anomalies described earlier in this chapter, although it does involve a problem with inserting data.

By the same token, if a customer doesn't want one item in a series, then you must remove all the rows for that customer for that series from the table. If the customer still wants the remaining items in the series, then you have a deletion anomaly.

As you might guess, you can solve the problem by breaking the table into two smaller tables, eliminating the unnecessary duplicated data, and the insertion and deletion anomalies:

```
series_subscription (customer_numb, series)
```

```
series_content (series, item_numb)
```

The official definition for 5NF is as follows:

- The relation is in fourth normal form.
- All join dependencies are implied by the candidate keys.

A *join dependency* occurs when a table can be put together correctly by joining two or more tables, all of which contain only attributes from the original table. The original *selections* relation does have a join dependency, because it can be created by joining the *series subscription* and *series content relations*. The join is valid only because of the rule that requires a customer to order all items in a series.

A join dependency is implied by candidate keys when all possible projections from the original relation that form a join dependency each contain a candidate key for the original relation. For example, the following projections can be made from the *selections* relation:

A: (`customer_numb`, `series`)

B: (`customer_numb`, `item_numb`)

C: (`series`, `item_numb`)

We can regenerate the *selections* relation by combining any two of the preceding relations. Therefore, the join dependencies are A + B, A + C, B + C, and A + B + C. Like other relational algebra operations, the join theoretically removes duplicate rows, so although the raw result of the join contains extra rows, they will be removed from the result, producing the original table.

Note: One of the problems with 5NF is that as the number of columns in a table increases, the number of possible projections increases exponentially. It can therefore be very difficult to determine 5NF for a large relation.

However, each of the projections does not contain a candidate key for the *selections* relation. All three columns from the original relation are required for a candidate key. Therefore, the relation is not in 5NF. When we break down the selections relation into *series_selections* and *series_content*, we eliminate the join dependencies, ensuring that the relations are in 5NF.

Sixth Normal Form

Normalization theory has been very stable for more than 45 years. However, in the late 1990s, C. J. Date, one of the foremost experts in database theory, proposed a sixth normal form, particularly to handle situations in which there is temporal data. This is technically not a project-join normal form, as were all of those discussed earlier in this chapter.

Consider the following relation:

`customer (id, valid_interval, street, city, state, zip, phone)`

The intent of this relation is to maintain a history of a customer's locations and when they were valid (starting date to ending date). Depending on the circumstances, there may be a great deal of duplicated data in this relation (for example, if only the phone number changed) or very little (for example, if there is a move to a new state with a new phone number). Nonetheless, there is only one functional dependency in the relation:

`id + valid_interval ->> street, city, state, zip, phone`

There are no transitive dependencies, no overlapping candidate keys, no multivalued dependencies, and all join dependencies are implied by the candidate key(s). The relation is therefore in fifth normal form.

Sixth normal form was created to handle the situation where temporal data vary independently to avoid unnecessary duplication. The result is tables that cannot be decomposed any further; in most cases, the tables include the primary key and a single non-key attribute. The sixth normal form tables for the sample *customer* relation would be as follows:

```
street_addresses (id, valid_interval, street)

cities (id, valid_interval, city)

states (id, valid_interval, state)

zip_codes (id, valid_interval, zip)

phone_numbers (id, valid_interval, phone)
```

The resulting tables eliminate the possibility of redundant data, but introduce some time consuming joins to find a customer's current address or to assemble a history for a customer. For this reason alone, you may decide that it makes sense to leave the relation in 5NF and not decompose it further.

Going to sixth normal form may also introduce the need for a *circular inclusion constraint*. There is little point in including a street address for a customer unless a city, state, and zip code exist for the same date interval. The circular inclusion constraint would therefore require that if a row for any given interval and any given customer ID exists in any of *street_addresses*, *cities*, *states*, or *zip_codes*, matching rows must exist in all of those tables. Today's relational DBMSs do not support circular inclusion constraints nor are they included in the current SQL standard. If such a constraint is necessary, it will need to be enforced through application code.

For Further Reading

There are many books available that deal with the theory of relational databases. You can find useful supplementary information in the following:

Date, C.J., 2012. Database Design and Relational Theory: Formal Forms and All That Jazz. O'Reilly Media.

Date, C. J. On DN/NF Normal Form. http://www.dbdebunk.com/page/page/621935.htm

Date, C.J., Darwen, H., Lorentzos, N., 2002. Temporal Data and the Relational Model. Morgan Kaufmann.

Earp, R., 2007. Database Design Using Entity-Relationship Diagrams. Taylor & Francis.

Halpin, T., Morgan, T., 2008. Information Modeling and Relational Databases, third ed. Morgan Kaufman.

Hillyer, M. An Introduction to Database Normalization. http://dev.mysql.com/tech-re-sources/articles/intro-to-normalization.html

Olivé, A., 2007. Conceptual Modeling of Information Systems. Springer.

Pratt, P.J., Adamski, J.J., 2007. Concepts of Database Management, sixth ed. Course Technology.

Ritchie, C., 2008. Database Principles and Design, third ed. Cengage Learning Business Press.

Chapter

8

Database Design and Performance Tuning

How long are you willing to wait for a computer to respond to your request for information? 30 seconds? 10 seconds? 5 seconds? In truth, we humans are not very patient at all. Even five seconds can seem like an eternity, when you are waiting for something to appear on the screen. A database that has a slow response time to user queries usually means that you will have dissatisfied users.

Slow response times can be the result of any number of problems. You might be dealing with a client workstation that is not properly configured, a poorly written application program, a query involving multiple join operations, a query that requires reading large amounts of data from disk, a congested network, or even a DBMS that is not robust enough to handle to the volume of queries submitted to it.

One of the duties of a *database administrator* (DBA) is to optimize database performance (also known as *performance tuning*). This includes modifying the design—where possible, without compromising data integrity—to avoid performance bottlenecks, especially involving queries.

For the most part, a DBMS takes care of storing and retrieving data based on a user's commands without human intervention. The strategy used to process a data manipulation request is handled by the DBMS's *query optimizer*, a portion of the program that determines the most efficient sequence of relational algebra operations to perform a query.

Although most of the query optimizer's choices are out of the hands of a database designer or application developer, you can influence the behavior of the query optimizer and also optimize database performance to some extent with database design elements. In this chapter, you will be introduced to several such techniques.

Note: In Chapters 6 and 7 we discussed the impact of joins on queries as part of the theory of relational database design. You will learn about SQL syntax to avoid joins in Chapter 17.

Indexing

Indexing is a way of providing a fast access path to the values of a column or a concatenation of columns. New rows are typically added to the bottom of a table, resulting in a relatively random order of the values in any given column. Without some way of ordering the data, the only way the DBMS can search a column is by sequentially scanning each row from top to bottom. The larger a table becomes, the slower a sequential search will be.

Note: On average, in a table of N rows, a sequential search will need to examine N/2 rows to find a row that matches a query predicate. However, the only way for the DBMS to determine that no rows match the predicate is to examine all N rows. A table with 1000 rows requires, on average, looking at 500 rows; an unsuccessful search requires consulting all 1000 rows. However, the fast searching techniques provided by some indexes require looking at about 6 rows to find a matching row in that table of 1000 rows; an unsuccessful search requires consulting about 10 rows.

The alternative to indexing for ordering the rows in a table is sorting. A *sort* physically alters the position of rows in a table, placing the rows in order, starting with the first row in the table. Most SQL implementations do sort the virtual tables that are created as the result of queries when directed to do so by the SQL query. However, SQL provides no way to sort base tables … and there is good reason for this. Regardless of the sorting method used, as a table grows large (hundreds of thousands to millions of rows) sorting takes an enormously long time. Keeping a table in sorted order also means that, on average, half the rows in the table will need to be moved to make room for a new row. In addition, searching a sorted base table takes longer than searching an index, primarily because the index search requires less disk access. The overhead in maintaining indexes is far less than that required to sort base tables whenever a specific data order is needed.

The conceptual operation of an index is diagrammed in Figure 8.1. (The different weights of the lines have no significance other than to make it easier for you to follow the crossed lines.) In this illustration, you are looking at *Antique Opticals' item* relation and an index that provides fast access to rows in the table, based on the item's title. The index itself contains an ordered list of keys (the titles), along with the locations of the associated rows in the item table. The rows in the *item* table are in relatively random order. However, because the index is in alphabetical order by title, it can

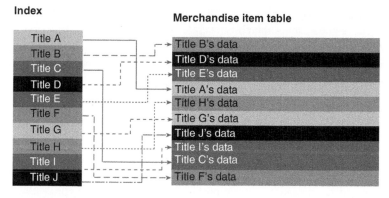

Index

Merchandise item table

Title A	Title B's data
Title B	Title D's data
Title C	Title E's data
Title D	Title A's data
Title E	Title H's data
Title F	Title G's data
Title G	Title J's data
Title H	Title I's data
Title I	Title C's data
Title J	Title F's data

■ **FIGURE 8.1** How an index works.

be searched quickly to locate a specific title. Then, the DBMS can use the information in the index to go directly to the correct row or rows in the *item* table, thus avoiding a slow sequential search of the base table's rows.

Once you have created an index, the DBMS's query optimizer will use the index whenever it determines that using the index will speed up data retrieval. You never need to access the index again yourself, unless you want to delete it.

When you create a primary key for a table, the DBMS automatically creates an index for that table using the primary key column or columns in the primary key as the index key. The first step in inserting a new row into a table is therefore verification that the index key (the primary key of the table) is unique in the index. In fact, uniqueness is enforced by requiring the index entries to be unique, rather than by actually searching the base table. This is much faster than attempting to verify uniqueness directly on the base table because the ordered index can be searched much more rapidly than the unordered base table.

Deciding Which Indexes to Create

You have no choice as to whether the DBMS creates indexes for your primary keys; you get them regardless of whether you want them. In addition, you can create indexes on any column or combination of columns you want. However, before you jump headfirst into creating indexes on every column in every table, there are some trade-offs to consider:

- Indexes take up space in the database. Given that disk space is relatively inexpensive today, this is usually not a major drawback.
- When you insert, modify, or delete data in indexed columns, the DBMS must update the index as well as the base table. This may slow down data modification operations, especially if the tables have a lot of rows.
- Indexes can significantly speed up access to data.

The trade-off is therefore generally between update speed and retrieval speed. A good rule of thumb is to create indexes for foreign keys and for other columns that are used frequently for queries that apply logical criteria to data. If you find that update speed is severely affected, you may choose at a later time to delete some of the indexes you created.

You should also try to avoid indexes on columns that contain *nondiscriminatory data*. Nondiscriminatory columns have only a few values throughout the entire table, such as Boolean columns that contain only true and false. Gender (male or female) is also nondiscriminatory. Although you may search on a column containing nondiscriminatory data—for example, a search for all open orders—an index will not provide much performance enhancement, because the DBMS must examine so many keys to complete the query.

Clustering

The slowest part of a DBMS's actions is retrieving data from or writing data to a disk. If you can cut down on the number of times the DBMS must read from or write to a disk, you can speed up overall database performance.

The trick to doing this is understanding that a database must retrieve an entire disk page of data at one time. The size of a page varies from one computing platform to another—it can be anywhere from 512 bytes to 4 K, with 1 K being typical on a PC—but data always travel to and from disk in page-sized units. Therefore, if you can get data that are often accessed together stored on the same disk page (or pages that are physically close together), you can speed up data access. This process is known as *clustering*, and is available with many large DBMSs (for example, Oracle).

Note: The term "clustering" has another meaning in the SQL standard. It refers to a group of catalogs (which in turn are groups of schemas) manipulated by the same DBMS. It has yet again another meaning when we talk about distributed databases, where it refers to a networked group of commodity PCs maintaining the same database. The use of the term in this section, however, is totally distinct from the SQL and distributed database meanings.

In practice, a cluster is designed to keep together rows related by matching primary and foreign keys. To define the cluster, you specify a column or columns on which the DBMS should form the cluster and the tables that should be included. Then, all rows that share the same value of the column or columns on which the cluster is based are stored as physically close together as possible. As a result, the rows in a table may be scattered across several disk pages, but matching primary and foreign keys are usually on the same disk page.

Clustering can significantly speed up join performance. However, just as with indexes, there are some trade-offs to consider when contemplating creating clusters:

- Because clustering involves physical placement of data in a file, a table can be clustered on only one column or combination of columns.
- Clustering can slow down performance of operations that require a scan of the entire table because clustering may mean that the rows of any given table are scattered throughout many disk pages.
- Clustering can slow down insertion of data.
- Clustering can slow down modifying data in the columns on which the clustering is based.

Partitioning

Partitioning is the opposite of clustering. It involves the splitting of large tables into smaller ones so that the DBMS does not need to retrieve as much data at any one time. Consider, for example, what happens to *Antique Opticals'* *order* and *order item* tables over time. Assuming that the business is reasonably successful, those tables (especially *order item*) will become very large. Retrieval of data from those tables will therefore begin to slow down. It would speed up retrieval of open orders if filled orders and their items could be separated from open orders and their items.

There are two ways to partition a table, horizontally and vertically. *Horizontal partitioning* involves splitting the rows of a table between two or more tables with identical structures. *Vertical partitioning* involves splitting the columns of a table, placing them into two or more tables linked by the original table's primary key. As you might expect, there are advantages and disadvantages to both.

Horizontal Partitioning

Horizontal partitioning involves creating two or more tables with exactly the same structure, and splitting rows between those tables. *Antique Opticals* might use this technique to solve the problem with the *order* and *order items* tables becoming increasingly large. The database design might be modified as follows:

open_order (<u>order_numb</u>, customer_numb, order_date)

open_order_item (<u>order_numb</u>, <u>item_numb</u>, quantity, shipped?)

filled_order (<u>order_numb</u>, customer_numb, order_date)

filled_order_item (<u>order_numb</u>, <u>item_numb</u>, quantity, shipped?)

Whenever all items in an open order have shipped, an application program deletes rows from the *open order* and *open order item* table and inserts them into the *filled order* and *filled order item* tables. The *open order* and *open order item* tables remain relatively small, speeding up both retrieval and modification performance. Although retrieval from *filled order* and *filled order line* will be slower, *Antique Opticals* uses those tables much less frequently.

The drawback to this solution occurs when *Antique Opticals* needs to access all of the orders and/or order items, at the same time. A query whose result table includes data from both sets of open and filled tables must actually be two queries connected by the union operator. (Remember that the union operation creates one table by merging the rows of two tables with the same structure.) Performance of such a query will be worse than that of a query of either set of tables individually. Nonetheless, if an analysis of *Antique Opticals*' data access patterns reveals that such queries occur rarely and that most retrieval involves the set of tables for open orders, then the horizontal partitioning is worth doing.

The only way you can determine whether horizontal partitioning will increase performance is to examine the ways in which your database applications access data. If there is a group of rows that are accessed together significantly more frequently than the rest of the rows in a table, then horizontal partitioning may make sense.

Vertical Partitioning

Vertical partitioning involves creating two or more tables with selected columns and all rows of a table. For example, if *Antique Opticals* accesses the titles and prices of their merchandise items more frequently than the other columns in the *item* table, the *item* table might be partitioned as follows:

```
item_title (item_numb, title, price)

item_detail (item_numb, distributor, release_date, …)
```

The benefit of this design is that the rows in the smaller *item title* table will be physically closer together; the smaller table will take up fewer disk pages and thus support faster retrieval.

Queries that require data from both tables must join the tables over the item number. Like most joins, this will be a relatively slow operation. Therefore, vertical partitioning makes sense only when there is a highly skewed access pattern of the columns of a table. The more often a small, specific group of columns is accessed together, the more vertical partitioning will help.

For Further Reading

Alapati, S., Kuhn, D., Padfield, B., 2013. Oracle database 12c performance tuning recipes: a problem-solution approach. Apress.

Andrews, T., 2012. DB2 SQL tuning tips for z/OS developers. IBM Press.

Atonini, C., 2008. Troubleshooting oracle performance. Apress.

Gulutzan, P., Pelzer, T., 2002. SQL performance tuning. Addison-Wesley Professional.

IBM Redbooks, 2006. A deep blue view of DB2 performance. IBM.com/Redbooks.

Meade, K., 2014. Oracle SQL performance tuning and optimization: it's all about the cardinalities. CreateSpace Independent Publishing Platform.

Mittra, S.S., 2002. Database performance tuning and optimization. Springer.

Nevarez, B., 2014. Microsoft SQL server 2014 query tuning & optimization. McGraw-Hill Education.

Shasha, D., Bonnet, P., 2002. Database tuning: principles, experiments, and troubleshooting techniques. Morgan Kaufmann.

Schwartz, B., Zaitsev, P., Tkachenko, V., Zawony, J.D., Lentz, A., Balling, D.J., 2008. High performance MySQL: optimization, backups replication, and more. O'Reilly.

Tow, D., 2003. SQL tuning. O'Reilly.

Winand, M., 2012. SQL performance explained: everything developers need to know about SQL performance. Markus Winand.

Codd's Rules for Relational DBMSs

In October 1985, E. F. Codd published a series of two articles in the computer industry weekly called *Computerworld*. The first article laid out 12 (or 13, depending on how you count them) criteria to which a "fully relational" database should adhere. The second article compared current mainframe products to those rules, producing a flurry of controversy over whether it was important the DBMSs be theoretically rigorous, or that they simply work effectively.

Note: If you read Appendix A, then you will be aware of a product based on the simple network data model called IDMS/R. When Codd rated IDMS/R—which was then being marketed as a relational DBMS—it met none (0) of the 12 rules. DB/2, IBM's flagship relational product, met 10 of the rules.

To help you understand the issues raised and why Codd's rules for relational databases for the most part make sense, in this chapter we will look at those criteria along with the implications of their implementation. Should you then choose not to adhere to one or more of the rules, you will be doing so with full understanding of the consequences. In some cases, the consequences are minimal; in others, they may significantly affect the integrity of the data in a database.

Rule 0: The Foundation Rule

Before getting into specifics, Codd wanted to ensure that a relational DBMS was truly using the relational data model and relational actions (for example, relational algebra) to process data:

> *"A relational database management system must manage its stored data using only its relational capabilities."*

This basic rule excludes products that have non-relational engines underlying tools and/or query languages that allow users to function as if the product were relational. Products such as IDMS/R, mentioned in the note above, were eliminated at this point.

Rule 1: The Information Rule

The first criterion for databases deals with the data structures that are used to store data and represent data relationships:

> *"All information in a relational database is represented explicitly at the logical level in exactly one way—by values in tables."*

The purpose of this rule is to require that relations (two-dimensional tables) be the *only* data structure used in a relational database. Therefore, products that require hard-coded links between tables are not relational.

At the time Codd's article was published, one of the most widely used mainframe products was IDMS/R, a version of IDMS that placed a relational-style query language on top of a simple network database. The simple network data model requires data structures, such as pointers or indexes, to represent data relationships. Therefore, IDBMS/R, although being marketed as relational, was not relational according to the very first rule of a relational database. It was this product that was at the heart of the "who cares about rules if my product works" controversy.

Regardless of which side you take in this particular argument, there are several very good reasons why creating a database from nothing but tables is a good idea:

- Logical relationships are very flexible. In a simple network or hierarchical database, the only relationships that can be used for retrieval are those that have been predetermined by the database designer who wrote the schema. However, because a relational database represents its relationships through matching data values, the join operation can be used to implement relationships on the fly, even those that a database designer may not have anticipated.
- Relational database schemas are very flexible. You can add, modify, and remove individual relations without disturbing the rest of the schema. In fact, as long as you are not changing the structure of tables currently being used, you can modify the schema of a live database. However, to modify the schema of a simple network or hierarchical database, you must stop all processing of data and regenerate the entire schema. In many cases, modifying the database design also means recreating all the physical files (using a dump and load process) to correspond to the new design.
- The meaning of tabular data is well understood by most people. For example, you usually don't need specialized training to teach people that all the data in a row apply to the same item.

Note: DBMSs that require you to specify "relationships between files" when you design a database fail this first rule. If you read Appendix A, then you know that a number of PC-only products work in this way and that although they are marketed as relational, they really use the simple network data model. Keep in mind that the ER diagrams for simple networks and 3NF relational database are identical. The differences come in how the relationships between the entities are represented. In a simple network, it is with hard-coded relationships; in a relational database, it is with primary key–foreign key pairs.

When Codd originally wrote his rules, databases couldn't store anything other than text and numbers. Today, many DBMSs store images, audio, and video in a variety of formats or store the path names (or URL) to media in external files. Technically, path names or URLs of external files are pointers to something other than tables and therefore would seem to cause a DBMS to violate this rule. However, the spirit of the rule is that relationships between entities—the logical relationships in the database—are represented by matching data values, without the use of pointers of any kind to indicate entity connections.

Note: This is not the only rule that needs to be stretched a bit to accommodate graphics in a database environment. See also rule 5 later in this chapter.

Rule 2: The Guaranteed Access Rule

Given that the entire reason we put data into a database is to get the data out again, we must be certain that we can retrieve every single piece of data:

> *"Each and every datum (atomic value) in a relational database is guaranteed to be logically accessible by resorting to a combination of table name, primary key value, and column name."*

This rule states that you should need to know only three things to locate a specific piece of data: the name of the table, the name of the column, and the primary key of the row containing the data.

Note: With today's DBMSs, the definition of a table name can mean many things. For example, if you are working with IBM's DB/2, a table name is the table creator's loginName.tableName. If you are working with Oracle, then a complete table name may include a catalog name, schema name, and Oracle owner name, as well as the name of the individual table.

There is no rule in this set of 12 rules that specifically states that each row in a relation must have a unique primary key. However, a relation cannot adhere to the guaranteed access rule unless it does have unique primary keys. Without unique primary keys, you will be able to retrieve *some* row with the primary key value used in a search, but not necessarily the exact row you want. Some data may therefore be inaccessible without the ability to uniquely identify rows.

Early relational DBMSs did not require primary keys at all. You could create and use tables without primary key constraints. Today, however, SQL will allow you to create a table without a primary key specification, but most DBMSs will not permit you to enter data into that table.

Note: A DBMS that requires "relationships between files" cannot adhere to this rule because you must specify the file in which data reside to locate data.

Rule 3: Systematic Treatment of Null Values

As you know, null is a special database value that means "unknown." Its presence in a database brings special problems during data retrieval. Consider, for example, what happens if you have an *employee* relation that contains a column for salary. Assume that the salary is null for some portion of the rows. What, then, should happen if someone queries the table for all people who make more than $60,000? Should the rows with null be retrieved or should they be left out?

When the DBMS evaluates a null against the logical criterion of salary value greater than 60,000, it cannot determine whether the row containing the null meets the criteria. Maybe it does; maybe it doesn't. For this reason, we say that relational databases use *three-valued logic*. The result of the evaluation of a logical expression is either true, false, or maybe.

Codd's third rule therefore deals with the issue of nulls:

> *"Null values (distinct from the empty character string or a string of blank characters or any other number) are supported in the fully relational DBMS for representing missing information in a systematic way, independent of data type."*

First, a relational DBMS must store the same value for null in all columns and rows where the user does not explicitly enter data values. The value used for null must be the same, regardless of the data type of the column. Note that null is not the same as a space character or zero; it has its own, distinct ASCII or UNICODE value. However, in most cases when you see a query's result table on the screen, nulls do appear as blank.

Second, the DBMS must have some consistent, known way of handling those nulls when performing queries. Typically, you will find that rows with nulls are not retrieved by a query such as the salary greater than 60,000 example unless the user explicitly asks for rows with a value of null. Most relational DBMSs today adhere to a three-valued logic truth table to determine retrieval behavior when they encounter nulls.

The inclusion of nulls in a relation can be extremely important. They provide a consistent way to distinguish between valid data such as a 0, and missing data. For example, it makes a great deal of difference to know that the balance in an account payable is 0 instead of unknown. The account with 0 is something we like to see; the account with an unknown balance could be a significant problem.

Note: The concept of unknown values is not unique to relational databases. Regardless of the data model it uses, a DBMS must contend with the problem of how to behave when querying against a null.

Rule 4: Dynamic Online Catalog Based on the Relational Model

Earlier in this book, you read about relational database data dictionaries. Codd very clearly specifies that those dictionaries (which he calls *catalogs*) should be made up of nothing but relations:

> *"The data base description is represented at the logical level in the same way as ordinary data, so that authorized users can apply the same relational language to the interrogation as they apply to regular data."*

One advantage of using the same data structures for the data dictionary as you do for data tables is that you have a consistent way to access all elements of the database. You need to learn only one query language. This also simplifies the DBMS itself, since it can use the same mechanism for handling data about the database (*metadata*) as it can data about the organization.

When you purchase a DBMS, it comes with its own way of handling a data dictionary. There is rarely anything you can do to change it. Therefore, the major implication of this particular rule comes in selecting relational software: You want to look for something that has a data dictionary that is made up of nothing but tables.

Note: Because of the way in which their schemas were implemented, it was rare for a prerelational DBMS to have an online data dictionary.

Rule 5: The Comprehensive Data Sublanguage Rule

A relational database must have some language that can maintain database structural elements, modify data, and retrieve data. Codd included the following rule that describes his ideas about what such a language should do:

> *"A relational system may support several languages and various modes of terminal use (for example, fill-in-the-blanks mode). However, there must be at least one language whose statements are expressible, per some well-defined syntax, as character strings and that is comprehensive in supporting all of the following items:*

> - *Data definition*
> - *View definition*
> - *Data manipulation (interactive and by program)*
> - *Integrity constraints*
> - *Transaction boundaries (begin, commit and rollback)"*

The current SQL language does meet all of these rules. (Versions earlier than SQL-92 did not include complete support for primary keys and referential integrity.) Given that most of today's relational DBMSs use SQL as their primary data manipulation language, there would seem to be no issue here.

However, a DBMS that does not support SQL, but uses a graphic language, would technically not meet this rule. Nonetheless, there are several products today whose graphic language can perform all the tasks Codd has listed, without a command-line syntax. Such DBMSs might not be theoretically "fully relational," but, since they can perform all the necessary relational tasks, you lose nothing by not having the command-line language.

Note: Keep in mind the time frame in which Codd was writing. In 1985, the Macintosh—whose operating system legitimized the graphic user interface—was barely a year old. Most people still considered the GUI-equipped computers to be little more than toys.

Rule 6: The View Updating Rule

As you will read in more depth in Chapter 21 some views can be used to update data. Others—those created from more than one base table or view, those that do not contain the primary keys of their base tables, and so on—often cannot be used for updating. Codd's sixth rule speaks only about those that meet a DBMS's criteria for updatability:

> *"All views that are theoretically updatable are also updatable by the system."*

This rule simply means that if a view meets the criteria for updatability, a DBMS must be able to handle that update and propagate the updates back to the base tables.

Note: DBMSs that used prerelational data models included constructs similar in concept to views. For example, CODASYL DBMSs included "subschemas," which allowed an application programmer to construct a subset of a schema to be used by a specific end user or by an application program.

Rule 7: High-Level Insert, Update, Delete

Codd wanted to ensure that a DBMS could handle multiple rows of data at a time, especially when data were modified. Therefore, the seventh rule requires that a DBMS's data manipulation facilities be able to insert, update, and delete more than one row with a single command:

> *"The capability of handling a base relation or a derived relation as a single operand applies not only to the retrieval of data but also to the insertion, update, and deletion of data."*

SQL provides this capability for today's relational DBMSs. What does it bring you? Being able to modify more than one row with a single command simplifies data manipulation logic. Rather than needing to scan a relation row by row to locate rows for modification, for example, you can specify logical criteria that identify rows to be affected and let the DBMS find the rows for you.

Rule 8: Physical Data Independence

One of the benefits of using a database system rather than a file processing system is that a DBMS isolates the user from physical storage details. The physical data independence rule speaks to this issue:

> *"Applications and terminal activities remain logically unimpaired whenever any changes are made in either storage representation or access methods."*

This means that you should be able to move the database from one disk volume to another, change the physical layout of the files, and so on, without any impact on the way in which application programs and end users interact with the tables in the database.

Most of today's DBMSs give you little control over the file structures used to store data on a disk. (Only the very largest mainframe systems allow systems programmers to determine physical storage structures.) Therefore, in a practical sense, physical data independence means that you should be able to move the database from one disk volume or directory to another, without affecting the logical design of the database and, therefore, the application programs and interactive users remain unaffected. With a few exceptions, most of today's DBMSs do provide physical data independence.

Note: Prerelational DBMSs generally fail this rule to a greater or lesser degree. The older the data model, the closer it was tied to its physical data storage. The tradeoff, however, is performance. Hierarchical systems are much faster than relational systems when processing data in tree traversal order. The same can be said for a CODASYL database. When traversing in set order, access will be faster than row-by-row access within a relational database. The tradeoff is flexibility to perform ad hoc queries, something at which relational systems excel.

Rule 9: Logical Data Independence

Logical data independence is a bit more subtle than physical data independence. In essence, it means that if you change the schema—perhaps adding or removing a table or adding a column to a table—then other parts of the schema that should not be affected by the change remain unaffected:

> *"Application programs and terminal activities remain logically unimpaired when information-preserving changes of any kind that theoretically permit unimpairment are made to the base tables."*

As an example, consider what happens when you add a table to a database. Since relations are logically independent of one another, adding a table should have absolutely no impact on any other table. To adhere to the logical data independence rule, a DBMS must ensure that there is indeed no impact on other tables.

On the other hand, if you delete a table from the database, such a modification is not "information preserving." Data will almost certainly be lost when the table is removed. Therefore, it is not necessary that application programs and interactive users be unaffected by the change.

Rule 10: Integrity Independence

Although the requirement for unique primary keys is a corollary to an earlier rule, the requirement for nonnull primary keys and for referential integrity is very explicit:

> *"Integrity constraints specific to a particular relational data base must be definable in the relational data sublanguage and storable in the catalog, not in the application programs.*

A minimum of the following two integrity constraints must be supported:

1. *Entity integrity: No component of a primary key is allowed to have a null value.*
2. *Relational integrity: For each distinct non-null foreign key value in a relational data base, there must exist a matching primary key value from the same domain."*

Notice that the rule requires that the declaration of integrity constraints must be a part of whatever language is used to define database structure. In addition, integrity constraints of any kind must be stored in a data dictionary that can be accessed while the database is being used.

When IBM released its flagship relational database—DB/2—one of the two things users complained about was the lack of referential integrity support. IBM and other DBMS vendors at that time omitted referential integrity because it slowed down performance. Each time you modify a row of data, the DBMS must go to the data dictionary, search for an integrity rule, and perform the test indicated by the rule, all before performing an update. A referential integrity check of a single column can involve two or more disk accesses, all of which takes more time than simply making the modification directly to the base table.

However, without referential integrity, the relationships in a relational database very quickly become inconsistent. Retrieval operations therefore do not necessarily retrieve all data because the missing cross-references cause joins to omit data. In that case, the database is unreliable and virtually unusable. (Yes, IBM added referential integrity to DB/2 fairly quickly!)

Note: One solution to the problem of a DBMS not supporting referential integrity was to have application programmers code the referential integrity checks into application programs. This certainly works, but it puts the burden of integrity checking in the wrong place. It should be an integral part of the database, rather than left up to an application programmer.

Note: Most DBMSs using prerelational data models provided some types of integrity constraints, including domain constraints, unique entity identifiers, and required values (non-null). CODASYL could also enforce mandatory relationships, something akin to referential integrity.

Rule 11: Distribution Independence

As you will remember from Chapter 1 a distributed database is a database where the data themselves are stored on more than one computer. The database is therefore the union of all its parts. In practice, the parts are not unique, but contain a deal of duplicated data.

Nonetheless, according to rule 11:

"A relational DBMS has distribution independence."

In other words, a distributed database must look to the user like a centralized database. Application programs and interactive users should not be required to know where data are stored, including the location of multiple copies of the same data.

DBMS vendors have been working on distributed DBMS software since the late 1970s. However, current relational DBMSs do not truly meet this rule. Even the most sophisticated distributed DBMS software requires in some circumstances that the user indicate some location information when retrieving data.

Rule 12: Nonsubversion Rule

The final rule might be subtitled the "no cheating rule."

"If a relational system has a low-level (single-record-at-a-time) language that low-level language cannot be used to subvert or bypass the integrity rules or constraints expressed in the higher level relational language (multiple-records-at-a-time)."

Many DBMS products during the 1980s had languages that could directly access rows in tables separate from SQL, which operates on multiples rows at a time. This rule states that there must be no way to use that direct-access language to get around the constraints stored in the data dictionary. The integrity rules must be observed without exception.

For Further Reading

The original articles outlining Codd's rules can't be found online for free access. (Those two issues are missing from Computerworld's Google Books archive.) However, you may be able to find them on paper, or in a paper replica (for example, microfilm or microfiche) at a library. The full text of the articles is available on LexisNexis Academic as well.

Codd, EF. Is Your DBMS Really Relation? Computerworld, October 14, 1985.
Codd, EF. Does Your DBMS Run by the Rules? Computerworld, October 21, 1985.

Part

III

Relational Database Design Practice

In this part of the book, you will read about some of the practical techniques we use when working with relational database designs. You will be introduced to the SQL language statements needed to create relational schemes and their contents. You will also see how a CASE tool can help design and document a database. In addition, this part contains three complete relational design case studies to provide further examples of the database design process.

Chapter

10   Introduction to SQL

SQL[1] is a database definition and database manipulation language that has been implemented by virtually every relational database management system (DBMS) intended for multiple users, partly because it has been accepted by ANSI (the American National Standards Institute) and ISO (International Standards Organization) as a standard query language for relational databases.

The chapter presents an overview of the environment in which SQL exists. We will begin with a bit of SQL history so you will know where it came from and where it is heading. Then, you will read about the way in which SQL commands are processed and the software environments in which they function.

A Bit of SQL History

SQL was developed by IBM at its San Jose Research Laboratory in the early 1970s. Presented at an ACM conference in 1974, the language was originally named SEQUEL (Structured English Query Language) and pronounced "sequel." The language's name was later shortened to SQL.

Although IBM authored SQL, the first SQL implementation was provided by Oracle Corporation (then called Relational Software Inc.). Early commercial implementations were concentrated on midsized UNIX-based DBMSs, such as Oracle, Ingres, and Informix. IBM followed in 1981 with SQL/DS, the forerunner to DB2, which debuted in 1983.

---

[1]Whether you say "sequel" or "S-Q-L" depends on how long you've been working with SQL. Those of us who have been working in this field for longer than we'd like to admit often say "sequel," which is what I do. When I started using SQL, there was no other pronunciation. That is why you'll see "a SQL" (a sequel) rather than "an SQL" (an es-que-el) throughout this book. Old habits die hard! However, many people do prefer the acronym.

ANSI published the first SQL standard (SQL-86) in 1986. An international version of the standard issued by ISO appeared in 1987. A significant update to SQL-86 was released in 1989 (SQL-89). Virtually all relational DBMSs that you encounter today support most of the 1989 standard.

In 1992, the standard was revised again (SQL-92), adding more capabilities to the language. Because SQL-92 was a superset of SQL-89, older database application programs ran under the new standard with minimal modifications. In fact, until October 1996, DBMS vendors could submit their products to NIST (National Institute for Standards and Technology) for verification of SQL standard compliance. This testing and certification process provided significant motivation for DBMS vendors to adhere to the SQL standard. Although discontinuing standard compliance testing saves the vendors money, it also makes it easier for products to diverge from the standard.

The SQL-92 standard was superseded by SQL:1999, which was once again a superset of the preceding standard. The primary new features of SQL:1999 supported the object-relational data model, which is discussed in Chapter 27 of this book.

The SQL:1999 standard also adds extensions to SQL to allow scripts or program modules to be written in SQL or to be written in another programming language, such as C++ or Java and then invoked from within another SQL statement. As a result, SQL becomes less "relational," a trend decried by some relational purists.

Note: Regardless of where you come down on the relational theory argument, you will need to live with the fact that the major commercial DBMSs, such as Oracle and DB/2, have provided support for the object-relational data model for some time now. The object-relational data model is a fact of life, although there certainly is no rule that says that you must use those features, should you choose not to do so.

Even the full SQL:1999 standard does not turn SQL into a complete, stand-alone programming language. In particular, SQL lacks I/O statements. This makes perfect sense, since SQL should be implementation and operating system independent. However, the full SQL:1999 standard does include operations such as selection and iteration that make it *computationally complete*. These language features, which are more typical of general-purpose programming languages, are used when writing stored procedures and triggers:

■ Triggers: A *trigger* is a script that runs when a specific database action occurs. For example, a trigger might be written to execute when data are inserted or deleted.

- Stored procedures: A *stored procedure* is a script that runs when it is called by an application program written in a general-purpose programming language or another SQL language module.

Triggers and stored procedures are stored in the database itself, rather than being a part of an application program. The scripts are, therefore, available to all application programs written to interact with the database.

The SQL standard has been updated four times since the appearance of SQL:1999, in versions named SQL:2003, SQL:2006, SQL:2008, and SQL:2011. As well as fleshing out the capabilities of the core relational capabilities and extending object-relational support, these revisions have added support for XML (Extensible Markup Language). XML is a platform-independent method for representing data using text files. SQL's XML features are introduced in Chapter 26.

Conformance Levels

The SQL in this book is based on the more recent versions of the SQL standard (SQL:2003 through SQL:2011). However, keep in mind that SQL:2011 (or whatever version of the language you are considering) is simply a standard, not a mandate. Various DBMSs exhibit different levels of conformance to the standard. In addition, the implementation of language features usually lags behind the standard. Therefore, although SQL:2011 may be the latest version of the standard, no DBMS meets the entire standard and most are based on earlier versions.

Note: In one sense, the SQL standard is a moving target. Just as DBMSs look like they're going to catch up to the most recent standard, the standard is updated. DBMS developers scurry to implement new features and, as soon as they get close, the standard changes again.

Conformance to early versions of the standard (SQL-92 and earlier) was measured by determining whether the portion of the language required for a specific level of conformance were supported. Each feature in the standard was identified by a *leveling rule*, indicating at which conformance level it was required. At the time, there were three conformance levels:

- Full SQL-92 conformance: all features in the SQL-92 standard are supported.
- Intermediate SQL-92 conformance: all features required for intermediate conformance are supported.
- Entry SQL-92: conformance: all features required for entry level conformance are supported.

In truth, most DBMSs were only entry level compliant, and some supported a few of the features at higher conformance levels. The later standards define conformance in a different way, however.

The standard itself is documented in nine parts (parts 1, 2, 3, 4, 9, 10, 11, 13, 14). Core conformance is defined as supporting the basic SQL features (Part 2, Core/Foundation) as well as features for definition and information schemas (Part 11, SQL/Schemata). A DBMS can claim conformance to any of the remaining parts individually, as long as the product meets the conformance rules presented in the standard.

In addition to language features specified in the standard, there are some features from earlier standards that, although not mentioned in the 2006, 2008, and 2011 standards, are widely implemented. This includes, for example, support for indexes.

SQL Environments

There are two general ways in which you can issue a SQL command to a database:

- Interactive SQL, in which a user types a single command and sends it immediately to the database: The result of an interactive query is a table in main memory (a *virtual table*). In mainframe environments, each user has one result table at a time, which is replaced each time a new query is executed; PC environments sometimes allow several. As you read in Chapter 6, result tables may not be legal relations—because of nulls, they may have no primary key—but that is not a problem because they are not part of the database, but exist only in main memory.
- Embedded SQL, in which SQL statements are placed in an application program: The interface presented to the user may be form-based or command-line based. Embedded SQL may be *static*, in which case the entire command is specified at the time the program is written. Alternatively, it may be *dynamic*, in which case the program builds the statement using user input and then submits it to the database.

In addition to the two methods for writing SQL syntax, there are also a number of graphic query builders. These provide a way for a user who may not know the SQL language to "draw" the elements of a query. Some of these programs are report writers (for example, Crystal Reports[2]) and are not intended for data modification or for maintaining the structure of a database.

---

[2]For more information, see www.crystalreports.com.

Interactive SQL Command Processors

At the most general level, we can describe working with an interactive SQL command processor in the following way:

- Type the SQL command.
- Send the command to the database and wait for the result.

In this era of the graphic user interface (GUI), command line environments like that in Figure 10.1 seem rather primitive. Nonetheless, the SQL command line continues to provide basic access to relational databases and is used extensively when developing a database.

```
                                    Terminal — edb-psql — 127×23
edb=#
edb=#
edb=# select * from customer;
 customer_numb | first_name | last_name |       street       |    city     | state_province | zip_postcode | contact_phone
---------------+------------+-----------+--------------------+-------------+----------------+--------------+---------------
             1 | Janice     | Jones     | 125 Center Road    | Anytown     | NY             | 11111        | 518-555-1111
             2 | Jon        | Jones     | 25 Elm Road        | Next Town   | NJ             | 18888        | 209-555-2222
             3 | John       | Doe       | 821 Elm Street     | Next Town   | NJ             | 18888        | 209-555-3333
             4 | Jane       | Doe       | 852 Main Street    | Anytown     | NY             | 11111        | 518-555-4444
             5 | Jane       | Smith     | 1919 Main Street   | New Village | NY             | 13333        | 518-555-5555
             6 | Janice     | Smith     | 800 Center Road    | Anytown     | NY             | 11111        | 518-555-6666
             7 | Helen      | Brown     | 25 Front Street    | Anytown     | NY             | 11111        | 518-555-7777
             8 | Helen      | Jerry     | 16 Main Street     | Newtown     | NJ             | 18886        | 518-555-8888
             9 | Mary       | Collins   | 301 Pine Road, Apt. 12 | Newtown | NJ             | 18886        | 518-555-9999
            10 | Peter      | Collins   | 18 Main Street     | Newtown     | NJ             | 18886        | 518-555-1010
            11 | Edna       | Hayes     | 209 Circle Road    | Anytown     | NY             | 11111        | 518-555-1110
            12 | Franklin   | Hayes     | 615 Circle Road    | Anytown     | NY             | 11111        | 518-555-1212
            13 | Peter      | Johnson   | 22 Rose Court      | Next Town   | NJ             | 18888        | 209-555-1212
            14 | Peter      | Johnson   | 881 Front Street   | Next Town   | NJ             | 18888        | 209-555-1414
            15 | John       | Smith     | 881 Manor Lane     | Next Town   | NJ             | 18888        | 209-555-1515
(15 rows)

edb=#
```

■ **FIGURE 10.1 A typical SQL command line environment.**

A command line environment also provides support for *ad hoc queries*, queries that arise at the spur of the moment, and are not likely to be issued with any frequency. Experienced SQL users can usually work faster at the command line than with any other type of SQL command processor.

The down side to the traditional command line environment is that it is relatively unforgiving. If you make a typing error or an error in the construction of a command, it may be difficult to get the processor to recall the command so that it can be edited and resubmitted to the database. In fact, you may have no other editing capabilities except the backspace key.

The SQL command examples that you will see throughout this book were all tested in a command line environment. As you are learning to create your own queries, this is, in most cases, the environment in which you will be working.

GUI Environments

There are actually two strategies used by GUI environments to provide access to a SQL database. The first is to simply provide a window into which you can type a command, just as you would do from the command line (for example, Figure 10.2, which shows a query tool for Postgres). Such environments usually make it easier to edit the command, supporting recall of the command and full-screen editing features.

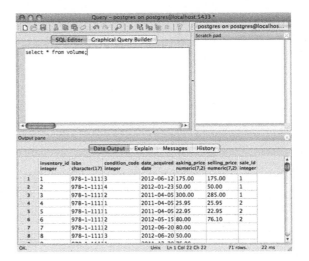

■ **FIGURE 10.2 Typing a SQL command into a window.**

The other strategy is to provide a "query builder," an environment in which the user is guided through the construction of the query (for example, Figure 10.3). The query builder presents the user with lists of the legal command elements. Those lists change as the query is built so that the user also constructs legal syntax. The query builder type of SQL command

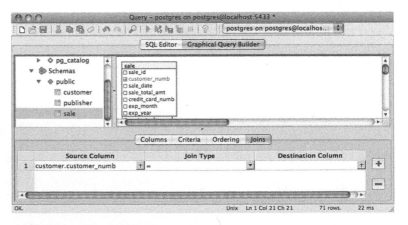

■ **FIGURE 10.3 A "query builder" environment.**

environment makes it much easier for many users to construct correct SQL statements, but it is also slower than working directly at the command line.

The Embedded SQL Dilemma

Embedding SQL in a general-purpose programming language presents an interesting challenge. The host languages (for example, Java, C++, JavaScript) have compilers or interpreters that don't recognize SQL statements as legal parts of the language. The solution is to provide SQL support through an application library that can be linked to a program. Program source code is passed through a precompiler that changes SQL commands into calls to library routines. The modified source code will then be acceptable to a host language compiler or interpreter.

In addition to the problem of actually compiling an embedded SQL program, there is a fundamental mismatch between SQL and a general-purpose programming language: Programming languages are designed to process data one row at a time, while SQL is designed to handle many rows at a time. SQL therefore includes some special elements so that it can process one row at a time when a query has returned multiple rows.

Elements of a SQL Statement

There are certainly many options for creating a SQL command. However, they are all made up of the same elements:

- Keywords: Each SQL command begins with a keyword—such as SELECT, INSERT, or UPDATE—that tells the command processor the type of operation that is to be performed. The remainder of the keywords precede the tables from which data are to be taken, indicate specific operations that are to be performed on the data, and so on.
- Tables: A SQL command includes the names of the tables on which the command is to operate.
- Columns: A SQL command includes the names of the columns that the command is to affect.
- Functions: A *function* is a small program that is built into the SQL language. Each function does one thing. For example, the AVG function computes the average of numeric data values. You will see a number of SQL functions discussed throughout this book.

Keywords and tables are required for all SQL commands. Columns may be optional, depending on the type of operation being performed. Functions are never required for a legal SQL statement, but, in some cases may be essential to obtaining a desired result.

For Further Reading

Chamberlin, DD, Raymond FB. SEQUEL: a structured english query language. 1974. http://www.almaden.ibm.com/cs/people/chamberlin/sequel-1974.pdf

Programmers Stack Exchange. Sequel vs. S-Q-L. http://programmers.stackexchange.com/questions/108518/sequel-vs-s-q-l

O'Reilly Media. History of the SQL Standard from SQL in a nutshell, 2nd ed. (entire book: http://users.atw.hu/sqlnut/index.html). http://users.atw.hu/sqlnut/sqlnut2-chp-1-sect-2.html

Chapter

11

Using SQL to Implement a Relational Design

As a complete data manipulation language, SQL contains statements that allow you to insert, modify, delete, and retrieve data. However, to a database designer, the portions of SQL that support the creation of database structural elements are of utmost importance. In this chapter, you will be introduced to the SQL commands that you will use to create and maintain the tables that make up a relational database.

Some of the structural elements in a relational database are created with SQL retrieval commands embedded in them. We will therefore defer a discussion of those elements until Chapter 21.

The actual file structure of a database is implementation dependent, as is the procedure needed to create database files. Therefore, the discussion in this chapter assumes that the necessary database files are already in place.

Note: You will see extensive examples of the use of the syntax presented in this chapter at the end of each of the three case studies that follow in this book.

Database Structure Hierarchy

The elements that describe the structure of a SQL:2011-compliant database are arranged in a hierarchy, diagrammed in Figure 11.1. The smallest units with which the DBMS works—columns and rows—appear in the center. These, in turn, are grouped into tables and views.

The tables and views that comprise a single logical database are collected into a schema. Multiple schemas are grouped into catalogs, which can then be grouped into clusters. A catalog usually contains information describing

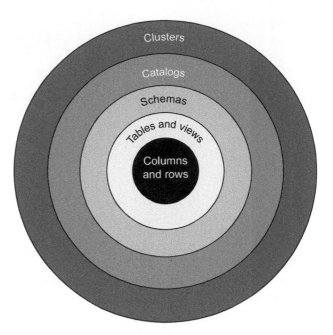

■ FIGURE 11.1   The SQL:2011 database structure hierarchy.

all the schemas handled by one DBMS. Catalog creation is implementation dependent and, therefore, not part of the SQL standard.

Prior to SQL-92, clusters often represented database files, and the clustering of database elements into files was a way to increase database performance by placing data accessed together in the same physical file. The SQL-92 and beyond concept of a cluster, however, is a group of catalogs that are accessible using the same connection to a database server.

Note: Don't forget that SQL is a dynamic language. The standard has been updated in 1999, 2003, 2006, and 2011.

In current versions of SQL, none of the groupings of database elements are related to physical storage structures. If you are working with a centralized mainframe DBMS, you may find multiple catalogs stored in the same database file. However, on smaller or distributed systems, you are likely to find one catalog or schema per database file or to find a catalog or schema split between multiple files.

Clusters, catalogs, and schemas are not required elements of a database environment. In a small installation where there is one collection of tables serving a single purpose, for example, it may not even be necessary to create a schema to hold them.

Naming and Identifying Structural Elements

The way in which you name and identify database structural elements is, in some measure, dictated by the structure hierarchy:

- Column names must be unique within the table.
- Table names must be unique within the schema.
- Schema names must be unique within their catalog.
- Catalog names must be unique within their cluster.

When a column name appears in more than one table in a SQL statement—as it often does, when there are primary key–foreign key references—the user must specify the table from which a column should be taken (even if it makes no difference which table is used). The general form for qualifying duplicate column names is:

```
table_name.column_name
```

If an installation has more than one schema, then a user must also indicate the schema in which a table resides:

```
schema_name.table_name.column_name
```

This naming convention means that two different schemas can include tables with the same name.

By the same token, if an installation has multiple catalogs, a user will need to indicate the catalog from which a database element comes:

```
catalog_name.schema_name.table_name.column_name
```

The names that you assign to database elements can include the following:

- Letters
- Numbers
- Underscores (_)

SQL names can be up to 128 characters long. According to the SQL standard, they should not be case sensitive. In fact, many SQL command processors convert names to all upper- or lowercase before submitting a SQL statement to a DBMS for processing. However, there are always exceptions, so you should check your DBMS's naming rules before creating any structural elements.

Note: Some DBMSs also allow pound signs (#) and dollar signs ($) in element names, but neither is recognized by SQL statements, so their use should be avoided.

Schemas

To a database designer, a schema represents the overall, logical design of a complete database. As far as SQL is concerned, however, a schema is nothing more than a container for tables, views, and other structural elements. It is up to the database designer to place a meaningful group of elements within each schema.

A schema is not required to create tables and views. In fact, if you are installing a database for an environment in which there is likely to be only one logical database, then you can just as easily do without one. However, if more than one database will be sharing the same DBMS and the same server, then organizing database elements into schemas can greatly simplify the maintenance of the individual databases.

Creating a Schema

To create a schema, you use the CREATE SCHEMA statement. In its simplest form, it has the syntax

```
CREATE SCHEMA schema_name
```

as in

```
CREATE SCHEMA antique_opticals;
```

Note: The majority of SQL command processors require a semicolon at the end of each statement. However, that end-of-statement marker is not a part of the SQL standard and you may encounter DBMSs that do not use it. We will use it in this book at the end of statements that could be submitted to a DBMS. It does not appear at the end of command "templates" that show the elements of a command.

By default, a schema belongs to the user who created it (the user ID under which the schema was created). The owner of the schema is the only user ID that can modify the schema, unless the owner grants that ability to other users.

To assign a different owner to a schema, you add an AUTHORIZATION clause:

```
CREATE SCHEMA schema_name AUTHORIZATION owner_user_ID
```

For example, to assign the *Antique Opticals* schema to the user ID DBA, someone could use:

```
CREATE SCHEMA antique_opticals AUTHORIZATION dba;
```

When creating a schema, you can also create additional elements at the same time. To do so, you use braces to group the CREATE statements for the other elements, as in:

```
CREATE SCHEMA schema_name AUTHORIZATION owner_user_id
{
// other CREATE statements go here
}
```

This automatically assigns the elements within the braces to the schema.

Identifying the Schema You Want to Use

One of the nicest things about a relational database is that you can add or delete database structural elements at any time. There must therefore be a way to specify a current schema for new database elements after the schema has been created initially with the CREATE SCHEMA statement.

One way to do this is with the SET SCHEMA statement:

```
SET SCHEMA schema_name
```

To use SET SCHEMA, the user ID under which you are working must have authorization to work with that schema.

Alternatively, you can qualify the name of a database element with the name of the schema. For example, if you are creating a table, then you would use something like

```
CREATE TABLE schema_name.table_name
```

For those DBMSs that do not support SET SCHEMA, this is the only way to attach new database elements to a schema after the schema has been created.

Domains

As you know, a domain is an expression of the permitted values for a column in a relation. When you define a table, you assign each column a data type (example, character, or integer) that provides a broad domain. A DBMS will not store data that violate that constraint.

The SQL-92 standard introduced the concept of user-defined domains, which can be viewed as user-defined data types that can be applied to columns in tables. (This means you have to create a domain before you can assign it to a column!)

Domains can be created as part of a CREATE SCHEMA statement, which has the following syntax:

```
CREATE DOMAIN domain_name data_type
CHECK (expression_to_validate_values)
```

The CHECK clause is actually a generic way of expressing a condition that data must meet. It can include a retrieval query to validate data against other data stored in the database, or it can include a simple logical expression. In that expression, the keyword VALUE represents the data being checked.

For example, if *Antique Opticals* wanted to validate the price of a disc, someone might create the following domain:

```
CREATE DOMAIN price numeric (6,2)
CHECK (VALUE >= 19.95);
```

After creating this domain, a column in a table can be given the data type of price. The DBMS will then check to be certain that the value in that column is always greater than, or equal to, 19.95. (We will leave a discussion of the data type used in the preceding SQL statement until we cover creating tables in the next section of this chapter.)

The domain mechanism is very flexible. Assume, for example, that you want to ensure that telephone numbers are always stored in the format XXX-XXX-XXXX. A domain to validate that format might be created as:

```
CREATE DOMAIN telephone char (12)
CHECK (SUBSTRING (VALUE FROM 4 FOR 1 = '-') AND
       SUBSTRING (VALUE FROM 8 FOR 1 = '-'));[1]
```

When a user attempts to store a value in a column to which the *telephone* domain has been assigned, the DBMS performs two SUBSTRING functions. The first looks at the fourth character in the string to determine whether it is a -. The second examines the character at position 8. The data will be accepted only if both conditions are met.

You can use the CREATE DOMAIN statement to give a column a default value. For example, the following statement sets up a domain that holds either Y or N, and defaults to Y:

```
CREATE DOMAIN boolean char (1)
DEFAULT = 'Y'
CHECK (UPPER(VALUE) = 'Y' OR UPPER(VALUE) = 'N');[2]
```

---

[1]The SUBSTRING function extracts characters from text data, beginning at the character following FROM. The number of characters to extract appears after the FOR.

[2]As you might guess, the UPPER function converts characters to upper case. Although SQL names may not be case sensitive, data are!

Tables

The most important structure within a relational database is the table. As you know, tables contain just about everything, including business data and the data dictionary.

SQL divides tables into three categories:

- *Permanent base tables*: Permanent base tables are tables whose contents are stored in the database, and remain permanently in the database, unless they are explicitly deleted.
- *Global temporary tables*: Global temporary tables are tables for working storage that are destroyed at the end of a SQL session. The definitions of the tables are stored in the data dictionary, but their data are not. The tables must be loaded with data each time they are going to be used. Global temporary tables can be used only by the current user, but they are visible to an entire SQL session (either an application program or a user working with an interactive query facility).
- *Local temporary tables*: Local temporary tables are similar to global temporary tables. However, they are visible only to the specific program module in which they are created.

Temporary base tables are subtly different from views, which assemble their data by executing a SQL query. You will read more about this difference and how temporary tables are created and used later in this chapter.

Most of the tables in a relational database are permanent base tables. You create them with the CREATE TABLE statement:

```
CREATE TABLE table_name
(    column1_name column1_data_type
     column1_constraints,
     column2_name column2_data_type
     column2_constraints, …
     table_constraints)
```

The constraints on a table include declarations of primary and foreign keys. The constraints on a column include whether values in the column are mandatory, as well as other constraints you may decide to include in a CHECK clause.

Column Data Types

Each column in a table must be given a data type (or a user-defined domain). Although data types are somewhat implementation dependent, most DBMSs that support SQL include the following predefined data types:

- INTEGER (abbreviated INT): a positive or negative whole number. The number of bits occupied by the value is implementation dependent. In most cases, integers are either 32 or 64 bits.

- SMALLINT: a positive or negative whole number. A small integer is usually half the size of a standard integer. Using small integers when you know you will need to store only small values can save space in the database.
- NUMERIC: a fixed-point positive or negative number. A numeric value has a whole number portion and a fractional portion. When you create it, you must specify the total length of the number (including the decimal point), and how many of those digits will be to the right of the decimal point (its *precision*). For example

```
NUMERIC (6,2)
```

creates a number in the format XXX.XX. The DBMS will store exactly two digits to the right of the decimal point.
- DECIMAL: a fixed-point positive or negative number. A decimal number is similar to a numeric value. However, the DBMS may store more digits to the right of the decimal point than you specify. Although there is no guarantee that you will get the extra precision, its use can provide more accurate results in computations.
- REAL: a "single-precision" floating point value. A floating point number is expressed in the format:

```
XX.XXXXX * 10YY
```

where YY is the power to which 10 is raised. Because of the way in which computers store floating point numbers, a real number may not be an exact representation of a value, but only a close approximation. The range of values that can be stored is implementation dependent, as is the precision. You therefore cannot specify a size for a real number column.
- DOUBLE PRECISION (abbreviated DOUBLE): a "double-precision" floating point number. The range and precision of double precision values are implementation dependent, but generally both will be greater than single-precision real numbers.
- FLOAT: a floating point number for which you can specify the precision. The DBMS will maintain at least the precision that you specify. (It may be more.)
- BOOLEAN: a true/false value. The BOOLEAN data type was introduced in the SQL:1999 standard, but is not supported by all DBMSs. If your DBMS does not include BOOLEAN, the best alternative is usually a one-character text column with a CHECK clause restricting values to Y and N.
- BIT: storage for a fixed number of individual bits. You must indicate the number of bits, as in

```
BIT (n)
```

where *n* is the number of bits. (If you do not, you will have room for only one bit.)

- BIT VARYING: storage for a varying number of bits up to a specified maximum, as in

```
BIT VARYING (n)
```

where *n* is the maximum number of bits. In some DBMSs, columns of this type can be used to store graphic images.

- DATE: a date.
- TIME: a time.
- TIMESTAMP: the combination of a date and a time.
- CHARACTER (abbreviated CHAR): a fixed-length space to hold a string of characters. When declaring a CHAR column, you need to indicate the width of the column:

```
CHAR (n)
```

where *n* is the amount of space that will be allocated for the column in every row. Even if you store less than *n* characters, the column will always take up *n* bytes—or n × 2 bytes, if you are storing UNICODE characters—and the column will be padded with blanks to fill up empty space. The maximum number of characters allowed is implementation dependent (usually 256 or more).

- CHARACTER VARYING (abbreviated VARCHAR): a variable length space to hold a string of characters. You must indicate the maximum width of the column—

```
VARCHAR (n)
```

—but the DBMS stores only as many characters as you insert, up to the maximum *n*. The overall maximum number of characters allowed is implementation dependent (usually 256 or more).

- INTERVAL: a date or time interval. An interval data type is followed by a qualifier that specifies the size of the interval and, optionally, the number of digits. For example:

```
INTERVAL YEAR
INTERVAL YEAR (n)
INTERVAL MONTH
INTERVAL MONTH (n)
INTERVAL YEAR TO MONTH
INTERVAL YEAR (n) TO MONTH
INTERVAL DAY
INTERVAL DAY (n)
INTERVAL DAY TO HOUR
INTERVAL DAY (n) TO HOUR
INTERVAL DAY TO MINUTE
INTERVAL DAY (n) TO MINUTE
INTERVAL MINUTE
INTERVAL MINUTE (n)
```

In the preceding examples, *n* specifies the number of digits. When the interval covers more than one date and/or time unit, such as YEAR TO MONTH, you can specify a size for only the first unit. Year–month intervals can include days, hours, minutes, and/or seconds.

■ BLOB (Binary Large Object): a block of binary code (often a graphic) stored as a unit and retrievable only as a unit. In many cases, the DBMS cannot interpret the contents of a BLOB (although the application that created the BLOB can do so). Because BLOB data are stored as undifferentiated binary, BLOB columns cannot be searched directly. Identifying information about the contents of a BLOB must be contained in other columns of the table, using data types that can be searched.

In Figure 11.2 you will find bare-bones CREATE TABLE statements for the *Antique Opticals* database. These statements include only column names and data types. SQL will create tables from statements in this format, but because the tables have no primary keys, many DBMSs will not allow you to enter data.

Default Values

As you are defining columns, you can designate a default value for individual columns. To indicate a default value, you add a DEFAULT keyword to the column definition, followed by the default value. For example, in the *orders* relation the order date column defaults to the current system date. The column declaration is therefore written:

```
order_date date DEFAULT CURRENT_DATE;
```

Notice that this particular declaration is using the SQL value CURRENT_DATE. However, you can place any value after DEFAULT that is a valid instance of the column's data type.

NOT NULL Constraints

The values in primary key columns must be unique and not null. In addition, there may be other columns for which you want to require a value. You can specify such columns by adding NOT NULL after the column declaration. Since *Antique Opticals* wants to ensure that an order date is always entered, the complete declaration for that column in the *orders* table is

```
order_date date NOT NULL DEFAULT CURRENT_DATE;
```

Primary Keys

There are two ways to specify a primary key:

■ Add a PRIMARY KEY clause to a CREATE TABLE statement. The keywords PRIMARY KEY are followed by the names of the primary key column or columns, surrounded by parentheses.

```
CREATE TABLE customer
      (customer_numb int,
      customer_first_name varchar (15),
      customer_last_name varchar (15),
      customer_street varchar (30),
      customer_city varchar (15),
      customer_state char (2),
      customer_zip char (10),
      customer_phone char (12));

CREATE TABLE distributor
      (distributor_numb int,
      distributor_name varchar (15),
      distributor_street varchar (30),
      distributor_city varchar (15),
      distributor_state char (2),
      distributor_zip char (10),
      distributor_phone char (12),
      distributor_contact_person varchar (30),
      contact_person_ext char (5));

CREATE TABLE item
      (item_numb int,
      item_type varchar (15),
      title varchar (60),
      distributor_numb int,
      retail_price numeric (6,2),
      relase_date date,
      genre varchar (20),
      quant_in_stock int);

CREATE TABLE order
      (order_numb int,
      customer_numb int,
      order_date date,
      credit_card_numb char (16),
      credit_card_exp_date char (5),
      order_complete boolean,
      pickup_or_ship char (1));

CREATE TABLE order_line
      (order_numb int,
      item_numb int,
      quantity int,
      discount_percent int,
      selling_price numeric (6,2),
      line_cost numeric (7,2),
      shipped boolean,
      shipping_date date);
```

■ FIGURE 11.2 Initial CREATE TABLE statements for the *Antique Opticals* database (continues).

```
CREATE TABLE purchase
      (purchase_date date,
      customer_numb int,
      items_received boolean),
      customer_paid boolean);

CREATE TABLE purchase_item
      (purchase_date date,
      customer_numb int,
      item_numb int,
      condition char (15),
      price_paid numeric (6,2));

CREATE TABLE actor
      (actor_numb int,
      actor_name varchar (60));

CREATE TABLE performance
      (actor_numb int,
      item_numb int,
      role varchar (60));

CREATE TABLE producer
      (producer_name varchar (60),
      studio varchar (40));

CREATE TABLE production
      (producer_name varchar (60),
      item_numb int);
```

■ **FIGURE 11.2** (*cont.*)

■ Add the keywords PRIMARY KEY to the declaration of each column that is part of the primary key. Use a CONSTRAINT clause if you want to name the primary key constraint.

In Figure 11.3, you will find the CREATE TABLE statement for the *Antique Opticals* database, including both PRIMARY KEY and CONSTRAINT clauses. Notice that in those tables that have concatenated primary keys, all the primary key columns have been included in a PRIMARY KEY clause.

Foreign Keys

As you know, a foreign key is a column (or combination of columns) that is exactly the same as the primary of some table. When a foreign key value matches a primary key value, we know that there is a logical relationship between the database objects represented by the matching rows.

```
CREATE TABLE customer
       (customer_numb int PRIMARY KEY,
        customer_first_name varchar (15),
        customer_last_name varchar (15),
        customer_street varchar (30),
        customer_city varchar (15),
        customer_state char (2),
        customer_zip char (10),
        customer_phone char (12));

CREATE TABLE distributor
       (distributor_numb int PRIMARY KEY,
        distributor_name varchar (15),
        distributor_street varchar (30),
        distributor_city varchar (15),
        distributor_state char (2),
        distributor_zip char (10),
        distributor_phone char (12),
        distributor_contact_person varchar (30),
        contact_person_ext char (5));

CREATE TABLE item
       (item_numb int CONSTRAINT item_pk PRIMARY KEY,
        item_type varchar (15),
        title varchar (60),
        distributor_numb int,
        retail_price numeric (6,2),
        relase_date date,
        genre varchar (20),
        quant_in_stock int);

CREATE TABLE order
       (order_numb int,
        customer_numb int,
        order_date date,
        credit_card_numb char (16),
        credit_card_exp_date char (5),
        order_complete boolean,
        pickup_or_ship char (1)
        PRIMARY KEY (order_numb));

CREATE TABLE order_line
       (order_numb int,
        item_numb int,
        quantity int,
        discount_percent int,
```

■ **FIGURE 11.3   CREATE TABLE** statements for the *Antique Opticals* database including primary key declarations (continues).

```
            selling_price numeric (6,2),
            line_cost numeric (7,2),
            shipped boolean,
            shipping_date date
            PRIMARY KEY (order_numb, item_numb));

CREATE TABLE purchase
        (purchase_date date,
        customer_numb int,
        items_received boolean,
        customer_paid boolean
        PRIMARY KEY (purchase_date, customer_numb));

CREATE TABLE purchase_item
        (purchase_date date,
        customer_numb int,
        item_numb int,
        condition char (15),
        price_paid numeric (6,2)
        PRIMARY KEY (purchase_date, customer_numb, item_numb));

CREATE TABLE actor
        (actor_numb int PRIMARY KEY,
        actor_name varchar (60));

CREATE TABLE performance
        (actor_numb int,
        item_numb int,
        role varchar (60)
        PRIMARY KEY (actor_numb, item_numb));

CREATE TABLE producer
        (producer_name varchar (60) CONSTRAINT producer_pk PRIMARY KEY,
        studio varchar (40));

CREATE TABLE production
        (producer_name varchar (60),
        item_numb int
        PRIMARY KEY (producer_name, item_numb));
```

■ **FIGURE 11.3** (*cont.*)

One of the major constraints on a relation is referential integrity, which states that every nonnull foreign key must reference an existing primary key value. To maintain the integrity of the database, it is vital that foreign key constraints be stored within the database's data dictionary so that the DBMS can be responsible for enforcing those constraints.

To specify a foreign key for a table, you add a FOREIGN KEY clause:

```
FOREIGN KEY foreign_key_name (foreign_key_columns)
REFERENCES primary_key_table (primary_key_columns)
    ON UPDATE update_option
    ON DELETE delete_option
```

Each foreign key–primary key reference is given a name. This makes it possible to identify the reference at a later time, in particular, so you can remove the reference if necessary.

Note: Some DBMSs, such as Oracle, do not support the naming of foreign keys, in which case you would use preceding syntax without the name.

The names of the foreign key columns follow the name of the foreign key. The REFERENCES clause contains the name of the primary key table being referenced. If the primary key columns are named in the PRIMARY KEY clause of their table, then you don't need to list the primary key columns. However, if the columns aren't part of a PRIMARY KEY clause, you must list the primary key columns in the REFERENCES clause.

The final part of the FOREIGN KEY specification indicates what should happen when a primary key value being referenced by a foreign key value is updated or deleted. There are three options that apply to both updates and deletions and one additional option for each:

- SET NULL: Replace the foreign key value with null. This isn't possible when the foreign key is part of the primary key of its table.
- SET DEFAULT: Replace the foreign key value with the column's default value.
- CASCADE: Delete or update all foreign key rows.
- NO ACTION: On update, make no modifications of foreign key values.
- RESTICT: Do not allow deletions of primary key rows.

The complete declarations for the *Antique Opticals* database tables, which include foreign key constraints, can be found in Figure 11.4. Notice that, although there are no restrictions on how to name foreign keys, the foreign keys in this database have been named to indicate the tables involved. This makes them easier to identify, if you need to delete or modify a foreign key at a later date.

Additional Column Constraints

There are additional constraints that you can place on columns in a table beyond primary and foreign key constraints. These include requiring unique values and predicates in CHECK clauses.

```
CREATE TABLE customer
      (customer_numb int PRIMARY KEY,
      customer_first_name varchar (15),
      customer_last_name varchar (15),
      customer_street varchar (30),
      customer_city varchar (15),
      customer_state char (2),
      customer_zip char (10),
      customer_phone char (12));

CREATE TABLE distributor
      (distributor_numb int PRIMARY KEY,
      distributor_name varchar (15),
      distributor_street varchar (30),
      distributor_city varchar (15),
      distributor_state char (2),
      distributor_zip char (10),
      distributor_phone char (12),
      distributor_contact_person varchar (30),
      contact_person_ext char (5));

CREATE TABLE item
      (item_numb int  CONSTRAINT item_pk PRIMARY KEY,
      item_type varchar (15),
      title varchar (60),
      distributor_numb int,
      retail_price numeric (6,2),
      relase_date date,
      genre varchar (20),
      quant_in_stock int);

CREATE TABLE order
      (order_numb int,
      customer_numb int,
      order_date date,
      credit_card_numb char (16),
      credit_card_exp_date char (5),
      order_complete boolean,
      pickup_or_ship char (1)
      PRIMARY KEY (order_numb)
      FOREIGN KEY order2customer (customer_numb)
      REFERENCES customer
            ON UPDATE CASCADE
            ON DELETE RESTRICT);
```

■ FIGURE 11.4 The complete CREATE TABLE statements for the *Antique Opticals* database (continues).

```
CREATE TABLE order_line
      (order_numb int,
      item_numb int,
      quantity int,
      discount_percent int,
      selling_price numeric (6,2),
      line_cost numeric (7,2),
      shipped boolean,
      shipping_date date
      PRIMARY KEY (order_numb, item_numb)
      FOREIGN KEY order_line2item (item_numb)
      REFERENCES item
            ON UPDATE CASCADE
            ON DELETE RESTRICT
      FOREIGN KEY order_line2order (order_numb)
      REFERENCES order
            ON UPDATE CASCADE
            ON DELETE CASCADE);

CREATE TABLE purchase
      (purchase_date date,
      customer_numb int,
      items_received boolean,
      customer_paid boolean
      PRIMARY KEY (purchase_date, customer_numb)
      FOREIGN KEY purchase2customer (customer_numb)
      REFERENCES customer
            ON UPDATE CASCADE)
            ON DELETE RESTRICT);

CREATE TABLE purchase_item
      (purchase_date date,
      customer_numb int,
      item_numb int,
      condition char (15),
      price_paid numeric (6,2)
      PRIMARY KEY (purchase_date, customer_numb, item_numb)
      FOREIGN KEY purchase_item2purchase (purchase_date, customer_numb
            ON UPDATE CASCADE
            ON DELETE CASCADE
      FOREIGN KEY purchase_item2item (item_numb)
      REFERENCES item
            ON UPDATE CASCADE
            ON DELETE RESTRICT);

CREATE TABLE actor
      (actor_numb int PRIMARY KEY,
      actor_name varchar (60))
```

■ **FIGURE 11.4 (*cont.*)**

```
CREATE TABLE performance
      (actor_numb int,
      item_numb int,
      role varchar (60)
      PRIMARY KEY (actor_numb, item_numb)
      FOREIGN KEY performance2actor (actor_numb)
      REFERENCES actor
            ON UPDATE CASCADE
            ON DELETE CASCADE
      FOREIGN KEY performance2item (item_numb)
      REFERENCES item
            ON UPDATE CASCADE
            ON DELETE CASCADE);

CREATE TABLE producer
      (producer_name varchar (60) CONSTRAINT producer_pk PRIMARY KEY,
      studio varchar (40));

CREATE TABLE production
      (producer_name varchar (60),
      item_numb int
      PRIMARY KEY (producer_name, item_numb)
      FOREIGN KEY production2producer (producer_name)
      REFERENCES producer
            ON UPDATE CASCADE
            ON DELETE CASCADE
      FOREIGN KEY production2item
      REFERENCES item
            ON UPDATE CASCADE
            ON DELETE CASCADE);
```

■ **FIGURE 11.4** (*cont.*)

Requiring Unique Values

If you want to ensure that the values in a non-primary key column are unique, then you can use the UNIQUE keyword. UNIQUE verifies that all non-null values are unique. For example, if you were storing social security numbers in an employee table that used an employee ID as the primary key, you could also enforce unique social security numbers with

```
ssn char (11) UNIQUE
```

The UNIQUE clause can also be placed at the end of the CREATE TABLE statement, along with the primary key and foreign key specifications. In that case, it takes the form

```
UNIQUE (column_names)
```

Check Clauses

The CHECK clause to which you were introduced earlier in the chapter, in the "Domains" section, can also be used with individual columns to declare column-specific constraints. To add a constraint, you place a CHECK clause after the column declaration, using the keyword VALUE in a predicate to indicate the value being checked.

For example, to verify that a column used to hold true-false values is limited to T and F, you could write a CHECK clause as

```
CHECK (UPPER(VALUE) = 'T' OR UPPER(VALUE) = 'F')
```

Modifying Database Elements

With the exception of tables, database elements are largely unchangeable. When you want to modify them, you must delete them from the database and create them from scratch. In contrast, just about every characteristic of a table can be modified without deleting the table, using the ALTER TABLE statement.

Adding Columns

To add a new column to a table, use the ALTER TABLE statement with the following syntax:

```
ALTER TABLE table_name
ADD column_name column_data_type column_constraints
```

For example, if *Antique Opticals* wanted to add a telephone number column to the producer table, they would use

```
ALTER TABLE producer
ADD producer_phone char (12);
```

To add more than one column at the same time, simply separate the clauses with commas:

```
ALTER TABLE producer
ADD producer_phone char (12),
ADD studio_street char (30),
ADD studio_city char (15),
ADD studio_state char (2),
ADD studio_zip char (10);
```

Adding Table Constraints

You can add table constraints, such as foreign keys, at any time. To do so, include the new constraint in an ALTER TABLE statement:

```
ALTER TABLE table_name
ADD table_constraint
```

Assume, for example, that *Antique Opticals* created a new table named *states*, and included in it all the two-character US state abbreviations. The company would then need to add a foreign key reference to that table from the customer, distributor, and producer tables:

```
ALTER TABLE customer
ADD FOREIGN KEY customer2states (customer_state)
    REFERENCES states (state_name);

ALTER TABLE distributor
ADD FOREIGN KEY distributor2states (distributor_state)
    REFERENCES states (state_name);

ALTER TABLE producer
ADD FOREIGN KEY producer2states (studio_state)
    REFERENCES states (state_name);
```

When you add a foreign key constraint to a table, the DBMS verifies that all existing data in the table meet that constraint. If they do not, the ALTER TABLE statement will fail.

Modifying Columns

You can modify columns by changing any characteristic of the column, including the data type, size, and constraints.

Changing Column Definitions

To replace a complete column definition, use the MODIFY command with the current column name and the new column characteristics. For example, to change the customer number in *Antique Opticals' customer* table from an integer to a character column, they would use

```
ALTER TABLE customer
MODIFY customer_numb char (4);
```

When you change the data type of a column, the DBMS will attempt to convert any existing values to the new data type. If the current values cannot be converted, then the table modification will not be performed. In general, most columns can be converted to character. However, conversions from a character data type to numbers, dates, and/or times require that existing data represent legal values in the new data type.

Given that the DBMS converts values whenever it can, changing a column data type may seem like a simple change, but it isn't. In this particular example, the customer number is referenced by foreign keys and therefore the foreign key columns must be modified as well. You need to remove the foreign key constraints, change the foreign key columns, change the primary key column, and then add the foreign key constraints back to the tables containing the foreign keys. Omitting the changes to the foreign keys will make it impossible to add any rows to those foreign key tables because integer customer numbers will never match character customer numbers. Moral to the story: before changing column characteristics, consider the effect of those changes on other tables in the database.

Changing Default Values

To add or change a default value only (without changing the data type or size of the column), include the DEFAULT keyword:

```
ALTER TABLE order_line
MODIFY discount_percent DEFAULT 0;
```

Changing Null Status

To switch between allowing nulls and not allowing nulls, without changing any other characteristics, add NULL or NOT NULL as appropriate:

```
ALTER TABLE customer
MODIFY customer_zip NOT NULL;
```

or

```
ALTER TABLE customer
MODIFY customer_zip NULL;
```

Changing Column Constraints

To modify a column constraint without changing any other column characteristics, include a CHECK clause:

```
ALTER TABLE item
MODIFY retail_price
    CHECK (VALUE >= 12.95);
```

Deleting Table Elements

You can also delete structural elements from a table as needed, without deleting the entire table:

- To delete a column:
  ```
  ALTER TABLE order_line
  DELETE line_cost;
  ```
- To delete a CHECK table constraint (a CHECK that has been applied to an entire table, rather than to a specific column):
  ```
  ALTER TABLE customer
  DELETE CHECK;
  ```

- To remove the UNIQUE constraint from one or more columns:

  ```
  ALTER TABLE item
  DELETE UNIQUE (title);
  ```

- To remove a table's primary key:

  ```
  ALTER TABLE customer
  DELETE PRIMARY KEY;
  ```

  Although you can delete a table's primary key, keep in mind that if you do not add a new one, you will not be able to modify any data in that table.

- To delete a foreign key:

  ```
  ALTER TABLE item
  DELETE FOREIGN KEY item2distributor;
  ```

Renaming Table Elements

You can rename both tables and columns:

- To rename a table, place the new table name after the RENAME keyword:

  ```
  ALTER TABLE order_line
  RENAME line_item;
  ```

- To rename a column, include both the old and new column names, separated by the keyword TO:

  ```
  ALTER TABLE item
  RENAME title TO item_title;
  ```

Deleting Database Elements

To delete a structural element from a database, you "drop" the element. For example, to delete a table you would type:

```
DROP TABLE table_name
```

Dropping a table (or any database structural element, for that matter) is irrevocable. In most cases, the DBMS will not bother to ask you "are you sure?" but will immediately delete the structure of the table and all of its data, if it can. A table deletion will fail, for example, if it has foreign keys referencing it and one or more of the foreign key constraints contain ON DELETE RESTRICT. Dropping a table or view will also fail if the element being dropped is currently in use by another user.

Note: There is one exception to the irrevocability of a delete. If an element is deleted during a program-controlled transaction and the transaction is rolled back, the deletion will be undone. Undoing transactions is covered in Chapter 22.

You can remove the following elements from a database with the DROP statement:

- Tables
- Views

  ```
  DROP VIEW view_name
  ```

- Indexes

  ```
  DROP INDEX index_name
  ```

- Domains

  ```
  DROP DOMAIN domain_name
  ```

For Further Reading

The Web sites in the following citations provide extensive SQL tutorials that you can use as references when needed.

SQLcourse.com. Creating Tables. http://www.sqlcourse.com/create.html

tutorialspoint. SQL – Constraints. http://www.tutorialspoint.com/sql/sql-constraints.htm

tutorialspoint. SQL – DROP or DELETE Table. http://www.tutorialspoint.com/sql/sql-drop-table.htm

w3schools.com. The SQL CREATE DATABASE Statement. http://www.w3schools.com/sql/sql_create_db.asp

w3schools.com. The SQL CREATE TABLE Statement. http://www.w3schools.com/sql/sql_create_table.asp

12 Using CASE Tools for Database Design

A *CASE* (computer-aided software engineering) tool is a software package that provides support for the design and implementation of information systems. By integrating many of the techniques used to document a system design—including the data dictionary, data flows, and entity relationships—CASE software can increase the consistency and accuracy of a database design. They can also ease the task of creating the diagrams that accompany a system design.

There are many CASE tools on the market. The actual "look" of the diagrams is specific to each particular package. However, the examples presented in this chapter are typical of the capabilities of most CASE tools.

Note: The specific CASE software used in Chapters 13–15 is MacA&D by Excel Software (www.excelsoftware.com). (There's also a Windows version.) Other such packages that are well suited to database design include Visio (www.microsoft.com) and Visible Analyst (www.visible.com).

A word of warning is in order about CASE tools before we proceed any further. A CASE tool is exactly that—a tool. It can document a database design and it can provide invaluable help in maintaining the consistency of a design. Although some current CASE tools can verify the integrity of a data model, they cannot design the database for you. There is no software in the world that can examine a database environment and identify the entities, attributes, and relationships that should be represented in a database. The model created with CASE software is therefore only as good as the analysis of the database environment provided by the people using the tool.

CASE Capabilities

Most CASE tools organize the documents pertaining to a single system into a "project." As you can see in Figure 12.1, by default, a typical project supports the following types of documents:

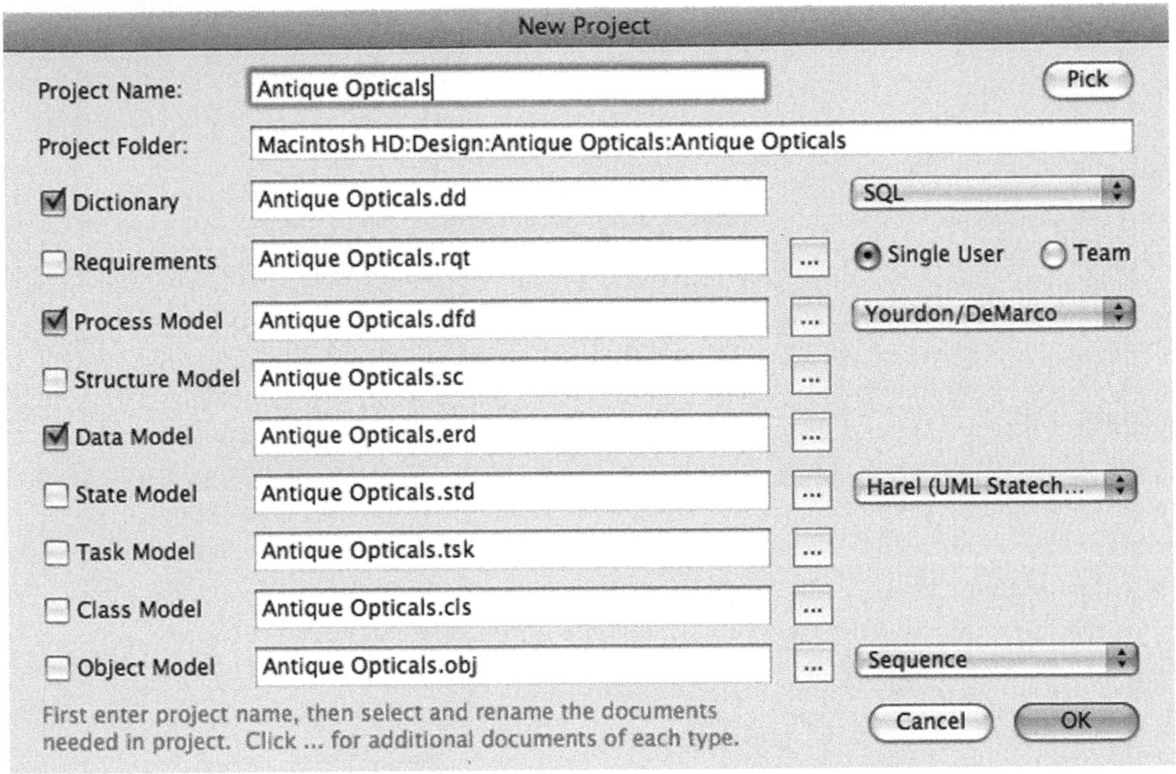

■ FIGURE 12.1 CASE software project documents.

- Data dictionary: In most CASE tools, the data dictionary forms the backbone of the project, providing a single repository for all processes, entities, attributes, and domains used anywhere throughout the project.
- Requirements: CASE tool requirements documents store the text descriptions of product specifications. They also make it possible to arrange requirements in a hierarchy, typically from general to specific.
- Data flow diagrams (DFD): As you read in Chapter 4, DFDs document the way in which data travel throughout an organization, indicating who handles the data. Although it isn't necessary to create a DFD, if your only goal with the project is to document a database design DFDs

can often be useful in documenting the relationships between multiple organization units and the data they handle. Data flow diagrams can, for example, help you determine whether an organization needs a single database or a combination of databases.

- Structure charts: Structure charts are used to model the structure of application programs that will be developed using structured programming techniques. The charts show the relationship between program modules.
- Data models: Data models are the ER diagrams about which you have been reading. The ER diagram on which the examples in this chapter are based can be found in Figure 12.2.
- Screen prototypes: Drawings of sample screen layouts are typically most useful for documenting the user interface of application programs. However, they can also act as a crosscheck to ensure that a database design is complete by allowing you to verify that everything needed to generate the sample screen designs is present in the database.
- State models: State models, documented in state transition diagrams, indicate the ways in which data change as they move through the information system.
- Task diagrams: Task diagrams are used to help plan application programs in which multiple operations (tasks) occur at the same time. They are therefore not particularly relevant to the database design process.
- Class diagrams: Class diagrams are used when performing object-oriented, rather than structured, analysis and design. They can also be used to document an object-oriented database design.
- Object diagrams: Object diagrams are used during object-oriented analysis to indicate how objects communicate with one another by passing messages.

Many of the diagrams and reports that a CASE tool can provide are designed to follow a single theoretical model. For example, the ER diagrams that you have seen earlier in this book might be based on the Chen model, or the Information Engineering model. Any given CASE tool will support some selection of diagramming models. You must therefore examine what a particular product supports before you purchase it to ensure that it provides exactly what you need.

ER Diagram Reports

In addition to providing tools for simplifying the creation of ER diagrams, many CASE tools can generate reports that document the contents of an ERD. For example, in Figure 12.3, you can see a portion of a report that

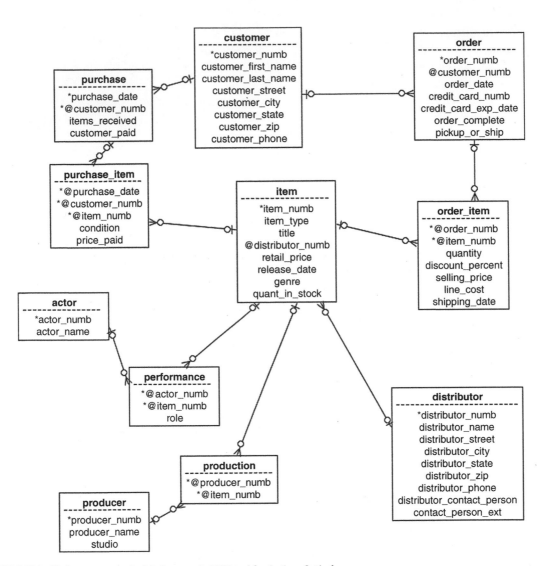

■FIGURE 12.2 ER diagram created with the sample CASE tool for *Antique Opticals*.

provides a description of each entity and its attributes, including the attribute's data type. The "physical" line contains the name that the database element will have in SQL CREATE TABLE statements; it can be different than the element's data dictionary entry name.[1] For many designers, this type of report actually constitutes a paper-based data dictionary.

---

[1]The ## at the end of each Physical line is a terminator used by the CASE tool; it isn't part of the name of the entity or attribute.

```
***************************************************

Entity: actor

Language: SQL
Physical: actor##

Attributes:

...*actor_numb
Language: SQL
DataType: INTEGER
Physical: actor_numb##

...actor_name
Language: SQL
DataType: long_name
Physical: actor_name##


***************************************************
```

■ **FIGURE 12.3   Part of an entity specification report.**

A CASE tool can also translate the relationships in an ER diagram into a report, such as that in Figure 12.4. The text in the report describes the *cardinality* of each relationship in the ERD (whether the relationship is one-to-one, one-to-many, or many-to-many) and can therefore be very useful for pinpointing errors that may have crept into the graphic version of the diagram.

Data Flow Diagrams

There are two widely used styles for DFDs: Yourdon/DeMarco (which has been used throughout this book), and Gene & Sarson.

The Yourdon/DeMarco style, which you can see in Figure 12.5, uses circles for processes. (This particular example is for a small taxi company that rents its cabs to drivers.) Data stores are represented by parallel lines. Data flows are curved or straight lines, with labels that indicate the data that are moving along that pathway. External sources of data are represented by rectangles.

In concept, the Gene & Sarson style is very similar: It varies primarily in style. As you can see in Figure 12.6, the processes are round-cornered rectangles as opposed to circles. Data stores are open-ended rectangles rather than parallel lines. External sources of data remain as rectangles and data flows use only straight lines. However, the concepts of numbering the processing and exploding each process with a child diagram that shows further detail is the same, regardless of which diagramming style you use.

actor is associated with zero or more instances of performance.
performance is associated with zero or one instance of actor.

customer is associated with zero or more instances of order.
order is associated with zero or one instance of customer.

customer is associated with zero or more instances of purchase.
purchase is associated with zero or one instance of customer.

distributor is associated with zero or more instances of item.
item is associated with zero or one instance of distributor.

item is associated with zero or more instances of order_item.
order_item is associated with zero or one instance of item.

item is associated with zero or more instances of performance.
performance is associated with zero or one instance of item.

item is associated with zero or more instances of production.
production is associated with zero or one instance of item.

item is associated with zero or more instances of purchase_item.
purchase_item is associated with zero or one instance of item.

order is associated with zero or more instances of order_item.
order_item is associated with zero or one instance of order.

producer is associated with zero or more instances of production.
production is associated with zero or one instance of producer.

purchase is associated with zero or more instances of purchase_item.
purchase_item is associated with zero or one instance of purchase.

■ FIGURE 12.4 A relation specification report.

As mentioned earlier, DFDs are very useful in the database design process for helping a designer to determine whether an organization needs a single, integrated database or a collection of independent databases. For example, it is clear from the taxi company's DFDs that an integrated database is required. Of the four processes shown in the diagram, three use data from both the cab data store and the drive and shift data store. (Only the maintenance process uses just one data store.) You will see examples of using DFDs in this way in one of the case studies in the following three chapters.

The Data Dictionary

From a database designer's point of view, the ER diagram and its associated data dictionary are the two most important parts of CASE software. Since you were introduced to several types of ER diagrams in Chapter 4, we will not repeat them here, but instead focus on the interaction of the diagrams and the data dictionary.

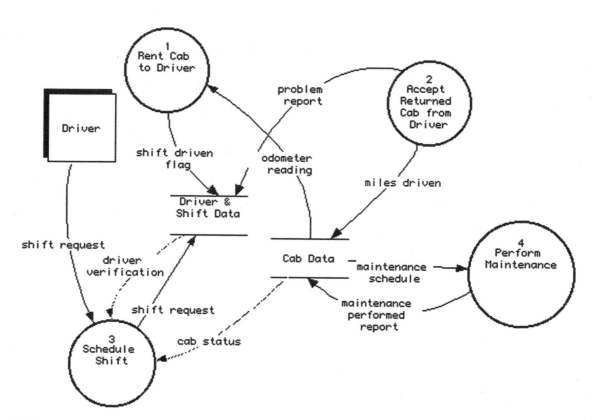

■FIGURE 12.5 Yourdon/Marco style DFD.

A data dictionary provides a central repository for documenting entities, attributes, and domains. In addition, by linking entries in the ER diagram to the data dictionary you can provide enough information for the CASE tool to generate the SQL CREATE statements needed to define the structure of the database.

The layout of a data dictionary varies with the specific CASE tool, as does the way in which entries are configured. In the CASE tool used for examples in this chapter, entities are organized alphabetically, with the attributes following the entity name. Entity names are red; attributes are blue. (Of course, you can't see the colors in this black-and-white book, so you'll have to take my word for it.) Domain names appear alphabetically among the entities. Each relationship in the related ERD also has an entry. Because each item name begins with "Relation," all relationship entries sort together in the data dictionary.

When you select an entity name, the display shows the entity's name, composition (the attributes in the entity), definition (details needed to generate

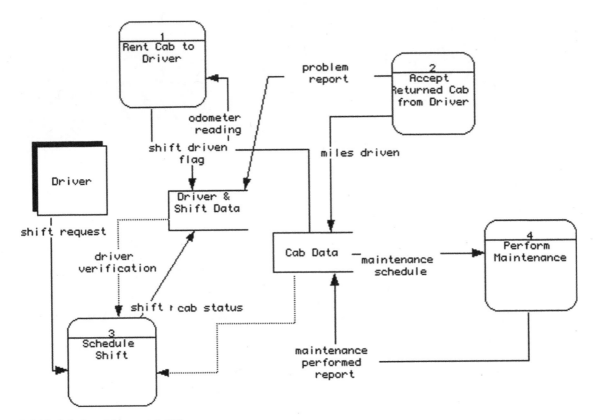

■ FIGURE 12.6 Gene & Sarson style DFD.

SQL, and so on), and type of database element (in the References section). Figure 12.7, for example, shows the information stored in the data dictionary for *Antique Opticals' customer* relation. All of the information about the entity (and all other entries, for that matter) is editable, but because the format is specific to the CASE tool, be careful when making changes unless you know exactly how entries should appear.

Attribute entries (Figure 12.8) are similar to entity entries, but have no data in the composition section. Attribute definitions can include the attribute's data type, a default value, and any constraints that have been placed on that attribute. In most cases, these details are entered through a dialog box, relieving the designer of worrying about specific SQL syntax.

Relationships (Figure 12.9) are named by the CASE tool. Notice that the definition indicates which entities the relationship relates, as well as which

■ **FIGURE 12.7** Definition of an entity in a data dictionary window.

is at the "many" end of the relationship (the child) and which is at the "one" end (the parent).

Many relational DBMSs now support the definition of custom domains. Such domains are stored in the data dictionary (Figure 12.10), along with their definitions. Once a domain has been created and is part of the data

■FIGURE 12.8 Definition of an attribute in a data dictionary window.

dictionary, it can be assigned to attributes. If a database administrator needs to change a domain, it can be changed once in the data dictionary and propagated automatically to all attributes entries that use it.

The linking of data dictionary entries to an ER diagram has another major benefit: The data dictionary can examine its entries and automatically identify

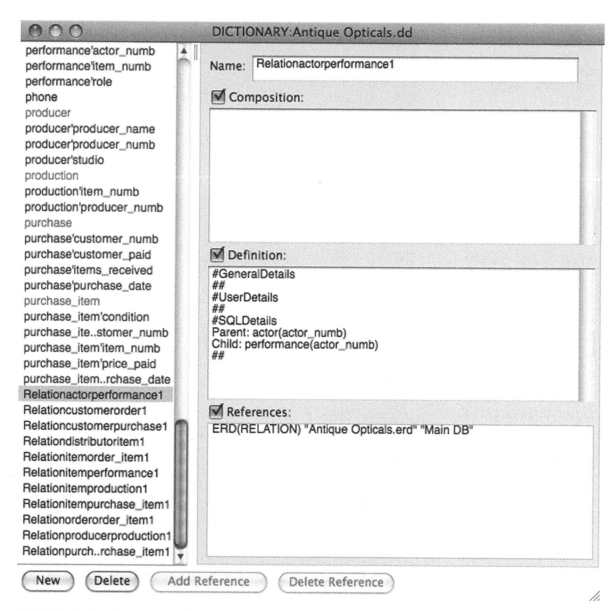

■ FIGURE 12.9 Data dictionary entry for a relationship between two entities in an ERD.

foreign keys. This is yet another way in which the consistency of attribute definitions enforced by a CASE tool's data dictionary can support the database design process.

Note: Mac A&D is good enough at identifying foreign keys to pick up concatenated foreign keys.

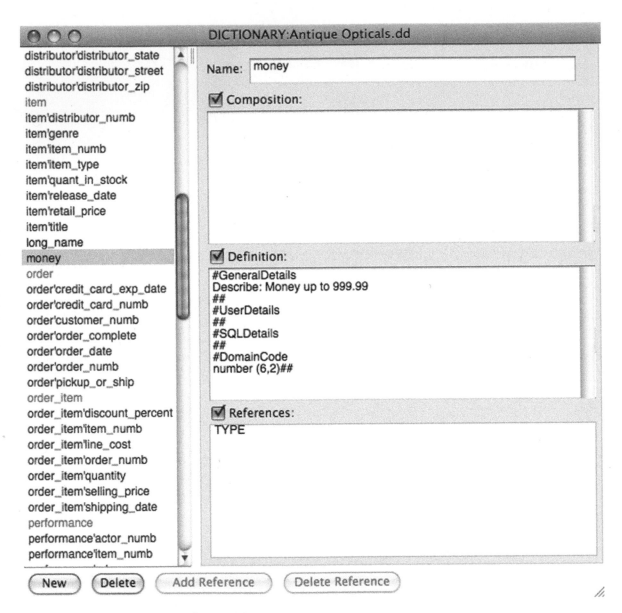

Keep in mind that a CASE tool is not linked dynamically with a DBMS. Although data definitions in the data dictionary are linked to diagrams, changes made to the CASE tool's project will not affect the DBMS. It is up to the database administrator to make the actual changes to the database.

Code Generation

The end product of most database design efforts is a set of SQL CREATE TABLE commands. If you are using CASE software, and the software contains a complete data dictionary, then the software can generate the SQL for you. You will typically find that a given CASE tool can tailor the SQL syntax to a range of specific DBMSs. In most cases, the code will be saved in a text file, which you can then use as input to a DBMS.

Note: Most of today's CASE tools will also generate XML for you. XML provides a template for interpreting the contents of files containing data and therefore isparticularly useful when you need to transfer schemas and data between DBMSs with different SQL implementations, or between DBMSs that do not use SQL at all. XML has become so important for data exchange that it is covered in Chapter 26.

The effectiveness of the SQL that a CASE tool can produce, as you might expect, depends on the completeness of the data dictionary entries. To get truly usable SQL, the data dictionary must contain:

- Domains for every attribute.
- Primary key definitions (created as attributes, are added to entities in the ER diagram).
- Foreign key definitions (created as attributes, are added to entities in ER diagram or by the CASE tool after the ER diagram is complete).
- Any additional constraints that are to be placed on individual attributes or on the entity as a whole.

Sample Input and Output Designs

Sample input and output designs form part of the system documentation, especially in that they help document requirements. They can also support the database designer by providing a way to double-check that the database can provide all the data needed by application programs. Many CASE tools therefore provide a way to draw and label sample screen and report layouts.

Most of today's CASE tools allow multiple users to interact with the same project. This means that interface designers can work with the same data dictionary that the systems analysts and database designers are building, ensuring that all the necessary data elements have been handled.

For example, one of the most important things that the person scheduling cab reservations for the taxi company needs to know is which cabs are not reserved for a given date and shift. A sample screen, such as that in Figure 12.11, will do the trick.[2] The diagram shows what data the user needs to enter (the shift date and the shift name). It also shows the output (cab numbers). The names of the fields on the sample screen design can be linked to the data dictionary.

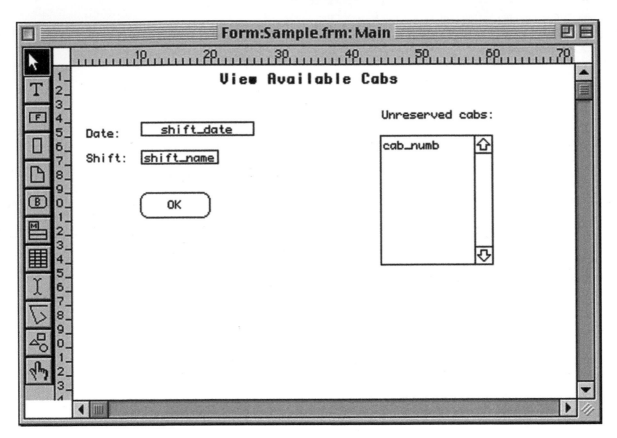

■FIGURE 12.11 Sample screen design.

A CASE tool can be used to model an entire application program. The "browse" tool at the very bottom of the tool bar in Figure 12.11 switches into browse mode, in which buttons and menus become active. Users can make choices from pull-down menus that can be linked to other forms. Buttons can also trigger the opening of other forms. Users can click into data entry

---

[2]In the interest of complete disclosure, you should know that when Mac A&D was ported from Mac OS 9 to Mac OS X, the screen and report design module wasn't included. (It is now available as a stand-alone product.) Therefore, the sample screen designs that you will see in this chapter and in Chapter 13 are from an older version of the product.

fields and tab between fields. Users can therefore not only see the layout and output screen and documents, but also navigate through an application.

The Drawing Environment

To this point, you've been reading about the way in which the functions provided by CASE software can support the database design effort. In this last section we will briefly examine the tools you can expect to find as part of CASE software, tools with which you can create the types of documents you need.

Because many of the documents you create with CASE software are diagrams, the working environment of a CASE tool includes a specialized drawing environment. For example, in Figure 12.12, you can see the drawing tools provided by the sample CASE tool for creating ER diagrams. (Keep in mind that each CASE tool will differ somewhat in the precise layout of its drawing tool bars, but the basic capabilities will be similar.)

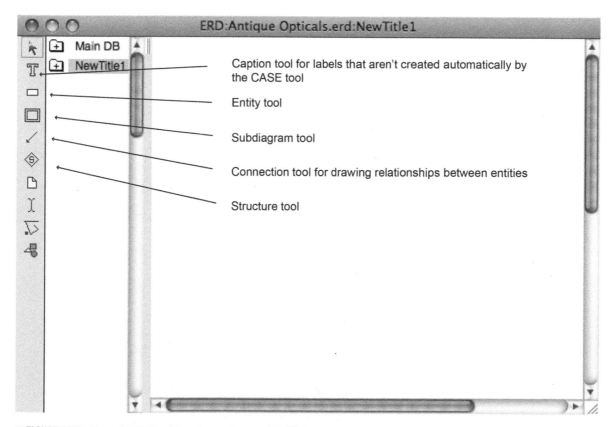

■ **FIGURE 12.12 Example CASE tool drawing environment for ER diagrams.**

The important thing to note is that the major shapes needed for the diagrams—for ER diagrams, typically just the entity and relationship line—are provided as individual tools. You therefore simply click the tool you want to use in the tool bar and draw the shape in the diagram, much like you would if you were working with a general-purpose object graphics program.

For Further Reading

To learn more about the Yourdon/DeMarco method of structure analysis using DFDs, see either of the following:

DeMarco, T., Flauger, P.J., 1985. Structured analysis and system specification. Prentice-Hall.

Yourdon, E., 2000. Modern structured analysis. Prentice Hall PTR.

13 Database Design Case Study #1: Mighty-Mite Motors

It is not unusual for a database designer to be employed to reengineer the information systems of an established corporation. As you will see from the company described in this chapter, information systems in older companies have often grown haphazardly, with almost no planning and integration. The result is a hodgepodge of data repositories that cannot provide the information needed for the corporation to function because they are isolated from one another. In such a situation, it is the job of the database designer to examine the environment as a whole and to focus on the integration of data access across the corporation, as well as the design of one or more databases that will meet individual department needs.

On the bright side, an organization such as Mighty-Mite Motors, which has a history of data processing of some kind, knows quite well what it needs in information systems, even if the employees are unable to articulate those needs immediately. There will almost certainly be a collection of paper forms and reports that the organization uses regularly to provide significant input to the systems design process.

Corporate Overview

Might-Mite Motors, Inc. (MMM) is a closely held corporation, established in 1980, that manufactures and markets miniature rideable motor vehicles for children. Products include several models of cars, trucks, all-terrain vehicles, and trains (see Figure 13.1). Vehicles are powered by car batteries and achieve speed of about 5 mph.

At this time, MMM is organized into three divisions: Product Development, Manufacturing, and Marketing and Sales. Each division is headed by a

Mighty-Mite Motors

Product Catalog

Winter Holiday Season 2020

■ FIGURE 13.1 Might-Mite Motors product catalog (continues).

Model #001

001

All Terrain Vehicle: Accelerator in the handgrip lets young riders reach speeds of up to 5 mph. Vehicle stops immediately when child removes his or her hand from the handlegrips. Can carry one passenger up to 65 lbs. **Suggested retail price: $124.95**

Model #002

002

4-Wheel Drive Cruiser: Two-pedal drive system lets vehcile move forward at 2 1/2 mph on hard surfaces, plus reverse. Electronic speed reduction for beginners. Includes one 6v battery and one recharger. Ages 3–7 (can carry two passengers up to 40 lbs each). **Suggested retail price: $249.99**

■FIGURE 13.1 (*cont.*)

Model #003

003

Classic roadster: Sounds include engine start-up, rev, shifting gears, and idle. Two forward speeds—2 1/2 mph and 5 mph; reverses at 2 1/2 mph. High-speed lockout. On/off power pedal. Power-Lock electric brake. Includes two 6v batteries and recharger. Ages 3–7 (carries two passengers up to 60 lbs each). **Suggested retail price: $189.95**

Model #004

004

Sports car #1: Two-forward speeds, 2 1/2 and 5 mph. Reverses at 2 1/2 mph. High-speed lockout. Power-Lock electric brake. Includes two 6v batteries and one recharger. Ages 3–6 (carries two passengers up to 90 lbs. total).
Suggested retail price: $249.95

Model #005

005

Sports car #2: Phone lets child pretend to talk while he or she drives. Two forward speeds—2 1/2 mph and 5 mph; reverses at 2 1/2 mph. High-speed lockout. Power-Lock electric brake. Includes two 6v batteries and one recharger. Ages 3–6 (carries two passengers up to 90 lbs. total).
Suggested retail price: $249.95

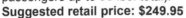

■**FIGURE 13.1** *(cont.)*

Model #008

006

Turbo-Injected Porche: Working stick shift—3 mph and 5 mph froward; 3 mph reverse. High-speed lockout. Adjustable seat. Doors, trunk, and hood open. Simulated car phone. Includes one 18v battery and recharger. Ages 3–8 (carries two passengers up to 120 lbs. total)
Suggested retail price: $299.95

Model #007

007

Indy car: Dual motors for cruising on a variety of surfaces, even up hills. Two forward speeds (2 1/2 and 5 mph), plus reverse (2 1/2 mph). Adjustable seat. Includes two 6v batteries and recharger. Ages 3–7 (carries on passenger up to 80 lbs.)
Suggested retail price: $269.95

Model #008

008

2-Ton Pickup: Metallic teal color. Simulated chrome engine covers and headlight with over-sized wheels. 2 1/2 mph forward speed. Includes on 6v battery and recharger. Ages 3–7 (carries one passenger up to 65 lbs).
Suggested retail price: $189.95

■ FIGURE 13.1 *(cont.)*

Model #008

009

Santa Fe Train: Soundly engineered for a little guy or gal. A hand-operated on/off button controls the 6v battery-operated motor. Reaches speeds to 5 mph. Includes a battery powered "whoo whoo" whistle to greet passersby. Ride on 76" x 168" oval track (sold separately) or on carpet or sidewalk, indoors or outdoors. Plastic body and flooboard; steel axles and coupling pins. Brigh red, blue and yellow body featrues a large lift-up seat and trailing car for storage. Includes battery and chargers. Ages 3–6.
Suggested retail price: $159.95

Model #010

Oval track: Measures 76" × 168."
Suggested retail price: $39.95

Model #011

6 Pieces Straight track: Six straight track section 19" each (total 109")..
Suggested retail price: $19.95

Model #012

012

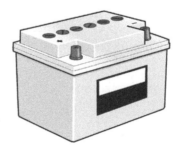

Rechargable battery (6v): For use with 6v or 12v vehicles. For 12v vehicles, use two. To charge, use charger included with vehicle.
Suggested retail price: $27.95

■FIGURE 13.1 *(cont.)*

vice president, who reports directly to the CEO. (An organization chart appears in Figure 13.2. The solid lines represent existing positions; dotted lines represent positions that will be added as part of the reengineering project.) All these divisions are housed in a single location that the corporation owns outright.

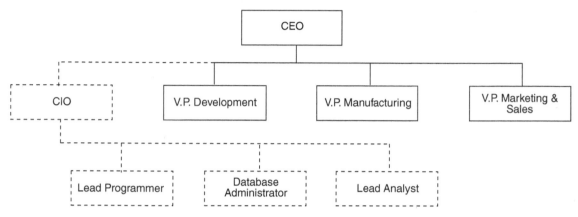

■ FIGURE 13.2 Might-Mite Motors organization chart.

Product Development Division

The Product Development division is responsible for designing and testing new and redesigned products. The division employs design engineers who use computer-aided design (CAD) software to prepare initial designs for new or redesigned vehicles. Once a design is complete, between one and 10 prototypes are built. The prototypes are first tested in-house using robotic drivers/passengers. After refinement, the prototypes are tested by children in a variety of settings. Feedback from the testers is used to refine product designs and to make decisions about which designs should actually be manufactured for mass marketing.

Manufacturing Division

The Manufacturing division is responsible for producing product for mass market sales. Manufacturing procures its own raw materials and manages its own operations, including personnel (hiring, firing, scheduling) and assembly line management. Manufacturing maintains the inventory of products ready for sale. It also handles shipping of products to resellers, based on sales information received from Marketing and Sales.

Marketing and Sales Division

MMM sells directly to toy stores and catalog houses; the corporation has never used distributors. Marketing and Sales employs a staff of 25 sales people who make personal contacts with resellers. Salespeople are responsible for distributing catalogs in their territories, visiting and/or calling potential resellers, and taking reseller orders. Order accounting is handled by Marketing and Sales. As noted earlier, Marketing and Sales transmits shipping information to Manufacturing, which takes care of actual product delivery.

Current Information Systems

MMM's information systems are a hodgepodge of computers and applications that have grown up with little corporate planning. The Product Development division relies primarily on stand-alone CAD workstations. In contrast to the sophistication of the CAD machines, testing records are kept and analyzed manually. Product Development employs product designers (some of whom function as project leaders) and clerical support staff, but no information systems personnel. Attempts to have clerical staff develop simple database applications to store data about children who test new and redesigned products and the results of those tests have proved futile. It has become evident that Product Development needs information systems professionals, and although the division is willing to hire IT staff, corporate management has decided to centralize the IT staff, rather than add to a decentralized model.

Manufacturing uses a stand-alone server to track purchases and inventory levels of raw materials, personnel scheduling, manufacturing line scheduling, and finished product inventory. Each of the applications running on the server were custom-written by outside consultants in COBOL, many years ago; the most significant maintenance they have had was when they were ported from the department's original minicomputer to the server, about 15 years ago. The data used by a Manufacturing application are contained in files that do not share information with any of the other applications. Manufacturing employs one COBOL programmer, who will be retiring shortly, and a system administrator. Although the programmer is talented, the most he can do is fix superficial user interface issues and repair corrupted data files; he was not part of the original program development and does not understand the functioning of much of the application code, which was poorly written and even more poorly documented. The applications no longer meet the needs of the Manufacturing division and management has determined that it isn't cost effective to write new applications to access the existing data files.

Marketing and Sales, which wasn't computerized until 1987, has a local area network consisting of one server and 15 workstations. The server provides shared applications, such as word processing and spreadsheets. It also maintains a marketing and sales database that has been developed using a PC-based product. The database suffers from several problems, including a limit of 10 users at one time and concurrency control problems that lead to severe data inconsistencies. The marketing and sales database was developed by the division's two IT employees at the time, both of whom have since left the company. No current staff understands the software. Regardless of the amount of time spent trying to maintain the database, inaccurate data continue to be introduced.

The Marketing and Sales network is not connected to the Internet. Sales people must therefore transmit hard copies of their orders to the central office, where the orders are manually keyed into the existing database. Some of the sales people do have laptop computers, but because the network has no Internet connection, the sales people cannot connect to it when they are out of the office.

Reengineering Project

Because MMM seems to have lost its strategic advantage in the marketplace, the CEO has decided to undertake a major systems reengineering project. The overall thrust of the project is to provide an information system that will support better evaluation of product testing, better analysis of sales patterns, better control of the manufacturing process, and enhanced communications options throughout the corporation. New information systems will be based on a client/server model and include one or more databases running on an Internet-connected network of servers, workstations, and PCs. The ultimate goal is to create a Web site for the company so resellers can place orders online.

New Information Systems Division

The first step in the reengineering project is to establish an information technology division. This new division will also be housed in the corporate headquarters, along with the three existing divisions. To accommodate the new division, MMM will be constructing a 10,000 square foot addition to its building.

MMM is in the process of searching for a Chief Information Officer (CIO). This individual, who will report directly to the CEO, will manage the new division and be responsible for overseeing the reengineering of information systems that will handle all of the corporation's operations, as well as the creation, implementation, and maintenance of the company's Web presence.

All current IT personnel (those who work for the Manufacturing, and Marketing and Sales divisions) will be transferred to the new IT division. The division will hire (either internally or externally) three management-level professionals: a Lead Programmer (responsible for overseeing application development), a Database Administrator (responsible for database design and management), and a Lead Analyst (responsible for overseeing systems analysis and design efforts). The company will investigate various solutions for the development of the Web site, with an eye to determining whether it should be done in-house or outsourced to a consulting firm.

Basic System Goals

The CEO has defined the following goals for the reengineering project:

- Develop a corporation-wide data administration plan that includes a requirements document detailing organizational functions that require technology support and the functions that the reengineered system will provide.
- Provide an application roadmap that documents all application programs that will be needed to support corporate operations.
- Investigate alternatives for developing and hosting a Web site that will allow online orders. Conduct a cost-benefit analysis of those alternatives before beginning development.
- Document all databases to be developed for the corporation. This documentation will include ER diagrams and data dictionaries.
- Create a timeline for the development of applications and their supporting databases.
- Specify hardware changes and/or acquisitions that will be necessary to support the reengineered information systems.
- Plan and execute a security strategy for an expanded corporate network that will include both internal and external users.
- Implement the planned systems.

Note: It is important to keep in mind that the implementation of a Web presence for the company is relatively independent of the database design. The Web application will require the same data as all the other types of data entry. Concerns about hosting and security are rarely the job of the database designer.

Current Business Processes

To aid the systems analysts in their assessment of MMM's information systems needs, the CEO of MMM asked all existing division heads to document the way in which information is currently processed. This documentation, which also includes some information about what an improved system should do, provides a starting point for the redesign of both business and IT processes.

Sales and Ordering Processes

MMM receives orders at its plant in two ways: either by telephone directly from customers or from members of the sales staff who have visited customers in person. Orders from the remote sales staff usually arrive by fax or overnight courier.

Each order is taken on a standard order form (Figure 13.3). If the order arrives by fax, it will already be on the correct form. Telephone orders are written directly onto the form. Several times a day, a clerk enters the orders into the existing database. Unfortunately, if the sales office is particularly busy, order entry may be delayed. This backup has a major impact on production line scheduling and thus on the company's ability to fill orders. The new information system must streamline the order entry process, including online order entry, electronic transmission of order data from the field, and the direct entry of in-house orders.

The in-house sales staff has no access to the files that show the current finished-goods inventory. They are therefore unable to tell customers when their orders will ship. They can, however, tell customers how many orders are ahead of theirs to be filled and, based on general manufacturing timetables, come up with an approximation of how long it will take to ship a given order. Therefore, another goal of the information systems reengineering project is to provide better company-wide knowledge of how long it will take to fill customer orders.

Manufacturing, Inventory, and Shipping Processes

The MMM Manufacturing division occupies a large portion of the MMM facility. The division controls the actual manufacturing lines (three assembly lines), a storage area for finished goods, a storage area for raw materials, and several offices for supervisory and clerical staff.

The manufacturing process is triggered when a batch of order forms is received each morning by the manufacturing office. The batch consists of all orders that were entered into the sales database the previous working day. A secretary takes the individual order forms, and completes a report summarizing the number ordered by model (Figure 13.4). This report is then given to the Manufacturing Supervisor, whose responsibility it is to schedule which model will be produced on each manufacturing line, each day.

Mighty-Mite Motors

Customer Order Form

Customer #:

Order date:

Name:

Street:

City: State: Zip:

Voice phone #:   Fax:

First name: Contact person   Last name:

Item #	Quantity	Unit Price	Line Total

Order total:

■ **FIGURE 13.3** Mighty-Mite Motors order form.

```
┌─────────────────────────────────────────────────────────┐
│              Mighty-Mite Motors                          │
│                Order Summary                             │
│                                                          │
│               MM/DD/YYYY                                 │
│                                                          │
│     Model #              Quantity Ordered                │
│      001                      75                         │
│      002                     150                         │
│      004                      80                         │
│      005                      35                         │
│      008                     115                         │
│      009                      25                         │
│      010                      25                         │
│      011                      15                         │
└─────────────────────────────────────────────────────────┘
```

■ **FIGURE 13.4 Mighty-Mite Motors order summary report format.**

The scheduling process is somewhat complex, because the Manufacturing Supervisor must take into account previously placed orders, which have determined the current manufacturing schedule, and current inventory levels, as well as the new orders. The availability of raw materials and the time it takes to modify a manufacturing line to produce a different model also enter into the scheduling decision. This is one function that MMM's management understands will be almost impossible to automate; there is just too much human expertise involved to translate into an automatic process. However, it is vital that the Manufacturing Supervisor have access to accurate, up-to-date information about orders, inventory, and the current time schedule so that judgments can be made based on as much hard data as possible.

As finished vehicles come off the assembly line, they are packed for shipping, labeled, and sent to finished goods storage. Each shipping carton contains one vehicle, which is marked with its model number, serial number, and date of manufacturing. The Shipping Manager, who oversees finished goods storage and shipping, ensures that newly manufactured items are entered into the shipping inventory files.

The Shipping Manager receives customer order forms after the order report has been completed. (Photocopies of the order forms are kept in the Marketing and Sales office as backup.) The orders are placed in a box in reverse chronological order so that the oldest orders can be filled first. The Shipping Manager checks orders against inventory levels by looking at the inventory level output screen (Figure 13.5). If the manager sees that there is enough inventory to fill an order, then the order is given to a shipping clerk for processing. If there isn't enough inventory, then the order is put back in the box, where it will be checked again the following day. Under this system, no partial orders are filled, because they would be extremely difficult

```
┌──────────────────────────────────────────────────────┐
│          Current Finished Goods Inventory Levels       │
│                     MM/DD/YYYY                          │
│                                                         │
│          Model #                    Number on Hand      │
│                                                         │
│            001                          215             │
│            002                           35             │
│            003                          180             │
│            004                          312             │
│            005                           82             │
│            006                            5             │
│            007                          212             │
│            008                          189             │
│            009                           37             │
│            010                          111             │
│            011                          195             │
│            012                           22             │
└──────────────────────────────────────────────────────┘
```

■ FIGURE 13.5 Mite-Mite Motors inventory screen layout.

to track. (The reengineered information system should allow handling of partial shipments.)

Shipping clerks are given orders to fill. They create shipping labels for all vehicles that are part of a shipment. The cartons are labeled and set aside for pickup by UPS. The shipping clerks create UPS manifests, ensure that the items being shipped are removed from the inventory file, and return the filled orders to the Shipping Manager. The orders are then marked as filled and returned to Marketing and Sales. The reengineered information system should automate the generation of pick-lists, packing slips, and updating of finished-goods inventory.

MMM's raw materials inventory is maintained on a just-in-time basis. The Manufacturing Supervisor checks the line schedule (Figure 13.6) and the current raw materials inventory (Figure 13.7) daily to determine what raw materials need to be ordered. This process relies heavily on the Manufacturing Supervisor's knowledge of which materials are needed for which model vehicle. MMM's CEO is very concerned about this process because the Manufacturing Supervisor, while accurate in scheduling the manufacturing line, is nowhere near as accurate in judging raw materials needs. The result is that occasionally manufacturing must stop because raw materials have run out. The CEO would therefore like to see ordering of raw materials triggered automatically. The new information system should keep track of the raw materials needed to produce each model and, based on the line schedule and a reorder point established for each item, generate orders for items when needed.

Raw materials are taken from inventory each morning as each manufacturing line is set up for the day's production run. The inventory files are

```
                        Line Schedule
                         MM/DD/YYYY

MM/DD/YYYY
            Line #1: Model 008              300 units
            Line #2: Model 002              150 units
            Line #3: Model 010              200 units

MM/DD/YYYY
            Line #1: Model 008              200 units
            Line #2: Model 003              400 units
            Line #3: Model 005              300 units

MM/DD/YYYY
            Line #1: Model 008              250 units
            Line #2: Model 006              100 units
            Line #3: Model 002              300 units

                  :
                  :
                  :


Total production scheduled:
            Model 002                       450 units
            Model 003                       400 units
            Model 005                       300 units
            Model 006                       100 units
            Model 008                       750 units
            Model 010                       200 units
```

■ **FIGURE 13.6** **Mighty-Mite Motors line schedule report format.**

```
            Current Raw Materials Inventory Levels
                        MM/DD/YYYY

        Item #   Item                 QOH

        001      Plastic #3           95 lbs.
        002      Red dye 109          25 gals.
        003      Wheel 12"            120 each
        004      Plastic #4           300 lbs.
        005      Yellow dye 110       5 gals.
        006      Yellow dye 65        30 gals.
        007      Strut 15"            99 each
        008      Axle 24"             250 each
        009      Blu dye 25           18 gals.
        010      Plastic #8           350 lbs.
        011      Cotter pin: small    515 each
        012      Cotter pin: medium   109 each


                                      Next screen
```

■ **FIGURE 13.7** **Mighty-Mite Motors raw materials inventory screen layout.**

modified immediately after all raw materials have been removed from storage for a given manufacturing line. There is no way to automate the reduction of inventory; however, the new information system should make it very easy for nontechnical users to update inventory levels.

Product Testing and Support Function

MMM's top management makes decisions about which model vehicles to produce, based on data from three sources: product testing, customer registrations, and problem reports.

Customer registrations are received on cards packaged with sold vehicles (Figure 13.8). Currently, the registration cards are filed by customer name.

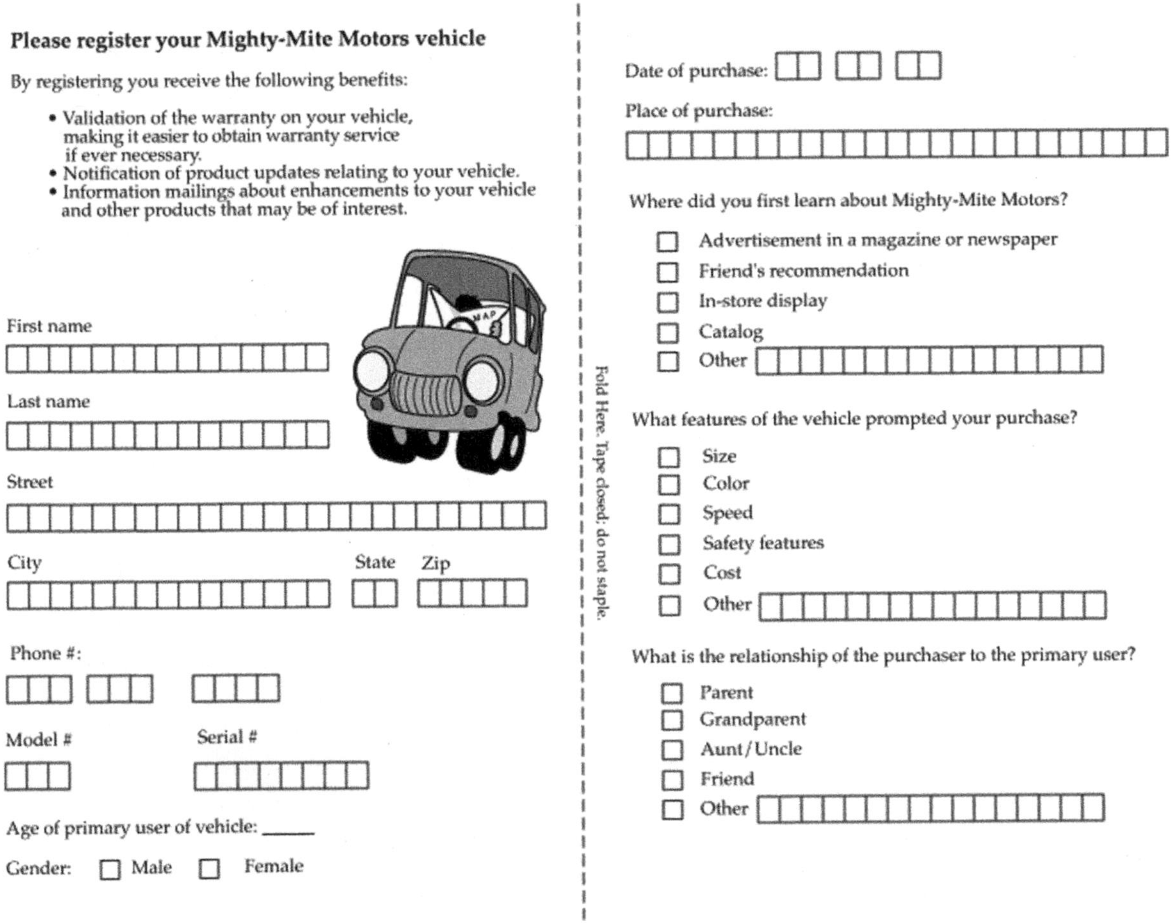

Please register your Mighty-Mite Motors vehicle

By registering you receive the following benefits:

- Validation of the warranty on your vehicle, making it easier to obtain warranty service if ever necessary.
- Notification of product updates relating to your vehicle.
- Information mailings about enhancements to your vehicle and other products that may be of interest.

First name

Last name

Street

City State Zip

Phone #:

Model # Serial #

Age of primary user of vehicle: _____

Gender: ☐ Male ☐ Female

Fold Here. Tape closed; do not staple.

Date of purchase:

Place of purchase:

Where did you first learn about Mighty-Mite Motors?

- ☐ Advertisement in a magazine or newspaper
- ☐ Friend's recommendation
- ☐ In-store display
- ☐ Catalog
- ☐ Other

What features of the vehicle prompted your purchase?

- ☐ Size
- ☐ Color
- ☐ Speed
- ☐ Safety features
- ☐ Cost
- ☐ Other

What is the relationship of the purchaser to the primary user?

- ☐ Parent
- ☐ Grandparent
- ☐ Aunt/Uncle
- ☐ Friend
- ☐ Other

■ FIGURE 13.8 Mighty-Mite Motors purchase registration form.

However, MMM would also like access to these data by model and serial number to make it easier to notify customers if a recall occurs. Management would also like summaries of the data by model purchased, age of primary user, gender of primary user, and who purchased the vehicle for the child.

Problem reports (Figure 13.9) are taken by customer support representatives who work within the product testing division. These reports include the serial number and model experiencing problems, along with the date and type of problem. Currently, the problem descriptions are nonstandard, made up of whatever terms the customer support representative happens to use. It is therefore difficult to summarize problem reports to get an accurate picture of which models are experiencing design problems that should be corrected. MMM would therefore like to introduce a standardized method for describing problems, probably through a set of problem codes. The result should be regular reports on the problems reported for each model that can be used to help make decisions about which models to continue, which to discontinue, which to redesign, and which to recall.

MMM does not repair its own products. When a problem report is received, the customer is either directed to return the product to the store where it was purchased for an exchange (during the first 30 days after purchase) or directed to an authorized repair center in the customer's area. In the latter case, the problem report is faxed to the repair center, so that it is waiting when the customer arrives. MMM does not plan to change this procedure because it currently provides quick, excellent service to customers and alleviates the need for MMM to stock replacement parts. However, the fax transmissions could be replaced with electronic data sent over the Internet.

Product test results are recorded on paper forms (Figure 13.10). After a testing period is completed, the forms are collated manually to produce a summary of how well a new product performed. MMM would like the test results stored within an information system so that the testing report can be produced automatically, saving time and effort. Such a report will be used to help decide which new models should be placed in production.

Designing the Database

The most effective approach to the design of a database (or collection of databases) for an environment as diverse as that presented by Mighty-Mite Motors usually involves breaking the design into components indicated by the organization of the company. As the design evolves, the designer can examine the entities and the relationships to determine where parts of the organization will need to share data. Working on one portion of the

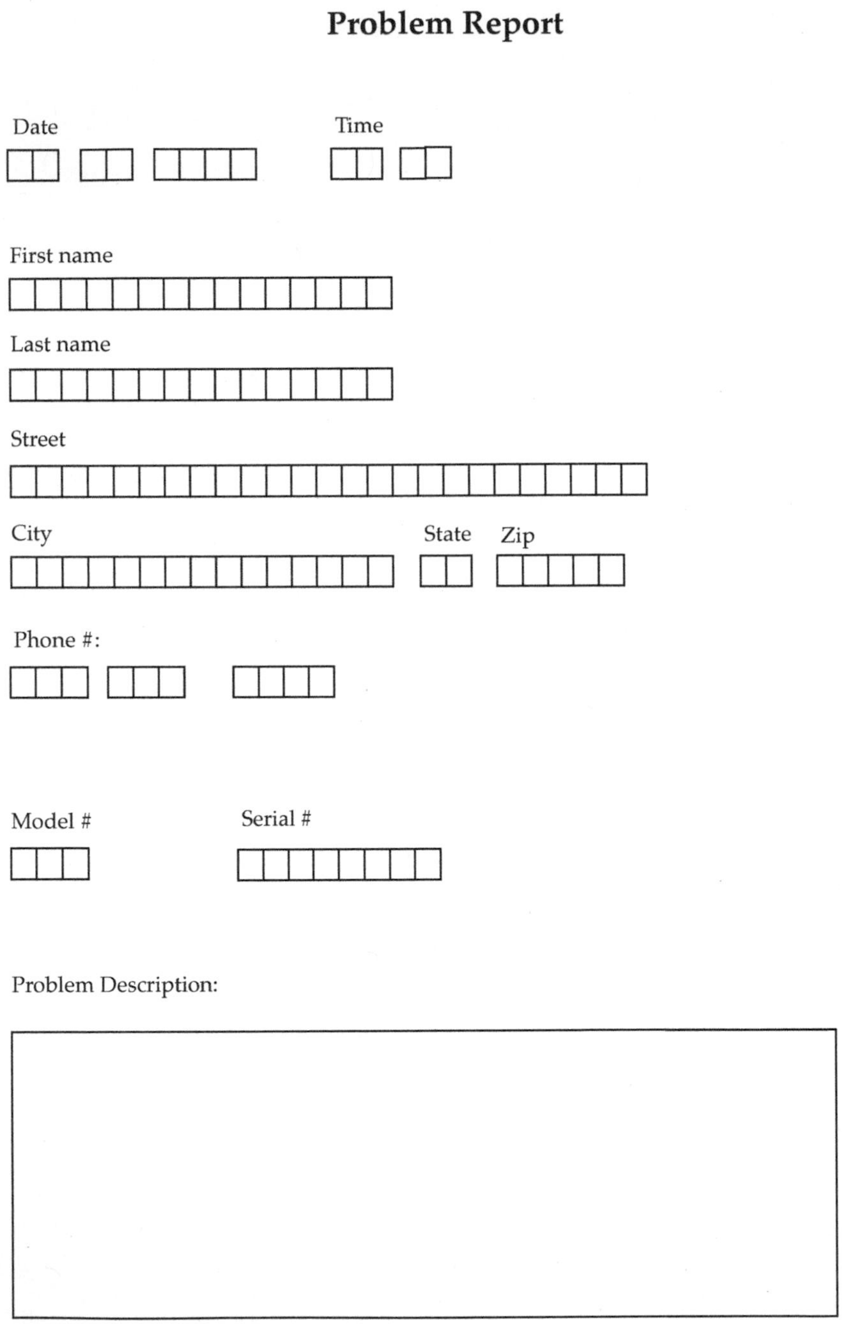

Problem Report

Date   Time

First name

Last name

Street

City   State   Zip

Phone #:

Model #   Serial #

Problem Description:

■ FIGURE 13.9 Mighty-Mite Motors problem report.

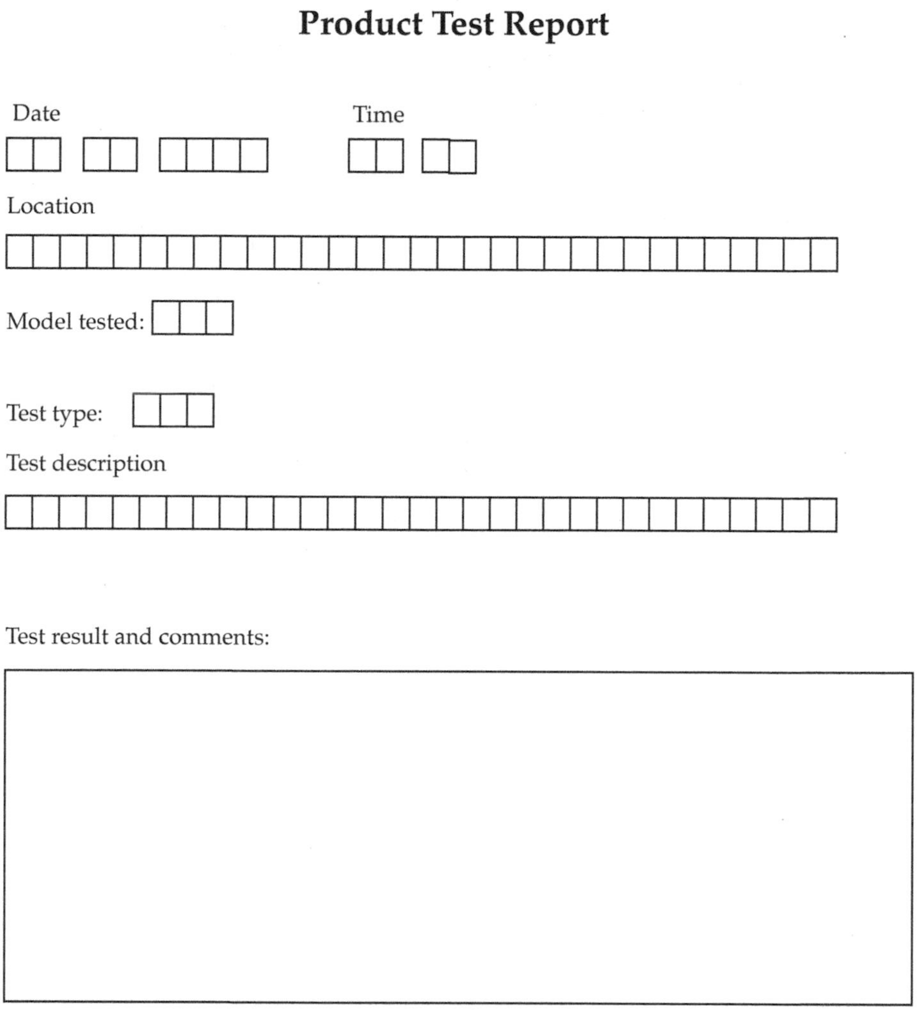

Product Test Report

Date   Time

□□   □□□   □□□□   □□   □□

Location

□□

Model tested: □□□

Test type: □□□

Test description

□□

Test result and comments:

■ **FIGURE 13.10** **Mighty-Mite Motors product test report.**

design at a time also simplifies dealing with what might at first seem to be an overwhelmingly large database environment. Paying special attention for the needs for shared data helps ensure that shared data are consistent and suitable for all required uses.

A systems analysis indicates that the MMM database environment falls into the following areas:

■ Manufacturing (including finished goods inventory and raw materials ordering).

- Sales to toy stores, and shipping of products ordered.
- Purchase registrations.
- Testing.
- Problem handling.

Examining the Data Flows

During the systems analysis, a data flow diagram can be of enormous use in identifying where data are shared by various parts of an organization. The top-level DFD (the *context diagram* in Figure 13.11) actually tells us very little. It indicates that there are three sources outside the company provide data: customers (the stores to which the company sells), purchasers (the individuals who purchase products from the stores), and raw materials suppliers. Somewhere, all those data are used by a general process named "Manufacture and Sell Products" to keep the company in business.

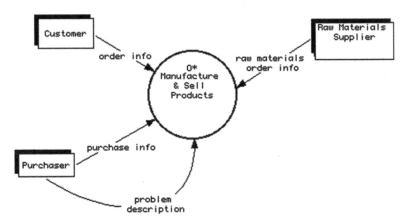

■FIGURE 13.11 Context DFD for Mighty-Mite Motors.

However, the level 1 DFD (Figure 13.12) is much more telling. As the data handling processes are broken down, five data stores emerge:

- Raw materials: This data store holds both the raw materials inventory and the orders for raw materials.
- Product data: The product data store contains data about the products being manufactured, product testing results, and the finished goods inventory.
- Customer orders: This data store contains customer information, as well as order data.

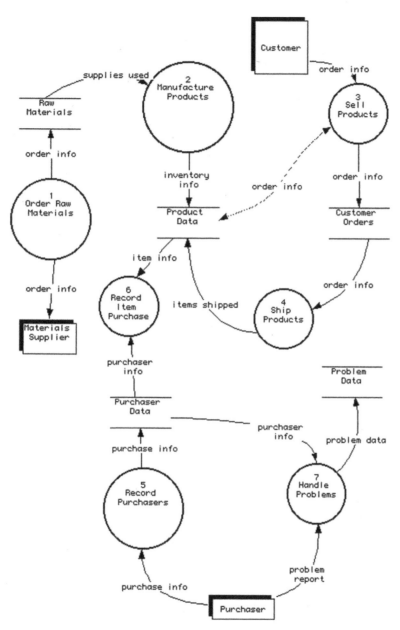

■ FIGURE 13.12 Level 1 DFD for Mighty-Mite Motors.

- Purchaser data: The purchaser data store contains information about the individuals who purchase products and the products they have purchased.
- Problem data: This final data store contains problem reports.

As you examine the processes that interact with these five data stores, you will find a number of processes that manipulate data in more than one data store, as well as data stores that are used by more than one process:

- The raw materials data store is used by the raw materials ordering and the manufacturing processes.
- Product data are used by manufacturing, sales, shipping, and product registration.
- Customer order data are used by sales and shipping.
- The purchases data store is used by purchaser registration and problem handling.
- The problem data store, used only by problem handling, is the only data store not shared by multiple processes.

The raw materials ordering process is the only process that uses only a single data store. Nonetheless, the level 1 DFD makes it very clear that there is no instance in which a single process uses a single data store without interaction with other data stores and processes. Given that each process in the DFD probably represents all or part of an application program, this suggests that the database designer should consider either a single database or a set of small databases, along with software to facilitate the interchange of data.

The DFD makes it very clear that the need for the integration of the various data stores is very strong. In addition, Mighty-Mite Motors is a relatively small business and therefore a single database that manages all needed aspects of the company will not grow unreasonably large. It will also be more cost effective and perform better than multiple databases that use some type of middleware to exchange data. Ultimately, the database designer may decide to distribute the database onto multiple servers, placing portions of it that are used most frequently in the division where that use occurs. The database design, however, will be the same, regardless of whether the final implementation is centralized or distributed. The essential decision is to create a single database rather than several smaller, interrelated databases that must exchange data.

The ER Diagram

The systems analyst preparing the requirements document for the Mighty-Mite Motors reengineering project has had two very good sources of information about exactly what needs to be stored in the database: the employees of the company and the paper documents that the company has been using. The document that is given to the database designer is therefore quite complete.

The design needs to capture all the information on the paper documents. Some documents are used only for input (for example, the product registration form or the order form). Others represent reports that an application program must be able to generate (for example, the line schedule report). Although the current documents do not necessarily represent all the outputs application programs running against the database will eventually prepare, they do provide a good starting place for the design. Whenever the designer has questions, he or she can then turn to Might-Mite's employees for clarification.

Working from the requirements document prepared by the systems analyst, along with the paper input and output documents, the database designer puts together the ER diagram. Because there are so many entities, all of which interconnect, the diagram is very wide. It has therefore been split into three pieces so you can see it. As you look at each piece, keep in mind that entities that appear on more than one piece represent the connection between the three illustrations.

The first part (found in Figure 13.13) contains the entities for raw materials and manufacturing. This portion of the data model is dealing with three many-to-many relationships:

- *material_order* to *raw_material* (resolved by the composite entity *material_order_line*),
- *raw_material* to *model* (resolved by the composite entity *material_needed*),
- *manufacturing_line* to *model* (resolved by the composite entity *line_schedule*).

The second portion of the ERD (Figure 13.14) contains entities for product testing and sales. (Remember that in this instance, the customers are toy stores rather than individual purchasers.) There are two many-to-many relationships:

- *test_type* to *model* (resolved by the *test* entity),
- *order* to *model* (resolved by the *order_line* composite entity).

The test entity is somewhat unusual for a composite entity. It is an activity that someone performs and, as such, has an existence outside the database. It is not an entity created just to resolve a many-to-many relationship.

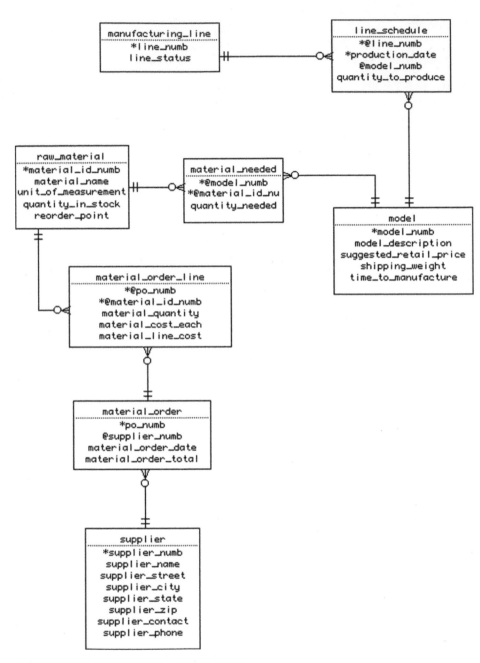

■ **FIGURE 13.13** Might-Mite Motors ERD (part 1).

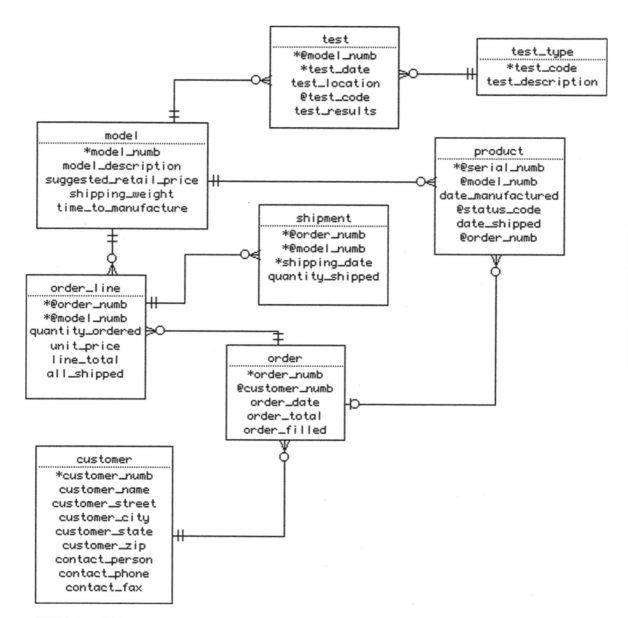

■ FIGURE 13.14 Might-Mite Motors ERD (part II).

At this point, the diagrams become a bit unusual because of the need to keep track of individual products rather than simply groups of products of the same model. The *model* entity, which you first saw in Figure 13.13, represents a type of vehicle manufactured by Mighty-Mite Motors. However, the *product* entity, which first appears in Figure 13.14, represents a single vehicle that is uniquely identified by a serial number. This means that the relationships between an order, the line items on an order, and the models and products are more complex than for most other sales database designs.

The *order* and *line_item* entities are fairly typical. They indicate how many of a given model are required to fill a given order. The *shipment* entity then indicates how many of a specific model are shipped on a specific date. However, the database must also track the order in which individual products are shipped. As a result, there is a direct relationship between the *product* entity and the *order* entity in addition to the relationships between *order_line* and *model*. In this way, Mighty-Mite Motors will know exactly where each product has gone. At the same time, the company will be able to track the status of orders (in particular, how many units of each model have yet to ship).

The final portion of the ERD (Figure 13.15) deals with the purchasers and problem reports. There are two many-to-many relationships:

- *problem_type* to *product* (resolved with the entity *problem_report*),
- *purchase* to *feature* (resolved with the composite entity *purchase_feature*).

As with the test entity that you saw earlier, the *problem_report* entity acts like a composite entity to resolve a many-to-many relationship, but is really a simple entity. It is an entity that has an existence outside the database and was not created simply to take care of the M:N relationship.

Note: Calling an entity "problem_report" can be a bit misleading. In this case, the word "report" does not refer to a piece of paper, but to the action of reporting a problem. A "problem_report" is therefore an activity rather than a document. In fact, the printed documentation of a problem report will probably include data from several entities, including the product, problem_report, purchase, and owner entities.

If you look closely at the diagram, you'll notice that there is a one-to-one relationship between the product and purchase entities. The handling of the data supplied by a purchaser on the product registration card presents an interesting dilemma for a database designer. Each product will be registered by only one purchaser. (Even if the product is later sold or given to someone else, the new owner will not have a registration card to send in.) There will be only one set of registration data for each product, at first thought suggesting that all the registration data should be part of the *product* entity.

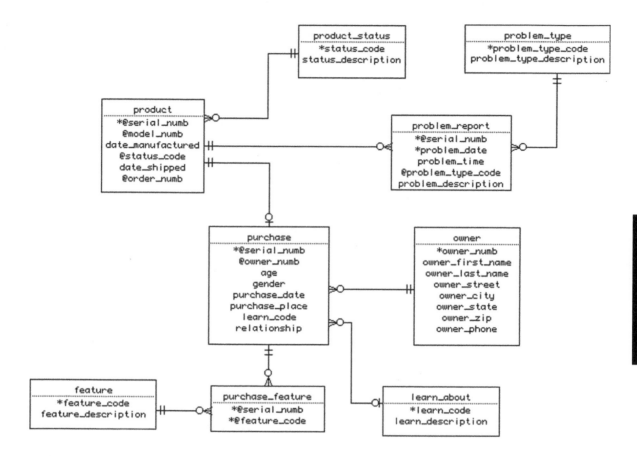

■FIGURE 13.15 Mighty-Mite Motors ERD (part III).

However, there is a lot of registration data—including one repeating group (the features for which the purchaser chose the product, represented by the *feature* and *purchase_feature* entities)—and the product is involved in a number of relationships that have nothing to do with product registration. If the DBMS has to retrieve the registration data along with the rest of the product data, database performance will suffer. It therefore makes sense in this case to keep the purchase data separate and to retrieve it only when absolutely needed.

Note: One common mistake made by novice database designers is to create an entity called "registration card." It is important to remember that the card itself is merely an input document. What is crucial is the data the card contains and the entity that the data describe, rather than the medium on which the data are supplied.

Creating the Tables

The tables for the Mighty-Mite Motors database can come directly from the ER diagram. They are as follows:

model (model_numb, model_description, suggested_retail_price, shipping_weight, time_to_manufacture)

test (model_numb, test_date, test_location, test_code, test_results)

test_types (test_code, test_description)

customers (customer_numb, customer_name, customer_street, customer_city, customer_state, customer_zip, contact_person, contact_phone, contact_fax)

orders (order_numb, customer_numb, order_date, order_total, order_filled)

order_line (order_numbzu, model_numb, quantity_ordered, unit_price, line_total, all_shipped)

shipments (order_numb, model_numb, quantity_shipped)

product (serial_numb, model_numb, date_manufactured, status_code, order_numb, date_shipped)

raw_material (material_id_numb, material_name, unit_of_measurement, quantity_in_stock, reorder_point)

supplier (supplier_numb, supplier_name, supplier_street, supplier_city, supplier_state, supplier_zip, supplier_contact, supplier_phone)

material_order (po_numb, supplier_numb, material_order_date, material_order_total)

material_order_line (po_numb, material_id_numb, material_quantity, material_cost_each, material_line_cost)

manufacturing_line (line_numb, line_status)

line_schedule (line_numb, production_date, model_numb, quantity_to_produce)

owner (owner_numb, owner_first_name, owner_last_name, owner_street, owner_city, owner_state, owner_zip, owner_phone)

purchase (serial_numb, owner_numb, age, gender, purchase_date, purchase_price, learn_code, relationship)

purchase_feature (serial_numb, feature_code)

learn_about (learn_code, learn_description)

feature (feature_code, feature_description)

problem_report (serial_numb, problem_date, problem_time, problem_type_code, problem_details)

problem_type (problem_type_code, problem_type_description)

Generating the SQL

Assuming that the designers of the Mighty-Mite Motors database are working with a CASE tool, then generating SQL statements to create the database can be automated. For example, in Figure 13.16 you will find the SQL generated by Mac A&D from the ER diagram you saw earlier in this chapter.

```
CREATE TABLE model
(
      model_numb INTEGER,
      model_description VARCHAR (40),
      suggested_retail_price NUMBER (6,2),
      shipping_weight NUMBER(6,2),
      time_to_manufacture TIME,
      PRIMARY KEY (model_numb)
);
CREATE TABLE test_type
(
      test_code INTEGER,
      test_description VARCHAR (40),
      PRIMARY KEY (test_code)
);

CREATE TABLE test
(
      test_date DATE,
      test_location VARCHAR (40),
      test_code INTEGER,
      test_results VARCHAR (256),
      PRIMARY KEY (model_numb, test_date),
      FOREIGN KEY (model_numb) REFERENCES model,
      FOREIGN KEY (test_code) REFERENCES test_type
);

CREATE TABLE customer
(
      customer_numb INTEGER,
      customer_name VARCHAR (40),
      customer_street VARCHAR (50),
      customer_city VARCHAR (50),
      customer_state CHAR (2),
      customer_zip CHAR (10),
      contact_person VARCHAR (30),
      contact_phone CHAR (12),
      contact_fax CHAR (12),
      PRIMARY KEY (customer_numb)
);
```

■ **FIGURE 13.16 SQL statements needed to create the Mighty-Mite Motors database (continues).**

```
CREATE TABLE order
(
     order_numb INTEGER,
     customer_numb INTEGER,
     order_date DATE,
     order_total NUMBER (8,2),
     order_filled BOOLEAN,
     PRIMARY KEY (order_numb),
     FOREIGN KEY (customer_numb) REFERENCES customer
);
CREATE TABLE order_line
(
     order_numb INTEGER,
     model_numb INTEGER,
     quantity_ordered INTEGER,
     unit_price NUMBER (6,2),
     line_total NUMBER (8,2),
     all_shipped BOOLEAN,
     PRIMARY KEY (order_numb, model_numb),
     FOREIGN KEY (order_numb) REFERENCES order,
     FOREIGN KEY (model_numb) REFERENCES model
);
CREATE TABLE shipment
(
     order_numb INTEGER,
     model_numb INTEGER,
     shipping_date DATE,
     quantity_shipped INTEGER,
     PRIMARY KEY (order_numb, model_numb, shipping_date),
     FOREIGN KEY (order_numb, model_numb) REFERENCES order_line
);
CREATE TABLE product
(
     serial_numb INTEGER,
     model_numb INTEGER,
     date_manufactured DATE,
     status_code INTEGER,
     date_shipped DATE,
     order_numb INTEGER,
     PRIMARY KEY (serial_numb),
     FOREIGN KEY (model_numb) REFERENCES model,
     FOREIGN KEY (status_code) REFERENCES product_status,
     FOREIGN KEY (order_numb) REFERENCES order
);
CREATE TABLE product_status
(
     status_code INTEGER,
     status_description VARCHAR (40),
     PRIMARY KEY (status_code)
);
```

■ **FIGURE 13.16** *(cont.)*

```
CREATE TABLE raw_material
(
      material_id_numb INTEGER,
      material_name VARCHAR (40),
      unit_of_measurement CHAR (12),
      quantity_in_stock INTEGER,
      reorder_point INTEGER,
      PRIMARY KEY (material_id_numb)
);
CREATE TABLE material_needed
(
      model_numb INTEGER,
      material_id_numb INTEGER,
      quantity_needed INTEGER,
      PRIMARY KEY (model_numb, material_id_numb),
      FOREIGN KEY (model_numb) REFERENCES model,
      FOREIGN KEY (material_id_numb) REFERENCES raw_material
};
CREATE TABLE supplier
(
      supplier_numb INTEGER,
      supplier_name VARCHAR (40),
      supplier_street VARCHAR (50),
      supplier_city VARCHAR (50),
      supplier_state CHAR (2),
      supplier_zip CHAR (10),
      supplier_phone CHAR (12),
      PRIMARY KEY (supplier_numb)
};
CREATE TABLE material_order
(
      po_numb INTEGER,
      supplier_numb INTEGER,
      material_order_date DATE,
      material_order_total NUMBER (8,2),
      PRIMARY KEY (po_numb),
      FOREIGN KEY (supplier_numb) REFERENCES supplier
);
CREATE TABLE material_order_line
(
      po_numb INTEGER,
      material_id_numb INTEGER,
      material_quantity INTEGER,
      material_cost_each NUMBER (6,2),
      material_line_cost NUMBER (8,2),
      PRIMARY KEY (po_numb, material_id_numb),
      FOREIGN KEY (po_numb) REFERENCES material_order,
      FOREIGN KEY (material_id_numb) REFERENCES raw_material
}
```

■ FIGURE 13.16 (*cont.*)

```
CREATE TABLE manufacturing_line
(
        line_numb INTEGER,
        line_status CHAR (12),
        PRIMARY KEY (line_numb)
);

CREATE TABLE line_schedule
(
        line_numb INTEGER,
        production_date DATE,
        model_numb INTEGER,
        quantity_to_product INTEGER
        PRIMARY KEY (line_numb, production_date),
        FOREIGN KEY (lne_numb) REFERENCES manufacturing_line,
        FOREIGN KEY (model_numb) REFERENCES model
);

CREATE TABLE owner
(
        owner_numb INTEGER,
        owner_street VARCHAR (50),
        owner_city VARCHAR (50),
        owner_state CHAR (2),
        owner_zip CHAR (10),
        owner_phone CHAR (10),
        PRIMARY KEY (owner_numb)
};

CREATE TABLE purchase
(
        serial_numb INTEGER,
        owner_numb INTEGER,
        age INTEGER,
        gender CHAR (1),
        purchase_date DATE,
        purchase_place VARCHAR (50),
        learn_code INTEGER,
        relationship CHAR (10),
        PRIMARY KEY (serial_numb),
        FOREIGN KEY (serial_numb) REFERENCES product,
        FOREIGN KEY (owner_numb) REFERENCES owner
        FOREIGN KEY (learn_code) REFERENCES learn_about
);

CREATE TABLE feature
(
        feature_code INTEGER,
        feature_description VARCHAR (40),
        PRIMARY KEY (feature_code)
);
```

■ FIGURE 13.16 *(cont.)*

```
CREATE TABLE purchase_feature
(
      serial_numb INTEGER,
      feature_code INTEGER,
      PRIMARY KEY (serial_numb, feature_code),
      FOREIGN KEY (serial_numb) REFERENCES product,
      FOREIGN KEY (feature_code) REFERENCES feature
};

CREATE TABLE learn_about
(
      learn_code INTEGER,
      learn_description VARCHAR (50),
      PRIMARY KEY (learn_code)
};

CREATE TABLE problem_type
(
      problem_type_code INTEGER,
      problem_type_description VARCHAR (50),
      PRIMARY KEY (problem_type_code)
);

CREATE TABLE problem_report
(
      serial_numb INTEGER,
      problem_date DATE,
      problem_time TIME,
      problem_type_code INTEGER,
      problem_details VARCHAR (50),
      PRIMARY KEY (serial_numb, problem_date),
      FOREIGN KEY (serial_numb) REFERENCES product,
      FOREIGN KEY (product_type_code) REFERENCES problem_type
};
```

■ **FIGURE 13.16** *(cont.)*

14 Database Design Case Study #2: East Coast Aquarium

Many-to-many relationships are often the bane of the relational database designer. Sometimes, it is not completely clear that you are dealing with that type of relationship. However, failure to recognize the many-to-many can result in serious data integrity problems.

The organization described in this chapter actually needs two databases that don't share data, the larger of which is replete with many-to-many relationships. In some cases, it will be necessary to create additional entities for composite entities to reference merely to ensure data integrity.

Perhaps the biggest challenge facing a database design working for East Coast Aquarium is the lack of complete specifications. As you will read, the people who will be using the application programs created to manipulate the aquarium's two new databases have only a general idea of what they need the programs to do. Unlike Mighty-Mite Motors—which had the history of working from a large collection of existing forms, documents, and procedures—East Coast Aquarium has nothing of that sort.

Organizational Overview

The East Coast Aquarium is a nonprofit organization dedicated to the study and preservation of marine life. Located on the Atlantic coast in the heart of a major northeastern US city, it provides a wide variety of educational services to the surrounding area. The aquarium is supported by donations, memberships, charges for private functions, gift shop revenues, class fees, and the small admission fees it charges to the public. Research activities are funded by federal and private grants. To help keep costs down, many of the public service jobs (leading tours, staffing the admissions counter, running the gift shop) are handled by volunteers.

The aquarium grounds consist of three buildings: the main facility, a dolphin house, and a marina where the aquarium's research barge is docked.

The centerpiece of the main building is a three-story center tank that is surrounded by a spiral walkway. The sides of the tank are transparent so that visitors can walk around the tank, observing the residents at various depths.

Note: If you happen to recognize the layout of this aquarium, please keep in mind that only the physical structure of the environment is modeled after anything that really exists. The way in which the organization functions is purely a product of my imagination, and no comment, either positive or negative, is intended with regard to the real-world aquarium.

The height of the tank makes it possible to simulate the way in which habitats change as the ocean depth changes. Species that dwell on the ocean floor, coral reef fish, and sand bar dwellers therefore are all housed in the same tank, interacting in much the same way as they would in the ocean.

The remaining space on the first floor of the main building (Figure 14.1) includes the gift shop and a quarantine area for newly arrived animals. The latter area is not accessible to visitors.

The second floor (Figure 14.2) contains a classroom and the volunteer's office. Small tanks containing single-habitat exhibits are installed in the outside walls. These provide places to house species that have special habitat requirements or that don't coexist well with other species.

The third floor (Figure 14.3) provides wall space for additional small exhibits. It also houses the aquarium's administrative offices.

East Coast Aquarium has two very different areas in which it needs data management. The first is in the handling of its animals—where they are housed in the aquarium, the source and location from where they came, what they are to be fed, problems that occur in the tanks, and so on. The second area concerns the volunteers, including who they are, what they have been trained to do, and when they are scheduled to work. For this particular organization, the two data environments are completely separate: They share no data. A database designer who volunteers to work with the aquarium staff will therefore prepare two database designs, one to be used by the volunteer staff in the volunteer's office and another to be used by the administrative and animal-care staff through the aquarium grounds.

Animal Tracking Needs

Currently, East Coast Aquarium uses a general-purpose PC accounting package to handle its data processing needs. The software takes care of

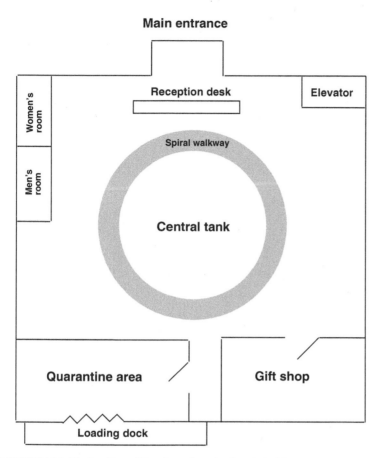

■ FIGURE 14.1   The first floor of East Coast Aquarium's main building.

payroll as well as purchasing, accounts payable, and accounts receivable. Grant funds are managed by special-purpose software designed to monitor grant awards and how they are spent.

Although the accounting and grant management packages adequately handle the aquarium's finances, there is no data processing that tracks the actual animals housed in the aquarium. The three people in charge of the animals have expressed a need for the following:

■ An "inventory" of which species are living in which locations in the aquarium. Some species can be found in more than one tank and several tanks in addition to the central tank contain more than one species. For larger animals, such as sharks and dolphins, the head animal keeper would like a precise count. However, for small fish that

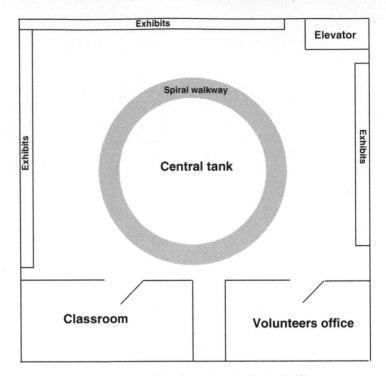

■ FIGURE 14.2 The second floor of East Coast Aquarium's main building.

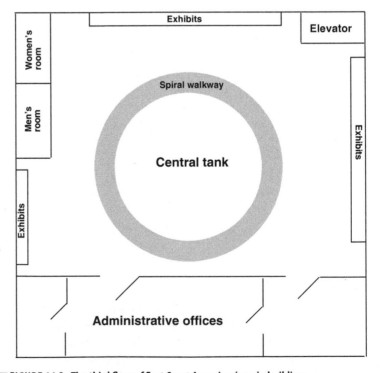

■ FIGURE 14.3 The third floor of East Coast Aquarium's main building.

are often eaten by large fish and that breed in large numbers, only an estimate is possible. The animal handling staff would like to be able to search for information about animals using either the animal's English name or its Latin name.

- Data about the foods each species eats, including how much should be fed at what interval. The head animal keeper would like to be able to print out a feeding instruction list every morning to give to staff. In addition, the animal-feeding staff would like to store information about their food inventory. Although purchasing of food is handled by the administrative office, the head animal keeper would like an application program to decrement the food inventory automatically by the amount fed each day and to generate a tickle request whenever the stock level of a type of food drops below the reorder point. This will make it much easier to ensure that the aquarium does not run short of animal food.

- Data about the sizes, locations, and habitats of the tanks on the aquarium grounds. Some tanks, such as the main tank, contain more than one habitat and the same habitat can be found in more than one tank.

- Data about tank maintenance. Although the main tank is fed directly from the ocean, the smaller tanks around the walls of the main building are closed environments, much like a saltwater aquarium might be at home. This means that the pH and salinity of the tanks must be monitored closely. The head animal keeper therefore would like to print out a maintenance schedule each day as well as be able to keep track of what maintenance is actually performed.

- Data about the habitats in which a given species can live. When a new species arrives at the aquarium, the staff can use this information to determine which locations could possibly house that species.

- Data about where species can be obtained. If the aquarium wants to increase the population of a particular species and the increase cannot be generated through in-house breeding, then the staff would like to know which external supplier can be contacted. Some of the suppliers sell animals; others, such as zoos or other aquariums, will trade or donate animals.

- Problems that arise in the tanks. When animals become ill, the veterinarian wants to be able to view a history of both the animal and the tank in which it is currently living.

- Data about orders placed for animals, in particular, the shipments in which animals arrive. Since any financial arrangements involved in securing animals are handled by the administrative office, these data indicate only how many individuals of each species are included on a given order or shipment.

The shipment and problem data are particularly important to the aquarium. When animals first arrive, they are not placed immediately into the general population. Instead, they are held in special tanks in the quarantine area at the rear of the aquarium's first floor. The length of the quarantine is determined by the species.

After the quarantine period has passed and the animals are declared disease free, they can be placed on exhibit in the main portion of the aquarium. Nonetheless, animals do become ill after they have been released from quarantine. It is therefore essential that records are kept of the sources of animals so that patterns of illness can be tracked back to specific suppliers. By the same token, patterns of illnesses in various species housed in the same tank can be an indication of serious problems with the environment in the tank.

The Volunteer Organization

The volunteer organization (the Friends of the Aquarium) is totally separate from the financial and animal-handling areas of the aquarium. Volunteers perform tasks that do not involve direct contact with animals, such as leading tours, manning the admissions desk, and running the gift shop. The aquarium has provided office space and a telephone line for the volunteer coordinator and her staff. Beyond that, the Friends of the Aquarium organization has been on its own to secure office furniture and equipment.

The recent donation of a PC now makes it possible for the volunteers to input some of the volunteer data online, although the scheduling is still largely manual. Currently, the scheduling processing works in the following way:

- The person on duty in the volunteer's office receives requests for volunteer services from the aquarium's administrative office. Some of the jobs are regularly scheduled (for example, staffing the gift shop and the admissions desk). Others are ad hoc, such as the request by a schoolteacher to bring a class of children for a tour.
- The volunteer doing the scheduling checks the list of volunteers to see who is trained to do the job requested. Each volunteer's information is recorded in a data file that contains the volunteer's contact data, along with the volunteer's skills. A skill is a general expression of something the volunteer knows how to do, such as lead a tour for elementary school children. The volunteer's information also includes an indication of when that person is available to work.
- The volunteer doing the scheduling searches the file for those people who have the required skill and have indicated that they are available at the required time. Most volunteer's work on a regularly scheduled

basis, either at the admissions desk or in the gift shop. However, for ad hoc jobs, the person doing the scheduling must start making telephone calls until someone who is willing and able to do the job is found.

- The volunteer is scheduled for the job by writing in the master scheduling notebook. As far as the volunteer coordinator is concerned, a job is an application of a skill. Therefore, a skill is knowing how to lead a tour for elementary school students, while a job that applies that skill is leading a tour for Mrs Brown's third graders at 10 am on Thursday.

One of the things that is very difficult to do with the current scheduling process is to keep track of the work record of each individual volunteer. The aquarium holds a volunteer recognition luncheon once a year and the volunteer organization would like to find an easy way to identify volunteers who have put in an extra effort so that they can be recognized at that event. In contrast, the volunteer organization would also like to be able to identify volunteers who rarely participate—the people who stay on the volunteer rolls only to get free admission to the aquarium—as well as people who make commitments to work but do not show up. (The latter are actually far more of a problem than the former.)

The Volunteers Database

In terms of scope, the volunteers database is considerably smaller than the animal tracking database. It therefore makes sense to tackle that smaller project first. The database designer will create an application prototype and review it with the users. When the users are satisfied and the designers feel they have detailed information to actually design a database, they will move on to the more traditional steps of creating an ER diagram, tables, and SQL statements.

Note: As you will see, there is a lot involved in creating a prototype. It requires very detailed, intensive work, and produces a number of diagrams and/or application program shells. We will therefore look at the volunteers prototype in full, but, in the interest of length, we will look at only selected aspects of the animal tracking prototype.

Creating the Application Prototype

Given that the specifications of the database are rather general, the first step is to create a prototype of an application program interface. It begins with the opening screen and its main menu bar (Figure 14.4). As you can see, when in browse mode, the CASE tool allows users and designers to pull down the menus in the menu bar.

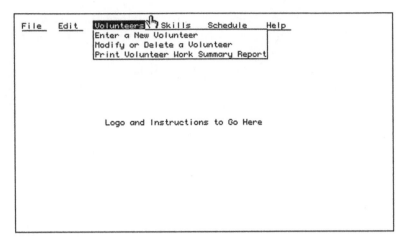

■ FIGURE 14.4 **Main menu prototype for the volunteers application.**

The complete menu tree (with the exception of the Help menu, whose contents are determined by the user interface guidelines of the operating system on which the application is running) can be found in Figure 14.5. Looking at the menu options, users can see that their basic requirements have been fulfilled. The details, however, must be specified by providing users with specific input and output designs.

Main menu

File	Edit	Volunteers	Skills	Schedule
Close	Cut	Enter a new volunteer	Create new skills	Find available volunteers
Page setup...	Copy	Modify or delete a volunteer	Assign skills to volunteers	Schedule volunteer to work
Print...	Paste	Print volunteer work summary		Record volunteer attendance
Quit	Clear			Print daily schedule

■ FIGURE 14.5 **Menu tree of the volunteers database prototype application.**

Each menu option in the prototype's main menu has therefore been linked to a screen form. For example, to modify or delete a volunteer, a user must first *find* the volunteer's data. Therefore, the Modify or Delete a Volunteer menu option leads to a dialog box that lets the user either enter a volunteer number or select a volunteer by name and phone number from a list (Figure 14.6). With the prototype, clicking the Find button opens the modify/delete form (Figure 14.7). Users can click in the data entry fields and tab between them, but the buttons at the right of the window are not functional.

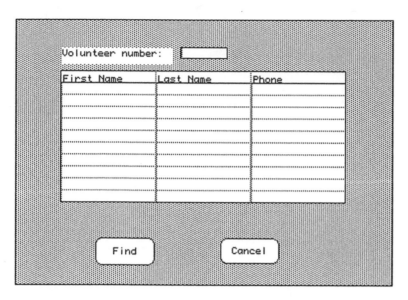

■ FIGURE 14.6 Prototype of a dialog box for finding a volunteer for modifications.

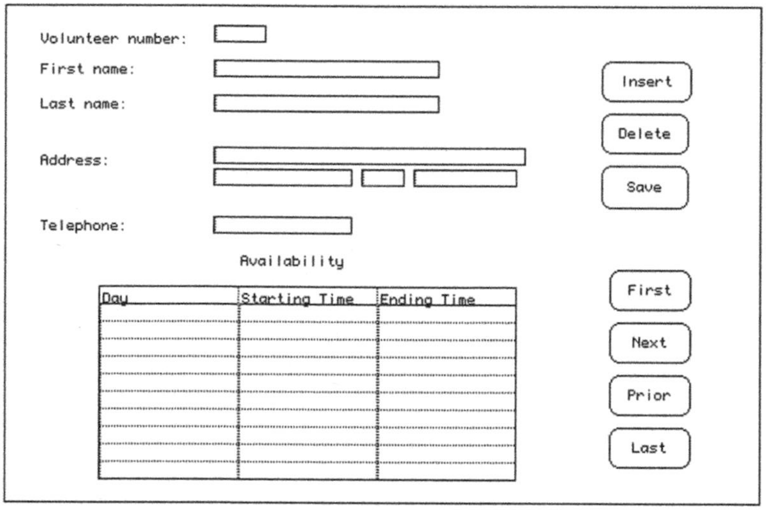

■ FIGURE 14.7 Prototype of form for modifying and deleting a volunteer.

While in browse mode, the CASE tool presents a form as it would appear to the user. However, in design mode, a database designer can see the names of the fields on the form (for example, Figure 14.8). These field names suggest attributes that will be needed in the database.

In the case of the volunteer data, it is apparent to the designers that there are at least two entities (and perhaps three) involved with the data that describe a

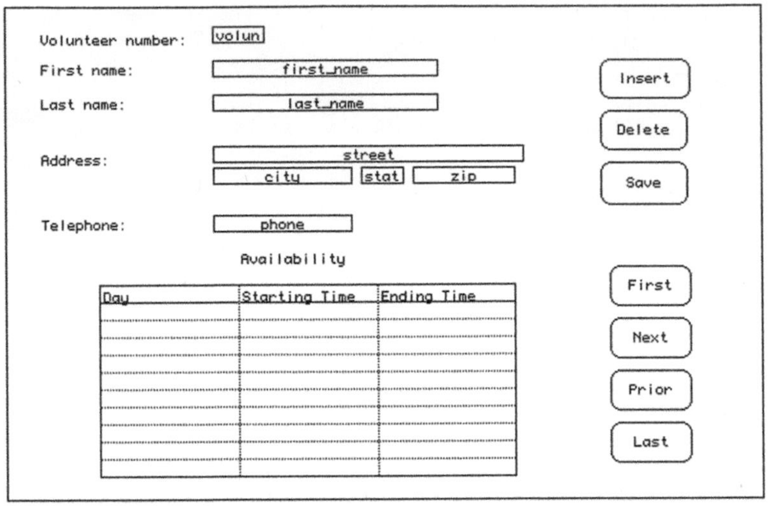

FIGURE 14.8 Prototype data modification form showing field names.

volunteer. The first entity is represented by the single-valued fields occupying the top half of the form (volunteer number, first name, last name, city, state, zip, and phone). However, the availability data—day of the week, starting time, and ending time—are multi-valued and therefore must be given an entity of their own. This also implies that there will be a one-to-many relationship between a volunteer and a period of time during which he or she is available.

Note: Should you choose, the field names of a screen prototype can become part of the data dictionary. However, if the field names do not ultimately correspond to column names, their inclusion may add unnecessary complexity to the data dictionary.

The remainder of the prototype application and its forms are designed and analyzed in a similar way:

- The volunteer work summary report has been designed to let the user enter a range of dates that the report will cover (see Figure 14.9). The report itself (Figure 14.10) is a control-break report that displays the work performed by each volunteer, along with the total hours worked and the number of times the volunteer was a "no show." The latter number was included because the volunteer coordinator had indicated that it was extremely important to know which volunteers consistently signed up to work and then didn't report when scheduled.

The need to report the "no shows" tells the designers that the schedule table needs to include a Boolean column that indicates whether a person

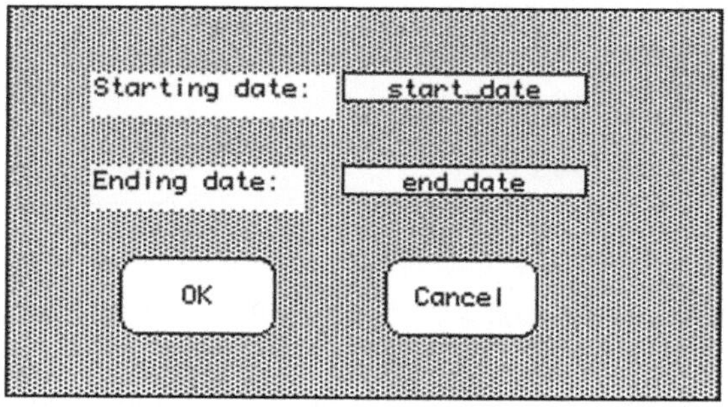

■ FIGURE 14.9 A dialog box layout for entering dates for the work summary report.

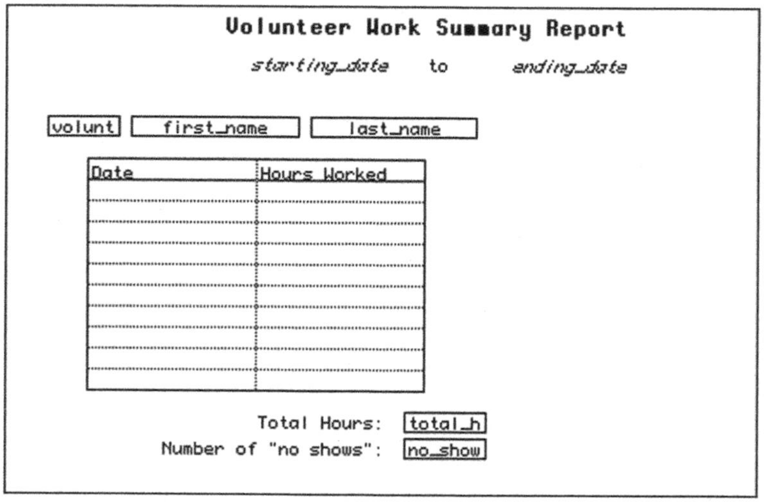

■ FIGURE 14.10 Prototype layout for the work summary report.

showed up for a scheduled shift. The report layout also includes some computed fields (total hours worked and number of no shows) that contain data that do not need to be stored, but can be generated when the report is displayed.

■ Entering a new skill into the master list requires only a simple form (Figure 14.11). The end user sees only the description of a skill. However, the database designers know that the best way to handle unstructured blocks of text is to assign each description a skill number, which can then be used as a foreign key throughout the database. Users, however, do not necessarily need to know that a skill number is being used; they will always see just the text descriptions.

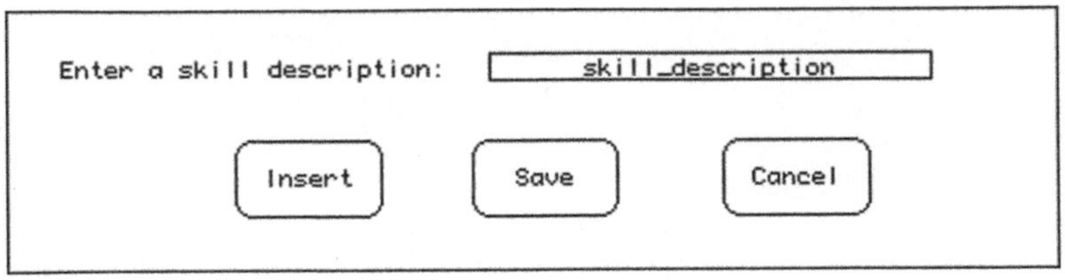

■ FIGURE 14.11 Entering a new skill.

■ To assign skills to a volunteer, the end user must first find the volunteer. The application can therefore use a copy of the dialog box in Figure 14.6. In this case, however, the Find button leads to the form in Figure 14.12.

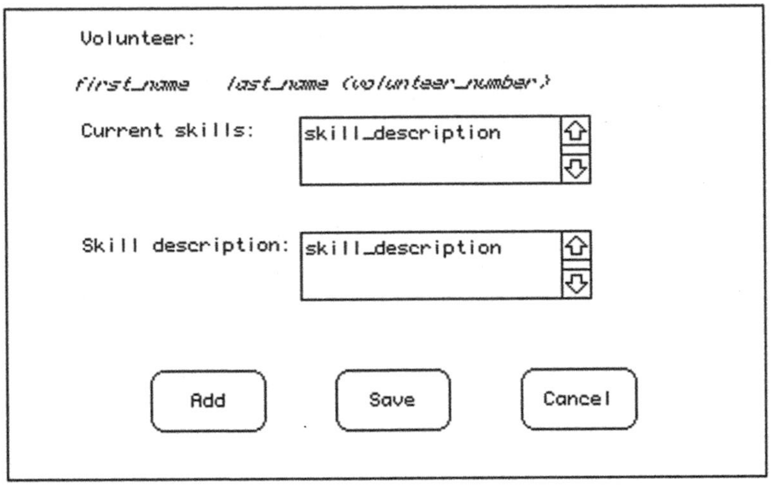

■ FIGURE 14.12 Assigning skills to a volunteer.

A database designer will recognize quickly that there is a many-to-many relationship between a skill and a volunteer. There are actually three entities behind Figure 14.12: the skill, the volunteer, and the composite entity that represents the relationship between the two. The skill entry form displays data from the volunteer entity at the top, data from the composite entity in the current skills list, and all skills not assigned from the skills table in the skill description list. Of course, the actually foreign key used in the composite entity is a skill number, but the user sees only the result of a join back to the skills table that retrieves the skill description.

Note: Database integrity constraints will certainly prevent anyone from assigning the same skill twice to the same volunteer. However, it is easier if the user can see currently assigned skills. Then, the application can restrict what appears in the skill description list to all skills not assigned to that volunteer. In this case, it is a matter of user interface design, rather than database design.

■ To find the volunteers available to perform a specific job, the volunteer's application needs a form something like Figure 14.13. The end user enters the date and time of the job and chooses the skill required by the job. Clicking the Search button fills in the table at the bottom of the form with the names and phone numbers of volunteers who are theoretically available.

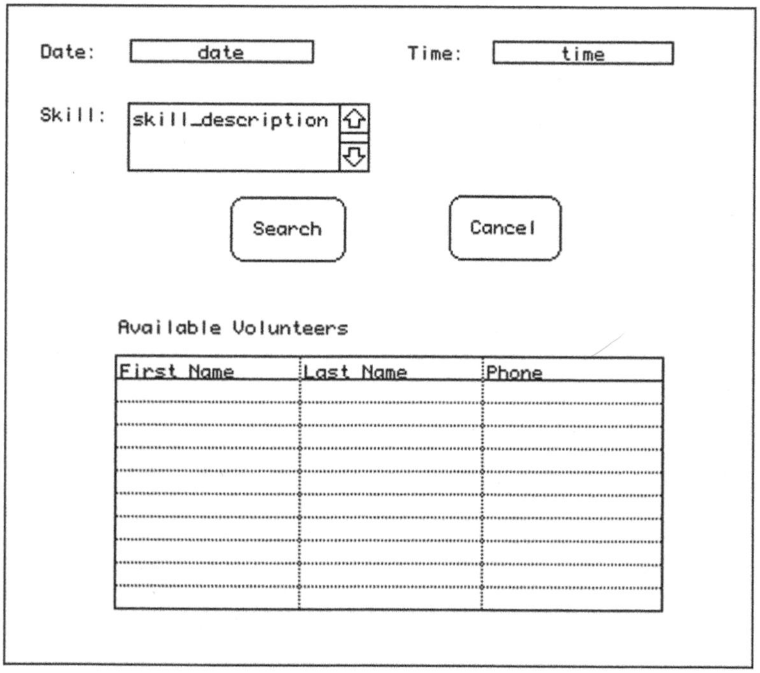

■FIGURE 14.13 Finding available volunteers.

Of all the outputs produced by this application, finding available volunteers is probably the most difficult to implement. The application program must not only work with overlapping intervals of time, but also consider both when a volunteer indicates he or she will be available and when a volunteer is already scheduled to work. In most cases, however, a database designer does not have to write the application program code. The designer needs only to ensure that the data necessary to produce the output are present in the database.

Note: A smart database designer, however, would discuss any output that involves something as difficult as evaluating overlapping time intervals with application programmers to ensure that the output is feasible, not only in terms of data manipulation, but in terms of performance as well. There is no point in specifying infeasible output in a design.

- Once the person doing the volunteer scheduling has located a volunteer to fill a specific job, then the volunteer's commitment to work needs to become a part of the database. The process begins by presenting the user with a Find Volunteer dialog box like that in Figure 14.6. In this case, the Find button is linked to the Schedule Volunteer window (Figure 14.14). A database designer will recognize that this is not all the data the needs to be stored about a job, however. In particular, someone will need to record whether the volunteer actually appeared to do the scheduled job on the day of the job; this cannot be done when the job is scheduled initially.

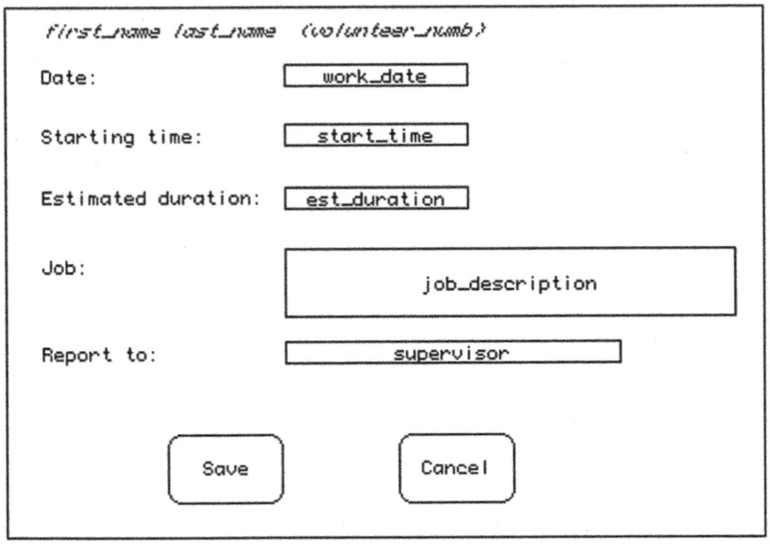

first_name last_name (volunteer_numb)

Date: work_date

Starting time: start_time

Estimated duration: est_duration

Job: job_description

Report to: supervisor

Save   Cancel

■FIGURE 14.14 Scheduling a volunteer to perform a job.

- To record attendance, an end user first locates the volunteer using a Find Volunteer dialog box (Figure 14.6), which then leads to a display of the jobs the volunteer has been scheduled to work in reverse chronological order (see Figure 14.15). For those jobs that have not been worked, the End Time and Worked? columns will be empty. The user can then scroll the list to find the job to be modified and enter

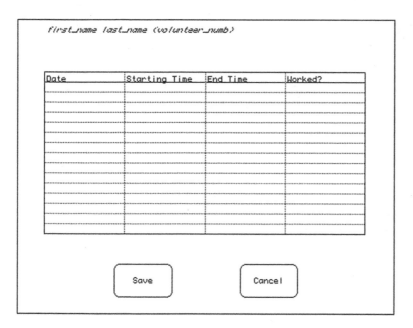

■ FIGURE 14.15 Recording jobs worked.

values for the two empty columns. The fields on this form, plus those on the job scheduling form, represent the attributes that will describe the job entity.

■ To print a daily schedule, an end user first uses a dialog box to indicate the date for which a schedule should be displayed (Figure 14.16). The application program then assembles the report (Figure 14.17). To simplify working with the program, the application developers should probably allow users to double-click on any line in the listing to open the form in Figure 14.15 for the scheduled volunteer. However, this capability will have no impact on the database design.

Creating the ER Diagram

From the approved prototype of the application design and conversations with the volunteers who do volunteer scheduling, the database designers can gather enough information to create a basic ER diagram for the volunteers organization. The designers examine each screen form carefully to ensure that the database design provides the attributes and relationships necessary to generate the output.

At first, the ER diagram (Figure 14.18) may seem overly complex. However, two of the entities—*state* and *day*—are present for referential integrity

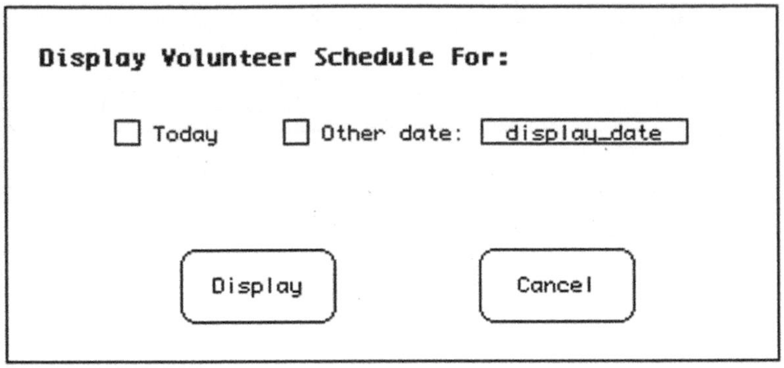

■ FIGURE 14.16 Choosing a date for schedule display.

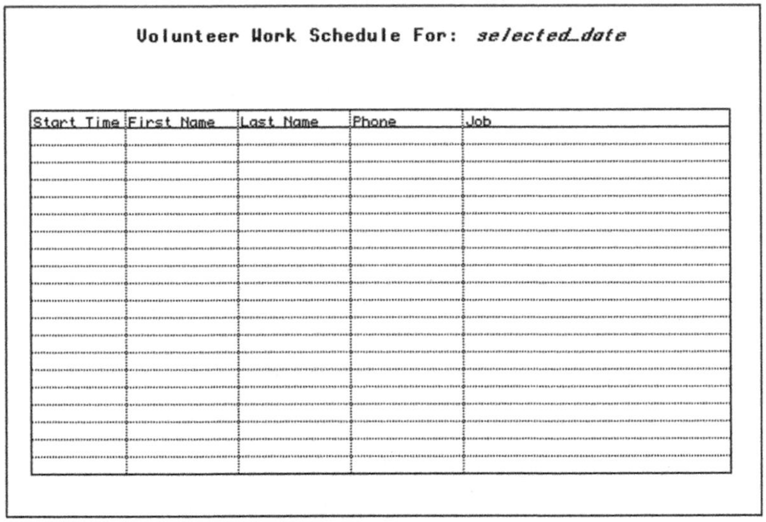

■ FIGURE 14.17 Volunteer work schedule.

purposes, ensuring that abbreviations for state and day names are entered consistently. The relationships between a volunteer, jobs, and skills also aren't quite as simple as they might seem at first, in part because there are several many-to-many relationships:

- There is a many-to-many relationship between volunteers and skills, which is handled by the *skills_known* entity.
- Because a job may require more than on volunteer, there is a many-to-many relationship between volunteers and jobs that is handled by the *volunteer_scheduled* entity.

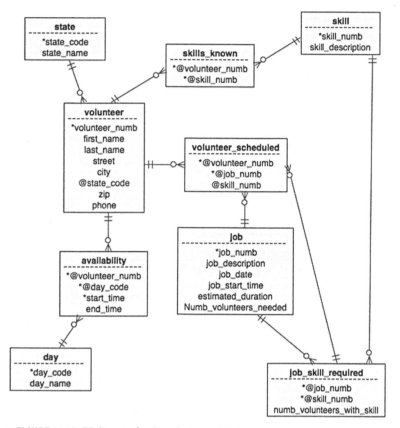

■FIGURE 14.18 ER diagram for the volunteers database.

- A job may require more than one skill and a skill is used on many jobs. The many-to-many relationship between a job and a skill is therefore handled by the *job_skill_required* entity.

Making the situation a bit more complex is that the meaning of the M:M relationship between *job* and *skill* (through *job_skill_required*) is used differently than the relationship between *volunteer_scheduled* and *job_skill_required*. A row is added to *job_skill_required* for each skill required by a job; these data are available when the job is requested. As volunteers are scheduled for the job, rows are added to *volunteer_scheduled*, creating the relationship between that entity and *job_skill_required*. (This is essential for determining the correct volunteers still needed to be scheduled for specific skills for a specific job.) The foreign key in *volunteer_scheduled* uses one column from the table's primary key (*job_numb*) and one non-key attribute (*skill_numb*). Nonetheless, that concatenation is exactly the same as the primary key of the *job_skill_required* table (same columns with the same meaning).

Designing the Tables

The ER diagram in Figure 14.18 produces the following tables:

volunteer (<u>volunteer_numb</u>, first_name, last_name, street,
    city, state_code, zip, phone)

state (<u>state_code</u>, state_name)

availability (<u>volunteer_numb</u>, <u>day_code</u>, <u>start_time</u>, end_time)

day (<u>day_code</u>, day_name)

skill (<u>skill_numb</u>, skill_description)

skills_known (<u>volunteer_numb</u>, <u>skill_numb</u>)

job (<u>job_numb</u>, job_description, job_date, job_start_time,
    estimated_duration, numb_volunteers_needed)

job_skill_required (<u>job_numb</u>, <u>skill_numb</u>,
    numb_volunteers_with_skill)

volunteer_scheduled (<u>volunteer_numb</u>, <u>job_numb</u>, skill_numb)

Generating the SQL

The nine tables that make up the volunteers database can be created with the SQL in Figure 14.19. Notice that some of the attributes in the volunteers table have been specified as NOT NULL. This constraint ensures that at least a name and phone number are available for each volunteer.

```
CREATE TABLE skill
(
  skill_numb integer,
  skill_description char (50),
  CONSTRAINT PK_skill PRIMARY KEY (skill_numb)
);

CREATE TABLE job
(
  job_numb integer,
  job_description varchar (256),
  job_date date,
  job_start_time time,
  estimated_duration interval,
  numb_volunteers_needed integer,
  CONSTRAINT PK_job PRIMARY KEY (job_numb)
);
```

■ FIGURE 14.19 SQL statements needed to create the tables for the volunteers database (continues).

```
CREATE TABLE job_skill_required
(
  job_numb integer,
  skill_numb integer,
  numb_volunteers_with_skill integer,
  CONSTRAINT PK_job_skill_required PRIMARY KEY (job_numb,skill_numb),
  CONSTRAINT Relationjobjob_skill_required1 FOREIGN KEY ()
     REFERENCES job,
  CONSTRAINT Relationskilljob_skill_required1 FOREIGN KEY ()
     REFERENCES skill
);

CREATE TABLE state
(
  state_code char (2),
  state_name char (15),
  CONSTRAINT PK_state PRIMARY KEY (state_code)
);

CREATE TABLE volunteer
(
  volunteer_numb integer,
  first_name char (15) NOT NULL,
  last_name char (15) NOT NULL,
  street char (50),
  city char (30),
  state_code char (2),
  zip char (10),
  phone char (10) NOT NULL,
  CONSTRAINT PK_volunteer PRIMARY KEY (volunteer_numb),
  CONSTRAINT Relationstatevolunteer1 FOREIGN KEY (state_code)
     REFERENCES state
);

CREATE TABLE volunteer_scheduled
(
  volunteer_numb integer,
  job_numb integer,
  skill_numb integer,
  CONSTRAINT PK_volunteer_scheduled PRIMARY KEY
     (volunteer_numb,job_numb),
  CONSTRAINT Relationvolunteervolunteer_scheduled1 FOREIGN KEY ()
     REFERENCES volunteer,
  CONSTRAINT Relationjobvolunteer_scheduled1 FOREIGN KEY ()
     REFERENCES job,
  CONSTRAINT Relationjob_skill_requiredvolunteer_scheduled1
     FOREIGN KEY () REFERENCES job_skill_required
);

CREATE TABLE skills_known
(
  volunteer_numb integer,
  skill_numb integer,
  CONSTRAINT PK_skills_known PRIMARY KEY (volunteer_numb,skill_numb),
  CONSTRAINT Relationvolunteerskills_known1 FOREIGN KEY
     (VOLUNTEER_NUMB) REFERENCES volunteer,
  CONSTRAINT Relationskillskills_known1 FOREIGN KEY (skill_numb)
     REFERENCES skill
);
```

■ FIGURE 14.19 (cont.)

```
CREATE TABLE day
(
  day_code char (3),
  day_name char (10),
  CONSTRAINT PK_day PRIMARY KEY (day_code)
);

CREATE TABLE availability
(
  volunteer_numb integer,
  day_code char (3),
  start_time time,
  end_time time,
  CONSTRAINT PK_availability PRIMARY KEY
      (volunteer_numb,day_code,start_time),
  CONSTRAINT Relationvolunteeravailability1 FOREIGN KEY
      (volunteer_numb) REFERENCES volunteer,
  CONSTRAINT Relationdayavailability1 FOREIGN KEY (day_code)
      REFERENCES day
);
```

■ FIGURE 14.19 (*cont.*)

The Animal Tracking Database

The animal tracking database is considerably bigger than the volunteers database. The application that will manipulate that database therefore is concomitantly larger, as demonstrated by the menu tree in Figure 14.20. (The File and Edit menus have been left off so the diagram will fit across the width of the page. However, they are intended to be the first and second menus from the left, respectively. A Help menu can also be added along the right side.)

The functionality requested by the animal handlers falls generally into four categories: the locations (the tanks) and their habitats, the species, the food,

Main menu

Locations	Species	Feeding	Sources
Add/modify/delete tank info	Add/modify/delete species	Add/modify/delete types of food	Add/modify/delete source
Add/modify/delete habitat info	Transfer species	Update food inventory	Add/modify/delete arriving shipment
Assign habitats to tanks	Find current species location	Print food reorder report	
Find a habitat	Find sources for species	Add/modify/delete feeding instructions	
Add/modify/delete maintenance info	Find where species can live	Print daily feeding schedule	
Add/modify/delete required maintenance	Add/modify/delete problem type	Print daily feeding schedule	
Add/modify/delete maintenance performed	Add/modify/delete problem type		
Print a maintenance schedule	Add/modify/delete problem occurrence		
	Add/modify/delete problem solutions		
	Print problem summary report		

■ FIGURE 14.20 Menu tree for the animal tracking application.

and the sources of animals. The organization of the application interface, therefore, was guided by those groups.

Highlights of the Application Prototype

The screen and report layouts designed for the animal tracking application provide a good starting place for the database designers to identify the entities and attributes needed in the database. As with the volunteers application, there is not necessarily a one-to-one correspondence between an entity and an output.

Note: One of the common mistakes made when designing the interface of database application programs is to use one data entry form per table. Users do not look at their environments in the same way as a database designer, however, and often the organization imposed by tables does not make sense to the users. Another benefit of prototyping is therefore that it forces database and application designers to adapt to what the users really need, rather than the other way around.

Food Management

One of the important functions mentioned by the aquarium's animal handlers was management of the aquarium feeding schedule (including what *should* be fed and what *was* fed), and the food inventory. First, they wanted a daily feeding schedule that could be printed and carried with them as they worked (for example, Figure 14.21). They also wanted to be able to record that feeding had occurred so that an updated feeding schedule could take prior feedings into account. Knowing that each species may eat more than one type of food and that each type of food can be eaten by many species, a database designer realizes that there are a number of entities required to implement what the users need:

- An entity that describes each species.
- An entity that describes each tank in the aquarium.
- An entity that describes a type of food.
- A composite entity between the *species* and *location* entities to record where a specific species can be found.
- A composite entity between a species and a type of food, recording which food a species eats, how much it eats, and how often it is fed.
- A composite entity between a species and a type of food, recording which food was fed to an animal, when it was fed, and how much it was fed.

Food inventory management—although it sounds like a separate application to the animal handlers—actually requires nothing more than the food entity. The food entity needs to store data about how much food is currently in stock (modified by data from the entity that describes what was fed and by manual entries made when shipments of food arrive) and a reorder point.

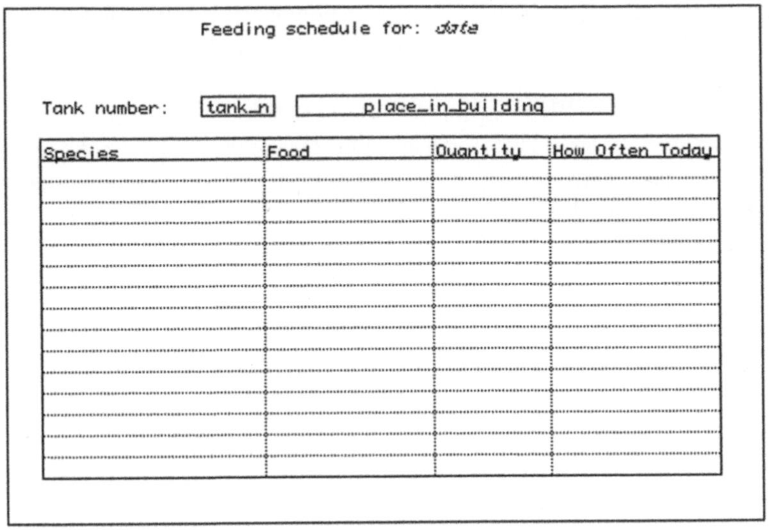

■ FIGURE 14.21 Daily feeding schedule.

Handling Arriving Animals

When a shipment of animals arrives at the aquarium, animal handlers first check the contents of the shipment against the shipment's paperwork. They then take the animals and place them in the aquarium's quarantine area. The data entry form that the animal handlers will use to store data about arrivals therefore includes a place for entering an identifier for the tank in which the new animals have been placed (Figure 14.22). Given that the aquarium staff needs to be able to locate animals at any time, this suggests that the quarantine tanks should be handled no differently from the exhibit tanks and that there is only one entity for a tank.

After the quarantine period has expired and the animals are certified as healthy, they can be transferred to another location in the building. This means an application program must delete the species from their current tank (regardless of whether it is a quarantine tank or an exhibit tank) and insert data for the new tank. The screen form (Figure 14.23) therefore lets the user identify the species and its current location using popup menus. The user also uses a popup menu to identify the new location. To the database designer, this translates into the modification of one row (if the species is new to the exhibit tank) or the modification of one row and the deletion of another (if some of the species already live in the exhibit tank) in the table that represents the relationship between a species and a tank. All the database designer needs to do, however, is to provide the table; the application program will take care of managing the data modification.

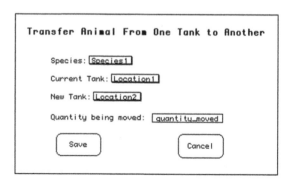

■ FIGURE 14.22 Recording the arrival of a shipment of animals.

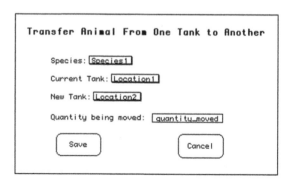

■ FIGURE 14.23 Moving a species between tanks.

Problem Analysis

The health of the animals in the aquarium is a primary concern of the animal handlers. They are therefore anxious to be able to analyze the problems that occur in the tanks for patterns. Perhaps a single species is experiencing more problems than any other; perhaps an animal handler is not paying as much attention to the condition of the tanks for which he or she is responsible.

The animal handlers want the information in Figure 14.24 included in the problem summary report. What cannot be seen from the summary screen created by the CASE tool is that the data will appear as a control-break layout. For example, each tank number will appear only once; each species will appear once for each tank in which it was the victim of a problem. By the same token, each type of problem will appear once for each tank and species it affected. Each type of problem also will appear once for each tank and species it affected. Only the problem solutions will contain data for every row in the sample output table.

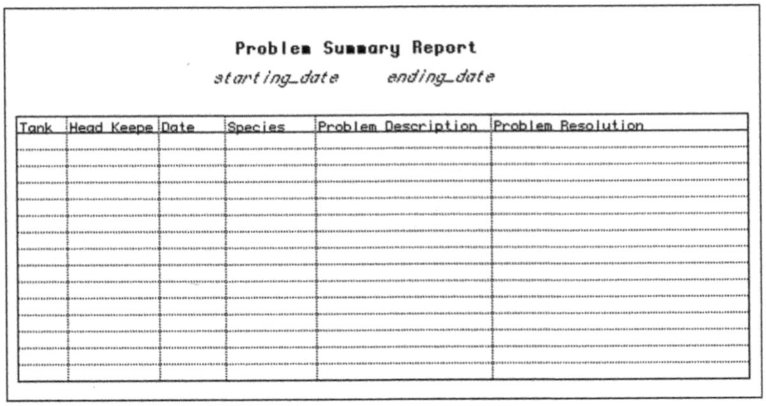

■ FIGURE 14.24 Problem summary report.

To a database designer, the form in Figure 14.24 suggests the need for five entities:

■ The species.
■ The tank.
■ The type of problem.
■ A problem occurrence (a type of problem occurring in one tank and involving one species).
■ Problem solutions (one or more solutions tried for one problem occurrence). There may be many solutions to a single problem occurrence.

One of the best ways to handle problems is to avoid them. For this reason, the animal handlers also want to include maintenance data in their database. To move data entry simpler for the end users, the form for entering required maintenance (Figure 14.25) lets a user select a tank and then enter as many maintenance activities as needed.

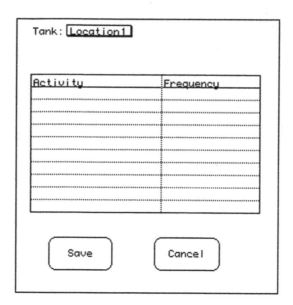

■ **FIGURE 14.25   Entering required maintenance.**

A database designer views such a form as requiring three entities: the tank, the maintenance activity, and the maintenance required for this tank (a composite entity between the tank and maintenance activity entities).

Creating the ER Diagram

After refining the entire application prototype (and giving it a far more attractive design than the rather dull output produced by the CASE tool), the database designers for the East Coast Aquarium generate a large interconnected ER diagram. (Part I can be found in Figure 14.26; part II appears in Figure 14.27.) As you can see, when examining both diagrams, the centerpiece is the *species* entity, which participates in seven different relationships.

There are at least 11 many-to-many relationships represented by this design:

- Species to location
- Location to habitat
- Species to habitat
- Location to maintenance activity for required maintenance
- Location to maintenance activity for maintenance performed
- Location to problem
- Species to problem
- Species to food

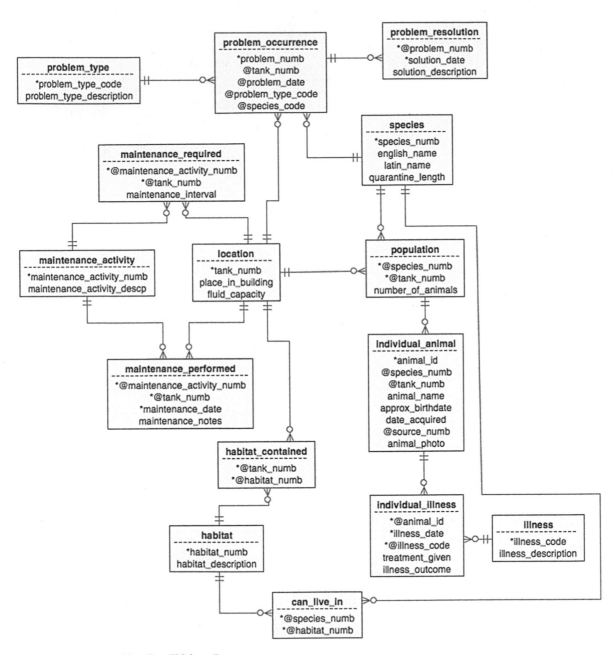

■FIGURE 14.26 Animal handling ERD (part I).

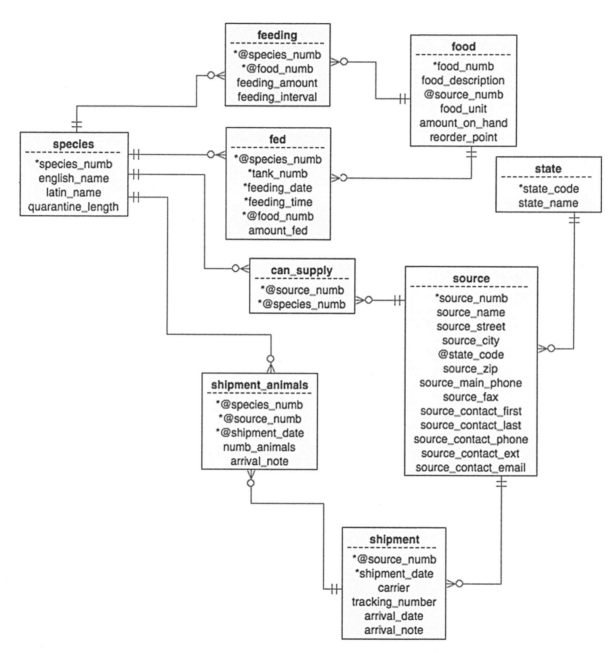

■ FIGURE 14.27 Animal handling ERD (part II).

- Species to source for ability of source to supply the species
- Shipment to species
- Illness to individual animal for tracking the condition of mammals and other large animals

The relationships involving location, problem, and species are particularly interesting. On the surface, there appears to be a many-to-many relationship between a tank and a type of problem. By the same token, there appears to be another many-to-many relationship between a species and a type of problem. The problem is that if the database maintained the two separate relationships, each with its own individual composite entity, then it will be impossible to determine which species was affected by which problem, in which tank. To resolve the issue, the designer uses a three-way composite entity—*problem_occurrence*— that relates three parent entities (*location*, *problem*, and *species*) rather than the traditional two. Semantically, a problem occurrence is one type of problem affecting one species in one location and therefore identifying it in the database requires all three parent entities.

In contrast, why is there no three-way composite entity between species, location, and habitat? As with the preceding example, there is a many-to-many relationship between species and location, and a many-to-many relationship between habitat and location. The answer, once again, lies in the meaning of the relationships. Were we to create a single composite entity relating all three entities, we would be asserting that a given species lives in a given habitat, in a given location. However, the animal handlers at the aquarium know that this type of data is not valid, particularly because if an animal lives in a tank with many habitats, it may move among multiple habitats. Instead, the relationship between species and habitat indicates all habitats in which a species can live successfully; the relationship between location and habitat indicates the habitats present in a tank.

The remainder of the many-to-many relationships are the typical two-parent relationships that you have been seeing throughout this book. The only aspect of these relationships that is the least bit unusual is the two relationships between maintenance activity and location. Each relationship has a different meaning (scheduled maintenance versus maintenance actually performed). The design therefore must include two composite entities, one to represent the meaning of each individual relationship.

Note: There is no theoretical restriction to the number of relationships that can exist between the same parent entities. As long as each relationship has a different meaning, there is usually justification for including all of them in a database design.

Creating the Tables

The ER diagrams translate to the following tables:

species (species_numb, English_name, latin_name,
    quarantine_length)

location (tank_numb, place_in_building, fluid_capacity)

population (species_numb, tank_numb, number_of_animals)

individual_animal (animal_id, species_numb, tank_numb,
    animal_name, approx_birthdate, source_numb, animal_photo)

illness (illness_code, illness_description)

individual_illness (animal_id, illness_date, illness_code,
    treatment_given, illness_outcome)

habitat (habitat_numb, habitat_description)

habitat_contained (tank_numb,habitat_numb)

can_live_in (species_numb, habitat_numb)

problem_type (problem_type_code, problem_type_description)

problem_occurrence (problem_numb, tank_numb, problem_date,
    problem_type_code, species_code)

problem_resolution (problem_numb, solution_date,
    solution_description)

maintenance_activity (maintenance_activity_numb,
    maintenance_activity_desc)

maintenance_required (maintenance_activity_numb, tank_numb,
    maintenance_interval)

maintenance_performed (maintenance_activity_numb, tank_numb,
    maintenance_date, maintenance_notes)

food (food_numb, food_description, source_numb, food_unit,
    amount_on_hand, reorder_point)

feeding (species_numb, food_numb, feeding_amount,
    feeding_interval)

fed (species_numb, tank_numb, feeding_date, feeding_time,
    food_numb, amount_fed)

```
state (state_code, state_name)

source (source_numb, source_name, source_street, source_city,
        state_code, source_zip, source_main_phone, source_fax,
        source_contact_first, source_contact_last,
        source_contact_phone, source_contact_ext,
        source_contact_email)

can_supply (source_numb, species_numb)

shipment (source_numb, shipment_nate, carrier,
        tracking_number, arrival_date, arrival_note)

shipment_animals (species_numb, source_numb, shipment_date,
        numb_animals, arrival_note)
```

Choosing a primary key for the *problem_occurrence* table presents a bit of a dilemma. Given that a problem occurrence represents a relationship between a problem type, tank, and species, the theoretically appropriate primary key is a concatenation of the problem type, tank number, species number, and problem date. However, this is an extremely awkward primary key to use as a foreign key in the *problem_resolution* table. Although it is unusual to give composite entities arbitrary unique keys, in this case it makes good practical sense.

There are several tables in this design that are "all key" (made up of nothing but the primary key). According to the CASE tool used to draw the ER diagram, this represents an error in the design. However, there is nothing in relational database theory that states that all-key relations are not allowed. In fact, they are rather common when they are needed to represent a many-to-many relationship that has no accompanying relationship data.

Generating the SQL

The SQL CREATE statements that generate the animal tracking database for East Coast Aquarium can be found in Figure 14.28. Because of the large number of composite entities, there are also a large number of foreign keys. Other than that, the SQL presents no unusual features.

```
CREATE TABLE state
(
  state_code char (2),
  state_name varchar (20),
  CONSTRAINT PK_STATE PRIMARY KEY (state_code)
);

CREATE TABLE source
(
  source_numb integer,
  source_name char (15),
  source_street varchar (500,
  source_city varchar (50),
  state_code char (2),
  source_zip char (10),
  source_main_phone char (10),
  source_fax char (10),
  source_contact_first char (15),
  source_contact_last char (15),
  source_contact_phone char (10),
  source_contact_ext char (5),
  source_contact_email varchar (256),
  CONSTRAINT PK_SOURCE PRIMARY KEY (source_numb),
  CONSTRAINT Relationstatesource1 FOREIGN KEY () REFERENCES STATE
);

CREATE TABLE shipment
(
  source_numb integer,
  shipment_date date,
  carrier varchar (30),
  tracking_number char (20),
  arrival_date date,
  arrival_note varchar (50,
  CONSTRAINT PK_SHIPMENT PRIMARY KEY (source_numb,shipment_date)
);

CREATE TABLE species
(
  species_numb integer,
  engish_name varchar (256),
  latin_name varchar (256),
  quarantine_length integer,
  CONSTRAINT PK_species PRIMARY KEY (species_numb)
);
```

■ FIGURE 14.28 SQL statements prepared by a CASE tool for the animal tracking database (continues).

```
CREATE TABLE shipment_animals
(
  species_numb integer,
  source_numb integer,
  shipment_date date,
  numb_animals integer,
  arrival_note varchar (256),
  CONSTRAINT PK_SHIPMENTANIMALS PRIMARY KEY (species_numb,source_numb,shipment_date)
);

CREATE TABLE can_supply
(
  source_numb integer,
  species_numb integer,
  CONSTRAINT PK_CAN_SUPPLY PRIMARY KEY (source_numb,species_numb),
  CONSTRAINT Relationspeciescan_supply1 FOREIGN KEY ()
      REFERENCES species,
  CONSTRAINT Relationsourcecan_supply1 FOREIGN KEY () REFERENCES SOURCE
);

CREATE TABLE food
(
  food_numb integer,
  food_description varchar (256),
  source_numb integer,
  food_unit char (10),
  amount_on_hand integer,
  reorder_point integer,
  CONSTRAINT PK_food PRIMARY KEY (food_numb)
);

CREATE TABLE fed
(
  species_numb integer,
  feeding_date date,
  feeding_time time,
  tank_numb integer,
  food_numb integer,
  amount_fed integer,
  CONSTRAINT PK_fed PRIMARY KEY
      (species_numb,tank_numb,feeding_date,feeding_time,food_numb),
  CONSTRAINT Relationspeciesfed1 FOREIGN KEY () REFERENCES species,
  CONSTRAINT Relationfoodfed1 FOREIGN KEY () REFERENCES food
);
```

■ **FIGURE 14.28** (*cont.*)

```
CREATE TABLE feeding
(
  species_numb integer,
  food_numb integer,
  feeding_amount integer,
  feeding_interval interval,
  CONSTRAINT PK_feeding PRIMARY KEY (species_numb,food_numb),
  CONSTRAINT Relationspeciesfeeding1 FOREIGN KEY () REFERENCES species,
  CONSTRAINT Relationfoodfeeding1 FOREIGN KEY () REFERENCES food
);
CREATE TABLE location
(
  tank_numb integer,
  place_in_building char (6),
  fluid_capacity integer,
  CONSTRAINT PK_location PRIMARY KEY (tank_numb)
);
CREATE TABLE problem_type
(
  problem_type_code integer,
  problem_type_description varchar(256),
  CONSTRAINT PK_problem_type PRIMARY KEY (problem_type_code)
);
CREATE TABLE problem_occurrence
(
  problem_numb integer,
  tank_numb integer,
  problem_date date,
  problem_type_code integer,
  species_code integer,
  CONSTRAINT PK_problem_occurrence PRIMARY KEY (problem_numb),
  CONSTRAINT Relationproblem_typeproblem_occurrence1 FOREIGN KEY ()
      REFERENCES problem_type,
  CONSTRAINT Relationproblem_occurrencelocation1 FOREIGN KEY ()
      REFERENCES location,
  CONSTRAINT Relationspeciesproblem_occurrence1 FOREIGN KEY ()
      REFERENCES species
);
CREATE TABLE problem_resolution
(
  problem_numb integer,
  solution_date date,
  solution_description varchar (256),
  CONSTRAINT PK_problem_resolution## PRIMARY KEY
      (problem_numb,solution_date),
  CONSTRAINT Relationproblem_occurrenceproblem_resolution1
      FOREIGN KEY () REFERENCES problem_occurrence
);
```

■ FIGURE 14.28 *(cont.)*

```
CREATE TABLE habitat
(
  habitat_numb integer,
  habitat_description varchar (256),
  CONSTRAINT PK_habitat PRIMARY KEY (habitat_numb)
);

CREATE TABLE can_live_in
(
  species_numb integer,
  habitat_numb integer,
  CONSTRAINT PK_can_live_in PRIMARY KEY (species_numb,habitat_numb),
  CONSTRAINT Relationhabitatcan_live_in1 FOREIGN KEY ()
      REFERENCES habitat
);

CREATE TABLE habitat_contained
(
  tank_numb integer,
  habitat_numb integer,
  CONSTRAINT PK_habitat_contained PRIMARY KEY (tank_numb,habitat_numb),
  CONSTRAINT Relationlocationhabitat_contained1 FOREIGN KEY ()
      REFERENCES location,
  CONSTRAINT Relationhabitathabitat_contained1 FOREIGN KEY ()
      REFERENCES habitat
);

        CREATE TABLE maintenance_activity
(
  maintenance_activity_numb integer,
  maintenance_activity varchar (256),
  CONSTRAINT PK_maintenance_activity
        PRIMARY KEY (maintenance_activity_numb)
);

CREATE TABLE maintenance_performed
(
  maintenance_activity_numb integer,
  tank_numb integer,
  maintenance_date date,
  maintenance_notes varchar (256),
  CONSTRAINT PK_maintenance_performed PRIMARY KEY
        (maintenance_activity_numb,tank_numb,maintenance_date),
  CONSTRAINT Relationmaintenance_activitymaintenance_performed1
        FOREIGN KEY () REFERENCES maintenance_activity,
  CONSTRAINT Relationlocationmaintenance_performed1 FOREIGN KEY ()
        REFERENCES location
);
```

■ **FIGURE 14.28** *(cont.)*

```
CREATE TABLE maintenance_required
(
  maintenance_activity_numb integer,
  tank_numb integer,
  maintenance_interval interval,
  CONSTRAINT PK_maintenance_required PRIMARY KEY
        (maintenance_activity_numb,tank_numb),
  CONSTRAINT Relationmaintenance_requiredmaintenance_activity1
        FOREIGN KEY () REFERENCES maintenance_activity,
  CONSTRAINT Relationlocationmaintenance_required1 FOREIGN KEY ()
        REFERENCES location
);

CREATE TABLE illness
(
  illness_code integer,
  illness_description varchar (256),
  CONSTRAINT PK_illness PRIMARY KEY (illness_code)
);

CREATE TABLE population
(
  species_numb integer,
  tank_numb integer,
  number_of_animals integer,
  CONSTRAINT PK_population PRIMARY KEY (species_numb,tank_numb),
  CONSTRAINT Relationspeciespopulation1 FOREIGN KEY ()
        REFERENCES species,
  CONSTRAINT Relationlocationpopulation1 FOREIGN KEY ()
        REFERENCES location
);

CREATE TABLE individual_animal
(
  animal_id integer,
  species_numb integer,
  tank_numb integer,
  animal_name varchar (50),
  approx_birthdate char (10),
  date_acquired date,
  source_numb integer,
  animal_photo blob,
  CONSTRAINT PK_individual_animal PRIMARY KEY (animal_id),
  CONSTRAINT Relationpopulationindividual_animal1 FOREIGN KEY ()
        REFERENCES population
);
```

■ **FIGURE 14.28** *(cont.)*

```
CREATE TABLE individual_illness
(
  animal_id integer,
  illness_date date,
  illness_code integer,
  treatment_given varchar (256),
  illness_outcome varchar (256),
  CONSTRAINT PK_individual_illness
        PRIMARY KEY (animal_id,illness_date,illness_code),
  CONSTRAINT Relationindividual_animalindividual_illness1
        FOREIGN KEY () REFERENCES individual_animal,
  CONSTRAINT Relationillnessindividual_illness1
        FOREIGN KEY () REFERENCES illness
);
```

■ FIGURE 14.28 (*cont.*)

Chapter
15 Database Design Case Study #3: SmartMart

Many retail chains today maintain both a Web and a brick-and-mortar presence in the marketplace. Doing so presents a special challenge for inventory control because the inventory is shared between physical stores and Web sales. The need to allow multiple shipping addresses and multiple payment methods within a single order also adds complexity to Web selling. Online shopping systems also commonly allow users to store information about multiple credit cards.

To familiarize you with what is necessary to maintain the data for such a business, we'll be looking at a database for SmartMart, a long-established retailer with 325 stores across North America that has expanded into Web sales. SmartMart began as a local grocery store, but over the years has expanded to carry clothing, sundries, home furnishings, hardware, and electronics. Some stores still have grocery departments; others carry just "dry" goods.

In addition to the retail stores, SmartMart maintains four regional warehouses that supply the stores as well as ship products ordered over the Web.

The Merchandising Environment

SmartMart has three major areas for which it wants an integrated database: in-store sales, Web sales, and some limited Human Resources needs. The sales data must be compatible with accounting systems to simplify data transfer. In addition, both the in-store sales and Web sales applications must use the same data about products.

Product Requirements

The products that SmartMart sells are stocked throughout the company's stores, although every store does not carry every product. The database must therefore include data about the following:

- Products
- Stores
- Departments within stores
- Products stocked within a specific department
- Current sales promotions for a specific product

The store and department data will need to be integrated with the database's Human Resources data.

In-Store Sales Requirements

The data describing in-store sales serve two purposes: accounting and inventory control. Each sale (whether paid with cash or credit) must decrement inventory and provide an audit trail for accounting.

Retaining data about in-store sales is also essential to SmartMart's customer service reputation. The company offers a 15-day return period, during which a customer can return any product with which he or she is not satisfied. Store receipts therefore need to identify entire sales transactions, in particular which products were purchased during a specific transaction.

Because the company operates in multiple US states, there is a wide variety of sales tax requirements. Which products are taxed varies among states, as well as the sales tax rates. The database must therefore include sales tax where necessary as a part of an in-store transaction.

The database must distinguish between cash and credit transactions. The database will not store customer data about cash transactions, but must retain card numbers, expiration dates, and customer names on credit sales.

Web Sales Requirements

Web sales add another layer of complexity to the SmartMart data environment. The Web application must certainly have access to the same product data as the in-store sales, but must also integrate with a shopping cart application.

To provide the most flexibility, SmartMart wants to allow customers to store multiple shipping addresses, to ship to multiple addresses on the same order, and to store multiple credit card data from which a customer can choose when checking out. In addition, customers are to be given a choice as to whether to pick up their order or have it shipped. The Web application must therefore have access to data about which stores are in a customer's area and which products are available at each store, the same inventory information used by in-store applications.

Finally, the Web application must account for backorders and partial shipments. This means that a shipment is not the same as a Web order, whereas an in-store sale delivers its items at one time. (Should an in-store customer want to purchase an item that is not in stock, the item will be handled as if it were a Web order.)

Personnel Requirements

Although a complete personnel database is beyond the scope of this case, SmartMart's management does want to be able to integrate some basic HR functions into the database, especially the scheduling of "sales associates" to specific departments in specific stores. The intent is to eventually be able use an expert system to analyze sales and promotion data to determine staffing levels and to move employees among the stores in a region as needed.

Putting Together an ERD

As you might expect, the SmartMart ERD is fairly large. It therefore has been broken into three parts to make it easier to see and understand.

Stores, Products, and Employees

As you can see in Figure 15.1 (the first third of the ERD), the SmartMart database begins with four "foundation" entities (entities that are only at the "one" end of 1:M relationships): *employee*, *store*, *warehouse*, and *product*.

The *store* and *warehouse* entities, at least at this time, have exactly the same attributes. It certainly would be possible to use a single entity representing any place products were kept. This would remove some of the complexity that arises when locating a product. However, there is no way to be certain that the data stored about a store and a warehouse will remain the same over the life of the database. Separating them into two entities after the database has been in use for some time would be very difficult and time

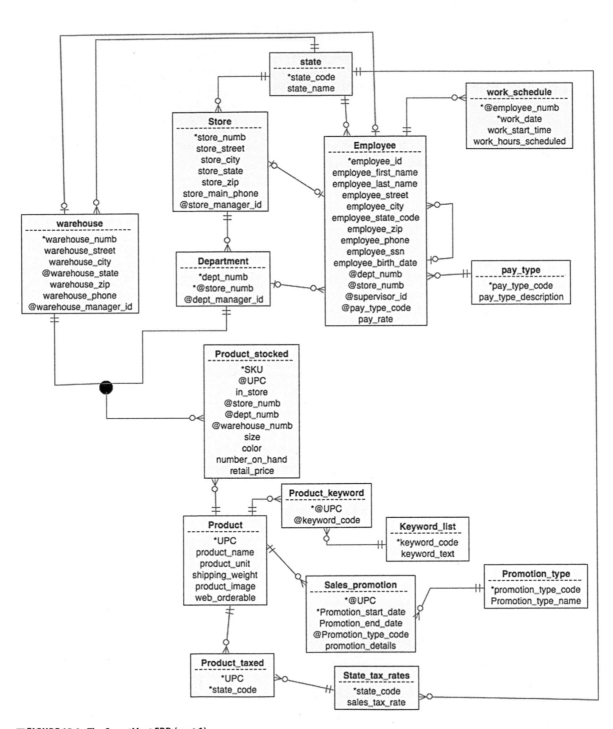

■ FIGURE 15.1 The SmartMart ERD (part 1).

consuming. Therefore, the choice was made to handle them as two distinct entities from the beginning.

Reference Entities

There are also several entities that are included for referential integrity purposes (*state*, *keyword_list*, *pay_type*, *promotion_type*). These entities become necessary because the design attempts to standardize text descriptions by developing collections of acceptable text descriptions and then using a numbering scheme to link the descriptions to places where they are used. There are two major benefits to doing this.

First, when the text descriptions, such as a type of pay (for example, hourly versus salaried), are standardized, searches will be more accurate. Assume, for example, that the pay types haven't been standardized. An employee who is paid hourly might have a pay type of "hourly," "HOURLY," "hrly," and so on. A search that retrieves all rows with a pay type of "hourly" will miss any rows with "HOURLY" or "hrly," however.

Second, using integers to represent values from the standardized list of text descriptions saves space in the database. Given the relative low price of disk storage, this usually isn't a major consideration.

The drawback, of course, is that when you need to search on or display the text description, the relation containing the standardized list and the relation using the integers representing the terms must be joined. Joins are relatively slow activities, but, in this case, the reference relation containing the master list of text descriptions will be relatively small; the join uses integer columns, which are quick to match. Therefore, unless for some reason the reference relation becomes extremely large, the overhead introduced by the join is minimal.

Circular Relationships

If you look closely at the *employee* entity in Figure 15.1, you'll see a relationship that seems to relate the entity to itself. In fact, this is exactly what that circular relationship does. It represents the idea that a person who supervises other employees is also an employee: The *supervisor_id* attribute is drawn from the same domain as *employee_id*. Each supervisor is related to many employees and each employee has only one supervisor.

There is always a temptation to create a separate *supervisor* entity. Given that a supervisor must also be an employee, however, the *supervisor* entity would contain data duplicated from the *employee* entity. This means that we introduce unnecessary duplicated data into the database and run a major risk of data inconsistencies.

Note: To retrieve a list of supervisors and who they supervise, someone using SQL would join a copy of the employee table to itself, matching the supervisor_id column in one table to the employee_id column in the other. The result table would contain data for two employees in each row (the employee and the employee's supervisor) that could be manipulated—in particular, sorted—for output, as needed.

Mutually Exclusive Relationships

There is one symbol on the ERD in Figure 15.1 that has not been used before in this book: the small circle that sits in the middle of the relationships between a stocked product, a department (in a store), and a warehouse. This type of structure indicates a *mutually exclusive* relationship. A given product can be stocked in a store or in a warehouse, but not both. (This holds true for this particular data environment because a product stocked represents physical items to be sold.)

The structure of the *product_stocked* entity reflects its participation in this type of relationship. In particular, it contains a Boolean column (*in_store*) that holds a value of true if the product is stocked in a store; a value of false indicates that the product is stocked in a warehouse. The value of the *in_store* attribute will then tell a user whether to use the *warehouse_numb* column or the concatenation of the *store_numb* column with the *dept_numb* attribute to find the actual location of an item.

One-to-one Relationships

Earlier in this book, you read that true one-to-one relationships are relatively rare. There are, however, three of them visible in Figure 15.1. All involve employees that manage something: a store, a department within a store, or a warehouse. A corporate unit may have one manager at a time, or it may have no manager; an employee may be the manager of one corporate unit or the manager of none. It is the rules of this particular database environment that make the one-to-one relationships valid.

In-store Sales

The second part of the ERD (Figure 15.2) deals with in-store sales. The data that are common to cash and credit sales are stored in the *in_store_sale* entity. These data are all that are needed for a cash sale. Credit sales, however, require data about the credit card used (the *credit_sale_details* entity). Notice that there is therefore a one-to-one relationship between *in_store_sale* and *credit_sale_details*. The two-entity design is not

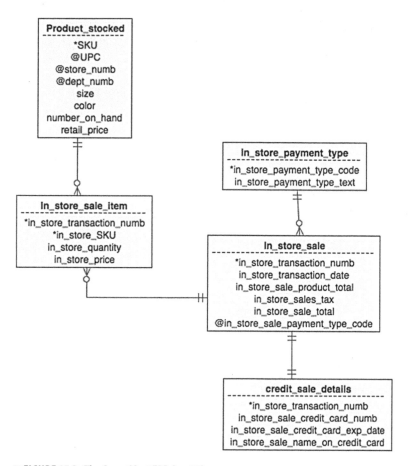

required for a good database design, but has been chosen for performance reasons with the assumption that although currently there are more credit/debit than cash transactions, the data retrieval is very skewed, requiring customer data far more frequently than credit card details. It therefore is a way of providing horizontal partitioning for an access pattern that is "unbalanced." In other words, a small proportion of the queries of sales data will need credit data.

After SmartMart's database has been in production for some time, the database administrator can look at the actual proportion of retrievals that need the credit card details. If a large proportion of the retrievals include the credit/debit data, then it may make sense to combine *in_store_sale* and *credit_sale_details* into a single entity and simply leave the credit detail columns as null for cash sales. Although some space will be wasted, the combined design avoids the need to perform a lengthy join when retrieving data about a credit sale.

Web Sales

The third portion of the ERD (Figure 15.3) deals with Web sales. Each Web sale uses only one credit card, but a Web customer may keep more than

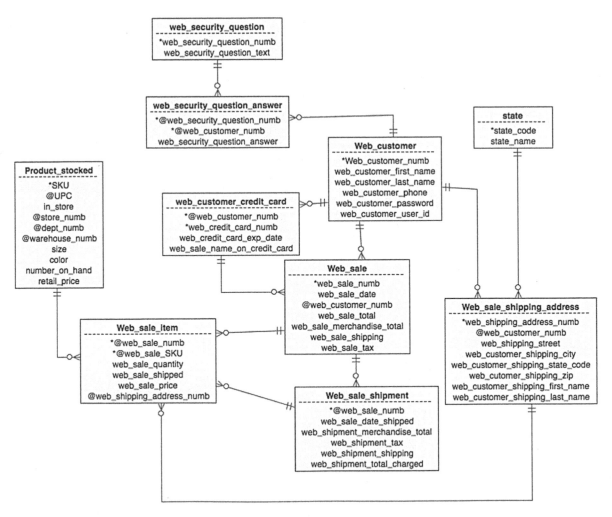

■ FIGURE 15.3 The SmartMart ERD (part 3).

one credit card number within SmartMart's database. A customer may also keep more than one shipping address; multiple shipping addresses can be used within the same order. (Multiple credit cards for a single order are not supported.)

At first glance, it might appear that the three relationships linking *web_customer*, *web_sale*, and *web_customer_credit_card* form a circular relationship. However, the meaning of the relationships is such that the circle does not exist:

- The direct relationship between *web_customer* and *web_customer_credit_card* represents the cards that a web customer has allowed to be stored in the SmartMart database. The credit card data are retrieved when the customer is completing a purchase. He or she chooses one for the current order.
- The relationship between *web_customer* and *web_sale* connects a purchase to a customer.
- The relationship between *web_customer_credit_card* and *web_sale* represents the credit card used for a specific order.

It can be difficult to discern such subtle differences in meaning from a simple ERD. There are two solutions: define the meaning of the relationships in the data dictionary or add relationship names to the ERD.

The *web_sale_shipping_address* entity is used to display addresses from which a user can choose. However, because items within the same shipment can be sent to different addresses, there is a many-to-many relationship between *web_sale* and *web_sale_shipping_address*. The *web_sale_item* resolves that many-to-many relationship into two one-to-many relationships.

The relationship between *web_sale*, *web_sale_item*, and *web_sale_shipment* is ultimately circular, as it appears in the ERD. However, at the time the order is placed, there are no instances of the *web_sale_shipment* entity because no items have shipped. The circle is closed when items actually ship. SmartMart's database can handle multiple shipments for a single order. However, each item on an order is sent to the customer in a single shipment. How do we know this? Because here is a 1:M relationship between a web sale and a web sale shipment (a sale may have many shipments) and a 1:M relationship between a shipment and an item on the order (each item is shipped as part of only one shipment).

Creating the Tables

The ERDs you have just seen produce the following tables, listed in alphabetical order:

credit_sale_details (<u>in_store_transaction_numb</u>,
        in_store_sale_credit_card_numb, in_store_exp_date,
        in_store_sale_name_on_credit_card)

department (<u>dept_numb</u>, store_numb, dept_manager_id)

employee (<u>employee_id</u>, employee_first_name, employee_last_name,
        employee_street, employee_city, employee_state_code,
        employee_zip, employee_phone, employee_ssn,
        employee_birth_date, dept_id, store_numb, supervisor_id,
        pay_type_code, pay_rate)

in_store_payment_type (<u>in_store_payment_type_code</u>,
        in_store_payment_type_text)

in_store_sale (<u>in_store_transaction_numb</u>,
        in_store_transaction_date, in_store_sale_product_total,
        in_store_sales_tax, in_store_total,
        in_store_payment_type_code)

in_store_sale_item (<u>in_store_sale_transaction_numb</u>,
        <u>in_store_SKU</u>, in_store_quantity, in_store_price)

keyword_list (<u>keyword_code</u>, keyword_text)

pay_type (<u>pay_type_code</u>, pay_type_description)

product (<u>UPC</u>, product_name, product_unit, shipping_weight,
        product_image, web_orderable)

product_keyword (<u>UPC</u>, <u>keyword_code</u>)

product_stocked (<u>SKU</u>, UPC, in_store, store_numb, dept_numb,
        warehouse_numb, size, color, number_on_hand, retail_price)

product_taxed (<u>UPC</u>, <u>state_code</u>)

promotion_type (<u>promotion_type_code</u>, promotion_type_name)

sales_promotion (<u>UPC</u>, promotion_start_date, promotion_end_date,
        promotion_type_code, promotion_details)

state (<u>state_code</u>, state_name)

state_tax_rates (<u>state_code</u>, sales_tax_rate)

store (<u>store_numb</u>, store_street, store_city, store_state_code,
        store_zip, store_main_phone, store_manager_id)

```
warehouse (warehouse_id, warehouse_street, warehouse_city,
    ware_house_state_code, warehouse_zip, warehouse_phone,
    warehouse_manager_id)

web_customer (web_customer_numb, web_customer_first_name,
    web_customer_last_name, web_customer_phone,
    web_customer_password, web_customer_user_id)

web_customer_credit_card (web_customer_numb,
    web_credit_card_numb, web_credit_card_exp_date,
    web_sale_name_on_credit_card)

web_sale (web_sale_numb, web_sale_date, web_customer_numb,
    web_sale_total, web_sale_merchandise_total,
    web_sale_shipping,web_sale_tax)

web_sale_item (web_sale_numb, web_sale_SKU,
    web_sale_quantity, web_sale_shipped, web_sale_price,
    web_shipping_address_numb)

web_sale_shipment (web_sale_numb, web_sale_date_shipped,
    web_shipment_merchandise_total, web_shipment_tax,
    web_shipment_shipping, web_shipment_total_charged)

web_sale_shipping_address (web_shipping_address_numb,
    web_customer_numb, web_shipping_street,
    web_shipping_city, web_shipping_state_code,
    web_customer_zip, web_customer_shipping_first_name,
    web_customer_shipping_last_name)

web_security_question (web_security_question_numb,
    web_security_question_text)

web_security_question_answer (web_security_question_numb,
    web_customer_numb, web_security_answer_text)

work_schedule (employee_id, work_date, work_start_time,
    work_hours_scheduled)
```

Because of the circulation relationship between a supervisor, who must be an employee, and an employee being supervised, the employee table contains a foreign key that references the primary key of its own table: *supervisor_id* is a foreign key referencing *employee_id*. There is nothing wrong with this type of design. The definition of a foreign key states only that the foreign key is the same as the primary key of some table; it does not rule out the foreign key referencing the primary key of its own table.

Generating the SQL

The case tool that generated the SQL misses some very important foreign keys—the relationships between employees and various other entities—because the two columns don't have the same name. Therefore, the database designer must add the constraints manually to the foreign key tables' CREATE TABLE statements:

```
employee table: FOREIGN KEY (supervisor_id)
     REFERENCES employee (employee_id)

warehouse table: FOREIGN KEY (warehouse_manager_id)
     REFERENCES employee (employee_id)

department table: FOREIGN KEY (department_manager_id)
     REFERENCES employee (employee_id)

store table: FOREIGN KEY (store_manager_id)
     REFERENCES employee (employee_id)
```

The manual foreign key insertions could have been avoided, had the manager IDs in the warehouse, department, and store tables been given the name *employee_id*. However, it is more important in the long-run to have the column names reflect the meaning of the columns.

There is also one foreign key missing of the two needed to handle the mutually exclusive relationship between a product stocked and either a department (in a store) or a warehouse. The foreign key from *product_stocked* to department is present, but not the reference to the warehouse table. The database designer must, therefore, add the following to the *product_stocked* table:

```
FOREIGN KEY (warehouse_numb)
     REFERENCES warehouse (warehouse_numb)
```

Won't there be a problem with including the two constraints, if only one can be valid for any single row in *product_stocked*? Not at all. Remember that referential integrity constraints are only used when the foreign key is not null. Therefore, a product stocked in a warehouse will have a value in its *warehouse_numb* column, but null in the *store_numb* and *dept_numb* columns. The reverse is also true: A product stocked in a store will have values in its *store_numb* and *dept_numb* columns, but null in the *warehouse_numb* column.

The foreign key relationships to the *state* reference relation must also be added manually, because the foreign key columns do not have the same name as the primary key column in the *state* table. Whether to use the same name throughout the database (*state_name*) is a design decision. If all tables that contain a state use the same name, foreign keys will be added automatically by the CASE tool. However, depending on the way in which the states are used, it may be difficult to distinguish among them, if the column names are all the same (Figure 15.4).

```
CREATE TABLE state
(
  state_code char (2),
  state_name char (15),
  CONSTRAINT PK_state PRIMARY KEY (state_code),
  CONSTRAINT RelationstateState_tax_rates1 FOREIGN KEY ()
      REFERENCES state_tax_rates
);

CREATE TABLE warehouse
(
  warehouse_id integer,
  warehouse_street char (50),
  warehouse_city char (3),
  wharehouse_state_code char (2),
  warehouse_zip char (10),
  warehouse_phone char (12),
  warehouse_manager_id integer,
  CONSTRAINT PK_warehouse PRIMARY KEY (warehouse_id)
);

CREATE TABLE state_tax_rates
(
  state_code char (2),
  sales_tax_rate number (5,20),
  CONSTRAINT PK_state_tax_rates PRIMARY KEY (state_code),
  CONSTRAINT RelationstateState_tax_rates1 FOREIGN KEY ()
      REFERENCES state
);

CREATE TABLE product
(
  UPC char (15),
  product_name varchar (256),
  product_unit char (10),
  shipping_weight integer,
  product_image blob,
  web_orderable boolean,
  CONSTRAINT PK_product PRIMARY KEY (UPC)
);

CREATE TABLE product_taxed
(
  UPC integer,
  state_code integer,
  CONSTRAINT PK_product_taxed PRIMARY KEY (UPC,state_code),
  CONSTRAINT RelationProductProduct_taxed1 FOREIGN KEY ()
      REFERENCES product,
  CONSTRAINT RelationState_tax_ratesProduct_taxed1 FOREIGN KEY ()
      REFERENCES state_tax_rates
);
```

■ **FIGURE 15.4   SQL CREATE statements for the SmartMart database (continues).**

```
CREATE TABLE In_store_payment_type
(
  in_store_payment_type_code integer,
  in_store_payment_type_text char (10),
  CONSTRAINT PK_In_store_payment_type PRIMARY KEY
      (in_store_payment_type_code)
);

CREATE TABLE web_customer
(
  web_customer_numb integer,
  web_customer_first_name char (15),
  web_customer_last_name INTEGER,
  web_customer_phone char (12),
  web_customer_password char (15),
  web_customer_user_id char (15),
  CONSTRAINT PK_web_customer PRIMARY KEY (web_customer_number)
);

CREATE TABLE web_sale_shipping_address
(
  web_shipping_address_numb integer,
  web_customer_numb integer,
  web_shipping_street char (50),
  web_customer_shipping_city char (50),
  web_customer_shipping_state_code char (2),
  eb_cutomer_shipping_zip char (10),
  web_customer_shipping_first_name char (15),
  web_customer_shipping_last_name char (15),
  CONSTRAINT PK_web_sale_shipping_address
      PRIMARY KEY (web_shipping_address_numb),
  CONSTRAINT RelationWeb_customerWeb_sale_shipping_address1
      FOREIGN KEY () REFERENCES web_customer,
  CONSTRAINT RelationstateWeb_sale_shipping_address1
      FOREIGN KEY () REFERENCES state
);

CREATE TABLE web_customer_credit_card
(
  web_customer_numb integer,
  web_credit_card_numb char (16),
  web_credit_card_exp_date date,
  web_sale_name_on_credit_card varchar (50),
  CONSTRAINT PK_web_customer_credit_card
      PRIMARY KEY (web_customer_numb,web_credit_card_numb),
  CONSTRAINT RelationWeb_customerweb_customer_credit_card1
      FOREIGN KEY () REFERENCES web_customer
);
```

■ FIGURE 15.4 (*cont.*)

```
CREATE TABLE web_sale
(
  web_sale_numb integer,
  web_sale_date date,
  web_customer_numb integer,
  web_sale_total number (7,2),
  web_sale_merchandise_total number (6,2),
  web_sale_shipping number (6,2),
  web_sale_tax number (6,2),
  CONSTRAINT PK_web_sale PRIMARY KEY (web_sale_numb),
  CONSTRAINT RelationWeb_customerWeb_sale1 FOREIGN KEY ()
      REFERENCES web_customer,
  CONSTRAINT Relationweb_customer_credit_cardWeb_sale1
      FOREIGN KEY () REFERENCES web_customer_credit_card
);

CREATE TABLE web_sale_shipment
(
  web_sale_numb inter,
  web_sale_date_shipped date,
  web_shipment_merchandise_total number(7,2),
  web_shipment_tax number (6,2),
  web_shipment_shipping number (6,2),
  web_shipment_total_charged number (6,2),
  CONSTRAINT PK_web_sale_shipment PRIMARY KEY (web_sale_numb),
  CONSTRAINT RelationWeb_saleWeb_sale_shipment1
      FOREIGN KEY () REFERENCES web_sale
);

CREATE TABLE pay_type
(
  pay_type_code integer,
  pay_type_description varhar (10),
  CONSTRAINT PK_pay_type PRIMARY KEY (pay_type_code)
);
```

■ **FIGURE 15.4** (*cont.*)

```
CREATE TABLE employee
(
  employee_id integer,
  employee_first_name varchar (15),
  employee_last_name integer,
  employee_street varchar (50),
  employee_city varchar (50),
  employee_state_code char (2),
  employee_zip char (10),
  employee_phone char (12),
  employee_ssn char (11),
  employee_birth_date date,
  dept_id integer,
  store_numb integer,
  supervisor_id integer,
  pay_type_code integer,
  pay_rate number (10,2),
  CONSTRAINT PK_employee PRIMARY KEY (employee_id),
  CONSTRAINT RelationEmployeeDepartment1
      FOREIGN KEY () REFERENCES department,
  CONSTRAINT Relationpay_typeEmployee1
      FOREIGN KEY () REFERENCES pay_type,
  CONSTRAINT RelationEmployeestate1
      FOREIGN KEY () REFERENCES state
);

CREATE TABLE department
(
  dept_numb integer,
  store_numnb integer,
  dept_manager_id integer,
  CONSTRAINT PK_department PRIMARY KEY (dept_numb,store_numnb),
  CONSTRAINT RelationStoreDepartment1 FOREIGN KEY () REFERENCES Store
);

CREATE TABLE store
(
  store_numb integer,
  store_street char (50),
  store_city char (50),
  store_state_code char (2),
  store_zip char (10),
  store_main_phone char (12),
  store_manager_id integer,
  CONSTRAINT PK_Store PRIMARY KEY (store_numb)
);
```

■ FIGURE 15.4 (*cont.*)

```
CREATE TABLE work_schedule
(
  employee_numb integer,
  work_date date,
  work_start_time time,
  work_hours_scheduled integer,
  CONSTRAINT PK_work_schedule PRIMARY KEY (employee_numb,work_date),
  CONSTRAINT RelationEmployeeWork_schedule2
      FOREIGN KEY () REFERENCES employee
);

CREATE TABLE credit_sale_details
(
  in_store_transaction_numb integer,
  in_store_sale_credit_card_numb char (16),
  in_store_exp_date date,
  in_store_sale_name_on_credit_card varchar (50),
  CONSTRAINT PK_credit_sale_details
      PRIMARY KEY (in_store_transaction_numb)
);

CREATE TABLE promotion_type
(
  promotion_type_code integer,
  promotion_type_name INTEGER,
  CONSTRAINT PK_Promotion_type PRIMARY KEY (promotion_type_code)
);

CREATE TABLE keyword_list
(
  keyword__code integer,
  keyword_text varchar (50),
  CONSTRAINT PK_keyword_list PRIMARY KEY (keyword__code)
);

CREATE TABLE product_keyword
(
  UPC char (15),
  keyword_code integer,
  CONSTRAINT PK_product_keyword PRIMARY KEY (UPC),
  CONSTRAINT RelationKeyword_listProduct_keyword1
      FOREIGN KEY () REFERENCES keyword_list
);
```

■ FIGURE 15.4 *(cont.)*

```
CREATE TABLE sales_promotion
(
  UPC char (15),
  promotion_start_date date,
  promotion_end_date date,
  promotion_type_code integer,
  promotion_details char (50),
  CONSTRAINT PK_sales_promotion PRIMARY KEY (UPC,promotion_start_date),
  CONSTRAINT RelationProductSales_promotion1
      FOREIGN KEY () REFERENCES product
);

CREATE TABLE In_store_sale
(
  in_store_transaction_numb integer,
  in_store_transaction_date date,
  in_store_sale_product_total number (8,2),
  in_store_sales_tax number (6,2),
  in_store_sale_total number (8,2),
  in_store_sale_payment_type_code integer,
  CONSTRAINT PK_In_store_sale PRIMARY KEY (in_store_transaction_numb),
  CONSTRAINT RelationIn_store_salecredit_sale_details1
      FOREIGN KEY () REFERENCES credit_sale_details,
  CONSTRAINT RelationIn_store_payment_typeIn_store_sale1
      FOREIGN KEY () REFERENCES In_store_payment_type
);

CREATE TABLE product_stocked
(
  SKU char (15),
  UPC char (15),
  in_store boolean,
  store_ numb integer,
  dept_numb integer,
  warehouse_numb integer,
  size char (10),
  color char (15),
  number_on_hand integer,
  retail_price number (7,2),
  CONSTRAINT PK_product_stocked PRIMARY KEY (SKU),
  CONSTRAINT RelationProductProduct_stocked1
      FOREIGN KEY () REFERENCES product,
  CONSTRAINT RelationDepartmentProduct_stocked1
      FOREIGN KEY () REFERENCES department
);
```

■ **FIGURE 15.4** *(cont.)*

```
CREATE TABLE In_store_sale_item
(
  in_store_transaction_numb integer,
  in_store_SKU integer,
  in_store_quantity integer,
  in_store_price number (7,2)0,
  CONSTRAINT PK_In_store_sale_item
      PRIMARY KEY (in_store_transaction_numb,in_store_SKU),
  CONSTRAINT RelationProduct_stockedIn_store_sale_item1
      FOREIGN KEY () REFERENCES product_stocked,
  CONSTRAINT RelationIn_store_saleIn_store_sale_item1
      FOREIGN KEY () REFERENCES In_store_sale
);

CREATE TABLE web_sale_item
(
  web_sale_numb integer,
  web_sale_SKU char (15),
  web_sale_quantity integer,
  web_sale_shipped boolean,
  web_sale_price number (6,2),
  web_shipping_address_numb integer,
  CONSTRAINT PK_web_sale_item PRIMARY KEY (web_sale_numb,web_sale_SKU),
  CONSTRAINT RelationProduct_stockedWeb_sale_item1
      FOREIGN KEY () REFERENCES product_stocked,
  CONSTRAINT RelationWeb_saleWeb_sale_item1
      FOREIGN KEY () REFERENCES web_sale,
  CONSTRAINT RelationWeb_sale_shipmentWeb_sale_item1
      FOREIGN KEY () REFERENCES web_sale_shipment,
  CONSTRAINT RelationWeb_sale_shipping_addressWeb_sale_item1
      FOREIGN KEY () REFERENCES web_sale_shipping_address
);

CREATE TABLE web_security_question
(
  web_security_question_numb integer,
  web_security_question_text varchar (256),
  CONSTRAINT PK_web_security_question PRIMARY KEY
      (web_security_question_numb)
);

CREATE TABLE web_security_question_answer
(
  web_security_question_numb integer,
  web_customer_numb integer,
  web_security_question_answer_text varchar (256),
  CONSTRAINT PK_web_security_question_answer PRIMARY KEY
      (web_security_question_numb,web_customer_numb)
  CONSTRAINT RelationWeb_security_questionWeb_security_question_answer1
      FOREIGN KEY () REFERENCES web_security_question
  CONSTRAINT RelationWeb_customerWeb_security_question_answer1
      FOREIGN KEY () REFERENCES web_customer
);
```

■ **FIGURE 15.4** *(cont.)*

Part

IV

Using Interactive SQL to Manipulate a Relational Database

This part of the book goes in depth into the uses and syntax of interactive SQL. You will learn to create a wide variety of queries, as well as perform data modification. In this part, you will read about the impact that equivalent syntaxes may have on the performance of your queries. Finally, you will learn about creating additional database structural elements that require querying in their syntax.

Chapter

16

Simple SQL Retrieval

As we've said several times earlier, retrieval is what databases are all about: We put the data in so we can get them out in some meaningful way. There are many ways to formulate a request for data retrieval, but when it comes to relational databases, SQL is the international standard. It may not seem very "modern" because it's a text-based language, but it's the best we have when it comes to something that can be used in many environments.

Note: Yes, SQL is a standard and, in theory, implementations should be the same. However, although the basic syntax is the same, the "devil is in the details," as the old saying goes. For example, some implementations require a semicolon to terminate a statement, but others do not. You will therefore find notes throughout the SQL chapters warning you about areas where implementations may differ. The only solution is to use product documentation to verify the exact syntax used by your DBMS.

SQL has one command for retrieving data: SELECT. This is nowhere as restrictive as it might seem. SELECT contains syntax for choosing columns, choosing rows, combining tables, grouping data, and performing some simple calculations. In fact, a single SELECT statement can result in a DBMS performing any or all of the relational algebra operations.

The basic syntax of the SELECT statement has the following general structure:

```
SELECT column1, column2 …
FROM table1, table2 …
WHERE predicate
```

The SELECT clause specifies the columns you want to see. You specify the tables used in the query in the FROM clause. The optional WHERE clause can contain a wide variety of criteria that identify which rows you want to retrieve.

Note: Most SQL command processors are not case sensitive when it comes to parts of a SQL statement. SQL keywords, table names, column names, and so on can be in any case you choose. However, most DBMSs are case sensitive when it comes to matching data values. Therefore, whenever you place a value in quotes for SQL to match, you must match the case of the stored data. In this book, SQL keywords will appear in uppercase letters; database components such as column and table names will appear in lowercase letters.

In addition to these basic clauses, SELECT has many other syntax options. Rather than attempt to summarize them all in a single general statement, you will learn to build the parts of a SELECT gradually throughout this and the next few chapters of this book.

Note: The SQL queries you see throughout the book are terminated by a semicolon (;). This is not part of the SQL standard, but is used by many DBMSs so that you can type a command on multiple lines. The SQL command processor doesn't execute the query until it encounters the semicolon.

Note: The examples in this chapter and the remaining SQL retrieval chapters use the rare book store database introduced in Chapter 6.

Revisiting the Sample Data

In Chapter 6 you were introduced to the rare book store database and the sample data with which the tables have been populated. The sample data are repeated here for easier reference when reading Chapters 16–19.

Table 6.1: Publisher

```
publisher_id |                    publisher_name
-------------+-------------------------------------------------------
           1 | Wiley
           2 | Simon & Schuster
           3 | Macmillan
           4 | Tor
           5 | DAW
```

Table 6.2: Author

```
author_numb |                  author_last_first
------------+---------------------------------------------------
          1 | Bronte, Charlotte
          2 | Doyle, Sir Arthur Conan
          3 | Twain, Mark
          4 | Stevenson, Robert Louis
          5 | Rand, Ayn
          6 | Barrie, James
          7 | Ludlum, Robert
          8 | Barth, John
          9 | Herbert, Frank
         10 | Asimov, Isaac
         11 | Funke, Cornelia
         12 | Stephenson, Neal
```

Table 6.3: Condition codes

```
condition_code |             condition_description
---------------+-------------------------------------------------
             1 | New
             2 | Excellent
             3 | Fine
             4 | Good
             5 | Poor
```

Choosing Columns

One of the characteristics of a relation is that you can view any of the columns in any order you choose. SQL therefore lets you specify the columns you want to see, and the order in which you want to see them, using the relational algebra project operation to produce the final result table.

Retrieving All Columns

To retrieve all the columns in a table, viewing the columns in the order in which they were defined when the table was created, you can use an asterisk (*) rather than listing each column. For example, to see all the works that the rare book store has handled, you would use

```
SELECT *
FROM work;
```

Table 6.4: Work

```
work_numb | author_numb |                      title
----------+-------------+----------------------------------------------------
       1 |          1 | Jane Eyre
       2 |          1 | Villette
       3 |          2 | Hound of the Baskervilles
       4 |          2 | Lost World, The
       5 |          2 | Complete Sherlock Holmes
       7 |          3 | Prince and the Pauper
       8 |          3 | Tom Sawyer
       9 |          3 | Adventures of Huckleberry Finn, The
       6 |          3 | Connecticut Yankee in King Arthur's Court, A
      13 |          5 | Fountainhead, The
      14 |          5 | Atlas Shrugged
      15 |          6 | Peter Pan
      10 |          7 | Bourne Identity, The
      11 |          7 | Matarese Circle, The
      12 |          7 | Bourne Supremacy, The
      16 |          4 | Kidnapped
      17 |          4 | Treasure Island
      18 |          8 | Sot Weed Factor, The
      19 |          8 | Lost in the Funhouse
      20 |          8 | Giles Goat Boy
      21 |          9 | Dune
      22 |          9 | Dune Messiah
      23 |         10 | Foundation
      24 |         10 | Last Foundation
      25 |         10 | I, Robot
      26 |         11 | Inkheart
      27 |         11 | Inkdeath
      28 |         12 | Anathem
      29 |         12 | Snow Crash
      30 |          5 | Anthem
      31 |         12 | Cryptonomicon
```

Table 6.5: Books

isbn	work_numb	publisher_id	edition	binding	copyright_year
978-1-11111-111-1	1	1	2	Board	1857
978-1-11111-112-1	1	1	1	Board	1847
978-1-11111-113-1	2	4	1	Board	1842
978-1-11111-114-1	3	4	1	Board	1801
978-1-11111-115-1	3	4	10	Leather	1925
978-1-11111-116-1	4	3	1	Board	1805
978-1-11111-117-1	5	5	1	Board	1808
978-1-11111-118-1	5	2	19	Leather	1956
978-1-11111-120-1	8	4	5	Board	1906
978-1-11111-119-1	6	2	3	Board	1956
978-1-11111-121-1	8	1	12	Leath	1982
978-1-11111-122-1	9	1	12	Leather	1982
978-1-11111-123-1	11	2	1	Board	1998
978-1-11111-124-1	12	2	1	Board	1989
978-1-11111-125-1	13	2	3	Board	1965
978-1-11111-126-1	13	2	9	Leath	2001
978-1-11111-127-1	14	2	1	Board	1960
978-1-11111-128-1	16	2	12	Board	1960
978-1-11111-129-1	16	2	14	Leather	2002
978-1-11111-130-1	17	3	6	Leather	1905
978-1-11111-131-1	18	4	6	Board	1957
978-1-11111-132-1	19	4	1	Board	1962
978-1-11111-133-1	20	4	1	Board	1964
978-1-11111-134-1	21	5	1	Board	1964
978-1-11111-135-1	23	5	1	Board	1962
978-1-11111-136-1	23	5	4	Leather	2001
978-1-11111-137-1	24	5	4	Leather	2001
978-1-11111-138-1	23	5	4	Leather	2001
978-1-11111-139-1	25	5	4	Leather	2001
978-1-11111-140-1	26	5	1	Board	2001
978-1-11111-141-1	27	5	1	Board	2005
978-1-11111-142-1	28	5	1	Board	2008
978-1-11111-143-1	29	5	1	Board	1992
978-1-11111-144-1	30	1	1	Board	1952
978-1-11111-145-1	30	5	1	Board	2001
978-1-11111-146-1	31	5	1	Board	1999

Table 6.6: Volume (continues)

inventory_id	isbn	condition_code	date_acquired	asking_price	selling_price	sale_id
1	978-1-11111-111-1	3	12-JUN-19 00:00:00	175.00	175.00	1
2	978-1-11111-131-1	4	23-JAN-20 00:00:00	50.00	50.00	1
7	978-1-11111-137-1	2	20-JUN-19 00:00:00	80.00		
3	978-1-11111-133-1	2	05-APR-18 00:00:00	300.00	285.00	1
4	978-1-11111-142-1	1	05-APR-18 00:00:00	25.95	25.95	2
5	978-1-11111-146-1	1	05-APR-18 00:00:00	22.95	22.95	2
6	978-1-11111-144-1	2	15-MAY-19 00:00:00	80.00	76.10	2
8	978-1-11111-137-1	3	20-JUN-20 00:00:00	50.00		
9	978-1-11111-136-1	1	20-DEC-19 00:00:00	75.00		
10	978-1-11111-136-1	2	15-DEC-19 00:00:00	50.00		
11	978-1-11111-143-1	1	05-APR-20 00:00:00	25.00	25.00	3
12	978-1-11111-132-1	1	12-JUN-20 00:00:00	15.00	15.00	3
13	978-1-11111-133-1	3	20-APR-20 00:00:00	18.00	18.00	3
15	978-1-11111-121-1	2	20-APR-20 00:00:00	110.00	110.00	5
14	978-1-11111-121-1	2	20-APR-20 00:00:00	110.00	110.00	4
16	978-1-11111-121-1	2	20-APR-20 00:00:00	110.00		
17	978-1-11111-124-1	2	12-JAN-21 00:00:00	75.00		
18	978-1-11111-146-1	1	11-MAY-20 00:00:00	30.00	30.00	6
19	978-1-11111-122-1	2	06-MAY-20 00:00:00	75.00	75.00	6
20	978-1-11111-130-1	2	20-APR-20 00:00:00	150.00	120.00	6
21	978-1-11111-126-1	2	20-APR-20 00:00:00	110.00	110.00	6
22	978-1-11111-139-1	2	16-MAY-20 00:00:00	200.00	170.00	6
23	978-1-11111-125-1	2	16-MAY-20 00:00:00	45.00	45.00	7
24	978-1-11111-131-1	3	20-APR-20 00:00:00	35.00	35.00	7
25	978-1-11111-126-1	2	16-NOV-20 00:00:00	75.00	75.00	8
26	978-1-11111-133-1	3	16-NOV-20 00:00:00	35.00	55.00	8
27	978-1-11111-141-1	1	06-NOV-20 00:00:00	24.95		
28	978-1-11111-141-1	1	06-NOV-20 00:00:00	24.95		
29	978-1-11111-141-1	1	06-NOV-20 00:00:00	24.95		
30	978-1-11111-145-1	1	06-NOV-20 00:00:00	27.95		
31	978-1-11111-145-1	1	06-NOV-20 00:00:00	27.95		
32	978-1-11111-145-1	1	06-NOV-20 00:00:00	27.95		
33	978-1-11111-139-1	2	06-OCT-20 00:00:00	75.00	50.00	9
34	978-1-11111-133-1	1	16-NOV-20 00:00:00	125.00	125.00	10
35	978-1-11111-126-1	1	06-OCT-20 00:00:00	75.00	75.00	11
36	978-1-11111-130-1	3	06-DEC-19 00:00:00	50.00	50.00	11
37	978-1-11111-136-1	3	06-DEC-19 00:00:00	75.00	75.00	11
38	978-1-11111-130-1	2	06-APR-20 00:00:00	200.00	150.00	12
39	978-1-11111-132-1	3	06-APR-20 00:00:00	75.00	75.00	12
40	978-1-11111-129-1	1	06-APR-20 00:00:00	25.95	25.95	13
41	978-1-11111-141-1	1	16-MAY-20 00:00:00	40.00	40.00	14
42	978-1-11111-141-1	1	16-MAY-20 00:00:00	40.00	40.00	14
43	978-1-11111-132-1	1	12-NOV-20 00:00:00	17.95		
44	978-1-11111-138-1	1	12-NOV-20 00:00:00	75.95		
45	978-1-11111-138-1	1	12-NOV-20 00:00:00	75.95		
46	978-1-11111-131-1	3	12-NOV-20 00:00:00	15.95		
47	978-1-11111-140-1	3	12-NOV-20 00:00:00	25.95		
48	978-1-11111-123-1	2	16-AUG-20 00:00:00	24.95		
49	978-1-11111-127-1	2	16-AUG-20 00:00:00	27.95		
50	978-1-11111-127-1	2	06-JAN-21 00:00:00	50.00	50.00	15
51	978-1-11111-141-1	2	06-JAN-21 00:00:00	50.00	50.00	15
52	978-1-11111-141-1	2	06-JAN-21 00:00:00	50.00	50.00	16

Table 6.6: Volume (*cont.*)

inventory_id	isbn	condition_ code	date_acquired	asking_price	selling_price	sale_id
53	978-1-11111-123-1	2	06-JAN-21 00:00:00	40.00	40.00	16
54	978-1-11111-127-1	2	06-JAN-21 00:00:00	40.00	40.00	16
55	978-1-11111-133-1	2	06-FEB-21 00:00:00	60.00	60.00	17
56	978-1-11111-127-1	2	16-FEB-21 00:00:00	40.00	40.00	17
57	978-1-11111-135-1	2	16-FEB-21 00:00:00	40.00	40.00	18
59	978-1-11111-127-1	2	25-FEB-21 00:00:00	35.00	35.00	18
58	978-1-11111-131-1	2	16-FEB-21 00:00:00	25.00	25.00	18
60	978-1-11111-128-1	2	16-DEC-20 00:00:00	50.00	45.00	
61	978-1-11111-136-1	3	22-OCT-20 00:00:00	50.00	50.00	19
62	978-1-11111-115-1	2	22-OCT-20 00:00:00	75.00	75.00	20
63	978-1-11111-130-1	2	16-JUL-20 00:00:00	500.00		
64	978-1-11111-136-1	2	06-MAR-20 00:00:00	125.00		
65	978-1-11111-136-1	2	06-MAR-20 00:00:00	125.00		
66	978-1-11111-137-1	2	06-MAR-20 00:00:00	125.00		
67	978-1-11111-137-1	2	06-MAR-20 00:00:00	125.00		
68	978-1-11111-138-1	2	06-MAR-20 00:00:00	125.00		
69	978-1-11111-138-1	2	06-MAR-20 00:00:00	125.00		
70	978-1-11111-139-1	2	06-MAR-20 00:00:00	125.00		
71	978-1-11111-139-1	2	06-MAR-20 00:00:00	125.00		

Because this query is requesting all rows in the table, there is no WHERE clause. As you can see in Figure 16.1, the result table labels each column with its name.

Note: The layouts of the printed output of many SQL queries in this book have been adjusted so that it will fit across the width of the pages. When you actually view listings on the screen, each row will be in a single horizontal line. If a listing is too wide to fit on the screen or a terminal program's window, either each line will wrap as it reaches the right edge of the display, or you will need to scroll.

Table 6.7: Customer

customer_ numb	first_ name	last_ name	street	city	state_ province	zip_ postcode	contact_ phone
1	Janice	Jones	125 Center Road	Anytown	NY	11111	518-555-1111
2	Jon	Jones	25 Elm Road	Next Town	NJ	18888	209-555-2222
3	John	Doe	821 Elm Road	Next Town	NJ	18888	209-555-3333
4	Jane	Doe	852 Main Street	Anytown	NY	11111	518-555-4444
5	Jane	Smith	1919 Main Street	New Village	NY	13333	518-555-5555
6	Janice	Smith	800 Center Road	Anytown	NY	11111	518-555-6666
7	Helen	Brown	25 Front Street	Anytown	NY	11111	518-555-7777
8	Helen	Jerry	16 Main Street	Newtown	NJ	18886	518-555-8888
9	Mary	Collins	301 Pine Road, Apt. 12	Newtown	NJ	18886	518-555-9999
10	Peter	Collins	18 Main Street	Newtown	NJ	18886	518-555-1010
11	Edna	Hayes	209 Circle Road	Anytown	NY	11111	518-555-1110
12	Franklin	Hayes	615 Circle Road	Anytown	NY	11111	518-555-1212
13	Peter	Johnson	22 Rose Court	Next Town	NJ	18888	209-555-1212
14	Peter	Johnson	881 Front Street	Next Town	NJ	18888	209-555-1414
15	John	Smith	881 Manor Lane	Next Town	NJ	18888	209-555-1515

Table 6.8: Sale

sale_id	customer_ numb	sale_date	sale_total_ amt	credit_card_ numb	exp_month	exp_year
3	1	15-JUN-21 00:00:00	58.00	1234 5678 9101 1121	10	18
4	4	30-JUN-21 00:00:00	110.00	1234 5678 9101 5555	7	17
5	6	30-JUN-21 00:00:00	110.00	1234 5678 9101 6666	12	17
6	12	05-JUL-21 00:00:00	505.00	1234 5678 9101 7777	7	16
7	8	05-JUL-21 00:00:00	80.00	1234 5678 9101 8888	8	16
8	5	07-JUL-21 00:00:00	90.00	1234 5678 9101 9999	9	15
9	8	07-JUL-21 00:00:00	50.00	1234 5678 9101 8888	8	16
10	11	10-JUL-21 00:00:00	125.00	1234 5678 9101 1010	11	16
11	9	10-JUL-21 00:00:00	200.00	1234 5678 9101 0909	11	15
12	10	10-JUL-21 00:00:00	200.00	1234 5678 9101 0101	10	15
13	2	10-JUL-21 00:00:00	25.95	1234 5678 9101 2222	2	15
14	6	10-JUL-21 00:00:00	80.00	1234 5678 9101 6666	12	17
15	11	12-JUL-21 00:00:00	75.00	1234 5678 9101 1231	11	17
16	2	25-JUL-21 00:00:00	130.00	1234 5678 9101 2222	2	15
17	1	25-JUL-21 00:00:00	100.00	1234 5678 9101 1121	10	18
18	5	22-AUG-21 00:00:00	100.00	1234 5678 9101 9999	9	15
2	1	05-JUN-21 00:00:00	125.00	1234 5678 9101 1121	10	18
1	1	29-MAY-21 00:00:00	510.00	1234 5678 9101 1121	10	18
19	6	01-SEP-21 00:00:00	95.00	1234 5678 9101 7777	7	16
20	2	01-SEP-21 00:00:00	75.00	1234 5678 9101 2222	2	15

Using the * operator to view all columns is a convenient shorthand for interactive SQL when you want a quick overview of data. However, it can be troublesome when used in embedded SQL (SQL inside a program of some sort) if the columns in the table are changed. In particular, if a column is added to the table and the application is not modified to handle the new column, then the application may not work properly. The * operator also displays the columns in the order in which they appeared in the CREATE statement that set up the table. This may simply not be the order you want.

Retrieving Specific Columns

In most SQL queries, you will want to specify exactly which column or columns you want retrieved and perhaps the order in which you want them to appear. To specify columns, you list them following SELECT in the order in which you want to see them. For example, a query to view the names and phone numbers of all of our store's customers is written

```
SELECT first_name,last_name,contact_phone
FROM customer;
```

```
work_numb | author_numb |                      title
--------- +------------ +--------------------------------------------
        1 |           1 | Jane Eyre
        2 |           1 | Villette
        3 |           2 | Hound of the Baskervilles
        4 |           2 | Lost World, The
        5 |           2 | Complete Sherlock Holmes
        7 |           3 | Prince and the Pauper
        8 |           3 | Tom Sawyer
        9 |           3 | Adventures of Huckleberry Finn, The
        6 |           3 | Connecticut Yankee in King Arthur's Court, A
       13 |           5 | Fountainhead, The
       14 |           5 | Atlas Shrugged
       15 |           6 | Peter Pan
       10 |           7 | Bourne Identity, The
       11 |           7 | Matarese Circle, The
       12 |           7 | Bourne Supremacy, The
       16 |           4 | Kidnapped
       17 |           4 | Treasure Island
       18 |           8 | Sot Weed Factor, The
       19 |           8 | Lost in the Funhouse
       20 |           8 | Giles Goat Boy
       21 |           9 | Dune
       22 |           9 | Dune Messiah
       23 |          10 | Foundation
       24 |          10 | Last Foundation
       25 |          10 | I, Robot
       26 |          11 | Inkheart
       27 |          11 | Inkdeath
       28 |          12 | Anathem
       29 |          12 | Snow Crash
       30 |           5 | Anthem
       31 |          12 | Cryptonomicon
```

■ FIGURE 16.1 Viewing all columns in a table.

The result (see Figure 16.2) shows all rows in the table for just the three columns specified in the query. The order of the columns in the result table matches the order in which the columns appeared after the SELECT keyword.

Removing Duplicates

Unique primary keys ensure that relations have no duplicate rows. However, when you view only a portion of the columns in a table, you may end up with duplicates. For example, executing the following query produced the result in Figure 16.3:

```
SELECT customer_numb, credit_card_numb
FROM sale;
```

```
 first_name | last_name | contact_phone
------------+-----------+---------------
 Janice     | Jones     | 518-555-1111
 Jon        | Jones     | 209-555-2222
 John       | Doe       | 209-555-3333
 Jane       | Doe       | 518-555-4444
 Jane       | Smith     | 518-555-5555
 Janice     | Smith     | 518-555-6666
 Helen      | Brown     | 518-555-7777
 Helen      | Jerry     | 518-555-8888
 Mary       | Collins   | 518-555-9999
 Peter      | Collins   | 518-555-1010
 Edna       | Hayes     | 518-555-1110
 Franklin   | Hayes     | 518-555-1212
 Peter      | Johnson   | 209-555-1212
 Peter      | Johnson   | 209-555-1414
 John       | Smith     | 209-555-1515
```

■ FIGURE 16.2 Choosing specific columns.

```
 customer_numb |   credit_card_numb
---------------+----------------------
             1 | 1234 5678 9101 1121
             1 | 1234 5678 9101 1121
             1 | 1234 5678 9101 1121
             1 | 1234 5678 9101 1121
             2 | 1234 5678 9101 2222
             2 | 1234 5678 9101 2222
             2 | 1234 5678 9101 2222
             4 | 1234 5678 9101 5555
             5 | 1234 5678 9101 9999
             5 | 1234 5678 9101 9999
             6 | 1234 5678 9101 6666
             6 | 1234 5678 9101 7777
             6 | 1234 5678 9101 6666
             8 | 1234 5678 9101 8888
             8 | 1234 5678 9101 8888
             9 | 1234 5678 9101 0909
            10 | 1234 5678 9101 0101
            11 | 1234 5678 9101 1231
            11 | 1234 5678 9101 1010
            12 | 1234 5678 9101 7777
```

■ FIGURE 16.3 A result table with duplicate rows.

Duplicates appear because the same customer used the same credit card number for more than one purchase. Keep in mind that, although this table with duplicate rows is not a legal relation, that doesn't present a problem for the database because it is not stored in the base tables.

To remove duplicates from a result table, you insert the keyword DISTINCT following SELECT:

```
SELECT DISTINCT customer_numb, credit_card_numb
FROM sale;
```

The result is a table without the duplicate rows (see Figure 16.4). Although a legal relation has no duplicate rows, most DBMS vendors have implemented SQL retrieval so that it leaves the duplicates. As you read earlier the primary reason is performance. To remove duplicates, a DBMS must sort the result table by every column in the table. It must then scan the table from top to bottom, looking at every "next" row to identify duplicate rows that are next to one another. If a result table is large, the sorting and scanning can significantly slow down the query. It is therefore up to the user to decide whether to request unique rows.

```
 customer_numb |    credit_card_numb
---------------+----------------------
            1 | 1234 5678 9101 1121
            2 | 1234 5678 9101 2222
            4 | 1234 5678 9101 5555
            5 | 1234 5678 9101 9999
            6 | 1234 5678 9101 6666
            6 | 1234 5678 9101 7777
            8 | 1234 5678 9101 8888
            9 | 1234 5678 9101 0909
           10 | 1234 5678 9101 0101
           11 | 1234 5678 9101 1010
           11 | 1234 5678 9101 1231
           12 | 1234 5678 9101 7777
```

■ FIGURE 16.4   **The result table in Figure 16.3 with the duplicates removed.**

Ordering the Result Table

The order in which rows appear in the result table may not be what you expect. In some cases, rows will appear in the order in which they are physically stored. However, if the query optimizer uses an index to process the query, then the rows will appear in index key order. If you want row ordering to be consistent and predictable, you will need to specify how you want the rows to appear.

```
author_numb |                author_last_first
------------+-------------------------------------------------------
          1 | Bronte, Charlotte
          2 | Doyle, Sir Arthur Conan
          3 | Twain, Mark
          4 | Stevenson, Robert Louis
          5 | Rand, Ayn
          6 | Barrie, James
          7 | Ludlum, Robert
          8 | Barth, John
          9 | Herbert, Frank
         10 | Asimov, Isaac
         11 | Funke, Cornelia
         12 | Stephenson, Neal
```

■ **FIGURE 16.5 The unordered result table.**

When you want to control the order of rows in a result table, you add an ORDER BY clause to your SELECT statement.

For example, if you issue the query

```
SELECT *
FROM author;
```

to get an alphabetical list of authors, you will see the listing in Figure 16.5. The author numbers are in numeric order because that was the order in which the rows were added, but the author names aren't alphabetical. Adding the ORDER BY clause sorts the result in alphabetical order by the *author_first_last* column (see Figure 16.6):

```
SELECT *
FROM author
ORDER BY author_last_first;
```

The keywords ORDER BY are followed by the column or columns on which you want to sort the result table. When you include more than one column, the first column represents the outer sort, the next column a sort within it. For example, assume that you issue the query

```
SELECT zip_postcode, last_name, first_name
FROM customer
ORDER BY zip_postcode, last_name;
```

```
author_numb |         author_last_first
------------+-------------------------------------------------------
         10 | Asimov, Isaac
          6 | Barrie, James
          8 | Barth, John
          1 | Bronte, Charlotte
          2 | Doyle, Sir Arthur Conan
         11 | Funke, Cornelia
          9 | Herbert, Frank
          7 | Ludlum, Robert
          5 | Rand, Ayn
         12 | Stephenson, Neal
          4 | Stevenson, Robert Louis
          3 | Twain, Mark
```

■ **FIGURE 16.6**   The result table from Figure 16.5 sorted in alphabetical order by author name.

```
zip_postcode | last_name | first_name
-------------+-----------+-----------
11111        | Brown     | Helen
11111        | Doe       | Jane
11111        | Hayes     | Edna
11111        | Hayes     | Franklin
11111        | Jones     | Janice
11111        | Smith     | Janice
13333        | Smith     | Jane
18886        | Collins   | Mary
18886        | Collins   | Peter
18886        | Jerry     | Helen
18888        | Doe       | John
18888        | Johnson   | Peter
18888        | Johnson   | Peter
18888        | Jones     | Jon
18888        | Smith     | John
```

■ **FIGURE 16.7**   Sorting output by two columns.

The result (see Figure 16.7) first orders by the zip code, and then sorts by
the customer's last name within each zip code. If we reverse the order of the
columns on which the output is to be sorted, as in

```
SELECT zip_postcode, last_name, first_name
FROM customer
ORDER BY last_name, zip_postcode;
```

```
zip_postcode | last_name | first_name
-------------+-----------+-----------
 11111       | Brown     | Helen
 18886       | Collins   | Peter
 18886       | Collins   | Mary
 11111       | Doe       | Jane
 18888       | Doe       | John
 11111       | Hayes     | Franklin
 11111       | Hayes     | Edna
 18886       | Jerry     | Helen
 18888       | Johnson   | Peter
 18888       | Johnson   | Peter
 11111       | Jones     | Janice
 18888       | Jones     | Jon
 11111       | Smith     | Janice
 13333       | Smith     | Jane
 18888       | Smith     | John
```

■ FIGURE 16.8 Reversing the sort order of the query in Figure 16.7.

the output (see Figure 16.8) then sorts first by last name, and then by zip code within each last name.

Choosing Rows

As well as viewing any columns from a relation, you can also view any rows you want. We specify row selection criteria in a SELECT statement's WHERE clause.

In its simplest form, a WHERE clause contains a logical expression against which each row in a table is evaluated. If a row meets the criteria in the expression, then it becomes a part of the result table. If the row does not meet the criteria, then it is omitted. The trick to writing row selection criteria is, therefore, knowing how to create logical expressions against which data can be evaluated.

Predicates

As you read earlier, a logical expression that follows WHERE is known as a predicate. It uses a variety of operators to represent row selection criteria. If a row meets the criteria in a predicate (in other words, the logical expression evaluates as true), then the row is included in the result table. If the row doesn't meet the criteria (the logical expression evaluates as false), then the row is excluded.

Relationship Operators

In Table 16.1 you can see the six operators used to express data relationships. To write an expression using one of the operators, you surround it with two values. In database queries, such expressions have either a column name on one side and a literal value on the other, as in

```
cost > 1.95
```

or column names on both sides:

```
numb_on_hand <= reorder_point
```

Table 16.1 The Relationship Operators

Operator	Meaning	Examples
=	Equal to	`cost = 1.95` `numb_in_stock = reorder_point`
<	Less than	`cost < 1.95` `numb_in_stock < reorder_point`
<=	Less than or equal to	`cost <= 1.95` `numb_in_stock <= reorder_point`
>	Greater than	`cost > 1.95` `numb_in_stock >= reorder_point`
>=	Greater than or equal to	`cost >= 1.95` `numb_in_stock >= reorder_point`
!= or < > [1]	Not equal to	`cost != 1.95` `numb_in_stock != reorder_point`

[1] *Check the documentation that accompanies your DBMS to determine whether the "not equal to" operator is != or < >.*

The first expression asks the question "Is the cost of the item greater than 1.95?" The second asks "Is the number of items in stock less than or equal to the reorder point?"

The way in which you enter literal values into a logical expression depends on the data type of the column to which you are comparing the value:

- Numbers: type numbers without any formatting. In other words, leave out dollar signs, commas, and so on. You should, however, put decimal points in the appropriate place in a number with a factional portion.
- Characters: type characters surrounded by quotation marks. Most DBMSs accept pairs of either single or double quotes. If your

characters include an apostrophe (a single quote), then you should use double quotes. Otherwise, use single quotes.

■ Dates: type dates in the format used to store them in the database. This will vary from one DBMS to another.

■ Times: type times in the format used to store them in the database. This will vary from one DBMS to another.

When you are using two column names, keep in mind that the predicate is applied to each row in the table individually. The DBMS substitutes the values stored in the columns in the same row, when making its evaluation of the criteria. You can, therefore, use two column names when you need to examine data that are stored in the same row but in different columns. However, you cannot use a simple logical expression to compare the same column in two or more rows.

The DBMS also bases the way it evaluates data on the type of data:

■ Comparisons involving numeric data are based on numerical order.

■ Comparisons involving character data are based on alphabetical order.

■ Comparisons involving dates and times are based on chronological order.

Logical Operators

Sometimes a simple logical expression is not enough to identify the rows you want to retrieve; you need more than one criterion. In that case, you can chain criteria together with logical operators. For example, assume that you want to retrieve volumes that you have in stock that cost more than $75, and that are in excellent condition. The conditions are coded (2 = excellent). The predicate you need is, therefore, made up of two simple expressions:

```
condition_code = 2
asking_price > 75
```

A row must meet both of these criteria to be included in the result table. You therefore connect the two expressions with the logical operator AND into a single complex expression:

```
condition_code = 2 AND asking_price > 75
```

Whenever you connect two simple expressions with AND, a row must meet *both* of the conditions to be included in the result.

You can use the AND operators to create a predicate that includes a range of dates. For example, if you want to find all sales that were made in Aug. and Sep. of 2019, the predicate would be written:[1]

```
sale_date >= '01-Aug-2019' AND sale_date <= '30-Sep-2019'
```

The same result would be generated by

```
Sale_date > '31-Jul-2019' AND sale_date < '1-Oct-2019'
```

To be within the interval, a sale date must meet both individual criteria.

You will find a summary of the action of the AND operators in Table 16.2. The labels in the columns and rows represent the result of evaluating the single expressions on either side of the AND. As you can see, the only way to get a true result for the entire expression is for both simple expressions to be true.

Table 16.2 AND Truth Table

AND	True	False
True	True	False
False	False	False

If you want to create an expression from which a row needs to meet only one condition from several conditions, then you connect simple expressions with the logical operator OR. For example, if you want to retrieve volumes that cost more than $125 or less than $50, you would use the predicate

```
asking_price > 125 OR asking_price < 50
```

Whenever you connect two simple expressions with OR, a row needs to meet only one of the conditions to be included in the result of the query. When you want to create a predicate that looks for dates outside an interval,

---

[1]This date format is a fairly generic one that is recognized by many DMBSs. However, you should consult the documentation for your DBMS to determine exactly what will work with your product.

you use the OR operator. For example, to see sales that occurred prior to Mar. 1, 2019 or after Dec. 31, 2019, the predicate is written

```
sale_date < '01-Mar-2019' OR sale_date > '31-Dec-2019'
```

You can find a summary of the OR operation in Table 16.3. Notice that the only way to get a false result is for both simple expressions surrounding OR to be false.

Table 16.3 OR Truth Table

OR	True	False
True	True	True
False	True	False

There is no limit to the number of simple expression you can connect with AND and OR. For example, the following expression is legal:

```
condition_code >= 3 AND selling_price < asking_price
    AND selling_price > 75
```

Negation

The logical operator NOT (or !) inverts the result of logical expression. If a row meets the criteria in a predicate, then placing NOT in front of the criteria *excludes* the row from the result. By the same token, if a row does not meet the criteria in a predicate, then placing NOT in front of the expression *includes* the row in the result. For example,

```
NOT (asking_price <= 50)
```

retrieves all rows where the cost is not less than or equal to $50 (in other words, greater than $50[2]). First the DBMS evaluates the value in the *asking_price* column against the expression *asking_price* $<=$ 50. If the row meets the criteria, then the DBMS does nothing. If the row does not meet the criteria, it includes the row in the result.

---

[2]It is actually faster for the DBMS to evaluate *asking_price* $>$ 50 because it involves only one action (is the asking price greater than 50) rather than three: Is the asking price equal to 50? Is the asking price less than 50? Take the opposite of the result of the first two questions.

The parentheses in the preceding example group the expression to which NOT is to be applied. In the following example, the NOT operator applies only to the expression *asking_price <= 50.*

```
NOT (asking_price <= 50) AND selling_price < asking_price
```

NOT can be a bit tricky when it is applied to complex expressions. As an example, consider this expression:

```
NOT (asking_price <= 50 AND selling_price < asking_price)
```

Rows that have both an asking price of less than or equal to $50, and a selling price that was less than the asking price will meet the criteria within parentheses. However, the NOT operator excludes them from the result. Those rows that have either an asking price of more than $50 or a selling price greater than or equal to the asking price will fail the criteria within the parentheses, but will be included in the result by the NOT. This means that the expression is actually the same as

```
asking_price > 50 OR selling_price >= asking_price
```

or

```
NOT (asking_price <= 50) OR NOT (selling_price < asking_price)
```

Precedence ad Parentheses

When you create an expression with more than one logical operation, the DBMS must decide on the order in which it will process the simple expressions. Unless you tell it otherwise, a DBMS uses a set of default *rules of precedence.* In general, a DBMS evaluates simple expressions first, followed by any logical expressions. When there is more than one operator of the same type, evaluation proceeds from left to right.

As a first example, consider this expression:

```
asking_price < 50 OR condition_code = 2 AND selling_price >
    asking_price
```

If the asking price of a book is $25, its condition code is 3, and the selling price was $20, the DBMS will exclude the row from the result. The first simple expression is true; the second is false. An OR between the first two produces a true result, because at least one of the criteria is true. Then the DBMS performs an AND between the true result of the first portion and the result of the third simple expression (false). Because we are combining a true result and a false result with AND, the overall result is false. The row is therefore excluded from the result.

We can change the order in which the DBMS evaluates the logical operators and, coincidentally, the result of the expression, by using parentheses to group the expressions that are to have higher precedence:

```
asking_price < 50 OR (condition_code = 2 AND selling_price >
     asking_price)
```

A DBMS gives highest precedence to the parts of the expression within parentheses. Using the same sample data from the preceding paragraph, the expression within parentheses is false (both simple expressions are false). However, the OR with the first simple expression produces true, because the first simple expression is true. Therefore, the row is included in the result.

Special Operators

SQL predicates can include a number of special operators that make writing logical criteria easier. These include BETWEEN, LIKE, IN, and IS NULL.

Note: There are additional operators that are used primarily with subqueries, SELECT statements in which you embed one complete SELECT within another. You will be introduced to them in Chapter 17.

Between

The BETWEEN operator simplifies writing predicates that look for values that lie within an interval. Remember the example you saw earlier in this chapter using AND to generate a date interval? Using the BETWEEN operator, you could rewrite that predicate as

```
sale_date BETWEEN '01-Aug-2021' AND '30-Sep-2021'
```

Any row with a sale date of Aug. 1, 2021 through Sep. 30, 2021 will be included in the result.

If you negate the BETWEEN operator, the DBMS returns all rows that are outside the interval. For example,

```
sale_date NOT BETWEEN '01-Aug-2021' AND '30-Sep-2021'
```

retrieves all rows with dates *prior* to Aug. 1, 2019 and *after* Sep. 31, 2021. It does not include 01-Aug-2021 or 30-Sep-2021. NOT BETWEEN is therefore a shorthand for the two simple expressions linked by OR that you saw earlier in this chapter.

Like

The LIKE operator provides a measure of character string pattern matching by allowing you to use placeholders (wildcards) for one or more characters. Although you may find that the wildcards are different in your particular DBMS, in most case, % stands for zero, one, or more characters and _ stands for zero or one character.

The way in which the LIKE operator works is summarized in Table 16.4. As you can see, you can combine the two wildcards to produce a variety of begins with, ends with, and contains expressions.

Table 16.4 Using the LIKE Operator

Expression	Meaning
`LIKE 'Sm%'`	Begins with *Sm*
`LIKE '%ith'`	Ends with *ith*
`LIKE '%ith%'`	Contains *ith*
`LIKE 'Sm_'`	Begins with *Sm* and is followed by at most one character
`LIKE '_ith'`	Ends with *ith* and is preceded by at most one character
`LIKE '_ith_'`	Ontains *ith* and begins and ends with at most one additional character
`LIKE '%ith_'`	Contains *ith*, begins with any number of characters, and ends with at most one additional character
`LIKE '_ith%'`	Contains *ith*, begins with at most one additional character, and ends with any number of characters

As with BETWEEN you can negate the LIKE operator:

```
last_name NOT LIKE 'Sm%'
```

Rows that are like the pattern are therefore excluded from the result.

One of the problems you may run into when using LIKE is that you need to include the wildcard characters as part of your data. For example, what can you do if you want rows that contain 'nd_by'? The expression you want is

```
column_name LIKE '%nd_by%'
```

The problem is that the DBMS will see the _ as a wildcard, rather than as characters in your search string. The solution was introduced in SQL-92, providing you with the ability to designate an *escape character*.

An escape character removes the special meaning of the character that follows. Because many programming languages use \ as the escape character, it is a logical choice for pattern matching, although it can be any character that is not part of your data. To establish the escape character, you add the keyword ESCAPE, followed by the escape character, to your expression:

```
column_name LIKE '%nd\_by%' ESCAPE '\'
```

In

The IN operator compares the value in a column against a set of values. IN returns true if the value is within the set. For example, assume that a store employee is checking the selling price of a book and wants to know if it is $25, $50, or $60. Using the IN operator, the expression would be written:

```
selling_price IN (25,50,60)
```

This is shorthand for

```
selling_price = 25 OR selling_price = 50 OR selling_price = 60
```

Therefore, any row whose price is one of those three values will be included in the result. Conversely, if you write the predicate

```
selling_price NOT IN (25,50,60)
```

the DBMS will return the rows with prices other than those in the set of values. The preceding expression is therefore the same as

```
selling_price != 25 AND selling_price != 50 AND selling_price !=60
```

or

```
NOT (selling_price = 25 OR selling_price = 50 OR selling_proce = 60)
```

Note: The most common use of IN and NOT IN is with a subquery, where the set of values to which data are compared are generated by an embedded SELECT. You will learn about this is Chapter 17.

Is Null

As you know, null is a specific indicator in a database. Although columns that contain nulls appear empty when you view them, the database actually stores a value that represents null, so that an unknown value can be distinguished from, for example, a string value containing a blank. As a user, however, you will rarely know exactly what a DBMS is using internally for null. This means that you need some special way to identify null in a predicate, so you can retrieve rows containing nulls. That is where the IS NULL operator comes in.

For example, an expression to identify all rows for volumes that have not been sold is written as

```
sale_date IS NULL
```

Conversely, to find all volumes that have been sold, you could use

```
sale_date IS NOT NULL
```

Performing Row Selection Queries

To perform SQL queries that select specific rows, you place a predicate after the SQL keyword WHERE. Depending on the nature of the predicate, the intention of the query may be to retrieve one or more rows. In this section, you therefore will see some SELECT examples that combine a variety of row selection criteria. You will also see how those criteria are combined in queries with column selection, and with sorting of the output.

Using a Primary Key Expression to Retrieve One Row

A common type of SQL retrieval query uses a primary key expression in its predicate to retrieve exactly one row. For example, if someone at the rare book store wants to see the name and telephone number of customer number 6, then the query is written

```
SELECT first_name, last_name, contact_phone
FROM customer
WHERE customer_numb = 6;
```

The result is the single row requested by the predicate.

```
first_name | last_name | contact_phone
-----------+-----------+---------------
Janice     | Smith     | 518-555-6666
```

If a table has a concatenated primary key, such as the employee number and child name for the *dependents* table you saw earlier in the book, then a primary key expression needs to include a complex predicate in which each column of the primary key appears in its own simple logical expression. For example, if you wanted to find the birthdate of employee number 0002's son John, you would use following query:

```
SELECT child_birth_date
FROM dependents
WHERE employee_number = '0002' AND child_name = 'John';
```

In this case, the result is simply

```
child_birth_date
----------------
2-Dec-1999
```

Retrieving Multiple Rows

Although queries with primary key expressions are written with the intention of retrieving only one row, more commonly SQL queries are designed to retrieve multiple rows.

Using Simple Predicates

When you want to retrieve data based on a value in a single column, you construct a predicate that includes just a simple logical expression. For example, to see all the books ordered on sale number 6, an application program being used by a store employee would use

```
SELECT isbn
FROM volume
WHERE sale_id = 6;
```

The output (see Figure 16.9) displays a single column for rows where the *sale_id* is 6.

```
isbn
------------------
978-1-11111-146-1
978-1-11111-122-1
978-1-11111-130-1
978-1-11111-126-1
978-1-11111-139-1
```

■ **FIGURE 16.9** Displaying a single column from multiple rows using a simple predicate.

Using Complex Predicates

When you want to see rows that meet two or more simple conditions, you use a complex predicate in which the simple conditions are connected by AND or OR. For example, if someone wanted to see the books on order number 6 that sold for less than the asking price, the query would be written

```
SELECT isbn
FROM volume
WHERE sale_id = 6 AND selling_price < asking_price;
```

Only two rows meet the criteria:

```
isbn
------------------
978-1-11111-130-1
978-1-11111-139-1
```

By the same token, if you wanted to see all sales that took place prior to Aug. 1, 2021, and for which the total amount of the sale was less than $100, the query would be written[3]

---

[3]Whether you need quotes around date expressions depends on the DBMS.

```
SELECT sale_id, sale_total_amt
FROM sale
WHERE sale_date < '1-Aug-2021' AND sale_total_amt < 100;
```

It produces the result in Figure 16.10.

```
 sale_id | sale_total_amt
---------+----------------
       3 |          58.00
       7 |          80.00
       8 |          90.00
       9 |          50.00
      13 |          25.95
      14 |          80.00
      15 |          75.00
```

■ **FIGURE 16.10 Retrieving rows using a complex predicate including a date.**

Note: Don't forget that the date format required by your DMBS may be different from the one used in examples in this book.

Alternatively, if you needed information about all sales that occurred prior to or on Aug. 1, 2021 that totaled more than 100, along with sales that occurred after Aug. 1, 2019 that totaled less than 100, you would write the query

```
SELECT sale_id, sale_date, sale_total_amt
FROM sale
WHERE (sale_date <= '1-Aug-2021' AND sale_total_amt > 100) OR
(sale_date > '1-Aug-2021' AND sale_total_amt < 100);
```

Notice that although the AND operator has precedence over OR and, therefore, the parentheses are not strictly necessary, the predicate in this query includes parentheses for clarity. Extra parentheses are never a problem—as long as you balance every opening parenthesis with a closing parenthesis—and you should feel free to use them whenever they help make it easier to understand the meaning of a complex predicate. The result of this query can be seen in Figure 16.11.

Note: The default output format for a column of type date in PostgreSQL (the DBMS used to generate the sample queries) includes the time. Because no time was entered (just a date), the time displays as all 0s.

Using Between and Not Between

As an example of using one of the special predicate operators, consider a query where someone wants to see all sales that occurred between Jul. 1, 2019 and Aug. 31, 2019. The query would be written

```
 sale_id |       sale_date       | sale_total_amt
---------+-----------------------+----------------
       4 | 30-JUN-21 00:00:00 |          110.00
       5 | 30-JUN-21 00:00:00 |          110.00
       6 | 05-JUL-21 00:00:00 |          505.00
      10 | 10-JUL-21 00:00:00 |          125.00
      11 | 10-JUL-21 00:00:00 |          200.00
      12 | 10-JUL-21 00:00:00 |          200.00
      16 | 25-JUL-21 00:00:00 |          130.00
       2 | 05-JUN-21 00:00:00 |          125.00
       1 | 29-MAY-21 00:00:00 |          510.00
      19 | 01-SEP-21 00:00:00 |           95.00
      20 | 01-SEP-21 00:00:00 |           75.00
```

■ **FIGURE 16.11** Using a complex predicate that includes multiple logical operators.

```
SELECT sale_id, sale_date, sale_total_amt
FROM sale
WHERE sale_date BETWEEN '1-Jul-2021' AND '31-Aug-2021';
```

It produces the output in Figure 16.12.

```
 sale_id |       sale_date       | sale_total_amt
---------+-----------------------+----------------
       6 | 05-JUL-21 00:00:00 |          505.00
       7 | 05-JUL-21 00:00:00 |           80.00
       8 | 07-JUL-21 00:00:00 |           90.00
       9 | 07-JUL-21 00:00:00 |           50.00
      10 | 10-JUL-21 00:00:00 |          125.00
      11 | 10-JUL-21 00:00:00 |          200.00
      12 | 10-JUL-21 00:00:00 |          200.00
      13 | 10-JUL-21 00:00:00 |           25.95
      14 | 10-JUL-21 00:00:00 |           80.00
      15 | 12-JUL-21 00:00:00 |           75.00
      16 | 25-JUL-21 00:00:00 |          130.00
      17 | 25-JUL-21 00:00:00 |          100.00
      18 | 22-AUG-21 00:00:00 |          100.00
```

■ **FIGURE 16.12** Using BETWEEN to retrieve rows in a date range.

The inverse query retrieves all orders not placed between Jul. 1, 2019 and Aug. 31, 2019 is written

```
SELECT sale_id, sale_date, sale_total_amt
FROM sale
WHERE sale_date NOT BETWEEN '1-Jul-2019' AND '31-Aug-2019';
```

and produces the output in Figure 16.13.

```
sale_id |      sale_date       | sale_total_amt
--------+----------------------+----------------
      3 | 15-JUN-21 00:00:00 |            58.00
      4 | 30-JUN-21 00:00:00 |           110.00
      5 | 30-JUN-21 00:00:00 |           110.00
      2 | 05-JUN-21 00:00:00 |           125.00
      1 | 29-MAY-21 00:00:00 |           510.00
     19 | 01-SEP-21 00:00:00 |            95.00
     20 | 01-SEP-21 00:00:00 |            75.00
```

■ FIGURE 16.13 Using NOT BETWEEN to retrieve rows outside a date range.

If we want output that is easier to read, we might ask the DBMS to sort the result by sale date:

```
SELECT sale_id, sale_date, sale_total_amt
FROM sale
WHERE sale_date NOT BETWEEN '1-Jul-2021' AND '31-Aug-2021'
ORDER BY sale_date;
```

producing the result in Figure 16.14.

```
sale_id |      sale_date       | sale_total_amt
--------+----------------------+----------------
      1 | 29-MAY-21 00:00:00 |           510.00
      2 | 05-JUN-21 00:00:00 |           125.00
      3 | 15-JUN-21 00:00:00 |            58.00
      5 | 30-JUN-21 00:00:00 |           110.00
      4 | 30-JUN-21 00:00:00 |           110.00
     19 | 01-SEP-21 00:00:00 |            95.00
     20 | 01-SEP-21 00:00:00 |            75.00
```

■ FIGURE 16.14 Output sorted by date.

Nulls and Retrieval: Three-Valued Logic

The predicates you have seen to this point omit one important thing: the presence of nulls. What should a DBMS do when it encounters a row that contains null, rather than a known value? As you know, the relational data model doesn't have a specific rule as to what a DBMS should do, but it does require that the DBMS act consistently when it encounters nulls.

Consider the following query as an example:

```
SELECT inventory_id, selling_price
FROM volume
WHERE selling_price < 100;
```

The result can be found in Figure 16.15. Notice that every row in the result table has a value of selling price, which means that rows for unsold items—those with null in the selling price column—are omitted.

```
inventory_id | selling_price
-------------+---------------
           2 |         50.00
           4 |         25.95
           5 |         22.95
           6 |         76.10
          11 |         25.00
          12 |         15.00
          13 |         18.00
          18 |         30.00
          19 |         75.00
          23 |         45.00
          24 |         35.00
          25 |         75.00
          26 |         55.00
          33 |         50.00
          35 |         75.00
          36 |         50.00
          37 |         75.00
          39 |         75.00
          40 |         25.95
          41 |         40.00
          42 |         40.00
          50 |         50.00
          51 |         50.00
          52 |         50.00
          53 |         40.00
          54 |         40.00
          55 |         60.00
          56 |         40.00
          57 |         40.00
          59 |         35.00
          58 |         25.00
          60 |         45.00
          61 |         50.00
          62 |         75.00
```

■ FIGURE 16.15 Retrieval based on a column that includes rows with nulls.

The DBMS can't ascertain what the selling price for unsold items will be: maybe it will be less than $100, or maybe it will be greater than or equal to $100.

The policy of most DBMSs is to exclude rows with nulls from the result. For rows with null in the selling price column, the *maybe* answer to "Is selling price less than 100" becomes *false*. This seems pretty straightforward, but what happens when you have a complex logical expression of which one portion returns *maybe*? The operation of AND, OR, and NOT must be expanded to take into account that they may be operating on a *maybe*.

The three-valued logic table for AND can be found in Table 16.5. Notice that something important hasn't changed: the only way to get a true result is for both simple expressions linked by AND to be true. Given that most DBMSs exclude rows where the predicate evaluates to *maybe*, the presence of nulls in the data will not change what an end user sees.

Table 16.5 Three-Valued AND Truth Table

AND	True	False	Maybe
True	True	False	Maybe
False	False	False	False
Maybe	Maybe	False	Maybe

The same is true when you look at the three-valued truth table for OR (see Table 16.6). As long as one simple expression is true, it does not matter whether the second returns true, false, or maybe. The result will always be true.

Table 16.6 Three-Valued OR Truth Table

OR	True	False	Maybe
True	True	True	True
False	True	False	Maybe
Maybe	True	Maybe	Maybe

If you negate an expression that returns *maybe*, the NOT operator has no effect. In other words, NOT (MAYBE) is still *maybe*.

To see the rows that return *maybe*, you need to add an expression to your query that uses the IS NULL operator. For example, the easiest way to see which volumes have not been sold is to write a query like:

```
SELECT inventory_id, isbn, selling_price
FROM volume
WHERE selling_price IS NULL;
```

The result can be found in Figure 16.16. Note that the selling price column is empty in each row. (Remember that you typically can't see any special value for null.) Notice also that the rows in this result table are all those excluded from the query in Figure 16.15.

```
 inventory_id |         isbn        | selling_price
--------------+---------------------+---------------
            7 | 978-1-11111-137-1 |
            8 | 978-1-11111-137-1 |
            9 | 978-1-11111-136-1 |
           10 | 978-1-11111-136-1 |
           16 | 978-1-11111-121-1 |
           17 | 978-1-11111-121-1 |
           27 | 978-1-11111-141-1 |
           28 | 978-1-11111-141-1 |
           29 | 978-1-11111-141-1 |
           30 | 978-1-11111-145-1 |
           31 | 978-1-11111-145-1 |
           32 | 978-1-11111-145-1 |
           43 | 978-1-11111-132-1 |
           44 | 978-1-11111-138-1 |
           45 | 978-1-11111-138-1 |
           46 | 978-1-11111-131-1 |
           47 | 978-1-11111-140-1 |
           48 | 978-1-11111-123-1 |
           49 | 978-1-11111-127-1 |
           63 | 978-1-11111-130-1 |
           64 | 978-1-11111-136-1 |
           65 | 978-1-11111-136-1 |
           66 | 978-1-11111-137-1 |
           67 | 978-1-11111-137-1 |
           68 | 978-1-11111-138-1 |
           69 | 978-1-11111-138-1 |
           70 | 978-1-11111-139-1 |
           71 | 978-1-11111-139-1 |
```

■ **FIGURE 16.16** Using IS NULL to retrieve rows containing nulls.

Four-Valued Logic

Codd's 330 rules for the relational data model include an enhancement to three-valued logic that he called *four-valued logic*. In four-valued logic, there are actually two types of null: "null and it doesn't matter that it's null" and "null and we've really got a problem because it's null." For example, if a company sells internationally, then it probably has a column for the country of each customer. Because it is essential to know a customer's country, a null in the *country* column would fall into the category of "null and we've really got a problem." In contrast, a missing value in a *company name* column would be quite acceptable in a customer table for rows that represented individual customers. Then the null would be "null and it doesn't matter that it's null." Four-valued logic remains purely theoretical at this time, however, and hasn't been widely implemented. (In fact, as far as I know, only one DBMS uses four-valued logic: FirstSQL.)

Chapter

17

Retrieving Data from More Than One Table

As you learned in the first part of this book, logical relationships between entities in a relational database are represented by matching primary and foreign key values. Given that there are no permanent connections between tables stored in the database, a DBMS must provide some way for users to match primary and foreign key values when needed using the join operation.

In this chapter, you will be introduced to the syntax for including a join in a SQL query. Throughout this chapter you will also read about the impact joins have on database performance. At the end, you will see how subqueries (SELECTs within SELECTs) can be used to avoid joins and in some cases, significantly decrease the time it takes for a DBMS to complete a query.

SQL Syntax for Inner Joins

There are two types of syntax you can use for requesting the inner join of two tables. The first, which we have been calling the "traditional" join syntax, is the only way to write a join in the SQL standards through SQL-89. SQL-92 added a join syntax that is both more flexible and easier to use. (Unfortunately, it hasn't been implemented by some commonly used DBMSs.)

Traditional SQL Joins

The traditional SQL join syntax is based on the combination of the product and restrict operations that you read about in Chapter 6. It has the following general form:

```
SELECT columns
FROM table1, table2
WHERE table1.primary_key = table2.foreign_key
```

Listing the tables to be joined after FROM requests the product. The join condition in the WHERE clause's predicate requests the restrict that identifies the rows that are part of the joined tables. Don't forget that if you leave off the join condition in the predicate, then the presence of the two tables after FROM simply generates a product table.

Note: If you really, really, really want a product, use the CROSS JOIN operator in the FROM clause.

Note: Even if you use the preceding syntax, it is highly unlikely today that the DBMS will actually perform a product followed by a restrict. Most current DMBSs have far faster means of processing a join. Nonetheless, a join is still just about the slowest common SQL operation. This is really unfortunate, because a relation database environment will, by its very nature, require a lot of joins.

For example, assume that someone wanted to see all the orders placed by a customer whose phone number is 518-555-1111. The phone number is part of the *customer* table; the purchase information is in the *sale* table. The two relations are related by the presence of the customer number in both (primary key of the *customer* table; foreign key in *sale*). The query to satisfy the information request, therefore, requires an equi-join of the two tables over the customer number, the result of which can be seen in Figure 17.1:

```
SELECT first_name, last_name, sale_id, sale_date
FROM customer, sale
WHERE customer.customer_numb = sale.customer_numb
      AND contact_phone = '518-555-1111';
```

```
 first_name | last_name | sale_id |     sale_date
------------+-----------+---------+--------------------
  Janice    | Jones     |       3 | 15-JUN-21 00:00:00
  Janice    | Jones     |      17 | 25-JUL-21 00:00:00
  Janice    | Jones     |       2 | 05-JUN-21 00:00:00
  Janice    | Jones     |       1 | 29-MAY-21 00:00:00
```

■ FIGURE 17.1 Output from a query containing an equi-join between a primary key and a foreign key.

There are two important things to notice about the preceding query:

- The join is between a primary key in one table and a foreign key in another. As you will remember, equi-joins that don't meet this pattern are frequently invalid.
- Because the *customer_numb* column appears in more than one table in the query, it must be qualified in the WHERE clause by the name of the table from which it should be taken. To add a qualifier, precede the name of a column by its name, separating the two with a period.

Note: With some large DBMSs, you must also qualify the names of tables you did not create with the user ID of the account that did create the table. For example, if user ID DBA created the customer table, then the full name of the customer number column would the DBA.customer.customer_numb. Check your product documentation to determine whether your DBMS is one of those that requires the user ID qualifier.

How might a SQL query optimizer choose to process this query? Although we cannot be certain because there is more than one order of operations that will work, it is likely that the restrict operation to choose the customer with a telephone number of 518-555-1111 will be performed first. This cuts down on the amount of data that needs to be manipulated for the join. The second step probably will be the join operation because doing the project to select columns for display will eliminate the column needed for the join.

SQL-92 Join Syntax

The SQL-92 standard introduced an alternative join syntax that is both simpler and more flexible than the traditional join syntax. If you are performing a natural equi-join, there are three variations of the syntax you can use, depending on whether the column or columns over which you are joining have the same name and whether you want to use all matching columns in the join.

Note: Despite the length of time that has passed since the introduction of this revised join syntax, not all DBMSs support all three varieties of the syntax. You will need to consult the documentation of your particular product to determine exactly which syntax you can use.

Joins Over All Columns with the Same Name

When the primary key and foreign key columns you are joining have the same name and you want to use all matching columns in the join condition, all you need to do is indicate that you want to join the tables, using the following general syntax:

```
SELECT column(s)
FROM table1 NATURAL JOIN table2
```

The query we used as an example in the preceding section could therefore be written as

```
SELECT first_name, last_name, sale_id, sale_date
FROM customer NATURAL JOIN sale
WHERE contact_phone = '518-555-1111';
```

Note: Because the default is a natural equi-join, you will obtain the same result if you simply use JOIN instead of NATURAL JOIN. In fact, we rarely use the word NATURAL in queries.

The SQL command processor identifies all columns in the two tables that have the same name and automatically performs the join over those columns.

Joins Over Selected Columns

If you don't want to use all matching columns in a join condition, but the columns still have the same name, you specify the names of the columns over which the join is to be made by adding a USING clause:

```
SELECT column(s)
FROM table1 JOIN table2 USING (column)
```

Using this syntax, the sample query would be written

```
SELECT first_name, last_name, sale_id, sale_date
FROM customer JOIN sale USING (customer_numb)
WHERE contact_phone = '518-555-1111';
```

Joins Over Columns with Different Names

When the columns over which you are joining table don't have the same name, then you must use a join condition similar to that used in the traditional SQL join syntax:

```
SELECT column(s)
FROM table1 JOIN table2 ON join_condition
```

Assume that the rare book store database used the name *buyer_numb* in the *sale* table (rather than duplicate *customer_numb* from the customer table). In this case, the sample query will appear as

```
SELECT first_name, last_name, sale_id, sale_date
FROM customer JOIN sale
ON customer.customer_numb = sale.customer_numb
WHERE contact_phone = '518-555-1111';
```

Joining Using Concatenated Keys

All of the joins you have seen to this point have been performed using a single matching column. However, on occasion, you may run into tables where you are dealing with concatenated primary and foreign keys. As an example, we'll return to the four tables from the small accounting firm database that we used in Chapter 6 when we discussed how joins over concatenated keys work:

```
accountant (acct_first_name, acct_last_name, date_hired,
    office_ext)

customer (customer_numb, first_name, last_name, street,
    city, state_province, zip_postcode, contact_phone)

project (tax_year, customer_numb, acct_first_name,
    acct_last_name)

form (tax_year, customer_numb, form_id, is_complete)
```

To see which accountant worked on which forms during which year, a query needs to join the *project* and *form* tables, which are related by a concatenated primary key. The join condition needed is

```
project.tax_year || project.customer_numb =
    form.tax_year || form.customer_numb
```

The || operator represents concatenation in most SQL implementations. It instructs the SQL command processor to view the two columns as if they were one and to base its comparison on the concatenation rather than individual column values.

The following join condition produces the same result because it pulls rows from a product table where *both* the customer ID numbers and the tax years are the same:

```
project.tax_year = form.tax_year AND
    project.customer_numb = form.customer_numb
```

You can therefore write a query using the traditional SQL join syntax in two ways:

```
SELECT acct_first_name, acct_last_name, form.tax_year,
    form.form_ID
FROM project, form
WHERE project.tax_year || project.customer_numb =
    form.tax_year || form.customer_numb;
```

or

```
SELECT acct_first_name, acct_last_name, form.tax_year,
    form.form_ID
FROM project, form
WHERE project.tax_year = form.tax_year
    AND project.customer_numb = form.customer_numb;
```

If the columns have the same names in both tables and are the only matching columns, then the SQL-92 syntax

```
SELECT acct_first_name, acct_last_name, form.tax_year,
    form.form_ID
FROM project JOIN form;
```

has the same effect as the preceding two queries.

When the columns have the same names but aren't the only matching columns, then you must specify the columns in a USING clause:

```
SELECT acct_first_name, acct_last_name, form.tax_year,
    form.form_ID
FROM project JOIN form USING (tax_year, form_ID);
```

Alternatively, if the columns don't have the same name you can use the complete join condition, just as you would if you were using the traditional join syntax. For this example only, let's assume that the accounting firm prefaces each duplicated column name with an identifier for its table. The relations in the sample query would therefore look something like this:

```
account (acct_first_name, acct_last_name, …)
project (p_customer_numb, p_tax_year, …)
form (f_customer_numb, f_taxYear, form_ID, …)
```

The sample query would then be written:

```
SELECT acct_first_name, acct_last_name, form.f_tax_year,
      form.form_ID
FROM project JOIN form ON
      project.p_tax_year || project.p_customer_numb =
      form.f_tax_year || form.f_customer_numb;
```

or

```
SELECT acct_first_name, acct_last_name, form.f_tax_year,
      form.form_ID
FROM project JOIN form ON p_project.tax_year = f_form.tax_year
      AND p_project.customer_numb = f_form.customer_numb;
```

Notice that in all forms of the query, the tax year and form ID columns in the SELECT clause are qualified by a table name. It really doesn't matter from which the data are taken, but because the columns appear in both tables the SQL command processor needs to be told which pair of columns to use.

Joining More Than Two Tables

What if you need to join more than two tables in the same query? For example, someone at the rare book store might want to see the names of the people who have purchased a volume with the ISBN of 978-1-11111-146-1. The query that retrieves that information must join *volume* to *sale* to find the sales on which the volume was sold. Then, the result of the first join must be joined again to *customer* to gain access to the names.

Using the traditional join syntax, the query is written

```
SELECT first_name, last_name
FROM customer, sale, volume
WHERE volume.sale_id = sale.sale_id AND
      sale.customer_numb = customer.customer_numb
AND isbn = '978-1-11111-136-1';
```

With the simplest form of the SQL-92 syntax, the query becomes

```
SELECT first_name, last_name
FROM customer JOIN sale JOIN volume
WHERE isbn = '978-1-11111-136-1';
```

Both syntaxes produce the following result:

```
first_name | last_name
-----------+-----------
Mary       | Collins
Janice     | Smith
```

Keep in mind that the join operation can work on only two tables at a time. If you need to join more than two tables, you must join them in pairs. Therefore, a join of three tables requires two joins, a join of four tables requires three joins, and so on.

SQL-92 Syntax and Multiple-Table Join Performance

Although the SQL-92 syntax is certainly simpler than the traditional join syntax, it has another major benefit: It gives you control over the order in which the joins are performed. With the traditional join syntax, the query optimizer is in complete control of the order of the *joins*. However, in SQL-92, the joins are performed from left to right, following the order in which the *joins* are placed in the FROM clause.

This means that you sometimes can affect the performance of a query by varying the order in which the joins are performed.[1] Remember that the less data the DBMS has to manipulate, the faster a query including one or more joins will execute. Therefore, you want to perform the most discriminatory joins first.

As an example, consider the sample query used in the previous section. The *volume* table has the most rows, followed by *sale* and then *customer*. However, the query also contains a highly discriminatory *restrict* predicate that limits the rows from that table. Therefore, it is highly likely that the DBMS will perform the restrict on *volume* first. This means that the query is likely to execute faster if you write it so that *sale* is joined with *volume* first, given that this join will significantly limit the rows from *sale* that need to be joined with *customer*.

---

[1] This holds true only if a DBMS has implemented the newer join syntax according to the SQL standard. A DBMS may support the syntax without its query optimizer using the order of tables in the FROM clause to determine join order.

In contrast, what would happen if there was no restrict predicate in the query and you wanted to retrieve the name of the customer for every book ordered in the database? The query would appear as

```
SELECT first_name, last_name
FROM customer JOIN sale JOIN volume;
```

First, keep in mind that this type of query, which is asking for large amounts of data, will rarely execute as quickly as one that contains predicates to limit the number of rows. Nonetheless, if will execute a bit faster if *customers* is joined to *sale* before joining to *volume*. Why? Because the joins manipulate fewer rows in that order.

Assume that there are 20 customers, 100 sales, and 300 volumes sold. Every sold item in *volume* must have a matching row in *sale*. Therefore, the result from that join will be at least 300 rows long. Those 300 rows must be joined to the 20 rows in *customer*. However, if we reverse the order, then the 20 rows in *customer* are joined to 100 rows in *sale*, producing a table of 100 rows, which can then be joined to *volume*. In either case, we are stuck with a join of 100 rows to 300 rows, but when the *customer* table is handled first, the other join is 20 to 100 rows, rather than 20 to 300 rows.

Finding Multiple Rows in One Table: Joining a Table to Itself

One of the limitations of a restrict operation is that its predicate is applied to only one row in a table at a time. This means that a predicate such as

```
isbn = '0-131-4966-9' AND isbn = '0-191-4923-8'
```

and the query

```
SELECT first_name, last_name
FROM customer JOIN sale JOIN volume
WHERE isbn = '978-1-11111-146-1'
      AND isbn = '978-1-11111-122-1';
```

will always return 0 rows. No row can have more than one value in the *isbn* column!

What the preceding query is actually trying to do is locate customers who have purchased two specific books. This means that there must be at least two rows for a customer's purchases in *volume*, one for each for each of the books in question.

Given that you cannot do this type of query with a simple restrict predicate, how can you retrieve the data? The technique is to join the *volume* table to itself over the sale ID. The result table will have two columns for the book's ISBN, one for each copy of the original table. Those rows that have both the ISBNs that we want will finally be joined to the *sale* table (over the sale ID) and *customer* (over customer number) tables so that the query can project the customer's name.

Before looking at the SQL syntax, however, let's examine the relational algebra of the joins so you can see exactly what is happening. Assume that we are working with the subset of the *volume* table in Figure 17.2. (The sale ID and the ISBN are the only columns that affect the relational algebra; the rest have been left off for simplicity.) Notice first that the result of our sample query should display the first and last names of the customer who made purchase number 6. (It is the only order that contains both of the books in question.)

```
sale_id |         isbn
--------+--------------------
      1 | 978-1-11111-111-1
      1 | 978-1-11111-133-1
      1 | 978-1-11111-131-1
      2 | 978-1-11111-142-1
      2 | 978-1-11111-144-1
      2 | 978-1-11111-146-1
      3 | 978-1-11111-133-1
      3 | 978-1-11111-132-1
      3 | 978-1-11111-143-1
      4 | 978-1-11111-121-1
      5 | 978-1-11111-121-1
      6 | 978-1-11111-139-1
      6 | 978-1-11111-146-1
      6 | 978-1-11111-122-1
      6 | 978-1-11111-130-1
      6 | 978-1-11111-126-1
      7 | 978-1-11111-125-1
      7 | 978-1-11111-131-1
      8 | 978-1-11111-126-1
      8 | 978-1-11111-133-1
      9 | 978-1-11111-139-1
     10 | 978-1-11111-133-1
```

■ **FIGURE 17.2 A subset of the *volume* table.**

The first step in the query is to join the table in Figure 17.2 to itself over the sale ID, producing the result table in Figure 17.3. The columns that come from the first copy have been labeled T1; those that come from the second copy are labeled T2.

The two rows in black are those that have the ISBNs for which we are searching. Therefore, we need to follow the join with a restrict that says something like

```
WHERE isbn (from table 1) = '978-1-11111-146-1'
   AND isbn (from table 2) = '978-1-11111-122-1'
```

The result will be a table with one row in it (the second of the two black rows in Figure 17.3).

```
sale_id (T1)|          isbn          | sale_id (T2)|          isbn
------------+------------------------+-------------+------------------
          1 | 978-1-11111-111-1 |             1 | 978-1-11111-133-1
          1 | 978-1-11111-111-1 |             1 | 978-1-11111-131-1
          1 | 978-1-11111-111-1 |             1 | 978-1-11111-111-1
          1 | 978-1-11111-131-1 |             1 | 978-1-11111-133-1
          1 | 978-1-11111-131-1 |             1 | 978-1-11111-131-1
          1 | 978-1-11111-131-1 |             1 | 978-1-11111-111-1
          1 | 978-1-11111-133-1 |             1 | 978-1-11111-133-1
          1 | 978-1-11111-133-1 |             1 | 978-1-11111-131-1
          1 | 978-1-11111-133-1 |             1 | 978-1-11111-111-1
          2 | 978-1-11111-142-1 |             2 | 978-1-11111-144-1
          2 | 978-1-11111-142-1 |             2 | 978-1-11111-146-1
          2 | 978-1-11111-142-1 |             2 | 978-1-11111-142-1
          2 | 978-1-11111-146-1 |             2 | 978-1-11111-144-1
          2 | 978-1-11111-146-1 |             2 | 978-1-11111-146-1
          2 | 978-1-11111-146-1 |             2 | 978-1-11111-142-1
          2 | 978-1-11111-144-1 |             2 | 978-1-11111-144-1
          2 | 978-1-11111-144-1 |             2 | 978-1-11111-146-1
          2 | 978-1-11111-144-1 |             2 | 978-1-11111-142-1
          3 | 978-1-11111-143-1 |             3 | 978-1-11111-133-1
          3 | 978-1-11111-143-1 |             3 | 978-1-11111-132-1
          3 | 978-1-11111-143-1 |             3 | 978-1-11111-143-1
          3 | 978-1-11111-132-1 |             3 | 978-1-11111-133-1
          3 | 978-1-11111-132-1 |             3 | 978-1-11111-132-1
          3 | 978-1-11111-132-1 |             3 | 978-1-11111-143-1
          3 | 978-1-11111-133-1 |             3 | 978-1-11111-133-1
          3 | 978-1-11111-133-1 |             3 | 978-1-11111-132-1
          3 | 978-1-11111-133-1 |             3 | 978-1-11111-143-1
          5 | 978-1-11111-121-1 |             5 | 978-1-11111-121-1
          4 | 978-1-11111-121-1 |             4 | 978-1-11111-121-1
          6 | 978-1-11111-146-1 |             6 | 978-1-11111-139-1
          6 | 978-1-11111-146-1 |             6 | 978-1-11111-126-1
          6 | 978-1-11111-146-1 |             6 | 978-1-11111-130-1
```

■ **FIGURE 17.3** The result of joining the table in Figure 17.2 to itself (continues).

At this point, the query can join the table to *sale* over the sale ID to provide access to the customer number of the person who made the purchase. The result of that second join can then be joined to *customer* to obtain the customer's name (Franklin Hayes). Finally, the query projects the columns the user wants to see.

Correlation Names

The challenge facing a query that needs to work with multiple copies of a single table is to tell the SQL command processor to make the copies of the table. We do this by placing the name of the table more than once on the FROM line, associating each instance of the name with a different alias. Such aliases for table names are known as *correlation names* and take the syntax

```
FROM table_name AS correlation_name
```

```
   6 | 978-1-11111-146-1 |        6 | 978-1-11111-122-1
   6 | 978-1-11111-146-1 |        6 | 978-1-11111-146-1
   6 | 978-1-11111-122-1 |        6 | 978-1-11111-139-1
   6 | 978-1-11111-122-1 |        6 | 978-1-11111-126-1
   6 | 978-1-11111-122-1 |        6 | 978-1-11111-130-1
   6 | 978-1-11111-122-1 |        6 | 978-1-11111-122-1
   6 | 978-1-11111-122-1 |        6 | 978-1-11111-146-1
   6 | 978-1-11111-130-1 |        6 | 978-1-11111-139-1
   6 | 978-1-11111-130-1 |        6 | 978-1-11111-126-1
   6 | 978-1-11111-130-1 |        6 | 978-1-11111-130-1
   6 | 978-1-11111-130-1 |        6 | 978-1-11111-122-1
   6 | 978-1-11111-130-1 |        6 | 978-1-11111-146-1
   6 | 978-1-11111-126-1 |        6 | 978-1-11111-139-1
   6 | 978-1-11111-126-1 |        6 | 978-1-11111-126-1
   6 | 978-1-11111-126-1 |        6 | 978-1-11111-130-1
   6 | 978-1-11111-126-1 |        6 | 978-1-11111-122-1
   6 | 978-1-11111-126-1 |        6 | 978-1-11111-146-1
   6 | 978-1-11111-139-1 |        6 | 978-1-11111-139-1
   6 | 978-1-11111-139-1 |        6 | 978-1-11111-126-1
   6 | 978-1-11111-139-1 |        6 | 978-1-11111-130-1
   6 | 978-1-11111-139-1 |        6 | 978-1-11111-122-1
   6 | 978-1-11111-139-1 |        6 | 978-1-11111-146-1
   7 | 978-1-11111-125-1 |        7 | 978-1-11111-131-1
   7 | 978-1-11111-125-1 |        7 | 978-1-11111-125-1
   7 | 978-1-11111-131-1 |        7 | 978-1-11111-131-1
   7 | 978-1-11111-131-1 |        7 | 978-1-11111-125-1
   8 | 978-1-11111-126-1 |        8 | 978-1-11111-133-1
   8 | 978-1-11111-126-1 |        8 | 978-1-11111-126-1
   8 | 978-1-11111-133-1 |        8 | 978-1-11111-133-1
   8 | 978-1-11111-133-1 |        8 | 978-1-11111-126-1
   9 | 978-1-11111-139-1 |        9 | 978-1-11111-139-1
  10 | 978-1-11111-133-1 |       10 | 978-1-11111-133-1
```

■ FIGURE 17.3 *(cont.)*

For example, to instruct SQL to use two copies of the *volume* table you
might use

```
FROM volume AS T1, volume AS T2
```

The AS is optional. Therefore, the following syntax is also legal:

```
FROM volume T1, volume T2
```

In the other parts of the query, you refer to the two copies using the correlation names rather than the original table name.

*Note: You can give any table a correlation name; its use is not restricted
to queries that work with multiple copies of a single table. In fact, if a table
name is difficult to type and appears several times in a query, you can
save yourself some typing and avoid problems with typing errors by giving
the table a short correlation name.*

Performing the Same-Table Join

The query that performs the same-table join needs to specify all of the relational algebra operations you read about in the preceding section. It can be written using the traditional join syntax, as follows:

```
SELECT first_name, last_name
FROM volume T1, volume T2, sale, customer
WHERE t1.isbn = '978-1-11111-146-1'
      AND T2.isbn = '978-1-11111-122-1'
      AND T1.sale_id = T2.sale_id
      AND T1.sale_id = sale.sale_id
      AND sale.customer_numb = customer.customer_numb;
```

There is one very important thing to notice about this query. Although our earlier discussion of the relational algebra indicated that the same-table join would be performed first, followed by a restrict and the other two joins, there is no way using the traditional syntax to indicate the joining of an intermediate result table (in this case, the same-table join). Therefore, the query syntax must join *sale* to either T1 or T2. Nonetheless, it is likely that the query optimizer will determine that performing the same-table join followed by the restrict is a more efficient way to process the query than joining *sale* to T1 first.

If you use the SQL-92 join syntax, then you have some control over the order in which the joins are performed:

```
SELECT first_name, last_name
FROM volume T1 JOIN volume T2 ON (T1.sale_id = T2.sale_id)
     JOIN sale JOIN customer
WHERE t1.isbn = '978-1-11111-146-1'
     AND T2.isbn = '978-1-11111-122-1';
```

The SQL command processor will process the multiple joins in the FROM clause from left to right, ensuring that the same-table join is performed first.

You can extend the same table join technique you have just read about to find as many rows in a table you need. Create one copy of the table with a correlation name for the number of rows the query needs to match in the FROM clause and join those tables together. In the WHERE clause, use a predicate that includes one restrict for each copy of the table. For example, to retrieve data that have four specified rows in a table, you need four copies of the table, three joins, and four expressions in the restrict predicate. The general format of such a query is

```
SELECT column(s)
FROM table_name T1 JOIN table_name T2
     JOIN table_name T3 JOIN table_name T4
WHERE T1.column_name = value AND T2.column_name = value
     AND T3.column_name = value
     AND T3.column_name = value
```

Outer Joins

As you read in Chapter 6, an outer join is a join that includes rows in a result table even though there may not be a match between rows in the two tables being joined. Whenever the DBMS can't match rows, it places nulls in the columns for which no data exist. The result may therefore not be a legal relation because it may not have a primary key. However, because a query's result table is a virtual table that is never stored in the database, having no primary keys doesn't present a data integrity problem.

To perform an outer join using the SQL-92 syntax, you indicate the type of join in the FROM clause. For example, to perform a left outer join between the *customer* and *sale* tables, you could type

```
SELECT first_name, last_name, sale_id, sale_date
FROM customer LEFT OUTER JOIN sale;
```

The result appears in Figure 17.4. Notice that five rows appear to be empty in the *sale_id* and *sale_date* columns. These five customers haven't

first_name	last_name	sale_id	sale_date
Janice	Jones	1	29-MAY-21 00:00:00
Janice	Jones	2	05-JUN-21 00:00:00
Janice	Jones	17	25-JUL-21 00:00:00
Janice	Jones	3	15-JUN-21 00:00:00
Jon	Jones	20	01-SEP-21 00:00:00
Jon	Jones	16	25-JUL-21 00:00:00
Jon	Jones	13	10-JUL-21 00:00:00
John	Doe		
Jane	Doe	4	30-JUN-21 00:00:00
Jane	Smith	18	22-AUG-21 00:00:00
Jane	Smith	8	07-JUL-21 00:00:00
Janice	Smith	19	01-SEP-21 00:00:00
Janice	Smith	14	10-JUL-21 00:00:00
Janice	Smith	5	30-JUN-21 00:00:00
Helen	Brown		
Helen	Jerry	9	07-JUL-21 00:00:00
Helen	Jerry	7	05-JUL-21 00:00:00
Mary	Collins	11	10-JUL-21 00:00:00
Peter	Collins	12	10-JUL-21 00:00:00
Edna	Hayes	15	12-JUL-21 00:00:00
Edna	Hayes	10	10-JUL-21 00:00:00
Franklin	Hayes	6	05-JUL-21 00:00:00
Peter	Johnson		
Peter	Johnson		
John	Smith		

■ FIGURE 17.4 The result of an outer join.

made any purchases. Therefore, the columns in question are actually null. However, most DBMSs have no visible indicator for null; it looks as if the values are blank. It is the responsibility of the person viewing the result table to realize that the empty spaces represent nulls rather than blanks.

The SQL-92 outer join syntax for joins has the same options as the inner join syntax:

- If you use the syntax in the preceding example, the DBMS will automatically perform the outer join on all matching columns between the two tables.
- If you want to specify the columns over which the outer join will be performed, and the columns have the same names in both tables, add a USING clause:

```
SELECT first_name, last_name, sale_id, sale_date
FROM customer LEFT OUTER JOIN sale USING (customer_numb);
```

- If the columns over which you want to perform the outer join do not have the same name, then append an ON clause that contains the join condition:

```
SELECT first_name, last_name
FROM customer T1 LEFT OUTER JOIN sale T2
    ON (T1.customer_numb = T2.customer_numb);
```

Note: The SQL standard also includes an operation known as the UNION JOIN. It performs a FULL OUTER JOIN on two tables and then throws out the rows that match, placing all those that don't match in the result table. The UNION JOIN hasn't been widely implemented.

Table Constructors in Queries

SQL standards from SQL-92 forward allow the table on which a SELECT is performed to be a virtual table rather than just a base table. This means that a DBMS should allow a complete SELECT (what is known as a *subquery*) to be used in a FROM clause to prepare the table on which the remainder of the query will operate. Expressions that create tables for use in SQL statements in this way are known as *table constructors*.

Note: When you join tables in the FROM clause you are actually generating a source for a query on the fly. What is described in this section is just an extension of that principle.

For example, the following query lists all volumes that were purchased by customers 6 and 10:

```
SELECT isbn, first_name, last_name
FROM volume JOIN (SELECT first_name, last_name, sale_id
    FROM sale JOIN customer
WHERE customer.customer_numb = 6 or customer.customer_numb = 10)
```

The results can be found in Figure 17.5. Notice that the row selection is being performed in the subquery that is part of the FROM clause. This forces the SQL command processor to perform the subquery prior to performing the join in the outer query. Although this query could certainly be written in another way, using the subquery in the FROM clause gives a programmer using a DBMS with a query optimizer that uses the FROM clause order additional control over the order in which the relational algebra operations are performed.

```
       isbn        | first_name | last_name
-------------------+------------+----------
978-1-11111-121-1 | Janice     | Smith
978-1-11111-130-1 | Peter      | Collins
978-1-11111-132-1 | Peter      | Collins
978-1-11111-141-1 | Janice     | Smith
978-1-11111-141-1 | Janice     | Smith
978-1-11111-128-1 | Janice     | Smith
978-1-11111-136-1 | Janice     | Smith
```

■ FIGURE 17.5   **Using a table constructor in a query's FROM clause.**

Avoiding Joins with Uncorrelated Subqueries

As we discussed earlier in this chapter, with some DBMSs you can control the order in which joins are performed by using the SQL-92 syntax and being careful with the order in which you place joins in the FROM clause. However, there is a type of SQL syntax—a *subquery*—that you can use with any DBMS to obtain the same result, but often avoid performing a join altogether.[2]

A subquery (or *subselect*) is a complete SELECT statement embedded within another SELECT. The result of the inner SELECT becomes data used by the outer.

Note: Subqueries have other uses besides avoiding joins, which you will see throughout the rest of this book.

---

[2]Even a subquery may not avoid joins. Some query optimizers actually replace subqueries with joins when processing a query.

A query containing a subquery has the following general form:

```
SELECT column(s)
FROM table
WHERE operator (SELECT column(s))
      FROM table
      WHERE …)
```

There are two general types of subqueries. In an *uncorrelated subquery*, the SQL command processor is able to complete the processing of the inner SELECT before moving to the outer. However, in a *correlated subquery*, the SQL command processor cannot complete the inner query without information from the outer. Correlated subqueries usually require that the inner SELECT be performed more than once and therefore can execute relatively slowly. The same is not true for uncorrelated subqueries which can be used to replace join syntax and therefore may produce faster performance.

Note: You will see examples of correlated subqueries beginning in Chapter 18.

Using the IN Operator

As a first example, consider the following query

```
SELECT sale_date, customer_numb
FROM sale JOIN volume
WHERE isbn = '978-1-11111-136-1';
```

which produces the following output:

```
 sale_date           | customer_numb
---------------------+----------------
 10-JUL-21 00:00:00 |             9
 01-SEP-21 00:00:00 |             6
```

When looking at the preceding output, don't forget that by default the DBMS adds the time to the display of a date column. In this case, there is no time included in the stored data, so the time appears as all zeros.

We can rewrite the query using subquery syntax as

```
SELECT sale_date, customer_numb
FROM sale
WHERE sale_id IN (SELECT sale_id
      FROM volume
      WHERE isbn = '978-1-11111-136-1');
```

The inner SELECT retrieves data from the *volume* table, and produces a set of sale IDs. The outer SELECT then retrieves data from *sale* where the sale ID is in the set of values retrieved by the subquery.

The use of the IN operator is actually exactly the same as the use you read about in Chapter 16. The only difference is that, rather than placing the set of values in parentheses as literals, the set is generated by a SELECT.

When processing this query, the DBMS never joins the two tables. It performs the inner SELECT first and then uses the result table from that query when processing the outer SELECT. In the case in which the two tables are very large, this can significantly speed up processing the query.

Note: You can also use NOT IN with subqueries. This is a very powerful syntax that you will read about in Chapter 18.

Using the ANY Operator

Like IN, the ANY operator searches a set of values. In its simplest form, ANY is equivalent to IN:

```
SELECT sale_date, customer_numb
FROM sale
WHERE sale_id = ANY (SELECT sale_id
      FROM volume
      WHERE isbn = '978-1-11111-136-1');
```

This syntax tells the DBMS to retrieve rows from *sale*, where the sale ID is "equal to any" of those retrieved by the SELECT in the subquery.

What sets ANY apart from IN is that the = can be replaced with any other relationship operator (for example, < and >). For example, you could use it to create a query that asked for all customers who had purchased a book with a price greater than the average cost of a book. Because queries of this type require the use of SQL summary functions, we will leave their discussion until Chapter 19.

Nesting Subqueries

The SELECT that you use as a subquery can have a subquery. In fact, if you want to rewrite a query that joins more than two tables, you will need to nest subqueries in this way. As an example, consider the following query that you saw earlier in this chapter:

```
SELECT first_name, last_name
FROM customer, sale, volume
WHERE volume.sale_id = sale.sale_id AND
      sale.customer_numb = customer.customer_numb
      AND isbn = '978-1-11111-136-1';
```

It can be rewritten as

```
SELECT first_name, last_name
FROM customer
WHERE customer_numb IN
      (SELECT customer_numb
      FROM sale
      WHERE sale_id = ANY
            (SELECT sale_id
            FROM volume
            WHERE isbn = '978-1-11111-136-1'));
```

Note that each subquery is surrounded completely by parentheses. The end of the query therefore contains two closing parentheses next to each other. The rightmost) closes the outer subquery; the) to its left closes the inner subquery.

The DBMS processes the innermost subquery first, returning a set of sale IDs that contains the sales on which the ISBN in question appears. The middle SELECT (the outer subquery) returns a set of customer numbers for rows where the sale ID is any of those in the set returned by the innermost subquery. Finally, the outer query displays information about customers whose customer numbers are in the set produced by the outer subquery.

In general, the larger the tables in question (in other words, the more rows they have), the more performance benefit you will see if you assemble queries using subqueries rather than joins. How many levels deep can you nest subqueries? There is no theoretical limit. However, once a query becomes more than a few levels deep, it may become hard to keep track of what is occurring.

Replacing a Same-Table Join with Subqueries

The same-table join that you read about earlier in this chapter can also be replaced with subqueries. As you will remember, that query required a join between *sale* and *customer* to obtain the customer name, a join between *sale* and *volume*, and a join of the *volume* table to itself to find all sales that contained two desired ISBNs. Because there were three joins in the original query, the rewrite will require one nested subquery for each join.

```
SELECT last_name, first_name
FROM customer
WHERE customer_numb IN
      (SELECT customer_numb
      FROM sale
      WHERE sale_id IN
            (SELECT sale_id
            FROM volume
            WHERE isbn = '978-1-11111-146-1'
            AND sale_id IN
                  (SELECT sale_id
                  FROM volume
                  WHERE isbn = '978-1-11111-122-1')));
```

The innermost subquery retrieves a set of sale IDs for the rows on which an ISBN of '978-1-11111-122-1' appears. The next level subquery above it retrieves rows from *volume* where the sale ID appears in the set retrieved by the innermost subquery and the ISBN is '978-1-11111-146-1'. These two subqueries, therefore, replace the same-table join.

The set of sale IDs is then used by the outermost subquery to obtain a set of customer numbers for the sales whose numbers appear in the result set of the two innermost subqueries. Finally, the outer query displays customer information for the customers whose numbers are part of the outermost subquery's result set.

Notice that the two innermost subqueries are based on the same table. To process this query, the DBMS makes two passes through the *volume* table—one for each subquery—rather than joining a copy of the table to itself. When a table is very large, this syntax can significantly speed up performance because the DBMS does not need to create and manipulate a duplicate copy of the large table in main memory.

Chapter
18

Advanced Retrieval Operations

To this point, the queries you have read about combine and extract data from relations in relatively straightforward ways. However, there are additional operations you can perform on relations that, for example, answer questions such as "show me the data that are not ..." or "show me the combination of data that are ...". In this chapter, you will read about the implementation of additional relational algebra operations in SQL that will perform such queries, as well as performing calculations and using functions that you can use to obtain information about the data you retrieve.

Union

Union is one of the few relational algebra operations whose name can be used in a SQL query. When you want to use a union, you write two individual SELECT statements joined by the keyword UNION:

```
SELECT column(s)
FROM table(s)
WHERE predicate
UNION
SELECT column(s)
FROM table(s)
WHERE predicate
```

The columns retrieved by the two SELECTs must have the same data types and sizes and be in the same order. For example, the following is legal as long as the customer numbers are the same data type (for example, integer), and the customer names are the same data type and length (for example, 30-character strings):

```
SELECT customer_numb, customer_first, customer_last
FROM some_table
UNION
SELECT cust_no, first_name, last_name
FROM some_other_table
```

Notice that the source tables of the two SELECTs don't need to be the same, nor do the columns need to have the same names. However, the following is not legal:

```
SELECT customer_first, customer_last
FROM some_table
UNION
SELECT cust_no, cust_phone
FROM some_table
```

Although both SELECTS are taken from the same table and the two base tables are therefore union compatible, the result tables returned by the two SELECTs are *not* union compatible[1] and the union therefore cannot be performed. The *cust_no* column has a domain of INT and therefore doesn't match the CHAR domain of the *customer_first* column. The *customer_last* and *cust_phone* columns do have the same data type, but they don't have the same size: *customer_last* has space for more characters. If even one corresponding set of columns don't match, the tables aren't union compatible.

Performing Union Using the Same Source Tables

A typical use of UNION in interactive SQL is a replacement for a predicate with an OR. As an example, consider this query:

```
SELECT first_name, last_name
FROM customer JOIN sale JOIN volume
WHERE isbn = '978-1-11111-128-1'
UNION
SELECT first_name, last_name
FROM customer JOIN sale JOIN volume
WHERE isbn = '978-1-11111-143-1';
```

It produces the following output:

```
first_name  | last_name
------------+-----------
Janice      | Jones
Janice      | Smith
```

---

[1] Don't forget that SQL's definition of union compatibility is different from the relational algebra definition. SQL unions require that the tables have the same number of columns. The columns must match in data type and in size. Relational algebra, however, requires that the columns be defined over the same domains, without regard to size (which is an implementation detail.)

The DBMS processes the query by performing the two SELECTs. It then combines the two individual result tables into one, eliminating duplicate rows. To remove the duplicates, the DBMS sorts the result table by every column in the table and then scans it for matching rows placed next to one another. (That is why the rows in the result are in alphabetical order by the author's first name.) The information returned by the preceding query is the same as the following:

```
SELECT first_name, last_name
FROM customer JOIN sale JOIN volume
WHERE isbn = '978-1-11111-128-1'
     OR isbn = '978-1-11111-143-1';
```

However, there are two major differences. First, when you use the complex predicate that contains OR, most DBMSs retain the duplicate rows. In contrast, the query with the UNION operator removes them automatically.

The second difference is in how the queries are processed. The query that performs a union makes two passes through the *volume* table, one for each of the individual SELECTs, making only a single comparison with the ISBN value in each row. The query that uses the OR in its predicate makes only one pass through the table, but must make two comparisons when testing most rows.[2]

Which query will execute faster? If you include a DISTINCT in the query with an OR predicate, then it will return the same result as the query that performs a union. However, if you are using a DBMS that does not remove duplicates automatically and you can live with the duplicate rows, then the query with the OR predicate will be faster.

Note: If you want a union to retain all rows—including the duplicates—use UNION ALL instead of UNION.

Performing Union Using Different Source Tables

Another common use of UNION is to pull together data from different source tables into a single result table. Suppose, for example, we wanted to obtain a list of books published by Wiley and books that have been purchased by customer number 11. A query to obtain this data can be written as

---

[2]Some query optimizers do not behave in this way. You will need to check with either a DBA or a system programmer (someone who knows a great deal about the internals of your DBMS) to find out for certain.

```
SELECT author_last_first, title
FROM work, book, author, publisher
WHERE work.author_numb = author.author_numb
      AND work.work_numb = book.work_numb
      AND book.publisher_id = publisher.publisher_id
      AND publisher_name = 'Wiley'
UNION
SELECT author_last_first, title
FROM work, book, author, sale, volume
WHERE customer_numb = 11
      AND work.author_numb = author.author_numb
      AND work.work_numb = book.work_numb
      AND book.isbn = volume.isbn
      AND volume.sale_id = sale.sale_id;
```

To process this query, the result of which appear in Figure 18.1, the DBMS performs each separate SELECT and then combines the individual result tables.

```
          author_last_first        |              title
----------------------------------+-----------------------------------
  Barth, John                      | Giles Goat Boy
  Bronte, Charlotte                | Jane Eyre
  Funke, Cornelia                  | Inkdeath
  Rand, Ayn                        | Anthem
  Rand, Ayn                        | Atlas Shrugged
  Twain, Mark                      | Adventures of Huckleberry Finn, The
  Twain, Mark                      | Tom Sawyer
```

■ FIGURE 18.1 The result of a union between result tables coming from different source tables.

Alternative SQL-92 Union Syntax

The SQL-92 standard introduced an alternative means of making two tables union compatible: the CORRESPONDING BY clause. This syntax can be used when the two source tables have some columns with the same names. However, the two source tables need not have completely the same structure.

To use CORRESPONDING BY, you SELECT * from each of the source tables, but then indicate the columns to be used for the union in the CORRESPONDING BY clause:

```
SELECT *
FROM table1
WHERE predicate
UNION CORRESPONDING BY (columns_for_union)
SELECT *
FROM table2
WHERE predicate
```

For example, the query to retrieve the names of all customers who have ordered two specific books could be rewritten

```
SELECT *
FROM volume JOIN sale JOIN customer
WHERE isbn = '978-1-11111-128-1'
UNION CORRESPONDING BY (first_name, last_name)
SELECT *
FROM volume JOIN sale JOIN customer
WHERE isbn = '978-1-11111-128-1';
```

To process this query, the DBMS performs the two SELECTs, returning all columns in the tables. However, when the time comes to perform the union, it throws away all columns except those in the parentheses following BY.

Negative Queries

Among the most powerful database queries are those phrased in the negative, such as "show me all the customers who have not made a purchase in the past year." This type of query is particularly tricky, because it is asking for data that are not in the database. (The rare book store has data about customers who *have* purchased, but not those who have not.) The only way to perform such a query is to request the DBMS to use the difference operation.

Traditional SQL Negative Queries

The traditional way to perform a query that requires a difference is to use subquery syntax with the NOT IN operator. To do so, the query takes the following general format:

```
SELECT column(s)
FROM table(s)
WHERE column NOT IN (SELECT column
     FROM table(s)
     WHERE predicate)
```

The outer query retrieves a list of all things of interest; the subquery retrieves those that meet the necessary criteria. The NOT IN operator then acts to include all those from the list of all things that *are not* in the set of values returned by the subquery.

As a first example, consider the query that retrieves all books that are not in stock (no rows exist in *volume*):

```
SELECT title
FROM book, work
WHERE book.work_numb = work.work_numb
        AND isbn NOT IN (SELECT isbn
        FROM volume);
```

The outer query selects those rows in *books* (the list of all things) whose ISBNs are not in *volume* (the list of things that *are*). The result in Figure 18.2 contains the nine books that do not appear at least once in the *volume* table.

```
title
-----------------------------------------------------
 Jane Eyre
 Villette
 Hound of the Baskervilles
 Lost World, The
 Complete Sherlock Holmes
 Complete Sherlock Holmes
 Tom Sawyer
 Connecticut Yankee in King Arthur's Court, A
 Dune
```

■ FIGURE 18.2 The result of the first SELECT that uses a NOT IN subquery.

As a second example, we will retrieve the titles of all books for which we don't have a new copy in stock, the result of which can be found in Figure 18.3:

```
SELECT title
FROM work, book
WHERE work.work_numb = book.work_numb
AND book.isbn NOT IN (SELECT isbn
        FROM volume
        WHERE condition_code = 1);
```

In this case, the subquery contains a restrict predicate in its WHERE clause, limiting the rows retrieved by the subquery to new volumes (those with a

title	isbn
Jane Eyre	978-1-11111-111-1
Jane Eyre	978-1-11111-112-1
Villette	978-1-11111-113-1
Hound of the Baskervilles	978-1-11111-114-1
Hound of the Baskervilles	978-1-11111-115-1
Lost World, The	978-1-11111-116-1
Complete Sherlock Holmes	978-1-11111-117-1
Complete Sherlock Holmes	978-1-11111-118-1
Tom Sawyer	978-1-11111-120-1
Connecticut Yankee in King Arthur's Court, A	978-1-11111-119-1
Tom Sawyer	978-1-11111-121-1
Adventures of Huckleberry Finn, The	978-1-11111-122-1
Matarese Circle, The	978-1-11111-123-1
Bourne Supremacy, The	978-1-11111-124-1
Fountainhead, The	978-1-11111-125-1
Atlas Shrugged	978-1-11111-127-1
Kidnapped	978-1-11111-128-1
Treasure Island	978-1-11111-130-1
Sot Weed Factor, The	978-1-11111-131-1
Dune	978-1-11111-134-1
Foundation	978-1-11111-135-1
Last Foundation	978-1-11111-137-1
I, Robot	978-1-11111-139-1
Inkheart	978-1-11111-140-1
Anthem	978-1-11111-144-1

■ **FIGURE 18.3 The result of the second SELECT that uses a NOT IN subquery.**

condition code value of 1). The outer query then copies a book to the result table if the ISBN is *not* in the result of the subquery.

Notice that in both of the sample queries there is no explicit syntax to make the two tables union compatible, something required by the relational algebra *difference* operation. However, the outer query's WHERE clause contains a predicate that compares a column taken from the result of the outer query with the same column taken from the result of the subquery. These two columns represent the union compatible tables.

As a final example, consider a query that retrieves the names of all customers who have not made a purchase after 1-Aug-2021. When you are putting together a query of this type, your first thought might be to write the query as follows:

```
SELECT first_name, last_name
FROM customer JOIN sale
WHERE sale_date < '1-Aug-2021';
```

This query, however, won't work as you intend. First of all, the join eliminates all customers who have no purchases in the *sale* table, even though they should be included in the result. Second, the retrieval predicate identifies those customers who placed orders prior to 1-Aug-2021, but says nothing about who may or may not have made a purchase after that date. Customers may have made a purchase prior to 1-Aug-2021, on 1-Aug-2021, after 1-Aug-2021, or any combination of the preceding.

The typical way to perform this query correctly is to use a difference: the difference between all customers and those who *have* made a purchase after 1-Aug-2021. The query—the result of which can be found in Figure 18.4—appears as follows:

```
SELECT first_name, last_name
FROM customer
WHERE customer_numb NOT IN (SELECT customer_numb
      FROM sale
      WHERE sale_date >= '1-Aug-2021')
```

```
 first_name | last_name
------------+-----------
 Janice     | Jones
 John       | Doe
 Jane       | Doe
 Helen      | Brown
 Helen      | Jerry
 Mary       | Collins
 Peter      | Collins
 Edna       | Hayes
 Franklin   | Hayes
 Peter      | Johnson
 Peter      | Johnson
 John       | Smith
```

■ **FIGURE 18.4 The result of the third query using a NOT IN subquery.**

Negative Queries Using the EXCEPT Operator

The SQL-92 standard added an operator—EXCEPT—that performs a difference operation directly between two union compatible tables. Queries using EXCEPT look very much like a union:

```
SELECT first_name, last_name
FROM customer
EXCEPT
SELECT first_name, last_name
FROM customer, sale
WHERE customer.customer_numb = sale.customer_numb
AND sale_date >= '1-Aug-2021';
```

or

```
SELECT *
FROM customer
EXCEPT CORRESPONDING BY (first_name, last_name)
SELECT *
FROM customer, sale
WHERE customer.customer_numb = sale.customer_numb
AND sale_date >= '1-Aug-2021';
```

Using the first syntax, you include two complete SELECT statements that are joined by the keyword EXCEPT. The SELECTs must return union compatible tables. The first SELECT retrieves a list of all things (in this example, all customers); the second retrieves the things that *are* (in this example, customers with sales after 1-Aug-2021). The EXCEPT operator then removes all rows from the first table that appear in the second.

The second syntax retrieves all columns from both source tables but uses the CORRESPONDING BY clause to project the columns to make the two tables union compatible.

The EXISTS Operator

The EXISTS operator check the number of rows returned by a subquery. If the subquery contains one or more rows, then the result is true and a row is placed in the result table; otherwise, the result is false and no row is added to the result table.

For example, suppose the rare book store wants to see the titles of books that have been sold. To write the query using EXISTS, you would use

```
SELECT title
FROM book t1, work
WHERE t1.work_numb = work.work_numb
AND EXISTS (SELECT *
       FROM volume
       WHERE t1.isbn = volume.isbn
       AND selling_price > 0);
```

The preceding is a *correlated subquery*. Rather than completing the entire subquery and then turning to the outer query, the DBMS processes the query in the following manner:

1. Look at a row in *book*.
2. Use the ISBN from that row in the subquery's WHERE clause.
3. If the subquery finds at least one row in *volume* with the same ISBN, place a row in the intermediate result table. Otherwise, do nothing.
4. Repeat steps 1 through 3 for all rows in the *book* table.
5. Join the intermediate result table to *work*.
6. Project the *title* column.

The important thing to recognize here is that the DBMS repeats the subquery for every row in *book*. It is this repeated execution of the subquery that makes this a correlated subquery.

When you are using the EXISTS operator, it doesn't matter what follows SELECT in the subquery. EXISTS is merely checking to determine whether any rows are present in the subquery's result table. Therefore, it is easiest simply to use * rather than to specify individual columns.[3]

How will this query perform? It will probably perform better than a query that joins *book* and *volume*, especially if the two tables are large. If you were to write the query using an IN subquery—

```
SELECT title
FROM work, book
WHERE work.work_numb = book.work_numb
      AND isbn IN (SELECT isbn
      FROM volume);
```

—you would be using an uncorrelated subquery that returned a set of ISBNs that the outer query searches. The more rows returned by the uncorrelated subquery, the closer the performance of the EXISTS and IN queries will be. However, if the uncorrelated subquery returns only a few rows, it will probably perform better than the query containing the correlated subquery.

The EXCEPT and INTERSECT Operators

INTERSECT operates on the results of two independent tables and must be performed on union compatible tables. In most cases, the two source tables are each generated by a SELECT. INTERSECT is the relational algebra

---

[3] Depending on your DBMS, you may get better performance using 1 instead of *. This holds true for DB2 and just might work with others.

intersect operation, which returns all rows the two tables have in common. It is the exact opposite of EXCEPT.

As a first example, let's prepare a query that lists all of the rare book store's customers *except* those who have made purchases with a total cost of more than $500. One way to write this query is

```
SELECT first_name, last_name
FROM customer
EXCEPT
SELECT first_name, last_name
FROM customer JOIN sale
WHERE sale_total_amt > 500;
```

Note that those customers who have made multiple purchases, some of which are less than $500 and some of which are greater than $500, will be excluded from the result.

If we replace the EXCEPT with an INTERSECT—

```
SELECT first_name, last_name
FROM customer
INTERSECT
SELECT first_name, last_name
FROM customer JOIN sale
WHERE sale_total_amt > 500;
```

—the query returns the names of those who *have* made a purchase of over $500. As you can see in Figure 18.5, the query results are quite different.

Output from the query using EXCEPT	Output from the query using INTERSECT
first_name | last_name ------------+----------- Edna | Hayes Helen | Jerry Jane | Doe Jane | Smith Janice | Smith Jon | Jones Mary | Collins Peter | Collins	first_name | last_name ------------+----------- Franklin | Hayes Janice | Jones

■ FIGURE 18.5 Output of queries using EXCEPT and INTERSECT.

UNION Versus EXCEPT Versus INTERSET
One way to compare the operation of UNION, EXCEPT, and INTERSECT is to look at graphic representations, as in Figure 18.6. Each rectangle represents a table of data; the dark areas where the images overlap represent the rows returned by a query using the respective operation. As you can see, INTERSECT returns the area of overlap, EXCEPT returns everything EXCEPT the overlap, and UNION returns everything.

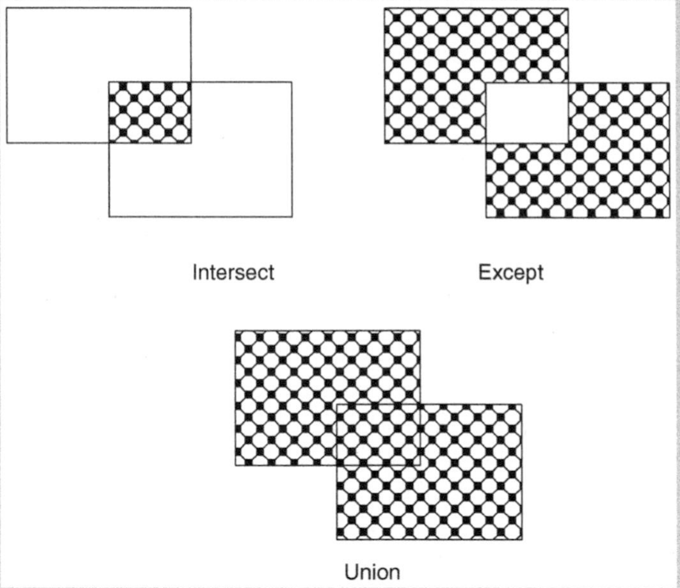

Intersect

Except

Union

■ FIGURE 18-6 Operation of the SQL INTERSECT, EXCEPT, and UNION operators.

Performing Arithmetic

Although SQL is not a complete programming language, it can perform some calculations. SQL recognizes simple arithmetic expressions involving column names and literal values. (When you are working with embedded SQL, you can also use host language variables. See Appendix B for details.) For example, if you wanted to compute a discounted price for a volume, the computation could be written

```
asking_price *.9
```

You could then incorporate this into a query as

```
SELECT isbn, asking_price,
     asking_price * .9 AS discounted_price
FROM volume
where sale_id = 6;
```

The result of the preceding query can be found in Figure 18.7.

```
isbn               | asking_price | discounted_price
-------------------+--------------+------------------
 978-1-11111-146-1 |        30.00 |           27.000
 978-1-11111-122-1 |        75.00 |           67.500
 978-1-11111-130-1 |       150.00 |          135.000
 978-1-11111-126-1 |       110.00 |           99.000
 978-1-11111-139-1 |       200.00 |          180.000
```

■ **FIGURE 18.7 Output of a query that includes a computed column.**

Arithmetic Operators

SQL recognizes the arithmetic operators in Table 18.1. Compared with a general-purpose programming language, this list is fairly limited. For example, there are no operators for exponentiation or modulo division. This means that if you need more sophisticated arithmetic manipulations, you will probably need to use embedded SQL to retrieve the data into host language variables and perform the arithmetic using the host programming language.

Table 18.1 SQL Arithmetic Operations

Operator	Meaning	Example
+	Unary +: preserve the sign of the value	`+balance`
−	Unary −: change the sign of the value	`-balance`
*	Multiplication: multiply two values	`balance * tax_rate`
/	Division: divide one value by another	`balance / numb_items`
+	Addition: add two values	`balance + new_charge`
−	Subtraction: subtract one value from another	`balance - payment`

Operator Precedence

The rows in Table 18.1 appear in the general order of the operators' precedence. (Both unary operators have the same precedence, followed by multiplication and division. Addition and subtraction have the lowest precedence.) This means that when multiple operations appear in the same expression, the DBMS evaluates them according to their precedence. For example, because the unary operators have the highest precedence, for the expression

```
-balance * tax_rate
```

the DBMS will first change the sign of the value in the *balance* column and then multiply it by the value in the *tax_rate* column.

When more than one operator of the same precedence appears in the same expression, they are evaluated from left to right. Therefore, in the expression

```
balance + new_charges - payments
```

the DBMS will first add the new charges to the balance and then subtract the payments from the sum.

Sometimes, the default precedence can produce unexpected results. Assume that you want to evaluate the expression

```
12 / 3 * 2
```

When the operators are evaluated from left to right, the DBMS divides 12 by 3 and then multiplies the 4 by 2, producing an 8. However, what if you really wanted to perform the multiplication first, followed by the division? (The result would be 2.)

To change the order of evaluation, you use parentheses to surround the operations that should be performed first:

```
12 / (3 * 2)
```

Just as when you use parentheses to change the order of evaluation of logical operators, whenever the DBMS sees a set of parentheses it knows to evaluate what is inside the parentheses first, regardless of the precedence of the operators.

Keep in mind that you can nest one set of parentheses within another:

```
12 / (3 * (1 + 2))
```

In this example, the DBMS evaluates the innermost parentheses first (the addition), moves to the outer set of parentheses (the multiplication), and finally evaluates the division.

There is no limit to how deep you can nest parentheses. However, be sure that each opening parenthesis is paired with a closing parenthesis.

String Manipulation

The SQL core standard contains one operator and several functions for manipulating character strings.

Concatenation

As you saw when we were discussing joins using concatenated foreign keys, the concatenation operator—| |—pastes one string on the end of another. It can be used to format output as well as to concatenate keys for searching. For example, the rare book store could get an alphabetical list of customer names formatted as *last, first* (see Figure 18.8) with:

```
SELECT last_name || ', ' || first_name AS cat_name
FROM customer
ORDER BY last_name, first_name;
```

```
cat_name
-----------------
 Brown, Helen
 Collins, Mary
 Collins, Peter
 Doe, Jane
 Doe, John
 Hayes, Edna
 Hayes, Franklin
 Jerry, Helen
 Johnson, Peter
 Johnson, Peter
 Jones, Janice
 Jones, Jon
 Smith, Jane
 Smith, Janice
 Smith, John
```

■ **FIGURE 18.8** The result of a concatenation.

Notice that the concatenation includes a literal string to place the comma and space between the last and first names. The concatenation operation knows nothing about normal English spacing; it simply places one string on the end of another. Therefore, it is up to the user to include any necessary spacing and punctuation.

UPPER and LOWER

When a DBMS evaluates a literal string against stored data, it performs a case-sensitive search. This means that upper- and lowercase letters are different:

'JONES' is not the same as 'Jones.' You can get around such problems using the UPPER and LOWER functions to convert stored data to a single case.

For example, assume that someone at the rare book store is not certain of the case in which customer names are stored. To perform a case-insensitive search for customers with a specific last name, the person could use

```
SELECT customer_numb, first_name, last_name
FROM customer
WHERE UPPER(last_name) = 'SMITH';
```

The result—

```
 customer_numb | first_name | last_name
---------------+------------+----------
             5 | Jane       | Smith
             6 | Janice     | Smith
            15 | John       | Smith
```

—includes rows for customers whose last names are made up of the characters S-M-I-T-H, regardless of case. The UPPER function converts the data stored in the database to uppercase before making the comparison in the WHERE predicate. You obtain the same effect by using LOWER instead of UPPER and placing the characters to be matched in lower case.

Mixed Versus Single Case in Stored Data

There is always the temptation to require that text data be stored as all uppercase letters to avoid the need to use UPPER and LOWER in queries. For the most part, this isn't a good idea. First, text in all uppercase is difficult to read. Consider the following two lines of text:

WHICH IS EASIER TO READ? ALL CAPS OR MIXED CASE?

Which is easier to read? All caps or mixed case?

Our eyes have been trained to read mixed upper- and lowercase letters. In English, for example, we use letter case cues to locate the start of sentences and to identify proper nouns. Text in all caps removes those cues, making the text more difficult to read. The "sameness" of all uppercase also makes it more difficult to differentiate letters and, thus, to understand the words.

Second, because professional documents are typed/printed in mixed case, all uppercase looks less professional and isn't suitable for most business documents. Finally, Internet text communications in all uppercase are considered to be shouting and this feeling that all uppercase is impolite carries over into any displayed or printed output.

TRIM

The TRIM function removes leading and/or trailing characters from a string. The various syntaxes for this function and their effects are summarized in Table 18.2. The blanks in the first four examples can be replaced with any characters you need to remove, as can the * in the last example.

Table 18.2 The Various Forms of the SQL TRIM Function

Function Format	Result	Action of the Sample
TRIM (' word ')	'word'	Default: removes both leading and trailing blanks
TRIM (BOTH ' ' FROM ' word ')	'word'	Removes leading and trailing blanks
TRIM (LEADING ' ' FROM ' word ')	'word'	Removes leading blanks
TRIM (TRAILING ' ' FROM ' word ')	'word'	Removes trailing blanks
TRIM (BOTH '*' FROM '*word*')	'word'	Removes leading and trailing *

You can place TRIM in any expression that contains a string. For example, if you are using characters to store a serial number with leading 0s (for example, 0012), you can strip those 0s when performing a search:

```
SELECT item_description
FROM items
WHERE TRIM (LEADING '0' FROM item_numb) = '25';
```

SUBSTRING

The SUBSTRING function extracts portions of a string. It has the following general syntax:

```
SUBSTRING (source_string, FROM starting_position
    FOR number_of_characters)
```

For example, if the rare book store wanted to extract the first character of a customer's first name, the function call would be written

```
SUBSTRING (first_name FROM 1 FOR 1)
```

The substring being created begins at the first character of the column and is one character long.

You could then incorporate this into a query with

```
SELECT SUBSTRING (first_name FROM 1 FOR 1) || '. '
    || last_name AS whole_name
FROM customer;
```

The results can be found in Figure 18.9.

```
whole_name
------------
J. Jones
J. Jones
J. Doe
J. Doe
J. Smith
J. Smith
H. Brown
H. Jerry
M. Collins
P. Collins
E. Hayes
F. Hayes
P. Johnson
P. Johnson
J. Smith
```

■ **FIGURE 18.9 Output of a query including the SUBSTRING function.**

Date and Time Manipulation

SQL DBMSs provide column data types for dates and times. When you store data using these data types, you make it possible for SQL to perform chronological operations on those values. You can, for example, subtract two dates to find out the number of days between them or add an interval to a date to advance the date a specified number of days. In this section, you will read about the types of date manipulations that SQL provides, along with a simple way to get current date and time information from the computer.

The core SQL standard specifies four column data types that relate to dates and times (jointly referred to as *datetime* data types):

- DATE: a date only,
- TIME: a time only.
- TIMESTAMP: a combination of date and time,
- INTERVAL: the interval between two of the preceding data types.

As you will see in the next two sections, these can be combined in a variety of ways.

Date and Time System Values

To help make date and time manipulations easier, SQL lets you retrieve the current date and/or time with the following three keywords:

- CURRENT_DATE: returns the current system date,
- CURRENT_TIME: returns the current system time

- CURRENT_TIMESTAMP: returns a combination of the current system date and time.

For example, to see all sales made on the current day, someone at the rare book store uses the following query:

```
SELECT first_name, last_name, sale_id
FROM customer JOIN sale
WHERE sale_date = CURRENT_DATE;
```

You can also use these system date and time values when performing data entry.

Date and Time Interval Operations

SQL dates and times can participate in expressions that support queries such as "how many days/months/years in between?" and operations such as "add 30 days to the invoice date." The types of date and time manipulations available with SQL are summarized in Table 18.3. Unfortunately, expressions involving these operations aren't as straightforward as they might initially appear. When you work with date and time intervals, you must also specify the portions of the date and/or time that you want.

Table 18.3 Datetime Arithmetic

Expression	Result
DATE ± integer	DATE
DATE ± time_interval	TIMESTAMP
DATE + time	TIMESTAMP
INVERVAL ± INTERVAL	INTERVAL
TIMESTAMP ± INTERVAL	TIMESTAMP
TIME ± time_interval	TIME
DATE - DATE	integer
TIME - TIME	INTERVAL
integer * INTERVAL	INTERVAL

Each datetime column will include a selection of the following fields:

- MILLENNIUM
- CENTURY
- DECADE
- YEAR
- QUARTER

- MONTH
- DAY
- HOUR
- MINUTE
- SECOND
- MILLISECONDS
- MICROSECONDS

When you write an expression that includes an interval, you can either indicate that you want the interval expressed in one of those fields (for example, DAY for the number of days between two dates) or specify a range of fields (for example, YEAR TO MONTH to give you an interval in years and months). The *start field* (the first field in the range) can be only YEAR, DAY, HOUR, or MINUTE. The second field in the range (the *end field*) must be a chronologically smaller unit than the start field.

Note: There is one exception to the preceding rule. If the start field is YEAR, then the end field must be MONTH.

To see the number of years between a customer's orders and the current date, someone at the rare book store might use

```
SELECT CURRENT_DATE - sale_date YEAR
FROM sale
WHERE customer_numb = 6;
```

To see the same interval expressed in years and months, the query would be rewritten as

```
SELECT CURRENT_DATE - sale_date YEAR TO MONTH
FROM sale
WHERE customer_numb = 6;
```

To add 7 days to an order date to give a customer an approximate delivery date, someone at the rare book store would write a query like

```
SELECT sale_date + INTERVAL '7' DAY
FROM sale
WHERE sale_id = 12;
```

Notice that when you include an interval as a literal you precede it with the keyword INTERVAL, put the interval's value in single quotes, and follow it with the datetime unit in which the interval is expressed.

OVERLAPS

The SQL OVERLAPS operator is a special-purpose keyword that returns true or false, depending on whether two datetime intervals overlap. This operator might be used in applications such as hotel booking systems to determine room availability: Does one customer's planned stay overlap another's?

The operator has the following general syntax:

```
SELECT (start_date1, end_date1)
OVERLAPS
(start_date2, end_date2)
```

An expression such as

```
SELECT (DATE '16-Aug-2021', DATE '31-Aug-2021')
OVERLAPS
(DATE '18-Aug-2021', DATE '9-Sep-2021');
```

produces the following result:

```
overlaps
----------
t
```

Notice that the dates being compared are preceded by the keyword DATE and surrounded by single quotes. Without the specification of the type of data in the operation, SQL doesn't know how to interpret what is within the quotes.

The two dates and/or times that are used to specify an interval can be either DATE, TIME, or TIMESTAMP values or they can be intervals. For example, the following query checks to see whether the second range of dates is within 90 days of the first start date and returns false:

```
SELECT (DATE '16-Aug-2021', INTERVAL '90 DAYS')
OVERLAPS
(DATE '12-Feb-2021', DATE '4-Jun-2021');
```

Note: Because the OVERLAPS operator returns a Boolean, it can be used as the logical expression in a CASE statement, about which you will read shortly.

EXTRACT

The EXTRACT operator pulls out a part of a date and/or time. It has the following general format:

```
EXTRACT (datetime_field FROM datetime_value)
```

For example, the query

```
SELECT EXTRACT (YEAR FROM CURRENT_DATE);
```

returns the current year.

In addition to the datetime fields you saw earlier in this section, EXTRACT also can provide the day of the week (DOW) and the day of the year (DOY).

CASE Expressions

The SQL CASE expression, much like a CASE in a general purpose programming language, allows a SQL statement to pick from among a variety of actions based on the truth of logical expressions. Like arithmetic and string operations, the CASE statement generates a value to be displayed and therefore is part of the SELECT clause.

The CASE expression has the following general syntax:

```
CASE
      WHEN logical condition THEN action
      WHEN logical condition THEN action
      :
      :
      ELSE default action
END
```

It fits within a SELECT statement in this way:

```
SELECT column1, column2,
CASE
      WHEN logical condition THEN action
      WHEN logical condition THEN action
      :
      :
      ELSE default action
END
FROM table(s)
WHERE predicate;
```

The CASE does not necessarily need to be the last item in the SELECT clause. The END keyword can be followed by a comma and other columns or computed quantities.

As an example, assume that the rare book store wants to offer discounts to users based on the price of a book. The more the asking price for the book, the greater the discount. To include the discounted price in the output of a query, you could use

```
SELECT isbn, asking_price,
CASE
      WHEN asking_price < 50 THEN asking_price * .95
      WHEN asking_price < 75 THEN asking_price * .9
      WHEN asking_price < 100 THEN asking_price * .8
      ELSE asking_price * .75
END
FROM volume;
```

The preceding query displays the ISBN and the asking price of a book. It then evaluates the first CASE expression following WHEN. If that condition is true, the query performs the computation, displays the discounted price, and exits the CASE. If the first condition is false, the query proceeds to the second WHEN, and so on. If none of the conditions are true, the query executes the action following ELSE. (The ELSE is optional.)

The first portion of the output of the example query appears in Figure 18.10. Notice that the value returned by the CASE construct appears in a column named *case*. You can, however, rename the computed column just as you would rename any other computed column by adding AS followed by the desired name.

```
        isbn         | asking_price |   case
---------------------+--------------+----------
 978-1-11111-111-1 |       175.00 | 131.2500
 978-1-11111-131-1 |        50.00 |   45.000
 978-1-11111-137-1 |        80.00 |   64.000
 978-1-11111-133-1 |       300.00 | 225.0000
 978-1-11111-142-1 |        25.95 | 2465.25
 978-1-11111-146-1 |        22.95 | 2180.25
 978-1-11111-144-1 |        80.00 |   64.000
 978-1-11111-137-1 |        50.00 |   45.000
 978-1-11111-136-1 |        75.00 |   60.000
 978-1-11111-136-1 |        50.00 |   45.000
 978-1-11111-143-1 |        25.00 | 2375.00
 978-1-11111-132-1 |        15.00 | 1425.00
 978-1-11111-133-1 |        18.00 | 1710.00
 978-1-11111-121-1 |       110.00 | 82.5000
 978-1-11111-121-1 |       110.00 | 82.5000
 978-1-11111-121-1 |       110.00 | 82.5000
```

■ FIGURE 18.10 Default output of a SELECT statement containing CASE.

The output of the modified statement—

```
SELECT isbn, asking_price,
CASE
     WHEN asking_price < 50 THEN asking_price * .95
     WHEN asking_price < 75 THEN asking_price * .9
     WHEN asking_price < 100 THEN asking_price * .8
     ELSE asking_price * .75
END AS discounted_price
FROM volume;
```

—can be found in Figure 18.11

```
       isbn          | asking_price | discounted_price
---------------------+--------------+------------------
978-1-11111-111-1    |    175.00    |      131.2500
978-1-11111-131-1    |     50.00    |       45.000
978-1-11111-137-1    |     80.00    |       64.000
978-1-11111-133-1    |    300.00    |      225.0000
978-1-11111-142-1    |     25.95    |     2465.25
978-1-11111-146-1    |     22.95    |     2180.25
978-1-11111-144-1    |     80.00    |       64.000
978-1-11111-137-1    |     50.00    |       45.000
978-1-11111-136-1    |     75.00    |       60.000
978-1-11111-136-1    |     50.00    |       45.000
978-1-11111-143-1    |     25.00    |     2375.00
978-1-11111-132-1    |     15.00    |     1425.00
978-1-11111-133-1    |     18.00    |     1710.00
978-1-11111-121-1    |    110.00    |       82.5000
978-1-11111-121-1    |    110.00    |       82.5000
978-1-11111-121-1    |    110.00    |       82.5000
```

■ FIGURE 18.11 CASE statement output using a renamed column for the CASE value.

Chapter

19

Working With
Groups of Rows

The queries you have seen so far in this book for the most part operate on one row at a time. However, SQL also includes a variety of keywords and functions that work on groups of rows—either an entire table or a subset of a table. In this chapter, you will read about what you can do to and with grouped data.

Note: Many of the functions that you will be reading about in this chapter are often referred to as SQL's OLAP functions.

Set Functions

The basic SQL *set,* or *aggregate*, *functions* (summarized in Table 19.1) compute a variety of measures based on values in a column in multiple rows. The result of using one of these set functions is a computed column that appears only in a result table.

The basic syntax for a set function is

```
function_name (input_argument)
```

You place the function call following SELECT, just as you would an arithmetic calculation. What you use for an input argument depends on which function you are using.

Note: For the most part, you can count on a SQL DBMS supporting COUNT, SUM, AVG, MIN, and MAX. In addition, many DBMSs provide additional aggregate functions for measures such as standard deviation and variance. Consult the DBMS's documentation for details.

COUNT

The COUNT function is somewhat different from other SQL set functions in that instead of making computations based on data values, it counts the

Table 19.1 SQL Set Functions

Function	Meaning
Functions implemented by most DBMSs	
COUNT	Returns the number of rows
SUM	Returns the total of the values in a column from a group of rows
AVG	Returns the average of the values in a column from a group of rows
MIN	Returns the minimum value in a column from among a group of rows
MAX	Returns the maximum value in a column from among a group of rows
Less widely implemented functions	
COVAR_POP	Returns a population's covariance
COVAR_SAMP	Returns the covariance of a sample
REGR_AVGX	Returns the average of an independent variable
REGR_AVGY	Returns the average of a dependent variable
REGR_COUNT	Returns the number of independent/dependent variable pairs that remain in a population after any rows that have null in either variable have been removed
REGR_INTERCEPT	Returns the Y-intercept of a least-squares-fit linear equation
REGR_R2	Returns the square of a the correlation coefficient R
REGR_SLOPE	Returns the slope of a least-squares-fit linear equation
REGR_SXX	Returns the sum of the squares of the values of an independent variable
REGR_SXY	Returns the product of pairs independent and dependent variable values
REGR_SYY	Returns the sum of the square of the values of a dependent variable
STDDEV_POP	Returns the standard deviation of a population
STDDEV_SAMP	Returns the standard deviation of a sample
VAR_POP	Returns the variance of a population
VAR_SAMP	Returns the variance of a sample

number of rows in a table. To use it, you place COUNT (*) in your query. COUNT's input argument is always an asterisk:

```
SELECT COUNT (*)
FROM volume;
```

The response appears as

```
count

-------

    71
```

To count a subset of the rows in a table, you can apply a WHERE predicate:

```
SELECT COUNT (*)
FROM volume
WHERE isbn = '978-1-11111-141-1';
```

The result—

```
Count
-------
    7
```

—tells you that the store has sold or has in stock seven books with an ISBN of 978-1-11111-141-1. It does not tell you how many copies of the book are in stock or how many were purchased during any given sale because the query is simply counting the number of rows in which the ISBN appears. It does not take into account data in any other column.

Alternatively, the store could determine the number of distinct items contained in a specific order, with a query like

```
SELECT COUNT (*)
FROM volume
WHERE sale_id = 6;
```

When you use * as an input parameter to the COUNT function, the DBMS includes all rows. However, if you wish to exclude rows that have nulls in a particular column, you can use the name of the column as an input parameter. To find out how many volumes are currently in stock, the rare book store could use

```
SELECT COUNT (selling_price)
FROM volume;
```

If every row in the table has a value in the *selling_date* column, then COUNT (*selling_date*) is the same as COUNT (*). However, if any rows contain null, then the count will exclude those rows. There are 71 rows in the *volume* table. However, the count returns a value of 43, indicating that 43 volumes have not been sold and therefore are in stock.

You can also use COUNT to determine how many unique values appear in any given column by placing the keyword DISTINCT in front of the column name used as an input parameter. For example, to find out how many different books appear in the *volume* table, the rare book store would use

```
SELECT COUNT (DISTINCT isbn)
FROM volume;
```

The result—27—is the number of unique ISBNs in the table.

SUM

If someone at the rare book store wanted to know the total amount of an order so that value could be inserted into the *sale* table, then the easiest way to obtain this value is to add up the values in the *selling_price* column:

```
SELECT SUM (selling_price)
FROM volume
WHERE sale_id = 6;
```

The result appears as

```
 sum
--------
 505.00
```

In the preceding example, the input argument to the SUM function was a single column. However, it can also be an arithmetic operation. For example, to find the total of a sale if the books are discounted 15 percent, the rare book store could use the following query:

```
SELECT SUM (selling_price * .85)
FROM volume
WHERE sale_id = 6;
```

The result—

```
  sum
----------
 429.2500
```

—is the total of the multiplication of the selling price times the selling discount.

If we needed to add tax to a sale, a query could then multiply the result of the SUM by the tax rate,

```
SELECT SUM (selling_price * .85) * 1.0725
FROM volume
WHERE sale_id = 6;
```

producing a final result of 429.2500.

Note: Rows that contain nulls in any column involved in a SUM are excluded from the computation.

AVG

The AVG function computes the average value in a column. For example, to find the average price of a book, someone at the rare book store could use a query like

```
SELECT AVG (selling_price)
FROM volume;
```

The result is 68.2313953488372093 (approximately $68.23).

Note: Rows that contain nulls in any column involved in an AVG are excluded from the computation.

MIN and MAX

The MIN and MAX functions return the minimum and maximum values in a column or expression. For example, to see the maximum price of a book, someone at the rare book store could use a query like

```
SELECT MAX (selling_price)
FROM volume;
```

The result is a single value: $205.00.

The MIN and MAX functions are not restricted to columns or expressions that return numeric values. If someone at the rare book store wanted to see the latest date on which a sale had occurred, then

```
SELECT MAX (sale_date)
FROM volume;
```

returns the chronologically latest date (in our particular sample data, 01-Sep-21).

By the same token, if you use

```
SELECT MIN (last_name)
FROM customer;
```

you will receive the alphabetically first customer last name (Brown).

Set Functions in Predicates

Set functions can also be used in WHERE predicates to generate values against which stored data can be compared. Assume, for example, that someone at the rare book store wants to see the titles and cost of all books that were sold that cost more than the average cost of a book.

The strategy for preparing this query is to use a subquery that returns the average cost of a sold book and to compare the cost of each book in the *volume* table to that average:

```
SELECT title, selling_price
FROM work, book, volume
WHERE work.work_numb = book.work_numb
      AND book.isbn = volume.isbn
      AND selling_price > (SELECT AVG (selling_price)
      FROM volume);
```

Although it would seem logical that the DBMS would calculate the average once and use the result of that single computation to compare to rows in the *volume*, that's not what happens. This is actually a correlated subquery; the DBMS recalculates the average for every row in *volume*. As a result, a query of this type will perform relatively slowly on large amounts of data. You can find the result in Figure 19.1.

Changing Data Types: CAST

One of the problems with the output of the SUM and AVG functions that you saw in the preceding section of this chapter is that they give you no control over the *precision* (number of places to the right of the decimal point) of the output. One way to solve that problem is to change the data type of the result to something that has the number of decimal places you want using the CAST function.

```
title                                              | selling_price
---------------------------------------------------+---------------
Jane Eyre                                          |        175.00
Giles Goat Boy                                     |        285.00
Anthem                                             |         76.10
Tom Sawyer                                         |        110.00
Tom Sawyer                                         |        110.00
Adventures of Huckleberry Finn, The                |         75.00
Treasure Island                                    |        120.00
Fountainhead, The                                  |        110.00
I, Robot                                           |        170.00
Fountainhead, The                                  |         75.00
Giles Goat Boy                                     |        125.00
Fountainhead, The                                  |         75.00
Foundation                                         |         75.00
Treasure Island                                    |        150.00
Lost in the Funhouse                               |         75.00
Hound of the Baskervilles                          |         75.00
```

■ FIGURE 19.1 Output of a query that uses a set function in a subquery.

CAST has the general syntax

CAST (*source_data* AS *new_data_type*)

To restrict the output of the average price of books to a precision of 2, you could then use

CAST (AVG (selling_price) AS DECIMAL (10,2))

and incorporate it into a query using

SELECT CAST (AVG (selling_price) AS DECIMAL (10,2))
FROM volume;

The preceding specifies that the result should be displayed as a decimal number with a maximum of 10 digits (including the decimal point) with two digits to the right of the decimal point. The result is 68.23, a more meaningful currency value than the original 68.2313953488372093.

Note: If you request more digits of precision than are available, the DBMS may add trailing 0s or it may simply show you all digits available without padding the result to the specified length.

CAST also can be used, for example, to convert a string of characters into a date. The expression

```
CAST ('10-Aug-2021' AS DATE)
```

returns a datetime value.

Valid conversions for commonly used data types are represented by the light gray boxes in Table 19.2. Those conversions that may be possible if certain conditions are met are represented by the dark gray boxes. In particular, if you are attempting to convert a character string into a shorter string, the result will be truncated.

Table 19.2 Valid Data Type Conversion for Commonly Used Data Types (Light Gray Boxes are Valid; Dark Gray Boxes May Be Valid)

Original data type	New data type						
	Integer or fixed point	Floating point	Variable length character	Fixed length character	Date	Time	Timestamp
Integer or fixed point							
Floating point							
Character (fixed or variable length)							
Date							
Time							
Timestamp							

Grouping Queries

SQL can group rows based on matching values in specified columns and compute summary measures for each group. When these *grouping queries* are combined with the set functions that you saw earlier in this chapter, SQL can provide simple reports without requiring any special programming.

Forming Groups

To form a group, you add a GROUP BY clause to a SELECT statement, followed by the columns whose values are to be used to form the groups. All rows whose values match on those columns will be placed in the same group.

For example, if someone at the rare book store wants to see how many copies of each book edition have been sold, he or she can use a query like

```
SELECT isbn, COUNT(*)
FROM volume
GROUP BY isbn
ORDER BY isbn;
```

The query forms groups by matching ISBNs. It displays the ISBN and the number of rows in each group (see Figure 19.2).

```
         isbn        | count
---------------------+-------
 978-1-11111-111-1 |    1
 978-1-11111-115-1 |    1
 978-1-11111-121-1 |    3
 978-1-11111-122-1 |    1
 978-1-11111-123-1 |    2
 978-1-11111-124-1 |    1
 978-1-11111-125-1 |    1
 978-1-11111-126-1 |    3
 978-1-11111-127-1 |    5
 978-1-11111-128-1 |    1
 978-1-11111-129-1 |    1
 978-1-11111-130-1 |    4
 978-1-11111-131-1 |    4
 978-1-11111-132-1 |    3
 978-1-11111-133-1 |    5
 978-1-11111-135-1 |    1
 978-1-11111-136-1 |    6
 978-1-11111-137-1 |    4
 978-1-11111-138-1 |    4
 978-1-11111-139-1 |    4
 978-1-11111-140-1 |    1
 978-1-11111-141-1 |    7
 978-1-11111-142-1 |    1
 978-1-11111-143-1 |    1
 978-1-11111-144-1 |    1
 978-1-11111-145-1 |    3
 978-1-11111-146-1 |    2
```

■ FIGURE 19.2 Counting the members of a group.

There is a major restriction that you must observe with a grouping query: You can display values only from columns that are used to form the groups. As an example, assume that someone at the rare book store wants to see the number of copies of each title that have been sold. A working query could be written

```
SELECT title, COUNT (*)
FROM volume, book, work
WHERE volume.isbn = book.isbn
      AND book.work_numb = work.work_numb
GROUP BY title
ORDER BY title;
```

The result appears in Figure 19.3. The problem with this approach is that the same title may have different ISBNs (for different editions), producing multiple entries for the same title. To ensure that you have a count for a title, including all editions, you will need to group by the work number. However, given the restriction as to what can be displayed, you won't be able to display the title.

title	count
Adventures of Huckleberry Finn, The	1
Anathem	1
Anthem	4
Atlas Shrugged	5
Bourne Supremacy, The	1
Cryptonomicon	2
Foundation	11
Fountainhead, The	4
Giles Goat Boy	5
Hound of the Baskervilles	1
I, Robot	4
Inkdeath	7
Inkheart	1
Jane Eyre	1
Kidnapped	2
Last Foundation	4
Lost in the Funhouse	3
Matarese Circle, The	2
Snow Crash	1
Sot Weed Factor, The	4
Tom Sawyer	3
Treasure Island	4

■ **FIGURE 19.3** Grouping rows by book title.

The solution is to make the DBMS do a bit of extra work: group by both the work number and the title. (Keep in mind that the title is functionally dependent on the work number, so there will always be only one title for each work number.) The DBMS will then form groups that have the same values in both columns. The result will be the same as that in Figure 19.3, using our sample data. We therefore gain the ability to display the title when grouping by the work number. The query could be written

```
SELECT work.work_numb, title, COUNT (*)
FROM volume, book, work
WHERE volume.isbn = book.isbn
     AND book.work_numb = work.work_numb
GROUP BY work_numb, title
ORDER BY title;
```

As you can see in Figure 19.4, the major difference between the two results is the appearance of the work number column.

work_numb	title	count
9	Adventures of Huckleberry Finn, The	1
28	Anathem	1
30	Anthem	4
14	Atlas Shrugged	5
12	Bourne Supremacy, The	1
31	Cryptonomicon	2
23	Foundation	11
13	Fountainhead, The	4
20	Giles Goat Boy	5
3	Hound of the Baskervilles	1
25	I, Robot	4
27	Inkdeath	7
26	Inkheart	1
1	Jane Eyre	1
16	Kidnapped	2
24	Last Foundation	4
19	Lost in the Funhouse	3
11	Matarese Circle, The	2
29	Snow Crash	1
18	Sot Weed Factor, The	4
8	Tom Sawyer	3
17	Treasure Island	4

■ FIGURE 19.4 Grouped output using two grouping columns.

You can use any of the set functions in a grouping query. For example, someone at the rare book store could generate the total cost of all sales with

```
SELECT sale_id, SUM (selling_price)
FROM volume
GROUP BY sale_id;
```

The result can be seen in Figure 19.5. Notice that the last line of the result has nulls for both output values. This occurs because those volumes that haven't been sold have null for the sale ID and selling price. If you wanted to clean up the output, removing rows with nulls, you could add a WHERE clause:

```
SELECT sale_id, SUM (selling_price)
FROM volume
WHERE NOT (sale_id IS NULL)
GROUP BY sale_id;
```

```
sale_id |   sum
--------+--------
      1 | 510.00
      2 | 125.00
      3 |  58.00
      4 | 110.00
      5 | 110.00
      6 | 505.00
      7 |  80.00
      8 | 130.00
      9 |  50.00
     10 | 125.00
     11 | 200.00
     12 | 225.00
     13 |  25.95
     14 |  80.00
     15 | 100.00
     16 | 130.00
     17 | 100.00
     18 | 100.00
     19 |  95.00
     20 |  75.00
        |
```

■ FIGURE 19.5 The result of using a set function in a grouping query.

In an earlier example we included the book title as part of the GROUP BY clause as a trick to allow us to display the title in the result. However, more commonly we use multiple grouping columns to create nested groups. For example, if someone at the rare book store wanted to see the total cost of purchases made by each customer per day, the query could be written

```
SELECT customer.customer_numb, sale_date,
       sum (selling_price)
FROM customer, sale, volume
WHERE customer.customer_numb = sale.customer_numb
      AND sale.sale_id = volume.sale_id
GROUP BY customer.customer_numb, sale_date;
```

Because the *customer_numb* column is listed first in the GROUP BY clause, its values are used to create the outer groupings. The DBMS then groups order by date *within* customer numbers. The default output (see Figure 19.6) is somewhat hard to interpret because the outer groupings are not in order. However, if you add an ORDER BY clause to sort the output by customer number, you can see the ordering by date within each customer (see Figure 19.7).

```
customer_numb |      sale_date      |   sum
--------------+---------------------+--------
            1 | 15-JUN-21 00:00:00  |   58.00
            6 | 01-SEP-21 00:00:00  |   95.00
            2 | 01-SEP-21 00:00:00  |   75.00
            5 | 22-AUG-21 00:00:00  |  100.00
            2 | 25-JUL-21 00:00:00  |  210.00
            1 | 25-JUL-21 00:00:00  |  100.00
            8 | 07-JUL-21 00:00:00  |   50.00
            5 | 07-JUL-21 00:00:00  |  130.00
           12 | 05-JUL-21 00:00:00  |  505.00
            8 | 05-JUL-21 00:00:00  |   80.00
            6 | 10-JUL-21 00:00:00  |   80.00
            2 | 10-JUL-21 00:00:00  |   25.95
            6 | 30-JUN-21 00:00:00  |  110.00
            9 | 10-JUL-21 00:00:00  |  200.00
           10 | 10-JUL-21 00:00:00  |  225.00
            4 | 30-JUN-21 00:00:00  |  110.00
           11 | 10-JUL-21 00:00:00  |  125.00
           11 | 12-JUL-21 00:00:00  |  100.00
            1 | 05-JUN-21 00:00:00  |  125.00
            1 | 29-MAY-21 00:00:00  |  510.00
```

■ FIGURE 19.6 Group by two columns (default row order).

```
customer_numb |      sale_date      |   sum
--------------+---------------------+--------
            1 | 29-MAY-21 00:00:00  |  510.00
            1 | 05-JUN-21 00:00:00  |  125.00
            1 | 15-JUN-21 00:00:00  |   58.00
            1 | 25-JUL-21 00:00:00  |  100.00
            2 | 10-JUL-21 00:00:00  |   25.95
            2 | 25-JUL-21 00:00:00  |  130.00
            2 | 01-SEP-21 00:00:00  |   75.00
            4 | 30-JUN-21 00:00:00  |  110.00
            5 | 07-JUL-21 00:00:00  |  130.00
            5 | 22-AUG-21 00:00:00  |  100.00
            6 | 30-JUN-21 00:00:00  |  110.00
            6 | 10-JUL-21 00:00:00  |   80.00
            6 | 01-SEP-21 00:00:00  |   95.00
            8 | 05-JUL-21 00:00:00  |   80.00
            8 | 07-JUL-21 00:00:00  |   50.00
            9 | 10-JUL-21 00:00:00  |  200.00
           10 | 10-JUL-21 00:00:00  |  225.00
           11 | 10-JUL-21 00:00:00  |  125.00
           11 | 12-JUL-21 00:00:00  |  100.00
           12 | 05-JUL-21 00:00:00  |  505.00
```

■ FIGURE 19.7 Grouping by two columns (rows sorted by outer grouping column).

Restricting Groups

The grouping queries you have seen to this point include all the rows in the table. However, you can restrict the rows that are included in grouped output using one of two strategies:

- Restrict the rows before groups are formed.
- Allow all groups to be formed and then restrict the groups.

The first strategy is performed with the WHERE clause in the same way we have been restricting rows to this point. The second requires a HAVING clause, which contains a predicate that applies to groups after they are formed.

Assume, for example, that someone at the rare book store wants to see the number of books ordered at each price over $75. One way to write the query is to use a WHERE clause to throw out rows with a selling price less than or equal to $75:

```
SELECT selling_price, count (*)
FROM volume
WHERE selling_price > 75
GROUP BY selling_price;
```

Alternatively, you could let the DBMS form the groups and then throw out the groups that have a cost less than or equal to $75 with a HAVING clause:

```
SELECT selling_price, count (*)
FROM volume
GROUP BY selling_price
HAVING selling_price > 75;
```

The result in both cases is the same (see Figure 19.8). However, the way in which the query is processed is different.

```
 selling_price | count
---------------+-------
         76.10 |     1
        110.00 |     3
        120.00 |     1
        125.00 |     1
        150.00 |     1
        170.00 |     1
        175.00 |     1
        285.00 |     1
```

■ FIGURE 19.8 Restrict groups to volumes that cost more than $75.

Windowing and Window Functions

Grouping queries have two major drawbacks: they can't show you individual rows at the same time they show you computations made on groups of rows and you can't see data from non-grouping columns unless you resort to the group making trick shown earlier. The more recent versions of the SQL standard (from SQL:2003 onward), however, include a new way to compute aggregate functions, yet display the individual rows within each group: *windowing*. Each window (or *partition*) is a group of rows that share some criteria, such as a customer number. The window has a *frame* that "slides" to present to the DBMS the rows that share the same value of the partitioning criteria. *Window functions* are a special group of functions that can act only on partitions.

Note: By default, a window frame includes all the rows as its partition. However, as you will see shortly, that can be changed.

Let's start with a simple example. Assume that someone at the rare book store wants to see the volumes that were part of each sale, as well as the average cost of books for each sale. A grouping query version wouldn't be able to show the individual volumes in a sale nor would it be able to display the ISBN or *sale_id* unless those two values were added to the GROUP BY clause. However, if the query were written using windowing—

```
SELECT sale_id, isbn, CAST (AVG(selling_price)
      OVER (PARTITION BY sale_id) AS DECIMAL (7,2))
FROM volume
WHERE sale_id IS NOT NULL;
```

—it would produce the result in Figure 19.9. Notice that the individual volumes from each sale are present, and that the rightmost column contains the average cost for the specific sale on which a volume was sold. This means that the *avg* column in the result table is the same for all rows that come from a given sale.

The query itself includes two new keywords: OVER and PARTITION BY. (The CAST is present to limit the display of the average to a normal money display format and therefore isn't part of the windowing expression.) OVER indicates that the rows need to be grouped in some way. PARTITION BY indicates the criteria by which the rows are to be grouped. This particular example computes the average for groups of rows that are separated by their sale ID.

To help us explore more of what windowing can do, we're going to need a sample table with some different types of data. Figure 19.10a shows you a table that describes sales representatives and the value of product they have sold in specific quarters. The names of the sales reps are stored in the table labeled as Figure 19.10b.

```
sale_id |         isbn         |   avg
--------+----------------------+--------
      1 | 978-1-11111-111-1 | 170.00
      1 | 978-1-11111-131-1 | 170.00
      1 | 978-1-11111-133-1 | 170.00
      2 | 978-1-11111-142-1 |  41.67
      2 | 978-1-11111-146-1 |  41.67
      2 | 978-1-11111-144-1 |  41.67
      3 | 978-1-11111-143-1 |  42.00
      3 | 978-1-11111-132-1 |  42.00
      3 | 978-1-11111-133-1 |  42.00
      3 | 978-1-11111-121-1 |  42.00
      5 | 978-1-11111-121-1 | 110.00
      6 | 978-1-11111-146-1 | 101.00
      6 | 978-1-11111-122-1 | 101.00
      6 | 978-1-11111-130-1 | 101.00
      6 | 978-1-11111-126-1 | 101.00
      6 | 978-1-11111-139-1 | 101.00
      7 | 978-1-11111-125-1 |  40.00
      7 | 978-1-11111-131-1 |  40.00
      8 | 978-1-11111-126-1 |  65.00
      8 | 978-1-11111-133-1 |  65.00
      9 | 978-1-11111-139-1 |  50.00
     10 | 978-1-11111-133-1 | 125.00
     11 | 978-1-11111-126-1 |  66.67
     11 | 978-1-11111-130-1 |  66.67
     11 | 978-1-11111-136-1 |  66.67
     12 | 978-1-11111-130-1 | 112.50
     12 | 978-1-11111-132-1 | 112.50
     13 | 978-1-11111-129-1 |  25.95
     14 | 978-1-11111-141-1 |  40.00
     14 | 978-1-11111-141-1 |  40.00
     15 | 978-1-11111-127-1 |  50.00
     15 | 978-1-11111-141-1 |  50.00
     16 | 978-1-11111-141-1 |  43.33
     16 | 978-1-11111-123-1 |  43.33
     16 | 978-1-11111-127-1 |  43.33
     17 | 978-1-11111-133-1 |  50.00
     17 | 978-1-11111-127-1 |  50.00
     18 | 978-1-11111-135-1 |  33.33
     18 | 978-1-11111-131-1 |  33.33
     18 | 978-1-11111-127-1 |  33.33
     19 | 978-1-11111-128-1 |  47.50
     19 | 978-1-11111-136-1 |  47.50
     20 | 978-1-11111-115-1 |  75.00
```

■ FIGURE 19.9 Output of a simple query using windowing.

```
(a)
quarterly_sales
 id | quarter | year | sales_amt
----+---------+------+-----------
  1 |       1 | 2020 |    518.00
  1 |       2 | 2020 |   1009.00
  1 |       3 | 2020 |   1206.00
  1 |       4 | 2020 |    822.00
  1 |       1 | 2021 |    915.00
  1 |       2 | 2021 |   1100.00
  2 |       1 | 2020 |    789.00
  2 |       2 | 2020 |   1035.00
  2 |       3 | 2020 |   1235.00
  2 |       4 | 2020 |   1355.00
  2 |       1 | 2021 |   1380.00
  2 |       2 | 2021 |   1400.00
  3 |       3 | 2020 |    795.00
  3 |       4 | 2020 |    942.00
  3 |       1 | 2021 |   1012.00
  3 |       2 | 2021 |   1560.00
  4 |       1 | 2020 |   1444.00
  4 |       2 | 2020 |   1244.00
  4 |       3 | 2020 |    987.00
  4 |       4 | 2020 |    502.00
  5 |       1 | 2020 |   1200.00
  5 |       2 | 2020 |   1200.00
  5 |       3 | 2020 |   1200.00
  5 |       4 | 2020 |   1200.00
  5 |       1 | 2021 |   1200.00
  5 |       2 | 2021 |   1200.00
  6 |       1 | 2020 |    925.00
  6 |       2 | 2020 |   1125.00
  6 |       3 | 2020 |   1250.00
  6 |       4 | 2020 |   1387.00
  6 |       1 | 2021 |   1550.00
  6 |       2 | 2021 |   1790.00
  7 |       1 | 2021 |   2201.00
  7 |       2 | 2021 |   2580.00
  8 |       1 | 2021 |   1994.00
  8 |       2 | 2021 |   2121.00
  9 |       1 | 2021 |    502.00
  9 |       2 | 2021 |    387.00
 10 |       1 | 2021 |    918.00
 10 |       2 | 2021 |   1046.00

(b)
rep_names

 id | first_name | last_name
----+------------+-----------
  1 | John       | Anderson
  2 | Jane       | Anderson
  3 | Mike       | Baker
  4 | Mary       | Carson
  5 | Bill       | Davis
  6 | Betty      | Esteban
  7 | Jack       | Fisher
  8 | Jen        | Grant
  9 | Larry      | Holmes
 10 | Lily       | Imprego
```

■ FIGURE 19.10 Quarterly sales tables for use in windowing examples.

Note: Every windowing query must have an OVER clause, but you can leave out the PARTITION BY clause—using only OVER—if you want all the rows in the table to be in the same partition.

Ordering the Partitioning

When SQL processes a windowing query, it scans the rows in the order they appear in the table. However, you control the order in which rows are processed by adding an ORDER BY clause to the PARTITION BY expression. As you will see, doing so can alter the result, producing a "running" average or sum.

Consider first a query similar to the first windowing example:

```
SELECT first_name, last_name, quarter, year, sales_amt,
    CAST (AVG (sales_amt
    OVER (PARTITION BY quarterly_sales.sales_id) AS DECIMAL (7,2))
FROM rep_names, quarterly_sales
WHERE rep_names.id = quarterly_sales.id;
```

As you can see in Figure 19.11, the output is what you would expect: Each line displays the average sales for the given sales representative. The DBMS adds up the sales for all quarters for the sales person and divides by the number of quarters. However, if we add an ORDER BY clause to force processing in quarter and year order, the results are quite different.

The query changes only a bit:

```
SELECT first_name, last_name, quarter, year, sales_amt
   CAST (AVG (sales_amt OVER (PARTITION BY quarterly_sales.sales_id
   ORDER BY year, quarter) AS DECIMAL (7,2))
FROM rep_names, quarterly_sales
WHERE rep_names_id = quarterly_sales.id
ORDER BY year, quarter;
```

However, in this case, the ORDER BY clause forces the DBMS to process the rows in year and quarter order. As you can see in Figure 19.12, the average column is now a moving average. What is actually happening is that the window frame is changing in the partition each time a row is scanned. The first row in a partition is averaged by itself. Then, the window frame expands to include two rows and both are included in the average. This process repeats until all the rows in the partition have been included in the average. Therefore, each line in the output of this version of the query gives you the average at the end of that quarter, rather than for all quarters.

Note: If you replace the AVG in the preceding query with the SUM function, you'll get a running total of the sales made by each sales representative.

```
 first_name | last_name | quarter | year | sales_amt |   avg
------------+-----------+---------+------+-----------+---------
 John       | Anderson  |       1 | 2020 |    518.00 |  928.33
 John       | Anderson  |       1 | 2021 |    915.00 |  928.33
 John       | Anderson  |       2 | 2020 |   1009.00 |  928.33
 John       | Anderson  |       2 | 2021 |   1100.00 |  928.33
 John       | Anderson  |       3 | 2020 |   1206.00 |  928.33
 John       | Anderson  |       4 | 2020 |    822.00 |  928.33
 Jane       | Anderson  |       1 | 2020 |    789.00 | 1199.00
 Jane       | Anderson  |       1 | 2021 |   1380.00 | 1199.00
 Jane       | Anderson  |       2 | 2020 |   1035.00 | 1199.00
 Jane       | Anderson  |       2 | 2021 |   1400.00 | 1199.00
 Jane       | Anderson  |       3 | 2020 |   1235.00 | 1199.00
 Jane       | Anderson  |       4 | 2020 |   1355.00 | 1199.00
 Mike       | Baker     |       1 | 2021 |   1012.00 | 1077.25
 Mike       | Baker     |       2 | 2021 |   1560.00 | 1077.25
 Mike       | Baker     |       3 | 2020 |    795.00 | 1077.25
 Mike       | Baker     |       4 | 2020 |    942.00 | 1077.25
 Mary       | Carson    |       1 | 2020 |   1444.00 | 1044.25
 Mary       | Carson    |       2 | 2020 |   1244.00 | 1044.25
 Mary       | Carson    |       3 | 2020 |    987.00 | 1044.25
 Mary       | Carson    |       4 | 2020 |    502.00 | 1044.25
 Bill       | Davis     |       1 | 2020 |   1200.00 | 1200.00
 Bill       | Davis     |       1 | 2021 |   1200.00 | 1200.00
 Bill       | Davis     |       2 | 2020 |   1200.00 | 1200.00
 Bill       | Davis     |       2 | 2021 |   1200.00 | 1200.00
 Bill       | Davis     |       3 | 2020 |   1200.00 | 1200.00
 Bill       | Davis     |       4 | 2020 |   1200.00 | 1200.00
 Betty      | Esteban   |       1 | 2020 |    925.00 | 1337.83
 Betty      | Esteban   |       1 | 2021 |   1550.00 | 1337.83
 Betty      | Esteban   |       2 | 2020 |   1125.00 | 1337.83
 Betty      | Esteban   |       2 | 2021 |   1790.00 | 1337.83
 Betty      | Esteban   |       3 | 2020 |   1250.00 | 1337.83
 Betty      | Esteban   |       4 | 2020 |   1387.00 | 1337.83
 Jack       | Fisher    |       1 | 2021 |   2201.00 | 2390.50
 Jack       | Fisher    |       2 | 2021 |   2580.00 | 2390.50
 Jen        | Grant     |       1 | 2021 |   1994.00 | 2057.50
 Jen        | Grant     |       2 | 2021 |   2121.00 | 2057.50
 Larry      | Holmes    |       1 | 2021 |    502.00 |  444.50
 Larry      | Holmes    |       2 | 2021 |    387.00 |  444.50
 Lily       | Imprego   |       1 | 2021 |    918.00 |  982.00
 Lily       | Imprego   |       2 | 2021 |   1046.00 |  982.00
```

■ FIGURE 19.11 Computing the windowed average without ordering the rows.

```
first_name | last_name | quarter | year | sales_amt |   avg
-----------+-----------+---------+------+-----------+---------
John       | Anderson  |       1 | 2020 |    518.00 |  518.00
John       | Anderson  |       2 | 2020 |   1009.00 |  763.50
John       | Anderson  |       3 | 2020 |   1206.00 |  911.00
John       | Anderson  |       4 | 2020 |    822.00 |  888.75
John       | Anderson  |       1 | 2021 |    915.00 |  894.00
John       | Anderson  |       2 | 2021 |   1100.00 |  928.33
Jane       | Anderson  |       1 | 2020 |    789.00 |  789.00
Jane       | Anderson  |       2 | 2020 |   1035.00 |  912.00
Jane       | Anderson  |       3 | 2020 |   1235.00 | 1019.67
Jane       | Anderson  |       4 | 2020 |   1355.00 | 1103.50
Jane       | Anderson  |       1 | 2021 |   1380.00 | 1158.80
Jane       | Anderson  |       2 | 2021 |   1400.00 | 1199.00
Mike       | Baker     |       3 | 2020 |    795.00 |  795.00
Mike       | Baker     |       4 | 2020 |    942.00 |  868.50
Mike       | Baker     |       1 | 2021 |   1012.00 |  916.33
Mike       | Baker     |       2 | 2021 |   1560.00 | 1077.25
Mary       | Carson    |       1 | 2020 |   1444.00 | 1444.00
Mary       | Carson    |       2 | 2020 |   1244.00 | 1344.00
Mary       | Carson    |       3 | 2020 |    987.00 | 1225.00
Mary       | Carson    |       4 | 2020 |    502.00 | 1044.25
Bill       | Davis     |       1 | 2020 |   1200.00 | 1200.00
Bill       | Davis     |       2 | 2020 |   1200.00 | 1200.00
Bill       | Davis     |       3 | 2020 |   1200.00 | 1200.00
Bill       | Davis     |       4 | 2020 |   1200.00 | 1200.00
Bill       | Davis     |       1 | 2021 |   1200.00 | 1200.00
Bill       | Davis     |       2 | 2021 |   1200.00 | 1200.00
Betty      | Esteban   |       1 | 2020 |    925.00 |  925.00
Betty      | Esteban   |       2 | 2020 |   1125.00 | 1025.00
Betty      | Esteban   |       3 | 2020 |   1250.00 | 1100.00
Betty      | Esteban   |       4 | 2020 |   1387.00 | 1171.75
Betty      | Esteban   |       1 | 2021 |   1550.00 | 1247.40
Betty      | Esteban   |       2 | 2021 |   1790.00 | 1337.83
Jack       | Fisher    |       1 | 2021 |   2201.00 | 2201.00
Jack       | Fisher    |       2 | 2021 |   2580.00 | 2390.50
Jen        | Grant     |       1 | 2021 |   1994.00 | 1994.00
Jen        | Grant     |       2 | 2021 |   2121.00 | 2057.50
Larry      | Holmes    |       1 | 2021 |    502.00 |  502.00
Larry      | Holmes    |       2 | 2021 |    387.00 |  444.50
Lily       | Imprego   |       1 | 2021 |    918.00 |  918.00
Lily       | Imprego   |       2 | 2021 |   1046.00 |  982.00
```

■ FIGURE 19.12 Computing the windowed average with row ordering.

If you don't want a running sum or average, you can use a *frame clause* to change the size of the window (which rows are included). To suppress the cumulative average in Figure 19.12, you would add ROWS BETWEEN UNBOUNDED PRECEDING AND CURRENT ROW following the columns by which the rows within each partition are to be ordered. The window frame clauses are summarized in Table 19.3.

Table 19.3 Window Frame Clauses

Frame clause	Action
RANGE UNBOUNDED PRECEDING (default) RANGE BETWEEN UNBOUNDED PRECEDING AND CURRENT ROW	Include all rows within the current partition through the current row, based on the ordering specified in the ORDER BY clause. If no ORDER BY clause, include all rows. If there are duplicate rows, include their values only once

RANGE BETWEEN UNBOUNDED PRECEDING
   AND UNBOUNDED FOLLOWING
ROWS BETWEEN UNBOUNDED PRECEDING
   AND UNBOUNDED FOLLOWING
	Include all rows in the partition

ROWS UNBOUNDED PRECEDING ROWS BETWEEN UNBOUNDED PRECEDING AND CURRENT ROW	Include all rows within the current partition through the current row, including duplicate rows

Specific Functions

The window functions built into SQL perform actions that are only meaningful on partitions. Many of them include ways to rank data, something that is difficult to do otherwise. They can also number rows and compute distribution percentages. In this section we'll look at some of the specific functions: what they can do for you, and how they work.

Note: Depending on your DBMS, you may find additional window functions available, some of which are not part of the SQL standard.

RANK

The RANK function orders and numbers rows in a partition based on the value in a particular column. It has the general format

```
RANK () OVER (partition_specifications)
```

For example, if we wanted to see all the quarterly sales data ranked for all the sales representatives, the query could look like the following:

```
SELECT first_name, last_name, quarter, year, sales_amt,
    RANK () OVER (ORDER BY sales_amt desc)
FROM rep_names, quarterly_sales
WHERE rep_names.id = quarterly_sales.id;
```

The output appears in Figure 19.13. Notice that, because there is no PARTITION BY clause in the query, all of the rows in the table are part of a single ranking.

```
 first_name | last_name | quarter | year | sales_amt | rank
------------+-----------+---------+------+-----------+------
 Jack       | Fisher    |       2 | 2021 |   2580.00 |   1
 Jack       | Fisher    |       1 | 2021 |   2201.00 |   2
 Jen        | Grant     |       2 | 2021 |   2121.00 |   3
 Jen        | Grant     |       1 | 2021 |   1994.00 |   4
 Betty      | Esteban   |       2 | 2021 |   1790.00 |   5
 Mike       | Baker     |       2 | 2021 |   1560.00 |   6
 Betty      | Esteban   |       1 | 2021 |   1550.00 |   7
 Mary       | Carson    |       1 | 2020 |   1444.00 |   8
 Jane       | Anderson  |       2 | 2021 |   1400.00 |   9
 Betty      | Esteban   |       4 | 2020 |   1387.00 |  10
 Jane       | Anderson  |       1 | 2021 |   1380.00 |  11
 Jane       | Anderson  |       4 | 2020 |   1355.00 |  12
 Betty      | Esteban   |       3 | 2020 |   1250.00 |  13
 Mary       | Carson    |       2 | 2020 |   1244.00 |  14
 Jane       | Anderson  |       3 | 2020 |   1235.00 |  15
 John       | Anderson  |       3 | 2020 |   1206.00 |  16
 Bill       | Davis     |       4 | 2020 |   1200.00 |  17
 Bill       | Davis     |       3 | 2020 |   1200.00 |  17
 Bill       | Davis     |       1 | 2021 |   1200.00 |  17
 Bill       | Davis     |       2 | 2021 |   1200.00 |  17
 Bill       | Davis     |       1 | 2020 |   1200.00 |  17
 Bill       | Davis     |       2 | 2020 |   1200.00 |  17
 Betty      | Esteban   |       2 | 2020 |   1125.00 |  23
 John       | Anderson  |       2 | 2021 |   1100.00 |  24
 Lily       | Imprego   |       2 | 2021 |   1046.00 |  25
 Jane       | Anderson  |       2 | 2020 |   1035.00 |  26
 Mike       | Baker     |       1 | 2021 |   1012.00 |  27
 John       | Anderson  |       2 | 2020 |   1009.00 |  28
 Mary       | Carson    |       3 | 2020 |    987.00 |  29
 Mike       | Baker     |       4 | 2020 |    942.00 |  30
 Betty      | Esteban   |       1 | 2020 |    925.00 |  31
 Lily       | Imprego   |       1 | 2021 |    918.00 |  32
 John       | Anderson  |       1 | 2021 |    915.00 |  33
 John       | Anderson  |       4 | 2020 |    822.00 |  34
 Mike       | Baker     |       3 | 2020 |    795.00 |  35
 Jane       | Anderson  |       1 | 2020 |    789.00 |  36
 John       | Anderson  |       1 | 2020 |    518.00 |  37
 Larry      | Holmes    |       1 | 2021 |    502.00 |  38
 Mary       | Carson    |       4 | 2020 |    502.00 |  38
 Larry      | Holmes    |       2 | 2021 |    387.00 |  40
```

■ **FIGURE 19.13** Ranking all quarterly sales.

Alternatively, you could rank each sales representative's sales to identify the quarters in which each representative sold the most. The query would be written

```
SELECT first_name, last_name, quarter, year, sales_amt,
    RANK () OVER (PARTITION BY quarterly_sales.id
        ORDER BY sales_amt DESC)
FROM rep_names, quarterly_sales
WHERE rep_names.id = quarterly_sales.id;
```

The output can be found in Figure 19.14.

Note: When there are duplicate rows, the RANK function includes only one of the duplicates. However, if you want to include the duplicates, use DENSE_RANK instead of RANK.

first_name	last_name	quarter	year	sales_amt	rank
John	Anderson	3	2020	1206.00	1
John	Anderson	2	2021	1100.00	2
John	Anderson	2	2020	1009.00	3
John	Anderson	1	2021	915.00	4
John	Anderson	4	2020	822.00	5
John	Anderson	1	2020	518.00	6
Jane	Anderson	2	2021	1400.00	1
Jane	Anderson	1	2021	1380.00	2
Jane	Anderson	4	2020	1355.00	3
Jane	Anderson	3	2020	1235.00	4
Jane	Anderson	2	2020	1035.00	5
Jane	Anderson	1	2020	789.00	6
Mike	Baker	2	2021	1560.00	1
Mike	Baker	1	2021	1012.00	2
Mike	Baker	4	2020	942.00	3
Mike	Baker	3	2020	795.00	4
Mary	Carson	1	2020	1444.00	1
Mary	Carson	2	2020	1244.00	2
Mary	Carson	3	2020	987.00	3
Mary	Carson	4	2020	502.00	4
Bill	Davis	1	2020	1200.00	1
Bill	Davis	2	2020	1200.00	1
Bill	Davis	3	2020	1200.00	1
Bill	Davis	4	2020	1200.00	1
Bill	Davis	1	2021	1200.00	1
Bill	Davis	2	2021	1200.00	1
Betty	Esteban	2	2021	1790.00	1
Betty	Esteban	1	2021	1550.00	2
Betty	Esteban	4	2020	1387.00	3
Betty	Esteban	3	2020	1250.00	4
Betty	Esteban	2	2020	1125.00	5
Betty	Esteban	1	2020	925.00	6
Jack	Fisher	2	2021	2580.00	1
Jack	Fisher	1	2021	2201.00	2
Jen	Grant	2	2021	2121.00	1
Jen	Grant	1	2021	1994.00	2
Larry	Holmes	1	2021	502.00	1
Larry	Holmes	2	2021	387.00	2
Lily	Imprego	2	2021	1046.00	1
Lily	Imprego	1	2021	918.00	2

■ FIGURE 19.14 **Ranking within partitions.**

Choosing Windowing or Grouping for Ranking

Given the power and flexibility of SQL's windowing capabilities, is there any time that you should use grouping queries instead? Actually, there just might be. Assume that you want to rank all the sales representatives based on their total sales rather than simply ranking within each person's sales. Probably the easiest way to get that ordered result is to use a query like the following:

```
SELECT id, SUM (sales_amt)
FROM quarterly_sales
GROUP BY id
ORDER BY SUM (sales_amt) DESC;
```

You get the following output:

```
 id |   sum
----+--------
  6 | 8027.00
  5 | 7200.00
  2 | 7194.00
  1 | 5570.00
  7 | 4781.00
  3 | 4309.00
  4 | 4177.00
  8 | 4115.00
 10 | 1964.00
  9 |  889.00
```

The highest ranking total sales are at the top of listing, the lowest ranking sales at the bottom. The output certainly isn't as informative as the windowed output because you can't include the names of the sales representatives, but it does provide the required information.

Yes, you could use a windowing function to generate the same output, but it still needs to include the aggregate function SUM to generate the totals for each sales representative:

```
SELECT id, SUM (SUM(sales_amt))
     OVER (PARTITION BY quarterly_sales.id)
FROM quarterly_sales
GROUP BY id
ORDER BY SUM (sales_amt) DESC;
```

It works, but it's more code and the presence of the GROUP BY clause still means that you can't include the names unless they are part of the grouping criteria. Using the GROUP BY and the simple SUM function just seems easier.

PERCENT_RANK

The PERCENT_RANK function calculates the percentage rank of each value in a partition relative to the other rows in the partition. It works in the same way as RANK, but rather than returning a rank as an integer, it returns the percentage point at which a given value occurs in the ranking.

Let's repeat the query used to illustrate RANK using PERCENT_RANK instead:

```
SELECT first_name, last_name, quarter, year, sales_amt,
    PERCENT_RANK () OVER (PARTITION BY quarterly_sales.id
            ORDER BY sales_amt DESC)
FROM rep_names, quarterly_sales
WHERE rep_names.id = quarterly_sales.id;
```

The output can be found in Figure 19.15. As you can see, the result is exactly the same as the RANK result in Figure 19.14, with the exception of the rightmost column, where the integer ranks are replaced by percentage ranks.

ROW_NUMBER

The ROW_NUMBER function numbers the rows within a partition. For example, to number the sales representatives in alphabetical name order, the query could be

```
SELECT first_name, last_name,
    ROW_NUMBER () OVER (ORDER BY last_name, first_name)
    AS row_numb
FROM rep_names;
```

As you can see from Figure 19.16, the result includes all 10 sales representatives, numbered and sorted by name (last name as the outer sort).

Note: The SQL standard allows a named ROW_NUMBER result to be placed in a WHERE clause to restrict the number of rows in a query. However, not all DBMSs allow window functions in WHERE clauses.

CUME_DIST

When we typically think of a cumulative distribution, we think of something like that in Table 19.4, where the actual data values are gathered into ranges. SQL, however, can't discern the data grouping that we would like and therefore must consider each value (whether it be an individual data row or a row of an aggregate function result) as a line in the distribution.

The CUME_DIST function returns a value between 0 and 1, which, when multiplied by 100, gives you a percentage. Each "range" in the distribution, however, is a single value. In other words, the frequency of each group is

```
first_name  | last_name  | quarter | year | sales_amt |       percent_rank
------------+------------+---------+------+-----------+-----------------------
John        | Anderson   |       3 | 2020 |   1206.00 |                      0
John        | Anderson   |       2 | 2021 |   1100.00 |                    0.2
John        | Anderson   |       2 | 2020 |   1009.00 |                    0.4
John        | Anderson   |       1 | 2021 |    915.00 |                    0.6
John        | Anderson   |       4 | 2020 |    822.00 |                    0.8
John        | Anderson   |       1 | 2020 |    518.00 |                      1
Jane        | Anderson   |       2 | 2021 |   1400.00 |                      0
Jane        | Anderson   |       1 | 2021 |   1380.00 |                    0.2
Jane        | Anderson   |       4 | 2020 |   1355.00 |                    0.4
Jane        | Anderson   |       3 | 2020 |   1235.00 |                    0.6
Jane        | Anderson   |       2 | 2020 |   1035.00 |                    0.8
Jane        | Anderson   |       1 | 2020 |    789.00 |                      1
Mike        | Baker      |       2 | 2021 |   1560.00 |                      0
Mike        | Baker      |       1 | 2021 |   1012.00 |       0.333333333333333
Mike        | Baker      |       4 | 2020 |    942.00 |       0.666666666666667
Mike        | Baker      |       3 | 2020 |    795.00 |                      1
Mary        | Carson     |       1 | 2020 |   1444.00 |                      0
Mary        | Carson     |       2 | 2020 |   1244.00 |       0.333333333333333
Mary        | Carson     |       3 | 2020 |    987.00 |       0.666666666666667
Mary        | Carson     |       4 | 2020 |    502.00 |                      1
Bill        | Davis      |       1 | 2020 |   1200.00 |                      0
Bill        | Davis      |       2 | 2020 |   1200.00 |                      0
Bill        | Davis      |       3 | 2020 |   1200.00 |                      0
Bill        | Davis      |       4 | 2020 |   1200.00 |                      0
Bill        | Davis      |       1 | 2021 |   1200.00 |                      0
Bill        | Davis      |       2 | 2021 |   1200.00 |                      0
Betty       | Esteban    |       2 | 2021 |   1790.00 |                      0
Betty       | Esteban    |       1 | 2021 |   1550.00 |                    0.2
Betty       | Esteban    |       4 | 2020 |   1387.00 |                    0.4
Betty       | Esteban    |       3 | 2020 |   1250.00 |                    0.6
Betty       | Esteban    |       2 | 2020 |   1125.00 |                    0.8
Betty       | Esteban    |       1 | 2020 |    925.00 |                      1
Jack        | Fisher     |       2 | 2021 |   2580.00 |                      0
Jack        | Fisher     |       1 | 2021 |   2201.00 |                      1
Jen         | Grant      |       2 | 2021 |   2121.00 |                      0
Jen         | Grant      |       1 | 2021 |   1994.00 |                      1
Larry       | Holmes     |       1 | 2021 |    502.00 |                      0
Larry       | Holmes     |       2 | 2021 |    387.00 |                      1
Lily        | Imprego    |       2 | 2021 |   1046.00 |                      0
Lily        | Imprego    |       1 | 2021 |    918.00 |                      1
```

■ FIGURE 19.15 Percent ranking within partitions.

```
first_name  | last_name  | row_numb
------------+------------+----------
Jane        | Anderson   |        1
John        | Anderson   |        2
Mike        | Baker      |        3
Mary        | Carson     |        4
Bill        | Davis      |        5
Betty       | Esteban    |        6
Jack        | Fisher     |        7
Jen         | Grant      |        8
Larry       | Holmes     |        9
Lily        | Imprego    |       10
```

■ FIGURE 19.16 Row numbering.

Table 19.4 A Cumulative Frequency Distribution

Sales amount	Frequency	Cumulative frequency	Cumulative percentage
$0–1999	2	2	20
$2000–3999	0	0	20
$4000–5999	5	7	70
$6000–7999	2	9	90
> $8000	1	10	100

always 1. As an example, let's create a cumulative frequency distribution of the total sales made by each sales representative. The SQL can be written

```
SELECT id, SUM (sales_amt),
    100 * (CUME_DIST() OVER (ORDER BY SUM (sales_amt)))
    AS cume_dist
FROM quarterly_sales
GROUP BY id
ORDER BY cume_dist;
```

As you can see in Figure 19.17, each range is a group of 1.

```
 id |   sum    | cume_dist
----+----------+-----------
  9 |   889.00 |        10
 10 |  1964.00 |        20
  8 |  4115.00 |        30
  4 |  4177.00 |        40
  3 |  4309.00 |        50
  7 |  4781.00 |        60
  1 |  5570.00 |        70
  2 |  7194.00 |        80
  5 |  7200.00 |        90
  6 |  8027.00 |       100
```

■ **FIGURE 19.17 A SQL-generated cumulative frequency distribution.**

NTILE

NTILE breaks a distribution into a specified number of partitions, and indicates which rows are part of which group. SQL keeps the numbers of rows in each group as equal as possible. To see how this works, consider the following query:

```
SELECT id, SUM (sales_amt),
    NTILE(2) OVER (ORDER BY SUM (sales_amt) DESC) as N2,
        NTILE(3) OVER (ORDER BY SUM (sales_amt) DESC) as N3, NTILE(4)
        OVER (ORDER BY SUM (sales_amt) DESC) as N4
FROM quarterly_sales
GROUP BY id;
```

For the result, see Figure 19.18. The columns labeled n2, n3, and n4 contain the results of the NTILE calls. The highest number in each of those columns corresponds to the number of groups into which the data have been placed, which is the same value used as an argument to the function call.

```
 id |    sum    | n2 | n3 | n4
----+-----------+----+----+----
  6 | 8027.00 |  1 |  1 |  1
  5 | 7200.00 |  1 |  1 |  1
  2 | 7194.00 |  1 |  1 |  1
  1 | 5570.00 |  1 |  1 |  2
  7 | 4781.00 |  1 |  2 |  2
  3 | 4309.00 |  2 |  2 |  2
  4 | 4177.00 |  2 |  2 |  3
  8 | 4115.00 |  2 |  3 |  3
 10 | 1964.00 |  2 |  3 |  4
  9 |  889.00 |  2 |  3 |  4
```

■ FIGURE 19.18 Using the NTILE function to divide data into groups.

Inverse Distributions: PERCENTILE_CONT and PERCENTILE_DISC

The SQL standard includes two inverse distribution functions—PERCENTILE_CONT and PERCENTILE_DISC—that are most commonly used to compute the median of a distribution. PERCENTILE_CONT assumes that the distribution is continuous, and interpolates the median as needed. PERCENTILE_DISC, which assumes a discontinuous distribution, chooses the median from existing data values. Depending on the data themselves, the two functions may return different answers.

The functions have the following general format:

```
PERCENTILE_cont/disc (0.5)
    WITHIN GROUP (optional ordering clause)
    OVER (optional partition and ordering clauses)
```

If you replace the 0.5 following the name of the function with another probability between 0 and 1, you will get the nth percentile. For example, 0.9 returns the 90th percentile. The functions examine the percent rank of the values in a partition until it finds the one that is equal to or greater than whatever fraction you've placed in parentheses.

When used without partitions, each function returns a single value. For example,

```
SELECT PERCENTILE_CONT (0.5) WITHIN GROUP
    (ORDER BY SUM (sales_amt) DESC) AS continuous,
        PERCENTILE_DISC (0.5) WITHIN
        GROUP (ORDER BY SUM (sales_amt DESC) as discontinuous
FROM quarterly_sales
GROUP BY id;
```

Given the sales data, both functions return the same value: 1200. (There are 40 values, and the two middle values are 1200. Even with interpolation, the continuous median computes to the same answer.)

If we partition the data by sales representative, then we can compute the median for each sales representative:

```
SELECT first_name, last_name, PERCENTILE_CONT (0.5) WITHIN GROUP
    (ORDER BY SUM (sales_amt) DESC) OVER (PARTITION BY id)
        AS continuous, PERCENTILE_DISC (0.5) WITHIN GROUP
        (ORDER BY SUM (sales_amt DESC) OVER (PARTITION BY id)
        AS discontinuous
FROM quarterly_sales JOIN rep_names
GROUP BY id
ORDER BY last_name, first_name;
```

As you can see in Figure 19.19, the result contains one row for each sales representative, including both medians.

```
 first_name | last_name | continuous | discontinuous
------------+-----------+------------+--------------
 John       | Anderson  |     962.0  |       915.0
 Jane       | Anderson  |    1295.0  |      1235.0
 Mike       | Baker     |     977.0  |       942.0
 Mary       | Carson    |    1115.5  |       987.0
 Bill       | Davis     |    1200.0  |      1200.0
 Betty      | Esteban   |    1318.5  |      1250.0
 Jack       | Fisher    |    2350.5  |      2201.0
 Jen        | Grant     |    2057.5  |      1994.0
 Larry      | Holmes    |     484.5  |       387.0
 Lily       | Imprego   |     982.0  |       918.0
```

■ **FIGURE 19.19 Continuous and discontinuous medians for partitioned data.**

Chapter 20

Data Modification

SQL includes commands for modifying the data in tables: INSERT, UPDATE, and DELETE. In many business environments, application programs provide forms-driven data modification, removing the need for end users to issue SQL data modification statements directly to the DBMS. (As you will see, this is a good thing because using SQL data modification statements are rather clumsy.) Nonetheless, if you are developing and testing database elements and need to populate tables and modify data, you will probably be working at the command line with the SQL syntax.

Note: This chapter is where it will make sense that we covered retrieval before data modification.

Inserting Rows

The SQL INSERT statement has two variations: one that inserts a single row into a table and a second that copies one or more rows from another table.

Inserting One Row

To add one row to a table, you use the general syntax

```
INSERT INTO table_name VALUES (value_list)
```

In the preceding form, the value list contains one value for every column in the table, in the order in which the columns were created. For example, to insert a new row into the *customer* table someone at the rare book store might use

```
INSERT INTO customer VALUES (8,'Helen','Jerry',
    '16 Main Street','Newtown','NJ','18886','209-555-8888');
```

There are two things to keep in mind when inserting data in this way:

■ The format of the values in the value list must match the data types of the columns into which the data will be placed. In the current example, the first column requires an integer. The remaining columns all require characters and therefore the values have been surrounded by single quotes.

■ When you insert a row of data, the DBMS checks any integrity constraints that you have placed on the table. For the preceding example, it will verify that the customer number is unique and not null. If the constraints are not met, you will receive an error message and the row will not be added to the table.

If you do not want to insert data into every column of a table, you can specify the columns into which data should be placed:

```
INSERT INTO table_name (column_list) VALUES (value_list)
```

There must be a one-to-one correspondence between the columns in the column list and the values in the value list because the DBMS matches them by their relative positions in the lists.

As an example, assume that someone at the rare book store wants to insert a row into the *book* table, but doesn't know the binding type. The SQL would then be written

```
INSERT INTO book (isbn, work_numb, publisher_id,
    edition, copyright_year)
    VALUES ('978-11111-100-1',16,2,12,1960);
```

There are five columns in the column list and therefore five values in the value list. The first value in the list will be inserted into the *isbn* column, the second value into the *work_numb* column, and so on. The column omitted from the lists—*binding*—will remain null. You therefore must be sure to place values at least in primary key columns. Otherwise, the DBMS will not permit the insertion to occur.

Although it is not necessary to list column names when inserting values for every column in a table, there is one good reason to do so, especially when embedding the INSERT statement in an application program. If the structure of the table changes—if columns are added, deleted, or rearranged—then an INSERT without column names will no longer work properly. By always specifying column names, you can avoid unnecessary program modifications as your database changes to meet your changing needs.

Placement of New Rows

Where do new rows go when you add them? That depends on your DBMS. Typically, a DBMS maintains a unique internal identifier for each row that is not accessible to users (something akin to the combination of a row number and a table identifier) to provide information about the row's physical storage location. These identifiers continue to increase in value.

If you were to use the SELECT * syntax on a table, you would see the rows in internal identifier order. At the beginning of a table's life, this order corresponds to the order in which rows were added to the table. New rows appear to go at the "bottom" of the table, after all existing rows. As rows are deleted from the table, there will be gaps in the sequence of row identifiers. However, the DBMS does not reuse them (to "fill in the holes") until it has used up all available identifiers. If a database is very old, very large, and/ or very active, the DBMS will run out of new identifiers and will then start to reuse those made available by deleted rows. In that case, new rows may appear anywhere in the table. Given that you can view rows in any order by using the ORDER BY clause, it should make absolutely no difference to an end user or an application program where a new row is added.

Copying Existing Rows

The SQL INSERT statement can also be used to copy one or more rows from one table to another. The rows that will be copied are specified with a SELECT, giving the statement the following general syntax:

```
INSERT INTO table_name SELECT complete_SELECT_statement
```

The columns in the SELECT must match the columns of the table. For the purposes of this example, we will add a simple table to the rare book store database:

```
summary (isbn, how_many)
```

This table will contain summary information gathered from the *volume* table. To add rows to the new table, the INSERT statement can be written:

```
INSERT INTO summary
SELECT isbn, COUNT (*)
FROM volume
GROUP BY isbn;
```

The result is 27 rows copied into the *summary* table, one for each unique ISBN in the *volume* table.

Note: Should you store summary data like that placed in the table created in the preceding example? The answer is "it depends." If it takes a long time to

generate the summary data and you use the data frequently, then storing it
probably makes sense. But if you can generate the summary data easily and
quickly, then it is just as easy not to store it and to create the data whenever
it is needed for output.

Updating Data

Although most of today's end users modify existing data using an on-screen
form, the SQL statements to modify the data must nonetheless be issued by
the program providing the form. For example, as someone at the rare book
store adds volumes to a sale, the *volume* table is updated with the selling
price and the sale ID. The selling price is also added to the total amount of
the sale in the *sale* table.

The SQL UPDATE statement affects one or more rows in a table, based on
row selection criteria in a WHERE predicate. UPDATE has the following
general syntax:

```
UPDATE table_name
SET column1 = new_value, column2 = new_value, …
WHERE row_selection_predicate
```

If the WHERE predicate contains a primary key expression, then the
UPDATE will affect only one row. For example, to change a customer's
address, the rare book store could use

```
UPDATE customer
SET street = '195 Main Street'
    city = 'New Town'
    zip = '11111'
WHERE customer_numb = 5;
```

However, if the WHERE predicate identifies multiple rows, each row that
meets the criteria in the predicate will be modified. To raise all $50 prices to
$55, someone at the rare book store might write a query as

```
UPDATE books
SET asking_price = 55
WHERE asking_price = 50;
```

Notice that it is possible to modify the value in a column being used to
identify rows. The DBMS will select the rows to be modified before making
any changes to them.

If you leave the WHERE clause off an UPDATE, the same modification will be applied to every row in the table. For example, assume that we add a column for sales tax to the *sale* table. Someone at the rare book store could use the following statement to compute the tax for every sale:

```
UPDATE sale
SET sales_tax = sale_total_amt * 0.075;
```

The expression in the SET clause takes the current value in the *sale_total_amt* column, multiplies it by the tax rate, and puts it in the *sales_tax* column.

Deleting Rows

Like the UPDATE statement, the DELETE statement affects one or more rows in a table based on row selection criteria in a WHERE predicate. The general syntax for DELETE is

```
DELETE FROM table_name
WHERE row_selection_predicate
```

For example, if a customer decided to cancel an entire purchase, then someone at the rare book store would use something like

```
DELETE FROM sale
WHERE customer_numb = 12 AND sale_date = '05-Jul-2021';
```

Assuming that all purchases on the same date are considered a single sale, the WHERE predicate identifies only one row. Therefore, only one row is deleted.

When the criteria in a WHERE predicate identify multiple rows, all those matching rows are removed. If someone at the rare book store wanted to delete all sales for a specific customer, then the SQL would be written

```
DELETE FROM sale
WHERE customer_numb = 6;
```

In this case, there are multiple rows for customer number 6, all of which will be deleted.

DELETE is a potentially dangerous operation. If you leave off the WHERE clause—

```
DELETE FROM sale
```

—you will delete every row in the table! (The table remains in the database without any rows.)

Deletes and Referential Integrity

The preceding examples of DELETE involve a table that has a foreign key in another table (*sale_id* in *volume*) referencing it. It also has a foreign key of its own (*customer_numb* referencing the primary key of *customer*). You can delete rows containing foreign keys without any effect on the rest of the database, but what happens when you attempt to delete rows that *do* have foreign keys referencing them?

Note: The statement in the preceding paragraph refers to database integrity issues and clearly misses the logical issue of the need to decrement the total sale amount in the sale table whenever a volume is removed from the sale.

Assume, for example, that a customer cancels a purchase. Your first thought might be to delete the row for that sale from the *sale* table. There are, however, rows in the *volume* table that reference that sale and if the row for the sale is removed from *sale*, there will be no primary key for the rows in *volume* to reference and referential integrity will be violated.

As you will remember from our discussion of creating tables with foreign keys, what actually happens in such a situation depends on what was specified when the table containing the primary key being referenced was created (SET NULL, SET DEFAULT, CASCADE, NO ACTION).

Deleting All Rows: TRUNCATE TABLE

The 2008 SQL standard introduced a new command—TRUNCATE TABLE—that removes all rows from a table more quickly than a DELETE, without a WHERE clause. This can be particularly useful when you are developing a database and need to remove test data but leave the table structure untouched. The command's general syntax is

```
TRUNCATE TABLE table_name
```

Like the DELETE without a WHERE clause, the table structure remains intact, and in the data dictionary.

There are some limits to using the command:

- It cannot be used on a table that has foreign keys referencing it.
- It cannot be used on a table on which indexed views are based.
- It cannot activate a trigger (a program module stored in the database that is initiated when a specific event, such as a delete, occurs).

Although DELETE and TRUNCATE TABLE seem to have the same effect, they do work differently. DELETE removes the rows one at a time and writes an entry into the database log file for each row. In contrast, TRUNCATE TABLE deallocates space in the database files, making the space formerly occupied by the truncated table's rows available for other use.

Inserting, Updating, or Deleting on a Condition: MERGE

The SQL:2003 standard introduced a very powerful and flexible way to insert, update, or delete data using the MERGE statement. MERGE[1] includes a condition to be tested and alternative sets of actions that are performed when the condition is or is not met. The model behind this statement is the merging of a table of transactions into a master table.

MERGE has the following general syntax:

```
MERGE INTO target_table_name
     USING source_table_name ON merge_condition
WHEN MATCHED THEN
     update/delete_specification
WHEN NOT MATCHED THEN
     insert specification
```

Notice that when the merge condition is matched (in other words, evaluates as true for a given row), an update and/or delete is performed. When the condition is not matched, an insert is performed. Either the MATCHED or NOT MATCHED clause is optional.

The target table is the table that will be affected by the changes made by the statement. The source table—which can be a base table or a virtual table generated by a SELECT—provides the source of the table. To help you understand how MERGE works, let's use the classic model of applying transactions to a master table. First, we need a transaction table:

```
transaction (sale_id, inventory_id, selling_price,
     sale_date, customer_numb)
```

The *transaction* table contains information about the sale of a single volume. (It really doesn't contain all the necessary columns for the *sale* table but it will do for this example.) If a row for the sale exists in the *sale* table, then the selling price of the volume should be added to existing sale total. However, if the sale is not in the *sale* table, then a new row should be created and the sale total set to the selling price of the volume. A MERGE statement that will do the trick might be written as

```
MERGE INTO sale S USING transaction T ON (S.sale_id = T.sale_id)
WHEN MATCHED THEN
     UPDATE SET sale_total_amt = sale_total_amt + selling_price
WHEN NOT MATCHED
     INSERT (sale_id, customer_numb, sale_date, sale_total_amt)
          VALUES (T.sale_id, T.customer_numb, T.sale_date,
          T.selling_price);
```

---

[1] Some DBMSs call this functionality UPSERT.

The target table is *sale*; the source table is *transaction*. The merge condition looks for a match between sale IDs. If a match is found, then the UPDATE portion of the command performs the modification of the *sale_total_amt* column. If no match is found, then the insert occurs. Notice that the INSERT portion of the command does not need a table name because the table affected by the INSERT has already been specified as the target table.

As we said earlier, the source table for a merge operation doesn't need to be a base table; it can be a virtual table created on the fly using a SELECT. For example, assume that someone at the rare book store needs to keep a table of total purchases made by each customer. The following table can be used to hold that data:

```
summary_stats (customer_numb, year, total_purchases)
```

You can find the MERGE statement below. The statement assembles the summary data using a SELECT that extracts the year from the sale date and sums the sale amounts. Then, if a summary row for a year already exists in *summary_stats*, the MERGE adds the amount from the source table to what is stored already in the target table. Otherwise, it adds a row to the target table.

```
MERGE INTO summary_stats AS S USING
     (SELECT customer_numb,
      EXTRACT (YEAR FROM sale_date) AS Y, sum
(sale_total_amt AS M) AS T
      FROM sale
      GROUP BY customer_numb, Y)
ON (CAST(S.customer_numb AS CHAR (4)
     || CAST (S.year AS CHAR(4) =
CAST(T.customer_numb AS CHAR (4) || CAST (T.year AS CHAR(4)
WHEN MATCHED
     UPDATE SET total_purchases = T.M
WHEN NOT MATCHED
     INSERT VALUES (customer_numb, Y, M);
```

As powerful as MERGE seems to be, the restriction of UPDATE/DELETE to the matched condition and INSERT to the unmatched prevent it from being able to handle some situations. For example, if someone at the rare book store wanted to archive all orders more than two years old, the process would involve creating a row for each sale that didn't exist in the archive table and then deleting the row from the *sale* table. (We're assuming that the delete cascades, removing all rows from *volume* as well.) The problem is that the delete needs to occur on the unmatched condition, which isn't allowed with the MERGE syntax.

Chapter

21

Creating Additional Structural Elements

Views

As you first read in Chapter 5, views provide a way to give users a specific portion of a larger schema with which they can work. Before you actually can create views, there are two things you should consider: which views you really need and whether the views can be used for updating data.

Deciding Which Views to Create

Views take up very little space in a database, occupying only a few rows in a data dictionary table. That being the case, you can feel free to create views as needed.

A typical database might include the following views:

- One view for every base table that is exactly the same as the base table, but with a different name. Then, you prevent end users from seeing the base tables and do not tell the end users the table names; you give end users access only to the views. This makes it harder for end users to attempt to gain access to the stored tables because they do not know their names. However, as you will see in the next section, it is essential for updating that there be views that do match the base tables.
- One view for each primary key–foreign key relationship over which you join frequently. If the tables are large, the actual syntax of the statement may include structures for avoiding the join operation, but still combining the tables.
- One view for each complex query that you issue frequently.
- Views as needed to restrict user access to specific columns and rows. For example, you might recreate a view for a receptionist that shows employee office numbers and telephone extensions, but leaves off home address, telephone number, and salary.

View Updatability Issues

A database query can apply any operations supported by its DBMS's query language to a view, just as it can to base tables. However, using views for updates is a much more complicated issue. Given that views exist only in main memory, any updates made to a view must be stored in the underlying base tables if the updates are to have any effect on the database.

Not every view is updatable, however. Although the rules for view updatability vary from one DBMS to another, you will find that many DBMSs share the following restrictions:[1]

- A view must be created from one base table or view, or if the view uses joined tables, only one of the underlying base tables can be updated.
- If the source of the view is another view, then the source view must also adhere to the rules for updatability.
- A view must be created from only one query. Two or more queries cannot be assembled into a single view table using operations such as union.
- The view must include the primary key columns of the base table.
- The view must include all columns specified as not null (columns requiring mandatory values).
- The view must not include any groups of data. It must include the original rows of data from the base table, rather than rows based on values common to groups of data.
- The view must not remove duplicate rows.

Creating Views

To create a view whose columns have the same name as the columns in the base tables from which it is derived, you give the view a name and include the SQL query that defines its contents:

```
CREATE VIEW view_name AS
     SELECT …
```

---

[1]MySQL views are updatable if they adhere to the rules stated in the text, as are many DB2 views; PostgreSQL views aren't updatable at all. However, you can update using views that don't meet the rules for updatability. If you write a trigger—a SQL procedure executed when some modification event occurs—using INSTEAD OF for a view, you can create an alternative for the modification command that works directly on the base tables. The user still performs the update command on the view, but, instead of doing the update, the DBMS activates the trigger to actually do the work. Triggers require SQL programming (see Appendix B). In addition, the syntax for INSTEAD OF triggers is highly implementation-dependent.

For example, if *Antique Opticals* wanted to create a view that included actions films, the SQL is written

```
CREATE VIEW action_films AS
    SELECT item_numb, title
    FROM item
    WHERE genre = 'action';
```

If you want to rename the columns in the view, you include the view's column names in the CREATE VIEW statement:

```
CREATE VIEW action_films (identifier, name)
    AS
    SELECT item_numb, title
    FROM item
    WHERE genre = 'action';
```

The preceding statement will produce a view with two columns named *identifier* and *name*. Note that if you want to change even one column name, you must include *all* the column names in the parentheses following the view name. The DBMS will match the columns following SELECT with the view column names by their positions in the list.

Views can be created from any SQL query, including those that perform joins, unions, and grouping. For example, to simplify looking at customers and their order totals, *Antique Opticals* might create a view like the following:

```
CREATE VIEW sales_summary AS
    SELECT customer_numb, order.order_numb, order.order_date,
      SUM (selling_price)
    FROM order_line JOIN order
    GROUP BY customer_number, orders.order_date,
      orders.order_numb;
```

The view table will then contain grouped data along with a computed column.

Temporary Tables

A temporary table is a base table that is not stored in the database, but instead exists only while the database session in which it was created is active. At first glance, this may sound like a view, but views and temporary tables are somewhat different:

- A view exists only for a single query. Each time you use the name of a view, its table is recreated from existing data.
- A temporary table exists for the entire database session in which it was created.
- A view is automatically populated with the data retrieved by the query that defines it.

- You must add data to a temporary table with SQL INSERT commands.
- Only views that meet the criteria for view updatability can be used for data modifications.
- Because temporary tables are base tables, all of them can be updated. (They can be updated, but keep in mind that any modifications you make won't be retained in the database.)
- Because the contents of a view are generated each time the view's name is used, a view's data are always current.
- The data in a temporary table reflect the state of the database at the time the table was loaded with data. If the data from which the temporary table was loaded are modified after the temporary table has received its data, then the contents of the temporary table may be out of sync with other parts of the database.

If the contents of a temporary table become outdated when source data change, why use a temporary table at all? Wouldn't it be better simply to use a view whose contents are continually regenerated? The answer lies in performance. It takes processing time to create a view table. If you are going to use data only once during a database session, then a view will actually perform better than a temporary table because you don't need to create a structure for it. However, if you are going to be using the data repeatedly during a session, then a temporary table provides better performance because it needs to be created only once. The decision therefore results in a trade-off: Using a view repeatedly takes more time, but provides continuously updated data; using a temporary table repeatedly saves time, but you run the risk that the table's contents may be out of date.

Creating Temporary Tables

Creating a temporary table is very similar to creating a permanent base table. You do, however, need to decide on the *scope* of the table. A temporary table may be *global*, in which case it is accessible to the entire application program that created it.[2] Alternatively, it can be *local*, in which case it is accessible only to the program module in which it was created.

To create a global temporary table, you add the keywords GLOBAL TEMPORARY to the CREATE TABLE statement:

```
CREATE GLOBAL TEMPORARY TABLE
    (remainder of CREATE statement)
```

---

[2]The term "application program" refers to a program written by programmers for end-users or to a command-line SQL command processor that a user is using interactively.

By the same token, you create a local temporary table with

```
CREATE LOCAL TEMPORARY TABLE
    (remainder of CREATE statement)
```

For example, if *Antique Opticals* was going to use the order summary information repeatedly, it might create the following temporary table instead of using a view:

```
CREATE GLOBAL TEMPORARY TABLE order_summary
    (customer_numb int,
    order_numb int,
    order_date date,
    order_total numeric (6,2),
    PRIMARY KEY (customer_numb, order_numb);
```

Loading Temporary Tables with Data

To place data in a temporary table, you use one or more SQL INSERT statements. For example, to load the order summary table created in the preceding section, you could type

```
INSERT INTO order_summary
    SELECT customer_numb, order.order_numb, order.order_date,
      SUM (selling_price)
    FROM order_line JOIN order
    GROUP BY customer_number, orders.order_date,
      orders.order_numb
```

You can now query and manipulate the *order_summary* table, just as you would a permanent base table.

Disposition of Temporary Table Rows

When you write embedded SQL (SQL statements coded as part of a program written in a high-level language such as C++ or Java), you have control over the amount of work that the DBMS considers to be a unit (a *transaction*). Although we will cover transactions in depth in Chapter 22, at this point you need to know that a transaction can end in one of two ways: It can be *committed* (changes made permanent) or it can be *rolled back* (its changes undone).

By default, the rows in a temporary table are purged whenever a transaction is committed. If you want to use the same temporary tables in multiple transactions, however, you can instruct the DBMS to retain the rows by including ON COMMIT PRESERVE ROWS to the end of the table creation statement:

```
CREATE GLOBAL TEMPORARY TABLE order_summary
    (customer_numb int,
    order_numb int,
    order_date date,
    order_total numeric (6,2),
    PRIMARY KEY (customer_numb, order_numb
    ON COMMIT PRESERVE ROWS);
```

Because a rollback returns the database to the state it was in before the transaction begins, a temporary table will also be restored to its previous state (with or without rows).

Common Table Expressions (CTEs)

A *common table expression* (CTE) is yet another way of extracting a subset of a database for use in another query. CTEs are like views in that they generate virtual tables. However, the definition of a CTE is not stored in the database, and it must be used immediately after it is defined.

To get started, let's look at a very simple example. The general format of a simple CTE is

```
WITH CTE_name (columns) AS
    (SELECT_statement_defining_table)
CTE_query
```

For example, a CTE and its query to view all of the rare book store's customers could be written

```
WITH customer_names (first, last) AS
    (SELECT first_name, last_name
     FROM customer)
SELECT *
FROM customer_names;
```

The result is a listing of the first and last names of the customers. This type of structure for a simple query really doesn't buy you much, except that the CTE isn't stored in the database like a view and doesn't require INSERT statements to populate it like a temporary table. However, the major use of CTEs is for *recursive queries*, queries that query themselves. (That may sound a bit circular and it is, intentionally.) The typical application of a recursive query using a CTE is to process hierarchical data, data arranged in a tree structure. It will allow a single query to access every element in the tree or to access subtrees that begin somewhere other than the top of the tree.

As an example, let's create a table that handles the descendants of a single person (in this case, John). As you can see in Figure 21.1, each node in the tree has at most one parent and any number of children. The numbers in the illustration represent the ID of each person.

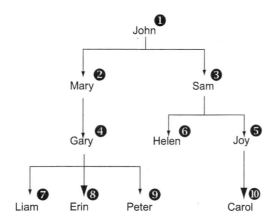

FIGURE 21.1 A tree structure that can be represented in a relational database, and traversed with a recursive query.

Relational databases are notoriously bad at handling this type of hierarchically structured data. The typical way to handle it is to create a relation, something like this:

```
genealogy (person_id, parent_id, person_name)
```

Each row in the table represents one node in the tree. For this example, the table is populated with the 10 rows in Figure 21.2. John, the node at the top of the tree, has no parent ID. The *parent_ID* column in the other rows is filled with the person ID of the node above it in the tree. (The order of the rows in the table is irrelevant.)

```
person_id | parent_id |          person_name
-----------+-----------+---------------------------------
        1 |           | John
        2 |         1 | Mary
        3 |         1 | Sam
        4 |         2 | Gary
        5 |         3 | Joy
        6 |         3 | Helen
        7 |         4 | Liam
        8 |         4 | Erin
        9 |         4 | Peter
       10 |         5 | Carol
```

■**FIGURE 21.2 Sample data for use with a recursive query.**

We can access every node in the tree by simply accessing every row in the table. However, what can we do if we want to process just the people who are Sam's descendants? There is no easy way with a typical SELECT to do that. However, a CTE used recursively will identify just the rows we want.

The syntax of a recursive query is similar to the simple CTE query, with the addition of the keyword RECURSIVE following WITH. For our particular example, the query will be written:

```
WITH RECURSIVE show_tree AS
      (SELECT
      FROM genealogy
      WHERE person_name = 'Sam'
      UNION ALL
      SELECT g.*
      FROM genealogy AS g, show_tree AS st
      WHERE g.parent_id = st.person_id)
SELECT *
FROM show_tree
ORDER BY person_name;
```

The result is

```
person_id | parent_id |          person_name
----------+-----------+-------------------------
       10 |         5 | Carol
        6 |         3 | Helen
        5 |         3 | Joy
        3 |         1 | Sam
```

The query that defines the CTE called *show_tree* has two parts. The first is a simple SELECT that retrieves Sam's row and places it in the result table as well as in an intermediate table that represents the current state of *show_tree*. The second SELECT (below UNION ALL) is the recursive part. It will use the intermediate table in place of *show_tree* each time it executes and add the result of each iteration to the result table. The recursive portion will execute repeatedly until it returns no rows.

Here's how the recursion will work in our example:

1. Join the intermediate result table to *genealogy*. Because the intermediate result table contains just Sam's row, the join will match Helen and Joy.
2. Remove Sam from the intermediate table and insert Helen and Joy.
3. Append Helen and Joy to the result table.

4. Join the intermediate table to *genealogy*. The only match from the join will be Carol. (Helen has no children, and Joy has only one.)
5. Remove Helen and Joy from the intermediate table and insert Carol.
6. Append Carol to the result table.
7. Join the intermediate table to *genealogy*. The result will be no rows, and the recursion stops.

CTEs cannot be reused; the declaration of the CTE isn't saved. Therefore, they don't buy you much for most queries. However, they are enormously useful if you are working with tree-structured data. CTEs and recursion can also be helpful when working with bill of materials data.

Creating Indexes

As you read in Chapter 7, an index is a data structure that provides a fast access path to rows in a table based on the value in one or more columns (the index key). Because an index stores key values in order, the DBMS can use a fast search technique to find the values, rather than being forced to search each row in an unordered table sequentially.

You create indexes with the CREATE INDEX statement:

```
CREATE INDEX index_name
ON table_name (index_key_columns)
```

For example, to create an index on the *title* column in *Antique Opticals item* table, you could use

```
CREATE INDEX item_title_index
ON item (title);
```

By default, the index will allow duplicate entries and keeps the entries in ascending order (alphabetical, numeric, or chronological, whichever is appropriate). To require unique indexes, add the keyword UNIQUE after CREATE:

```
CREATE UNIQUE INDEX item_title_index
ON item (title);
```

To sort in descending order, insert DESC after the column whose sort order you want to change. For example, *Antique Opticals* might want to create an index on the order date in the *order* relation in descending order so that the most recent orders are first:

```
CREATE INDEX order_order_date_index
ON order (order_date DESC);
```

If you want to create an index on a concatenated key, include all the columns that should be part of the index key in the column list. For example, the following creates an index organized by actor and item number:

```
CREATE INDEX actor_actor_item_index
ON actor (actor_numb, item_numb);
```

Although you do not need to access an index directly unless you want to delete it from the database, it helps to give indexes names that will tell you something about their tables and key columns. This makes it easier to remember them should you need to get rid of the indexes.

Database Implementation Issues

When the time comes to implement your relational database, you will probably discover that there are other decisions you need to make beyond the design of the tables. You will need to worry about concurrency control and database security; you may need to send your data to a data warehouse or exchange data with another system that requires an XML document as the transfer medium. In this last section of this book, we will look into all of those topics to round out your understanding of relational databases.

Chapter
22

Concurrency Control

For the most part, today's DBMSs are intended as shared resources. A single database may be supporting thousands of users at one time. We call this type of use *concurrent use*. However, although many users are working with the same database, it does not mean that more than one user is (or should be) working with exactly the same data as another at precisely the same moment.

It is physically impossible for two users to read or write exactly the same bit on a disk at precisely the same time. Operating systems and hardware disk controllers work together to ensure that only one read or write request is executed for any given disk location. This type of *concurrency control* is distinct from what occurs within a database environment. Database concurrency control is concerned with the logical consistency and integrity of a database; the physical concurrency control offered by the OS and the hardware is assumed to be in place.

In this chapter, we will begin by looking at the multiuser environment and then turn to the consistency and integrity problems that can occur when multiuser access is not controlled. Then, we will look at some solutions to those problems.

The Multiuser Environment

Any time you have more than one user interacting with the same database at the same time, you have a multiuser environment. The DBMS must be able to separate the actions of one user from another and group them into a logical whole. It must also be able to ensure the integrity of the database while multiple users are modifying data.

Transactions

A *transaction* is a unit of work submitted to a database by a single user. It may consist of a single interactive command or it may include many commands issued from within an application program. Transactions are important to multiuser databases because they either succeed or fail as a whole. For example, if you are entering data about a new customer and an order placed by that customer, you won't be able to save any of the information unless you satisfy all the constraints on all the tables affected by the modification. If any validation fails, the customer data, the order data, and the data about the items on the order cannot be stored.

A transaction can end in one of two ways: If it is successful, then the changes it made are stored in the database permanently—the transaction is *committed*—or if the transaction fails, all the changes made by transaction are undone, restoring the database to the state that it was in prior to the start of the transaction (a *rollback*). A transaction is an all-or-nothing unit. Either the entire transaction succeeds or the entire transaction fails and is undone. We therefore often call a transaction the *unit of recovery*.

Why might a transaction fail? There are several reasons:

- A transaction may be unable to satisfy constraints necessary for modifying data.

Note: In the interests of efficiency, some DBMSs commit all transactions that perform only data retrieval, even if the retrievals requested by the transactions returned no data.

- A transaction may time out. (See the discussion later in this chapter on Web database issues.)
- The network connection between the user and the database may go down.
- The server running the database may go down, for any reason.

The ACID Transaction Goal

One way to summarize the major goal of concurrency control is to say that a DBMS attempts to produce *ACID transactions*. ACID stands for atomicity, consistency, isolation, and durability:

- Atomicity: As mentioned in the preceding section, a transaction is a complete unit. It either succeeds as a whole or fails as a whole. A DBMS with atomic transactions never leaves a transaction partially completed, regardless of what caused the failure (data consistency problems, power failures, and so on).

- Consistency: Each transaction will leave the database in a consistent state. In other words, all data will meet all constraints that have been placed on the data. This means that a user or application program can be certain that the database is consistent at the start of a new transaction.
- Isolation: One of the most important things concurrency control can do is insure that multiple transactions running at the same time are isolated from one another. When two transactions run at the same time, the result should be the same as if one transaction ran first in its entirety, followed by the other. This should be true regardless of which transaction runs first. In that case, we say that the transactions are *serializable* (produce the same result when running concurrently as they would running in a series).
- Durability: Once committed, a transaction is forever. It will not be rolled back.

Logging and Rollback

To effect transaction rollback, a DBMS must somehow save the state of the database *before* a transaction begins. As a transaction proceeds, the DBMS must also continue to save data modifications as they are made. Most DBMSs write this type of transaction audit trail to a *log file*. Conceptually, a log file looks something like Figure 22.1.

Note: Throughout this section of this chapter, we will describe several things as "conceptual." This is because the exact procedure for performing some actions or the specific file structure in use depends on the DBMS. However, the effect of actions and/or file structures is as described.

When a transaction begins, it is given a number. Each time the transaction makes a change, the values prior to the change are written to a record in the log file. Records for transactions running concurrently are intermixed in the file. Therefore, the records for each transaction are connected into a linked list, with each record pointing to the next.

When a transaction commits, its changes are written to the database and its records purged from the log file. If a transaction fails for any reason, however, a rollback occurs conceptually in the following way:

1. Find the last record for the transaction in the log file.
2. Replace current values with the values in the log record.
3. Follow the pointer to the previous log record.
4. Repeat steps 2 and 3 until reaching the record that marks the start of the transaction.

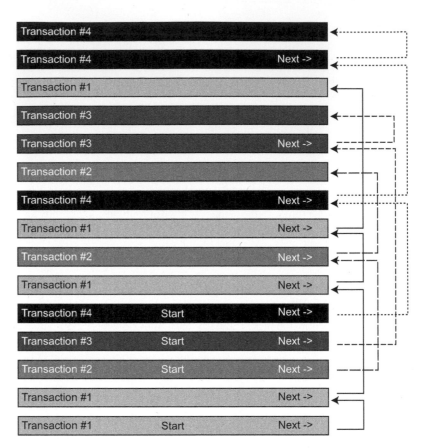

FIGURE 22.1 The conceptual structure of a database log file.

Note: Committing a transaction is final. By definition, a committed transaction is never rolled back.

There is one major problem with maintaining a log file: ensuring that all changes to the log file are actually written to disk. This is important because it is more efficient for a computer to wait until it has a complete unit of data to write before it actually accesses the disk than to write each time data are modified. Operating systems maintain disk I/O *buffers* in main memory to hold data waiting to be written. When a buffer is full, the write occurs. The buffering system is efficient because while memory—which is one of the computer's fastest components—fills several buffers, the disk can be taking its time with the writing. Once it finishes a write, the disk empties the next buffer in line. In this way, the slower device—the disk—is kept busy. However, a problem occurs when the computer fails for any reason. (Even a power outage can be at fault.) Whatever data were in the buffers at that time, waiting to be written, are lost. If those lost buffer contents happen to contain database log records, then the database and the log may well be inconsistent.

Note: The number and size of a computer's I/O buffers depends on the both hardware and the operating system. Typically, however, the buffers in today's machines are between 1 and 4K.

The solution is something known as a *checkpoint*. A checkpoint is an instant in time at which the database and the log file are known to be consistent. To take a checkpoint, the DBMS forces the OS to write the I/O buffers to disk, even if they aren't full. Both database changes and log file changes are forced to disk. The DBMS then writes a small file (sometimes called the "checkpoint file" or the "recovery file") that contains the location in the log file of the last log record when the checkpoint was taken.

There will always be some unit of time between checkpoints during which log records are written to the log file. If a system failure occurs, anything after the checkpoint is considered to be suspect because there is no way to know whether data modifications were actually written to disk. The more closely spaced the checkpoints, the less data will be lost due to system failure. However, taking a checkpoint consumes database processing and disk I/O time, slowing down overall database processing. It is therefore the job of a database administrator to find a checkpoint interval that balances safety and performance.

Recovery

Recovering a database after a system failure can be a tedious process. It not only has to take into account transactions that were partially completed, but those that committed after the last checkpoint was taken and whose records haven't yet been purged from the log file.

Conceptually, a recovery would work like this:

1. Find the latest checkpoint file.
2. Read the checkpoint file to determine the location of the last log record known to be written to disk in the log file.
3. Set up two lists for transactions: one for those that need to be *undone*, and another for those that need to be *redone*.
4. Starting at the last verified log file record, read from the back of the file to the front of the file, placing each transaction found in the *undo* list.
5. Stop at the beginning of the file.
6. Now read each record from the front to the back. Each time you encounter a commit record, you'll know that you've discovered a transaction that completed yet didn't have its log records purged from the log file. Because almost all of these transactions will be committed after the last checkpoint record, there is no way to ensure that any

changes made by these transactions were written to the database. Therefore, move these transactions to the *redo* list.

7. Undo any transactions for which there are no commit records.
8. Redo the suspect committed transactions.

No normal database processing can occur while the recovery operating is in progress. For large operations with many transactions in the log file, recovery may therefore take some time.

Problems with Concurrent Use

As mentioned earlier, the computer hardware and OS take care of ensuring that only one physical write occurs to a given storage location at one time. Why, then, might a database need additional concurrency control? The answer lies in the need for logical, in addition to physical, consistency of the database. To understand what can occur, let's look at some examples.

Lost Update #1

Assume, for example, that a small city has four community centers, each of which receives a single shipment of publicity materials for each city-wide event from the city's printer. To keep of track of what they have received and have in their storage rooms, each community center has a table in the database like the following:

```
publicity_materials (event_name, event_date,
      numb_posters_received, numb_brochures_received)
```

West Side Community Center has been accidentally left out of the delivery of posters for a special event on Saturday. The community center sends an e-mail to all the other community centers in the area, asking for 10–20 posters. Someone at the East Side Center calls in to say that they have 15 posters they can send. The West Side staff member who takes the call checks to see how many posters have been received, sees a 0, and then enters the 15 in the *publicity_materials* table.

About the same time, another call comes in from the North Side Center and is answered by a different staff member. North Side Center has 12 posters that can be sent. The second staff member queries the database and sees that there are 0 posters—the 15 posters from East Side Center haven't been stored as of yet—and therefore enters the 12 into the database. However, in the few seconds that elapse between viewing 0 posters and entering 12 posters, the 15 posters are stored in the database. The result is that the 12 overlays the existing value, wiping out the 15 that was just stored. West Side Community Center will be receiving 27 posters, but they don't know it. The second update wiped out the first. The unintentional loss of data when data are replaced by a newer value is the *lost update*.

You can see exactly how the first update to the database was lost if you look at the timeline in Figure 22.2. Notice first that the actions of the transactions (one for each user) overlap in time. We therefore say that the transactions are *interleaved*. One goal of concurrency control is to ensure that the result of interleaved transaction is the same as if the transactions ran one after the other.

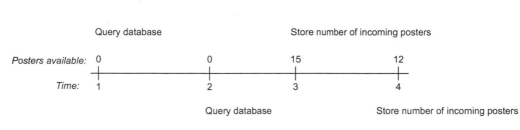

■ **FIGURE 22.2 Lost update.**

In this particular example, regardless of which transaction runs first, the correct answer should be 27: The second staff member should retrieve something other than 0 from the database and know that he or she would need to add the second group of posters to the first. But, that's not what happens without concurrency control. Instead, at time 4—when the second staff members stores 12 posters—the 0 that the staff member retrieved at time 2 is old data: The lost update occurs because the second transaction was based on old data.

Lost Update #2

A more subtle type of lost update occurs when an existing database value is modified rather than merely replaced. As an example, consider two travel agents, one in Philadelphia and the other in Boston. Both use the same airline reservations database. A customer calls the Boston travel agency and, as a part of a cross-country trip, needs three seats from Chicago to Denver on a specific date and at a specific time. The travel agent queries the database and discovers that exactly three seats are available on a flight that meets the customer's criteria. The agent reports that fact to the customer, who is waiting on the phone.

Meanwhile, a customer calls the travel agent in Philadelphia. This customer also needs three seats from Chicago to Denver on the same date and at the same time as the customer in Boston. The travel agent checks the database, and discovers that there are exactly three seats available. These are the same three seats the Boston travel agent just saw.

While the Philadelphia travel agent is talking to her customer, the Boston travel agent receives an OK from the other customer to book the seats. The number of available seats on the flight is modified from three to zero.

The Philadelphia travel agent has also received an OK to book the reservations and proceeds to issue a command that reserves another three seats. The problem, however, is that the Philadelphia travel agent is working from old information. There may have been three seats available when the database was queried, but they are no longer available at the time the reservations are made. As a result, the flight is now overbooked by three seats.

Note: Let's not get too carried away here. We all know that airlines often overbook flights intentionally, but, for the purposes of this example, assume that zero seats available means no more seats, period.

A summary of what is happening can be found in Figure 22.3. This lost update—just like the previous example—occurs because the Philadelphia travel agent is working with old data at time 4 when he or she books three seats.

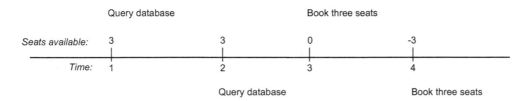

■ **FIGURE 22.3** A second lost update example.

There are two general strategies for handling the lost update problem:

■ Prevent a second transaction from viewing data that has been viewed previously and that might be modified.

- Prevent a second transaction from modifying data if the data has been viewed by another transaction.

The first can be accomplished using locking, the second with timestamping, both of which will be discussed shortly.

Inconsistent Analysis

The other major type of concurrency control problem is known as *inconsistent analysis*. As an example, assume that the West Side Community Center database contains the following relation to store data about attendance at special events:

events (event_name, event_date, total_attendance)

A staff member needs to produce a report that totals the attendance for all events during the past week. As she starts running the report, the table looks something like Figure 22.4. If the report were to run without being interleaved with any other transactions, the sum of the *total_attendance* column would be 495.

A second staff member needs to make some modifications to the attendance figures in the events table, correcting two errors. He changes the attendance

event_name	event_date	total_attendance
Knitting	10-1-20	15
Basketball	10-1-20	20
Open swim	10-1-20	30
Story hour	10-2-20	40
Soccer	10-2-20	35
Open swim	10-2-20	20
Knitting	10-3-20	20
Swim meet	10-3-20	80
Paper making	10-3-20	10
Book club	10-4-20	25
Open swim	10-4-20	20
Kids gym	10-5-20	10
Open swim	10-5-20	30
Handball tournament	10-6-20	50
Open swim	10-6-20	15
Story hour	10-7-20	35
Open swim	10-7-20	40

■ **FIGURE 22.4 The events table at the start of the attendance summary report transaction.**

at the basketball practice on 10-1-20 to 35. He also changes the attendance at the handball tournament on 10-6-20 from 50 to 55.

After the modifications are made, the attendance total is 515. If the report runs before the modifications, the result for the attendance total is 495; if the report runs after the modifications are made, the result for the total is 515. Either one of these results is considered correct because both represent the result of running the transactions one after the other.

However, look what happens when the transactions are interleaved. As you can see in Figure 22.5, the report transaction begins running first. After accessing each of the first 10 rows, the interim total is 295. At time 2, the update transaction begins and runs to completion. At time 4, the report completes its computations, generating a result of 500. Given our definition of a correct result, this is definitely incorrect.

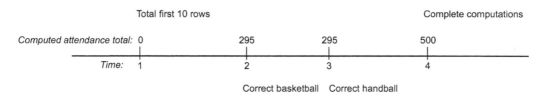

■ **FIGURE 22.5 An inconsistent analysis.**

The problem occurred because the update transaction changed the basketball practice attendance figure *after* the report had processed that row. Therefore, the change is never reflected in the report total.

We can solve the inconsistent analysis problem by

■ Preventing the update because another transaction has viewed the data.
■ Preventing the completion of the view-only transaction because data have been changed.

The first can be done with locking, the second with timestamping.

Dirty Reads

A *dirty read* occurs when a transaction reads and acts on data that have been modified by an update transaction that hasn't committed and is later rolled back. It is similar to an inconsistent analysis, but where the update transaction doesn't commit. To see how this might happen, consider Figure 22.6.

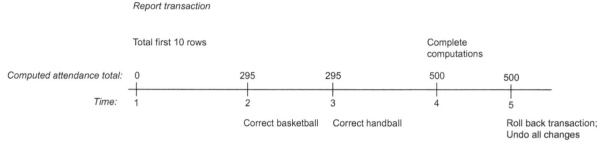

■FIGURE 22.6 A dirty read.

The report generating transaction starts first. It retrieves and totals the first 10 rows. Then the update transaction begins, making changes to both the basketball and handball totals. The report transaction runs again at time 4, reading the modified totals written to the database by the update transaction. The result, as it was with the inconsistent analysis example in the preceding section, is 500. However, at time 5 the update transaction is rolled back, restoring the original values in the table. The correct result should be 495.

As with an inconsistent analysis, a dirty read can be handled by preventing the update transaction from making its modifications at times 2 and 3, using locking or using timestamping to prevent the report from completing because the data "may" have been changed.

Nonrepeatable Read

A *nonrepeatable read* occurs when a transaction reads data for the second time and determines that the data are not the same as they were from the first read. To help understand how this occurs, let's change the community center reporting scenario just a bit. In this case, the report transaction must output two tables with events and their attendance, one ordered by date and the other by the name of the event. It will access the events table twice. When the update transaction runs between the two retrievals, the problem appears (Figure 22.7).

Notice that the total attendance for the first read by the report transaction is correct at that time (495). However, when the transaction reads the table again, the total is correct for the data as modified but not the same as the first read of the data.

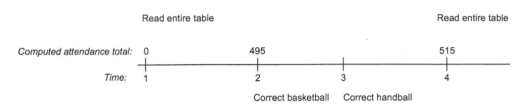

Report transaction

■ **FIGURE 22.7 A nonrepeatable read.**

The nonrepeatable read can be handled by preventing the update transaction from making its modifications because another transaction has already retrieved the data or by preventing the report transaction from completing because the data have been modified.

Phantom Read

A *phantom read* is similar to a nonrepeatable read. However, instead of data being changed on a second retrieval, new rows have been inserted by another transaction. For this example, the update transaction inserts a new row into the events table:

```
Open swim        10-8-20        25
```

Assuming that the report transaction is once again creating two output tables, the interaction might appear as in Figure 22.8. The report transaction's second pass through the table once again produces an incorrect result, caused by the row inserted by the interleaved update transaction.

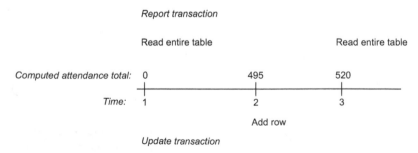

■ **FIGURE 22.8 A phantom read.**

As with other concurrency control issues that involve the interaction of update and retrieval transactions, the phantom read problem can be solved by preventing the insertion of the new row at time 2 or preventing the report transaction from completing at time 3 because the needed data have been changed.

Solution #1: Classic Locking

Locking is a method for giving a transaction control over some part of a database. It is the most widely used concurrency control practice today.

The portion of the database locked (the *granularity* of the lock) varies from one DBMS to another and depends to some extent on exactly what type of operation is being performed. The granularity can vary from a single row in a table to the entire database, although locking of single tables is very common.

Write or Exclusive Locks

To handle lost updates with locking, we need to prevent other transactions from accessing the data viewed by an update transaction because there is the possibility that the update transaction will modify everything it has retrieved.

Operation of Write/Exclusive Locks

The strongest type of lock is an *exclusive lock* (also known as a *write lock*). A transaction is given a write lock on a data element when it retrieves that element. Then, by definition, no other transaction can obtain a lock on that element until the transaction holding the write lock releases its lock. If a transaction needs a piece of data locked by another transaction, it must wait until it can obtain the needed lock.

To see how this solves the lost update at the West Side Community Center, look at Figure 22.9. At time 1, the first staff member queries the database to see how many posters are on hand. She not only sees that there are no posters, but her transaction also receives an exclusive lock on the poster data. Now when staff member 2's transaction attempts to query the database, the transaction must wait because it can't obtain the lock it needs to proceed. (Transaction 1 already holds the single possible write lock.)

Staff member 1 enters the 15 posters and her transaction commits, releasing the lock. Transaction 2 can now continue. It queries the database and now retrieves 15 for the second staff member. He is now working with current

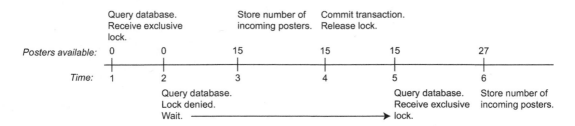

Staff member 1

■ **FIGURE 22.9 Using exclusive locks to solve a lost update problem.**

data and can decide not to accept the additional 12 posters or to add them to the existing 15, producing the correct result of 27. The write lock has therefore solved the problem of the lost update.

Problem with Write/Exclusive Locks: Deadlock

Although write locks can solve a lost update problem, they generate a problem of their own, a condition known as *deadlock*. Deadlock arises when two transactions hold locks that each other needs and therefore neither can continue. To see how this happens, let's look again at two travel agents, this time one in Boston and one in Los Angeles. The Boston travel agent is attempting to book a round trip from Boston to L.A. The Los Angeles travel agent is trying to book a trip from L.A. to Boston and back.

You can see the actions and locks of the two transactions in Figure 22.10. At time 1, the Boston travel agent retrieves data about the flights to Los

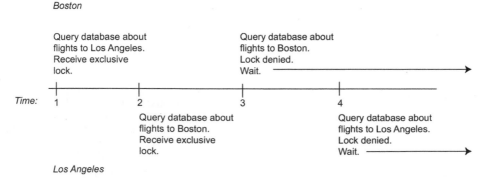

■ **FIGURE 22.10 Deadlock.**

Angeles and her transaction receives an exclusive lock on the data. Shortly thereafter (time 2), the Los Angeles travel agent queries the database about flights to Boston and his transaction receives an exclusive lock on the Boston flight data. So far, so good.

The trouble begins at time 3, when the Boston travel agent attempts to look for return flights from Los Angeles to Boston. The transaction cannot obtain a lock on the data and therefore must wait. At time 4, the Los Angeles travel agent tries to retrieve return flight data and cannot obtain a lock; the second transaction must wait as well. Each transaction is waiting for a lock on data that the other has locked and neither can continue. This is the deadlock.

In busy database systems, deadlock is inevitable. This means that a DBMS must have some way of dealing with it. There are two basic strategies:

- Detect and break: Allow deadlock to occur. When deadlock is detected, choose one transaction to be the "victim" and roll it back, releasing its locks. The rolled back transaction can then be restarted. The mix of transactions will be different when the victim is restarted and the same deadlock is unlikely to occur in the near future. In this case, all transactions start, but not every transactions runs to completion.
- Pre-declare locks: Require transactions to obtain all necessary locks before beginning. This ensures that deadlock cannot occur. Not all transactions start immediately, but every transaction that starts will finish.

Pre-declaration of locks is very difficult to implement because it is often impossible to know what a transaction will need to lock until the transaction is in progress. In contrast, detecting deadlock is actually quite straightforward. The DBMS maintains a data structure known as a *graph* to keep track of which transaction is waiting for the release of locks from which other transaction, as in Figure 22.11a. As long as the graph continues in a downward direction, everything is fine (the graph is *acyclic*). However, if a transaction ends up waiting for another transaction that is higher in the graph (the graphic become *cyclic*), as in Figure 22.11b, deadlock has occurred.

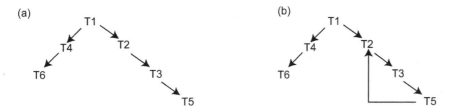

■ **FIGURE 22.11 Graphs to monitor transaction waits.**

In Figure 22.11a, T2 is waiting for something locked by T3; T5 is waiting for something locked by T3. When T5 completes and releases its locks, T3 can continue. As soon as T3 finishes, it will release its locks, letting T2 proceed. However, in Figure 22.11b, T5 is waiting for something locked by T2. T2 can't complete and release what T5 needs, because T2 is waiting for T3, which in turn is waiting for T5, which is waiting for T2, and so on endlessly. This circle of locks is the deadlock.

Because detecting deadlock is so straightforward, most DBMS that use classic locking for concurrency control also use the detect-and-break deadlock handling strategy.

Read or Shared Locks

Although a DBMS could use exclusive locks to solve the problem of inconsistent analysis presented earlier in this chapter, exclusive locks tie up large portions of the database, slowing performance and cutting down on the amount of concurrent access to the database. There is no reason, however, that multiple transactions can't view the same data, as long as none of the transactions attempt to update the data. A lock of this type—a *shared*, or *read*, lock—allows many transactions to read the same data, but none to modify it. In other words, as long as there is at least one shared lock on a piece of data, no transaction can obtain an exclusive lock for updating.

Let's look at how shared locks can solve the inconsistent analysis problem. Figure 22.12 diagrams the situation in which the report transaction begins first. The transaction retrieves 10 rows to begin totaling attendance, and receives a shared lock on the table. At time 2, the update transaction

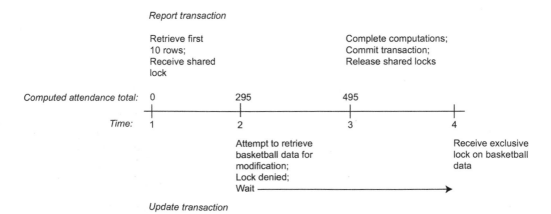

■ FIGURE 22.12 Using shared locks to prevent inconsistent analysis.

begins. However, when it attempts to obtain the exclusive lock it needs for data modification, it must wait because at least one other transaction holds a shared lock on the data. Once the report transaction completes (generating the correct result of 495), the shared locks are released, and the update transaction can obtain the locks it needs.

Now consider what happens if the update transaction starts first. In this case, it is the report transaction that has to wait because it cannot obtain shared locks as long as the modification has exclusive locks in place. As you can see from Figure 22.13, the report transaction produces a result of 515. However, under our rules of correctness for serializable transactions, this is as correct a result as the 495 that was produced when the report transaction started first.

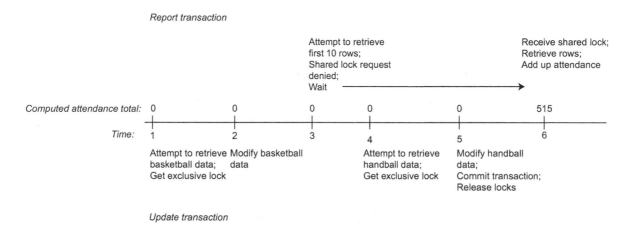

■ **FIGURE 22.13 The transaction from Figure 22.9 starting in the opposite order.**

Two-Phase Locking

In practice, the way in which locks are applied is a bit more complex than what you have just read. Some DBMSs use a variation of the exclusive and shared locking scheme known as *two-phase locking*. The intent is to allow as many shared locks as possible, thus increasing the amount of concurrent use permitted by a database.

Two-phase locking works by giving an update transaction a shared lock when it retrieves data and then upgrading the lock to an exclusive lock when the transaction actually makes a data modification. This helps increase the amount of concurrent use by keeping the amount of data tied up in exclusive locks to a minimum and by minimizing the time that exclusive locks are in place. The trade-off is that an update transaction may not be able to obtain an exclusive lock for data on which it holds a shared lock because other transactions hold shared locks on the same data. The update transaction will then be rolled back, causing it to release all its locks. It can then be restarted.

One major drawback to two-phase locking is that some processes may need to wait a long time before obtaining the exclusive locks they need to complete processing. This is not an issue for most business databases. However, real-time systems, such as those that monitor oil refineries, nuclear plants, and chemical factories, cannot tolerate delays in transaction processing. Therefore, many real-time databases cannot use two-phase locking.

Locks and Transaction Length

For locking to be effective, locks must be held until the end of transaction, releasing only when a transaction either commits or is rolled back. For interactive commands—for example, SQL commands being entered singly—a transaction usually lasts only a single command. However, application programs control the length of a transaction.

Some SQL implementations contain statements to indicate the start of a transaction (for example, START TRANSACTION). All, however, provide both COMMIT and ROLLBACK commands to terminate a transaction. The application program must intercept and interpret the code returned by the DBMS at the end of each SQL command to determine whether actions against the database have been successful.

The combination of the need to hold locks until a transaction ends, and programmer control over the length of an embedded SQL transaction means that a poorly written application program can have a major negative impact on database performance. A transaction that is too long, or that unnecessarily locks database resources, will impede the execution of concurrent transactions. It is, therefore, the responsibility of application developers to test their programs under concurrent use conditions to ensure that excessive locking is not occurring.

Solution #2: Optimistic Concurrency Control (Optimistic Locking)

A database that is used primarily for retrieval, with few updates, can also take advantage of a variation on locking known as *optimistic locking*. It is based on the idea that when there are few updates performed, there are relatively few opportunities for problems such as lost updates to occur.

An update transaction in an optimistic locking environment proceeds in the following manner:

- Find the data to be modified and place a copy in the transaction's work area in main memory.
- Make the change to data in the transaction's work area.
- Check the database to ensure that the modification won't conflict with any other transaction (for example, cause a lost update).
- If no conflicts are detected, write the modified data back to the database. If a conflict is detected, roll back the transaction and start it again.

The core of the process is determining whether there are conflicting transactions. An update transaction must therefore check all other transactions, looking for instances of retrieval of the same data. Therefore, optimistic locking performs well when there aren't too many other transactions to check and the number of conflicts is low. However, performance suffers if there are many concurrent update transactions and/or update conflicts.

Solution #3: Multiversion Concurrency Control (Timestamping)

Multiversion concurrency control, or *timestamping*, is a concurrency control method that does not rely on locking. Instead, it assigns a timestamp to each piece of data retrieved by a transaction and uses the chronological ordering of the timestamps to determine whether an update will be permitted.

Each time a transaction reads a piece of data, it receives a timestamp on that data. An update of the data will be permitted as long as no other transaction holds an earlier timestamp on the data. Therefore, only the transaction holding the earliest timestamp will be permitted to update, although any number of transactions can read the data.

Timestamping is efficient in environments where most of the database activity is retrieval because nothing blocks retrieval. However, as the proportion of update transactions increases, so does the number of transactions that are prevented from updating and must be restarted.

Transaction Isolation Levels

The SQL standard makes no determination of what concurrency control method a DBMS should use. However, it does provide a method for specifying how tight concurrency control should be in the face of the three "read phenomena" (dirty read, nonrepeatable read, phantom read). The inclusion of the relaxing of tight concurrency control is in response to the performance degradation that can occur when large portions of a database are locked. Despite the performance advantages, relaxing concurrency control can place a database at risk for data integrity and consistency problems.

There are four *transaction isolation levels* that provide increasingly strict concurrency control and solutions to the read phenomena:

- Serializable: Transactions must be serializable, as described in this chapter. This is the tightest isolation level.
- Read committed: Prevents a dirty read, but allows nonrepeatable reads and phantom reads. This means that a transaction can read all data from all committed transactions, even if the read may be inconsistent with a previous read.
- Repeatable read: Prevents dirty reads and nonrepeatable reads, but does not control for phantom reads.
- Read uncommitted: Virtually no concurrency control, making all three read phenomena possible.

The SQL standard allows a user to set the isolation level with one of the following:

```
SET TRANSACTION LEVEL SERIALIZABLE

SET TRANSACTION LEVEL READ COMMITTED

SET TRANSACTION LEVEL REPEATABLE READ

SET TRANSACTION LEVEL READ UNCOMMITTED
```

Some major DBMSs do not necessarily adhere to the standard exactly. Oracle, for example, provides only three isolation levels: serializable, read committed, and read only. The read only level restricts transactions to retrieval operations; by definition, a read-only transaction cannot modify data. The DB2 syntax uses SET CURRENT ISOLATION; with SQL Server, the statement is SET TRANSACTION ISOLATION LEVEL. Neither uses the precise syntax specified above. The moral to the story is that if you are going to manipulate isolation levels, check your DBMSs documentation for the specific syntax in use.

Web Database Concurrency Control Issues

Databases that allow access over the Web certainly face the same issues of concurrency control that non-Web databases face. However, there is also has another problem: The length of a transaction will vary considerably, both on the result of the inconsistent performance of the Internet and the tendency of a Web user to walk away from the computer for some period of time. How long should a transaction be kept open? When should a partially completed transaction be aborted and rolled back?

One way Web sites interacting with DBMSs handle the situation is by working with a unit known as a *session*. A session may contain multiple transactions, but a transaction is confined to only one session. The length of a session will vary, but usually will have a limit on the amount of time the session can remain idle. Once the limit has passed, the DBMS will end the session and abort any open transactions. This does not mean that the user necessarily loses all information generated during such a rolled back transaction. For example, some shopping cart applications store the items added to the cart as they are added. Even if the session is terminated by the DBMS, the items remain in the database (associated with the user's login name) so the shopping cart can be reconstructed, should the user visit the site again. Alternatively, a database application may use a cookie to store the contents of a shopping cart prior to ending a session, although a cookie may not be large enough to hold even partial data from a transaction.

Optimistic locking also works well over the Web. A transaction works with a copy of data to be modified that has been downloaded to the client computer over the Internet. The client communicates with the database only when it is time to write the update. A transaction that never completes leaves no dangling locks because no locks are placed until the DBMS determines that an update does not conflict with other transactions.

Distributed Database Issues

Distributed databases add yet another layer of complexity to concurrency control because there are often multiple copies of data, each of which is kept at a different location. This presents several challenges:

- To use classic locking, locks must be placed on all copies of a piece of data. What happens if some of the locks can be placed and others cannot?
- What happens if an instruction to commit a transaction modifying copies of the same data doesn't reach all parts of the database? Some transactions may commit and others hang without an end. Should the committed transactions be rolled back to keep the database consistent? That violates a basic precept of concurrency control: A committed transaction is never rolled back.

Early distributed DBMSs attempted to use timestamping for concurrency control. The overhead required to maintain the timestamps, however, was significant.

Today, most distributed DBMSs use some type of two-phase locking. To lessen the chance of needing to roll back a committed transaction, distributed databases also add a *two-phase commit*. During the first phase, the transaction that initiated the data modification sends a "prepare to commit" message to each copy that is locked. Each copy then responds with a "ready to commit" message. Once the transaction receives a "ready" message from each copy, it sends a "commit" message (the second phase). If some copies do not respond with a "ready" message, the transaction is rolled back at all locations.

Whichever type of concurrency control a distributed DBMS employs, the messages needed to effect the concurrency control can significantly increase the amount of network traffic among the database sites. There is also the issue of locks that aren't released by the local DBMS because no commit message was received from the remote DBMS placing the lock. Most distributed DBMSs therefore allow database administrators to set a limit to the time a transaction can sit idle. When a transaction "times out," it is rolled back and not restarted.

For Further Reading

Bernstein, P.A., Newcomer, E., 2009. Principles of Transaction Processing, second ed. Morgan Kaufmann, Boston.

Bernstein, P.A., Hadzilacos, V., Goodman, N., 1987. Concurrency Control and Recovery in Database Systems. Addison Wesley, Boston.

Sippu, S., Soisalon-Soininen, E., 2015. Transaction Processing: Management of the Logical Database and its Underlying Physical Structure. Springer, New York.

Thomasian, A., 2010. Database Concurrency Control: Methods, Performance, and Analysis. Springer.

Weikum, G., Vossen, G., 2001. Transactional Information Systems: Theory, Algorithms, and the Practice of Concurrency Control and Recovery. Morgan Kaufann.

Chapter
23

Database Security

In our current computing environment, we usually think that the instant world-spanning access provided by the Internet is a good thing. However, that access has a dark side: those who would inadvertently or purposefully violate the security of our data. Security has always been a part of relational database management, but now it has become one of the most important issues facing database administrators.

One way to look at security is to consider the difference between security and privacy. Privacy is the need to restrict access to data, whether they are trade secrets, data that can be used as a basis for identity theft, or personal information that by law must be kept private. Security is what you do to ensure privacy.

Many people view network security as having three goals:

- Confidentiality: ensuring that data that must be kept private, stay private.
- Integrity: ensuring that data are accurate. For a security professional, this means that data must be protected from unauthorized modification and/or destruction.
- Availability: ensuring that data are accessible whenever needed by the organization. This implies protecting the network from anything that would make it unavailable, including such events as power outages.

One of the things that makes data theft such a problem is that it is possible to steal data without anyone knowing that a theft has occurred. A good thief will be able to enter a target system, copy data, and get out without leaving a trace. Because copying digital data does not affect the source, examining the data won't reveal that any copying has occurred. An accomplished thief will also modify system log files, erasing any trace of the illegal entry. Although major data breaches are reported widely in the media, it's a safe bet to say that there have been several times as many that go undetected.

The popular media (television, newspapers, and so on) would have you believe that the cause of almost all computer security problems is the "hacker." However, if you ask people actually working in the field, they will tell you that many of the security breaches they encounter come from sources internal to an organization and in particular, employees. (At one point, more than half of security problems were caused by employees; this number has diminished as Internet intrusions have increased.) Therefore, this does mean that it won't be sufficient to secure a network against external intrusion attempts; you must pay as much attention to what is occurring within your organization as you do to external threats. Databases, in particular, are especially vulnerable to internal security threats because direct access is typically provided only to employees.

Sources of External Security Threats

The Internet has been both a blessing and a curse to those who rely on computer networks to keep an organization in business. The global network has made it possible for potential customers, customers, and employees to reach an organization through its Web site. But with this new access have come the enormous problems caused by individuals and groups attempting illegal entry into computer networks and the computer systems they support.

Physical Threats

We are so focused on security issues that come over a network that we tend to ignore physical threats to our database installation. Certainly, we need to worry about a disgruntled employee with a hammer, but there is more to physical security risks than that. The major issue today is physical access to a server by a knowledgeable data thief.

All servers have at least one user account that has access rights to the entire computer. When the servers are housed in a locked location, operators tend to leave the privileged user account logged in. It makes administration just a bit easier. The operators rely on the security on the server room door to keep unauthorized people out. The problem with this strategy is that sometimes physical barriers aren't sufficient; a knowledgeable data thief will be able to circumvent whatever lock has been placed on the server room door and gain physical access to the servers. If the privileged accounts are left logged in, all the thief needs to do is sit down at a machine and start extracting data.

Hackers and Crackers

External threats are initiated by people the general population calls "hackers." Initially, however, the term "hacker" referred to someone who could write an ingenious bit of software. In fact, the phrase "a good hack" meant a particularly clever piece of programming. As with many technological terms, however, the meaning changed when the term entered the mainstream and therefore today anyone who attempts illegal access to a computer network is called a hacker.

There are many ways to classify those who break into computer systems, depending on which source you are reading. However, most lists of the types of hackers include the following (although they may be given different names):

- *White hat hackers*: This group considers itself to be the "good guys." (Whether they actually are good guys is open to question, however.) Although white hat hackers may crack a system, they do not do it for personal gain. When they find a vulnerability in a network, some hardware, or a piece of software, they report it to the network owner, hardware vendor, or software vendor, whichever is appropriate. They do not release information about the system vulnerability to the public until the vendor has had a chance to develop and release a fix for the problem. White hat hackers might also be hired by an organization to test a network's defenses.

  White hat hackers are extremely knowledgeable about networking, programming, and existing vulnerabilities that have been found and fixed. They often write their own system cracking tools.

- *Script kiddies*: The script kiddies are hacker "wannabes." They have little, if any, programming skill and therefore must rely on tools written by others. Psychological profiles of script kiddies indicate that they are generally male, young (under 30), and not socially well-adjusted. They are looked down upon by most other hackers.

  Script kiddies usually do not target specific networks, but instead scan for any system that is vulnerable to attack. They might try to deface a Web site, delete files from a target system, flood network bandwidth with unauthorized packets, or in some other way commit what amounts to cyber vandalism. Script kiddies typically don't want to keep their exploits secret. In fact, many of those that are caught are trapped because they have been bragging about what they have done.

- *Black hat hackers*: Black hat hackers are motivated by greed or a desire to cause harm. They target specific systems, write their own tools, and generally attempt to get in and out of a target system without being detected. Because they are very knowledgeable, and their activities often undetectable, black hat hackers are among the most dangerous.

- *Cyberterrorists*: Cyberterrorists are hackers who are motivated by a political, religious, or philosophical agenda. They may propagate their beliefs by defacing Web sites that support opposing positions. Given the current global political climate, there is also a reasonable fear that cyberterrorists may attempt to disable networks that handle utilities such as nuclear plants and water systems.

Types of Attacks

When a hacker targets your network, what might you expect? There are a number of broad categories of attacks.

- *Denial of service*: A denial of service attack (DoS) attempts to prevent legitimate users from gaining access to network resources and, by extension, any database that uses the network. It can take the form of flooding a network or server with traffic so that legitimate messages can't get through or it can bring down a server. If you are monitoring traffic on your network, a DoS attack is fairly easy to detect. Unfortunately, it can be difficult to defend against and stop without disconnecting your network from the Internet.

- *Buffer overflow*: A buffer overflow attack takes advantage of a programming error in an application or system program. The hacker can insert his or her own code into a program and from there take control of a target system. Because they are the result of a programming error, buffer overflow conditions are almost impossible for a network engineer to detect. They are usually detected by hackers or the software vendor. The most common defense is a patch provided by that vendor.

  Closely related to the more general buffer overflow vulnerability, a *SQL injection attack* occurs when a hacker uses openings in SQL statements to insert and execute malicious code from a database application. Such attacks can be prevented by following specific syntax forms when embedding SQL in high-level programming languages. It is therefore important that application coding syntax rules be documented, updated, and readily accessible to application programmers.

- *Malware*: The term "malware" includes all types of malicious software, such as viruses, worms, and Trojan horses. The goal of a hacker in placing such software on a computer may be simple maliciousness or to provide access to the computer at a later date. Although there is a constantly escalating battle between those who write malware and those who write malware detection software, a good virus checker goes a long way to keeping network devices free from infection.

- *Social engineering*: A social engineering attack is an attempt to get system access information from employees using role-playing and misdirection. It is usually the prelude to an attempt to gain unauthorized access to the network. Because it is "no tech," social engineering is widely used, and can be very effective.

- *Brute force*: One way to gain access to a system is to run brute force login attempts. Assuming that a hacker knows one or more system login names, he can attempt to guess the passwords. By keeping and monitoring logs of who is attempting to log into a system, a network administrator can usually detect brute force break-in attacks.

Note: There is no gender discrimination intended with the use of the pronoun "he" when referring to hackers. The fact is that most hackers are male.

Sources of Internal Threats

Most internal threats come from two sources: employees and accidents. Employee threats may be intentional or accidental, as well.

Employee Threats

In most cases, employees know more about a network and the computers on it than any outsider. At the very least, they have legitimate access to user accounts. IT personnel, of course, have various levels of increased access. Intentional employee security threats include the following:

- Personnel who employ hacking techniques to upgrade their legitimate access to root/administrator access, allowing them to divulge trade secrets, steal money, and so on, for personal or political gain.
- Personnel who take advantage of legitimate access to divulge trade secrets, steal money, and so on, for personal or political gain.
- Family members of employees who are visiting the office and have been given access to company computers to occupy them while waiting.
- As mentioned earlier, personnel who break into secure machine rooms to gain physical access to mainframe and other large system consoles.
- Former employees, especially those who did not leave the organization willingly, who are interested in revenge. Attacks may be physical, actually damaging equipment, or traditional hacking attacks, usually resulting in damaged data.

As dangerous as the intentional employee security threat may be, employees can also cause a great deal of damage unintentionally, such as

- Becoming the victim of a social engineering attack, unknowingly helping a hacker gain unauthorized network access.

- Unintentionally revealing confidential information.
- Physically damaging equipment, resulting in data loss.
- Misusing a system, introducing inaccurate and/or damaged data or accidentally deleting or modifying data.
- Installing personal equipment on a network (for example, a wireless access point) that isn't included in the organization's security measures.

Most unintentional employee threats, theoretically, can be handled through employee education. For example, it seems logical that instructing employees not to write passwords on sticky notes that are then fixed to monitors would help prevent compromised passwords. However, when you are dealing with human beings, even the best education can be forgotten in the stress of getting a job done on time.

Employees certainly can unintentionally damage a network. In addition, true accidents also occur. A security plan will need to guard against data damage and loss caused by

- Electrical power fluctuations
- Hardware failures
- Natural disasters, such as fire and flood

Guarding against accidental network damage includes power protection (for example, surge protectors, and UPSs) and comprehensive backup schemes. When done well, backup takes significant planning and disaster recovery rehearsals.

External Remedies

External security measures are typically outside the responsibility of database administrators. However, you should be aware of what security protections external to the database are in place and, if they appear inadequate, know how to make your concerns and recommendations heard. In this section, we'll therefore look at security strategies that should be in place, external to the database, to provide a first line of defense.

Securing the Perimeter: Firewalls

A *firewall* is a piece of software that filters incoming and outgoing network traffic, and stops messages that violate the rules that define allowable traffic. It is typically placed between the Internet and an internal network. Its primary job is to eliminate as much undesirable network traffic as possible.

Note: You may hear a firewall spoken of as a piece of hardware. However, a firewall device is really a special-purpose computer that runs firewall software. Because the device is dedicated to the firewall application, it may be more powerful than firewall software that is added to a router or other network interconnection device.

If you look at Figure 23.1, you'll notice that the network looks very much like something that might be used by SmartMart from Chapter 15. Specifically, it includes a Web server that is exposed to the Internet through a router and a database server that is isolated from the Web server by a second firewall.

The first firewall—the one connected to the edge router—allows specific messages to pass, including those intended for the Web server and for destinations that represent legitimate network traffic (for example, e-mail and remote employees).

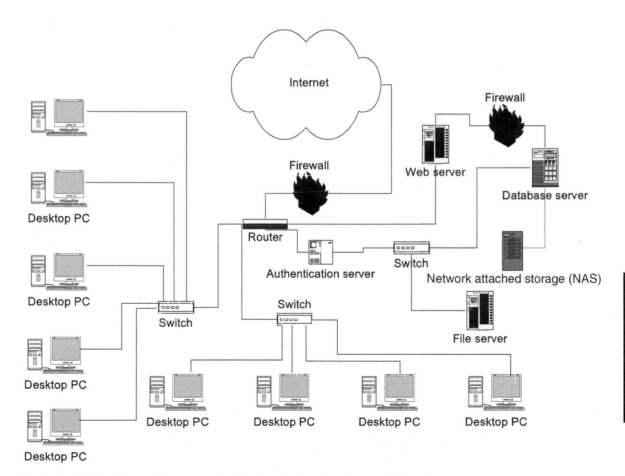

■ **FIGURE 23.1** Using firewalls to secure a network and create a DMZ to protect the database server.

The edge router will send all Web traffic to the Web server, preventing it from getting onto the internal network. However, because Web users need access to data stored on the database server, simply routing that traffic to the Web server doesn't provide protection for the database.

To protect the database, only messages from the Web server are permitted to interact with the database. A second firewall has therefore been placed between the two servers. The Web server is said to reside in a DMZ, a part of the network that is walled off from the internal network.

A Web transaction that involves access to the database server proceeds as follows:

1. User's browser generates a request for data stored in the database (for example, a page from a retail catalog) and transmits it to the company network.
2. The edge router passes the request to the Web server.
3. The Web server requests data from the database.
4. The firewall between the Web server and the database server passes the message because it comes from the Web server.
5. The database server retrieves the requested data and sends it back through the firewall to the Web server.
6. The Web server formats the data and sends a response to the user, whose browser displays the new Web page.

Notice that internal users have direct access to the Web server, without having to pass through the DMZ. The assumption is that internal users will be authorized for direct database access.

Handling Malware

Malware infecting a database server can be a serious problem. The result may be loss of data, loss of access to the database, or loss of control of the database server's hardware. Protection against malware is typically provided by "virus protection" software running on firewalls and the servers themselves.

Most current virus protection software handles worms, Trojan horses, and bots, as well as viruses. The most important thing to keep in mind, however, is that there is an ever-escalating battle between those who write malware and those who produce the virus protection software. As soon as a new threat is identified, the software developers rush to add the new malware to their protection database; the malware producers then write new malware that is typically more powerful and sophisticated than previous releases. You can never be completely safe from malware because there is always a lag, however short, between the detection of a new piece of malware and the updating of virus protection software to handle that malware. The best you can do is to update the database that accompanies your virus protection software regularly.

Buffer Overflows

Because a buffer overflow problem is a flaw in the way software is written, there is really nothing an organization without access to the source code and a staff of programmers can do to fix it. An organization must rely on the software developer to release updates (*patches*) to the code.

Patching is a cooperative operation, in that once the vendor has released a patch, it is up to organizations using the software to install the patch. Nonetheless, the best defense against buffer overflow vulnerabilities (and any other vulnerabilities caused by bugs in software) is to apply all available patches.

Patch management can become a nightmare for an IT staff. There are so many patches released for some types of software (for example, Microsoft Windows, in all its myriad versions) that it is difficult to know which patches are important, stable and, in a large organization, which patches have been applied to which machine. Nonetheless, to protect your database server (both the operating system and the DBMS), you will need to work with IT to ensure that all necessary patches have been applied.

Physical Server Security

Physical security requires a two-pronged approach: preventing physical access to the server and, should that fail, securing the administrative accounts. Actual physical methods include any or all of the following:

- Security cameras outside machine/server room doors to record who enters, exits, and loiters in the area.
- Smart locks on machine/server room doors that store the code of each individual who enters and exits, along with the date and time of an entry or exit. Smart locks can be equipped with biometric identification devices if desired. (These will be discussed shortly.)
- Removal of signs from machine/server room doors and hallways so that no one can locate hardware rooms by simply walking the hallways of the building.

The output produced by security cameras and smart locks must be examined regularly to determine if any unusual access patterns appear.

Should an unauthorized person manage to defeat the physical security, he will probably want to gain software access to a computer. (We are assuming that physical damage to the equipment is a rare goal of an intruder.) This means that the administrative accounts for each server must be secured. First, the accounts should never be left logged in. It may be more convenient for operators, but it makes the servers vulnerable to anyone who happens to walk by. Second, login attempts to the administrative accounts should be limited. For example, after three failed attempts to log in, the server should disallow further login attempts for some predetermined length of time.

User Authentication

Any user who is going to have direct access to a database first needs to be authenticated for access to the local area network. The forms that such authentication takes depend on the size and security risks of the network.

Positive user identification requires three things:

- Something the user knows
- Something the user has
- Something the user is

The first can be achieved with passwords, the second with physical login devices, and the third with biometrics.

User IDs and Passwords (What the User Knows)

The first line of defense for any network authentication scheme is the user ID and password. User IDs in and of themselves are not generally considered to be private; in fact, many are based on user e-mail addresses. The security, therefore, resides in the password. General security practice tells us the following about passwords:

- Longer passwords are better than shorter passwords.
- Passwords with a combination of letters, numbers, and special characters (for example, punctuation) are more secure then passwords that are all letters or numbers.
- User education is needed to ensure that users don't share their passwords with anyone, or write them down where others may find them.
- Passwords should be changed at regular intervals.

Although "general wisdom" dictates that passwords should be changed regularly, there are some problems with that policy. When users are forced to change their passwords, they often forget which password they have used. The solution is to write the password down, sometimes placing it in an insecure location such as the center drawer of a desk or even on a sticky note affixed to a monitor.

Login Devices (What User Has)

The second layer of user authentication is requiring that someone attempting to log in present a physical device that only an authorized user will have. The device has some way of making it unique to the user ID.

Login devices include access cards that a user must scan in some way before entering a password and devices that issue one-time passwords that the user keys in as well as a normal password. For example, Union Bank and Trust offers business customers a physical token that generates a single-user six-digit code every 60 seconds. The token itself is small enough to put on a keychain. Use of the code from the token is required for a variety of online financial transactions.[1]

Some authentication tokens require that the token be physically inserted into a computer connected directly to the network. For example, the eToken series from SafeNet consists primarily of devices that are to be plugged into a USB port to authenticate both the user and the user's location.[2]

The advantage of a login device is that it is small—usually small enough to attach to a keychain—so that there is little difficulty for the user to keep the device available. However, if the user doesn't have the device and needs access, there must be either an alternative form of authentication available or the user will not gain access.

Biometrics (Who the User Is)

Biometric identification—identification based on characteristics of a person's body—has long been a part of science fiction. The idea of retina prints, thumb prints, palm prints, and facial scans isn't particularly far-fetched, however. Today you can purchase a mouse with a thumb print reader that sends the print to a computer for authentication. You may need a fingerprint to unlock your smartphone or laptop. Extremely high security installations today can use retina, face, and palm prints to permit physical access; the readers are too large and expensive for mobile use.

VPNs

Remote access to a database is typical today. Users travel; users work from home. The days are long gone where remote users dialed into their work network using a modem and a standard telephone line. Most remote access reaches an internal network over the Internet. The problem facing a database

---

[1]http://www.bankatunion.com/home/business/online/goidtokens/goidtokensfaqs
[2]http://www.safenet-inc.com/data-protection/password-protection-applications/?aldn-true

administrator is ensuring that the data remain safe while traveling on the external network.

One commonly applied solution is a *virtual private network* (VPN). VPNs provide encryption for data transmissions over the Internet. Although there are several types of VPNs, many use a security protocol known as *IPSec*, including the VPNs that are built into desktop operating systems such as Windows and Mac OS X.

IPSec encrypts the data, turning it into something that is meaningless to anyone who does not have the secret encryption keys. Even if data are intercepted traveling over the Internet, they will be useless. We say that IPSec provides a secure *tunnel* for data (Figure 23.2.) One type of tunneling encrypts data only when they are actually on the Internet; the other provides *end-to-end* encryption where data are encrypted from the sending computer to the destination network.

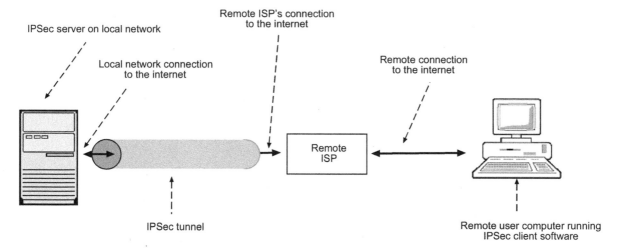

■ FIGURE 23.2 The architecture of an IPSec VPN.

To operate a VPN, the destination network must have a VPN server, a machine that receives all incoming VPN traffic and handles authenticating the VPN user. The VPN server acts as a gatekeeper to the internal network. Once authenticated, VPN users can interact with the destination network as if they were physically present at the network's location.

Combating Social Engineering

Social engineering isn't a technical attack at all—it's a psychological/ behavioral attack—and, therefore, can't be stopped by technical means. It requires employee education to teach employees to recognize this type of attack, and how to guard against it.

As an example, consider the following scenario: Jane Jones is the secretary for the R&D department of a high tech firm. Her boss, John Smith, often works at home. Ms. Jones has been with the company for many years, and she is a trusted employee. She knows the user names and passwords for her computer, Mr. Smith's desktop and laptop, and Mr. Smith's mainframe account.

One morning, Ms. Jones receives a telephone call. "Ms. Jones, this is James Doe from IT. I have some upgrades that I need to install on your computer and Mr. Smith's computer. I don't need to come to your office. I can do it over the network, if I have the user IDs and passwords."

"Oh, that sounds fine," says Ms. Jones. "I hate it when IT has to come by and interrupt my work to fix something. My user ID is …." And she gives Mr. Doe the user names and passwords, just as he requested.

Unfortunately, the man who claims to be James Doe isn't who he says he is. He's a hacker, and, with some simple research and a phone call, has received access to two corporate desktops. First, he checked the corporate directory online. It was simple to find the name of an IT employee, as well as the names of the head of R&D and his secretary. Then, all he had to do was to place his phone call to Ms. Jones. She cooperated, and he was in business.

The phony James Doe does install a file or two on each of the compromised computers. However, the files are actually a Trojan horse that he can activate later when he needs control of the compromised machines.

Ms. Jones made one critical error: she revealed user names and passwords. She felt comfortable doing so because she knew that someone named James Doe worked for IT. She had never thought that there would be a problem trusting someone from that department; the idea of an impersonator never crossed her mind.

There is no technological solution to a social engineering attack of this type. The best prevention is employee awareness. Training sessions with role playing to demonstrate how such attacks are perpetrated can be very helpful. A few simple policies will also go a long way:

- Never reveal your user ID or password to anyone, no matter who that person claims to be.
- If someone claims to be a corporate employee and asks for your user name and password, take their name, supervisor's name, and extension. Then hang up and call the supervisor to report the attempt to obtain a user ID and password.

- If someone claims to be a vendor representative (or anyone else who is not an employee) and asks for a user ID and password, hang up and notify IT security.

An organization should also take steps to restrict the information that it makes public, so that it becomes more difficult for a hacker to develop a convincing social engineering attack. For example, employee directories should not be available publicly. Instead, use titles (such as "IT Manager") in contact lists accessible to non-employees. Organizations with registered Internet domain names should also restrict the information available to those who perform a "whois" search on the domain name.

Handling Other Employee Threats

There are many things an organization can do to guard against other employee threats. They include the following:

- Develop and enforce policies and procedures for users who want to install their own hardware and software on corporate machines. Use network discovery and mapping software to monitor network hardware and detect any unauthorized equipment.
- Develop and enforce policies for users who wish to use personal computing devices on the company network.
- Conduct employee training sessions to familiarize employees with the organization's policies on the release of information.
- Document all organizational security policies, distribute to employees, and require employees to sign, indicating that they have read and accepted the policies.
- Require employees to take two consecutive weeks of vacation at least once every two years. If an employee is hacking the organization's information systems and covering up the unauthorized access, an absence of two weeks is likely long enough to expose what is occurring.
- When an employee is going to be fired, disable all of the employee's computer accounts prior to telling the employee about the termination.

Internal Solutions

To this point, the security measures we've discussed have all been applied outside the DBMS. They are put in place by network administrators, rather than database personnel. There are, however, at least two layers of security that a relational DBMS adds to whatever is supplied by the network.

Internal Database User IDs and Passwords

The user IDs and passwords we discussed earlier in this chapter are used to give a user access to a network. They do not necessarily (and probably shouldn't) give access to a database. Most of today's relational DBMSs provide their own user ID and password mechanism. Once a user has gained access to the network, he or she must authenticate again to gain direct access to the database (either at the command line or with an application program).

It is important to distinguish between direct access to the database and account access by Web customers. Someone making a purchase on a Web site does not interact directly with the database; only the Web server has that type of access. A Web user supplies a user name and password, both of which are probably stored in the database. The Web server sends a query to the DBMS to retrieve data that match the user ID/password pair. Assuming that a matching account is found, the Web server can then send a query to retrieve the Web user's account data. Web customers cannot issue ad hoc queries using a query language; they only can use the browser-based application provided for them. Therefore, there is little that the typical Web user can do to compromise the security of the database.

However, internal database users have direct access to database elements for which their account has been configured. They can formulate ad hoc queries at a command line to manipulate the tables or views to which they have access. The trick, then, is to tailor access to database elements based on what each user ID "needs to know." A relational database accomplishes this using an authorization matrix.

Authorization Matrices

Most DBMSs that support SQL use their data dictionaries to provide a level of security. Known as an *authorization matrix*, this type of security provides control of access rights to tables, views, and their components. Like other structural elements in the database, the authorization matrix is stored in tables along with the data dictionary.

Types of Access Rights

By default, the user who created a database element is the only user that has access to that element. Nonetheless, access rights can be *granted* to other users. There are six types of access right that you can grant:

- SELECT: allows a user to retrieve data from a table or view.
- INSERT: allows a user to insert new rows in a table or updatable view. Permission may be granted to specific columns, rather than the entire database element.

- UPDATE: allows a user to modify rows in a table or updatable view. Permission may be granted to specific columns, rather than the entire database element.
- DELETE: allows a user to delete rows from a table or updatable view.
- REFERENCES: allows a user to reference a table column as a foreign key in a table that that he or she creates. Permission may be granted to specific columns, rather than the entire database element.
- ALL PRIVILEGES: give a user all of the preceding rights to a table or view.

By default, granting access rights to another user does not give the user the right to pass those rights on to others. If, however, you add a WITH GRANT OPTION clause, you give the user the ability to grant the rights that he or she has to another user.

Using an Authorization Matrix

Whenever a user makes a request to the DBMS to manipulate data, the DBMS first consults the authorization matrix to determine whether the user has the rights to perform the requested action. If the DBMS cannot find a row with a matching user ID and table or view identifier, then the user has no right at all to the database element. If a row with a matching user ID and table identifier exists, then the DBMS checks for the specific rights that the user has to the table or view and either permits or disallows the requested database access.

Database Implementations

Access rights to tables and views are stored in the data dictionary. Although the details of the data dictionary tables vary from one DBMS to another, you will usually find access rights split between two system tables named something like *systableperm* and *syscolperm*. The first table is used when access rights are granted to entire tables or views; the second is used when rights are granted to specific columns within a table or view.

A *systableperm* table has a structure similar to the following:

```
systableperm (table_id, grantee, grantor,
    slsectauth, insertauth, deleteauth, updateauth,
    updatecols, referenceauth)
```

The columns represent:

- table_id: an identifier for the table or view
- grantee: the user ID to which rights have been granted
- grantor: the user ID granting the rights

- selectauth: the grantee's SELECT rights
- insertauth: the grantee's INSERT rights
- deleteauth: the grantee's INSERT rights
- updateauth: the grantee's UPDATE rights
- updatecols: indicates whether rights have been granted to specific columns, rather than the entire table or view. When this value is Y (yes), the DBMS must also look in *syscolperm* to determine whether a user has the rights to perform a specific action against the database.

The columns that hold the access rights take one of three values: Y (yes), N (no), or G (Yes with grant option).

Granting and Revoking Access Rights

When you create an element of database structure, the user name under which you are working becomes that element's owner. The owner has the right to do anything to that element; all other users have no rights at all. This means that if tables and views are going to be accessible to other users, you must grant them access rights.

Granting Rights

To grant rights to another user, a user that either created the database element (and, therefore, has all rights to it) or has GRANT rights issues a GRANT statement:

```
GRANT type_of_rights
ON table_or_view_name TO user_ID
```

For example, if the DBA of *Antique Opticals* wants to allow the accounting manager (who has a user ID of acctg_mgr) to access an order summary view, the DBA would type

```
GRANT SELECT
ON order_summary TO acctg_mgr;
```

To allow the accounting manager to pass those rights on to others, the DBA would need to add one line to the SQL:

```
GRANT SELECT
ON order_summary TO acctg_mgr;
WITH GRANT OPTION
```

If *Antique Opticals* wants to give some student interns limited rights to some of the base tables, the GRANT might be written:

```
GRANT SELECT, UPDATE (retail_price, distributor_name)
ON item TO intern1, intern2, intern3;
```

The preceding example grants SELECT rights to the entire table, but gives UPDATE rights on only two specific columns. Notice also that you can grant multiple rights in the same command, as well as the same group of rights, to more than one user. However, a single GRANT applies to only one table or view.

In most cases, rights are granted to specific user IDs. You can, however, make database elements accessible to anyone, giving rights to the special user ID PUBLIC. For example, the following statement gives every authorized user the rights to see the order summary view:

```
GRANT SELECT
ON order_summary TO PUBLIC;
```

Revoking Rights

To remove previously granted rights, use the REVOKE statement, whose syntax is almost the opposite of GRANT:

```
REVOKE access_rights
ON table_or_view_name FROM user_ID
```

For example, if *Antique Opticals'* summer interns have finished their work for the year, the DBA might want to remove their access from the database:

```
REVOKE SELECT, UPDATE (retail_price, distributor_numb)
ON item FROM intern1, intern2, intern3;
```

If the user from which you are revoking rights has the GRANT option for those rights, then you also need to make a decision about what to do if the user has passed on those rights. In the following case, the REVOKE option will be disallowed if the acctg_mgr user has passed on his or her rights:

```
REVOKE SELECT
ON order_summary FROM acctg_mgr
RESTRICT;
```

In contrast, the syntax

```
REVOKE SELECT
ON order_summary FROM acctg_mgr
CASCADE;
```

will remove the rights from the acctg_mgr ID, along with any user IDs to which acctg_mgr granted rights.

Who Has Access to What

The internal database security measures we have discussed to this point assume that we know which users should have access to which data. For example, does a bookkeeper need access to data from the last audit or should access to those data be restricted to the comptroller? Such decisions may not be as easy as they first appear. Consider the following scenario (loosely based on a real incident).

The Human Relations department for a small private college occupies very cramped quarters. Originally, personnel files were not converted to machine-readable form, but instead were stored in a half dozen locked four-drawer file cabinets stored in the reception area, behind the receptionist's desk. The receptionist kept the keys to the file cabinets and gave them to HR employees as needed.

The problem with this arrangement was that the receptionist, who was a long-time college employee, had a habit of peeking at the personnel files. She was known to have the juiciest gossip in the building at coffee break time.

One day, the receptionist came in to work and saw the file cabinets being moved out of the reception area. In their place, a PC had been placed on her desk. The new HR system was online and an IT staff member had come to train the receptionist. She was supplied with a word processor, access to the college faculty/staff directory, and an appointment scheduling application.

"How do I get to the personnel files?" she asked at the end of the training session.

"'You don't have that application," she was told.

"Why not?"

The IT staff member shrugged. "You'll have to ask the database administrator."

The receptionist was out the door, headed for IT.

She found the database administrator in his office.

"Why didn't I get the personnel application?" she asked.

"Because you don't need access to that information to do your job and legally we have to ensure the privacy of those data."

At this point, the receptionist was furious. "But I've always had access to the personnel files!" she shouted.

The scene degenerated from there.

The problem would appear to be that the HR receptionist should never have had access to the personnel files in the first place. However, it's a bit more complicated than that. Access to information makes people feel powerful. It's the "I know something you don't know" syndrome. Remove or restrict access and any many people feel that they have lost power and status in the organization.

One solution to this problem that some organizations have adopted is to appoint a committee to handle decisions of who has access to what. Users who feel that they need additional access appeal to the committee, rather than to a single individual. This protects the staff members making the decisions and provides broader input to the decision making process.

The other side of this issue is data sharing. Occasionally, you may run into employees who have control of data that need to be shared, but the employee is reluctant to release the data. A researcher who controls survey data, a district manager who handles data about the activities of salespeople in the field... Psychologically, the issue is the same as determining data access: Access to data and controlling data can make people feel powerful and important.

Data sharing can be mandated by a supervisor (if necessary, as a condition to continued employment). However, it is often better to try to persuade the data owner that there is benefit to everyone if the data are shared. By the same token, the committee that makes decisions about data access must also be willing to listen to the data owner's arguments in favor of keeping the data restricted and be willing to agree if the arguments are compelling.

Backup and Recovery

Every discussion of database security needs to spend at least some time looking at preparation for catastrophic failures. Disk drives develop bad sectors, making it impossible to read or write data; natural disasters can fill the server room with water. Earthquakes and fires happen.

When such failures occur, there is only one thing you can do: Revert to a backup copy. In this section, we'll look at making backups and how they fit into a disaster recovery scheme.

Backup

We don't usually think of backup as part of a security strategy, but, in some circumstances, it can be the most effective way to recover from security problems. If a server becomes so compromised by malware that it is impossible to remove (perhaps because virus protection software hasn't been developed for the specific malware), then a reasonable solution is to reformat any affected hard disks and restore the database from the most recent backup. Backups are also your only defense against physical damage to data storage, such as a failed hard disk.

Note: Some small databases are kept on solid state devices (SSDs). SSDs don't have the same failure points as magnetic disks, but they are subject to wear: A bit on an SSD can be written only so many times before it wears out. Therefore, a very volatile and/or old database stored on an SSD is vulnerable to media failure.

A backup copy is a usable fallback strategy only if you have a backup that isn't too old and you are certain that the backup copy is clean (in other words, not infected by malware).

How often should you make backup copies? The answer depends on the volatility of your data. In other words, how much do your data change? If the database is primarily for retrieval, with very little data modification, then a complete backup once a week and incremental backups every day may be sufficient. However, an active transaction database in which data are constantly being entered may need complete daily backups. It comes down to a decision of how much you can afford to lose versus the time and effort needed to make backups often.

Assuming that you have decided on a backup interval, how many backups should you keep? If you back up daily, is it enough to keep a week's worth? Or will less do or do you need more? In this case, it depends a great deal on the risk of malware. You want to keep enough backups that you can go far enough back in time to obtain a clean copy of the database (one without the malware). However, it is also true that malware may affect the server operating system without harming the database, in which case the most recent backup will be clean. Then you can fall back on the "three generations of backups" strategy, where you keep a rotation of "child," "father," and "grandfather" backup copies.

It used to be easy to choose backup media. Hard disk storage was expensive; tape storage was slow and provided only sequential retrieval, but it was cheap. We backed up to tape almost exclusively until the mid-2000s, when hard disk storage became large enough and cheap enough to be seen as a viable backup device. Some mainframe installations continue to use tape cartridges, but even large databases are quickly being migrated to disk backup media. Small systems, which once could back up to optical drives, now use disks as backup media almost exclusively.

The issue of backup has a psychological component, as well as a technical component: How can you be certain that backups are being made as scheduled? At first, this may not seem to be something to worry about, but consider the following scenario (which is a true story).

In the mid-1980s, a database application was installed for an outpatient psychiatry clinic that was affiliated with a major hospital in a major northeastern city. The application, which primarily handled patient scheduling, needed to manage more than 25,000 patient visits a year, split between about 85 clinicians. The database itself was placed on a server in a secured room.

The last patient appointment was scheduled for 5 pm. Most staff left at that time. However, the receptionist stayed until 6 pm to close up after the last patient left. Her job during that last hour included making a daily backup of the database.

About a month after the application went into day-to-day use, the database developer who installed the system received a frantic call from the office manager. There were 22 unexplained files on the receptionist's computer. The office manager was afraid that something was terribly wrong.

Something was indeed wrong, but not what anyone would have imagined. The database developer discovered that the unidentified files were temporary files left by the database application. Each time the application was launched from the server it downloaded the structure of the database and its application from the server and kept them locally until the client software was shut down. The presence of the temporary files meant that the receptionist wasn't quitting the application, but merely turning off her computer. If she wasn't quitting the database application properly, was she making backup copies?

As you can guess, she wasn't. The only backup that existed was the one that the database developer made the day the application was installed and data were migrated into the database. When asked why the backups weren't made, the receptionist admitted that it was just too much trouble.

The solution was a warning from the office manager and additional training in backup procedures. The office manager also monitored the backups more closely.

The moral to the story is that just having a backup strategy in place isn't enough. You need to make certain that the backups are actually being made.

Disaster Recovery

The term *disaster recovery* refers to the activities that must take place to bring the database back into use after it has been damaged in some way.

In large organizations, database disaster recovery will likely be part of a broader organizational disaster recovery plan. However, in a small organization, it may be up to the database administrator to coordinate recovery.

A disaster recovery plan usually includes specifications for the following:

- Where backup copies will be kept so that they will remain undamaged even if the server room is damaged.
- How new hardware will be obtained.
- How the database and its applications are to be restored from the backups.
- Procedures for handling data until the restored database is available for use.
- Lists of those affected by the database failure and procedures for notifying them when the failure occurs and when the database is available again.

The location of backup copies is vitally important. If they are kept in the server room, they are likely to be destroyed during a flood, fire, or earthquake, along with the server itself. At least one backup copy should therefore be stored off-site.

Large organizations often contract with commercial data storage facilities to handle their backups. The storage facility maintains temperature-controlled rooms to extend the life of backup media. They may also operate trucks that deliver and pick up the backup media so that the off-site backup remains relatively current.

For small organizations, it's not unheard of for an IT staff member to take backups home for safe keeping. This probably isn't the best strategy, given that the backup may not be accessible when needed. Some use bank safe deposit boxes for offsite storage, although those generally are only accessible during normal business hours. If a small organization needs 24/7 access to off-site backup copies, the expense of using a commercial facility may be justified.

When a disaster occurs, an organization needs to be up and running as quickly as possible. If the server room and its machines are damaged, there must be some other way to obtain hardware. Small organizations can simply purchase new equipment, but they must have a plan for where the new hardware will be located and how network connections will be obtained.

Large organizations often contract with *hot sites*, businesses that provide hardware that can run the organization's software. Hot sites store backup copies and guarantee that they can have the organization's applications up and running in a specified amount of time.

Once a disaster recovery plan has been written, it must be tested. Organizations need to run a variety of disaster recovery drills, simulating a range of system failures. It is not unusual to discover that what appears to be a good plan on paper doesn't work in practice. The plan needs to be modified as needed to ensure that the organization can recover its information systems should a disaster occur.

The Bottom Line: How Much Security Do You Need?

Many of the security measures described in this chapter are costly, such as adding user authentication measures beyond passwords and user IDs and contracting with a hot site. How important are high-end security measures? Should your organization invest in them?

The answer depends on a number of factors, but primarily on the type of data being protected:

- Are there laws governing the privacy of the data?
- Could the data be used as the basis for identity theft?
- Do the data represent trade secrets that could seriously compromise the organization's market position should they be disclosed?

The final question you must answer is how much risk you are willing to tolerate. Assume that it is affordable to install enough security to protect against about 80 percent of security threats. However, it may well cost as much as that entire 80 percent to achieve an additional one or two percent of protection. If you are willing (and able) to tolerate a 20 percent chance of a security breach, then the 80 percent security is enough. However, if that is too much risk, then you will need to take more security measures, regardless of cost.

For Further Reading

Bond, R., See, K.Y.-K., Wong, C.K.M., Chan, Y.-K.H., 2006. Understanding DB2 9 Security. IBM Press.

Clarke, J., 2009. SQL Injection attacks and Defense. Syngress.

Davis, M., 2009. Hacking Exposed Malware and Rootkits. McGraw-Hill Osborne Media.

Faragallah, O.S., et al., 2014. Multilevel Security for Relational Databases. Auerbach.

Gertz, M., Jajodia, S., 2007. Handbook of Database Security: Applications and Trends. Springer.

Kenan, K., 2005. Cryptography in the Database: The Last Line of Defense. Addison-Wesley Professional.

Litchfield, D., 2007. The Oracle Hacker's Handbook: Hacking and Defending Oracle. Wiley.

Litchfield, D., Anley, C, Heasman, B., Grindlay, et al., 2005. The Database Hacker's Handbook: Defending Database Servers. Wiley.

Natan, R.B., 2005. Implementing Database Security and Auditing. Digital Press.

Thuraisingham, B., 2005. Database and Applications Security: Integrating Information Security and Data Management. Auerbach Publications.

Welsh, T.R., 2009. A Manager's Guide to Handling Information Security Incidents. Auerbach.

Wright, J., Cache, J., 2015. Hacking Exposed Wireless, Third Edition: Wireless Security Secrets and Solutions. McGraw-Hill Education.

Chapter

24

Data Warehousing

A *data warehouse* is a repository of transaction and nontransaction data used for querying, reporting, and corporate decision-making. The data typically come from multiple sources. They are not used for day-to-day corporate operations and therefore once data have been stored, tend to change much less than the transactional/operational databases we have used as examples to this point.

Because of the cost associated with creating and maintaining a data warehouse, only very large organizations establish their own. Tables can grow to hold millions of rows; storage capacities have now moved into the petabyte range. Full-fledged data warehouses therefore require mainframe processing capabilities or large clusters of smaller servers.

Note: Who has data warehouses that large? eBay for one. The company has at least two data warehouses. The smaller is a mere 9.2 petabytes. The larger, which stores Web clicks along with other data, was more than 40 petabytes in 2013. Wal-Mart, Verizon, AT&T, and Bank of America also have data warehouses with storage measured in petabytes.

The software that manages a data warehouse typically is a relational DBMS.[1] However, data modeling is somewhat different, because the goals of the data warehouse are different from an operational transaction-based database. The purpose of this chapter is to acquaint you with how data warehouses fit into the information strategy of large organizations, as well as how and why their designs differ from the relational data model as it has been presented throughout this book.

---

[1] Most data warehouse software is commercial. However, Infobright has released an open-source product. For details, see http://pcworld.about.com/od/businesscenter/Infobright-Releases-Open-sourc.htm.

Scope and Purpose of a Data Warehouse

To better understand the difference between a data warehouse (or its smaller sibling, a *data mart*), let's return to SmartMart, the retailer whose operational database was presented in Chapter 15. SmartMart's operational system performs the following data management activities for the organization:

■ Tracks the location and stock level of inventory items
■ Stores in-store and Web sales data, including promotions applied at the time of purchase
■ Handles employee scheduling and work assignments (feeds into the payroll system)

The applications that run against the database answer queries such as

■ Where is a specific product in stock and how many are available?
■ What promotions apply to a product being purchased?
■ What items were ordered on a specific Web order?
■ Where and when is a specific employee working?

The queries provide information necessary for the day-to-day operations of the business. However, they aren't intended to provide the types of information that upper-level management needs to make strategic decisions, such as which products sell well in which parts of country, and to evaluate the results of previous decisions, such as which promotions generated a significant rise in sales and should be repeated. Although an operational database can provide summary reports for a district manager showing how the stores in his or her territory performed over various time periods, such reports are typically limited to only a few years and the type of information presented by the reports is fixed when the report application is developed.

Strategic planning and reviews of the implementation of strategic plans need to be able to "slice and dice" the data in a variety of ways. In other words, the queries need to allow data to be grouped by a variety of descriptions—sales by state, sales by promotion type, sales by zip code, sales by date, and so on—in an ad hoc manner. The data in an operational database may be offloaded to archival storage after a year or so to keep the database from becoming too large, but the data in a data warehouse are usually kept indefinitely.

Operational systems are usually accompanied by a variety of prewritten applications, such as those that run on point of sale terminals, and management summary reports, such as that described earlier. Very few users have ad hoc query access to the database. In contrast, there are few (if any)

prewritten applications for the data in a data warehouse. Users work with a query tool that makes it possible to explore data groupings however they choose and however the data might lead them.

The primary activity performed using a data warehouse is *data mining*, through which a user analyzes data to look for patterns in the data. For example, data mining can identify which products sell best in which parts of a company's market. The results can be used to tailor marketing campaigns to the location or to shift inventory levels to better match demand.

A data mining activity conducted by the 7-Eleven Corporation, for example, indicated that around 8 pm in the evening, sales of beer and diapers went up. When you think about it, the result makes some sense: Fathers are sent to the convenience store to get diapers in the early evening and, while there, pick up a six pack of beer. The corporation moved merchandise in the stores so that diapers were placed next to the beer coolers. As a result, beer sales went up significantly.

You have to be careful when data mining, because statistically you are bound to find "something" sooner or later. For example, a data mining activity discovered that individuals with higher incomes tended to own more expensive houses than those with lower incomes. This type of fact is certainly true, but of little practical use to anyone.

Because we continually add data to a data warehouse and rarely delete data, data warehouses tend to be extremely large databases, with tables containing millions and tens of millions of rows. The sheer volume of the data and the processing power needed to perform ad hoc queries against them require a mainframe or a cluster of smaller servers with the power of a mainframe, rather than a single desktop server. Although many desktop servers do rival mainframes in raw processing power, they can't handle the high volume of I/O that data warehouses require.

Data warehouses also support creating reports for a large business. For example, a company that manages many fast-food restaurants loads all transaction data into a data warehouse. The reports include charts of profit and loss for some or all restaurants, as well as summary reports (such as summaries of sales and the average customer check) for the company as a whole.[2]

Note: Data marts, the smaller versions of full-fledged data warehouses, can and often do run on desktop servers.

---

[2]For details, see http://www.xore.com/casestudies/case_study_fastfood.pdf.

Most of the large data warehouses in use today use relational DBMSs, such as DB/2 and Oracle, two of the few products able to handle the data volume.

Note: A new type of DBMSs has emerged to handle the large data sets used by data warehouses. These nonrelational databases are particularly good at managing distributed installations. For details, see Chapter 28.

Obtaining and Preparing the Data

Early in the evolution of data warehousing, general wisdom suggested that the data warehouse should store summarized data rather than the detailed data generated by operational systems. Experience has shown, however, that the data warehouse needs as much detail as the operational system. Storing the detail makes the data warehouse more flexible, allowing users to query in any way they choose. You can always produce summaries if you have the detail, but if you only have summarized data, such as totals and averages, you can't recreate the detail should you need it.

Most, but not all, of the data come from operational systems. Data may also come from outside sources. For example, a company such as Smart-Mart might want to include demographic data about geographic regions and would be more likely to purchase such data from a government entity rather than attempt to collect those data itself.

Although a data warehouse may store much of the same data as an operational database, there are some significant differences in the way the data are handled:

- Operational databases are generally updated in real time. For example, a sales transaction is entered into the database as the sale occurs. In contrast, data warehouses are typically loaded in batches at regular intervals, such as once a day.
- Operational systems are interested in the latest or current values of many data elements, such as a customer's current address and telephone. Data warehouses, however, want to see how data have changed over time and therefore need to keep historical data. This means that there may be multiple values for a customer's address; each value will then be associated with the dates the address was valid. (See the section *Dates and Data* later in this chapter for more information.)
- Missing values are acceptable in an operational database. For example, if the attribute color doesn't apply to an inventory item, then the value for that column in the product's row can simply be left null. However, nulls in a data warehouse can produce unpredictable or inaccurate

results. Assume that we want to know the percentage of products sold over the Web that aren't shipped, such as software that is downloaded. Such items have no shipping weight and, in the operational database, produce no problems when the shipping weight column remains null. But when the data warehouse software is counting the number of items that aren't shipped, the nulls aren't specific enough. A null might represent an item that isn't shipped, but might also represent a shipped item for which we don't know the shipping weight. Therefore, nulls in a data warehouse need to be replaced with specific values, such as "doesn't ship" in our example of the nonshipping inventory items.

Data warehouses typically obtain their data from multiple sources, be they operational systems or data obtained from outside the company. This generates a significant problem when the data sources don't represent duplicated data in the same way. For example, two operational systems (say, one from sales and one from marketing) may use different transaction identifiers, although many transactions appear in both databases. The software that loads the data warehouse must recognize that the transactions are the same and merge the data into a single entity.

Before they are loaded into a data warehouse, data must be modified so that they match whatever format is used in the data warehouse. In addition, duplicated data must be identified and coalesced; nulls must be replaced with specific values. These activities, along with procedures for cleaning the data (removing errors), are performed before the data are loaded.

The process of getting data into the data warehouse is known as *extract-transform-load* (ETL). It is virtually impossible to purchase complete software that will perform ETL processing because the sources of data for each data warehouse are so very different. In most cases, such software must be custom-developed for each warehouse. Much of the expense in setting up a data warehouse therefore comes from the writing and testing of the ETL software. Running data through the ETL software and maintaining the ETL software also consumes a large portion of IT staff effort in maintaining the data warehouse. This work takes place out of the users' sight, in the "back room" where the data are prepared.

Note: When all or most of the data that go into a data warehouse come from within an organization, the changes necessary to make data formatting consistent can either be made in the feeder systems or during the ETL process. If the organization has many operational systems—and, in particular, is working with legacy software—then it may not be feasible to modify the operational systems. However, many organizations can benefit from a project that makes data formatting consistent across multiple databases. The effort to make the changes may be worthwhile in and of itself, even without the benefits to the ongoing ETL process.

Data Modeling for the Data Warehouse

Because the purpose of a data warehouse differs from that of an operational system, there are differences in the types of tables that make up the design. The most commonly used data model used in data warehouses is *dimensional modeling*. As you will see, it takes its basic precepts from the relational data model, such as tables and a variety of keys. However, the tables are generally not normalized. In fact, they are really only in first normal form, because many tables contain data about multiple entities. They are nonetheless legal relations, because they are two-dimensional tables without repeating groups.

Dimensional Modeling Basics

Dimensional modeling uses two major types of tables: *fact tables* and *dimension tables*. Fact tables hold numeric data that can be summarized as needed; dimension tables hold the descriptive criteria by which a user can organize the data. As a first example, consider Figure 24.1. These tables support querying the data warehouse about inventory levels of products on any given date. They illustrate several of the characteristics of dimensional modeling that are different from pure relational design.

■ Natural keys, such as UPCs or ISBNs or invoice numbers, are not used as all or part of the primary keys. Instead, each row in a table is given a unique integer key. These keys speed up joins between the fact and dimension tables. For example, the primary key of the *dimension_date* table is an arbitrary integer rather than the date itself. When the natural keys are included in a table, they are known as *deprecated dimensions*. (Although they are natural keys, they are not referenced by any foreign keys in the data warehouse.)

■ Fact tables contain foreign keys and data that can be summarized. For example, the *fact_inventory_level* table contains foreign keys to the date, location, and product dimension tables. The summarizable data item is the quantity in stock. The primary key of the table is the concatenation of two or more of the foreign keys (all of which are arbitrary integer keys). Data warehouses use referential integrity to ensure that the arbitrary foreign keys, used in the fact tables, reference existing dimension table rows. However, unlike true relational databases, the dimensional model foreign keys are always meaningless. Data warehouses also enforce nonnull, unique primary keys.

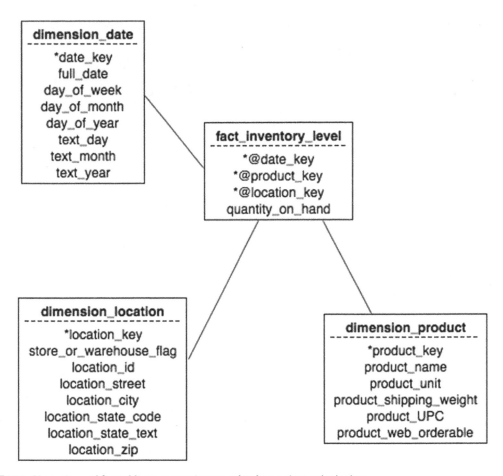

■ FIGURE 24.1 Dimension and fact tables to capture inventory levels at a given point in time.

- Dimension tables contain descriptive data. The *dimension_date* table, for example, has its unique integer key, along with attributes for the many ways in which a person might want to use a date in a query. There will be one row in a date dimension table for each date that might be used by any query against the data warehouse.

What can a user do with the dimensional model of the inventory levels? There are a variety of analyses that the model can satisfy, including the following:

- How do the inventory levels of product X vary from month to month?
- How do the inventory levels of product X vary from month to month and store to store?

- Which stores show the greatest/least inventory of product X after the winter holiday shopping season?
- Which products had more inventory in the warehouses for product X than in stores during the winter holiday season?
- Which warehouses had the total lowest inventory at the end of each month?

Dates and Data

Unlike operational databases, data warehouses keep track of data changes over time. For example, the SmartMart operational database is concerned about inventory levels at the current time; inventory levels a week ago aren't particularly relevant. However, the design in Figure 24.1 takes a snapshot of inventory levels at some specified date. The data warehouse will therefore contain many snapshots, making the analysis of inventory levels over time possible.

In some circumstances, this can present some problems to the data warehouse designer, especially where human data, such as addresses, are concerned. Consider, for example, the simple customer dimension in Figure 24.2. The problem with this design is that, over time, customers change their addresses and phone numbers. Analysis based on customer location during a specific time period may be incorrect if there are multiple addresses for the same customer.

```
dimension_customer
-----------------------------
         *customer_key
     customer_first_name
     customer_last_name
   customer_street_address
         customer_city
        customer_state
         customer_zip
        customer_phone
```

■ FIGURE 24.2 A simple customer dimension.

One solution is to include only the most recent address for a customer in the data warehouse. However, this makes it impossible to analyze sales by location, given that the address in the related customer row may not have been the address when the sale was made. Another solution is to add the dates during which an address was valid to the customer dimension table, as was done in Figure 24.3. There will then be one row in the table for each

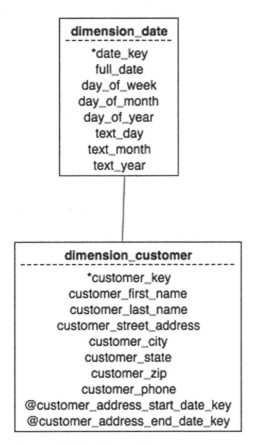

■ FIGURE 24.3 Including valid dates for an address.

address used by a customer when making purchases. Because each sale is related to the customer based on an arbitrary customer key rather than a concatenation of customer data, there will be no problem determining the correct address for a specific sale (see Figure 24.4). Queries based on location and date will then need to include logic to ensure that an address was valid during the time period of the analysis.

Data Warehouse Appliances

During the early 1980s, when relational databases were supplanting those based on older data models, several hardware vendors were attempting to sell special-purpose computers called *database machines*. The idea was to take a minicomputer and use it to run just a DBMS (with an OS that was specifically tailored to that purpose). It would be connected to another

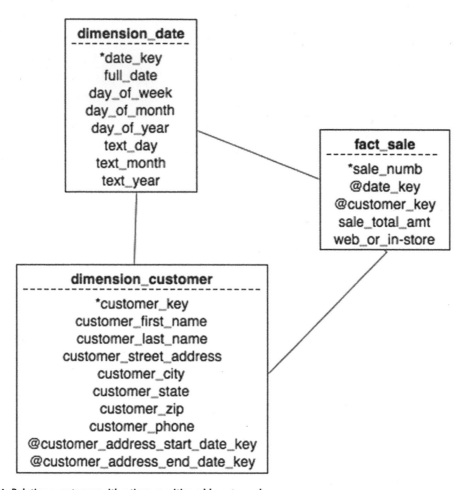

■ FIGURE 24.4 Relating a customer with a time-sensitive address to a sale.

computer in a master–slave relationship. Requests for database processing came first to the master machine, which passed them to the database machine. The database machine completed all database activity and sent the results back to the master computer, which, in turn, sent the data to the user. In theory, by offloading database processing to a dedicated machine overall system performance (including database performance) would improve. In practice, however, only database applications that were severely CPU-bound showed significant performance improvements when running on a database machine. The overhead needed to move queries and data to and from the database machine erased any performance gains that occurred from relieving the master computer's CPU of database work. By 1990, almost no one had heard of a database machine.

The rise of data warehouses has seen the reappearance of computers dedicated to database work. Today, the situation is very different because a dedicated database computer is really a special-purpose server that is connected directly to a network.

One such hardware configuration, for example, is being offered by Teradata.[3] The system is focused on high performance access, using a "shared-nothing" architecture. In other words, each processor has access to its own storage and pathways to reach that storage.

The benefit of such a preconfigured solution is that it simplifies setting up the data warehouse. An appliance such as Teradata's also means that the entire data warehouse infrastructure is supported by a single vendor, which many organizations prefer.

For Further Reading

Aggarwal, C., 2015. Data Mining: The Textbook. Springer.

Clampa, B., 2014. The Data Warehouse Workshop: Providing Practical Experience to the Aspiring ETL Developer. CreateSpace Independent Publishing.

Inmon, W.H., Linstedt, D., 2014. Data Architecture: A Primer for the Data Scientist: Big Data, Data Warehouse and Data Vault. Morgan Kaufmann.

Kimball, R., Ross, M., 2013. The Data Warehouse Toolkit: The Definitive Guide to Dimensional Modeling, third ed. Wiley.

Kimball, R., Ross, M., Thornwaite, W., Mundy, J., Becker, B., 2008. The Data Warehouse Lifecycle Toolkit, second ed. Wiley.

Laberge, R., 2011. The Data Warehouse Mentor: Practical Data Warehouse and Business Intelligence Insights. McGraw-Hill Osborne Media.

Tan, P.-N., Steinbach, M., Kumar, V., 2005. Introduction to Data Mining. Addison-Wesley.

Vaisman, A., Zimanyi, E., 2014. Data Warehouse Systems: Design and Implementation (Data-Centric Systems and Applications). Springer.

Westphal, C., 2008. Data Mining for Intelligence, Fraud & Criminal Detection: Advanced Analytics & Information Sharing Techniques. CRC.

Zaki, M.J., Meira, Jr., W., 2014. Data Mining and Analysis: Fundamental Concepts and Algorithms. Cambridge University Press.

---

[3]http://www.teradata.com/News-Releases/2015/Newest-Teradata-Data-Warehouse-Appliance-is-a-Powerhouse-for-the-Most-Demanding-Analytics/

Chapter
25

Data Quality

As early as the 1960s, there was an expression in computing that most people in the field agreed was true: "Garbage in, garbage out." (It was abbreviated GIGO and was pronounced "guy-go.") We worried about the effect of the quality of input data on the output of our programs. In the intervening years, during the rise of databases, GIGO was largely forgotten. Today, however, with some data warehouses exceeding a petabyte of data, the quality of that data has become extremely important once again.

Exactly what do we mean by data quality? To be useful, the data in a database must be accurate, timely, and available when needed. Data quality assures the accuracy and timeliness of data and, as you will see, it is much easier to ensure data quality *before* data get into a database than once they are stored.

Note: Much of what we do to ensure data quality is just plain common sense. In fact, you may find yourself saying "well, that's obvious" or "of course you would do that" as you read. The truth is, however, that as logical as many data quality procedures seem to be, some organizations simply overlook them.

Why Data Quality Matters

Why do we care so much about data quality? Because we need to be able to trust that what we retrieve from a database is reliable. We will be making both operational and strategic decisions based on what we retrieve from a database. The quality of those decisions is directly related to the quality of the data that underlies them.

Consider, for example, the decisions that a buyer makes for the clothing department of a retail chain such as SmartMart. Choices of what to stock for the winter holiday shopping season are made nine to 12 months in advance, based on what sold the previous year and the buyer's knowledge of clothing styles. The buyer therefore queries the operational database to create a report showing how much of each style sold at each store and on the Web. She can see that jeans sell well in one particularly store in a region, while another store sells more dress pants. She will then adjust her orders to reflect those sale patterns.

However, if the sales data are incorrect, she runs the risk of ordering the wrong type of merchandise for each store. SmartMart can certainly move inventory from one store another, but during the holiday shopping season, customers are often unable to wait for merchandise to arrive. They will either purchase a different item or go to another retailer. In the long run, SmartMart will lose sales.

We can probably come up with hundreds of scenarios in which inaccurate data cause problems for businesses: customers who can't be contacted because of out-of-date phone numbers or e-mail addresses, orders missing items that are never shipped, customers who aren't notified of recalls, and so on. The bottom line is that when we have problem data, business suffers.

Note: It is often better to have a database application crash than it is to have a report that contains inaccurate results. In the former case, it's clear that you have a problem; in the latter case, there may be no indication that the report is invalid, so you'll go ahead and use it, bad data and all.

Data quality problems arise from a wide range of sources, and have many remedies. Throughout the rest of this chapter we will look at variety of data quality ills, how they are likely to occur and what you can do to prevent them, or at least minimize their occurrence.

Recognizing and Handling Incomplete Data

One source of data quality problems is missing data. There are two general sources: data that are never entered into the database and data that are entered but deleted when they should not be.

Missing Rows

Missing rows occur for a number of reasons. One common reason is that someone has been using low-level data manipulation tools to "maintain" the database and, in the process, either deleted rows or missed rows when copying data from one table to another.

Note: The ability to manipulate rows in this way with a low-level tool violates one of Codd's rules for a relational database, which states that it should not be possible to circumvent integrity rules with low-level tools.

Missing rows can be very hard to detect if their absence doesn't violate referential integrity constraints. For example, it's impossible to detect that an item is missing from an order—until the customer contacts you about not receiving the item. It's not necessarily obvious, however, where the error has occurred. Any of the following might have happened:

- An item was lost in transmission from the customer's computer to the vendor's computer (Internet order) or a customer service representative didn't enter the item (phone or mail order).
- An error in one of the vendor's application programs missed entering the row.
- Someone maintaining the database with a low-level data manipulation tool accidentally deleted the item.

It's a relatively easy matter to enter the missing item and ship it to the customer. But what is to prevent the error from occurring again? To do that, we have to find the cause of the error and fix it. Because the possible causes are so diverse, it will be a long, difficult process. Ultimately, we can fix a bug in an application program and put policies in place that control the use of maintenance languages. We can even conduct additional training for data entry personnel to make them more careful with entering order items. We cannot control, however, packets lost on the Internet (or even more problematic, customers who insist that a product was on an order when it wasn't in the first place).

Missing Column Data

As you will recall, SQL is based on what we call three-valued logic. The result of a logical comparison between data and a search criterion can be true, false, or maybe. The maybe occurs when a column contains null because no determination can be made. Sometimes nulls are harmless—we don't care that the data are missing—but in other situations we wish we had the data. Currently, there is no way to distinguish between the two types of null, but some database theorists have proposed that DBMSs should support four-valued logic: true, false, maybe and it's OK, and maybe and it's not OK. It's nulls that fall into the latter category that cause problems with missing data. For example, assume that a customer table has a column for the customer's country. If the customer is in the country where the company is based, a null in the country column doesn't really matter. However, if the customer is in another country, then we need to know the country and leaving that value null leads to problems of undeliverable marketing mailings.

Missing column data can be prevented relatively easily by disallowing nulls in those columns that must have values.

Missing Primary Key Data

A relational database with tight integrity controls prevents data from entering a database because part of a primary key is null. From the viewpoint of data retrieval, this is a positive result because it ensures that every piece of data that makes it into the database is retrievable. However, the lack of a primary key may mean that a set of data are never stored in the database, despite the data being important to the business operating the database.

One situation in which this problem occurs is when entities that are only at the "one" end of relationships have no obvious primary key attribute and no arbitrary key has been created. The primary key is therefore created from the concatenation of two or more columns. For example, if an employee entity has no employee number attribute, then a primary key might be constructed of first name, last name, and phone number. If a phone number isn't available, the data can't be entered because there isn't a complete primary key; the data are never stored. In this case, the solution lies in the database design. Those "top" entities that do not have inherent primary keys should be given arbitrary primary keys. Those arbitrary keys then filter down through the design as parts of foreign keys and ensure that primary key values are available for all instances of all entities.

Recognizing and Handling Incorrect Data

Incorrect data are probably the worst type of problems to detect and prevent. Often, the errors aren't detected until someone external to an organization makes a complaint. Determining how the error occurred is equally difficult because, sometimes, the problems are one-of-a-kind.

Wrong Codes

Relational databases make significant use of coded data. The codes are defined in tables related to the tables where they are used through primary key–foreign key relationships. For example, we often store the names of US states as two-letter abbreviations and then use a table that contains the abbreviation and the full state name for validation and output (when the full state name is needed).

Coding, however, is a two-edged sword. Consider the following scenario: A company divides its products into categories, each of which is represented by a three-letter code. The codes are stored in a table with the code and a description of the product category (for example, PEN and "custom imprinted pens," WCP and "white cups," and so on). When the company decides to carry a new product, the application program used by the staff allows the user to make up a code and enter the code and its description. To make things easier for the user, the user doesn't need to explicitly enter the new code. During data entry, the application captures a failed referential integrity check, automatically asks the user for the code description, and creates the new row in the code table. The problem with this is that, if the user has mistyped a code for an existing product, the application handles it as a new product. Therefore, many codes for the same product could exist in the database. Searches on the correct code will not retrieve rows containing the incorrect codes.

The solution is to restrict the ability to enter new codes. In some organizations, only database administrators have the right to modify the master code tables. If a new product needs to be entered, the DBA assigns and enters the code prior to a clerical worker entering product data. Application programs then retrieve the list of codes and make it available to data entry personnel.

Wrong Calculations

One of the decisions that a database designer makes is whether to include calculated values in a database or to compute them as needed, on the fly. The decision depends on many factors, including the overhead to perform the calculations and how often they are used. We often, for example, compute and store line costs in a line items table:

```
line_items (order_numb, item_numb, quantity_ordered, line_cost)
```

The line cost is computed by retrieving the cost for each item from the *items* table (item number is the foreign key) and then multiplying it by the quantity ordered. The lookup of the price is quick and the computation is simple.

What happens, however, if the formula for computing the line cost is incorrect? Primarily, the total amount of the order (which is also often stored) will be incorrect. It is much more likely that someone will notice that the order total is incorrect, but it may require a bit more investigation to find the specific error and then to track down its source.

Many of the automatic calculations performed by a DBMS when data are modified are performed using *triggers*, small procedures stored in the database whose executions are triggered when specific actions occur (for example, storing a new row). An error in an automatic calculation therefore means examining not only application programs, but all relevant database triggers as well. Nonetheless, once an error in a computation has been identified and corrected, it is unlikely the exact problem will occur again.

Wrong Data Entered into the Database

We humans are prone to make typing mistakes. Despite all our best efforts at integrity constraints, we are still at the mercy of simple typos. If a user types "24 West 325th Street" rather than "325 West 24th Street," you can be sure that the customer won't receive whatever is being sent. The transposition of a pair of letters or digits in a postcode or zip code is all it takes to separate a customer from his or her shipment!

The typographical error is the hardest error to detect because we rarely know about it until a customer complains. The fix is usually easy: edit the data and replace the error with the correct values. However, determining how the error occurred is even tougher than finding the source of missing rows. Was it simply a one-time typing error, in which case an apology usually solves the problem, or is there some underlying application code problem that is causing errors?

The best strategy for separating typos from system errors is to keep logs of errors. Such logs should include the table, row, and column in which the error was detected, when the error was reported, and who was responsible for entering the erroneous data. The intent here is not to blame an employee, but to make it possible to see patterns that may exist in the errors. When multiple errors are in the same column in the same table, the evidence points toward an underlying system problem. When many errors are made by the same employee, the evidence points to an employee who may need more training. However, a random pattern in the errors points to one-of-a-kind typographical errors. (Whether the random errors are at a level that suggests the need for more training for all data entry personnel depends, of course, on the organization and the impact of the errors on the organization.)

Violation of Business Rules

A business often has rules that can be incorporated into a database so that they can be enforced automatically when data are modified. For example, a book club that bills its customers after shipping may place a limit on customer accounts. The orders table includes a trigger that adds the amount of a newly stored order to the total amount owed in the customer table. If the customer table has no constraint to limit the value in the total amount owed column, a customer could easily run up a balance beyond what the company allows.

Yes, it is possible to enforce such constraints through application programs. However, there is no guarantee that all data modification will be made using the application program. In all cases where business rules can be implemented as database constraints, you should do so. This relieves application programmers of the responsibility of enforcing constraints, simplifies application program logic, and ensures that the constraints are always enforced.

Recognizing and Handling Incomprehensible Data

Incomprehensible data are data that we can't understand. Unlike incorrect data, it is relatively easy to spot incomprehensible data, although finding the source of the problem may be as difficult as it is with incorrect data.

Multiple Values in a Column

Assume that you are working with a personnel database. The dependents table has the following structure:

```
dependents (employee_ID, child_first_name, child_birth_date)
```

The intent, of course, is that there will be one row in the table for each dependent of each employee. However, when you issue a query to retrieve the dependents of employee number 12, you see the following:

```
Employee_ID      child_first_name        child_birth_date
12               Mary, John, Sam         1-15-00
```

Clearly something is wrong with these data. As we discussed earlier in this book, putting multiple values in the same column not only violates the precepts of the relational data model, but makes it impossible to associate data values accurately. Does the birthdate apply to the first, second, or third dependent? Or does it apply to all three? (Triplets, perhaps?) There is no way to know definitively from just the data in the database.

Character columns are particularly vulnerable to multiple data values, especially where names are concerned because they must be left without constraints other than a length. You can't attach constraints that forbid blanks or commas because those characters may be part of a legitimate name. The only solution to this type of problem is user education: You must teach the people doing data entry that multiple values mean multiple rows.

Orphaned Foreign Keys

So much of the querying that we do of a relational database involves joins between primary and foreign keys. If we delete all foreign key references to a primary key, then the row containing the primary key simply doesn't appear in the result of a join. The same thing occurs if the primary key referenced by a foreign key is missing: The rows with the foreign keys don't appear in the result of a join. The former *may* be a problem, but the latter always is. For example, a customer with no orders in a database may be just fine, but orders that can't be joined to a customer table to provide customer identification will be a major headache.

A relational database must prevent these "orphaned" foreign keys from existing in the database and the solution should be provided when the foreign keys are defined. As you will remember from Chapter 11, the definition of a foreign key can contain an ON DELETE clause. Its purpose is to specify what should happen to the row containing a foreign key when its primary key reference is deleted. The DBMS can forbid the deletion, set foreign key values to null, or delete the foreign key row. Which one you choose, of course, depends on the specific needs of your database environment. Nonetheless, an ON DELETE clause should be set for every foreign key so that orphans never occur.

Recognizing and Handling Inconsistent Data

Inconsistent data are those that are correct and make sense but, when duplicated throughout the database and/or organization, aren't the same. We normalize relations to help eliminate duplicated data, but in large organizations there are often multiple databases that contain information about the same entities. For example, a retail company might have one database with customer information for use in sales and another for use in marketing. If the data are to be consistent, then the name and address of a customer must be stored in exactly the same way in both databases.

Note: The best way to handle inconsistent data is the same, regardless of the type of inconsistent data. The solution is, therefore, presented at the end of this section.

Inconsistent Names and Addresses

When names and addresses duplicate throughout an organization, it's tough to keep the data consistent. By their very nature, name and address columns have few constraints because the variation of the data in those columns is so great. Adding to the problem is the difficulty of detecting when such data are inconsistent: You rarely know until someone complains or there is a need to match data between databases.

Inconsistent Business Rules

Some business rules can be implemented as database constraints. When there are multiple data stores within an organization, those constraints may not be applied consistently. Assume, for example, that the highest salary paid by an organization is $125,000 annually. There is a central personnel database, and smaller personnel databases at each of six satellite offices. The central database contains all personnel data; satellite databases contain data for the site at which they are installed. The satellite databases were designed and installed at the same time. The salary column in the employee table has the correct CHECK clause to limit the salary value. However, IT ran into a problem with that check clause at headquarters because the CEO's salary was $1,500,000. Their solution was simply to modify the check clause to allow for the higher salary. The CEO is an exception to the rule, but once the CHECK clause was modified, *anyone* who was entered into the central database could be given a higher salary without violating a table constraint.

Now assume that the CEO hires a new manager for one of the satellite offices at a salary of $150,000. Someone on the human resources staff enters the new employee's information into the database. Because the constraint on the salary limit has been removed, the data are stored. However, when the update is propagated to the appropriate satellite database, the constraint on the employee table prevents the update. The organization is left with a distributed database in an inconsistent state.

Inconsistent Granularity

Granularity is the level of detail at which data are stored in a database. When the same data are represented in multiple databases, the granularity may differ. As an example, consider the following tables:

```
order_lines (order_numb, item_numb, quantity, cost)

order_lines (order_numb, item_numb, cost)
```

Both tables contain a cost attribute, but the meaning and use of the columns are different. The first relation is used in the sales database and includes details about how many of each item were ordered and the amount actually charged for each item (which may vary from what is in the items table). The second is used by marketing. Its cost attribute is actually the line cost (quantity * cost from the sales database). Two attributes with the same name therefore have different granularities. Any attempt to combine or compare values in the two attributes will be meaningless.

This type of problem needs to be handled at an organizational level rather than at the single database level. See the last part of this section for details.

Unenforced Referential Integrity

In the preceding section, we discussed the problem of orphaned foreign keys. They represent a violation of referential integrity that occurs *after* the data have been stored and can be handled with strict foreign key definitions when the tables are created. However, what happens if foreign key constraints are never added to a table definition? Foreign keys may then be orphaned as soon as they are added to the database because there is nothing to ensure that they reference existing primary keys.

As you might expect, the solution to this problem is straightforward: Ensure that referential integrity constraints are present for all foreign keys. Make this a policy that everyone who has the right to create tables in the database must follow.

Inconsistent Data Formatting

There are many ways to represent the same data, such as telephone numbers and dates. Do you surround an area code with parentheses or do you follow it with a hyphen? Do you store the area code in the same column as the rest of the phone number or is it stored in its own column? Do dates have two or four digit years? Does the month come first, the day, or the year? How are months represented (numbers, codes, full words)? There are so many variations for telephone numbers and dates that unless there is some standard set for formatting throughout an organization's data management, it may be nearly impossible for queries to match values across databases.

Preventing Inconsistent Data on an Organizational Level

There is no easy solution to preventing inconsistent data through an organization. It requires planning at the organizational level and a commitment by all those who are responsible for databases to work together and, above all, to communicate.

Fixing the Problem

A large organization with multiple databases should probably be involved in *data administration*, a process distinct from *database administration*. Data administration keeps track of where data are used throughout an organization and how the data are represented. It provides oversight for data at an organizational level, rather than at the database level. When the time comes to use the data in a database or application program, the developers can consult the *metadata* (data about data) that have been identified through the data administration process and then determine how the data should be represented to ensure consistency.[1]

---

[1]A discussion of data administration is beyond the scope of this book. If you would like to learn more, see the Inmon title in the For Further Reading section at the end of this chapter.

It is important to keep in mind, however, that even the best data administration can't totally protect against inconsistent names and addresses. Although organizational metadata can specify that the abbreviation for street is always "St." and that the title for a married woman is always stored as "Mrs.", there is no way to ensure that names and addresses are always spelled consistently. Human error will always be a factor. When that occurs, the best strategy may be just to smile sweetly to the complaining customer and fix the problem.

Employees and Data Quality

One recurrent theme throughout this chapter is that many data quality problems are the result of human error. They may be attributable to a single individual or to a group of employees as a whole. But how will you know? The database needs to keep track of who enters data. The easiest way to implement such audit trails is to add a column for an employee ID to each table for which you want to keep data entry data. Assuming that an employee must log in to the system with a unique user name before running any application programs, the application programs can tag rows with the employee ID without any employee intervention.

If you need to keep more detailed modification information, in particular maintaining an audit trail for each modification of a table, then you need a further modification of the database design. First, you give each row in each table a unique numeric identifier:

```
customer (customer_numb, customer_first_name,
    customer_last_name, customer_street, customer_city,
    customer_zip, customer_phone, row_ID)
```

The row ID is an integer that is assigned when a row is created. It is merely a sequence number that has no relationship to the row's position in the table, or to the customer number. The row ID continues to get larger as rows are entered to the table; row IDs for deleted rows are not reused.

Note: Should a table be old enough or large enough to run out of row IDs, row IDs for deleted rows can be reused or row IDs can be reassigned to the entire table in a contiguous sequence (perhaps using a larger storage space, such as a 64-bit rather than 32-bit integer). This is a rather lengthy process, because all foreign keys that reference those row IDs must be updated, as well.

The design must then include a table to hold the audit trail:

```
customer_mods (row_ID, modification_date, column_modified, employee_ID)
```

A search of this table will indicate who made a change to which column on which date in the customer table. Alternatively, row IDs can be unique throughout the database (rather than within each table), and all audit information kept in one table:

```
modifications (table_name, row_ID, modification_date,
    column_modified, employee_ID)
```

An even more detailed audit trail could include columns for the old value in the modified column and the new value.

Note: In many cases, databases that require an audit trail use application programs to handle the insertion of data into the audit trail tables. This helps insure that the audit data are entered accurately.

Some of today's DBMSs include audit trail capabilities. For example, once you've enabled audit trails with Oracle, you can use a SQL SELECT to pull data from a table named *audit_trail* that includes the columns *username*, *obj_name* (name of the database item affected), *action_name* (SQL command issued), and *sql_text* (the text of command issued).

For Further Reading

Batini, C., Scannapieco, M., 2006. Data Quality: Concepts, Methodologies and Techniques. Springer.

Fisher, C., Lauria, E., Chengalur-Smith, S., Wang, R., 2006. An Introduction to Data Quality. M.I.T. Information Quality Program.

Inmon, W.H., O'Neil, Bonnie, Fryman, Lowell, 2007. Business Metadata: Capturing Enterprise Knowledge. Morgan Kaufmann.

Jugulum, R., 2014. Competing with High Quality Data: Concepts, Tools, and Techniques for Building a Successful Approach to Data Quality. Wiley.

Maydancik, A., 2007. Data Quality Assessment. Technics Publications.

McGilvray, D., 2008. Executing Data Quality Projects: Ten Steps to Quality Data and Trusted Information. Morgan Kaufmann.

Olson, J.E., 2003. Data Quality: The Accuracy Dimension. Morgan Kaufmann.

Sebastian-Coleman, L., 2013. Measuring Data Quality for Ongoing Improvement: A Data Quality Assessment Framework. Morgan Kaufmann.

Part
VI

Beyond the Relational Data Model

Although most new databases today are based on the relational data model, there are some circumstances in which a relational database may not be the best choice. In this final part of the book you will read about some of those alternative choices, with an emphasis on deciding when one of them would be appropriate for your organization.

Chapter
26

XML Support

Extensible Markup Language (XML) is a way of representing data and data relationships in text files. Because such UNICODE[1] text files have become widespread and are usually platform independent, XML is being used heavily for data transfer, especially between databases and the Web.

As you will see, XML shares some characteristics with HTML. However, the two markup languages have very different goals. HTML is designed to give instructions to a browser about how to display a page. XML, in contrast, is designed to describe the structure of data and to facilitate moving that data from one place to another.

XML has been accepted by the Word Wide Web Consortium (W3C), and has become a de facto standard for cross-platform data transfers. Because it is an open source specification, a number of application programming languages have been built on top of it, such as XHTML, RSS, MathML, GraphML, Scalable Vector Graphics, and MusicXML.

Relational databases can use XML in three ways:

- Import XML documents and store the data in one or more relations: At this time, such functionality is not provided within the SQL standard. In practice, it requires program code that is specific to a particular DBMS and therefore is beyond the scope of this book.
- Format data stored in relations as XML for output: SQL/XML, which first appeared in the SQL:2003 standard, provides a group of functions for performing this output. The standard also includes detailed instructions for mapping SQL elements to XML.
- Store entire XML documents (or portions of documents) in a column of type XML. SQL provides this capability with the XML data type.

---

[1]UNICODE is the character encoding scheme that has replaced ASCII in many computing platforms. It includes ASCII, but uses two-byte rather than single-byte codes, allowing it to support characters from non-Roman alphabets.

This chapter covers the basics of the structure of XML documents. It then looks at the major SQL/XML functions, and the XML data type.

XML Basics

XML is a *markup language*. In other words, you place special coding in the text to identify data elements. It shares some contents with HTML, but at the same time is both more and less flexible. (As you will see, this is not a contradiction!)

Note: The following is not intended to be a complete primer on XML. It will, however, give you more than enough background to understand what SQL/XML can and cannot do.

XML Structure

XML data are organized in hierarchies. As an example, consider the hierarchies diagrammed in Figure 26.1, both of which are taken from the rare book store database. Notice that it takes two hierarchies to represent the entire database because a hierarchy does not allow a child element—an element at the "many" end of a 1:M relationship—to have two parent elements (elements at

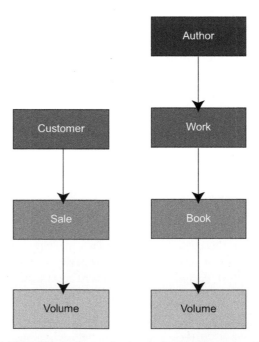

■ FIGURE 26.1 Hierarchies for the rare book store database for use in an XML document.

the "one" end of a 1:M relationship). Therefore, we can represent the relationship between a customer, a sale, and a volume, *or* the relationship between author, work, book, and volume, but not both within the same hierarchy.

Parent elements may have more than one type of child entity. As an example, consider the hierarchy in Figure 26.2. Each department has many salespeople working for it. A salesperson has many contacts (potential customers) but also makes many sales. Each sale is for one or more customers, and contains one or more items. This entire hierarchy can be represented as a whole in an XML document.

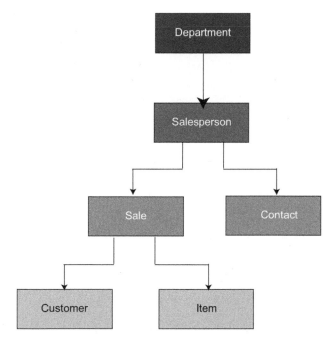

■ FIGURE 26.2 A hierarchy that includes parent elements with multiple child element types.

Because of their hierarchical structure, XML documents are said to be organized in tree structures. (You will discover later in this chapter that this botanical terminology turns up in other places in XML.)

Each hierarchy has a *root* element, the top element in the hierarchy. In Figure 26.1, there are two root elements—Author and Customer; Figure 26.2 has only one root element, Department.

Attributes

As well as having child elements, an element may have "attributes." An attribute is a single data value that describes an element. For example, in

Figure 26.2, a department might have its name and the name of its manager as attributes. In contrast, salespeople and the data that describe them are represented as child elements.

Attributes do have some limitations. First, they are single-valued; elements can be multivalued. Because they are a single value attached to an element, attributes can't be related to other attributes or elements. Attributes also make the structure of the XML more difficult to modify should the underlying structure of the data change.

XML Document Structure

An XML document really has a very simple structure: It is made up of nested pairs of tags. With the exception of the first line in the file, that's all there is to it. (If this were an e-mail rather than a book, a smiley face would go here.)

Tags

Elements and their data are identified by *tags* in the text file. These tags are similar to HMTL tags, but don't come from a fixed set of tags like those available for HTML. Each element begins with an opening tag—

`<element_name>`

—and ends with a closing tab:

`</element_name>`

Unlike HTML, which has some tags that don't come in pairs (for example, <LI>), all XML tags must be paired. Between its tags, an element has either a data value or other elements. Nested elements may, in turn, have data values or other elements.

As mentioned earlier, XML elements may have attributes, as well as elements, that are nested beneath them. An attribute is a single occurrence of a value that describes an element. Their values are placed within the element's opening tag:

`<element_name attribute_name = "attribute_value" …>`

Attribute values must be quoted.

If you have a pair of tags that have attributes but no nested elements (an *empty tag*), then you can get away with combining the two tags into one, placing the closing symbol (/) just before the closing symbol (>):

`<element_name element_data/>`

You can find a portion of an XML document that describes some of the data for the hierarchy in Figure 26.2 in Figure 26.3.

```
<?xml version "1.0" encoding="ISO-8859-1"?>
<department dept_name = "Hannover" manager_last_name = "Benson" manager_first_name
= "James">
    <salesperson>
    <first>John</first>
    <last>Doe</last>
    <ext>1234</ext>
        <sale>
            <sale_date>1-12-2012<sale_date>
            <sale_total>152</sale_total>
            <sale_numb>65</sale_numb>
            <customer>
                <cust_numb>12</cust_numb>
            </customer>
            <item>
                <item_numb>109</item_numb>
                <quantity>1</quantity>
                <sale_numb>65</sale_numb>
            </item>
            <item>
                <item_numb>85</item_numb>
                <quantity>1</quantity>
                <sale_numb>65</sale_numb>
            </item>
        </sale>
        <contact>
            <c_first>Mary</c_last>
            <c_last>Jones</c_last>
            <c_phone>555-525-1111</c_phone>
        </contact>
        <contact>
            <c_first>Sam</c_first>
            <c_last>Smith</c_last>
            <c_phone>555-999-1212</ c_phone >
        </contact>
    </salesperson>
</department>
```

■ **FIGURE 26.3 A portion of an XML document.**

Note: The indentation is not required and is included to make the code easier to read here. In fact, the indentation and spacing in some of the longer listings in this chapter have been changed in the interest of space preservation. Nonetheless, the structure of the documents has been maintained through the proper use of nested tags.

Declarations (Prologs)

Each XML document begins with a declaration (or prolog) that identifies the version of XML being used and optionally a character encoding scheme. The particular encoding specified in Figure 26.3 identifies a Western European (and thus also North American) scheme.

The declaration also optionally includes an attribute named STANDALONE. When its value is "yes," the document has no external references needed to understand its content. If the value is "no," then an application processing the XML document will need to consult outside resources to get complete information for understanding the document. Although some of the examples of declarations that you will see include this attribute, in practice it is not widely used.

The declaration is followed by the opening tag for the root element; the last line in the document is the closing tag for the root element. In between the root element tags, the document contains the elements describing the remainder of the data.

Being "Well-Formed"

As you read about XML and XML documents, especially in the context of interactions with databases, you will find references to *well-formed XML documents*. An XML document is well-formed if it meets all the XML syntax rules. Specifically, that means that:

- It has one and only one root element.
- Every element has a closing tag, or is an empty element.
- Tags are case sensitive.
- All elements are nested properly.
- All attribute values are quoted.

A well-formed XML document is much more likely to be acceptable by many different types of software running on many different platforms.

XML Schemas

To help validate the structure of an XML document, you can create an *XML schema*, a special type of XML document that contains definitions of document structure. An XML schema also defines data types for elements and attributes. It can also contain a number of domain constraints.

Note: XML schemas are a relatively recent addition to XML. The older description of the structure of an XML file is a DTD (Document Type Definition).

Unlike XML documents, XML schemas use pre-defined element tags and element attributes. An example can be found in Figure 26.4, which contains a schema that describes the structure of the XML in Figure 26.3.

```
<?xml version = "1.0"?>
<xs:schema>
    <xs:complexType name = "department">
        <xs:sequence>
            <xs:element name = "dept_name" type = "xs:string"/>
            <xs:element name = "manager_first_name" type = "xs:string"/>
        </xs:sequence>
        <xs:complexType name = "salesperson">
            <xs:sequence>
                <xs:element name = "first" type = "xs:string"/>
                <xs:element name = "last" type = "xs:string"/>
                <xs:element name = "ext" type = "xs:string"/>
            </xs:sequence>
            <xs:complexType name = "sale" mixed = "true">
                <xs:all>
                    <xs:element name = "sale_date" type = "xs:date"/>
                    <xs:element name = "sale_total" type = "xs:decimal"/>
                    <xs:element name = "sale_numb" type = "xs:string"/>
                </xs:all name = "item" mixed = "true">
                    <xs:sequence>
                        <xs:element name = "item_numb" type = "xs:integer"/>
                        <xs:element name = "quantity"  type = "xs:integer"/>
                        <xs:element name = "sale_numb" type = "xs:string"/>
                    </xs:sequence>
                </xs:complexType>
                <xs:complexType name = "customer" mixed = "true">
                    <xs:element name = "cust_numb" type = "xs:integer"/>
                </xs:complexType>
            </xs:complexType>
        <xs:complexType name = "contact">
            <xs:sequence>
                <xs:element name = "c_first" type = "xs:string"/>
                <xs:element name = "c_last" type = "xs:string"/>
                <xs:element name = "c_phone" type = "xs:string"/>
            </xs:sequence>
        </xs:complexType>
    </xs:complexType>
</xs:schema>
```

■ **FIGURE 26.4   An XML schema that describes the XML document in Figure 17.3.**

This schema contains the following elements:

- *xs:schema*: the root element.
- *xs:element*: a declaration of a root element. Each element has a name and a data type. XML includes string, integer, decimal, Boolean, date, and time types.
- *xs:complexType*: a group of elements that contain multiple data types.
- *xs:sequence* (an *indicator*): a group of elements that must appear in the order specified within the pair of sequence tags.

- *xs:all* (an indicator): a group of elements that can appear in any order specified within the pair of sequence tags. Each element can appear only once within the group.

SQL's ability to use XML schemas for validation is strongly implementation-dependent. You may find that you will have to use standalone software to determine whether an XML document is well-formed.

Note: There are a number of free Web sites that will check your XML for you, including http://www.w3schools.com/xml/xml_validator.asp, http://www.validome.org/xml/, and http://xmlgrid.net/validator.html.

SQL/XML

SQL/XML, the extensions that provide XML support from within the SQL language, entered the standard in 2003. This section covers those that are used frequently.

Note: XML standards now include a language called XQuery. It is separate from SQL, and appeals primarily to XML programmers who need to interact with data stored in a relational database. In contrast, SQL/XML tends to appeal to SQL programmers who need to generate XML documents.

XML Publishing Functions

SQL/XML's publishing functions extract data from tables and produce XML. You can therefore use a series of the functions—most usually within an embedded SQL application—to generate an entire XML document.

XMLCOMMENT

XML documents can include any comments needed. The XMLCOMMENT function has the general syntax:

```
XMLCOMMENT (source_string);
```

The source string can be a literal string or a string stored in a host language variable. The SQL statement

```
SELECT XMLCOMMENT ('High priced volumes');
```

produces the output

```
xmlcomment
----------------------------
<!--High priced volumes-->
```

Notice that the output string is now surrounded by the XML comment indicators.

XMLPARSE

The XMLPARSE function turns a string of text into XML. It is particularly useful when you need to store a string of text in a column of type XML. The function has the general format:

```
XMLPARSE (type_indicator content_string whitespace_option)
```

The type indicator takes one of two values: DOCUMENT (for a complete XML document) or CONTENT (for a small chunk of XML that doesn't represent an entire document). Most of the time, the DOCUMENT type is used in an embedded SQL program where an entire XML document can be stored in a host language string variable.

The content string cannot be generated with a SELECT within the XML-PARSE statement. The content string therefore must be either a literal or a host language variable. There is no reason, however, that the host language variable can't be loaded with a long string created by embedded SELECTs and/or other host language string manipulations.

The whitespace option tells SQL what to do with any empty space at the end of a string. Its value can be either STRIP WHITESPACE or PRESERVE WHITESPACE.

As a simple example, consider the following:

```
SELECT XMLPARSE
    (CONTENT 'Converting a literal to XML' STRIP WHITESPACE);
```

The output looks just like regular text because the interactive SQL command processor strips off the XML tags before displaying the result:

```
        xmlparse
----------------------------
Converting a literal to XML
```

XMLROOT

The XMLROOT function is a bit of a misnomer. Its definition says that it modifies an XML root node, but what it really does is create or modify an XML declaration at the very beginning of an XML document. The function has the following general syntax:

```
XMLROOT (XML_value, VERSION version, STANDALONE standalone_property)
```

The first parameter—*xml_value*—is the XML data for which you will be creating or modifying the prolog. You can then set its version (usually supplied as a literal string) and its standalone property.

The standalone property indicates whether all declarations needed for the XML document are contained within the document or whether declarations are contained in an external document. In most cases when you are using XML with a relational database, the standalone property will be set to *yes*.

The following example adds the prolog at the beginning of the XML, sets the version to 1.1, and the standalone property to *yes*—

```
SELECT XMLROOT (XMLPARSE (CONTENT '<content>abc</content>'),
    VERSION '1.1', STANDALONE YES);
```

—and produces the output

```
                        xmlroot
----------------------------------------------------------------
<?xml version="1.1" standalone="yes"?><content>abc</content>
```

XMLELEMENT

XMLELEMENT is one of two ways to generate content for an XML document. It has the following general syntax:

```
XMLELEMENT (NAME name_of_element,
    XMLATTRIBUTES (attribute_value AS attribute_name, …), content…)
```

Each element has a name that becomes the element's tag. Attributes are optional. The content may be

- A literal value (in quotes)
- Data from a database table
- Another XML element, typically generated with an embedded call to XMLELEMENT or XMLFOREST

As an example, let's create some XML that contains data about books (author, title, and ISBN):

```
SELECT XMLELEMENT (NAME "Books",
    XMLELEMENT (NAME "Author", author.author_last_first),
    XMLELEMENT (NAME "Title",work.title),
    XMLELEMENT (name "ISBN",book.isbn))
FROM author JOIN book JOIN work;
```

The function call is placed in a SELECT statement as one of the values that SELECT should return. The FROM clause identifies the tables from which data will be drawn. This particular example creates an XML element named *Books*. The contents of the element include three other elements—*Author, Title, ISBN*—each of which is created with an embedded call to XMLELEMENT. The SQL statement produces one element for each row retrieved by the query. In this case, the SELECT has no WHERE clause and therefore generates an element for every row in the joined table created by the FROM clause.

The output of this command can be found in Figure 26.5. Note that the spacing of the output has been adjusted by putting multiple tags on the same line so the output will take up less space. This isn't a problem because XML is text only; any spacing between tags is purely cosmetic.

```
<Books>      <Author>Bronte, Charlotte</Author>
      <Title>Jane Eyre</Title>
      <ISBN>978-1-11111-111-1</ISBN>      </Books>
<Books>      <Author>Bronte, Charlotte</Author>
      <Title>Jane Eyre</Title>
    <ISBN>978-1-11111-112-1</ISBN>      </Books>
<Books>      <Author>Bronte, Charlotte</Author>
      <Title>Villette</Title>
      <ISBN>978-1-11111-113-1</ISBN>      </Books>
<Books>      <Author>Doyle, Sir Arthur Conan</Author>
      <Title>Hound of the Baskervilles</Title>
      <ISBN>978-1-11111-114-1</ISBN>      </Books>
<Books>      <Author>Doyle, Sir Arthur Conan</Author>
      <Title>Hound of the Baskervilles</Title>
      <ISBN>978-1-11111-115-1</ISBN>      </Books>
<Books>      <Author>Doyle, Sir Arthur Conan</Author>
      <Title>Lost World, The</Title>
      <ISBN>978-1-11111-116-1</ISBN>      </Books>
<Books>      <Author>Doyle, Sir Arthur Conan</Author>
      <Title>Complete Sherlock Holmes</Title>
      <ISBN>978-1-11111-117-1</ISBN>      </Books>
<Books>      <Author>Doyle, Sir Arthur Conan</Author>
      <Title>Complete Sherlock Holmes</Title>
      <ISBN>978-1-11111-118-1</ISBN>      </Books>
<Books>      <Author>Twain, Mark</Author>
      <Title>Tom Sawyer</Title>
      <ISBN>978-1-11111-120-1</ISBN>      </Books>
<Books>      <Author>Twain, Mark</Author>
      <Title>Connecticut Yankee in King Arthur's Court, A</Title>
      <ISBN>978-1-11111-119-1</ISBN>      </Books>
```

■ **FIGURE 26.5** An XML fragment created with calls to XMLELEMENT (continues).

```
<Books>      <Author>Twain, Mark</Author>
    <Title>Tom Sawyer</Title>
    <ISBN>978-1-11111-121-1</ISBN>      </Books>
<Books>      <Author>Twain, Mark</Author>
    <Title>Adventures of Huckleberry Finn, The</Title>
    <ISBN>978-1-11111-122-1</ISBN>      </Books>
<Books>      <Author>Ludlum, Robert</Author>
    <Title>Matarese Circle, The</Title>
    <ISBN>978-1-11111-123-1</ISBN>      </Books>
<Books>      <Author>Ludlum, Robert</Author>
    <Title>Bourne Supremacy, The</Title>
    <ISBN>978-1-11111-124-1</ISBN>      </Books>
<Books>      <Author>Rand, Ayn</Author>
    <Title>Fountainhead, The</Title>
    <ISBN>978-1-11111-125-1</ISBN>      </Books>
<Books>      <Author>Rand, Ayn</Author>
    <Title>Fountainhead, The</Title>
    <ISBN>978-1-11111-126-1</ISBN>      </Books>
<Books>      <Author>Rand, Ayn</Author>
    <Title>Atlas Shrugged</Title>
    <ISBN>978-1-11111-127-1</ISBN>      </Books>
<Books>      <Author>Stevenson, Robert Louis</Author>
    <Title>Kidnapped</Title>
    <ISBN>978-1-11111-128-1</ISBN>      </Books>
<Books>      <Author>Stevenson, Robert Louis</Author>
    <Title>Kidnapped</Title>
    <ISBN>978-1-11111-129-1</ISBN>      </Books>
<Books>      <Author>Stevenson, Robert Louis</Author>
    <Title>Treasure Island</Title>
    <ISBN>978-1-11111-130-1</ISBN>      </Books>
<Books>      <Author>Barth, John</Author>
    <Title>Sot Weed Factor, The</Title>
    <ISBN>978-1-11111-131-1</ISBN>      </Books>
<Books>      <Author>Barth, John</Author>
    <Title>Lost in the Funhouse</Title>
    <ISBN>978-1-11111-132-1</ISBN>      </Books>
<Books>      <Author>Barth, John</Author>
    <Title>Giles Goat Boy</Title>
    <ISBN>978-1-11111-133-1</ISBN>      </Books>
<Books>      <Author>Herbert, Frank</Author>
    <Title>Dune</Title>
    <ISBN>978-1-11111-134-1</ISBN>      </Books>
<Books>      <Author>Asimov, Isaac</Author>
    <Title>Foundation</Title>
    <ISBN>978-1-11111-135-1</ISBN>      </Books>
<Books>      <Author>Asimov, Isaac</Author>
    <Title>Foundation</Title>
    <ISBN>978-1-11111-136-1</ISBN>      </Books>
<Books>      <Author>Asimov, Isaac</Author>
    <Title>Last Foundation</Title>
    <ISBN>978-1-11111-137-1</ISBN>      </Books>
```

■ **FIGURE 26.5** (*cont.*)

```
<Books>      <Author>Asimov, Isaac</Author>
      <Title>Foundation</Title>
      <ISBN>978-1-11111-138-1</ISBN>      </Books>
<Books>      <Author>Asimov, Isaac</Author>
      <Title>I, Robot</Title>
      <ISBN>978-1-11111-139-1</ISBN>      </Books>
<Books>      <Author>Funke, Cornelia</Author>
      <Title>Inkheart</Title>
      <ISBN>978-1-11111-140-1</ISBN>      </Books>
<Books>      <Author>Funke, Cornelia</Author>
      <Title>Inkdeath</Title>
      <ISBN>978-1-11111-141-1</ISBN>      </Books>
<Books>      <Author>Stephenson, Neal</Author>
      <Title>Anathem</Title>
      <ISBN>978-1-11111-142-1</ISBN>      </Books>
<Books>      <Author>Stephenson, Neal</Author>
      <Title>Snow Crash</Title>
      <ISBN>978-1-11111-143-1</ISBN>      </Books>
<Books>      <Author>Rand, Ayn</Author>
      <Title>Anthem</Title>
      <ISBN>978-1-11111-144-1</ISBN>      </Books>
<Books>      <Author>Rand, Ayn</Author>
      <Title>Anthem</Title>
      <ISBN>978-1-11111-145-1</ISBN>      </Books>
<Books>      <Author>Stephenson, Neal</Author>
      <Title>Cryptonomicon</Title>
      <ISBN>978-1-11111-146-1</ISBN>      </Books>
```

■ **FIGURE 26.5** (*cont.*)

XMLFOREST

The XMLFOREST function can be used to create elements that are part of a higher-level element. Its results are very similar to XMLELEMENT, although its syntax can be simpler than using multiple embedded XMLELEMENT calls. However, the result of XMLFOREST alone is not a valid XML document. We therefore often wrap a call to XMLELEMENT around XMLFOREST.

By itself, XMLFOREST has the following general syntax:

```
XMLFOREST (content AS element_name, …)
```

As an example, assume that we want to create an XML element for an inventory item, including the ISBN, asking price, and selling price. One way to code the element would be as follows:

```
SELECT XMLELEMENT (NAME "Inventory_item",
    XMLFOREST (volume.isbn, volume.asking_price,
        volume.selling_price)) "Volumes"
FROM volume
WHERE selling_price > 75;
```

Notice that the external function call is to XMLELEMENT to create the element named *inventory_item*. The content of the element is produced by a single call to XMLFOREST, which contains the three data values that are part of the inventory item element. Because there is no AS clause, the function uses the column names as the names of the data elements. You can find the output of the sample query in Figure 26.6.

```
<Inventory_item>
     <isbn>978-1-11111-111-1</isbn>
     <asking_price>175.00</asking_price>
     <selling_price>175.00</selling_price>        </Inventory_item>
<Inventory_item>
     <isbn>978-1-11111-133-1</isbn>
     <asking_price>300.00</asking_price>
<Inventory_item>
     <isbn>978-1-11111-144-1</isbn>
     <asking_price>80.00</asking_price>
     <selling_price>76.10</selling_price>         </Inventory_item>
<Inventory_item>
     <isbn>978-1-11111-121-1</isbn>
     <asking_price>110.00</asking_price>
     <selling_price>110.00</selling_price>        </Inventory_item>
<Inventory_item>
     <isbn>978-1-11111-121-1</isbn>
     <asking_price>110.00</asking_price>
     <selling_price>110.00</selling_price>        </Inventory_item>
<Inventory_item>
     <isbn>978-1-11111-130-1</isbn>
     <asking_price>150.00</asking_price>
     <selling_price>120.00</selling_price>        </Inventory_item>
<Inventory_item>
     <isbn>978-1-11111-126-1</isbn>
     <asking_price>110.00</asking_price>
     <selling_price>110.00</selling_price>        </Inventory_item>
<Inventory_item>
     <isbn>978-1-11111-139-1</isbn>
     <asking_price>200.00</asking_price>
     <selling_price>170.00</selling_price>        </Inventory_item>
<Inventory_item>
     <isbn>978-1-11111-133-1</isbn>
     <asking_price>125.00</asking_price>
     <selling_price>125.00</selling_price>        </Inventory_item>
<Inventory_item>
     <isbn>978-1-11111-130-1</isbn>
     <asking_price>200.00</asking_price>
     <selling_price>150.00</selling_price>        </Inventory_item>
```

■ **FIGURE 26.6** The results of using XMLFOREST to generate the contents of an XML attribute.

XMLATTRIBUTES

As you will remember from earlier in this chapter, an XML element can have attributes, data values that are part of the element tag. The XMLATTRIBUTES function is used to specify those attributes. Like XMLFOREST, it is most commonly used as part of an XMLELEMENT function call.

The function has the following general syntax:

XMLATTRIBUTES (*value* AS *attribute_name*)

If the attribute's value is a column in a database table, then the AS and the attribute name are optional. SQL will then use the column name as the attribute name.

As an example, let's create an XML element for books with selling prices of more than $75, the results of which appear in Figure 26.7. Notice that text values (eg, the ISBN) are in quotes.

```
SELECT XMLELEMENT (NAME "High_Priced",
    XMLATTRIBUTES (volume.isbn AS ISBN),
    XMLELEMENT (NAME "Asking_price", volume.asking_price),
    XMLELEMENT (NAME "Selling_price", volume.selling_price))
FROM volume
WHERE selling_price > 75;
```

```
<High_Priced isbn="978-1-11111-111-1">
     <Asking_price>175.00</Asking_price>
     <Selling_price>175.00</Selling_price>
</High_Priced>
<High_Priced isbn="978-1-11111-133-1">
     <Asking_price>300.00</Asking_price>
     <Selling_price>285.00</Selling_price>
</High_Priced>
<High_Priced isbn="978-1-11111-144-1">
     <Asking_price>80.00</Asking_price>
     <Selling_price>76.10</Selling_price>
</High_Priced>
<High_Priced isbn="978-1-11111-121-1">
     <Asking_price>110.00</Asking_price>
     <Selling_price>110.00</Selling_price>
</High_Priced>
<High_Priced isbn="978-1-11111-121-1">
     <Asking_price>110.00</Asking_price>
     <Selling_price>110.00</Selling_price>
</High_Priced>
```

■ **FIGURE 26.7 The results of using XMLATTRIBUTES to add attributes to an XML element (continues).**

```
<High_Priced isbn="978-1-11111-130-1">
    <Asking_price>150.00</Asking_price>
    <Selling_price>120.00</Selling_price></High_Priced>
<High_Priced isbn="978-1-11111-126-1">
    <Asking_price>110.00</Asking_price>
    <Selling_price>110.00</Selling_price>
</High_Priced>
<High_Priced isbn="978-1-11111-139-1">
    <Asking_price>200.00</Asking_price>
    <Selling_price>170.00</Selling_price>
</High_Priced>
<High_Priced isbn="978-1-11111-133-1">
    <Asking_price>125.00</Asking_price>
    <Selling_price>125.00</Selling_price>
</High_Priced>
<High_Priced isbn="978-1-11111-130-1">
    <Asking_price>200.00</Asking_price>
    <Selling_price>150.00</Selling_price>
</High_Priced>
```

■ **FIGURE 26.7** (*cont.*)

XMLCONCAT

The XML functions we have been discussing generate fragments of XML documents. To paste them together, you use the XMLCONCAT function. It has a relatively simple general syntax:

```
XMLCONCAT (XML_value, XML_value, …)
```

As an example, let's put a comment in front each of the elements that contain data about books with high selling prices:

```
SELECT XMLCONCAT (XMLCOMMENT ('This is a high-priced book'),
    XMLELEMENT (NAME "High_Priced",
        XMLATTRIBUTES (volume.isbn AS ISBN),
        XMLELEMENT (NAME "Asking_price", volume.asking_price),
        XMLELEMENT (NAME "Selling_price", volume.selling_price)))
FROM volume
WHERE selling_price > 75;
```

The results can be found in Figure 26.8. Line breaks have been added to make the result readable. Note, however, that SQL views each occurrence of the comment and the entire element as a single string of text and therefore inserts a line break only at the end of each element.

```
                                    xmlconcat
--------------------------------------------------------------------------
 <!--This is a high-priced book-->
     <High_x0020_Priced isbn="978-1-11111-111-1">
     <Asking_x0020_Price>175.00</Asking_x0020_Price>
     <Selling_x0020_Price>175.00</Selling_x0020_Price>
</High_x0020_Priced>
 <!--This is a high-priced book-->
     <High_x0020_Priced isbn="978-1-11111-133-1">
     <Asking_x0020_Price>300.00</Asking_x0020_Price>
     <Selling_x0020_Price>285.00</Selling_x0020_Price>
</High_x0020_Priced>
 <!--This is a high-priced book-->
     <High_x0020_Priced isbn="978-1-11111-144-1">
     <Asking_x0020_Price>80.00</Asking_x0020_Price>
     <Selling_x0020_Price>76.10</Selling_x0020_Price>
</High_x0020_Priced>
 <!--This is a high-priced book-->
     <High_x0020_Priced isbn="978-1-11111-121-1">
     <Asking_x0020_Price>110.00</Asking_x0020_Price>
     <Selling_x0020_Price>110.00</Selling_x0020_Price>
</High_x0020_Priced>
 <!--This is a high-priced book-->
     <High_x0020_Priced isbn="978-1-11111-121-1">
     <Asking_x0020_Price>110.00</Asking_x0020_Price>
     <Selling_x0020_Price>110.00</Selling_x0020_Price>
</High_x0020_Priced>
 <!--This is a high-priced book-->
     <High_x0020_Priced isbn="978-1-11111-130-1">
     <Asking_x0020_Price>150.00</Asking_x0020_Price>
     <Selling_x0020_Price>120.00</Selling_x0020_Price>
</High_x0020_Priced>
 <!--This is a high-priced book-->
     <High_x0020_Priced isbn="978-1-11111-126-1">
     <Asking_x0020_Price>110.00</Asking_x0020_Price>
     <Selling_x0020_Price>110.00</Selling_x0020_Price>
</High_x0020_Priced>
 <!--This is a high-priced book-->
     <High_x0020_Priced isbn="978-1-11111-139-1">
     <Asking_x0020_Price>200.00</Asking_x0020_Price>
     <Selling_x0020_Price>170.00</Selling_x0020_Price>
</High_x0020_Priced>
 <!--This is a high-priced book-->
     <High_x0020_Priced isbn="978-1-11111-133-1">
     <Asking_x0020_Price>125.00</Asking_x0020_Price>
     <Selling_x0020_Price>125.00</Selling_x0020_Price>
</High_x0020_Priced>
 <!--This is a high-priced book-->
     <High_x0020_Priced isbn="978-1-11111-130-1">
     <Asking_x0020_Price>200.00</Asking_x0020_Price>
     <Selling_x0020_Price>150.00</Selling_x0020_Price>
</High_x0020_Priced>
```

■ **FIGURE 26.8** The result of using XMLCONCAT to concatenate XML fragments.

Note: The x0020 that appears frequently in the output is the ASCII code for a blank.

The XML Data Type

You can declare a column in a table to be of type XML, just as you would with any other data type:

```
CREATE TABLE xmlstuff
    (seq_numb INT,
    xml_text XML,
    PRIMARY KEY (seq_numb));
```

The XML column can then be used to store fragments of XML or entire XML documents. However, doing so has several drawbacks:

- The contents of the column are not searchable with standard SQL commands.[2]
- The contents of the column cannot be used in predicates that require comparison operators such as > or =.
- The column cannot be indexed.

For that reason, tables that have XML columns need at least a unique sequence number to identify each row. You may also want to include a table that assigns keywords to each document, so there is some type of search capability. Such a table might be created with

```
CREATE TABLE keywords
    (seq_numb int,
    keyword char (30),
    PRIMARY KEY (seq_numb, keyword),
    FOREIGN KEY keywords2xmlstuff
        (seq_numb) REFERENCES xmlstuff);
```

As mentioned earlier in the discussion of XMLPARSE, you need to use that function to convert text into XML to store in an XML column. Because you can't generate an input string with a SELECT, the interactive INSERT is limited to XML fragments:

```
INSERT INTO xmlstuff
    VALUES (1, XMLPARSE
        (CONTENT 'This is a test' STRIP WHITE SPACE);
```

---

[2]Some current DBMSs support XQuery, a SQL extension that can be used to search XML data.

For complete document input, you will generally be working with an embedded SQL application.

If you want to look at the contents of an XML column, you can use an interactive SELECT. SQL strips the XML tags for output. The query

```
SELECT * FROM xmlstuff;
```

produces

```
 sequ_numb |     xml_text
-----------+----------------
         1 | this is a test
```

Note: You could store XML in a text column, tags and all. However, when you use an XML column, SQL will check the XML to see that it is well-formed.

XMLSERIALIZE

The XMLSERIALIZE function is essentially the opposite of XMLPARSE: it takes the contents of an XML column and converts it to a text string:

```
XMLSERIALIZE (type_indicator column_name AS character_type)
```

For example,

```
SELECT XMLSERIALIZE
    (DOCUMENT xmltext AS VARCHAR (256))
    FROM sql_stuff
    WHERE seq_numb = 16;
```

would extract the document from the row with the sequence number of 16, convert it to plain text (removing the tags), and display it on the screen. Because SQL removes the tags from interactive SELECT output, this function is particularly useful in an embedded SQL program.

For Further Reading

Fawcett, J., 2012. Beginning XML, fifth ed. Wrox.

Key, S., 2015. XML Programming Success in a Day: Beginner's Guide to Fast, Easy and Efficient Learning of XML Programming. CreativeSpace Independent Publishing Platform.

Ray, E.T., 2003. Learning XML, second ed. O'Reilly Media.

Walmsley, P., 2012. Definitive XML Schema, second ed. Prentice Hall.

Walmsley, P., 2015. XQUERY: Search Across a Variety of XML Data, second ed. O'Reilly Media.

Chapter 27

Object-Relational Databases

The relational data model has been a mainstay of business data processing for more than 30 years. Nothing has superseded it in the way the relational data model superseded the simple network data model. However, a newer data model—the object-oriented data model—has come into use as an alternative for some types of navigational data processing.

Note: To be completely accurate, the relational data model is the only data model that has a formal specification. The hierarchical data model and the OO data model do not. The closest thing the simple network data model has is the CODASYL specifications.

This chapter begins with an overview of some object-oriented concepts for readers who aren't familiar with the object-oriented paradigm. If you have object-oriented programming experience, then you can skip over the first parts of this chapter and begin reading with the section *The Object-Relational Data Model.*

The object-oriented paradigm was the brainchild of Dr Kristen Nygaard, a Norwegian who was attempting to write a computer program to model the behavior of ships, tides, and fjords. He found that the interactions were extremely complex and realized that it would be easier to write the program if he separated the three types of program elements and let each one model its own behavior against each of the others.

The object-oriented programming languages in use today (most notably C ++, Java, and JavaScript) are a direct outgrowth of Nygaard's early work. The way in which objects are used in databases today is an extension of object-oriented programming.

Note: This is in direct contrast to the relational data model, which was designed specifically to model data relationships, although much of its theoretical foundations are found in mathematical set theory.

Getting Started: Object-Orientation without Computing

To understand the role of objects in relational databases, you must first understand the object-oriented paradigm as it is used in object-oriented programming and pure object-oriented databases. The easiest way to do so is to begin with an example that has absolutely nothing to with programming at all.

Assume that you have a teenage daughter (or sister, whichever is more appropriate) named Jane and that your family is going to take a long car trip. Like many teens, Jane is less than thrilled about a trip with the family and, in particular, with spending so much time with her 12-year-old brother, especially since her parents have declared the trip a holiday from hand-held electronics. In self-defense, Jane needs something to keep her brother busy so he won't bother her as she reads while her parents are driving. She therefore decides to write up some instructions for playing solitaire games for him.

The first set of instructions is for the most common solitaire game, Klondike. As you can see in Figure 27.1, the deal involves seven piles of cards of increasing depth, with the top card turned over. The rest of the deck remains in the draw pile. Jane decides to break the written instructions into two main parts: information about the game and questions her brother might ask. She therefore produces instructions that look something like Figure 27.2. She also attached the illustration of the game's deal.

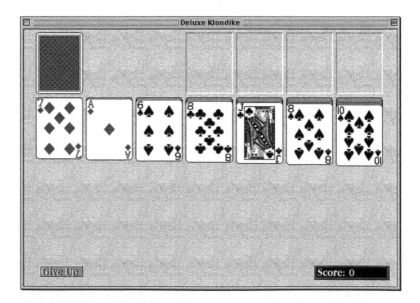

■ FIGURE 27.1 The starting layout for Klondike.

```
┌─────────────────────────────────────────────────────────────────────┐
│ Information about the game                                            │
│       Name: Klondike                                                  │
│       Illustration: See next page                                     │
│       Decks: One                                                      │
│       Dealing: Deal from left to right                                │
│               First pass: First card face up six cards down.          │
│               Second pass: First card face up on top of pile #2, five │
│                     cards down on remaining piles.                    │
│               Third pass: First card face up on top of pile #3; four  │
│                     cards down on remaining piles.                    │
│               …repeat pattern for total of seven passes.              │
│               Place remaining cards in draw pile, face down.          │
│       Playing: One or two cards can be turned from the draw pile      │
│               at a time. As encountered, put aces above layout. Build up │
│               from aces in suits. Build down on the deal, opposite suit │
│               colors. Can move from the middle of a stack moving card │
│               and all cards built below it.                           │
│               Move only kings into empty spots on the layout.         │
│               If turning one card, make only one pass through the draw │
│                     Pile.                                             │
│               If turning three cards, make as many passes as you like │
│                     through the draw pile.                            │
│       Winning: All cards built on top of their aces.                  │
│ Questions to Ask                                                      │
│       What is the name of the game?                                   │
│               Read Name section.                                      │
│       How many decks do I need?                                       │
│               Read Decks section.                                     │
│       What does the layout look like?                                 │
│               Read Illustration section.                              │
│       How do I deal the game?                                         │
│               Read Dealing section.                                   │
│       How do I play the game?                                         │
│               Read Playing section.                                   │
│       How do I know when I've won?                                    │
│               Read Winning section.                                   │
└─────────────────────────────────────────────────────────────────────┘
```

■ FIGURE 27.2 Instructions for playing Klondike.

The next game she tackles is Canfield. Like Klondike, it is played with one deck, but the deal and play are slightly different (see Figure 27.3). Jane uses the same pattern for the instructions as she did for Klondike because it cuts down the amount of writing she has to do (see Figure 27.4).

And finally, just to make sure her brother doesn't get too bored, Jane prepares instructions for Forty Thieves (see Figure 27.5). This game uses two decks of cards and plays in a very different way from the other two games (see Figure 27.6). Nonetheless, preparing the instructions for the third game is fairly easy because she has the template for the instructions down pat.

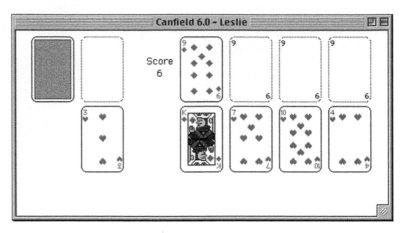

■ FIGURE 27.3 The starting deal for Canfield.

```
Information about the game
        Name: Canfield
        Illustration: See next page
        Decks: One
        Dealing: Deal four cards face up.
                Place one additional card above the first four as the
                        starting card for building suits.
                The remaining cards stay in the draw pile.
        Playing: Turn one card at a time, going through the deck as many
                        times as desired.
                Build down from deal, opposite suit colors.
                Can move cards from the middle of stack, moving card and
                        all cards built below it.
                Place cards of the same value as the initial foundation
                        card above the deal as encountered.
                Build up in suits from the foundation cards.
                Any card can be placed in any empty space in the deal.
        Winning: All cards built on top of the foundation cards.
Questions to Ask
        What is the name of the game?
                Read Name section.
        How many decks do I need?
                Read Decks section.
        What does the layout look like.
                Read Illustration section.
        How do I deal the game?
                Read Dealing section.
        How do I play the game?
                Read Playing section.
        How do I know when I've won?
                Read Winning section.
```

■ FIGURE 27.4 Instructions for playing Canfield.

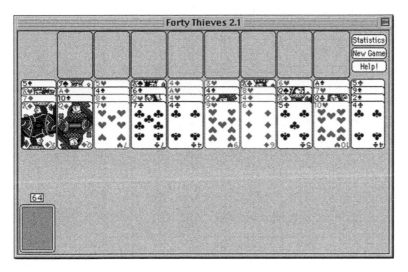

■ FIGURE 27.5 **The starting layout for Forty Thieves.**

```
Information about the game
     Name: Forty Thieves
     Illustration: See next page
     Decks: Two
     Dealing: Make 10 piles of four cards, all face up.
          Jog cards so that the values of all cards can be seen.
          Remaining cards stay in the draw pile.
     Playing: Turn one card at a time.
          Make only one pass through the draw pile.
          Build down in suits.
          Only the top card of a stack can be moved.
          As aces are encountered, place at top of deal and build up
               in suits from the aces.
          Any card can be moved into any open space in the layout.
     Winning: All cards built on top of their aces.
Questions to Ask
     What is the name of the game?
          Read Name section.
     How many decks do I need?
          Read Decks section.
     What does the layout look like.
          Read Illustration section.
     How do I deal the game?
          Read Dealing section.
     How do I play the game?
          Read Playing section.
     How do I know when I've won?
          Read Winning section.
```

■ FIGURE 27.6 **Instructions for playing Forty Thieves.**

After completing three sets of instructions, it becomes clear to Jane that having the template for the instructions makes the process extremely easy. Jane can use the template to organize any number of sets of instructions for playing solitaire. All she has to do is make a copy of the template and fill in the values for the information about the game.

Basic OO Concepts

Objects

If someone were writing an object-oriented computer program to manage the instructions for playing solitaire, each game would be known as an *object*. It is a self-contained element used by the program, conceptually similar to an instance of an entity. It has things that it knows about itself: its name, the illustration of the layout, the number of decks needed to play, how to deal, how to play, and how to determine when the game is won. In object-oriented terms, the values that an object stores about itself are known as *attributes* or *variables* or, occasionally, *properties*.

Each solitaire game object also has some things it knows how to do: explain how to deal, explain how to play, explain how to identify a win, and so on. In object-oriented programming terminology, actions that objects know how to perform are called *methods*, *services*, *functions*, *procedures*, or *operations*.

Note: It is unfortunate, but there is no single accepted terminology for the object-oriented paradigm. Each programming language or DBMS chooses which terms it will use. You therefore need to recognize all of the terms that might be used to describe the same thing.

An object is very security-minded. It typically keeps the things it knows about itself private and releases that information only through a method whose purpose is to share data values (an *accessor method)*. For example, a user or program using one of the game objects cannot access the contents of the Dealing variable directly. Instead, the user or program must execute the How Do I Deal the Game? method to see that data.

Objects also keep private the details of the procedures for the things they know how to do, but they make it easy for someone to ask them to perform those actions. Users or programs cannot see what is inside the methods. They see only the result of the method. This characteristic of objects is known as *information hiding* or *encapsulation*.

An object presents a public interface to other objects that might use it. This provides other objects with a way to ask for data values or for actions to be performed. In the example of the solitaire games, the questions that Jane's little brother can ask are a game's public interface. The instructions below each question represent the procedure to be used to answer the question. A major benefit of data encapsulation is that as long as the object's public interface remains the same, you can change the details of the object's methods without needing to inform any other objects that might be using those methods. For example, the card game objects currently tell the user to "read" the contents of an attribute. However, there is no reason that the methods couldn't be changed to tell the user to "print" the contents of an attribute. The user would still access the method in the same way, but the way in which the method operates would be slightly different.

An object requests data or an action by sending a *message* to another object. For example, if you were writing a computer program to manage the instructions for solitaire games, the program (an object in its own right) could send a message to the game object asking the game object to display the instructions for dealing the game. Because the actual procedures of the method are hidden, your program would ask for the instruction display and then you would see the instructions on the screen. However, you would not need to worry about the details of how the screen display was produced. That is the job of the game object rather than the object that is asking the game to do something.

An object-oriented program is made up a collection of objects, each of which has attributes and methods. The objects interact by sending messages to one another. The trick, of course, is figuring out which objects a program needs and the attributes and methods those objects should have.

Classes

The template on which the solitaire game instructions are based is the same for each game. Without data, it might be represented as in Figure 27.7. The nice thing about this template is that it provides a consistent way of organizing all the characteristics of a game. When you want to create the instructions for another game, you make a copy of the template and "fill in the blanks." You write the data values for the attributes. The procedures that make up the answers to the questions someone might ask about the game have already been completed.

In object-oriented terminology, the template on which similar objects like the solitaire game objects are based is known as a *class*. When a program creates an object from a class, it provides data for the object's variables. The object can then use the methods that have been written for its class. All of the objects created from the same class share the same procedures for their methods. They also have the same types of data, but the values for the data may differ, for example, just as the names of the solitaire games are different.

```
Information about the game
      Name:
      Illustration:
      Decks:
      Dealing:
      Playing:
      Winning:
Questions to Ask
      What is the name of the game?
            Read Name section.
      How many decks do I need?
            Read Decks section.
      What does the layout look like.
            Read Illustration section.
      How do I deal the game?
            Read Dealing section.
      How do I play the game?
            Read Playing section.
      How do I know when I've won?
            Read Winning section.
```

■ FIGURE 27.7 The solitaire game instruction template.

A class is also a data type. In fact, a class is an implementation of what is known as an *abstract data type*, which is just another term for a user-defined data type. The implication of a class being a data type is that you can use a class as the data type of an attribute in a relation.

Suppose, for example, you were developing a class to handle data about the employees in your organization. The attributes of the class might include the employee ID, the first name, the last name, and the address. The address itself is made up of a street, city, state, and zip. Therefore, you would probably create an address class with those attributes and then, rather than duplicating those attributes in the employee class, simply indicate that an object of the employee class will include an object created from the address class to contain the employee's address.

Types of Classes

There are three major types of classes used in an object-oriented program:

■ *Control classes*: Control classes neither manage data nor have visible output. Instead, they control the operational flow of a program. For example, *application classes* represent the programs themselves. In most cases, each program creates only one object from an application class. The application class's job includes starting the execution of the program, detecting menu selections (or other user interface events), and executing the correct program code to satisfy the user's requests.

- *Entity classes*: Entity classes are used to create objects that manage data. The solitaire game class, for example, is an entity class. Classes for people, tangible objects, and events (for example, business meetings) are entity classes. Most object-oriented programs have at least one entity class from which many objects are created. In fact, in its simplest sense, the object-oriented data model is built from the representation of relationships among objects created from entity classes.
- *Interface classes*: Interface classes handle the input and output of information. For example, if you are working with a graphic user interface, then each window and menu used by the program is an object created from an interface class.

In an object-oriented program, entity classes do not do their own input and output (I/O). Keyboard input is handled by interface objects that collect data and send it to entity objects for storage and processing. Screen and printed output is formatted by interface objects that get data for display from entity objects. When an entity object becomes part of a database, the DBMS takes care of the file I/O; the rest of the I/O is handled by application programs or DBMS utilities.

Why is it so important to keep data manipulation separate from I/O? Wouldn't it be simpler to let the entity object manage its own I/O? It might be simpler in the short run, but if you decided to change a screen layout, you would need to modify the entity class. If you keep them separate, then data manipulation procedures are independent of data display. You can change one without affecting the other. In a large program, this can not only save you a lot of time, but also help you avoid programming errors. In a database environment, the separation of I/O and data storage becomes especially critical because you do not want to modify data storage each time you decide to modify the look and feel of a program.

Many object-oriented programs also use a fourth type of class: a *container* class. Container classes exist to "contain," or manage, multiple objects created from the same class. Because they gather objects together, they are also known as *aggregations*. For example, if you had a program that handled the instructions for playing solitaire, then that program would probably have a container class that organized all the individual card game objects. The container class would keep the objects in some order, list them for you, and probably search through them as well. Many pure object-oriented DBMSs require container classes, known as *extents*, to provide access to all objects created from the same class. However, as you will see, container classes are not used when objects are integrated into a relational database.

Types of Methods

Several types of methods are common to most classes, including the following:

- *Constructors*: A constructor is a method that has the same name as the class. It is executed whenever an object is created from the class. A constructor, therefore, usually contains instructions to initialize an object's variables in some way.
- *Destructors*: A destructor is a method that is executed when an object is destroyed. Not all object-oriented programming languages support destructors, which are usually used to release system resources (for example, main memory allocated by the object). Java, in particular, does not use destructors because it cleans up memory by itself.
- *Accessors*: An accessor, also known as a *get method*, returns the value of a private attribute to another object. This is the typical way in which external objects gain access to encapsulated data.
- *Mutators*: A mutator, or *set method*, stores a new value in an attribute. This is the typical way in which external objects can modify encapsulated data.

The remaining methods defined for a class depend on the specific type of class, and the specific behaviors it needs to perform.

Method Overloading

One of the characteristics of a class is its ability to contain *overloaded* methods, methods that have the same name but require different data to operate. Because the data are different, the public interfaces of the methods are distinct.

As an example, assume that a human relations program has a container class named AllEmployees that aggregates all objects created from the Employee class. Programs that use the AllEmployees class create one object from the class and then relate all employee objects to the container using some form of program data structure.

To make the container class useful, there must be some way to locate specific employee objects. You might want to search by the employee ID number, by first and last name, or by telephone number. The AllEmployees class, therefore, contains three methods named "find." One of the three requires an integer (the employee number) as input, the second requires two strings (the first and last name), and the third requires a single string (the phone number). Although the methods have the same name, their public interfaces are different because the combination of the name and the required input data is distinct.

Many classes have overloaded constructors. One might accept interactive input, another might read input from a file, and a third might get its data by copying data from another object (a *copy constructor*). For example, most object-oriented environments have a Date class that supports initializing a date object with three integers (day, month, year), the current system date, another Date object, and so on.

The benefit of method overloading is that the methods present a consistent interface to the programmer. In the case of our example of the AllEmployees container class, whenever a programmer wants to locate an employee, he or she knows to use a method named "find." Then the programmer just uses whichever of the three types of data he or she happens to have. The object-oriented program locates the correct method by using the entire public interface (its *signature*), made up of the name and the required input data.

Class Relationships

The classes in an object-oriented environment aren't always independent. The basic object-oriented paradigm has two major ways to relate objects, distinct from any logical data relationships that might be included in a pure object-oriented database: inheritance and composition.

Inheritance

As a developer or database designer is working on an object-oriented project, he or she may run into situations where there is a need for similar—but not identical—classes. If these classes are related in a general to specific manner, then the developer can take advantage of one of the major features of the object-oriented paradigm, known as *inheritance*.

Inheriting Attributes

To see how inheritance works, assume that you are writing a program (or developing a database) to manage a pet shop. One of the entity classes you will use is Animal, which will describe the living creatures sold by the shop. The data that describe objects created from the Animal class include the English and Latin names of the animal, the animal's age, and the animal's gender. However, the rest of the data depend on what type of animal is being represented. For example, for reptiles, you want to know the length of the animal, but for mammals, you want to know the weight. And for fish, you don't care about the weight or length, but you do want to know the color. All the animals sold by the pet shop share some data, yet have pieces of data that are specific to certain subgroups.

You could diagram the relationship as in Figure 27.8. The Animal class provides the data common to all types of animals. The subgroups—Mammals, Reptiles, and Fish—*add* the data specific to themselves. They don't need to repeat the common data because they *inherit* them from Animal. In other words, Mammals, Reptiles, and Fish all include the four pieces of data that are part of Animal.

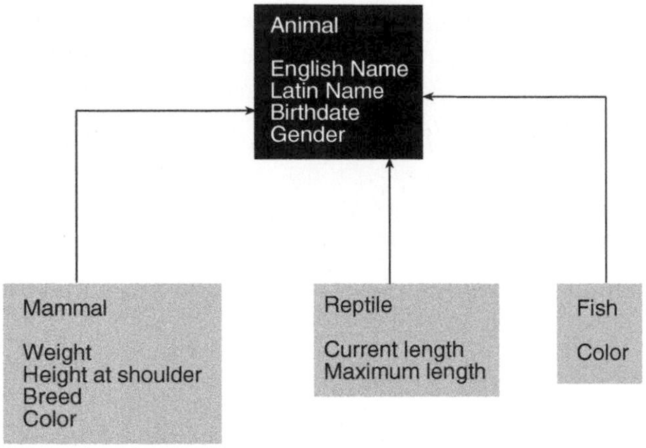

■ FIGURE 27.8   The relationship of classes for an object-oriented environment for a pet shop.

If you look closely at Figure 27.8, you'll notice that the lines on the arrows go from the subgroups to Animal. This is actually contrary to what is happening: The data from Animal are flowing down the lines into the subgroups. Unfortunately, the direction of the arrows is dictated by convention, even though it may seem counterintuitive.

In object-oriented terminology, the subgroups are known as *subclasses* or *derived classes*. The Animal class is a *superclass* or *base class*.

The trick to understanding inheritance is to remember that subclasses represent a more specific occurrence of their superclass. The relationships between a base class and its derived classes therefore can be expressed using the phrase "is a":

- A mammal is an animal.
- A reptile is an animal.
- A fish is an animal.

If the "is a" phrasing does not make sense in a given situation, then you are not looking at inheritance. As an example, assume that you are designing an object-oriented environment for the rental of equipment at a ski rental shop. You create a class for a generic merchandise item, and then subclasses for the specific types of items being rented, as in the top four rectangles in Figure 27.9. Inheritance works properly here because skis are a specific type of merchandise item, as well as boots and poles.

However, you run into trouble when you begin to consider the specific items being rented and the customer doing the renting (the renter). Although there is a logical database-style relationship between a renter and an item being rented, inheritance does not work because the "is a" test fails. A rented item is not a renter!

The situation with merchandise items and rental inventory is more complex. The Merchandise Item, Skis, Boots, and Poles classes represent descriptions of types of merchandise, but not physical inventory. For example, the ski shop may have many pairs of one type of ski in inventory and many pairs of boots of the same type, size, and width. Therefore, what is being rented is individual inventory items, represented by the Item Rented class. A given inventory item is either skis, boots, or poles. It can only be *one*, not all three as shown in Figure 27.9. Therefore, an item rented is not a pair of skis, a pair of boots, and a set of poles. (You also have the problem of having no class that can store the size or length of an item.)

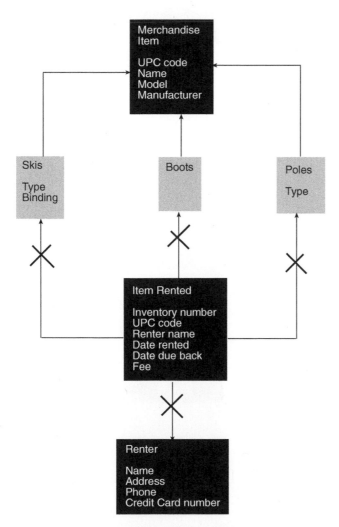

■ FIGURE 27.9 Inheritance and no inheritance in an object-oriented environment for a ski equipment rental.

The solution to the problem is to create a separate "rented item" class for each type of merchandise, as in Figure 27.10. When you are looking at this diagram, be sure to pay attention to the direction of the arrows. The physical layout of the diagram does not correspond to the direction of the inheritance. Remember that, by convention, the arrows point from the derived class to the base class.

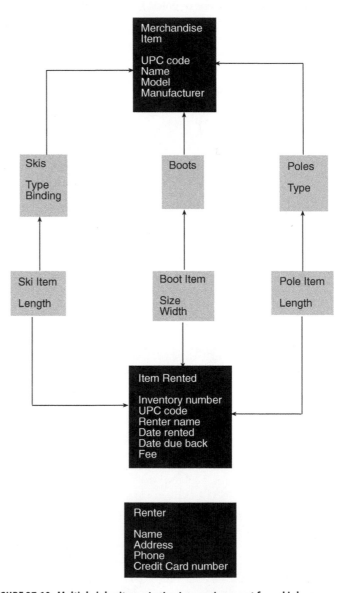

■ FIGURE 27.10 Multiple inheritance in the data environment for a ski shop.

The Ski Item class inherits information about the type of item it is from the Skis class. It also inherits information about an item being rented from the Item Rented class. A ski item "is a" pair of skis; a ski item "is a" rented item as well. Now the design of the classes passes the "is a" test for appropriate inheritance. (Note that it also gives you a class that can contain information such as the length and size of a specific inventory item.) The Renter class does not participate in the inheritance hierarchy at all.

Multiple Inheritance

When a class inherits from more than one base class, you have *multiple inheritance*. The extent to which multiple inheritance is supported in programming languages and DBMSs varies considerably from one product to another.

Abstract Classes

Not every class in an inheritance hierarchy is necessarily used to create objects. For example, in Figure 27.10, it is unlikely that any objects are ever created from the Merchandise Item or Item Rented classes. These classes are present simply to provide the common attributes and methods that their derived classes share.

Such classes are known as *abstract*, or *virtual*, classes. In contrast, classes from which objects are created are known as *concrete* classes.

Note: Many computer scientists use the verb "instantiate" to mean "creating an object from a class." For example, you could say that abstract classes are never instantiated. However, I find that term rather contrived (although not quite as bad as saying "we will now motivate the code" to mean we will now explain the code) and prefer to use the more direct "create an object from a class."

Inheriting Methods: Polymorphism

In general, methods are inherited by subclasses from their superclass. A subclass can use its base class's methods as its own. However, in some cases, it may not be possible to write a generic method that can be used by all subclasses. For example, assume that the ski rental shop's Merchandise Item class has a method named printCatalogEntry, the intent of which is to print a properly formatted entry for each distinct type of merchandise item. The subclasses of Merchandise Item, however, have attributes not shared by all subclasses and the printCatalogEntry method therefore must work somewhat differently for each subclass.

To solve the problem, the ski rental shop can take advantage of *polymorphism*, the ability to write different bodies for methods of the same name that belong to classes in the same inheritance hierarchy. The Merchandise Item class includes a *prototype* for the printCatalogEntry method, indicating just the method's pubic interface. There is no body for the method, no specifications of how the method is to perform its work (a *virtual method*). Each subclass then redefines the method, adding the program instructions necessary to execute the method.

The beauty of polymorphism is that a programmer can expect methods of the same name and same type of output for all the subclasses of the same base class. However, each subclass can perform the method according to its own needs. Encapsulation hides the details from all objects outside the class hierarchy.

Note: It is very easy to confuse polymorphism and overloading. Just keep in mind that overloading applies to methods of the same class that have the same name but different signatures, whereas polymorphism applies to several subclasses of the same base class that have methods with the same signature but different implementations.

Composition

Inheritance can be described as a general–specific relationship. In contrast, *composition* is a whole–part relationship. It specifies that one class is a component of another and is often read as "has a."

To help you understand how composition can be used, let's assume that the ski rental shop wants to offer packages of items for rent (skis, boots, and poles). The packages will come in three qualities—good, better, and best—based on the retail value of the items in the package.

As you can see in Figure 27.11, each package contains three types of merchandise items, so the package class "has a" boot, "has a" pole, and "has a" ski. An object created from this class would be used to indicate which types of items could be rented as a bundle. In contrast, the rented package class contains actual rental items and therefore indicates which specific inventory items have been rented together.

Some pure object-oriented DBMSs take composition to the extreme. They provide simple data types such as integers, real numbers, characters, and Booleans. Everything else in the database—even strings—is built by creating classes from these simple data types, using those classes to build more complex classes, and so on.

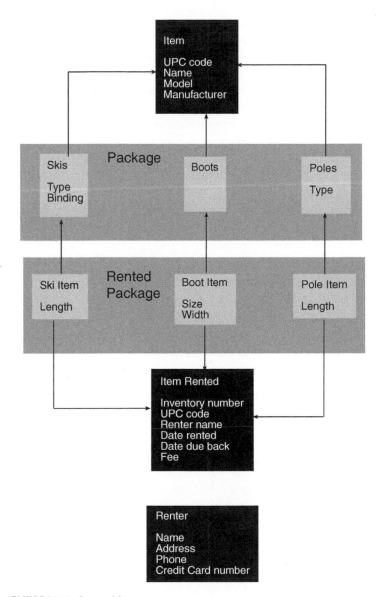

■ FIGURE 27.11   Composition.

Benefits of Object-Orientation

There are several reasons why the object-oriented paradigm has become so pervasive in programming. Among the perceived benefits are the following:

■ An object-oriented program consists of modular units that are independent of one another. These units can therefore be reused in multiple programs, saving development time. For example, if you have a well-debugged employee class, you can use it in any of your business programs that require data about employees.

- As long as a class's public interface remains unchanged, the internals of the class can be modified as needed without requiring any changes to the programs that use the class. This can significantly speed up program modification. It can also make program modification more reliable, as it cuts down on many unexpected side effects of program changes.

- An object-oriented program separates the user interface from data handling, making it possible to modify one independent of the other.

- Inheritance adds logical structure to a program by relating classes in a general to specific manner, making the program easier to understand and therefore easier to maintain.

Where Objects Work Better Than Relations

There are some database environments—especially those involving a great deal of inheritance—in which object-orientation is easier to implement than a relational design. To see why this is so, let's look at a hobby environment that just happens to be one of the best examples of the situation in question that I've ever encountered.

The database catalogs Yu-Gi-Oh cards (one of those animé related trading card games). The collector for whom this database and its application were developed has thousands of cards, some of which are duplicates. They are stored in three binders. Within each binder there may be several sections; the pages are numbered within each section.

There are three major types of cards: monsters, spell, and traps. The monster card in Figure 27.12 is fairly typical. Notice that it has a title, an "attribute" at the top right, a "level" (count the circles below the name), an "edition" (first, limited, or other), a set designation, a type (and optionally two subtypes), a description, attack points, and defense points. At the bottom left, there may be a code number, which is missing from some of the early cards.

A card with the same name may appear in many sets and the same set may have more than one card of the same name. What distinguishes them is their "rarity," determined by how the title is printed (black or white for common cards and silver or gold for rare cards) and how the image is printed (standard color printing or holofoil printing). There are a variety of combinations of printing to generate common, rare, super rare, ultra rare, and ultimate rare cards.

Note: If you want an interesting challenge before you see the relational design for this database, try to figure out the primary key for a card!

Most cards can be used for game play, but some have been banned from specific types of games. Others have caveats ("rulings") attached to them by the game's governing board that affect how the card can be used in a game.

■ FIGURE 27.12 A typical Yu-Gi-Oh monster card.

Spell cards that, as you might expect, can be used in the game to cast spells, share a number of attributes with the monster card, but don't have things such as type and subtypes. The third type of card, a trap, also shares some attributes with monsters, but is missing others and has a property that is unique to this type of card. Spells also have properties, but the list of possible properties differs between spells and traps.

You can find an ER diagram for the card database in Figure 27.13. As you might have guessed, there is an entity for the card, which has three subclasses, one for each specific type of card. There are also many holdings for each card.

To design the relational database, we create one relation for each entity, including the superclass (in this example, Card) and its subclasses (Monster card, Trap card, and Spell card). With an object-oriented DMBS, we would create objects only from the subclasses; no object would ever be created from the superclass. The subclasses "inherit" the attributes of their parent. For the relational database, we have to do that manually, using some type of primary key–foreign key relationship to connect the subclass tables to the parent table. Differences in where cards of a given name appear and how they are printed are handled by Holdings. Therefore, the design of the card database looks like this:

```
Card (InternalCardNUMB, Attribute, Banned?, CardDescription?,
    CardImage, CardName, CardNumber, CardType, Count, Limit,
    Ruling)

Monster card (InternalCardNumb, ATK, DEF, Level,
    MonsterSubtype1, MonsterSubtype2, MonsterType)

Trap card (InternalCardNumb, TrapType)

Spell card (InternalCardNumb, SpellType)

Holdings (InternalCardNumb, Code, Edition, Holofoil?,
    NamePrint, NumberOwned, Binder, Page, Section, Slot)
```

Why have both the trap and spell card relations if they have exactly the same attributes? At the current time, they could certainly be maintained in one relation. However, there are several reasons to keep them separate. First, there is no way to guarantee that they will always have the same attributes. If they are separated from the start, it will be easier to add attributes to one or the other if needed at some later date.

Second, the major reason this type of design doesn't perform as well as it might is because the details about a card always need to be looked up in another relation, joining on the internal card number. If we keep spell and trap data separate, the relations will remain smaller, and the joins will perform better.

Note: Here's the answer to the primary key challenge: A Holding actually represents one or more physical cards in the inventory. It has a name

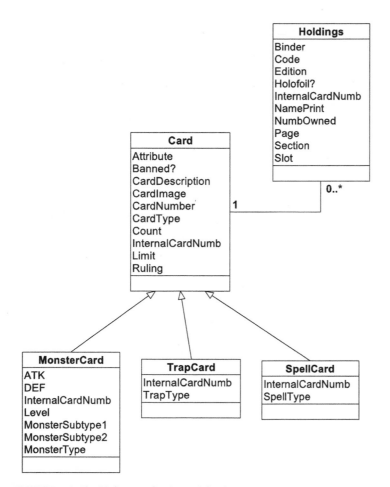

FIGURE 27.13 The ER diagram for the card database.

(represented by the internal card number) and a set designation. When cards of the same name are printed in different ways in the same set, they have different set designations. Therefore, the concatenation of the internal card number and the set designation uniquely identifies a card (although not a physical card in the inventory, given that there may be duplicate cards in the inventory). The only other alternative is to assign unique inventory numbers to each physical card and to use them. For some collectors, this may make sense, given that they would want to track the condition of each and every card.

There is an alternative design for this type of database: Rather than use one relation for each entity, create only a single relation in which many attributes may be null, depending on the type of card. Such a relation might look like this:

```
Card (InternalCardNumb, Attribute, Banned?, CardDescription,
      CardImage, CardName, CardNumber, CardType, Count,
      Limit, Ruling, ATK, DEF, Level, MonsterSubtype1,
      MonsterSubtype2, MonsterType, TrapType, spellType)
```

The CardType attribute indicates which of the type-specific attributes should have data. For example, if CardType contained "M" for Monster, you would expect to find data in the ATK, DEF, and level attributes but not the spell type or trap type. The supposed benefit of this design is that you avoid the joins to combine the separate relations of the earlier design. However, when a DBMS retrieves a row from this relation, it pulls in the entire row, empty fields and all. Practically, in a performance sense, you haven't gained much, and you're stuck with a design that can waste disk space.

Note: Personally, I prefer the multiple relation design because it's cleaner, wastes less space, and is much more flexible as the design of the relations need to change over time.

A pure-object oriented design for the same database would include the five entity classes, although the Card class would be an abstract class. It would also include a class to aggregate all objects created from subclasses of the Card class, letting users handle all cards, regardless of type, as a single type of object. The nature of these data—the major need for inheritance—suggests that an object-oriented database may well perform better than a relational database.

Limitations of Pure Object-Oriented DBMSs

When object-oriented DBMSs first appeared in the 1980s, some people predicted that they would replace relational DBMSs. That has not occurred for a number of reasons:

- Not all database environments can be represented efficiently by an object-oriented design.
- When implemented in a DBMS, object-oriented schemas are significantly more difficult to modify than relational schemas.

- There are no standards for object-oriented DBMSs, which means that each product has its own way of querying a database.
- Most object DBMSs do not have interactive query languages, which means that there is little support for ad-hoc queries.
- Because there are no standards for object-oriented DBMSs, moving from one DBMS to another often means redoing everything, from the design to application programs.

The Object-Relational Data Model

The *object-relational* (OR) data model—one of those known as *post-relational*—is a combination of the relational data model and some of the object-oriented concepts that—in the opinion of some database theorists and users—make up for shortcomings in the relational data model. The purpose of this discussion is to help you understand how OR designs differ from pure relational designs. With that in hand, you will be able to understand the strengths and weaknesses of SQL's support for object-related structures that are discussed later in this chapter.[1]

ER Diagrams for Object-Relational Designs

The Information Engineering, or IE, type of ER diagram does not lend itself to the inclusion of objects because it has no way to represent a class. Therefore, when we add objects to a relational database, we have to use another ERD style.

Although there are many techniques for object-oriented ERDs, one of the most commonly used is the Unified Modeling Language (UML). When used to depict a post-relational database design, UML looks a great deal like the IE style, but indicates relationships in a different way.

An example of an ER diagram using UML can be found in Figure 27.14. This design is of a purely object-oriented database and includes some elements that therefore won't appear in a hybrid design. It has been included here to give you an overview of UML so that you can better understand the portions of the modeling tool that we will be using later in this chapter.

---

[1]There have been some DBMSs that use only an object-oriented data model. However, over time they have not had significant market penetration. For more information, see "Whatever Happened to Object-Oriented Databases" (http://leavcom.com/articles/db_08_00.htm).

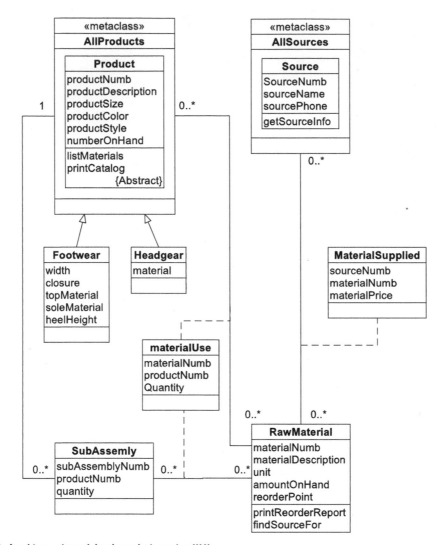

■ FIGURE 27.14 An object-oriented database design using UML.

The basic features of UML include the following:

■ A regular class is represented by a rectangle, divided into three parts (name, attributes, procedures).

■ An aggregate class (a *metaclass* in the diagram)—a class that collects all objects of a given class—is represented by a rectangle containing its name and the rectangles of the classes whose objects it aggregates. For example, in Figure 27.14, the Product and Source classes are within their aggregate classes, AllProducts and AllSources, respectively.

■ Relationships between entities are shown with lines with plain ends. The cardinality of a relationship is represented as *n*, *n..n*, or *n..**.

For example, if the cardinality is 1, it is simply written as 1. If the cardinality is 0 or more, it appears as 0..*; 1 or more appears as 1..*. Notice in Figure 27.14 that there are several direct many-to-many relationships, shown with 0..* at either end of the association line.

- Inheritance is shown by a line with an open arrow pointing toward the base class. In Figure 27.14, the Footwear and Headgear classes have such arrows pointing toward Product.

- What we call composite entities in a relational database are known as *association classes*. They are connected to the relationship to which they apply with a dashed line. As you can see in Figure 27.14, the MaterialSupplied and MaterialUse classes are each connected to at least one many-to-many relationship by the required dashed line.

In addition to the basic features shown in Figure 27.14, UML diagrams can include any of the following:

- An attribute can include information about its visibility (public, protected, or private), data type, default value, and domain. In Figure 27.15, for example, you can see four classes and the data types of their attributes. Keep in mind that, in an object-oriented environment, data types can be other classes. Therefore, the Source class uses an object of the TelephoneNumber class for its phoneNumber attribute, and an object of the Address class for its sourceAddress attribute. In turn, Source, Address, and TelephoneNumber all contain attributes that are objects of the String class.

String
length: INT theString: CHAR (256)
setString(char [ ]) getString(): String getLength(): INT

TelephoneNumber
areaCode: String exchange: String number: String
displayNumber() setPhoneNumber(String, String, String)

Address
street: String city: String state: String zip: String
displayAddress() getZip(): String getState(): String setStreet(char [ ]) setCity(char [ ]) setZip(char [ ])

Source
sourceNumb: INT sourceName: STRING sourcePhone: TelephoneNumber sourceAddress: Address
getSourceInfo(): String setName(char [ ]) setPhone(TelephoneNumber *) setAddress(Address *)

■ **FIGURE 27.15 UML classes showing attribute data types.**

- Procedures (officially called *operations* by UML) can include their complete program signature and return data type. If you look at Figure 27.15, for example, you can see each operation's name followed by the type of data it requires to perform its job (*parameters*). Together, the procedure's name and parameters make up the procedure's signature. If data are returned by the operation, then the operation's signature is followed by a colon and the data type of the return value, which may be an object of another class or a simple data type such as an integer.
- Solid arrows can be used at the end of associations to indicate the direction in which a relationship can be navigated.

Note: Pure object-oriented databases are navigational, meaning that traversal through the database is limited to following predefined relationships. Because of this characteristic, some theorists feel that the object-oriented data model is a step backwards rather than forward and that the relational data model continues to have significant advantages over any navigational data model.

There are three possible ways to use the arrows:
- Use arrows on the ends of all associations where navigation is possible. If an association has a plain end, then navigation is not possible in that direction. This would indicate, for example, a relationship between two objects that is not an inverse relationship, where only one of the two objects in a relationship contains the object identifier of a related object.
- Show no arrows at all, as was done in Figure 27.15. In that case, the diagram provides no information about how the database can be navigated.
- Show no arrows on associations that can be navigated in both directions, but use arrows on associations that can be navigated in only one direction. The drawback to this approach is that you cannot differentiate associations that can be navigated in both directions from associations that cannot be navigated at all.

- An association that ends in a filled diamond indicates a whole–part relationship. For example, if you were representing a spreadsheet in a database, the relationship between the spreadsheet and its cells could be diagrammed as in Figure 27.16. The filled diamond can also be used to show aggregation, instead of placing one object within another, as was done in Figure 27.14.

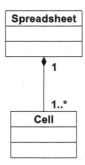

■ FIGURE 27.16   A UML representation of a whole–part relationship.

■ When an association is between more than two objects, UML uses a diamond to represent the relationship. If an association is present, it will be connected to the diamond, as in Figure 27.17. The four classes in the illustration represent entities from a poetry reading society's database. A "reading" occurs when a single person reads a single poem that was written by one or more poets. The association entity indicates when and where the reading took place.

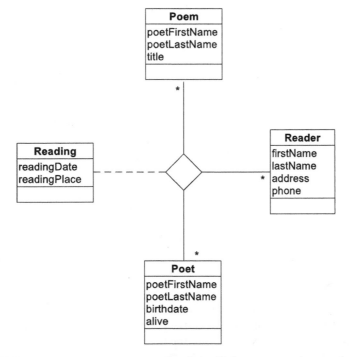

■ FIGURE 27.17   The UML representation of a relationship between more than two classes.

Features of the OR Data Model

There is no accepted standard for the object-relational data model. However, a commonly used model is based on the elements supported by recent SQL standards. As you will see, these features violate many of the rules applied to relational databases:

- A relational database should have no data structures other than tables. An OR database, however, allows an attribute to support a reference to a row in another table. These references are the internal object identifiers used by OO databases described earlier in this chapter. An OR database can use the relational concept of a primary key–foreign key relationship to indicate entity relationships. However, it is not required; references to rows can be used instead. The advantage to using row references rather than the relational method is improved performance because the joins needed to follow data relationships are unnecessary. The major drawback to using row references is that the integrity of the relationships can't be verified by the DBMS; referential integrity requires both primary and foreign key values.

- A relational database is limited to one value at the intersection of a single column and row. An OR database, however, can store more than one value in the same location. The values can be an array of the same type of data, a row of data (much like a table within a table), an unordered collection of data of different data types, or an entire object.

- Classes are implemented as *user-defined data types* (UDTs). A new UDT may inherit from an existing UDT, although multiple inheritance is not allowed. A UDT will have default accessor and mutator methods, as well as a default constructor, each of which can be overridden by a database programmer. There is nothing in the relational data model that prohibits UDTs. However, to be used in a relational database, a custom data type must hold only a single value.

- UDTs may have methods defined with them. Methods may be overloaded. Polymorphism is supported. Relational databases, however, have no concept of storing procedures with data.

SQL Support for the OR Data Model

The SQL:2003 standard introduced a variety of object-relational features. Although not all relational DBMSs support this part of the standard, SQL provides four column data types for OR storage, as well as support for UDTs. You will find at least some OR features in most of today's major DBMSs.

Note: There are some people who cling to the pure relational data model like a lifeline. However, in practice there is nothing that requires you to avoid SQL's OR features. If those features can help model your database environment, then those designing your database shouldn't be afraid to use them. Just be aware of the referential integrity issues that can arise when you store more than one piece of data in a single column in a single row.

Note: Some of the OR features covered in this chapter require programming. In those instances, this chapter assumes that you have programming experience. If you don't know how to program, then you can skim over that material.

An Additional Sample Database

For some of the examples in this chapter, we will be working with a classic home computer application: recipes. You can find the ERD in Figure 27.18. (It has been designed to illustrate OR concepts and therefore is probably missing elements that would be part of a commercial application.)

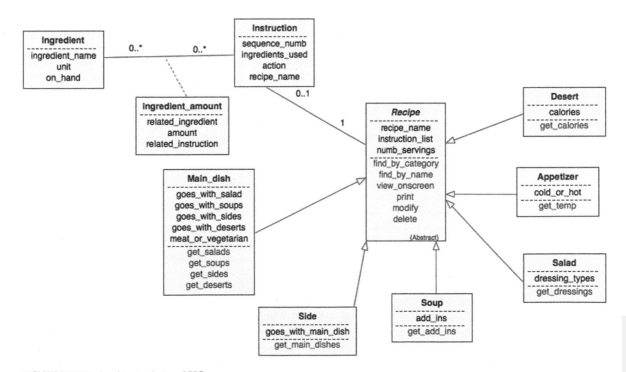

■ **FIGURE 27.18 An object-relational ERD.**

The *recipe* class is an abstract class that stores data common to all types of recipes. The six subclasses represent categories of recipes, each of which has at least one unique attribute.

The *ingredient, instruction*, and *ingredient_amount* classes are more traditional entities. A recipe has many instructions. Each instruction uses zero, one, or more ingredients. The *ingredient_amount* class therefore stores relationship data: the amount of a given ingredient used in a given instruction.

SQL Data Types for Object-Relational Support

SQL's OR features include three column data types for storing multiple values: ROW, ARRAY, and MULTISET. You can use these data types without using any of the other OR features (in particular, typed tables to store objects). Because they do not act as objects, these columns cannot have methods.

Row Type

A column declared as a ROW type holds an entire row of data (multiple pieces of data). This gives you the equivalent of a table within a table. The contents of the row—called *fields*—can be declared as built-in data types or UDTs.

As an example, we'll create a table for customers of the rare book store that stores the customer's address in a single column, using the ROW data type:

```
CREATE TABLE customer
    (first_name CHAR (20),
    last_name CHAR (20),
    address ROW (street CHAR (50), city CHAR (30),
        state CHAR (2), zip CHAR (10), phone CHAR (12)));
```

Notice that the ROW column is given a name, just as a single-valued column. The data type is followed by the contents of the row in parentheses. The row's fields are declared in the same way as any other SQL column (name followed by data type).

We use "dot" notation to access the individual fields in a column of type ROW. For example, to reference the *street* field in the *address* column without qualifying the table name you would use

```
address.street
```

When the SQL statement requires a table name (for example, for use in a join or for display by a query in which the field appears in multiple tables), you precede the field reference with the table name, as in

```
customer.address.street
```

Inserting values into a row column is only a bit different from the traditional INSERT statement. Consider the following example:

```
INSERT INTO customer VALUES
     ('John','Doe',
      ROW ('123 Main Street','Anytown','ST','11224'),
      '555-111-2233');
```

The data for the *address* column are preceded by the keyword ROW. The values follow in parentheses.

Array Type

An ARRAY is an ordered collection of elements. Like arrays used in programming, they are declared to have a maximum number of elements of the same type. That type can be a simple data type or a UDT. For example, we might want to store order numbers as part of a customer's data in a *customer* table:

```
CREATE TABLE customer
     (first CHAR (20),
      last CHAR (20),
      orders INT ARRAY[100],
      numb_orders INT,
      phone CHAR (12);
```

The array column is given a name and a data type, which are followed by the keyword ARRAY and the maximum number of elements the array should hold (the array's *cardinality*) in brackets. The array's data type can be one of SQL's built in data types or a UDT.

Access to values in an array is by the array's *index* (its position in the array order). Although you specify the maximum number of elements in an array counting from 1, array indexes begin at 0. An array of 100 elements therefore has indexes from 0 to 99. The sample *customer* table above includes a column (*numb_orders*) that stores the total number of elements in the array. The last used index will be *numb_orders – 1*.

You can input multiple values into an array at one time when you first insert a row:

```
INSERT INTO customer VALUES
    ('John','Doe', ARRAY (25,109,227,502,610),
    5, '555-111-2233');
```

The keyword ARRAY precedes the values in parentheses.

You can also insert or modify a specify array element directly:

```
INSERT INTO customer (first, last, orders[0],numb_orders,
    phone)
    VALUES ('John','Doe',25,1, '555-111-2233');
```

When you query a table and ask for display of an array column by name, without an index, SQL displays the entire contents of the array, as in:

```
SELECT orders
FROM customer
WHERE first = 'John' AND last = 'Doe';
```

Use an array index when you want to retrieve a single array element. The query

```
SELECT orders [numb_orders - 1]
FROM customer
WHERE first = 'John' AND last = 'Doe';
```

displays the last order stored in the array.

Processing each element in an array requires programming (a trigger, stored procedure, or embedded SQL). Declare a variable to hold the array index, initialize it to 0, and increment it by 1 each time an appropriate loop iterates—the same way you would process all elements in an array using any high-level programming language.

Note: Although many current DBMSs support arrays in columns, not all automatically perform array bounds checking. In other words, they do not necessarily validate that an array index is within the maximum number specified when the table was created. Check your software's documentation to determine whether array bounds constraints must be handled by an application program or can be left up to the DBMS.

Manipulating Arrays

Restrictions of content and access notwithstanding, there two operations that you can perform on arrays:

- Comparisons: Two arrays can be compared (for example, in a WHERE clause) if the two arrays are created from data types that can be compared. When making the comparison, SQL compares the elements in order. Two arrays A and B, therefore, are equivalent if A[0] = B[0], A[1] = B[1], and so on; all comparisons between all the pairs of values in the array must be true. By the same token, A > B if A[0] > B[0] throughout the arrays.
- Concatenation: Two arrays with compatible data types (data types that can be converted into a single data type) can be concatenated with the concatenation operator (∥). The result is another array, as in Figure 27.19. Notice that the data from array A have been converted to real numbers, because SQL will always convert to the format that has the highest precision.

(A)		(B)		(C)
16		96.05		16.00
52		295.82		52.00
109		303.00		109.00
85	∥	105.88	=	85.00
33		22.16		33.00
203		111.23		203.00
384		88.22		384.00
23		45.99		23.00
		18.62		96.05
		35.88		295.82
				303.00
				105.88
				22.16
				111.23
				88.22
				45.99
				18.62
				35.88

■ FIGURE 27.19 Concatenating arrays.

Multiset Type

A *multiset* is an unordered collection of elements of the same type. The following table contains a multiset to hold multiple phone numbers:

```
CREATE TABLE customer
    (first CHAR (20),
     last CHAR (20),
     orders INT ARRAY[100],
     phones CHAR (20) MULTISET;
```

You specify the contents of a multiset when you insert a row into a table, much like you do for an array. The only difference is the use of the keyword MULTISET to indicate that the values in parentheses are intended as a single group:

```
INSERT INTO customer (first, last, orders[0],numb_orders,phones)
   VALUES ('John','Doe',25,1, MULTISET ('555-111-2233','555-222-
1122'));
```

Because a multiset is unordered, you cannot access individual elements by position, as you do with array elements. You can, however, display the entire contents of the multiset by using its name in a query:

```
SELECT phones
FROM customer
WHERE first = 'John' AND last = 'Doe';
```

Updating a multiset is an all or nothing proposition. In other words, you can't pull one value out, or put in a single value. An UPDATE statement such as

```
UPDATE customer
    SET phones = MULTISET ('555-111-2233','555-333-1122');
```

replaces the entire contents of the *phones* column.

Manipulating Multisets

As with arrays, there are a few operations that can be performed on multisets with compatible data types:

■ Multisets can be compared, just as arrays. Multisets A and B will be true if they contain exactly the same elements.

- Union: The MULTISET UNION operator returns a multiset that contains all elements in the participating multisets. For example,

```
UPDATE some_table
  SET big_multiset = small_multiset1 MULTISET
      UNION small_multiset2
```

puts the two small multisets into the big multiset.
- Intersect: The MULTISET INTERSECT operator returns all elements that two multisets have in common. For example,

```
SELECT table1.multiset MULTISET
    INTERSECT table2.multiset
FROM table1 JOIN table2;
```

works on each row in the joined tables, returning the elements that the multisets in each row have in common.
- Difference: The MULTISET EXCEPT operation returns the difference between two multisets (all elements they *don't* have in common). The query

```
SELECT table1.multiset MULTISET
    EXCEPT table2.multiset
FROM table1 JOIN table2;
```

functions exactly like the previous example, but returns elements from each row that the multisets don't share.

The union, intersect, and difference operators have two options. If you include ALL after the operator, SQL includes duplicate elements in the result. To exclude duplicates, use DISTINCT.

User-Defined Data Types and Typed Tables

The more classic SQL object-oriented features are built from UDTs and typed tables. The UDT defines a class and the typed table provides a place to store objects from that class. What this means is that an instance of a UDT is not stored in the column to which the UDT has been assigned as a data type. Relations simply have no mechanism for handling multiple values at the intersection of a column and a row. Therefore, the objects are stored in their own typed table and a reference to those objects is placed in the relation using them, one reference per table row. Columns that will hold references to objects in another table are given a data type of REF.

In this section of this chapter you will first see UDTs used as domains, something you can do without using any other OR features in your database. Then, we will look at UDTs as classes and how references to objects are handled.

UDTs as Domains

A user-defined data type is a structured, named group of attributes of existing data types (either built-in types or other UDTs). In its simplest form, the UDT has the following general syntax:

```
CREATE TYPE type_name AS (column_definitions)
```

We could create a very simple type to hold a date, for example:

```
CREATE TYPE date_type AS
    (month int,
     day int,
     year int);
```

We could then specify *date_type* as the data type for a column in a table:

```
CREATE TABLE people
    (first CHAR (20),
     last CHAR (20),
     birthdate date_type);
```

You use dot notation to access the parts of the UDT. For example,

```
birthdate.year
```

refers to the year potion of the *date_type* UDT.

UDTs as Classes

More commonly, we use a UDT to define a class. For example, we could create a type for the *Ingredient* class with

```
CREATE TYPE ingredient_type AS OBJECT
    (ingredient_name CHAR (256),
     unit char (20),
     on_hand int);
```

Notice the AS OBJECT clause that has been inserted after the UDT's name. This indicates that rather than being used as the domain for a value in a table, this class will be used as the structure of a typed table.

Note: UDTs can have methods, just like a class created in an object-oriented programming language. We'll look at them at the end of this chapter.

Creating Typed Tables Using UDTs

Once you have created a class as a UDT, you then use that UDT to create a *typed table*:

```
CREATE TABLE table_name OF UDT_name
     REF IS reference_column_name (method_to_generate_row_ID)
```

SQL creates a table with one column for each column in the UDT on which the table is based, along with a column for the object ID. There are three options for creating the object ID of a row:

- The user generates the object ID (REF USING *existing_data_type*).
- The DBMS generates the object ID (REF IS *identifier_name* SYSTEM GENERATED).
- The object ID comes from the values in a list of attributes (REF FROM *attribute_list*).

You may want to use a primary key as a source for an object ID. Although this makes sense logically, it also provides the slowest retrieval performance.

By default, the object ID value is generated by the SQL command processor whenever a row is inserted into the typed table, using the method that was specified when the table was created. However, an insert operation can override the default object ID, placing a user-specified value into the ID column. Once created, the object ID cannot be modified.

To create the *ingredient* table, we could use

```
CREATE TABLE ingredient OF ingredient_type
     (REF IS ingredient_ID SYSTEM GENERATED);
```

Note: Only base tables or views can be typed tables. Temporary tables cannot be created from UDTs.

Inheritance

One of the most important OO features added to the SQL:2003 standard was support for inheritance. To create a *subtype* (a *subclass* or *derived class*, if you will), you create a UDT that is derived from another and then create a typed table of that subtype.

As a start, let's create the recipe type that will be used as the superclass for types of recipes:

```
CREATE TYPE recipe_type AS OBJECT
    (recipe_name CHAR (256),
     instruction_list instruction ARRAY[20],
     numb_servings INT)
    NOT INSTANTIABLE,
    NOT FINAL;
```

The two last lines in the preceding example convey important information about this class. *Recip_type* is an abstract class: Objects will never be created from it directly. We add NOT INSTANTIABLE to indicate this property.

By default, a UDT has a *finality* of FINAL. It cannot be used as the parent of a subtype. (In other words, nothing can inherit from it.) Because we want to use this class as a superclass, we must indicate that it is NOT FINAL.

To create the subtypes, we indicate the parent type, preceded by the keyword UNDER. The subtype declaration also includes any attributes (and methods) that are not in the parent type that need to be added to the subtype. For example, we could create the desert type with:

```
CREATE TYPE desert_type
    UNDER recipe_type (calories INT);
```

Because this type will be used to create objects, and because no other types will be derived from it, we can accept the defaults of INSTANTIABLE and FINAL.

Note: As you have just seen, inheritance can operate on UDTs. It can also be used with typed tables, where a typed table is created UNDER another.

Reference (REF) Type

Once you have a typed table, you can store references to the objects in that table in a column of type REF that is part of another table. For example, there is one REF column in the recipe database: the attribute in the *ingredient_amount* table (*related_ingredient*) that points to which ingredient is related to each occurrence of *ingredient_amount*.

To set up the table that will store that reference, use the data type REF for the appropriate column:

```
column_name REF UDT_being_referenced SCOPE IS typed_table_name
```

For example,

```
CREATE TABLE ingredient_amount
    (related_ingredient REF ingredient_type
     SCOPE IS ingredient, amount decimal (5,2));
```

creates a table with a column that stores a reference to an ingredient. The SCOPE clause specifies the table or view that is the source of the reference.

To insert a row into a table with a REF column, you must include a SELECT in the INSERT statement that locates the row whose reference is to be stored. As you would expect, the object being referenced must exist in its own table before a reference to it can be generated. We must therefore first insert an ingredient into the *ingredient* table:

```
INSERT INTO ingredient VALUES
    ('Unbleached flour', 'cups',25);
```

Then, we can insert a referencing row into *ingredient_amount*:

```
INSERT INTO ingredient_amount
    (SELECT REF (i)
     FROM ingredient i
     WHERE i.ingredient_name = 'Unbleached flour')
    VALUES (2.5);
```

Dereferencing for Data Access

An application program that is using the recipe database as its data store will need to use the reference stored in the *ingredient_amount* table to locate the name of the ingredient. The DEREF function follows a reference back to the table being referenced and returns data from the appropriate row. A query to retrieve the name and amount of an ingredient used in a recipe instruction could therefore be written:

```
SELECT DEREF(related_ingredient).ingredient_name, amount
FROM ingredient_amount
WHERE DEREF(related_instruction).recipe_name = 'French toast';
```

Note that the DEREF function accesses an entire row in the referenced table. If you don't specify otherwise, you will retrieve the values from every column in the referenced row. To retrieve just the value of a single column, we use "dot" notation. The first portion—

```
DEREF(related_ingredient)
```

—actually performs the dereference. The portion to the right of the dot specifies the column in the referenced row.

Some DBMSs provide a dereference operator (- >) that can be used in place of the DEREF function. The preceding query might be written:

```
SELECT related_ingredient->ingredient_name, amount
FROM ingredient_amount;
```

Methods

The UDTs that we have seen to this point have attributes, but not methods. It is certainly possible, however, to declare methods as part of a UDT and then to use SQL programming to define the body of the methods. Like classes used by OO programming languages such C + +, in SQL the body of a method is defined separately from the declaration of the UDT.

Note: SQL extensions for writing methods appear in Appendix B. To get the most out of it, you need to know a high-level programming language. If you don't program, you can just skim the rest of this section.

You declare a method after declaring the structure of a UDT. For example, we could add a method to display the instructions of a recipe with

```
CREATE TYPE recipe_type AS OBJECT
    (recipe_name CHAR (256),
     instruction_list instruction ARRAY[20],
     numb_servings INT)
     NOT INSTANTIABLE,
     NOT FINAL
     METHOD show_instructions ();
```

This particular method does not return a value and the declaration therefore does not include the optional RETURNS clause. However, a method to compute the cost of a recipe (if we were to include ingredient costs in the database) could be declared as

```
CREATE TYPE recipe_type AS OBJECT
    (recipe_name CHAR (256),
     instruction_list instruction ARRAY[20],
     numb_servings INT)
     NOT INSTANTIABLE,
     NOT FINAL
     METHOD show_instructions ()
     METHOD compute_cost ()
         RETURNS DECIMAL (5,2));
```

Methods can accept input parameters within the parentheses, following the method name. A method declared as

```
METHOD scale_recipe (IN numb_servings INT):
```

accepts an integer value as an input value. The parameter list can also contain output parameters (OUT) and parameters used for both input and output (INOUT).

Defining Methods

As mentioned earlier, although methods are declared when UDTs tables are declared, the bodies of methods are written separately. To define a method, use the CREATE METHOD statement:

```
CREATE METHOD method_name FOR UDT_name
BEGIN
    //body of method
END
```

A SQL-only method is written using the language constructs discussed in Appendix B.

Executing Methods

Executing a method uses notation:

```
typed_table_name.method_name (parameter_list );
```

Such an expression can be, for example, included in an INSERT statement to insert the method's return value into a column. It can also be included in another SQL method, trigger, or stored procedure. Its return value can then be captured across an assignment operator. Output parameters return their values to the calling routine, where they can be used as needed.

For Further Reading

Brown, P., 2000. Object-Relational Database Development: A Plumber's Guide. Prentice Hall PTR.

Date, C.J., Darwen, H., 1998. Foundation for Object/Relational Databases: The Third Manifesto. Addison-Wesley.

Dietrich, S.W., Urban, S.D., 2011. Fundamentals of Object Databases: Object-Oriented and Object-Relational Designs. Morgan and Claypool.

Melton, J., 2002. Advanced SQL: 1999: Understanding Object-Relational and Other Advanced Features. Morgan Kaufmann.

28

Relational Databases and "Big Data": The Alternative of a NoSQL Solution

Although relational database design theory has been relatively stable for the past 45 years, as you have read, other data models continue to be developed to handle changes in the data management environment. In particular, relational DBMSs can have trouble retrieving data with acceptable performance from extremely large data stores. These databases—often simply called *big data*—include massive installations, such as Amazon and Google.

The largest group of DBMSs designed to handle such huge amounts of data are known as *NoSQL DBMSs*. There doesn't seem to be any agreement on the origin of the "No" part of the name. There are certainly some products that use SQL in the background, so it doesn't necessarily mean that a NoSQL DBMS avoids SQL altogether. Some people insist that it means "not only SQL," which may indeed be the case. Regardless of the source of the name, however, NoSQL DBMSs have become very useful in data warehousing and in environments with enormous volumes of operational data.

In this chapter, we will look at the types of NoSQL databases and how they differ from relational databases. The goal is for you to understand enough about them so that you can recognize circumstances where a NoSQL solution might be appropriate. Keep in mind, however, that at the time this book was written, NoSQL databases were being used by less than 10 percent of even very large businesses.

Types of NoSQL Databases

Unlike the relational data model, there is no single NoSQL data model. There are, however, four commonly used types of NoSQL design.

Note: Much of what you read in this section is a generalization of each type of NoSQL design. Individual DBMSs often provide additional features to compensate for limitations of a particular type of storage.

Key-Value Store

A *key-value store* database assigns a unique key to a data value. The values are stored as an undifferentiated block and are retrieved by supplying the correct key. Because the data are seen as a single value, the data are not searchable. This pattern has some important implications:

- Retrieval by the key will be extremely fast.
- There is virtually no restriction on the type of data that can be stored. You could store text (for example, the HTML code for a Web page) or any type of multimedia binary (still images, audio, and video).
- To gain what appears to be search access to text data, the database designer must create indexes on the text. Keys are paired with text in the index and the search occurs on the index rather than the stored data.

Key-value store DBMSs use three commands taken from Web languages to manipulate the values in the database:

- PUT: inserts a key-value pair into the database
- GET: retrieves a value using a supplied key
- DELETE: removes a key-value pair from the database

Why would you want to use a database where you can't search the data? Anywhere you need to store and retrieve entire files. You could, for example, store an entire Web site where the key is a page's URL. When a user makes a request from a Web server to display a particular page, the Web server doesn't need access to the page's internal code; it just needs the HTML text as a unit. Therefore, the Web server submits the URL to the key-value store DBMS, which, in turn, uses the key to find the requested page. Any scripts, images, and videos used by the page could be stored and retrieved in the same way.

A key-value store database has no schema. In fact, the values associated with the keys do not need to be the same type of item. For example, one value could be a string of text, while another was a graphic image.

The biggest advantage to key-value store databases is extremely fast retrieval. However, if you need to be able to search within stored values rather than always retrieving by the key, this type of DBMS may not be a good fit for your data. Keep in mind that you can't update parts of a "value" while it's in the database. You must replace the entire value with a new copy if modifications are needed.

Key-value store databases are therefore best suited for applications where access is only through the key. They are being used for Web sites that include thousands of pages, large image databases, and large catalogs. They are also particularly useful for keeping Web app session information.

Document

A *document store* NoSQL database is very similar to a key-value store, but rather than storing "values," it stores "documents," which are made up of individual pieces of named data. Documents can be nested within documents.

Text data can be searched by creating indexes to the elements within the documents. Although not all documents need to have the same structure, the elements within a document can be named, making it possible to index on all items of the same name.

Document store databases do not require a schema, but each document does have a primary key, a value that uniquely identifies the document. The primary key index is a permanent feature of the database, but secondary indexes can be created and deleted as needed.

Document store databases work well for large on-line catalogs, for example. They provide fast access by a catalog number. However, the ability to build secondary indexes supports fast access using keywords such as those a user might use in a search.

Note: Some NoSQL products (for example, Amazon's DynamoDB) support both key-value and document stores. DynamoDB is completely cloud-based. You pay for the number of reads and writes you perform each month, as well as a fee for the amount of storage you use. Amazon handles all maintenance, including scaling the database when extra capacity becomes necessary.

Column

A *column-oriented* NoSQL database at first looks deceptively like a relational database: The concepts of columns and rows are present; data manipulation is provided by commands that are a variation on SQL syntax.[1]

---

[1] In my opinion, the problem with using something that is "like" SQL, but with a number of syntax differences, will lead to a lot of confusion, especially if users know standard SQL.

However, there are some major differences. In particular, column-oriented databases don't support joins.

In a relational database, each table has a fixed structure: Every row has space for every column. This is not the case in a column-oriented NoSQL database. Because the basic unit of storage is a column rather than a row, rows can be assigned different columns as needed. A column has a name (for example, first_name) that identifies the row within the column and a value (for example, "George") and, in many implementations, a timestamp. The timestamp not only anchors the data in time, but makes it easy to purge data that has been aggregated at any given point, as well as to keep multiple versions of the same data to track changes over time (*versioning*).

Columns are grouped into *column families*. When you place related columns in the same family, instances of those columns will be stored as physically close to each other as possible. You might, for example, create a column for each of street address, city, state, and zip. Then, you can group them into a column family with its own name (perhaps "address"). In contrast, most relational DBMSs try to store data in a single row together.

The biggest benefit of a column-oriented database is fast data aggregation. In other words, it will be extremely good at extracting data from a single column and providing summaries of that data. Google uses one, for example, to aggregate Web page visitation data. When the software has compiled the Web sites visited and the number of times each was visited, the data are archived.

Graph

A *graph* NoSQL database is made from *nodes* that are similar to rows in relational database tables. However, rather than using composite entities to show relationships and to store relationship data, graph databases use a representation of the relationships; the relationships can have properties, just like a composite entity stores relationship data. The result is something that looks like a mathematical directed graph.

The biggest advantage of the graph store is that joins aren't necessary. The pathways between related data exist within the database. As an example, consider the graph in Figure 28.1. It shows six instances of nodes from an *Antique Opticals* database.

The price charged the customer and the quantity ordered are properties of the Contains relationship. There is no composite entity between the order and the inventory item. To retrieve data, the DBMS follows the relationships stored in the database.

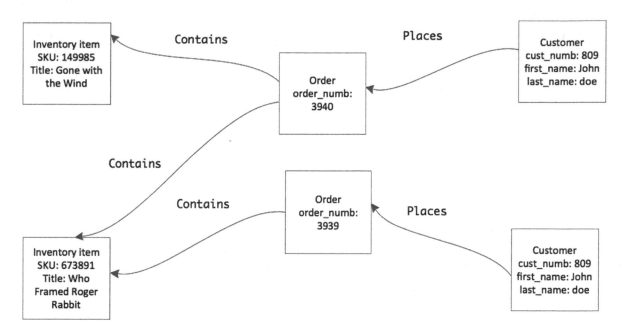

■ FIGURE 28.1 Instances of nodes in a NoSQL graph database.

Note: Graph databases are navigational, like the data models discussed in Appendix A, because access to data follows predefined paths. However, the stored relationships in the older data models cannot have properties.

Graph databases are well suited to large databases that must track networks of relationships. They are used by many online dating sites, as well as LinkedIn and Twitter. Avoiding the joins to traverse friend relationships can speed up performance significantly. In addition, they can be used effectively to plot routes (such as for a package delivery service).

Other Differences Between NoSQL Databases and Relational Databases

At this point, it should be clear that the designs of relational and NoSQL databases are very different. There are also major differences in the hardware architectures, the way in which data are accessed and manipulated, and transaction control.

Hardware Architecture Differences

In Chapter 1 we looked at a variety of hardware architectures that are used for relational database implementations. The most difficult to implement successfully is a distributed architecture, particularly because of the concurrency control challenges. However, NoSQL databases are designed to be distributed. They scale horizontally by adding more servers to a data storage cluster. Keep in mind that many NoSQL databases are hosted in the cloud, an environment in which distribution is relatively easy to achieve.

NoSQL distributed solutions can also be very cost effective. Rather than needing large machines with massive amounts of storage, they can be implemented on small, commodity servers, such as those you might buy for a LAN subnet. Run out of space? Just add another machine. Doing so is significantly cheaper than adding similar capacity to a mainframe. Some people argue that the total-cost-of-ownership of a mainframe can be less than a distributed cluster, but this doesn't take into account the idea of incremental upgrades. It costs less to add a small, single server to a cluster, than it does to add RAM or permanent storage to a mainframe.

Note: It certainly would be nice to have some real cost comparisons here, but it's very difficult to find current pricing for mainframe components. Although commodity server prices are widely advertised, mainframe prices are typically negotiated with each individual customer and kept secret.

There are two major types of NoSQL distributed architectures that can be used individually or together.

Sharding

Sharding is another word for what we called partitioning in Chapter 8. It splits the database into unique pieces, each of which is hosted on a different server. For best performance, you want to keep data that are accessed together in the same shard (in other words, on the same physical machine).

The physical arrangement of your servers depends, to some extent, on the specific NoSQL DBMS. As an example, let's look at one option for MongoDB, a document-oriented open-source product. (Please don't forget that this architecture is very specific to MongoDB and that each DBMS will require something a bit different.)

Note: MongoDB also supports a combination of sharding and replication, which we will look at in just a bit.

As you can see in Figure 28.2, there are three types of servers in a MongoDB sharded cluster:

- Query router: A cluster requires at least one query router. It runs a copy of the MongoDB software and acts as a director for data manipulation requests.

- Config router: Although a cluster can run with only one config router, Mongo suggests that a cluster use three. Each contains metadata about where data are stored.
- Shard: The shard machines are the storage locations for the data.

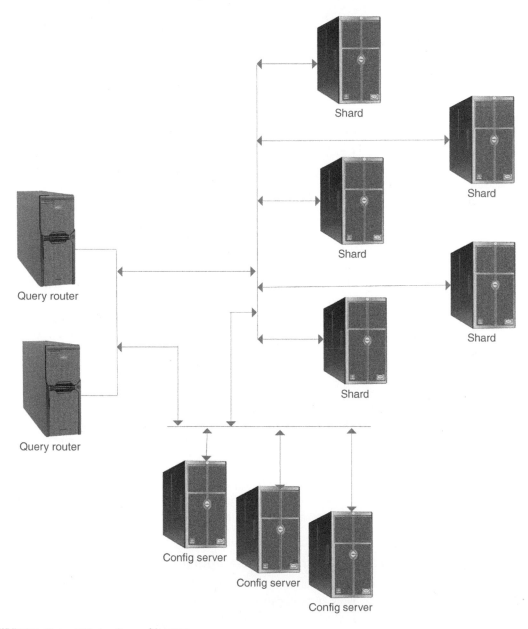

■ FIGURE 28.2 MongoDB's sharding architecture.

Data manipulation requests are sent to the query routers, which, in turn, use the metadata in the config routers to locate or place requested data. As each shard is a minimum of 64 Mb, sharding is truly intended for large databases.

Setting up a sharding environment is much more difficult than creating a NoSQL database on a single server. Doing so requires system programmer expertise in decisions such as the number of shards, the size of each shard, and the location of shards. It may also require selecting a *shard key* from which the location of a database element can be deduced by the DBMS. Shard keys must be unique, but because they contain location information, they aren't precisely the same as primary keys.

Replication

Replication means exactly what you might think: All or part of the database is replicated on more than one machine. If the copies are stored at remote locations, replication can provide faster retrieval for remote locations using those local data stores, as well as fault tolerance.

A replicated NoSQL database is subject to all of the problems of a distributed database that we discussed in Chapter 1. The biggest issue is consistency: How do you ensure that all the replicated copies are identical? As you will remember, locking isn't a particularly effective means of concurrency control in a distributed environment. NoSQL databases have therefore taken another tack to provide consistency. We'll look at it when we talk about BASE transactions later in this section.

Combining Sharding and Replication

Most NoSQL DBMSs support combining sharding and replication. As you can see in Figure 28.3, each shard is backed up by a second server that contains the copy of the shard.

A database that is both sharded and replicated will have more fault tolerance than a database that is sharded alone. However, it will need to deal with the concurrency control issues associated with distributed databases.

Data Access and Manipulation Techniques

We are rather spoiled with SQL. You don't need to be a programmer to work at the command line to perform sophisticated database interactions. If you don't want to type commands, there are many query tools that support

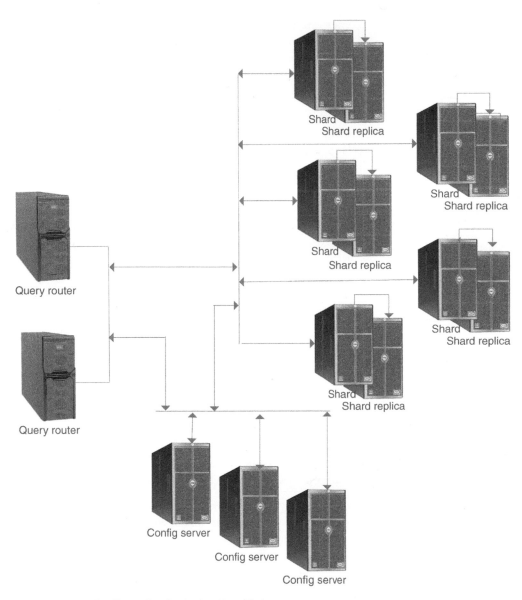

Shard
Shard replica

Shard
Shard replica

Shard
Shard replica

Shard
Shard replica

Query router

Query router

Shard
Shard replica

Config server

Config server

Config server

■ FIGURE 28.3 Combining sharding and replication in a MongDB cluster.

graphic or form-based query specification; the SQL is generated by the query tool, out of sight of the user. This works well because SQL is relatively standardized across relational DBMSs. The same can't be said for NoSQL products.

Virtually all current NoSQL products require configuration and data manipulation, either from a command line or from within an application program. This means that a company wanting to implement a NoSQL solution must have access to both systems and application programmers.

Transaction Control: BASE Transactions

One of the major goals of relational database transaction control is data consistency. As you read in Chapter 22, relational DBMSs typically enforce ACID transactions, ensuring that the database is internally consistent at all times. The main drawback is the overhead required by locking and the associated performance degradation. This is particularly problematic in distributed relational DBMSs.

With their emphasis on performance, many NoSQL DBMSs tolerate some data inconsistency, with the idea that eventually all the data will become consistent. Therefore, transaction control is BASE (Basic Availability, Soft State, and Eventual Consistency) rather than ACID.

With a relational database, we want serializable transactions (multiple transactions running interleaved produce the same result as they would if the transactions were run in a series rather than interleaved). The DBMS therefore locks portions of the database to prevent problems such as the lost update and inconsistent analysis.

Avoiding lost updates is essential in a transaction processing system. However, systems that are used primarily for querying, rather than a high volume of updates, can be allowed to suffer from lost updates. A report may be inaccurate for a while, until the writes catch up, but will reflect the modified data when it is rerun.

In a BASE concurrency control environment, no writes are blocked. The goal is to avoid locking to make the database as available as possible. Whereas ACID concurrency control is pessimistic (something might go wrong, so we to make sure that doesn't happen), BASE transaction control is optimistic (everything will become consistent in the end). BASE transaction control is also well suited to distributed databases because it doesn't worry about keeping replicated copies consistent at every moment.

Benefits of NoSQL Databases

Given the difficulty in setting up and manipulating data in a NoSQL database, what can a company gain from one? There are several major advantages when you are maintaining an extremely large database:

- Fast retrieval: Through keys and fast-access paths such as indexes, NoSQL databases can provide access that is much faster than a relational search. A NoSQL solution can allow direct retrieval of a single unit of data using a key, thus avoiding the retrieval of one or more entire tables of data.
- Cloud storage that relieves the database owner of hardware and DBMS maintenance: Using a cloud-based product is typically cheaper than maintaining a NoSQL solution within an organization's premises. When you use a cloud-based solution, you are paying for what you use, rather than paying for excess capacity that might be used some time in the future.
- Lower-cost incremental hardware upgrades: As mentioned earlier in this chapter, it costs much more to add storage to a mainframe (cost per Mb, be it RAM or permanent storage) than it does to add the equivalent storage by adding commodity PCs to a cluster.

Problems with NoSQL Databases

NoSQL databases are well suited to some very specific environments involving large amounts of data, but there a number of problems that those developing the databases will encounter:

- Lack of design standards: Unlike like the relational data model, there are no standards for NoSQL designs. Implementations are not consistent, even within the same type. Any solution that a business implements will be locked into a specific DBMS.
- Lack of access language standards: There are no query languages for NoSQL databases. Data manipulation is provided through application programs using an API (*application programmer interface*) embedded in a high-level programming language, such as Python, JavaScript, Java or C + +. Prior to SQL, this is how we gained access to database data. The lack of standards also makes it very costly for an organization to change NoSQL products, because all previous code will need to be modified in some way to account for the new API.
- Access restrictions: NoSQL databases are not well suited to ad hoc querying. This is a direct result of there being no interactive query

languages. They provide support for extremely large databases for which almost all queries can be anticipated and therefore coded into application programs.

Open Source NoSQL Products

If you want to play with NoSQL DBMSs, there are a number of open-source products that you can download. Unless stated otherwise, distributions are available for Windows, Mac OS X, and various flavors of UNIX:

DBMS	Type	Download Page
Apache CouchDB	Document	http://couchdb.apache.org
Apache HBase	Column	http://www.apache.org/dyn/closer.cgi/hbase/ (UNIX only)
LucidDB	Column	http://sourceforge.net/projects/luciddb/
Monetdb	Column	https://www.monetdb.org/Downloads
MongoDB	Document	https://www.mongodb.org/downloads
Neo4J	Graph	http://neo4j.com/download/ (Be certain to download the Community edition; the Enterprise edition is commercial.) (UNIX, including Mac OS X, only)
Redis	Key-value	http://redis.io/download (UNIX only)
Riak	Key-value	http://docs.basho.com/riak/latest/downloads/

For Further Reading

Alvina, H., 2015. RDBMS vs ORDBMS vs NoSQL. Lambert Academic Publishing.

Dayley, B., 2015. NoSQL with MongoDB in 25 Hours. Sams.

Fowler, A., 2015. NoSQL for Dummies. For Dummies.

Kemme, B., Jiménez-Peris, R., 2010. Database Replication. Morgan and Claypool.

McCreary, D., Kelly, A., 2014. Making Sense of NoSQL: A Guide for Managers and the Rest of Us. Manning.

Redmond, E., Wilson, J.R., 2012. Seven Databases in Seven Weeks: A Guide to Modern Databases and the NoSQL Movement. Pragmatic Bookshelf.

Sadalage, P.J., Fowler, M., 2012. NoSQL Distilled: A Brief Guide to the Emerging World of Polyglot Persistence. Addison-Wesley.

Sullivan, D., 2015. NoSQL for Mere Mortals. Addison-Wesley.

Vaish, G., 2013. Getting Started with NoSQL. Packt Publishing.

Part

VII

Appendices

Appendix A Historical Antecedents

In the beginning, there were data files… and from the need to manage the data stored in those files arose a variety of data management methods, most of which preceded the relational data model and, because of their shortcomings, paved the way for the acceptance of relational databases.

This appendix provides an overview of data management organizations used prior to the introduction of the relational data model. Although you do not need to read this appendix to understand the main body of this book, some of the case studies in Part III mention concepts discussed here. You will also find that NoSQL DBMSs (discussed in Chapter 28) share some characteristics with the older data models.

File Processing Systems

The first commercial computer—ENIAC—was designed to help process the 1960 census. Its designers thought that all computers could do was crunch numbers; the idea that computers could handle text data came later. Unfortunately, the tools available to handle data weren't particularly sophisticated. In most cases, all the computing staff had available was some type of storage (at first tapes and later disks) and a high-level programming language compiler.

Early File Processing

Early file processing systems were made up of a set of data files—most commonly text files—and application programs that manipulated those files directly, without the intervention of a DBMS. The files were laid out in a very precise, fixed format. Each individual piece of data (a first name, a last name, street address, and so on) was known as a *field*. Those data described a single entity and were collected into a *record*. A data file was therefore made up of a collection of records.

Each field was allocated a specific number of bytes. The fixed field lengths meant that no delimiters were required between fields or at the end of records, although some data files did include them. A portion of such a data file might appear like Figure A.1.

```
0      John       Smith      25 W. Main Street …
1      Jane       Johnson    120 #1m Lane …
2      Edward     Smith      44 Pine Heights …
3      Louis      Johnson    250 W. Main Street …
4      John       Jones      RR1 Box 250B …
5      Theresa    Jones      Anderson Road …
6      Thomas     Smith      12589 Highway 25 South …
7      Jan        Smith      48 Roxbury Court …
8      Edward     Jones      10101 Binary Road …
9      Emily      Johnson    202 Somerset Blvd …
10     Thomas     Johnson    25 N. Main Street …
11     Louis      Smith      918 Bayleaf Terrace …
```

■ FIGURE A.1 A portion of a fixed field length data file.

The programs that stored and retrieved data in the data files located data by their byte position in the file. Assuming that the first record in a file was numbered 0, a program could locate the start of any field with the computation:

```
record_number * record_length + starting_position_of_field
```

This type of file structure therefore was very easy to parse (in other words, separate into individual fields). It also simplified the process of writing the application programs that manipulated the files.

If the file was stored on tape, then access to the records was sequential. Such a system was well suited to batch processing *if* the records were in the order in which they needed to be accessed. If the records were stored on disk, then the software could perform direct access reads and writes. In either case, however, the program needed to know exactly where each piece of data was stored and was responsible for issuing the appropriate read and/or write commands.

Note: Some tape drives were able to read backwards to access data preceding the last written or read location. However, those that could not read backward needed to rewind completely and then perform a sequential scan beginning at the start of the tape to find data preceding the previous read/write location. Understandably, sequential access to data was unacceptably slow for interactive data processing.

These systems were subject to many problems, including all of those discussed in Chapter 3. In addition, programmers struggled with the following situations:

- Changing the layout of a data file (for example, changing the size of a field or record) required changing all of the programs that accessed that file, as well as rewriting the file to accommodate the new layout.
- Access was very fast when processing all records sequentially in the physical order of the file. However, searches for specific records based on some matching criteria also had to be performed sequentially, a very slow process. This held true even for files stored on disk.

The major advantage to a file processing system was that it was cheap. An organization that installed a computer typically had everything it needed: external storage and a compiler. In addition, a file processing system was relatively easy to create, in that it required little advance planning. However, the myriad problems resulting from unnecessary duplicated data, as well as the close coupling of programs and physical file layouts and the serious performance problems that arose when searching the file, soon drove data management personnel of the 1950s and 1960s to search for alternatives.

ISAM Files

Prior to the introduction of the database management system, programmers at IBM developed an enhanced file organization known as *indexed sequential access method* (ISAM), which supported quick sequential access for batch processing, but also provided indexes to fields in the file for fast access searches.

An ISAM file must be stored on disk. Initially, it is written to disk with excess space left in each cylinder occupied by the file. This allows records to be added in sequential key order. When a cylinder fills up, records are written to an overflow area and linked back to where they appear in the sequence in the file's primary storage areas (see Figure A.2).

Note: Hard drives write files to a single track on a single surface in a disk drive. When the track is full, then the drive writes to the same track on another surface. The same tracks on all the surfaces in a stack of platters in a disk drive are known as a cylinder. By filling a cylinder before moving to another track on the same surface, the disk drive can avoid moving the access arm to which read/write heads are attached, thus saving time in the read or write process.

When the overflow area fills up, the file must be *reblocked*. During the reblocking process, the file size is increased and records are rewritten, once

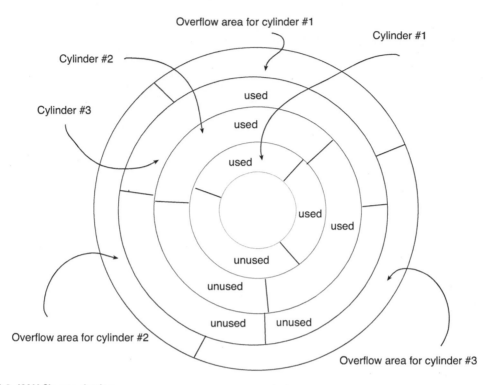

■FIGURE A.2 ISAM file organization.

again leaving expansion space on each cylinder occupied by the file. No data processing can occur using the file while reblocking is in progress.

Depending on the implementation, indexes to ISAM files may be stored in the same file as the data or in separate files. When the data files are stored separately, the functions that manipulate the files treat the indexes and data as if they were one logical file.

Note: Although ISAM files have largely fallen into disuse, the DBMS Informix (now owned by IBM) continues to use its own version of ISAM—c-isam—for data storage.

Limitations of File Processing

File processing, regardless of whether it uses simple data files or ISAM files, is awkward at best. In addition to the problems mentioned earlier in this section, there are two more major drawbacks to file processing.

First, file processing cannot support *ad hoc* queries (queries that arise at the spur of the moment, cannot be predicted, and may never arise again).

Because data files are created by the organization using them, there is no common layout to the files from one organization to another. There is therefore no reasonable way for a software developer to write a language that can query any data file; a language that could query file A probably wouldn't work with file B because there is no similarity between the layout of the files. Therefore, access is limited to preplanned queries and reports that are provided by application programs.

So much of today's data access requires ad hoc querying capabilities. Consider, for example, an ATM machine, perhaps the penultimate ad hoc query device. When you walk up to the machine, there is no way for the machine's software to predict which account you will access. Nor is there any way to predict who will use a particular machine nor what that person will request from the machine. Therefore, the software must be able to access data at any time, from any location, from any account holder, and perform any requested action.

Second, when a file processing system is made up of many files, there is no simple way either to validate cross references between the files or to perform queries that require data from multiple files. This cross-referencing issue is a major data integrity concern. If you store customer data in file A and orders in file B, you want the customer data in file B (even if it's only a customer number) to match the customer data in file B. Whenever data are duplicated, they must remain consistent. Unfortunately, when data are stored in multiple files, there is no easy way to perform this type of validation. The only way is to write a program that uses both files and explicitly verifies that the customer data in file B matches data in file A. Although this can certainly be done, file processing systems rarely perform this type of validation.

By the same token, queries or reports that require data to be extracted from multiple files are difficult to prepare. The application program that generates the output has to be created to read all necessary files, resulting in a program that is difficult to debug and maintain due to its complexity.

The solution is to look for some way to separate physical storage structures from logical data access. In other words, the program or user manipulating data shouldn't need to be concerned about physical placement of data in files, but should be able to express data manipulation requests in terms of how data logically relate to one another. This separation of logical and physical data organization is the hallmark of a database system.

File Processing on the Desktop

One of the problems with data management software written for PCs has been that both developers and users often didn't understand the exact meaning of the term database. As a result, the word was applied to any piece of software that managed data stored in a disk file, regardless of whether the software could handle logical data relationships.

The trend was started in the early 1980s by a product called *pfs:File*. The program was a simple file manager. You defined your fields and then used a default form for entering data. There was no way to represent multiple entities or data relationships. Nonetheless, the product was marketed as a database management system and the confusion in the marketplace began.

A number of products have fallen into this trap. One such product—*FileMaker Pro*—began as a file manager and has been upgraded to database status. The FileMaker company also introduced a product named *Bento* in 2008, which it advertised as a "personal database manager." Bento was a rather nice piece of software, but it wasn't a database management system; it was a file manager. After nearly 45 years, the confusion and the misuse of the term database persists.

You may often hear products such as those in the preceding paragraph described as "flat-file databases," despite the term "database" being a misnomer. Nonetheless, desktop file managers can be useful tools for applications such as maintaining a mailing list, customer contact list, and so on.

The issue here is not to be a database snob, but to ensure that consumers actually understand what they are buying and the limitations that actually accompany a file manager. This means that you must pay special attention to the capabilities of a product when you are considering a purchase.

The Hierarchical Data Model

The first true database model to be developed was the *hierarchical data model*, which appeared as the basis of a commercial product in 1966. Like the two network data models that followed, it was a *navigational data model*, meaning that access paths were constrained by predeclared pointer structures in the schema.

Characteristics of the Hierarchical Data Model

A database that is designed to use the hierarchical data model is restricted to one-to-many relationships. In addition, no child entity may have more than one parent entity. The implications of this last restriction are significant.

As an example, consider the ER diagram in Figure A.3, which contains two hierarchies, or *trees*. The first relates departments to their employees and their projects. The second relates employees to projects. There is a one-to-many relationship between an employee and a department, but a many-to-many relationship between projects and employees. The relationship between department and project is one-to-may.

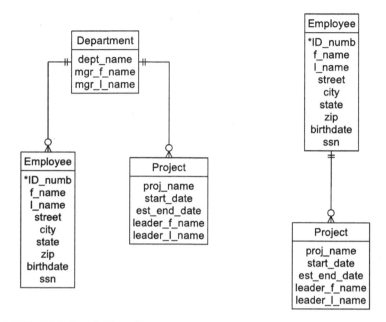

■**FIGURE A.3 Sample hierarchies.**

Ideally, we would like to be able to use a composite entity to handle the many-to-many relationship. Unfortunately, the hierarchical data model does not permit the inclusion of composite entities. (There is no way to give a single entity two parent entities.) The only solution is to duplicate entity occurrences. This means that a project occurrence must be duplicated for every employee that works on the project. In addition, the project and employee entities are duplicated in the department hierarchy as well.

By their very nature, hierarchies include a great deal of duplicated data. This means that hierarchical databases are subject to the data consistency problems that arise from unnecessary duplicated data.

There is another major limitation to the hierarchical data model. Access is only through the entity at the top of the hierarchy, the *root*. From each root occurrence, the access path is top-down and left to right. This means that the path

through the department hierarchy, for example, is through a department, to all its employees, and only then to the projects. For example, see Figure A.4, which contains two occurrences of the department/employee/project hierarchy. The arrows on the dashed lines represent the traversal order.

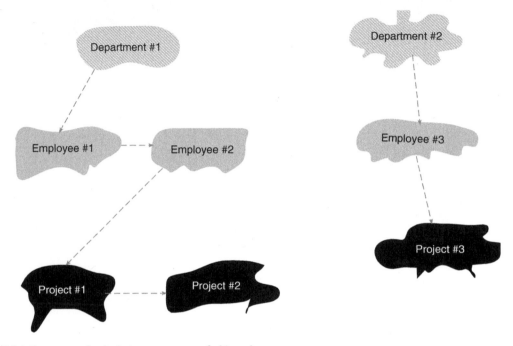

■ FIGURE A.4 Tree traversal order in two occurrences of a hierarchy.

The relationships between the entities in an occurrence of a hierarchy are maintained by pointers embedded in the data. As a result, traversing a hierarchy in its default order is very fast. However, if you need random access to data, then access can be extremely slow because you must traverse every entity occurrence in the hierarchy preceding a needed occurrence to reach the needed occurrence. Hierarchies are therefore well suited to batch processing in tree traversal order, but are not suitable for applications that require ad hoc querying.

The hierarchical model is a giant step forward from file processing systems, including those based on ISAM files. It allows the user to store and retrieve data based on logical data relationships. It therefore provides some independence between the logical and physical data storage, relieving application programmers to a large extent of the need to be aware of the physical file layouts.

IMS

The most successful hierarchical DBMS has been IMS, an IBM product. Designed to run on IBM mainframes, IMS has been handling high-volume transaction-oriented data processing since 1966. Today, IBM supports IMS legacy systems, but actively discourages new installations. In fact, many tools exist to help companies migrate from IMS to new products or to integrate IMS into more up-to-date software.

IMS does not adhere strictly to the theoretical hierarchal data mode. In particular, it does allow multiple parentage in some very restrictive situations. As an example, consider Figure A.5. There are actually two hierarchies in this diagram: the department to project hierarchy and the hierarchy consisting of just the employee.

Note: IMS refers to each hierarchy as a database and each entity as a segment.

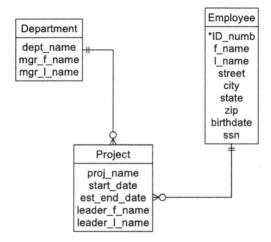

■ **FIGURE A.5 Two IMS hierarchies with permitted multiple parentage.**

The multiple parentage of the project entity is permitted because the second parent—the employee entity—is in another hierarchy and is at a higher level in the hierarchy. Despite the restrictions on multiple parentage, this easing of the rules goes a long way to removing unnecessary duplicated data.

IMS does not support a query language. All access is through application programs that are usually written in COBOL. Like a true hierarchical DBMS, it is therefore best suited to batch processing in tree traversal order. It has been heavily used in large businesses with heavy operational transaction processing loads, such as banks and insurance companies.

The Simple Network Data Model

At the same time IBM was developing IMS, other companies were working on DBMSs that were based on the simple network data model. The first DBMS based on this model appeared in 1967 (IDS from GE) and was welcomed because it directly addressed some of the limitations of the hierarchical data model. In terms of business usage, simple network databases had the widest deployment of any of the pre-relational data models.

Note: The network data models—both simple and complex—predate computer networks as we know them today. In the context of a data model, the term "network" refers to an interconnected mesh, such as a network of neurons in the brain or a television or radio network.

Characteristics of a Simple Network

A simple network database supports one-to-many relationship between entities. There is no restriction on multiple parentage, however. This means that the employees/departments/projects database we have been using as an example could be designed as in Figure A.6.

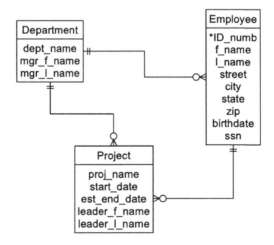

■ FIGURE A.6   A simple network data model.

In this example, the project acts as a composite entity between department and employee. In addition, there is a direct relationship between department and employee for faster access.

Given the restrictions of the hierarchical data model, the simple network was a logical evolutionary step. It removed the most egregious limitation of the hierarchical data model, that of no multiple parentage. It also further divorced the logical and physical storage, although as you will see shortly, simple network schemas still allowed logical database designers to specify some physical storage characteristics.

Simple network databases implement data relationships either by embedding pointers directly in the data or through the use of indexes. Regardless of which strategy is used, access to the data is restricted to the predefined links created by the pointers unless a fast access path has been defined separately for a particular type of entity. In this sense, a simple network is navigational, just like a hierarchical database.

There are two types of fast access paths available to the designer of a simple network. The first—*hashing*—affects the strategy used to place entity occurrences in a data file. When an entity occurrence is hashed into a data file, the DBMS uses a key (the value or one or more attributes) to compute a physical file locator (usually known as the *database key*). To retrieve the occurrence, the DBMS recomputes the hash value. Occurrences of related entities are then *clustered* around their parent entity in the data file. The purpose of this is twofold: It provides fast access to parent entities and puts child entities on the same disk page as their parents for faster retrieval. In the example we are using, a database designer might choose to hash department occurrences and cluster projects around their departments.

Note: A single entity occurrence can either be clustered or hashed; it can't be both because the two alternatives determine physical placement in a data file.

The second type of fast access path is an index, which provides fast direct access to entity occurrences containing secondary keys.

If occurrences are not hashed and have no indexes, then the only way to retrieve them is by traversing down relationships with parent entity occurrences.

To enable traversals of the data relationships, a simple network DBMS must keep track of where it is in the database. For every program running against the database, the DBMS maintains a set of *currency indicators*, each of which is a system variable containing the database key of the last entity occurrence accessed of a specific type. For example, there are currency indicators for each type of entity, for the program as a whole, and so on. Application programs can then use the contents of the currency indicators to perform data accesses relative to the program's previous location in the database.

Originally, simple network DBMSs did not support query languages. However, as the relational data model became more popular, many vendors added relational-style query languages to their products. If a simple network database is designed like a relational database, then it can be queried much like a relational database. However, the simple network is still underneath and the database is therefore still subject to the access limitations placed on a simple network.

Simple network databases are not easy to maintain. In particular, changes to the logical design of the database can be extremely disruptive. First, the database must be brought offline; no processing can proceed against it until the changes are complete. Once the database is down, then the following process occurs:

1. Back up all data or save the data in text files.
2. Delete the current schema and data files.
3. Compile the new database schema, which typically is contained in a text file, written in a *data definition language* (DDL).
4. Reallocate space for the data files.
5. Reload the data files.

In later simple network DBMSs, this process was largely automated by utility software, but considering that most simple network DBMSs were mainframe-based, they involved large amounts of data. Changes to the logical database could take significant amounts of time.

There are still simple network databases in use today as legacy systems. However, it would be highly unusual for an organization to decide to create a new database based on this data model.

CODASYL

In the mid-1960s, government and industry professionals organized into the Committee for Data Systems Languages (CODASYL). Their goal was to develop a business programming language, the eventual result of which was COBOL. As they were working, the committee realized that they had another output besides a programming language: the specifications for a simple network database. CODASYL spun off from the Database Task Group (DBTG), which in 1969 released its set of specifications.

The CODASYL specifications were submitted to the American National Standards Institute (ANSI). ANSI made a few modifications to the standard to further separate the logical design of the database from its physical storage layout. The result was two sets of very similar, but not identical, specifications.

Note: It is important to understand that CODASYL is a standard, rather than a product. Many products were developed to adhere to the CODASYL standards. In addition, there have been simple network DBMSs that employ the simple network data model but not the CODASYL standards.

A CODASYL DBMS views a simple network as a collection of two-level hierarchies known as *sets*. The database in Figure A.6 requires two sets: one for department → employee and department → project and the second for employee → project. The entity at the "one" end of the relationships is known as the *owner* of the set; entities at the "many" end of relationships are known as *members* of the set. There can be only one owner entity, but many member entities, of any set. The same entity can be an owner of one set and a member of another, allowing the database designer to build a network of many levels.

As mentioned in the previous section, access is either directly to an entity occurrence using a fast access path (hashing or an index) or in traversal order. In the case of a CODASYL database, the members of a set have an order that is specified by the database designer.

If an entity is not given a fast access path, then the only way to retrieve occurrences is through the owners of some set. In addition, there is no way to retrieve all occurrences of an entity unless all of those occurrences are members of the same set, with the same owner.

Each set provides a conceptual linked list, beginning with the owner occurrence, continuing through all member occurrences, and linking back to the owner. Like the occurrences of a hierarchy in a hierarchical database, the occurrences of a set are distinct and unrelated, as in Figure A.7.

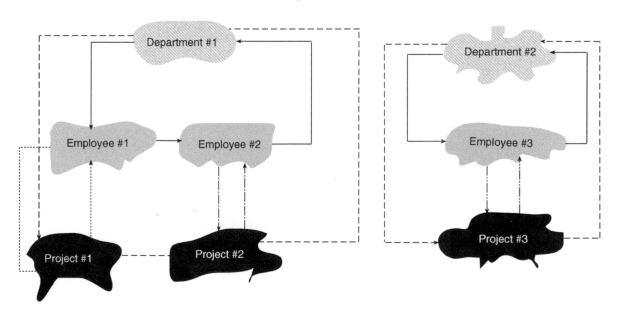

■ **FIGURE A.7** Occurrences of CODASYL sets.

Note: Early CODASYL DBMSs actually implemented sets as linked lists. The result was complex pointer manipulation in the data files, especially for entities that were members of multiple sets. Later products represented sets using indexes, with database keys acting as pointers to the storage locations of owner and member records.

The independence of set occurrences presents a major problem for entities that aren't a member of any set, such as the department occurrences in Figure A.7. To handle this limitation, CODASYL databases support a special type of set—often called a *system set*—that has only one owner occurrence, the database system itself. All occurrences of an entity that is a member of that set are connected to the single owner occurrence. Employees and projects would probably be included in a system set also to provide the ability to access all employees and all projects. The declaration of system sets is left up to the database designer.

Any DBMS that was written to adhere to either set of CODASYL standards is generally known as a CODASYL DBMS. This represents the largest population of simple network products that were marketed.

Arguably, the most successful CODASYL DBMS was IDMS, originally developed by Cullinet. IDMS was a mainframe product that was popular well into the 1980s. As relational DBMSs began to dominate the market, IDMS was given a relational-like query language and marketed as IDMS/R. Ultimately, Cullinet was sold to Computer Associates, which marketed and supported the product under the name CA-IDMS.

Note: Although virtually every PC DBMS in the market today claims to be relational, many are not. Some, such as FileMaker Pro, are actually simple networks. These are client/server products, robust enough for small business use. They allow multiple parentage with one-to-many relationships and represent those relationships with pre-established links between files. These are simple networks. This doesn't mean that they aren't good products, but simply that they don't meet the minimum requirements for a relational DBMS.

The Complex Network Data Model

The complex network data model was developed at the same time as the simple network. It allows direct many-to-many relationships without requiring the introduction of a composite entity. The intent of the data model's developers was to remove the restriction against many-to-many relationships imposed by the simple network data model. However, the removal of this restriction comes with a steep price.

There are at least two major problems associated with the inclusion of direct many-to-many relationships. Consider first the database segment in Figure A.8. Notice that there is no place to store data about the quantity of each item being ordered. The need to store relationship data is one reason why we replace many-to-many relationships with a composite entity and two one-to-many relationships.

Nonetheless, if we examine an occurrence diagram for Figure A.8 (see Figure A.9), you can see that there is no ambiguity in the relationships. However, assume that we add another entity to the design, as in Figure A.10. In this case each item can appear on many shipments and each shipment can contain many items.

The problem with this design becomes clear when you look at the occurrences in Figure A.11. Notice, for example, that it is impossible to determine the order to which Shipment #1 and Shipment #2 belong. After you follow the relationships from the shipment occurrence to Item #1, there is no way to know which order is correct.

There are two solutions to this problem. The first is to introduce an additional relationship to indicate which shipment comes from which order, as in Figure A.12. Although this is certainly a viable solution, the result is increased complexity for storing and retrieving data.

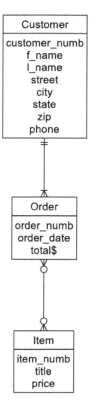

■ FIGURE A.8 A complex network lacking a place to store relationship data.

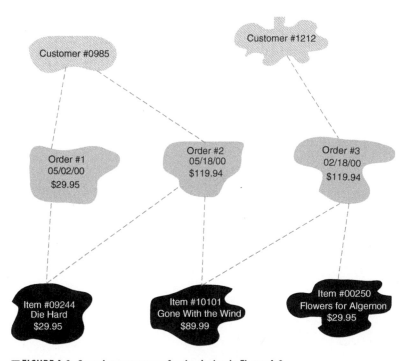

■ FIGURE A.9 Sample occurrences for the design in Figure A.8.

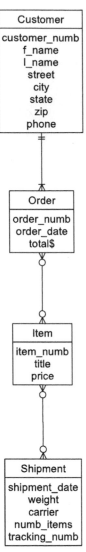

The other solution is to abandon the use of the complex network altogether and introduce composite entities to reduce all the many-to-many relationships to one-to-many relationships. The result, of course, is a simple network.

Note: A relational DBMS can represent all the relationships acceptable in a simple network—including composite entities—but does so in a non-navigational manner. Like a simple network, it can capture all of the meaning of a many-to-many relationship and still avoid data ambiguity.

Because of the complexity of maintaining many-to-many relationships and the possibility of logical ambiguity, there have been no widely successful commercial products based on the complex network data model. However, the data model remains in the literature, and provides some theoretical completeness to traditional data modeling.

■ FIGURE A.10 A complex network with ambiguous logical relationships.

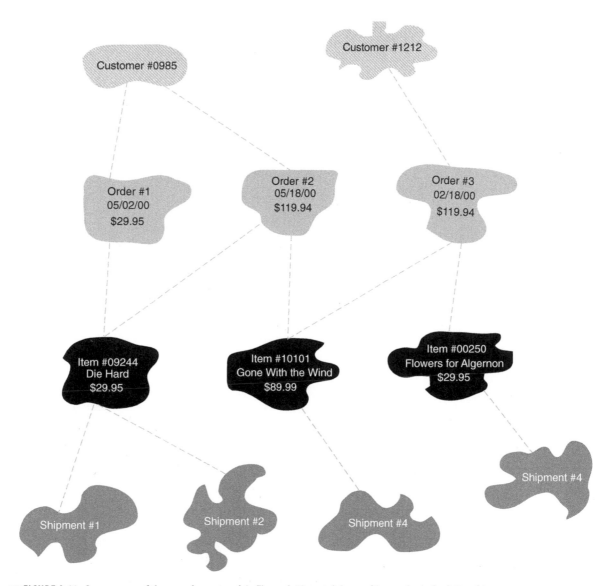

■ FIGURE A.11 Occurrences of the complex network in Figure A.10 containing ambiguous logical relationships.

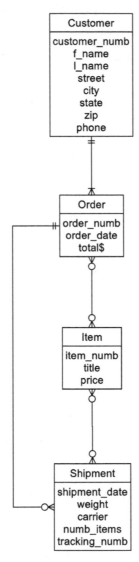

■ FIGURE A.12 Using an additional relationship to remove logical ambiguity in a complex network.

Appendix
B

SQL Programming

Although SQL is not a complete programming language—it lacks I/O statements—the standard does contain statements that perform typical programming language functions such as assignment, selection, and iteration for writing *persistent stored modules* (PSMs). Stored within the database, these can be executed as *triggers* (code that is executed when a specific event occurs) or as *stored procedures* (code that is executed with the SQL CALL statement).

In addition, SQL statements can be added to programs written in high-level programming languages to create stand-alone applications. This appendix looks at both types of SQL programming.

Note: This appendix does not attempt to teach programming concepts. To get the most out of it, you should be familiar with a general-purpose programming or scripting language such as COBOL, C, C++, Java, JavaScript, Python, or Perl.

SQL Language Programming Elements

The smallest unit of a SQL PSM is a *routine*. Typically, a routine will perform a single action, such as updating a total or inserting a row in a table. Routines are then gathered into *modules*.

There are three types of routines:

- Procedures: Procedures are executed with the SQL CALL statement. They do not return a value.
- Functions: Functions return a typed value and are used within other SQL statements (in particular, SELECT).
- Methods: Methods are used by SQL's object-relational extensions. They are written using the same programming elements as procedures and functions. Therefore, their structure is discussed in Chapter 27, but the techniques for creating method bodies can be found in this chapter.

To create a procedure, use the CREATE PROCEDURE statement:

```
CREATE PROCEDURE procedure_name (input_parameters)
LANGUAGE SQL
MODIFIES SQL DATA
BEGIN
     procedure_body
END
```

Function creation must include the type of data being returned and a RETURN statement:

```
CREATE FUNCTION function_name (input_parameters)
RETURNS return_data_type
LANGUAGE SQL
CONTAINS SQL
     function_body
RETURN return_value
```

Note: Functions that you write yourself are often called user-defined functions (UDFs) to distinguish them from functions such as SUM (sometimes called BIFs, for Built-In Functions) that are part of the SQL language.

Notice that the two preceding structures include statements that refer to the language and type of statements in the routine:

- LANGUAGE *language_name*: indicates the programming language used in the routine. In our examples, the language is SQL. If the LANGUAGE clause is not present, then the language defaults to SQL.
- Type of SQL statements contained in routine (one of the following):
  - CONTAINS SQL: indicates that the routine includes SQL statements that do not retrieve or modify data.
  - READS SQL DATA: indicates that the routine includes SQL statements that read data from a database, but that do not modify data.
  - MODIFIES SQL DATA: indicates that the routine modifies data using SQL commands. This also implies that the routine may be retrieving data.

The routine's contents may include SQL data modification statements (INSERT, UPDATE, and DELETE) along with SQL control structures.

SQL modules are created with the CREATE MODULE statement:

```
CREATE MODULE module_name
     module_contents
END MODULE
```

Like other SQL structural elements, routines, modules, and their contents are stored in the current schema. To remove a module or routine, you must therefore use

```
DROP ROUTINE routine_name
```

or

```
DROP MODULE module_name
```

Note: The interactive SELECT, which typically returns multiple rows, is useful only for display of a result table. To manipulate the data in a result table, you will need to use embedded SQL, which retrieves data into a virtual table and then lets you process the rows in that table one at a time. Dynamic SQL further extends programming with SQL by letting the user enter search values at run time. Both are discussed later in this appendix.

Within a module, SQL recognizes compound statements using BEGIN and END:

```
BEGIN
     one_or_more_executable_statements
END
```

As you might expect, compound statements can be nested as needed.

Variables and Assignment

SQL modules can maintain their own internal variables and perform assignment. Variables must be declared before they are used:

```
DECLARE variable_name data_type
```

Once a variable has been declared, you assign values to it across the assignment operator:

```
variable_name = value
```

For example, if you need to store a sales tax percentage, the routine could contain

```
DECLARE tax_rate NUMBER (6,3);
tax_rate = 0.075;
```

Important note: Depending on the DBMS, the assignment operator may be = or :-. Check your documentation to be sure.

Important note: Some DBMSs require a special character at the beginning of a variable name. For example, SQL Server requires @. Once again, the only way to be certain is to consult your DBMS's documentation.

Passing Parameters

Both functions and procedures can accept input parameters. A parameter list contains the names by which the parameters are to be referenced within the body of the routine and a declaration of their data types:

```
CREATE routine_type routine_name
    (parameter_1 parameter_1_data_type,
    parameter_2 parameter_2_data_type, … )
```

For example, to pass in a tax rate and a selling price to a function that computes sales tax, the function might be written

```
CREATE FUNCTION compute_tax (tax_rate NUMBER (6,3),
    selling_price NUMBER (7,2))
LANGUAGE SQL
RETURNS NUMBER
    RETURN selling_price * tax_rate;
```

Procedures can also use a parameter for output or for both input and output.

Note: Some DBMSs require/allow you to specify whether a parameter is for input, output, or both. If you are working with one of those implementations, each parameter in the parameter list must/can be labeled with IN, OUT, or INOUT.

Scope of Variables

Variables declared within SQL functions and procedures are local to the routine. Values passed in through a parameter list are declared in the parameter list and therefore become local variables. However, there are circumstances in which you may want to use variables declared outside the function or procedure (*host language variables*). In that case, there are two things you need to do:

■ Redeclare the host language variables using a SQL declare section.

```
BEGIN SQL DECLARE SECTION;
    redeclaration_of_host_language_variables;
END SQL DECLARE SECTION;
```

■ Place a colon in front of the name of each host language variable whenever it is used in the body of the SQL routine.

Selection

The SQL standard provides two selection structures: IF and CASE. Both function essentially like the analogous elements in general-purpose programming languages.

IF

In its simplest form, the SQL IF construct has the following structure:

```
IF boolean_expression THEN
     body_of_IF
END IF
```

Assume, for example, that the owner of the rare book store wants to give a discount on a total purchase to customers who order more than $100 on a single order. The code to do so could be written

```
IF sale_total_amt >= 100 THEN
     sale_total_amt = sale_total_amt * .9;
END IF;
```

As you would expect, the IF statement can be extended with ELSEIF and ELSE clauses:

```
IF boolean_expression THEN
     body_of_IF
ELSEIF boolean_expression THEN
     body_of_ELSEIF
:
ELSE
     body_of_ELSE
END OF
```

The ELSEIF clause is shorthand for the following:

```
IF boolean_expression THEN
     body_of_IF
ELSE
     IF boolean_expression THEN
          body_of_nested_IF
     END IF
END IF
```

A purchase from the rare book store that must be shipped is assessed shipping charges based on the number of volumes in the purchase. Assuming the number of volumes in the purchase is stored in *how_many*, an IF construct to assign those shipping charges might be written as

```
IF how_many <= 5 THEN
     shipping_charges = how_many * 2;
ELSEIF how_many <= 10 THEN
     shipping_charges = how_many * 1.5;
ELSE
     shipping_charges = how_many;
END IF
```

Note: Obtaining the count of the number of volumes in a single purchase requires embedded SQL.

CASE

The SQL CASE expression comes in two forms, one that chooses which statement to execute based on a single specified value and one that chooses based on logical expressions. (The syntaxes are essentially the same as the CASE statement that can be used in a SELECT clause.) In its simplest form, it has the general format:

```
CASE logical_expression
     WHEN value1 THEN executable_statement(s)
     WHEN value2 THEN executable_statement(s)
     WHEN value3 THEN executable_statement(s)
     :
     ELSE default
END CASE
```

For example, suppose T-shirt sizes are stored as integer codes, and you want to translate those sizes to words. The code could be written

```
DECLARE text_size CHAR (10)
CASE size
     WHEN 1 THEN text_size = 'Small'
     WHEN 2 THEN text_size = 'Medium'
     WHEN 3 THEN text_size = 'Large'
     WHEN 4 THEN text_size = 'Extra Large'
END CASE
```

The multiple condition version is a bit more flexible:

```
CASE
     WHEN logical_expression1  THEN executable_statement(s)
     WHEN logical_expression1  THEN executable_statement(s)
     WHEN logical_expression1  THEN executable_statement(s)
     :
     ELSE default
END CASE;
```

Someone could use this second version to compute a book discount based on selling price:

```
CASE
    WHEN asking_price < 50 THEN selling_price
        = asking_price * .9
    WHEN asking_price < 100 THEN selling_price
        = asking_price * .85
    WHEN asking_price < 150 THEN selling_price
        = asking_price * .75
    ELSE selling_price = asking_price * .5
END CASE;
```

Iteration

SQL has four statements that perform iteration—LOOP, WHILE, REPEAT, and FOR—that work somewhat differently from similar statements in general-purpose programming languages.

Note: The SQL FOR statement is not a general-purpose looping construct. Instead, it is designed to work with embedded SQL code that processes each row in a virtual table that has been created as the result of a SELECT. We will therefore defer a discussion of FOR until later in this appendix.

LOOP

The LOOP statement is a simple construct that sets up an infinite loop:

```
loop_name : LOOP
     body_of_loop
END LOOP
```

The condition that terminates the loop and a command to exit the loop must therefore be contained in the body of the loop. A typical structure therefore would be

```
loop_name: LOOP
     body_of_loop
     IF termination_condition
         LEAVE loop_name
END LOOP
```

Assume (for some unknown reason) that we want to total the numbers from 1 through 100. We could do it with a LOOP statement as follows:

```
DECLARE sum INT;
DECLARE count INT;
sum = 0;
count = 1;
sum_loop: LOOP
    sum = sum + count;
    count = count + 1;
    IF count > 100
        LEAVE sum_loop;
END LOOP;
```

Note: LEAVE can be used with any named looping construct. However, it is essential only for a LOOP structure because there is no other way to stop the iteration.

WHILE

The SQL WHILE is very similar to what you will find as part of a general-purpose programming language:

```
loop_name: WHILE boolean_expression DO
     body_of_loop
END WHILE
```

The loop name is optional.

As an example, assume that you wanted to continue to purchase items until all of your funds were exhausted, but that each time you purchased an item the price went up 10%. Each purchase is stored as a row in a table. Code to handle that could be written as

```
DECLARE funds NUMBER (7,2);
funds = 1000.00;
DECLARE price NUMBER (5,2);
price = 29.95;

WHILE :funds > :price = DO
     INSERT INTO items_purchased VALUES
     (6, CURRENT_DATE, :price);
     funds = funds - price;
     price = price * 1.1;
END WHILE;
```

Note: Whenever a host language (in this case SQL) variable is used in a SQL statement, it must be preceded by a colon, as in :price.

REPEAT

The SQL REPEAT statement is similar to the DO WHILE statement in high-level languages where the test for termination/continuation of the loop is at the bottom of the loop. It has the general format:

```
loop_name: REPEAT
     body_of_loop
UNTIL boolean_expression
END REPEAT
```

We could rewrite the example from the preceding section using a REPEAT in the following way:

```
DECLARE funds NUMBER (7,2);
funds = 1000.00;
DECLARE price NUMBER (5,2);
price = 29.95;

REPEAT
     INSERT INTO items_purchased VALUES
     (6, CURRENT_DATE, :price);
     funds = funds - price;
     price = price * 1.1;
UNTIL price > funds
END REPEAT;
```

Example #1: Interactive Retrievals

One of the things you might decide to do with a stored procedure is sim-plify issuing a query or series of queries. For example, suppose that the owner of the rare book store wants to see the sales that were made each day along with the total sales. A single interactive SQL command won't pro-duce both a listing of individual sales and a total. However, the two queries in Figure B.1 will do the trick. The user only needs to run the procedure to see the needed data.

```
CREATE PROCEDURE daily_sales
LANGUAGE SQL
READS SQL DATA
     SELECT first_name, last_name, sale_total_amt
     FROM sale JOIN customer
     WHERE sale_date = CURRENT_DATE;
     SELECT SUM(sale_total_amt)
     FROM sale
     WHERE sale_date = CURRENT_DATE;
END
```

■ **FIGURE B.1   A SQL procedure that contains multiple SELECT statements for display.**

Note: Without embedded SQL, we can only display data retrieved by a SE-LECT. We can't process the individual rows.

Example #2: Nested Modules

Procedures and functions can call other procedures and functions. For this example, let's assume that a column for the sales tax has been added to the *sale* table and prepare a procedure that populates the *sale* table and updates the *volume* table when a purchase is made (Figure B.2). The *sell_it* proce-dure uses the *compute_tax* function.

```
CREATE PROCEDURE sell_it (sale_numb INT, customer_id INT, book_id_char
      CHAR(17), price_paid NUMBER (7,2), tax_rate NUMBER (6,3))
LANGUAGE SQL
MODIFIES SQL DATA
BEGIN
      DECLARE tax NUMBER (6,3);
      tax = compute_tax (tax_rate, price_paid)
      IF (SELECT COUNT(*) FROM volume WHERE sale_id = sale_numb) < 1 THEN
            INSERT INTO sale (:sale_id, :customer_id, CURRENT_DATE,
                  :price_paid, amt, :sales_tax) VALUES (sale_numb,
                  customer_id, CURRENT_DATE, :price_paid, tax);
      END IF
      UPDATE volume
            SET selling_price = :price_paid,
            SET sale_id = :sale_numb;
END

CREATE PROCEDURE compute_tax (tax_rate NUMBER (6,3),selling_price (7,2))
LANGUAGE SQL
RETURNS NUMBER
      RETURN selling_price * tax_rate;
```

■ **FIGURE B.2 A SQL procedure that calls a user-defined function.**

Executing Modules as Triggers

A trigger is a module that is attached to a single table and executed in re-sponse to one of the following events:

- INSERT (either before or after an insert occurs)
- UPDATE (either before or after a modify occurs)
- DELETE (either before or after a delete occurs)

"Before" triggers are run prior to checking constraints on the table and prior to running the INSERT, UPDATE, or DELETE command. "After" triggers work on the table after the INSERT, UPDATE, or DELETE has been performed, using the table as it is changed by the command. A trigger can be configured to run once for every row in the table or just once for the entire table.

Note: It is possible to attach multiple triggers for the same event to the same table. The order in which they execute is implementation dependent. Some DBMSs execute them in alphabetical order by name; others execute them chronologically, with the first created being the first executed.

Before creating a trigger, you must create the function or procedure that is to be run. Once that is in place, you use the CREATE TRIGGER statement to attach the trigger to its table, and specify when it should be run:

```
CREATE TRIGGER trigger_name when_to_execute type_of_event
ON table_name row_or_table_specifier
EXECUTE PROCEDURE procedure_or_function_name
```

The *when_to_execute* value is either BEFORE or AFTER, the type of event is INSERT, MODIFY, or DELETE, and the *row_or_table_specifier* is either FOR EACH ROW or FOR EACH STATEMENT.

For example, to trigger the procedure that updates the *sale_total_amt* in the *sale* table whenever a volume is sold, someone at the rare book store could use

```
CREATE TRIGGER t_update_total AFTER UPDATE
ON volume FOR EACH STATEMENT
EXECUTE PROCEDURE p_update_total;
```

The trigger will then execute automatically whenever an update is performed on the *volume* table.

You remove a trigger with the DROP TRIGGER statement:

```
DROP TRIGGER trigger_name
```

However, it can be a bit tedious to continually drop a trigger when what you want to do is replace an existing trigger with a new version. To simply replace an existing trigger, use

```
CREATE OR MODIFY TRIGGER trigger_name …
```

instead of simply CREATE TRIGGER.

Executing Modules as Stored Procedures

Stored procedures are invoked with either the EXECUTE or CALL statement:

```
EXECUTE procedure_name (parameter_list)
```

or

```
CALL procedure_name (parameter_list)
```

Embedded SQL Programming

Although a knowledgeable SQL user can accomplish a great deal with an interactive command processor, much interaction with a database is through application programs that provide a predictable interface for nontechnologically sophisticated users. In this section, you will read about the preparation of programs that contain SQL statements and the special things you must do to fit SQL within a host programming language.

The Embedded SQL Environment

SQL statements can be embedded in a wide variety of host languages. Some are general-purpose programming languages, such as COBOL, C++, or

Java. Others are special-purpose database programming languages, such as the PowerScript language used by PowerBuilder or Oracle's SQL/Plus, which contains the SQL language elements discussed throughout this book as well as Oracle-specific extensions.

The way in which you handle source code depends on the type of host language you are using: Special-purpose database languages such as Power-Script or extensions of the SQL language (for example, SQL/Plus) need no special processing. Their language translators recognize embedded SQL statements and know what to do with them. However, general-purpose language compilers are not written to recognize syntax that isn't part of the original language. When a COBOL[1] or C++ compiler encounters a SQL statement, it generates an error.

The solution to the problem has several aspects:

- Support for SQL statements is provided by a set of program library modules. The input parameters to the modules represent the portions of a SQL statement that are set by the programmer.
- SQL statements embedded in a host language program are translated by a *precompiler* into calls to routines in the SQL library.
- The host language compiler can access the calls to library routines and therefore can compile the output produced by the precompiler.
- During the linking phase of program preparation, the library routines used to support SQL are linked to the executable file along with any other library used by the program.

Java and JDBC

Java is an unusual language in that it is pseudo-compiled. (Language tokens are converted to machine code at runtime by the Java virtual machine.) It also accesses databases in its own way: using a library of routines (an API) known as *Java Database Connectivity*, or JDBC. A JDBC driver provides the interface between the JDBC library and the specific DBMS being used.

JDBC does not require that Java programs be precompiled. Instead, SQL commands are created as strings that are passed as parameters to functions

---

[1]Many people think COBOL is a dead language. While few new programs are being written, there are literally billions of lines of code for business applications written in COBOL that are still in use. Maintaining these applications is becoming a major issue for many organizations because COBOL programmers are starting to retire in large numbers and young programmers haven't learned the language.

in the JDBC library. The process for interacting with a database using JDBC goes something like this:

1. Create a connection to the database.
2. Use the object returned in Step 1 to create an object for a SQL statement.
3. Store each SQL command that will be used in a string variable.
4. Use the object returned in Step 2 to execute one or more SQL statements.
5. Close the statement object.
6. Close the database connection object.

If you will be using Java to write database applications, then you will probably want to investigate JDBC. Many books have been written about using it with a variety of DBMSs.

To make it easier for the precompiler to recognize SQL statements, each one is preceded by EXEC SQL. The way in which you terminate the statement varies from one language to another. The typical terminators are summarized in Table B.1. For the examples in this book, we will use a semicolon as an embedded SQL statement terminator.

Table B.1 Embedded SQL Statement Terminators

Language	Terminator
Ada	Semicolon
C, C++	Semicolon
COBOL	END-EXEC
Fortran	None
MUMPS	Close parenthesis
Pascal	Semicolon
PL/1	Semicolon

Using Host Language Variables

General purpose programming languages require that you redeclare any host language variables used in embedded SQL statements. The declarations are bracketed between two SQL statements, using the following format:

```
EXEC SQL BEGIN DECLARE SECTION;
    declarations go here
EXEC SQL END DECLARE SECTION;
```

The specifics of the variable declarations depend on the host language being used. The syntax typically conforms to the host language's syntax for variable declarations.

When you use a host language variable in a SQL statement, you precede it by a colon so that it is distinct from table, view, and column names. For example, the following statement updates one row in the *customer* table with a value stored in the variable *da_new_phone*, using a value stored in the variable *da_which_customer* to identify the row to be modified:[2]

```
EXEC SQL UPDATE customer
    SET contact_phone = :da_new_phone
    WHERE customer_numb = :da_which_customer;
```

This use of a colon applies both to general purpose programming languages and to database application languages (even those that don't require a pre-compiler).

Note: The requirement for the colon in front of host language variables means that theoretically columns and host language variables could have the same names. In practice, however, using the same names can be confusing.

The host language variables that contain data for use in SQL statements are known as *dynamic parameters*. The values that are sent to the DBMS, for example, as part of a WHERE predicate, are known as *input parameters*. The values that accept data being returned by the DBMS, such as the data returned by a SELECT, are known as *output parameters*.

DBMS Return Codes

When you are working with interactive SQL, error messages appear on your screen. For example, if an INSERT command violates a table constraint, the SQL command processor tells you immediately. You then read the message and make any necessary changes to your SQL to correct the problem. However, when SQL is embedded in a program, the end user has no access to the SQL and therefore can't make any corrections. Technologically unsophisticated users also may become upset when they see the usually cryptic DBMS errors appearing on the screen. Programs in which SQL is embedded need to be able to intercept the error codes returned by the DBMS and to handle them before the errors reach the end user.

The SQL standard defines a status variable named SQLSTATE, a five-character string. The first two characters represent the class of the error. The rightmost three characters are the subclass, which provides further detail about the state of the database. For example, 00000 means that the SQL statement executed successfully. Other codes include a class of 22, which indicates a

---

[2]Keep in mind that this will work only if the value on which we are searching is a primary key and thus uniquely identifies the row.

data exception. The subclasses of class 22 include 003 (numeric value out of range) and 007 (invalid datetime format). A complete listing of the SQL-STATE return codes can be found in Table B.3 at the end of this appendix.

In most cases, an application should check the contents of SQLSTATE each time it executes a SQL statement. For example, after performing the update example you saw in the preceding section, a C++ program might do the following:

```
If (strcmp(SQLSTATE,'00000') == 0)
    EXEC SQL COMMIT;
else
{
    // some error handling code goes here
}
```

Retrieving a Single Row

When the WHERE predicate in a SELECT statement contains a primary key expression, the result table will contain at most one row. For such a query, all you need to do is specify host language variables into which the SQL command processor can place the data it retrieves. You do this by adding an INTO clause to the SELECT.

For example, if someone at the rare book store needed the phone number of a specific customer, a program might include

```
EXEC SQL SELECT contact_phone
INTO :da_phone_numb
FROM customers
WHERE customer_numb = 12;
```

The INTO clause contains the keyword INTO followed by the names of the host language variables in which data will be placed. In the preceding example, data are being retrieved from only one column and the INTO clause therefore contains just a single variable name.

Note: Many programmers have naming conventions that make working with host variables a bit easier. In this book, the names of host language variables that hold data begin with da_; indicator variables, to which you will be introduced in the next section, begin with in_.

If you want to retrieve data from multiple columns, you must provide one host language variable for each column, as in the following:

```
EXEC SQL SELECT first_name, last_name, contact_phone
INTO :da_first, :da_last, :da_phone
FROM customer
WHERE customer_numb = 12;
```

The names of the host language variables are irrelevant. The SQL command processor places data into them by position. In other words, data from the first column following SELECT is placed in the first variable following INTO, data from the second column following SELECT is placed in the second variable following INTO, and so on. Keep in mind that all host language variables are preceded by colons to distinguish them from the names of database elements.

After executing a SELECT that contains a primary key expression in its WHERE predicate, an embedded SQL program should check to determine whether a row was retrieved. Assuming we are using C or C++, the code might be written

```
if (strcmp(SQLSTATE,'00000') == 0)
{
    EXEC SQL COMMIT;
    // display or process data retrieved
)
else
{
    EXEC SQL COMMIT;
    // display error message
}
// continue processing
```

There are three things to note about the COMMIT statement in this code:

- The COMMIT must be issued *after* checking the SQLSTATE. Otherwise, the COMMIT will change the value in SQLSTATE.
- There is no need to roll back a retrieval transaction, so the code commits the transaction even if the retrieval fails.
- The COMMIT could be placed after the IF construct. However, depending on the length of the code that follows error checking, the transaction may stay open longer than necessary. Therefore, the repeated COMMIT statement is an efficient choice in this situation.

Indicator Variables

The SQLSTATE variable is not the only way in which a DBMS can communicate the results of a retrieval to an application program. Each host variable into which you place data can be associated with an *indicator variable*. When indicator variables are present, the DBMS stores a 0 to indicate that a data variable has valid data. Otherwise, it stores a -1 to indicate that the row contained a null in the specified column and that the contents of the data variable are unchanged.

To use indicator variables, first declare host language variables of an integer data type to hold the indicators. Then, follow each data variable in the INTO clause with the keyword INDICATOR, and the name of the indicator variable. For example, to use indicator variables with the customer data retrieval query:

```
EXEC SQL SELECT first_name, last_name, contact_phone
INTO :da_first INDICATOR :in_first, :da_last
      INDICATOR :in_last, :da_phone INDICATOR :in_phone
FROM customer
WHERE customer_numb = 12;
```

You can then use host language syntax to check the contents of each indicator variable to determine whether you have valid data to process in each data variable.

Note: The INDICATOR keyword is optional. Therefore, the syntax INTO :first :ifirst, :last :ilast, and so on, is acceptable.

Indicator variables can also be useful for telling you when character values have been truncated. For example, assume that the host language variable *first* has been declared to accept a 10-character string but that the database column *first_name* is 15 characters long. If the database column contains a full 15 characters, only the first 10 will be placed in the host language variable. The indicator variable will contain 15, indicating the size of the column (and the size to which the host language variable should have been set).

Retrieving Multiple Rows: Cursors

SELECT statements that may return more than one row present a bit of a problem when you embed them in a program. Host language variables can hold only one value at a time and the SQL command processor cannot work with host language arrays. The solution provides you with a pointer (a *cursor*) to a SQL result table that allows you to extract one row at a time for processing.

The procedure for creating and working with a cursor is as follows:

1. *Declare* the cursor by specifying the SQL SELECT to be executed. This does not perform the retrieval.
2. *Open* the cursor. This step actually executes the SELECT and creates the result table in main memory. It positions the cursor just above the first row in the result table.
3. *Fetch* the next row in the result table and process the data in some way.
4. Repeat step 3 until all rows in the result table have been accessed and processed.

5. *Close* the cursor. This deletes the result table from main memory, but does not destroy the declaration. You can therefore reopen an existing cursor, recreating the result table, and work with the data without redeclaring the SELECT.

If you do not explicitly close a cursor, it will be closed automatically when the transaction terminates. (This is the default.) If, however, you want the cursor to remain open after a COMMIT, then you add a WITH HOLD option to the declaration.

Even if a cursor is held from one transaction to another, its result table will still be deleted at the end of the database session in which it was created. To return that result table to the calling routine, add a WITH RETURN option to the declaration.

Note: There is no way to "undeclare" a cursor. A cursor's declaration disappears when the program module in which it was created terminates.

By default, a cursor fetches the "next" row in the result table. However, you may also use a *scrollable cursor* to fetch the "next, " "prior, " "first, " or "last" row. In addition, you can fetch by specifying a row number in the result table or by giving an offset from the current row. This eliminates, in large measure, the need to close and reopen the cursor to reposition the cursor above its current location.

Declaring a Cursor

Declaring a cursor is similar to creating a view in that you include a SQL statement that defines a virtual table. The DECLARE statement has the following general format in its simplest form:

```
DECLARE  cursor_name CURSOR FOR
SELECT  remainder_of_query
```

For example, assume that someone at the rare book store wanted to prepare labels for a mailing to all its customers. The program that prints mailing labels needs each customer's name and address from the database, which it can then format for labels. A cursor to hold the data might be declared as

```
EXEC SQL DECLARE address_data CURSOR FOR
SELECT first_name, last_name, street, city,
     state_province, zip_postcode
FROM customer;
```

The name of a cursor must be unique within the program module in which it is created. A program can therefore manipulate an unlimited number of cursors at the same time.

Scrolling Cursors

One of the options available with a cursor is the ability to retrieve rows in other than the default "next" order. To enable a scrolling cursor, you must indicate that you want scrolling when you declare the cursor by adding the keyword SCROLL after the cursor name:

```
EXEC SQL DECLARE address_data SCROLL CURSOR FOR
SELECT first_name, last_name, street, city,
    state_province, zip_postcode
FROM customer;
```

You will find more about using scrolling cursors a bit later in this chapter when we talk about fetching rows.

Enabling Updates

The data in a cursor are by default read only. However, if the result table meets all updatability criteria, you can use the cursor for data modification. (You will find more about the updatability criteria in the *Modification Using Cursors* section later in this appendix.)

To enable modification for a customer, add the keywords FOR UPDATE at the end of the cursor's declaration:

```
EXEC SQL DECLARE address_data SCROLL CURSOR FOR
SELECT first_name, last_name, street, city,
    state_province, zip_postcode
FROM customer
FOR UPDATE;
```

To restrict updates to specific columns, add the names of columns following UPDATE:

```
EXEC SQL DECLARE address_data SCROLL CURSOR FOR
SELECT first_name, last_name, street, city,
    state_province, zip_postcode
FROM customer
FOR UPDATE street, city, state_province, zip_postcode;
```

Sensitivity

Assume, for example, that a program for the rare book store contains a module that computes the average price of books and changes prices based on that average: If a book's price is more than 20% higher than the average, the price is discounted 10%; if the price is only 10% higher, it is discounted 5%.

A programmer codes the logic of the program in the following way:

1. Declare and open a cursor that contains the inventory IDs and asking prices for all volumes whose price is greater than the average. The SELECT that generates the result table is

```
SELECT inventory_id, asking_price
FROM volume
WHERE asking_price > (SELECT AVG (asking_price) FROM volume);
```

2. Fetch each row and modify its price.

The question at this point is: What happens in the result table as data are modified? As prices are lowered, some rows will no longer meet the criteria for inclusion in the table. More important, the average retail price will drop. If this program is to execute correctly, however, the contents of the result table must remain fixed once the cursor has been opened.

The SQL standard therefore defines three types of cursors:

- *Insensitive*: The contents of the result table are fixed.
- *Sensitive*: The contents of the result table are updated each time the table is modified.
- *Indeterminate* (*asensitive*): The effects of updates made by the same transaction on the result table are left up to each individual DBMS.

The default is indeterminate, which means that you cannot be certain that the DBMS will not alter your result table before you are through with it.

The solution is to request specifically that the cursor be insensitive:

```
EXEC SQL DECLARE address_data SCROLL INSENSITIVE CURSOR FOR
SELECT first_name, last_name, street, city,
    state_province, zip_postcode
FROM customer
FOR UPDATE street, city, state_province, zip_postcode;
```

Opening a Cursor

To open a cursor, place the cursor's name following the keyword OPEN:

```
EXEC SQL OPEN address_data;
```

Fetching Rows

To retrieve the data from the next row in a result table, placing the data into host language variables, you use the FETCH statement:

```
FETCH FROM cursor_name
INTO host_language_variables
```

For example, to obtain a row of data from the list of customer names and addresses, the rare book store's program could use

```
EXEC SQL FETCH FROM address_data
INTO :da_first, :da_last, :da_street, :da_city,
     :da_state_province, :da_zip_postcode;
```

Notice that, as always, the host language variables are preceded by colons to distinguish them from table, view, or column names. In addition, the host language variables must match the database columns as to data type. The FETCH will fail if, for example, you attempt to place a string value into a numeric variable.

If you want to fetch something other than the next row, you can declare a scrolling cursor and specify the row by adding the direction in which you want the cursor to move after the keyword FETCH:

- To fetch the first row

    ```
    EXEC SQL FETCH FIRST FROM address_data
    INTO :da_first, :da_last, :da_street, :da_city,
         :da_state_province, :da_zip_postcode;
    ```

- To fetch the last row

    ```
    EXEC SQL FETCH LAST FROM address_data
    INTO :da_first, :da_last, :da_street, :da_city,
         :da_state_province, :da_zip_postcode;
    ```

- To fetch the prior row

    ```
    EXEC SQL FETCH PRIOR FROM address_data
    INTO :da_first, :da_last, :da_street, :da_city,
         :da_state_province, :da_zip_postcode;
    ```

- To fetch a row specified by its position (row number) in the result table

    ```
    EXEC SQL FETCH ABSOLUTE 12 FROM address_data
    INTO :da_first, :da_last, :da_street, :da_city,
         :da_state_province, :da_zip_postcode;
    ```

    The preceding fetches the twelfth row in the result table.

- To fetch a row relative to and below the current position of the cursor

    ```
    EXEC SQL FETCH RELATIVE 5 FROM address_data
    INTO :da_first, :da_last, :da_street, :da_city,
         :da_state_province, :da_zip_postcode;
    ```

The preceding fetches the row five rows below the current position of the cursor (current position + 5).

- To fetch a row relative to and above the current position of the cursor

  ```
  EXEC SQL FETCH RELATIVE -5 FROM address_data
  INTO :da_first, :da_last, :da_street, :da_city,
       :da_state_province, :da_zip_postcode;
  ```

  The preceding fetches the row five rows above the current position of the cursor (current row − 5).

Note: If you use FETCH without an INTO clause, you will move the cursor without retrieving any data.

If there is no row containing data at the position of the cursor, the DBMS returns a "no data" error (SQLSTATE = "02000"). The general strategy for processing a table of data therefore is to create a loop that continues to fetch rows until a SQLSTATE of something other than "00000" occurs. Then you can test to see whether you've simply finished processing, or whether some other problem has arisen. In C/C++, the code would look something like Figure B.3.

```
EXEC SQL FETCH FROM address data
INTO :da_first, :da_last, :da_street, :da_city, :da_state_province,
     :da_zip_postcode;
while (strcmp (SQLSTATE, "00000") == 0)
{
      // Process one row's data in appropriate way
      EXEC SQL FETCH FROM address data
      INTO :da_first, :da_last, :da_street, :da_city, :da_state_province,
         :da_zip_postcode;
}
if (strcmp (SQLSTATE,"0200000") != 0)
{
      // Display error message and/or do additional checking
}
EXEC SQL COMMIT;
```

■**FIGURE B.3** Using a host language loop to process all rows in an embedded SQL result table.

Note: One common error that beginning programmers make is to write loops that use a specific error code as a terminating value. This can result in an infinite loop if some other error condition arises. We therefore typically write loops to stop on any error condition and then check to determine exactly which condition occurred.

Note: You can use indicator variables in the INTO clause of a FETCH statement, just as you do when executing a SELECT that retrieves a single row.

Closing a Cursor

To close a cursor, removing its result table from main memory, use

```
CLOSE cursor_name
```

as in

```
EXEC SQL CLOSE address_data;
```

Embedded SQL Data Modification

Although many of today's database development environments make it easy to create forms for data entry and modification, all those forms do is collect data. There must be a program of some type underlying the form to actually interact with the database. For example, whenever a salesperson at the rare book store makes a sale, a program must create the row in *sale* and modify the appropriate row in *volume*.

Data modification can be performed using the SQL UPDATE command to change one or more rows. In some cases, you can use a cursor to identify which rows should be updated in the underlying base tables.

Direct Modification

To perform direct data modification using the SQL UPDATE command, you simply include the command in your program. For example, if the selling price of a purchased volume is stored in the host language variable *da_selling_price*, the sale ID in *da_sale_id*, and the volume's inventory ID in *da_inventory_id*, you could update *volume* with

```
EXEC SQL UPDATE volume
SET selling_price = :da_selling_price,
    sale_id = :da_sale_id
WHERE inventory_id = :da_inventory_id;
```

The preceding statement will update one row in the table because its WHERE predicate contains a primary key expression. To modify multiple rows, you use an UPDATE with a WHERE predicate that identifies multiple rows, such as the following, which increases the prices by 2% for volumes with leather bindings:

```
EXEC SQL UPDATE volume
SET asking_price = asking_price * 1.02
WHERE isbn IN (SELECT isbn
      FROM book
      WHERE binding = 'Leather';
```

Indicator Variables and Data Modification

Indicator variables, which hold information about the result of embedded SQL retrievals, can also be used when performing embedded SQL modification.

Their purpose is to indicate that you want to store a null in a column. For example, assume that the rare book store has a program that stores new rows in the *volume* table. At the time a new row is inserted, there are no values for the selling price or the sale ID; these columns should be left null.

To do this, the program declares an indicator variable for each column in the table. If the data variable holds a value to be stored, the program sets the indicator variable to 0; if the column is to be left null, the program sets the indicator variable to -1.

Sample pseudocode for performing this embedded INSERT can be found in Figure B.4.

```
// Data variables
// Initialize all strings to null, all numeric variables to 0
string da_isbn = null, dat_date_acquired = null;
int da_inventory_id = 0, da_condition_code = 0, da_sale_id = 0;
float da_asking_price = 0, da_selling_price = 0;

// Indicator variables
// Initialize all to 0 except selling price and sale ID
    int in_isbn = 0,
        in_inventory_id = 0,
        in_asking_price = 0,
        in_selling_price = -1;
        in_sale_id = -1;

// Collect data from user, possibly using on-screen form
// Store data in data variables
// Check to see if anything other than the selling price and sale ID
// have no value

if (da_inventory == 0 or da_isbn == 0)
{
// Error handling goes here
    return;
}

if (stcmp(da_date_acquired), "") == 0) in_date_acquired = -1;
if (da_condition_code == 0) in_condition_code = -1;
// … continue checking each data variable and setting
// indicator variable if necessary

EXEC SQL INSERT INTO volume
    VALUES (:da_inventory INDICATOR :in_inventory_id,
            :da_isbn INDICATOR :in_isbn,
            :da_condition code INDICATOR :in_condition_code,
            :da_date_acquired INDICATOR :in_date_acquired,
            :da_asking_price INDICATOR :in_asking_price,
            :da_selling_price INDICATOR :in_selling_price,
            :da_sale_id INDICATOR :in_sale_id);

// Finish by checking SQLSTATE to see if insert worked to decide
// whether to commit or rollback
```

■ **FIGURE B.4** Using indicator variables to send nulls to a table.

Integrity Validation with the Match Predicate

The MATCH predicate is designed to be used with embedded SQL modification to let you test referential integrity before actually inserting data into tables. When included in an application program, it can help identify potential data modification errors.

For example, assume that a program written for the rare book store has a function that inserts new books into the database. The program wants to ensure that a work for the book exists in the database, before attempting to store the book. The application program might therefore include the following query:

```
EXEC SQL SELECT work_numb
FROM work JOIN author
WHERE (:entered_author, :entered_title)
      MATCH (SELECT author_first_last, title
             FROM work JOIN author);
```

The subquery selects all the rows in the join of the *work* and *author* tables and then matches the author and title columns against the values entered by the user, both of which are stored in host language variables. If the preceding query returns one or more rows, then the author and title pair entered by the customer exist in the *author* and *work* relations. However, if the result table has no rows, then inserting the book into *book* would produce a referential integrity violation and the insert should not be performed.

If a program written for the rare book store wanted to verify a primary key constraint, it could use a variation of the MATCH predicate that requires unique values in the result table. For example, to determine whether a work is already in the database, the program could use

```
EXEC SQL SELECT work_numb
FROM work JOIN author
WHERE UNIQUE (:entered_author, :entered_title)
      MATCH (SELECT author_first_last, title
             FROM work JOIN author);
```

By default, MATCH returns true if *any* value being tested is null or, when there are no nulls in the value being tested, a row exists in the result table that matches the values being tested. You can, however, change the behavior of MATCH when nulls are present:

- MATCH FULL is true if *every* value being tested is null or, when there are no nulls in the values being tested, a row exists in the result table that matches the values being tested.

■ MATCH PARTIAL is true if *every* value being tested is null or a row exists in the result table that matches the values being tested.

Note that you can combine UNIQUE with MATCH FULL and MATCH PARTIAL.

Modification Using Cursors

Updates using cursors are a bit different from updating a view. When you update a view, the UPDATE command acts directly on the view by using the view's name. The update is then passed back to the underlying base table(s) by the DBMS. In contrast, using a cursor for updating means you update a base table directly, but identify the row that you want to modify by referring to the row to which the cursor currently is pointing.

To do the modification, you use FETCH without an INTO clause to move the cursor to the row you want to update. Then, you can use an UPDATE command with a WHERE predicate that specifies the row pointed to by the cursor. For example, to change the address of the customer in row 15 of the *address_data* cursor's result table, a program for the rare book store could include

```
EXEC SQL FETCH ABSOLUTE 15 FROM address_data;
EXEC SQL UPDATE cutomer
    SET street = '123 Main Street',
    city = 'New Home'
    state_province = 'MA',
    zip_postcode = '02111'
    WHERE CURRENT OF address data;
```

The clause CURRENT OF *cursor_name* instructs SQL to work with the row in *customer* currently being pointed to by the named cursor. If there is no valid corresponding row in the *customer* table, the update will fail.

Deletion Using Cursors

You can apply the technique of modifying the row pointed to by a cursor to deletions, as well as updates. To delete the current row, you use

```
DELETE FROM table_name WHERE CURRENT OF cursor_name
```

The deletion will fail if the current row indicated by the cursor isn't a row in the table named in the DELETE. For example,

```
EXEC SQL DELETE FROM customers WHERE CURRENT OF address_data;
```

will probably succeed, but

```
EXEC SQL DELETE FROM volume WHERE CURRENT OF address_data;
```

will certainly fail, because the *volume* table isn't part of the *address_data* cursor (as declared in the preceding section of this chapter).

Dynamic SQL

The embedded SQL that you have seen to this point is "static," in that entire SQL commands have been specified within the source code. However, there are often times when you don't know exactly what a command should look like until a program is running.

Consider, for example, the screen in Figure B.5. The user fills in the fields on which he or she wishes to base a search of the rare book store's holdings. When the user clicks a Search button, the application program managing the window checks the contents of the fields on the window and uses the data it finds to create a SQL query.

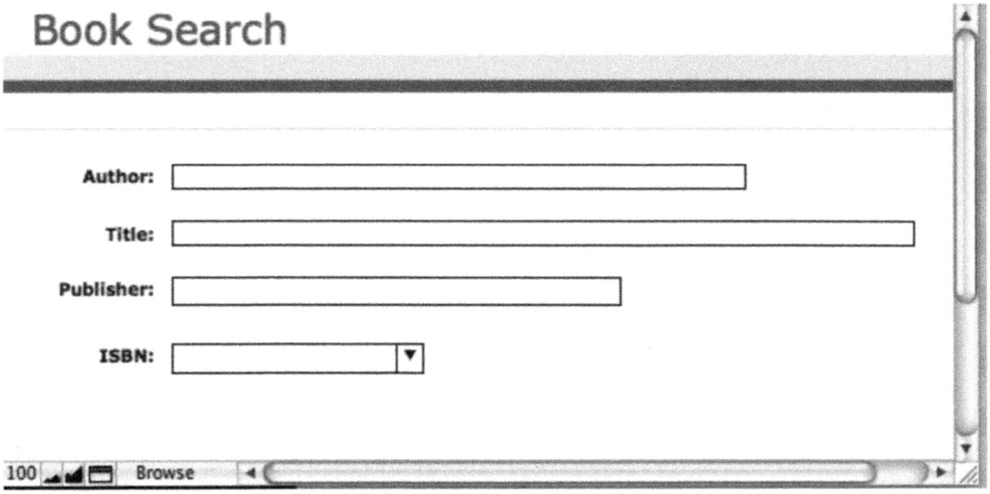

■ FIGURE B.5 A typical window for gathering information for a dynamic SQL query.

The query's WHERE predicate will differ, depending on which of the fields have values in them. It is therefore impossible to specify the query completely within a program. This is where dynamic SQL comes in.

Immediate Execution

The easiest way to work with dynamic SQL is the EXECUTE IMMEDIATE statement. To use it, you store a SQL command in a host language string variable and then submit that command for processing:

```
EXEC SQL EXECUTE IMMEDIATE variable_containing_command
```

For example, assume that a user fills in a data entry form with a customer number and the customer's new address. A program could process the update with code written something like the pseudocode in Figure B.6. Notice the painstaking way in which the logic of the code examines the values the user entered and builds a syntactically correct SQL UPDATE statement.

```
String theSQL;
theSQL = "UPDATE customer SET ";
Boolean needsComma = false;

If (valid_contents_in_street_field)
{
      theSQL = theSQL + "street = " + contents_of_street_field;
      needsComma = true;
}
if (valid_contents_in_state_field)
{
      if (needsComma)
            theSQL = theSQL + ", ";
      theSQL = theSQL + "state_province = " + contents_of_state_field;
      needsComma = true;
}
if (valid_contents_in_zip_field)
{
      if (needsComma)
            theSQL = theSQL + ", ";
      theSQL = theSQL + "zip_postcode = " + contents_of_zip_field;
      needsComma = true;
}
EXEC SQL EXECUTE IMMEDIATE :theSQL;
If (strcmp (SQLCODE, "00000"))
      EXEC SQL COMMIT;
else
{
      EXEC SQL ROLLBACK;
      // Display appropriate error message
}
```

■ FIGURE B.6 Pseudocode to process a dynamic SQL update.

By using the dynamic SQL, the program can update just those columns for which the user has supplied new data. (Columns whose fields on the data entry are left empty aren't added to the SQL statement.)

There are two major limitations to EXECUTE IMMEDIATE:

- The SQL command cannot contain input parameters or output parameters. This means that you can't use SELECT or FETCH statements.
- To repeat the SQL statement, the DBMS has to perform the entire immediate execution process again. You can't save the SQL statement, except as a string in a host language variable. This means that such statements execute more slowly than static embedded SQL statements because the SQL command processor must examine them for syntax errors at runtime rather than during preprocessing by a precompiler.

Each time you EXECUTE IMMEDIATE the same statement, it must be scanned for syntax errors again. Therefore, if you need to execute a dynamic SQL statement repeatedly, you will get better performance if you can have the syntax checked once and save the statement in some way.[3]

Dynamic SQL with Dynamic Parameters

If you want to repeat a dynamic SQL statement or if you need to use dynamic parameters (as you would to process the form in Figure B.5), you need to use a more involved technique for preparing and executing your commands.

The processing for creating and using a repeatable dynamic SQL statement is as follows:

1. *Store* the SQL statement in a host language string variable using host language variables for the dynamic parameters.
2. *Allocate* SQL *descriptor areas*.
3. *Prepare* the SQL statement. This process checks the statement for syntax and assigns it a name by which it can be referenced.
4. *Describe* one of the descriptor areas as input.

---

[3]A few DBMSs (for example, DB2 for Z/OS) get around this problem by performing dynamic statement caching (DSC), where the DBMS saves the syntax-scanned/prepared statement and retrieves it from the cache if used again.

5. *Set* input parameters, associating each input parameter with the input parameter descriptor.
6. (Required only when using a cursor) *Declare* the cursor.
7. (Required only when using a cursor) *Open* the cursor.
8. *Describe* another descriptor area as output.
9. *Set* output parameters, associating each output parameter with the output parameter descriptor.
10. (Required when not using a cursor) *Execute* the query.
11. (Required only when using a cursor) *Fetch* values into the output descriptor area.
12. (Required only when using a cursor) *Get* the output values from the descriptor area and process them in some way.
13. Repeat steps 11 and 12 until the entire result table has been processed.
14. Close the cursor.
15. If through with the statement, deallocate the descriptor areas.

There are a few limitations to the use of dynamic parameters in a statement of which you should be aware:

- You cannot use a dynamic parameter in a SELECT clause.
- You cannot place a dynamic parameter on both sides of a relationship operator such as <, >, or =.
- You cannot use a dynamic parameter as an argument in a summary function.
- In general, you cannot compare a dynamic parameter with itself. For example, you cannot use two dynamic parameters with the BETWEEN operator.

Dynamic Parameters with Cursors

Many dynamic queries generate result tables containing multiple rows. As an example, consider a query that retrieves a list of the customers of the rare book store who live in a given area. The user could enter a city, a state/province, a zip/postcode, or any combination of the three.

Step 1: Creating the Statement String

The first step in any dynamic SQL is to place the statement into a host language string variable. Pseudocode to generate the SQL query string for our example can be found in Figure B.7.

```
String theQuery;
Boolean hasWHERE = false;
String da_street = null, da_city = null, da_state_province = null,
      da_zip_postcode = null;

// Users search values into fields on screen form, which are
// then placed into the appropriate host language variables

theQuery = "SELECT first, last, street, city, state_province FROM CUSTOMER ";
if (da_street IS NOT NULL)
{
      theQuery = theQuery = "WHERE street = :da_street";
      hasWHERE = true;
}

if (da_city IS NOT NULL)
{
      if (!hasWHERE)
            theQuery = theQuery + "WHERE ";
      else
            theQuery = theQuery + ", ";
      theQuery = theQuery + " city = :da_city";
      hasWHERE = true;
}

if (da_state_province IS NOT NULL)
{
      if (!hasWHERE)
            theQuery = theQuery + "WHERE ";
      else
            theQuery = theQuery + ", ";
      theQuery = theQuery + " state_province = :date_state_province";
      hasWHERE = true;
}

if (da_zip_postcode IS NOT NULL)
{
      if (!hasWHERE)
            theQuery = theQuery + "WHERE ";
      else
            theQuery = theQuery + ", ";
      theQuery = theQuery +" state_postcode = :da_state_postcode";
}
```

■ **FIGURE B.7** Setting up a SQL query in a string for use with dynamic parameters.

Step 2: Allocating the Descriptor Areas

You allocate a descriptor area with the ALLOCATE DESCRIPTOR
statement:

```
ALLOCATE DESCRIPTOR descriptor_name
```

For our example, the statements would look something like

```
EXEC SQL ALLOCATE DESCRIPTOR 'input';
EXEC SQL ALLOCATE DESCRIPTOR 'output';
```

The names of the descriptor areas are arbitrary. They can be supplied as literals, as in the above example or they may be stored in host language string variables.

By default, the scope of a descriptor is local to the program module in which it was created. You can add the keyword GLOBAL after DESCRIPTOR, however, to create a global descriptor area that is available to the entire program.

Unless you specify otherwise, a descriptor area is defined to hold a maximum of 100 values. You can change that value by adding a MAX clause:

```
EXEC SQL ALLOCATE DESCRIPTOR GLOBAL 'input' MAX 10;
```

Step 3: Prepare the SQL Statement

Preparing a dynamic SQL statement for execution allows the DBMS to examine the statement for syntax errors and to perform query optimization. Once a query is prepared and stored with a name, it can be reused while the program is still running.

To prepare the statement for execution, use the PREPARE command:

```
PREPARE statement_identifier FROM variable_holding_command
```

The customer query command would be prepared with

```
EXEC SQL PREPARE sql_statement FROM :theQuery;
```

Steps 4 and 8: Describing Descriptor Areas

The DESCRIBE statement identifies a descriptor area as holding input or output parameters and associates it with a dynamic query. The statement has the following general form:

```
DESCRIBE INPUT|OUTPUT dynamic_statement_name
    USING DESCRIPTOR descriptor_name
```

The two descriptor areas for the customer list program will be written

```
EXEC SQL DESCRIBE INPUT sql_statement
    USING DESCRIPTOR 'input';
EXEC SQL DESCRIBE OUTPUT sql_staement
    USING DESCRIPTOR 'output';
```

Step 5: Setting Input Parameters

Each parameter—input or output—must be associated with an appropriate descriptor area. The SET DESCRIPTOR command needs four pieces of information for each parameter:

- A unique sequence number for the parameter. (You can start at 1 and count upward as you go.)
- The data type of the parameter, represented as an integer code. (See Table B.2 for the codes for commonly used data types.)

Table B.2 Selected SQL Data Type Codes

Data Type	Type Code
CHAR	1
VARCHAR	12
BLOB	30
BOOLEAN	16
DATE	9
DECIMAL	3
DOUBLE PRECISION	8
FLOAT	6
INT	4
INTERVAL	10
NUMERIC	2
REAL	7
SMALL INT	5

- The length of the parameter.
- A variable to hold the parameter's data.

The SET DESCRIPTOR statement has the following general syntax:

```
SET DESCRIPTOR descriptor_area_name VALUE sequence_number
    TYPE = type_code LENGTH = parameter_length
    DATA = variable_holding_parameter data
```

The code needed to set the input parameters for the address list query can be found in Figure B.8.

In addition to what you have just seen, there are two other descriptor characteristics that can be set:

- INDICATOR: identifies the host language variable that will hold an indicator value.

  ```
  INDICATOR = :host_language_indicator_variable
  ```

- TITLE: identifies the table column name associated with the parameter.

  ```
  TITLE = column_name
  ```

Steps 6 and 7: Declaring and Opening the Cursor

Declaring a cursor for use with a dynamic SQL statement is exactly the same as declaring a cursor for a static SQL statement. The cursor for the address list program therefore can be declared as

```
EXEC SQL DECLARE CURSOR addresses FOR theQuery;
```

Note: You can declare a scrolling cursor for use with dynamic SQL.

```
int da_street_type = 12, da_street_length = 30, da_city_type = 12,
      da_city_length = 30, da_state_province_type = 1,
      da_state_province = 2, da_zip_postcode_type = 12,
      da_zip_postcode_length = 12;

int value_count = 1;

if (da_street IS NOT NULL)
{
      EXEC SQL SET DESCRIPTOR 'input' VALUE :da_value_count TYPE =
:da_street_type
            LENGTH = :da_street_length DATA = :da_street;
      value_count++;
}

If (da_city IS NOT NULL)
{
EXEC SQL SET DESCRIPTOR 'input' VALUE :da_value_count TYPE = :da_city_type
      LENGTH = :da_city_length DATA = :da_city;
value_count++;
}

if (da_state_province IS NOT NULL)
{
      EXEC SQL SET DESCRIPTOR 'input' VALUE :da_value_count TYPE =
:da_state_province
            LENGTH = :da_state_province_length DATA = :da_state_province;
      value_count++;
}

if (da_zip_postcode IS NOT NULL)
{
      EXEC SQL SET DESCRIPTOR 'input' VALUE :da_value_count
TYPE = :da_zip_postcode_type LENGTH = :da_zip_postcode_length
            DATA = :da_zip_postcode;
}
```

■FIGURE B.8 Setting input parameters for a dynamic SQL query.

The OPEN statement is similar to the static OPEN, but it also needs to know which descriptor area to use:

```
EXEC SQL OPEN addresses USING DESCRIPTOR 'input';
```

Step 9: Setting the Output Parameters

The only difference between the syntax for setting the input and output parameters is that the output parameters are placed in their own descriptor area. The code can be found in Figure B.9.

```
int da_first_type = 12, da_first_length = 15, da_last_type = 12,
    da_last_length = 15;
// remaining variables have already been declared

EXEC SQL SET DESCRIPTOR 'output' VALUE 1 TYPE = :da_first_type
    LENGTH = :da_first_type_length DATA = :da_first;
EXEC SQL SET DESCRIPTOR 'output' VALUE 2 TYPE = :da_last_type
    LENGTH = :da_last_type_length DATA = :da_last;
EXEC SQL SET DESCRIPTOR 'output' VALUE 3 TYPE = :da_street_type
    LENGTH = :da_street_type_length DATA = :da_street;
EXEC SQL SET DESCRIPTOR 'output' VALUE 4 TYPE = :da_city_type
    LENGTH = :da_city_type_length DATA = :da_city;
EXEC SQL SET DESCRIPTOR 'output' VALUE 5 TYPE = :da_state_province_type
    LENGTH = :da_state_province_type_length DATA = :da_state_province;
EXEC SQL SET DESCRIPTOR 'output' VALUE 6 TYPE = :da_zip_postcode_type
    LENGTH = :da_zip_postcode_type_length DATA = :da_zip_postcode;
```

■ FIGURE B.9 Setting output parameters for a dynamic SQL query.

Be sure that the output parameters have sequence numbers that place them in the same order as the output columns in the prepared SELECT statement. When you pull data from the result table into the output descriptor area, the SQL command processor will retrieve the data based on those sequence numbers. If they don't match the order of the data, you won't end up with data in the correct host language variables.

Steps 11–13: Fetching Rows and Getting the Data

When you are using dynamic parameters, a FETCH creates a result table in main memory, just as it does with static SQL. Your code must then GET each parameter and pull it into the descriptor area. The end result is that the data from a row in the result table are available in the host language variables identified as holding data, as seen in Figure B.10.

```
EXEC SQL FETCH addresses INTO DESCRIPTOR 'output';
while (strcmp (SQLCODE = "00000")
{
    EXEC SQL GET DESCRIPTOR 'output' VALUE 1 :da_first = DATA;
    EXEC SQL GET DESCRIPTOR 'output' VALUE 2 :da_last = DATA;
    EXEC SQL GET DESCRIPTOR 'output' VALUE 3 :da_street = DATA;
    EXEC SQL GET DESCRIPTOR 'output' VALUE 4 :da_city = DATA;
    EXEC SQL GET DESCRIPTOR 'output' VALUE 5 :da_state_province = DATA;
    EXEC SQL GET DESCRIPTOR 'output' VALUE 6 :da_zip_postcode = DATA;
    // process the data in some way
    EXEC SQL FETCH addresses INTO DESCRIPTOR 'output';
}
```

■ FIGURE B.10 Fetching rows and getting data into host language variables.

Steps 14 and 15: Finishing Up

To finish processing the dynamic SQL query, you will close the cursor (if necessary)—

```
EXEC SQL CLOSE addresses;
```

—and deallocate the descriptor areas, freeing up the memory they occupy:

```
EXEC SQL DEALLOCATE DESCRIPTOR 'input';
EXEC SQL DEALLOCATE DESCRIPTOR 'output';
```

Dynamic Parameters without a Cursor

As you saw at the beginning of this section, using dynamic parameters is very similar to using static parameters, regardless of whether you are using a cursor. In fact, executing a query that returns a single row is much simpler. You can actually get away without using descriptor areas, although if the descriptor areas have been created, there is no reason you can't use them.

Statements without Cursors or a Descriptor Area

To execute a prepared statement that does not use either a cursor or a descriptor area, use the EXECUTE command in its simplest form:

```
EXECUTE statement_name
USING input_parameter_list
INTO output_parameter_list
```

The USING and INTO clauses are optional. However, you must include a USING clause if your statement has input parameters and an INTO clause if your statement has output parameters. The number and data types of the parameters in each parameter list must be the same as the number and data types of parameters in the query.

For example, assume that you have prepared the following query with the name *book_info*:

```
SELECT author, title
FROM work JOIN book
WHERE isbn = :da_isbn;
```

This query has one input parameter (*da_isbn*) and two output parameters (*da_author*) and (*da_title*). It can be executed with

```
EXEC SQL EXECUTE book_info
USING :da_isbn
INTO :da_author, :da_title;
```

Input parameters can be stored in host languages variables, as in the preceding example, or they can be supplied as literals.

Statements without Cursors but Using a Descriptor Area

If your parameters have already been placed in a descriptor area, then all you need to do to execute a statement that does not use a cursor is to add the name(s) of the appropriate descriptor area(s) to the EXECUTE statement:

```
EXEC SQL EXECUTE book_info
USING 'input'
INTO 'output';
```

SQLSTATE Return Codes

For your reference, the SQLSTATE return codes can be found in Table B.3.

Table B.3 SQLSTATE Return Codes (continues)

Class	Class Definition	Subclass	Subclass Definition
00	Successful completion	000	*None*
01	Warning	000	*None*
		001	Cursor operation conflict
		002	Disconnect error
		003	Null value eliminated in set function
		004	String data, right truncation
		005	Insufficient item descriptor area
		006	Privilege not revoked
		007	Privilege not granted
		008	Implicit zero-bit padding
		009	Search expression too long for information schema
		00A	Query expression too long for information schema
		00B	Default value too long for information schema
		00C	Result sets returned
		00D	Additional result sets returned
		00E	Attempt to return too many result sets
		00F	Statement too long for information schema
		010	Column cannot be mapped (XML)
		011	SQL-Java path too long for information schema
		02F	Array data, right truncation
02	No data	000	*None*
		001	No additional result sets returned
07	Dynamic SQL error	000	*None*
		001	Using clause does not match dynamic parameter
		002	Using clause does not match target specifications
		003	Cursor specification cannot be executed

(Continued)

Table B.3 SQLSTATE Return Codes (*cont.*)

Class	Class Definition	Subclass	Subclass Definition
		004	Using clause required for dynamic parameters
		005	Prepared statement not a cursor specification
		006	Restricted data type attribute violation
		007	Using clause required for result fields
		008	Invalid descriptor count
		009	Invalid descriptor index
		00B	Data type transform function violation
		00C	Undefined DATA value
		00D	Invalid DATA target
		00E	invalid LEVEL value
		00F	Invalid DATETIME_INVERTVAL_CODE
08	Connection exception	000	*None*
		001	SQL client unable to establish SQL connection
		002	Connection name in use
		003	Connection does not exist
		004	SQL server rejected establishment of SQL connection
		006	Connection failure
		007	Transaction resolution unknown
09	Triggered action exception	000	*None*
0A	Feature not supported	000	*None*
		001	Multiple server transactions
0D	Invalid target type specification	000	*None*
0E	Invalid schema name list specification	000	*None*
0F	Locator exception	000	*None*
		001	Invalid specification
0K	Resignal when handler not active	000	*None*
0L	Invalid grantor	000	*None*
0M	Invalid SQL-invoked procedure reference	000	*None*
0N	SQL/XML mapping error	000	*None*
		001	Unmappable XML name
		002	Invalid XML character
0P	Invalid role specification	000	*None*
0S	Invalid transform group name specification	000	*None*
0T	Target table disagrees with cursor specification	000	*None*
0U	Attempt to assign to non-updatable column	000	*None*
0V	Attempt to assign to ordering column	000	*None*

Table B.3 SQLSTATE Return Codes (*cont.*)

Class	Class Definition	Subclass	Subclass Definition
0W	Prohibited statement encountered during trigger execution	000	*None*
0X	Invalid foreign server specification	000	*None*
0Y	Pass-through specific condition	000	*None*
		001	Invalid cursor option
		002	Invalid cursor allocation
0Z	Diagnostics exception	001	Maximum number of stacked diagnostics area exceeded
		002	Stacked diagnostics accessed without active hander
10	XQuery error	000	*None*
20	Case not found for CASE statement	000	*None*
21	Cardinality violation	000	*None*
22	Data exception	000	*None*
		001	String data, right truncation
		002	Null value, no indicator
		003	Numeric value out of range
		004	Null value not allowed
		005	Error in assignment
		006	Invalid interval format
		007	Invalid datetime format
		008	Datetime field overflow
		009	Invalid time zone displacement value
		00B	Escape character conflict
		00C	Invalid use of escape character
		00D	Invalid escape octet
		00E	Null value in array target
		00F	Zero-length character string
		00G	Most specific type mismatch
		00H	Sequence generator limit exceeded
		00J	Nonidentical notations with the same name (XML)
		00K	Nonidentical unparsed entities with the same name (XML)
		00L	Not an XML document
		00M	Invalid XML document
		00N	Invalid XML content
		00P	Interval value out of range
		00Q	Multiset value overflow
		00R	XML value overflow
		00S	Invalid XML comment
		00T	Invalid XML processing instruction
		00U	Not an XQuery document node
		00V	Invalid XQuery context item

(Continued)

Table B.3 SQLSTATE Return Codes (*cont.*)

Class	Class Definition	Subclass	Subclass Definition
		00W	XQuery serialization error
		010	Invalid indicator parameter value
		011	Substring error
		012	Division by zero
		015	Interval field overflow
		017	Invalid data specified for datalink
		018	Invalid character value for cast
		019	Invalid escape character
		01A	Null argument passed to datalink constructor
		01B	Invalid regular expression
		01C	Null row not permitted in table
		01D	Datalink value exceeds maximum length
		01E	Invalid argument for natural logarithm
		01F	Invalid argument for power function
		01G	Invalid argument for width bucket function
		01J	XQuery sequence cannot be validated
		01K	XQuery document node cannot be validated
		01L	No XML schema found
		01M	Element namespace not declared
		01N	Global element not declared
		01P	No XML element with the specified QName
		01Q	No XML element with the specified namespace
		01R	Validation failure
		01S	invalid XQuery regular expression
		01T	Invalid XQuery option flag
		01U	Attempt to replace a zero-length string
		01V	Invalid XQuery replacement string
		021	Character not in repertoire
		022	Indicator overflow
		023	Invalid parameter value
		024	Unterminated C string
		025	Invalid escape sequence
		026	String data, length mismatch
		027	Trim error
		029	Noncharacter in UCS string
		02A	Null value in field reference
		02D	Null value substituted for mutator subject parameter
		02E	Array element error
		02F	Array data, right truncation
		02H	Invalid sample size
23	Integrity constraints violation	000	*None*
		001	Restrict violation

Table B.3 SQLSTATE Return Codes (*cont.*)

Class	Class Definition	Subclass	Subclass Definition
24	Invalid cursor state	000	*None*
25	Invalid transaction state	000	*None*
		001	Active SQL transaction
		002	Branch transaction already active
		003	Inappropriate access mode for branch transaction
		004	Inappropriate isolation level for branch transaction
		005	No active SQL transaction for branch transaction
		006	Read-only SQL transaction
		007	Schema and data statement mixing not supported
		008	Held cursor requires same isolation level
26	Invalid SQL statement name	000	*None*
27	Triggered data change violation	000	*None*
28	Invalid authorization specification	000	*None*
2A	Syntax error or access rule violation in direct SQL statement	000	*None*
2B	Dependent privilege descriptors still exist	000	*None*
2C	Invalid character set name	000	*None*
2D	Invalid transaction termination	000	*None*
2E	Invalid connection name	000	*None*
2F	SQL routine exception	000	*None*
		002	Modifying SQL data not permitted
		003	Prohibited SQL statement attempted
		004	Reading SQL data not permitted
		005	Function executed but no return statement
2H	Invalid collation name	000	*None*
30	Invalid SQL statement identifier	000	*None*
33	Invalid SQL descriptor name	000	*None*
34	Invalid cursor name	000	*None*
35	Invalid condition number	000	*None*
36	Cursor sensitivity exception	000	*None*
		001	Request rejected
		002	Request failed
37	Syntax error or access rule violation in dynamic SQL statement	000	*None*
38	External routine exception	000	*None*
		001	Containing SQL not permitted
		002	Modifying SQL not permitted
		003	Prohibited SQL statement attempted
		004	Reading SQL data not permitted
39	External routine invocation exception	000	*None*

(Continued)

Table B.3 SQLSTATE Return Codes (*cont.*)

Class	Class Definition	Subclass	Subclass Definition
		004	Null value not allowed
3B	Savepoint exception	000	*None*
		001	Invalid specification
		002	Too many
3C	Ambiguous cursor name	000	*None*
3D	Invalid catalog name	000	*None*
3F	Invalid schema name	000	*None*
40	Transaction rollback	000	*None*
		001	Serialization failure
		002	Integrity constraint violation
		003	Statement completion unknown
42	Syntax error or access rule violation	000	*None*
44	With check option violation	000	*None*
45	Unhandled user defined exception	000	*None*
46	Java DDL	000	*None*
		001	Invalid URL
		002	Invalid JAR name
		003	Invalid class deletion
		005	Invalid replacement
		00A	Attempt to replace uninstalled JAR
		00B	Attempt to remove uninstalled JAR
		00C	Invalid JAR removal
		00D	Invalid path
		00E	Self-referencing path
46	Java execution	000	*None*
		102	Invalid JAR name in path
		103	Unresolved class name
		110	Unsupported feature
		120	Invalid class declaration
		121	Invalid column name
		122	Invalid number of columns
		130	Invalid profile state
HV	FDW-specific condition	000	*None*
		001	Memory allocation error
		002	Dynamic parameter value needed
		004	Invalid data type
		005	Column name not found
		006	Invalid data type descriptors
		007	Invalid column name
		008	Invalid column number
		009	Invalid use of null pointer
		00A	Invalid string format

Table B.3 SQLSTATE Return Codes (*cont.*)

Class	Class Definition	Subclass	Subclass Definition
		00B	Invalid handle
		00C	Invalid option index
		00D	Invalid option name
		00J	Option name not found
		00K	Reply handle
		00L	Unable to create execution
		00M	Unable to create reply
		00N	Unable to establish connection
		00P	No schemas
		00Q	Schema not found
		00R	Table not found
		010	Function sequence error
		014	Limit on number of handles exceeded
		021	Inconsistent descriptor information
		024	Invalid attribute value
		090	Invalid string length or buffer length
		091	Invalid descriptor field identifier
HW	Datalink exception	000	*None*
		001	External file not linked
		002	External file already linked
		003	Referenced file does not exist
		004	Invalid write token
		005	Invalid datalink construction
		006	Invalid write permission for update
		007	Referenced file not valid
HY	CLI-specific condition	000	*None*
		001	Memory allocation error
		003	Invalid data type in application descriptor
		004	Invalid data type
		007	Associated statement is not prepared.
		008	Operation canceled
		009	Invalid use of null pointer
		010	Function sequence error
		011	Attribute cannot be set now
		012	Invalid transaction operation code
		013	Memory management error
		014	Limit on number of handles exceeded
		017	Invalid use of automatically-allocated descriptor handle
		018	Server declined the cancelation request
		019	Non-string data cannot be sent in pieces
		020	Attempt to concatenate a null value

(Continued)

Table B.3 SQLSTATE Return Codes (*cont.*)

Class	Class Definition	Subclass	Subclass Definition
		021	Inconsistent descriptor information
		024	Invalid attribute value
		055	Nonstring data cannot be used with string routine
		090	Invalid string length or buffer length
		091	Invalid descriptor field identifier
		092	Invalid attribute identifier
		093	Invalid datalink value
		095	Invalid FunctionID specified
		096	Invalid information type
		097	Column type out of range
		098	Scope out of range
		099	Nullable type out of rage
		103	Invalid retrieval code
		104	Invalid Length Precision value
		105	Invalid parameter mode
		106	Invalid fetch orientation
		107	Row value of range
		109	Invalid cursor position
		C00	Optional feature not implemented

Appendix
C

SQL Syntax Summary

This appendix contains a summary of SQL syntax used throughout this book. The first table (Table C.1) describes SQL statements, arranged alphabetically by command. The notation is as follows:

- Keywords that must be typed exactly as they appear are in uppercase characters, such as REFERENCES.
- Parts of commands that are determined by the user appear in italics and name the item that must be supplied, such as *table_name.*
- Optional portions of a command are surrounded by brackets ([and]).
- Portions of commands that form a single clause are grouped within braces ({ and }).
- Sets of options from which you choose one or more are separated by vertical lines (|).
- Portions of commands that may be repeated as needed are followed by an ellipsis (…).

The second table (Table C.2) describes SQL built-in functions discussed in this book, including input data types. In Table C.3 you will find SQL operators covered in the text.

Table C.1 SQL Statements (continues)

Allocate space for a descriptor area for a dynamic SQL statement

```
ALLOCATE DESCRIPTOR descriptor_name
     [ WITH MAX number_of_parameters ]
```

Change the specifications of a domain

```
ALTER DOMAIN domain_name
     { SET DEFAULT default_value }
     | { DROP DEFAULT }
     | { ADD constraint_definition_clause }
     | { DROP CONSTRAINT constraint_name }
```

Change the specifications of a table

```
ALTER TABLE table_name
     { ADD [COLUMN] column_defintion }
     | { ALTER [COLUMN]
          {SET DEFAULT default_value }
          | { DROP DEFAULT }
          | { DROP [COLUMN] column_name RESTRICT | CASCADE }
     | { ADD table_constraint_definition_clause }
     | { DROP CONSTRAINT constraint_name RESTRICT | CASCADE }
```

Declare host language variables for use in an embedded SQL statement

```
BEGIN DECLARE SECTION
     Declarations
END DECLARE SECTION
```

Close an embedded SQL cursor

```
CLOSE cursor_name
```

Commit a transaction, making its changes permanent

```
COMMIT [ WORK ]
```

Connect to a database, specify its cluster, catalog, and schema if necessary

```
CONNECT TO {cluster.catalog.schema.database_name
     { [ AS connection_name ] }
     { [ USER user_name
       | DEFAULT ] }
```

Create an assertion, a constraint that is not attached to a specific table

```
CREATE ASSERTION assertion_name
     CHECK ( check_predicate )
          [ { INITIALLY DEFERRED } | { INITIALLY IMMEDIATE } ]
          [ DEFERRABLE | { NOT DEFERRABLE } ]
```

Create a domain

```
CREATE DOMAIN domain_name
     [ AS ] data_type
          [ DEFAULT default_value ]
          CHECK ( check_clause )
          { [ INITIALLY DEFERRED ] | [ INITIALLY IMMEDIATE ] }
          [ DEFERRABLE | { NOT DEFERRABLE } ]
```

Table C.1 SQL Statements (*cont.*)

Define a method for a UDT

```
CREATE METHOD method_name FOR UDT_name
BEGIN
     // body of method
END
```

Create an index

```
CREATE INDEX index_name ON table_name (index_key_column_list)
```

Note: Indexes are no longer part of the SQL standard, but are still supported by most relational DBMSs.

Create a schema

```
CREATE SCHEMA { schema_name
     | AUTHORIZATION authorization_ID
     | schema_name AUTHORIZATION authorization_ID }
```

Create a table

```
CREATE [ [ GLOBAL | LOCAL ] TEMPORARY ] table_name
     ( { column_name { data_type | domain_name } [ column_size ]
     [ column_constraint … ] , …
     [ DEFAULT default_value ]
     [ table_constraint ], …
     [ ON COMMIT DELETE | PRESERVE ROWS ] )
```

Create a UDT

```
CREATE TYPE type_name AS [ OBJECT ](column_definitions)
     [ INSTANTIABLE | { NOT INSTANTIABLE } ]
     [ FINAL | { NOT FINAL } ]
     [ { METHOD method_name (parameter_list) }, … ]
```

Create a typed table

```
CREATE TABLE table_name OF UDT_name
     [ UNDER supertype_name (added_column_list) ]
     [ REF IS reference_column_name
          ( { REF USING existing_data_type }
          | { REF IS identifier_name SYSTEM GENERATED }
          | { REF FROM attribute_list } ) ]
```

Create a database user account and password

```
CREATE USER | LOGIN implementation_specific_syntax
```

Note: Creating user accounts is not part of the SQL standard, and much of the syntax is implementation dependent.

Create a view

```
CREATE VIEW view_name [ (column_list ) ]
     AS (complete_SELECT_statement
     [ WITH [ CASCADED | LOCAL ] CHECK OPTION ]
```

Remove a dynamic SQL descriptor area from main memory

```
DEALLOCATE DESCRIPTOR descriptor_name
```

Declare a cursor for processing an embedded SQL SELECT that returns multiple rows

```
DECLARE CURSOR cursor_name [ INSENSITIVE ] [ SCROLL ] CURSOR FOR
     (complete_SELECT_statement)
     [ FOR ( { READ ONLY } | UPDATE [ OF column_name, … ] ) ]
  | prepared_dynamic_SQL_statement_name
```

Table C.1 SQL Statements (*cont.*)

Delete rows from a table
```
DELETE FROM table_name
     [ { WHERE row_selection_predicate }
     | { WHERE CURRENT OF cursor_name } ]
```

Describe the dynamic parameters in a prepared dynamic SQL statement for a descriptor area
```
DESCRIBE [ INPUT | OUTPUT ]
     Prepared_dyamic_SQL_statement_name
     USING SQL DESCRIPTOR descriptor_name
```

Disconnect from a database
```
DISCONNECT connection_identifier
```

Remove an assertion from a schema
```
DROP ASSERTION assertion_name
```

Remove a domain from a schema
```
DROP DOMAIN domain_name CASCADE | RESTRICT
```

Remove an index from a schema
```
DROP INDEX index_name
```

Remove a schema from a catalog
```
DROP SCHEMA schema_name CASCADE | RESTRICT
```

Remove a table from a schema
```
DROP TABLE table_name CASCADE | RESTRICT
```

Remove a view from a schema
```
DROP VIEW view_name CASCADE | RESTRICT
```

Execute an embedded SQL statement
```
EXEC SQL complete_SQL_statement
```

Execute a prepared dynamic SQL statement
```
EXECTUE [ GLOBAL | LOCAL ] prepared_dynamic_SQL_statement
     [ INTO { parameter, … }
     | { SQL DESCRIPTOR [ GLOBAL | LOCAL ] descriptor_name } ]
     [ USING { parameter, … }
     | { SQL DESCRIPTOR [ GLOBAL | LOCAL ] descriptor_name } ]
```

Execute a dynamic SQL statement immediately, without a separate preparation step
```
EXECUTE IMMEDIATE SQL_statement_text_literal_or_variable
```

Retrieve a row from an open cursor's result table
```
FETCH [ [ NEXT | PRIOR | FIRST | LAST | ABSOLUTE | { RELATIVE
row_number } ]
     FROM cursor_name
     INTO host_language_variable, …
```

Retrieve information from a dynamic SQL descriptor area
```
GET DESCRIPTOR descriptor_name
     { host_langague_variable = COUNT | KEY_TYPE | DYNAMIC_FUNCTION |
DYNAMIC_FUNCTION_CODE | TOP_LEVEL_COUNT }
     |   VALUE descriptor_number { host_language_variable = descriptor_
field }, …
```

Table C.1 SQL Statements (*cont.*)

Note: Descriptor field types most commonly used are TYPE (data type of parameter), DATA (actual value of parameter), and INDICATOR (value of indicator variable associated with parameter).

Grant access rights to other users

```
GRANT { ALL PRIVILEGES }
        | SELECT
        | DELETE
        | INSERT [ (column_name, …) ]
        | UPDATE [ (column_name, …) ]
        | REFERENCES { (column_name, …) }
        | USAGE
    ON { [ TABLE ] table_name }
        | { DOMAIN domain_name }
    TO { user_id, … } | PUBLIC
    [ WITH GRANT OPTION ]
```

Insert new rows into a table

```
INSERT INTO table_name
    [ {column_name, …) ]
    { VALUES (value1, value2, …) }
    | complete_SELECT_statement
    | DEFAULT VALUES
```

Conditionally update, delete, or insert data from one table into another

```
MERGE INTO target_table_name USING source_table_name ON merge_condition
WHEN MATCHED THAN
    Update/delete specifications
WHEN NOT MATCHED THEN
    insert specification
```

Open a cursor, executing the SELECT and positioning the cursor at the first row

```
OPEN cursor_name
    [ { USING host_language_variable_or_literal, … }
    | { SQL DESCRIPTOR descriptor_name } ]
```

Prepare a dynamic SQL statement for execution

```
PREPARE [ GLOBAL | LOCAL ]
    prepared_dynamic_SQL_statement_name
    FROM SQL_statement_text_literal_or_variable
```

Remove access rights from a user

```
REMOVE [GRANT OPTION FOR ]
        { ALL PRIVILEGES }
        | SELECT
        | DELETE
        | UPDATE
        | REFERENCES
        | USAGE
    ON [ TABLE ] table_name
        | DOMAIN domain_name
    FROM PUBLIC | { user_id, … }
    CASCADE | RESTRICT
```

(Continued)

Table C.1 SQL Statements (*cont.*)

Roll back a transaction
```
ROLLBACK [ WORK ]
```

Retrieve rows from a table
```
SELECT [DISTINCT]
            { { summary_function, … }
            | { data_manipulation_expression, … }
            | { column_name, … } }
      FROM { { table_name [ AS ] [ correlation_name ] }
            | joined_tables
            | complete_SELECT_statement }
      [ WHERE row_selection_predicate ]
      [ GROUP BY column_name, … ]
            [ HAVING group_selection_predicate ]
      [ UNION | INTERSECT | EXCEPT [CORRESPONDING BY (column_name, …) ]
            complete_SELECT_statement ]
      [ ORDER BY (column_name [ ASC | DESC ], …) ]
```

Retrieve rows from a common table expression (CTE)
```
WITH [ RECURSIVE ] CTE_name (column_list) AS
      (SELECT_statement_defining_table
complete_SELECT_using_result_of_CTE_query
```

Choose the current catalog
```
SET CATALOG catalog_name
```

Choose an active connection
```
SET CONNECTION connection_name | DEFAULT
```

Choose when constraints are checked
```
SET CONSTRAINTS MODE { constraint_name, … | ALL }
      DEFFERED | IMMEDIATE
```

Store values in a SQL descriptor area
```
SET DESCRIPTOR [ GLOBAL | LOCAL ]
            descriptor_name { COUNT = integer_value }
      | {VALUE descriptor_number { descriptor_field = value, …}, …}
```

Choose the current schema
```
SET SCHEMA schema_name
```

Choose the characteristics of the next transaction
```
SET TRANSACTION
      { ISOLATION LEVEL
            { READ UNCOMMITED }
            | { READ COMMITTED }
            | { REPEATABLE READ }
            | { SERIALIZABLE } }
      | { READ ONLY } | { READ WRITE }
```

Begin a transaction
```
START TRANSACTION transaction_mode
```

Table C.1 SQL Statements (*cont.*)

Remove all rows from a table leaving the table structure intact
```
TRUNCATE TABLE table_name
```
Change the data in a table
```
UPDATE table_name
    SET { column_name = { value
                        | NULL
                        | DEFAULT }, … }
        [ { WHERE row_selection_predicate }
        | { WHERE CURRENT OF cursor_name } ]
```

Table C.2 SQL Functions

Function	Returns	Input Data
AVG ( )	Average of values	Numeric values
COUNT (*)	Number of rows in a result set	none
LOWER ( )	Convert to lowercase	Character value
MAX ( )	Maximum value	Number, character, or datetime values
MIN ( )	Minimum value	Number, character, or datetime values
SUBSTRING ( )	Portion of a character string	Character value
SUM ( )	Sum of values	Numeric values
TRIM ( )	Remove trailing blanks	Character value
UPPER ( )	Convert to uppercase	Character value
XMLATTRIBUTES	Create XML element attributes	Attribute value, attribute name
XML COMMENT ( )	Append comment to XML document string	Character value
XMLCONCAT ( )	Concatenate XML fragments	Character values containing XML text
XMLELEMENT ( )	Create an XML element	Element name, optional attributes, content of element
XMLFOREST ( )	Create nested XML element	Element content, element name
XMLPARSE ( )	Convert text to XML	Element type, content of element
XMLROOT ( )	Modify XML Prolog	XML character string, XML version, stand-alone property
XMLSERIALIZE ( )	Covert an XML string to text	Character string formatted as XML

Table C.3 SQL Operators

Operator	Use	Operates on:
Arithmetic	Compute arithmetic quantities	
+	Preserve the sign of a value	Numeric value
-	Change the sign of a value	Numeric value
*	Multiply two values	Numeric values
/	Divide one value by another	Numeric values
+	Add two values	Numeric values
-	Subtract one value from another	Numeric values
Comparison	Compare two values	
=	Equality	Any compatible data types
>	Greater than	Any compatible data types
> =	Greater than or equal to	Any compatible data types
<	Less than	Any compatible data types
< =	Less than or equal to	Any compatible data types
!= or <>	Note equal to	Any compatible data types
Logical		
AND	Determine if two expressions are true	Expressions returning a Boolean value
OR	Determine if at least one of two expressions is true	Expressions returning a Boolean value
NOT	Change the truth value	Expression returning a Boolean value
= or :=	Assignment	Any compatible data types
||	Concatenate two strings	Character strings
Specialty operators		
BETWEEN	Determine if a value falls inside an interval	Numeric, characters, or datetime values
DISTINCT	Remove duplicate rows	Table
EXCEPT	Find the difference between two tables	Tables
EXISTS	Determine if a subquery result table contains at least one row	Table
EXTRACT	Pull out portion of a datetime	Datetime
IN	Determine if a value is in a set	Any set of values of the same datatype
INTERSECT	Find rows in common of two tables	Tables
IS NULL	Determine if a value is null	Any data type
IS NOT NULL	Determine if a value is not null	Any data type
JOIN	Combine two tables horizontally	Tables
LIKE	Perform string pattern matching	Character value
MULTISET EXCEPT	Find elements unique to each of two multisets	Multisets
MULTISET INTERSECT	Find elements common to two multisets	Multisets
MULTISET UNION	Combine two multisets vertically	Multisets
NOT IN	Determine if a value is not in a set of values	Any sets of values of the same data type
OVERLAPS	Determine if two datetime intervals overlap	Datetimes
UNION	Combine to tables vertically	Tables

Glossary

1:1 Shorthand for a one-to-one relationship.

1:M Shorthand for a one-to-many relationship.

A

Abstract class A class from which no objects are created.

Abstract data type In an object-oriented environment, a user-defined data type; a class.

Accessor method A function that returns the values of private data stored about an object.

Aggregate function A SQL function—for example, AVG and SUM—that computes a variety of measures based on values in one or more numeric columns.

Aggregation In an object-oriented environment, a class that manages objects created from another class.

All-key relation A relation in which every column is part of the primary key.

American National Standards Institute (ANSI) The US body that approves standards for many items, including the SQL data manipulation language.

Array In a SQL database, an ordered collection of elements of the same data type, stored in a single column and row of a table.

Assertion A constraint that is not attached to a table, but is instead a distinct database object. It therefore can be used to enforce rules that apply to multiple tables or to verify that tables are not empty.

Attribute Data that describes an entity; the formal term for a column in a relation.

Authorization matrix A database system table that contains information about which users have access to which parts of the database. The DBMS consults the authorization matrix before performing user data manipulation requests.

B

Base class A class at the "general" end of an inheritance relationship; a parent class.

Base table Relations whose data are physically stored in a database.

Before-image file A file that contains images of every action taken by a transaction and is used to undo actions when a transaction is rolled back.

Binary large object (BLOB) A column data type specifying that the column will show the contents of a file (text and/or graphics) in its binary representation, without being searchable or readable in any way by the DBMS.

Black hat hackers Hackers who break into a computer system for profit or with a desire to do harm.

Buffer overflow attack An attempt to gain unauthorized control over a computer system by exploiting a programming error in an application or system program.

C

Candidate key A column or combination of columns that can be used as the primary key of a relation.

Cardinality (of a relationship) The type of relationship (one-to-one, one-to-many, or many-to-many).

Case sensitive Aware of the difference between upper- and lower-case letters.

Catalog Another term for a data dictionary.

Class A declaration of data and methods that describe a single entity and that will be used as a template to create objects.

Circular inclusion constraint A constraint on a relation that specifies that if a row is added to a specific table, rows must be added to one or more other tables.

Client/server architecture System architecture where processing tasks are shared between server and client computers.

Cluster (noSQL) A collection of commodity computers that are networked together to store a single database.

Cluster (SQL) A group of catalogs. Cluster definition is specific to a given DBMS.

Clustering Physically storing foreign key rows close to the primary key rows they reference to improve database performance.

CODASYL database A database that adheres to the CODASYL database standard.

Column homogeneous A property of a relation stating that all the values in a given column are taken from the same domain.

Commit (a transaction) End a transaction by making its changes permanent.

Committee on Data Systems Languages (CODASYL) A committee of government and industry technologists that developed the COBOL programming language and a standard for a simple network database.

Common table expression (CTE) A virtual table created by a SQL query that is used as the data source for another query. Unlike a view, the definition of a CTE is not stored in the database and must be used immediately after it is created.

Complex network data model A navigational data model that permits direct many-to-many relationships as well as one-to-many and one-to-one relationships.

Composite entity An entity that exists to represent the relationship between two other entities. It may have relationship data as attributes.

Composition A relationship between two classes where objects created from one class are part of objects created from the other.

Computer-aided software engineering (CASE) tool A software package that provides specialized tools for software and database modeling diagrams.

Concatenated foreign key A foreign key made up of two or more columns that references a concatenated primary key.

Concatenated identifier An entity identifier made up of a combination of values from multiple attributes.

Concatenated primary key A primary key made up of the combination of two or more columns.

Concatenation Combining two strings by placing one at the end of the other.

Concrete class A class from which objects are created.

Concurrency control Mechanisms to ensure that a database remains consistent and accurate during concurrent use.

Concurrent execution The simultaneous handling of multiple transactions by a single database.

Concurrent use Multiple users working with the same database at the same time.

Conforming parser Software that can read an XML document to determine whether the document is well-formed.

Connect (to a database) Establish a user session with a database.

Container class In an object-oriented environment, a class that manages groups of objects created from another class.

Constraint A rule to which data in a database must adhere.

Constructor In an object-oriented environment, a method that is executed automatically every time an object is created from a class.

Context diagram The top-level diagram in a data flow diagram that shows the environmental context in which the information system exists.

Control class A class that controls the operational flow of an object-oriented program.

Correlated subquery A subquery that a DBMS cannot process completely before turning to the outer query. The DBMS must execute the subquery repeatedly for every row in the outer query.

Correlation name An alias for a table used in a SQL query.

Currency indicator A system value kept by a navigational database to indicate a transaction's current position in the database hierarchy.

Cyberterrorists Hackers who are motivated by a political, religious, or philosophical agenda.

Cylinder The same track on all surfaces in a stack of platters in a hard disk.

D

Data definition language A special purpose computer language used to define the schema of a navigational database.

Data dictionary A repository that describes the data stored in a database along with definitions of data relationships.

Data dictionary driven A property of relational databases in which all access to stored data is preceded by access to the data dictionary to determine if the requested data elements exist and if the user has the access rights to perform the requested action.

Data flow The path taken by data as they are processed throughout an organization.

Data flow diagram (DFD) A graphic method for documenting the flow of data within an organization.

Data mart A small data warehouse.

Data model The formal way of expressing relationships in a database.

Data store A place where data are stored.

Data warehouse A repository of transaction and nontransaction data used for querying, reporting, and corporate decision making.

Database A collection of data and information about the relationships among those data.

Database administrator (DBA) A person who has the responsibility for maintaining a database.

Database key In a CODASYL database, an internal pointer to the physical storage location of a record occurrence in a file.

Database management system (DBMS) Software that manages the storage and retrieval of data stored in a database.

Declaration (in an XML document) A statement at the beginning of an XML document that identifies the XML version being used and, optionally, a character encoding scheme.

Deadlock A problem that occurs as a result of exclusive/writing locking where two or more transactions become stalled waiting for the release of locks held by each other.

Deletion anomaly A problem with the design of a relation such that deleting data about one entity in a row causes a part of the primary key to become null, requiring the deletion of the entire row, which may contain data that need to be retained.

Denial of service attack An attack on a computer system that attempts to prevent legitimate users from gaining access to network resources and, by extension, any database that uses that network.

Derived class A class at the "specific" end of an inheritance relationship; a child class.

Destructor In an object-oriented environment, a method that is run each time an object is destroyed (removed from main memory).

Determinant An attribute upon which other attributes are functionally dependent.

Difference A relational algebra operation that returns the rows found in one table but not in another.

Dimension table A table in a data warehouse that contains descriptive information for grouping data stored in fact tables.

Dimensional modeling The most frequently used data model for data warehouses.

Dirty read A problem with uncontrolled concurrent use of a database where a transaction acts on data that have been modified by an update transaction that hasn't committed and is later rolled back.

Disconnect (from a database) Terminate a user session with a database.

Distributed database A database where portions of the database are stored on computers at physically distributed locations. The entire database is the sum of all the parts.

Disaster recovery Activities that must take place to bring the database back into use after it has been damaged in some way.

Distribution independence A constraint on a distributed database that specifies that the database should look and act like a centralized database to users.

Divide A relational algebra operation that searches for multiple rows in a table.

Domain A specification of permissible values for an attribute.

Domain constraint A rule that requires that all values of an attribute come from a specified domain.

Drop Delete an element of database structure from a database.

E

Embedded SQL SQL statements placed within a host language, allowing SQL to be executed by application programs.

Entity Something about which we store data.

Entity class In an object-oriented environment, a class that is used to create objects that manipulate data.

Entity identifier A value (or combination of values) that uniquely identifies each occurrence of an entity in a database.

Entity integrity A constraint on a relation that states that no part of the primary key can be null.

Entity-relationship diagram (ERD) A graphic technique for representing entity relationships.

Entity-relationship (ER) model A technique for representing entity relationships that is independent of any specific data model and any specific software.

Equi-join A join based on matching identical values.

Escape character A character, usually \, that removes the special meaning of whatever follows in a literal string.

Evolutionary prototyping A form of prototyping in which successive prototypes of the software are modified based on user feedback, eventually converging on the production system.

Exclusive lock A lock that gives the transaction holding the lock the exclusive right to read and write a portion of the database.

Extensible markup language (XML) A platform-independent markup language for specifying the structure of data in a text document used for both data storage and the transfer of data.

Extract-transform-load The process of taking data from operational databases (and optionally external sources), modifying the data to meet the requirements of a data warehouse, and loading the data into the warehouse.

F

Fact table A table used in dimensional modeling to contain summarizable facts.

Field In a file processing system, the smallest unit of meaningful data, such as a first name or street address.

File processing system A system that handles data by storing them in data files and then manipulating the files through application programs.

Firewall A piece of software that filters incoming and outgoing network traffic and stops messages that violate the rules that define allowable traffic.

Foreign key (FK) An attribute (or combination of attributes) in a relation that is the same as the primary key of another relation. A foreign key may be a non-key attribute in its own relation or it may be part of a concatenated primary key.

Frame (in a windowing query) A portion of a windowing query's window that "slides" to present to the DBMS the rows that share the same value of the partitioning criteria.

Function A small program that performs one task and returns a single value. It may be built into the SQL language or written by a user, database administrator, or application programmer.

Functional dependency A relationship between two attributes (or a concatenation of attributes and another attribute) in a relation such that for every unique value of the second attribute, the table contains only one value of the first attribute (or concatenation of attributes). The first attribute, however, may be associated with multiple values of the second attribute.

G

Get method A function that returns the values of private data stored about an object.

Grant Give access rights to database elements to users. The user that creates a database element has all rights to that element. Other users have no access unless they are specifically granted access rights.

Granularity (of a lock) The size of the portion of a database to which a lock is applied.

Grouping query A query that groups rows of data based on common values in one or more columns and that optionally computes summary values from each group.

H

Hashing A technique for providing fast access to data based on a key value by determining the physical storage location of those data.

Hierarchical data model A legacy data model where all relationships are one-to-many or one-to-one and entities at the "many" end of a relationship can be related to only one entity at the "one" end of the relationship.

Hierarchy A structure for data relationships where all relationships are one-to-many and no child entity may have more than one parent entity.

Horizontal portioning Splitting the rows of a table between multiple tables with the same structure to improve database performance.

I

Identifier chain The fully qualified name of an element in a SQL database, including the catalog, schema, table, and column of the element.

Immutable Unable to be changed. Wherever possible, primary keys should be immutable as long the row containing the key is in the database.

Inconsistent analysis A problem that occurs from uncontrolled concurrent use of a database where a transaction produces incorrect output because another transaction was concurrently modifying data being retrieved.

Index A data structure in a database that provides a logical ordering of data based on key values.

Indexed sequential access method (ISAM) A physical file storage technique that also provides indexes to data based on a key for fast access on that key.

Inheritance A general to specific relationship between classes in an object-oriented environment.

Inner join An equi-join.

Insertion anomaly A problem with the design of a relation such that all data for a complete primary key are not available, preventing data from being stored in the relation.

Instance (of an entity) A group of attributes that describes a single real-world occurrence of an entity.

Instance (of a relation) A relation that contains at least one row of data.

Interactive SQL Individual SQL statements entered from the keyboard and processed immediately.

Interface class In an object-oriented environment, a class that handles input and output operations.

Interleaved execution The interleaving of the actions of two or more concurrent database transactions.

Intersect A relational algebra operation that returns all rows common to two tables.

IPSec A type of security used by a virtual private network.

Isolation level The degree to which a transaction can view data modified by other transactions running concurrently.

J

Join A relational algebra operation that combines two relations horizontally by matching values between the two tables. Most valid joins involve matching primary key values to foreign key values.

Join dependency The most general form of dependency between attributes in a relation such that a table can be put together correctly by joining two or more tables, all of which contain only attributes from the original table.

L

Legacy database A database using a prerelational data model that is still in use.

Locking Restricting access to parts of a database to specific transactions to provide concurrency control.

Logging The process of keeping an audit trail of changes made by a transaction to be used to undo the transaction should it need to be rolled back.

Lost update A problem that occurs during uncontrolled concurrent use of a database where an update made by one transaction wipes out the effect of an update made by a concurrent transaction.

M

Malware Unwanted software—such as a virus, worm, or Trojan horse—that is inadvertently loaded onto a computer and causes disruption of computer functioning.

Mandatory relationship A relationship between two entities in a database such that an instance of the second entity cannot exist in the database unless it is related to an instance of the first entity.

Many-to-many relationship (M:M or M:N) A relationship between two entities in a database such that each instance of the first entity can be related to many instances of the second and each instance of the second entity can be related to many instances of the first.

Markup language A set of special codes placed inside a text document to identify the elements of the document and optionally to give instructions to software using the document.

Message Requests for data manipulation sent from one object to another.

Metadata Data about data; the data stored in a data dictionary.

Method (class) A program module that acts on objects created from a class in an object-oriented program.

Method (SQL) A program module that is part of a user-defined data type that is used to create objects.

Modification anomaly A problem that occurs when duplicated data become inconsistent when not all occurrences of the same value are modified at the same time.

Module A group of SQL routines.

Multiset In a SQL database, an unordered collection of elements of the same data type that is stored in a single column and row.

Multivalued attribute An attribute that can contain more than one value at a time.

Multivalued dependency A general case of a functional dependency where a determinant determines a small group of values (as opposed to a single value) for each of two or more unrelated attributes.

Multi-version concurrency control A concurrency control method in which data retrievals and modifications are marked with the time they occur. Modifications are allowed if no other transaction holds an earlier timestamp on the data.

Mutually exclusive relationship A relationship between entities such that an instance of an entity can be related to an instance of either a second or third entity, but not both.

Mutator method A function that modifies the values of private data stored about an object.

N

Natural equi-join An equi-join.

Natural identifiers Entity identifiers that are unique by nature, such as invoice numbers.

Navigational data model A data model where relationships between entities are represented by physical data structures (for example, pointers or indexes) that provide the only paths for data access.

Nonprocedural A process that specifies "what" but not "how," leaving the manner in which the result is obtained up to the DBMS.

Non-repeatable read A problem with uncontrolled concurrent use of a database that occurs when a transaction reads data for the second time and determines that the data are not the same as they were from the first read.

Normal form A set of theoretical rules to which a relation must conform.

Normalization The process of designing relations to adhere to increasingly stringent sets of rules to avoid problems with poor database design.

NoSQL Arguably, "not only SQL"; a collection of postrelational data models that do not use SQL and that are intended for fast retrieval from extremely large databases.

Null A database value, distinct from a blank or zero, meaning "unknown."

O

Object An instance of a self-contained element used by an object-oriented program, containing data that describe the specific element and links to program modules that operate on the element.

Object-oriented analysis A method for viewing the interaction of data and manipulations of data that is based on the object-oriented programming paradigm.

Object-oriented paradigm A programming and database framework in which the elements in the environment are conceptualized as entities (classes). Data and programs for each class are stored together.

Object-Oriented Programming (OOP) A method for structuring a program so that it adheres to the precepts of the object-oriented paradigm.

Object-relational (OR) An environment in which object-oriented principles (for example, classes as domains) are made part of a relational database system.

One-to-many relationship (1:M) A relationship between two entities in a database such that one instance of an entity can be related to many instances of a second entity and the second entity can be related to only one instance of the first.

One-to-one (1:1) relationship A relationship between two entities in a database such that each instance of an entity is related to no more than one instance of the other entity.

Online analytical processing (OLTP) Data processing systems that are used in support of high-level organizational decision making.

Online transaction processing (OLTP) Data processing systems that handle the day-to-day operations of an organization.

Optimistic locking A concurrency control method that allows all modifications but then rolls back transactions if other transactions have modified the data.

Outer join A join that preserves all rows from both source tables. Where a new row cannot be formed by combining rows, the outer join places nulls in empty columns.

Overloading In an object-oriented environment, two methods of the same class that have the same name but different signatures (input parameters and data types).

P

Page The size of the block of data that a computer (and therefore a database) transfers between disk and main memory at one time.

Partition (in a windowing query) A set of rows for which an aggregate function will compute a summary value.

Performance tuning Making changes to the design of a database to enhance database performance.

Persistent stored module (PSM) A SQL program module that is stored within a database. It may be a trigger or a stored procedure.

Phantom read A problem with uncontrolled concurrent use of a database that occurs when a transaction reads data for the second time and determines that new rows have been inserted by another transaction.

Physical schema The underlying physical storage of a database, managed by the DBMS.

Polymorphism The redefinition of the body of a superclass method inherited by a subclass. The polymorphic method retains the same signature.

Post-relational A collection of data models developed since the introduction of the relational data model. Data models typically included in this category include object-relational, object-oriented, and NoSQL.

Precedence The order in which a DBMS evaluates operators in a predicate when multiple operators are present.

Precision The number of digits to the right of a decimal point in a number.

Predicate A statement of logical criteria against which data are evaluated during a query.

Primary key (PK) A column or combination of columns whose value uniquely identifies each row in a relation.

Procedural A process that is expressed in a step-by-step manner. It specifies "how" as well as "what."

Procedure A SQL routine that is stored in a database and executed with the SQL CALL statement. It does not return a value.

Process (in a DFD) Something that is done to data.

Product The relational algebra operation that combines two tables by forming all possible combination of rows; the Cartesian product of two tables.

Project The relational algebra operation that creates a projection of a relation.

Projection A subset of a relation created by copying selected columns and all rows in those columns.

Prolog (of an XML document) A statement at the beginning of an XML document that identifies the XML version being used and optionally a character encoding scheme.

Prototyping A form of system development where developers prepare models of a system that are not fully functional. User feedback is used to modify the prototype or to develop a final system.

Q

Query optimizer A portion of a DBMS that determines the most efficient sequence of relational algebra operations to use to satisfy a query.

R

Read lock Control over a portion of the database given to one or more transactions that prevents other transactions from modifying the data while the locks are in place.

Reblocking In an ISAM file, rewriting the file to leave physical space on each track occupied by the file to allow the addition of records in key sequence order.

Record In a file processing system, a collection of data that describe one instance of an entity.

Recovery The process of restoring a database from a damaged or inconsistent state so that it becomes operational again.

Recursive query A query that queries itself.

Referential integrity A constraint on a relation that states that every non-null foreign key value must match an existing primary key value.

Relation The definition of a two-dimensional table with columns and rows. There is no more than one value at the intersection of each column and row (no repeating groups).

Relational algebra The set of theoretical operations used to manipulate data in a relation.

Relational calculus A set of nonprocedural operations used to manipulate relations.

Relational data model A paradigm for describing the structure of a database in which entities are represented as tables and relationships between the entities are represented by matching data.

Relationship data Data that apply to the relationship between two entities rather than to the entities themselves.

Repeating group A multivalued attribute that must be removed before the data in the group can be stored in a relational database.

Replication In a NoSQL environment, placing identical copies of a database on multiple servers.

Requirements document A document prepared as the output of a systems analysis describing the information requirements of a new or modified information system.

Restrict The more recent term for the relational algebra operation that chooses rows from a table based on evaluating data against logical criteria (a *predicate*).

Revoke Remove previously granted access rights from a user.

Roll back (a transaction) Undo the changes made by a transaction, restoring the database to the state it was in before the transaction began.

Root (of an XML hierarchy) The top node in a hierarchy, providing a single point of access to the hierarchy.

Routine The smallest unit of a SQL PSM. Typically, it performs a single action, such as updating a total or inserting a row in a table.

S

Schema The overall logical plan of a database.

Script kiddies Hackers who use prewritten software to break into computer systems.

Scope (of a temporary table) The visibility of a temporary table. Local temporary tables can be seen only by the program module that created them. Global temporary tables can be seen by the entire database session.

Select The original relational algebra term for *restrict*; the SQL command to retrieve data from a database.

Serial execution A sequence of executing concurrent transactions in which one transaction runs from start to finish before a second transaction begins.

Serializable A condition in which interleaved transactions produce the same result as they would had they run in a series.

Service-oriented architecture (SOA) A method for organizing a company's entire information system functions so that all information components are viewed as services that are provided to the organization.

Session A block of time during which a user interacts with a database.

Set In a CODASYL database, a two-level hierarchy representing one or more one-to-many relationships.

Set function A SQL function—for example, AVG or SUM—that computes a variety of measures based on values in one or more numeric columns.

Set method A function that modifies the values of private data stored about an object.

Shard In a NoSQL environment, placing unique parts of a database on multiple servers.

Sharding In a NoSQL environment, maintaining a database that has been broken into shards.

Shared lock Control over a portion of the database given to one or more transactions that prevents other transactions from modifying the data while the locks are in place.

Simple network data model A legacy data model where all relationships are one-to-many or one-to-one; a navigational data model where relationships are represented with physical data structures such as pointers.

Single-valued attribute An attribute that contains only one value at any given time.

Social engineering A nontechnological method for gaining unauthorized access to a computer system by tricking people into revealing access information.

Sorting Physically reordering the rows in a table based on the values in one or more columns.

Spiral methodology A more formal form of prototyping that uses a gradual process in which each cycle further refines the system, bringing it closer to the desired end point.

SQL injection attack An attack against a database system launched through an application program containing embedded SQL.

Stored procedure A SQL program module that is invoked by an application program using the SQL CALL command. Stored procedures are stored in the database they manipulate.

Structured design life cycle The classic model for developing an information system. It involves a sequence of activities that define and develop a new or modified system. It works best in environments where information needs are well known.

Subclass A class at the "specific" end of an inheritance relationship; a child class.

Subquery A complete SELECT statement that is part of another SELECT.

Substring A portion of a string.

Superclass A class at the "general' end of an inheritance relationship; a parent class.

System set In a CODASYL database, a special set with only one owner occurrence that is used to collect all occurrences of a single entity.

Systems analysis Conduct a needs assessment to determine what a new or modified information system should do.

T

Table A term used synonymously with *relation* in the *relational data model*.

Tag The markup device in an XML file. XML tags exist in pairs, with an opening tag before the element being identified and a closing tag after it.

Temporary table A relation whose contents are not stored in the database, but that exists only during the database session in which it was created.

Θ-join (theta-join) A join that combines two tables on some condition, which may be equality or something else such as greater than or less than.

Three-schema architecture A view of a database environment in which the logical schema provides an interface between the physical schema and user views of the database.

Three-valued logic A set of logical truth tables that include the values true, false, and unknown.

Throwaway prototyping A type of prototyping in which the prototype software is demonstrated and evaluated and then discarded. The production system is developed from scratch, based on feedback to the prototype.

Timestamping A concurrency control method in which data retrievals and modifications are marked with the time they occur. Modifications are allowed if no other transaction holds an earlier timestamp on the data.

Transaction A unit of work presented to a database.

Transitive dependency A set of functional dependencies where an attribute that is a candidate key for its relation determines a second attribute and the second attribute determines a third, producing a functional dependency between the first and third as well.

Tree In the hierarchical data mode, a single entity hierarchy.

Trigger A SQL program module that is executed when a specific data modification activity occurs. Triggers are stored in the database they manipulate.

Truncate (a table) Remove all rows from a table, leaving the structure of the table in the database's data dictionary.

Tuple The formal term for a row in a relation.

Two-phase locking A concurrency control method that begins by giving transactions shared/read locks on data and then upgrades the locks to exclusive/write locks only when the transaction is ready to modify data.

Typecast Change the data type of a value for output or use in a SQL program.

Typed table A table created as a class using a user-defined data type to define the structure of the objects to be stored in the table. Each row contains one object.

U

Uncorrelated subquery A subquery that a DBMS can process completely before processing the query in which the subquery is contained.

Unified modeling language (UML) A style of ER diagramming.

Union A relational algebra operation that combines two tables by merging their rows into the same structure.

Union compatible A property of two tables where all columns in both tables are drawn from the same logical domains.

Unit of recovery A transaction, so called because a transaction either succeeds or fails as a whole.

Updatability A property of a view that indicates whether it can be used to perform updates that can then be propagated to the base table from which it was derived.

Update anomaly A problem that occurs when duplicated data become inconsistent when not all occurrences of the same value are modified at the same time.

User-defined data type (UDT) In a SQL database, a declaration of a structured data type that can be used as the domain of a column or as an object.

V

Vertical partitioning Storing a relation as two or more tables that are projections of the original relation to improve database performance.

View A virtual table that is constructed by executing a named query that is stored as part of a database.

Virtual class A class from which no objects are created.

Virtual private network (VPN) A method providing remote access to local area networks that uses the Internet and encrypts transmissions for security.

Virtual table A table whose data exist only in main memory rather than being stored physically in the database.

W

Wait state A hold placed by a DBMS on the execution of a transaction because the transaction is unable to obtain a needed lock on a database element, usually because the element is locked by another transaction. The transaction must wait until the lock can be placed.

Waterfall method An alternative name for the traditional structured systems development life cycle based on the idea that one step falls into another.

Weak entity An entity whose instances cannot exist in a database unless a related instance of another entity is present and related to it.

Well-formed (XML document) An XML document that conforms to the syntax rules for a correct document.

White hat hackers Hackers who break into computer systems and then report vulnerabilities to the software owner or developer. Their motives are usually to help make systems more secure.

Window A set of rows for which an aggregate function will compute a summary value.

Windowing A SQL technique for computing aggregate measures for groups of rows that also displays the individual rows in each group.

Windowing function A function that computes an aggregate measure about a partition in a windowing query.

Write lock A lock that gives the transaction holding the lock the exclusive right to read and write a portion of the database.

X

Extended (Extensible) Markup Language (XML) A way of representing data and data relationships in text files, typically for data exchange between software of different types.

XML schema A document without data that specifies the structure of an XML document.

Subject Index